SCRIPTURE AND HERMENEUTICS SERIES

VOLUME 6

READING LUKE

Interpretation, Reflection, Formation

The Scripture and Hermeneutics Series

Series Editors
Craig Bartholomew
Anthony Thiselton

Consultant Editors
Ann Holt
Karl Möller

Editorial Advisory Board
James Catford
Fred Hughes
Tremper Longman III
Francis Martin
Gordon McConville
Christopher Seitz
Janet Martin Soskice
Nick Wolterstorff

VOLUME 6

READING LUKE

Interpretation, Reflection, Formation

———————————— *editors* ————————————

CRAIG G. BARTHOLOMEW • JOEL B. GREEN
• ANTHONY C. THISELTON

UNIVERSITY OF
GLOUCESTERSHIRE

PATERNOSTER PRESS

bible society

REDEEMER
University College

BAYLOR
UNIVERSITY

ZONDERVAN™

GRAND RAPIDS, MICHIGAN 49530 USA

First published 2005 jointly
in the UK by Paternoster Press, an imprint of Authentic Media,
9 Holdom Avenue, Bletchley, Milton Keynes, MK1 1QR, UK
Website: www.authenticmedia.co.uk
and in the United States of America by Zondervan
5300 Patterson Ave SE, Grand Rapids, Michigan 49530

09 08 07 06 05 04   7 6 5 4 3 2 1

British Library Cataloguing in Publication Data
A catalogue record for this book is available from the British Library
ISBN 1-84227-070-2

Library of Congress Cataloging-in-Publication Data
Reading Luke : interpretation, reflection, formation / edited by
Craig G. Bartholomew, Joel B. Green, Anthony C. Thiselton.
    p. cm. — (Scripture and hermeneutics series ; v. 6)
Includes bibliographical references and indexes.
ISBN 13: 978-0-310-23416-6 (hardcover : alk. paper) —
ISBN 10: 0-310-23416-6 (hardcover : alk. paper)
    1. Bible. N.T. Luke — Criticism, interpretation, etc.
I. Bartholomew, Craig G., 1961- II. Green, Joel B., 1956- III. Thiselton, Anthony C. IV. Series.
BS2595.52.R43 2005
226.4'06—dc22   2005012037

UK edition cover design by Gert Swart and Zak Benjamin, South Africa
Typeset by WestKey Ltd, Falmouth, Cornwall
Printed in the United States of America
Printed on acid free paper

Contents

Introduction and Preview

Narrative, History and Theology

Language, Parables, and Ways or Levels of Reading Luke

Issues in Reception History and Reception Theory

Preface

From its inception the Scripture and Hermeneutics Seminar has been motivated by the conviction that attention to hermeneutics will be valuable only insofar as it leads us more deeply into the biblical text. In all five volumes published thus far we have kept actual exegesis clearly in mind as the goal of our hermeneutical reflections but never so overtly as with this volume. *Reading Luke* represents the Seminar's concern to bring all its work to bear on a particular biblical text as an unequivocal signal that healthy biblical hermeneutics will always lead us deeply into exegesis. We had considerable discussion about which text to focus on and eventually decided on Luke's Gospel – our consultation at Jesus College in Oxford in September 2004 confirmed again and again that Luke was a good choice – so many central interpretative and hermeneutical issues surface in a reading of this text.

I am most grateful to Anthony Thiselton and Joel Green for their help in editing this volume. Anthony has also written a superb introductory essay which not only surveys the history of the interpretation of Luke but also connects all the chapters in this volume into the key hermeneutical issues and relates this volume to the five previous ones in the Scripture and Hermeneutics Series. Joel has not only contributed a chapter but also provides a stimulating *Afterword* in which he reflects on continuing work on Luke that needs to be done.

Once again the American and the British editions have different covers. Each edition has a small version of the other cover on its back inside flap of the cover. The American edition features Carvaggio's *The Supper at Emmaus*, which is discussed in the chapter by Parsons and Hornik. Gert Swart and Zak Benjamin have produced a stunning portrait of Christ for the cover of the UK edition. Both images serve to remind us that Scripture, and especially the Gospels, are the field in which we find hid the Christ. Healthy Scriptural interpretation will cause us to rise again and again in the presence of Christ. Indeed Scripture is the means by which he gives himself to us. A stimulating smorgasbord awaits in this volume and our prayer is that it will contribute to fresh work on Luke as part of Holy Scripture so that God's people might hear more clearly God's address through this wonderful gospel.

Craig Bartholomew,
Ancaster, Canada,
May 2005

Contributors

Craig Bartholomew is the H. Evan Runner Professor of Philosophy and Professor of Theology and Religion at Redeemer University College, Ancaster, Canada as well as Visiting Professor in Biblical Hermeneutics at University of Chester. He is the author of *Reading Ecclesiastes* and co-author of *The Drama of Scripture*. Craig heads up the Scripture and Hermeneutics Seminar.

François Bovon is the Frothingham Professor of the History of Religion at Harvard University Divinity School and Professeur Honoraire at the University of Geneva. He has been president of the Swiss Society of Theology, the Studiorum Novi Testamenti Societas and the Association pour l'Étude de la Literature Apocryphe Chrétienne. His publications include a major commentary on the Gospel of Luke, *Luke the Theologian*, and *Acta Philippi*. He has also published several collections of essays in French, German and English, and he is an ordained minister of the Église Réformée du Canton de Vaud (Switzerland) and the Église Protestante de Genève.

Michael Goheen is the Geneva Professor of Worldview and Religious Studies at Trinity Western University, Canada. He is the author of *'As The Father Has Sent Me, I Am Sending You': J.E. Lesslie Newbigin's Missionary Ecclesiology* and co-author of *The Drama of Scripture*. He has also published a range of articles on mission in Western culture, worldview, and gospel and culture.

Joel B. Green is Vice President of Academic Affairs and Provost, and Professor of New Testament Interpretation, at Asbury Theological Seminary. He has written and edited numerous books, including *The Theology of the Gospel of Luke* (New International Commentary on the New Testament); *What about the Soul? Neuroscience and Christian Anthropology and Salvation*. He has co-authored *Introducing the New Testament: Its Literature and Theology* and *Recovering the Scandal of the Cross: Atonement in New Testament and Contemporary Contexts*.

Andrew Gregory is an Anglican priest who is a research fellow at Keble College, Oxford. He is a series editor for *Oxford Early Christian Gospel Texts* (for which he is preparing a volume on the so-called Jewish-Christian Gospels) and for *The Oxford Apostolic Fathers*. He has contributed to *The Reception of the New Testament in the Apostolic Fathers*, and *Trajectories through the New Testament and the Apostolic Fathers*, both of which he co-edited with Christopher Tuckett, and is the author of *The Reception of Luke and Acts in the Period before Irenaeus*.

Scott Hahn is Professor of Theology and Scripture at the Franciscan University of Steubenville. He also holds the Chair of Biblical Theology and Liturgical Proclamation at St. Vincent Seminary (USA). He is Founder and President of the St. Paul Center for Biblical Theology and director of the Institute of Applied Biblical Studies. He is the general editor of the Ignatius Catholic Study Bible and author of over a dozen books, including *The Lamb's Supper; Lord Have Mercy; Swear to God; Understanding the Scriptures* and, most recently, *Letter and Spirit*.

Robby Holt is a doctoral student with University of Chester. His research, 'Seeking Corporate Maturity: Praying Communities of the Gospel into Gospel Discernment', focuses upon Pauline prayer reports. Robby preaches and teaches in local churches in his hometown of Chattanooga (USA).

Heidi J. Hornik is Professor of Italian Renaissance and Baroque Art History at Baylor University (USA). She has published extensively in art historical journals such as *Paragone* and *Artibus et Historia* on the artist Michele Tosini (1503–77). Her work has included discovering the artist's testament and a fresco chapel in a private villa located in Chianti. Together with her husband Mikeal C. Parsons she has written *Illuminating Luke: The Public Ministry of Christ in Italian Renaissance and Baroque Painting* (forthcoming); *Illuminating Luke: The Infancy Narrative in Italian Renaissance Painting*; and has co-edited *Interpreting Christian Art*.

I. Howard Marshall is Emeritus Professor of New Testament at the University of Aberdeen. His publications include *The Gospel of Luke* (New International Greek Testament Commentary); *The Pastoral Epistles* (International Critical Commentary); and *New Testament Theology: Many Witnesses, One Gospel*. He has also edited the revised version of *Moulton and Geden: Concordance to the Greek New Testament*.

David P. Moessner is Professor of Biblical Theology at the University of Dubuque Theological Seminary. He is the author of *Lord of the Banquet* and editor of *Jesus and the Heritage of Israel* (Vol. 1 of *Luke the Interpreter of Israel*). He is also co-executive editor of the *Supplements to Novum Testamentum* as well as author of numerous articles on the New Testament and early Christianity.

John Nolland is Academic Dean at Trinity College, Bristol. His publications include commentaries on Luke in the Word Biblical Commentary Series and on Matthew in the New International Greek Testament Commentary Series (forthcoming) as well as numerous articles. John is an Anglican priest.

Mikeal C. Parsons is Professor and Macon Chair in Religion at Baylor University. In addition to numerous journal articles, he is co-author of *Illuminating Luke: The Public Ministry of Christ in Italian Renaissance and Baroque Painting* (forthcoming); *Illuminating Luke: The Infancy Narrative in Italian Renaissance Painting*; and *Acts: A Handbook on the Greek Text*. He is also the author of *The Departure of Jesus in Luke-Acts* and *Rethinking the Unity of Luke-Acts*. He currently serves as editor of *Perspectives in Religious Studies*.

Charles Scobie taught at McGill University, Montreal, and was head of the Department of Religious Studies and Cowan Professor of Religious Studies at Mount Allison University (Canada) until his retirement in 1998. He is a past president of the Canadian Society of Biblical Studies. His most recent book is *The Ways of Our God: An Approach to Biblical Theology*.

F. Scott Spencer is Professor of New Testament at the Baptist Theological Seminary at Richmond, Virginia (USA). His publications include *The Portrait of Philip in Acts: A Study of Roles and Relations* and *Journeying Through Acts: A Literary-Cultural Reading*. He currently serves as co-chair of the Acts Consultation for the Society of Biblical Literature.

Anthony C. Thiselton is Emeritus Professor of Christian Theology at the University of Nottingham and Research Professor of Christian Theology at University of Chester. He is also Canon Theologian of Leicester Cathedral and of Southwell Minster. His books include *The Two Horizons*; *New Horizons in Hermeneutics*; *Interpreting God and the Postmodern Self*; *The Promise of Hermeneutics* (co-author); *The First Epistle to the Corinthians: A Commentary on the Greek Text*; and *Thiselton on Hermeneutics: Collected Works* (forthcoming). He holds three doctorates and is a past president of the Society for the Study of Theology.

Max Turner is Professor of New Testament Studies at the London School of Theology and a Baptist minister. He is editor of the Two Horizons Commentary series and consultant editor of Paternoster's Studies in Pentecostal and Charismatic Issues. His publications include *Linguistics and Biblical Interpretation*; *Power from on High: The Spirit in Israel's Restoration and Witness*; *The Holy Spirit and Spiritual Gifts: Then and Now* and *Baptism in the Holy Spirit*.

David Wenham teaches New Testament at Wycliffe Hall, University of Oxford (UK). His publications include *The Rediscovery of Jesus' Eschatological Discourse*; *Paul: Follower of Jesus or Founder of Christianity?*; *Introducing the Gospels and Acts* (co-author); and *Paul and Jesus: The True Story*. He is also involved in parish ministry.

Stephen I. Wright is director of the College of Preachers (UK) and Associate Lecturer at Spurgeon's College, London. He is the author of *The Voice of Jesus: Studies in the Interpretation of Six Gospel Parables* and *Tales Jesus Told: An Introduction to the Narrative Parables of Jesus*. He is an Anglican priest.

Abbreviations

AB	Anchor Bible
ABD	*Anchor Bible Dictionary*
ABR	*Australian Biblical Review*
ABRL	Anchor Bible Reference Library
ACCS	Ancient Christian Commentary on Scripture
AGJU	Arbeiten zur Geschichte des antiken Judentums und des Urchristentums
AJT	*Asia Journal of Theology*
AnGr	Analecta Gregoriana
ANQ	*Andover Newton Quarterly*
ANRW	*Aufstieg und Niedergang der römischen Welt: Geschichte und Kultur Roms im Spiegel der neueren Forschung*
ANTC	Abingdon New Testament Commentaries
AThR	*Anglican Theological Review*
BAGD	Bauer, Arndt, Gingrich, and Danker's *Greek-English Lexicon of the New Testament and Other Early Christian Literature*
BBR	*Bulletin for Biblical Research*
BDAG	Bauer, Danker, Arndt and Gingrich's *Greek-English Lexicon of the New Testament and Other Early Christian Literature* (3rd edn, 1999)
BECNT	Baker Exegetical Commentary on the New Testament
BETL	Bibliotheca ephemeridum theologicarum lovaniensium
BGBE	Beiträge zur Geschichte der biblischen Exegese
BIW	The Bible in Its World
BJRL	*Bulletin of the John Rylands University Library of Manchester*
BSac	*Bibliotheca sacra*
BTB	*Biblical Theology Bulletin*
BZNW	Beihefte zur Zeitschrift für die neutestamentliche Wissenschaft
CBET	Contributions to Biblical Exegesis and Theology
CBQ	*Catholic Biblical Quarterly*
CBR	Currents in Biblical Research
Comm	*Communio*
CSR	*Christian Scholars Review*
CSCO	Corpus scriptorium christianorum orientalium
CurTM	*Currents in Theology and Mission*

DBT	*Dictionary of Biblical Theology*
DJG	*Dictionary of Jesus and the Gospels*
EAPR	*East Asian Pastoral Review*
EKKNT	Evangelisch-katholischer Kommentar zum Neuen Testament
ETL	*Ephemerides theologicae lovanienses*
EvQ	*Evangelical Quarterly*
ExAud	*Ex auditu*
ExpTim	*Expository Times*
FRLANT	Forschungen zur Religion und Literatur des Alten und Neuen Testaments
GNS	*Good News Studies*
Greg	*Gregorianum*
GTA	Göttinger theologischer Arbeiten
HBT	*Horizons in Biblical Theology*
HPR	*Homiletic and Pastoral Review*
HTKNT	Herders theologischer Kommentar zum Neuen Testament
HTR	*Harvard Theological Review*
HTS	Harvard Theological Studies
HvTSt	*Hervormde Teologiese Studies*
IDB	*The Interpreter's Dictionary of the Bible*
Int	*Interpretation*
IRM	*International Review of Mission*
ISBE	*International Standard Bible Encyclopedia*
ISBL	Indiana Studies in Biblical Literature
JBL	*Journal of Biblical Literature*
JETS	*Journal of the Evangelical Theological Society*
JPT	*Journal of Pentecostal Theology*
JSNT	*Journal for the Study of the New Testament*
JSNTSup	Journal for the Study of the New Testament: Supplement Series
JTSA	*Journal of Theology for Southern Africa*
KEK	Kritisch-exegetischer Kommentar über das Neue Testament
L&N	*Greek-English Lexicon of the New Testament: Based on Semantic Domains* (ed. J.P. Louw and E.A. Nida)
LCBI	Literary Currents in Biblical Interpretation
LCL	Loeb Classical Library
LTQ	*Lexington Theological Quarterly*
MSt	*Mission Studies*
NETR	*Near East School of Theology Theological Review*
NICNT	New International Commentary on the New Testament
NIDNTT	*New International Dictionary of New Testament Theology*
NIGTC	New International Greek Testament Commentary
NovT	*Novum Testamentum*
NTD	Das Neue Testament Deutsch

NTL	New Testament Library
NTOA	Novum Testamentum et Orbis Antiquus
NTS	*New Testament Studies*
NTT	New Testament Theology
OBO	Orbis biblicus et orientalis
PRSt	*Perspectives in Religious Studies*
PSB	*Princeton Seminary Bulletin*
RB	*Revue biblique*
RBL	*Review of Biblical Literature*
RHPR	*Revue d'histoire et de philosophie religieuses*
RivB	*Rivista biblica italiana*
RSQ	*Rhetoric Society Quarterly*
RSR	*Recherches de science religieuse*
SBLDS	SBL Dissertation Series
SBLMS	Society of Biblical Literature Monograph Series
SBT	Studies in Biblical Theology
SemeiaSt	Semeia Studies
SHM	Studies in the History of Mission
SHS	Scripture and Hermeneutics Series
SJT	*Scottish Journal of Theology*
SNT	Studien zum Neuen Testament
SNTSMS	Society for New Testament Studies Monograph Series
SNTSU	Studien zum Neuen Neuen Testament und seiner Umwelt
SP	Sacra pagina
StABH	Studies in American Biblical Hermeneutics
StPatr	Studia patristica
StudBibTh	*Studia Biblica et Theologica*
TBT	*The Bible Today*
TJ	*Trinity Journal*
TJT	*Toronto Journal of Theology*
TS	*Theological Studies*
TU	Texte und Untersuchungen
TynBul	*Tyndale Bulletin*
VE	*Vox evangelica*
VT	*Vetus Testamentum*
WBC	Word Biblical Commentary
WMANT	Wissenschaftliche Monographien zum Alten und Neuen Testament
WUNT	Wissenschaftliche Untersuchungen zum Neuen Testament
ZKT	*Zeitschrift für katholische Theologie*
ZKunstG	*Zeitschrift für Kunstgeschichte*
ZMR	*Zeitschrift für Missionswissenschaft und Religionswissenschaft*
ZNW	*Zeitschrift für die neutestamentliche Wissenschaft und die Kunde der älteren Kirche*
ZTK	*Zeitschrift für Theologie und Kirche*

The Artists

Zak Benjamin, Painter and Printmaker

Calvin Seerveld has thus characterized Zak Benjamin's style: '... bright gaiety and humour combined with ethereal seriousness. Like the unusual world of *One Hundred Years of Solitude* (Gabriel García Márquez), the paintings hold together, as natural, the most outlandish realities. Bold naiveté of forms and colours, stories of mysteries and conflict, trouble and healing – with a difference: friendly, zany, readable, provoking the viewer to look again ... a wholesome pleasure in the grit of life.'

Benjamin's friendship with sculptor Gert Swart is grounded in their mutual struggle to discover what it means to make contemporary art as Christians in post-apartheid South Africa.

His work is represented in collections internationally. He is married and lives in Vereeniging, South Africa, and has two daughters and two granddaughters.

http://zakbenjaminartist.homestead.com/index.html

Gert Swart

Gert Swart was born in Durban, South Africa, where he qualified and worked as a public health inspector before studying fine art for two years at the Natal Technikon. He now resides in Pietermaritzburg, South Africa, and works as a sculptor. He is married to Istine Rodseth.

Gert's most important solo exhibition of this period was staged at the Tatham Art Gallery in 1997. This exhibition, titled 'Contemplation: A body of work by Gert Swart', expressed the redemption of an individual as a metamorphosis from the curse of death to the hope of resurrection and how this transition affects the individual's relationship to society, nature and God.

One of Swart's most significant commissions of the past decade was a monument erected on the battlefield at Isandlwana in 1999. Although the battle of Isandlwana is known for its stunning defeat of a colonial army by an unconventional army, only monuments to fallen British soldiers had been erected on it in the past. It was a privilege to be involved in redressing this injustice and a challenge to design a monument that honours the fallen Zulu warriors but does not glorify war.

Recently Gert was commissioned by the Evangelical Seminary of Southern Africa (ESSA) to make a cross that would reflect the violence and suffering experienced in Southern Africa, particularly in the province of KwaZulu – Natal, RSA. While being a stark depiction of the cross as a brutal means of execution, the ESSA Cross is primarily a powerful symbol of hope: of the saving grace of God.

Gert met Zak Benjamin at a Christian Arts Festival over a decade ago. He and Benjamin were among the founder members of the Christian Worldview Network initiated by Craig Bartholomew. They enjoy a rich friendship that is currently finding expression in the joint design of book covers for this series in collaboration with Craig. This design project is the fruit of Craig's concern for Christian artists and his friendship with Gert and Zak.

http://gertswartsculptor.homestead.com/index.html

Introduction and Preview

1

The Hermeneutical Dynamics of 'Reading Luke' as Interpretation, Reflection and Formation
Anthony C. Thiselton

Hermeneutics and Lukan Studies

Whatever the sometimes unexpected twists and turns in the modern history of its interpretation, Luke–Acts has become increasingly ripe for hermeneutical enquiry. A relatively predictable discussion of Luke's aims, theological concerns and status as a historian had been prevalent over the first half of the twentieth century, but this changed dramatically from around 1954, when Hans Conzelmann published his controversial but hugely influential *Die Mitte der Zeit: Studien zur Theologie des Lukas.*[1] Stephen Wilson admirably sums up the impact of this study upon Lukan studies. He writes: 'Before this, Luke was thought of as a sort of homely old Hellenist: doctor, author, friend of Paul. He was seen as a man of wide sympathies but no great theological depth.'[2] After this, 'Luke is a man with a theological axe to grind. He is pictured as one who has systematically manipulated and recast his sources down to the smallest detail, in order to squeeze them into his overall theological framework'.[3]

The era of 'Luke the Historian': Hermeneutical implications

In the nineteenth century, Schleiermacher had regarded Luke as no more than the compiler and arranger of documents. In the early twentieth century, some stressed Luke's standing as a reliable historian in opposition to the scepticism of H.S. Reimarus in the eighteenth century and D.F. Strauss in the nineteenth,

---

[1] Conzelman, *The Theology of St Luke.*
[2] Wilson, 'Eschatology', 330. A slightly edited version also appears in Wilson, *Gentiles*, 59 and 59–87.
[3] Wilson, 'Eschatology' and *Gentiles*, 59.

who had cast extreme doubt on such reliability. Adolf von Harnack came to view Luke as an early historian, revising his dating to before 70 C.E., but for Harnack this was part of a theological liberal agenda that viewed 'doctrine' as a Greek intrusion upon the simple teaching of the 'liberal' Jesus who was essentially a teacher, who (with Luke) had little or nothing to do with theology or proclamation. In hermeneutical terms, Luke conveyed flat didactic axioms about the love of God and the brotherhood of humankind.

With the development of source criticism, B.H. Streeter's theory about 'Proto-Luke' and Vincent Taylor's postulation of this and an 'L' source behind Luke's distinctive material formed part of an attempt to establish pre-Lukan apostolic traditions on which *Luke's reliability* could rest. This work had little significance for hermeneutics. Interests lay more in the origins and transmission of Luke's material than in theology or meaning.

Henry J. Cadbury's *The Making of Luke-Acts* (1927; 2nd edn, 1958) brought a new phase within the 'historical' approach.[4] On one side Cadbury writes, 'This is not … an apology or a commentary, least of all is it a work of edification.'[5] Luke's heroes, he observes, are 'the makers of history'.[6] This seems to suggest a supposedly value-neutral account of Luke as a collection of sources. However, Cadbury was one of the first to recognize that history in this context normally embodies what later writers will call a *narrative plot*. He declares, 'The vindication of Christ and the Christian movement is a pragmatic motive frequently visible especially in the Acts of the Apostles.'[7] Like most 'histories', Luke-Acts exhibits a coherent structure, not simply raw facts. Cadbury anticipates a plot-like structure: enemies are confounded, setbacks are reversed, God's justice is vindicated.[8] The more the movement is attacked, the more powerful it grows. Such is his sensitivity to literary structure that he considers it more important to acknowledge the 'reality, interest, and attention to the later stage of history which the making of Luke-Acts represents' than to construct hypotheses about sources.[9]

This phase is now germane to hermeneutics, including issues about narrative, history and theology. The five chapters that form Part II of this volume also address these themes. Narrative plot constitutes a powerful vehicle for identity-*formation*, both communal and individual, as Joel Green convincingly demonstrates. Yet how are we to *interpret* the clear concern for history and for historical sources to which the prologue of Luke (Lk. 1:1–4) transparently

---

[4] Cadbury, *Making*.
[5] Cadbury, *Making*, v.
[6] Cadbury, *Making*, 21.
[7] Cadbury, *Making*, 37.
[8] Cadbury, *Making*, 38.
[9] Cadbury, *Making*, 368.

refers? David Wenham is not alone in making much of the role of the pro-logue. Charles Talbert, Howard Marshall, Loveday Alexander and many others address this issue.[10] On the other hand, Scott Spencer is clearly con-cerned lest a 'historical' paradigm of interpretation robs Luke-Acts of its con-fessional and formational character as divine address.

In the second half of the twentieth century, many writers explicitly reject any pitting of 'history' against 'theology' or narrative. C.K. Barrett insists that *Luke would not have understood the distinction between 'historian' and 'preacher'.*[11] Howard Marshall urges that Luke's 'view of theology led him to write a his-tory'.[12] 'We shall fail to do justice to his work if we do not think of him as a historian', but he is nonetheless a theologian.[13] 'Proclamation' and 'narrative' may be *more but not less* than 'history'.[14] All of these modes may communicate *kerygma* that is *formative* for Christian identity. David Moessner detects in Luke-Acts a *narrative structure* that not only embodies 'plot', but also functions as a communicative act at various levels. He calls attention to a triple hermeneutic that involves authorial intent, the dynamics of the text itself and its effect upon readers. This triple model received careful discussion in the second volume of this Scripture and Hermeneutics series, *After Pentecost: Language and Biblical Interpretation.*[15] This model invites interpretation and reflection but also recog-nizes the *formative* power of texts in their context. We review Moessner's model below.

The era of Conzelmann and redaction criticism: Further hermeneutical implications

It is easy to move from traditional questions about what is distinctive to Luke to a distinctively Lukan 'point of view'. Conzelmann identified Luke's point of view as addressing the delay of the parousia in the second-generation church. He argued that Luke reshaped earlier concerns about eschatological immi-nence. In a later study Conzelmann relates this to the pastoral epistles: 'The world becomes a place where the church is at home, a notion which Paul sharply rejected.'[16] The alleged change in theological outlook is radical: 'He [Luke] does not merely want to complement but to replace his predecessors. He offers not a contribution to the tradition but *the* tradition.'[17]

---

[10] See, e.g., Alexander, *Preface*; Brown, 'Prologue'; and Marshall, *Luke*, 37–41.
[11] Barrett, *Luke*, esp. 40–46.
[12] Marshall, *Luke*, 52.
[13] Marshall, *Luke*, 52.
[14] Marshall, *Luke,* 51–52.
[15] Thiselton, '"Behind" and "In Front of" the Text'.
[16] Conzelmann, 'Luke's Place', 302–303.
[17] Conzelmann, 'Luke's Place', 305 (italics his).

Conzelmann, therefore, portrays Luke as a *creative theologian*, and Luke–Acts as formative for a transition in the very nature of the church. But this does not mean that Luke is now thought no longer to be a 'historian'. Ernst Käsemann had observed a year or so before the publication of Conzelmann's work, 'One does not write a history of the church if one daily expects the end of the world.'[18] Conzelmann did not entirely follow Käsemann's thesis that Luke belonged to 'the era of the beginnings of early Catholicism (*Frühkatholizismus*)'.[19] Nevertheless, he agreed that Acts presented the story of Jesus as 'something absolutely in the past ... mere history indeed ... the sacred past'.[20]

In spite of the wide initial acceptance of his main claims, many believed that Conzelmann had attempted to base a radical interpretation of Luke's concerns on a mere handful of dubious exegetical claims. Yet his work found acceptance on the part of those who already drove a wedge between Luke and Paul. Vielhauer wrote of Luke, 'His distance from Paul is just as clear as his nearness to the apologists.'[21] By 1960, the interpretation of Luke–Acts and Luke's place within the New Testament era had become a burning issue. In 1966 W.C. van Unnik made the celebrated comment that 'This part of the New Testament has become ... a storm centre.'[22]

Van Unnik posed some seminal questions that remain relevant today. (1) Has the delay of the parousia really wrought the 'havoc' alleged by Conzelmann, Haenchen, Martin Werner and others, who see it as a catalyst for a new conception of the Christian faith?[23] (2) What is the real meaning of salvation history (*Heilsgeschichte*)? 'I cannot see why "history of salvation" is such a bad thing. Is not Luke often measured by a one-sided conception of Paulinism?'[24] In *hermeneutical* terms, must we limit the hermeneutical dynamics of Paul to *existential address and challenge alone,* and those of Luke–Acts merely to *reflection upon the founding of a religion?* Are not *both* Luke and Paul concerned with the unfolding of God's purposes of salvation expressed in terms of a *narrative of events* anchored in God's created, public, world? Do not Luke and Paul both see creation and the world as *God's theatre of salvation?* Van Unnik also asks: (3) What is Luke's relation to the Old Testament? (4) What is the role of those called 'witnesses' in Luke–Acts? (5) Does not Luke *structure* his 'history' in certain ways? (6) Is not more work needed on Luke's relation to the era of 1 Clement and Justin?[25] These resonate with issues addressed in this volume.

[18] Käsemann, *Essays*, 28; from an oral lecture of 1953.
[19] Käsemann, *Essays*, 29.
[20] Käsemann, *Essays*, 29.
[21] Vielhauer, 'On the "Paulinism" of Acts', 37 (originally published in 1951).
[22] Van Unnik, 'Luke–Acts', 18.
[23] Van Unnik. 'Luke–Acts', 28; cf. Werner, *Christian Dogma*, esp. 31–119.
[24] Van Unnik, 'Luke–Acts', 28.
[25] Van Unnik, 'Luke–Acts', 29.

Luke presents no merely static portrait of history, salvation or the church, but draws his reader in to participate actively in a dynamic, onward-moving, structured narrative, as W.C. Robinson and several contributors to this volume argue convincingly. Luke-Acts exhibits, in Paul Ricœur's language, 'the dynamic of emplotment'. Luke does not seek to 'replace' Mark or pre-Lukan traditions but to offer a 're-figuration' of the narrative of God's saving acts in terms that 'speak' and draw his readers in as *participating actors* rather than spectators, in a narrative drama.[26] Configuration and re-figuration play a significant role in the narrative hermeneutics of Paul Ricœur and Joel Green.[27]

Ricœur observes, 'The composition of the plot is grounded in a pre-understanding of the world in action.'[28] *Plot* makes possible both the 'discordance' within extended time of memory, attention and hope, and at the same time the 'concordance' of a temporal logic brings integration and coherence for interpretation and understanding. 'Plot is ... a synthesis of the heterogeneous'.[29] But this 'concordance' does not detract from 'the constitutive dynamism of the narrative configuration.'[30]

The critique of Conzelmann may be extended. He has arbitrarily selected certain features in Luke as 'key texts', or key omissions, to which he has given disproportionate weight. These include Luke's omission of Mark 10:1 (Jesus' travel 'beyond Jordan'); Luke 12:35–48 ('my master delays'); and the most notorious example, Luke 16:16. Paul Minear observes, 'Rarely has a scholar placed so much weight on so dubious an interpretation of so difficult a logion.'[31] Charles Talbert offers a careful reappraisal of the slender exegesis on the basis of which Conzelmann's redactional conclusions rest.[32]

Our main concern relates to the *hermeneutical* impact of this for reading Luke. Charles Talbert again hits the nail on the head: 'Is it really true that the Jesus tradition in the third gospel does not have the character of personal address, so that it cannot throw the person himself [i.e., Luke's reader] into question ... demanding of him a decision?'[33] It is false to claim that while the Pauline Epistles engage readers in *formative* existential challenge, Luke merely

---

[26] Ricœur, *Time*, I, 53; cf. 5–87.

[27] The terms are explicit in Joel Green's chapter below, and later in the present chapter, but they are implicit in Green, *The Theology of the Gospel of Luke*, 16–31, esp. 23; cf. also Green, *The Gospel of Luke*, 1–20, and Ricœur, *Time*, I, throughout.

[28] Ricœur, *Time*, 54.

[29] Ricœur, *Time*, 66.

[30] Ricœur, *Time*, 66.

[31] Cited in Wilson, 'Lukan Eschatology', 334.

[32] Talbert, 'Redactional Quest'.

[33] Talbert, 'Redactional Quest', 203.

presents a tale about the past inviting *reflection without participation*. Paul also demands *reflection;* he appeals to reason alongside Scripture.[34] On the other hand, while Luke, too, demands *interpretation* and *reflection* at various levels, Luke-Acts draws readers into active participation in a narrative emplotment that effects individual and communal *formation*.

The post-Conzelmann era: Resonances with themes in hermeneutics also explored in this volume

The last twenty-five or thirty years have witnessed an increasing concern with literary theory, especially with narratology, together with a diversity of theological emphases and further debates about faith and history. There is also a degree of scepticism toward less disciplined excesses of redaction criticism, including that of Conzelmann, although many also recognize that Conzelmann's work served to call attention to certain relevant theological features in Luke, including certain continuities of traditions. Conzelmann's emphasis on the church in Luke-Acts has encouraged further work in ecclesiology. François Bovon observes, 'This is why Lucan studies have taken a new direction. The dissertations concerning the Eucharist, the ministries, the Church, etc., are multiplying. Salvation history, so vigorously defended by O. Cullmann in the peak of the storm, frightens less now.'[35]

U. Luck (1960)
Ulrich Luck explores first of all the role of the prologues in Luke's Gospel (Lk. 1:1–4, esp. v. 4). The terminology allows both a historical and kerygmatic dimension. As Bovon observes, Paul uses the Greek word κατηχέω, 'to let resound', or in the passive 'to find out', to denote Christian instruction.[36] Bovon infers from this wording, 'Luke is thus not only a historian but also an evangelist and witness.'[37] He brings together the *kerygmatic content* and *historical confirmation* of the Christian message.[38] This is relevant to moderating Scott Spencer's hermeneutical critique below of David Wenham. Luke seeks to *combine* an emphasis upon *kerygma* (Spencer) with a concern for *history* (Wenham).

---

[34] See the arguments of Stowers, 'Use and Abuse'; Bornkamm, *Christian Experience*, 29–46; and Thiselton, *First Corinthians*, 151–57; cf. also 13–17, 20–22, 46–52 and 1216–19.

[35] Bovon, *Luke the Theologian*, 11.

[36] Bovon, *Luke 1*, 24.

[37] Bovon, *Luke 1*, 24.

[38] Luck, 'Kerygma'.

W.C. Robinson (1962)

W.C. Robinson writes with concern that resonates closely with several, perhaps even many, of the chapters in this volume.[39] The German translation (1964) bears the subtitle *Ein Gespräch mit H. Conzelmann,* but the differences here are greater than the similarities. Robinson offers an incisive critique of Conzelmann where the latter overplays his hand, but the major significance of Robinson's study for hermeneutics (and thus for this volume) is his emphasis upon the *dynamic forward-movement* of the Luke-Acts narrative. Luke does not portray a merely static 'period of salvation' that simply waits for some distant end time. The promises of God empower and motivate this dynamic movement, in continuity with Old Testament expectations. In accordance with Isaiah 40:3, the coming of the kingdom or the visitation of God takes the form of 'the way of the Lord'. But for Luke this 'way' is announced to the Gentiles.[40]

This 'dynamic' dimension finds expression regularly in the chapters in this volume. More specifically, against Conzelmann's more static view of geography as symbolic domains, Robinson sees the journey to Jerusalem as a travel motif, and notably travel to non-Jewish areas serves as a missionary motif concerning work among the Gentiles.[41] The gospel gives prominence to a 'travel plan' appointed by God. The Father has set times or periods 'by his own authority' (Acts 1:7). Luke's geography concerns a journey in terms of a *temporal* rather than merely spatial dimension, and follows the plan and purpose of God.

In hermeneutical terms this has affinities with the 'missional' hermeneutic explored by Michael W. Goheen with reference to David Bosch's proposal, as well as some points of contact with the arguments of Scott Hahn. Most especially, it anticipates many affinities with Charles Scobie's chapter on the journey motif as a hermeneutical key to Luke-Acts. We shall explore these points of contact further when we consider these chapters in more detail below. F. Bovon puts forward three criticisms of Robinson's thesis, including the argument that the citation of Isaiah 40:3 (LXX) is too fragile a foundation for the weight that Robinson places upon it.[42] However, this does not detract from the dynamic dimension and emphasis on mission that shape reading Luke-Acts, as Goheen and Scobie seek to demonstrate.

Helmut Flender (1965; ET 1967)

Helmut Flender examines the continuity between Israel and the church in Luke-Acts, and seeks to give due weight both to the uniqueness of Christ and

---

[39] Robinson, *Der Weg des Herrn,* also, *The Way of the Lord.* See further, Robinson, 'Theological Context'.

[40] Robinson, *The Way of the Lord,* 36–39.

[41] Robinson, *The Way of the Lord,* 34.

[42] Bovon, *Luke the Theologian,* 37–38.

salvation in the proclamation of the church. 'Luke ... discovers a *via media* between the gnostic denial and the early catholic canonization of history. His solution is to give simultaneous expression to the supernatural mystery and the earthly visibility of Christ and his history.'[43] He retains certain affinities with Conzelmann, for example, the view that Luke cannot 'reproduce' the theology of the apostolic age.[44] Nevertheless, Flender sees history in Luke as dynamic and ongoing, and his approach concerns 'the history of the world' as 'the new world of God which Christ brought', a world 'open for the action of God'.[45]

Luke's theology reveals a subtle dialectic between the gospel of Christ and an affirmation of the world as the public domain in which the Christian message 'penetrates the social structure of the old world'. Here Flender views the Lukan writings as *'unusually fruitful for the problem of hermeneutics'*.[46] Against Conzelmann, Luke's theology does not become 'crystallized, and salvation objectified'.[47] Luke planned his gospel on more 'levels' than most readers recognize. Christ is both the proclaimer and the proclaimed.[48]

Jacob Jervell (1972)
Jacob Jervell explores the missionary call to reach the Gentiles, but he disengages this from any notion of turning away from the Jews.[49] The Christian church is *not* the *'new'* Israel, but *takes its place as part of the true Israel.* Acts 1–5 makes this clear. Jervell rejects Conzelmann's notion that Acts 1–5 reflects an idealized and unrepeatable past period of the church. Addressing what Michael Goheen (see below) calls 'missional' issues, he asks, 'Why does the church carry on the Gentile mission?'[50] In sum, 'The conversion of the Gentiles is itself a fulfilment of the promises to Israel, so that the apostolic mission to Jews turns out indirectly to be the Gentile mission ... In ... Jewish Christians the unity and continuity of salvation history were evident.'[51] Although Goheen develops his own 'missional' hermeneutic in Luke in distinctive ways, the role of the 'metanarrative' of the Old Testament and divine promise shares certain themes and agenda with Jervell.

---

[43] Flender, *St. Luke*, 167.
[44] Flender, *St. Luke*, 163.
[45] Flender, *St. Luke*, 164–65.
[46] Flender, *St. Luke*, 2 and 165 (italics mine); cf. further 8–35.
[47] Flender, *St. Luke*, 3.
[48] Flender, *St. Luke*, 164; see also 36–89; cf. 90–162.
[49] Jervell, *People of God*.
[50] Jervell, *People of God*, 41.
[51] Jervell, *People of God*, 68.

I. Howard Marshall (1970, 1978)

Howard Marshall has often been categorized as re-establishing the 'history' approach discussed in our first section.[52] However, this is only partly the case. The genius of his work of 1970 is well summed up in the title *Luke: Historian and Theologian*. Marshall explicitly rejects any relation of mutual exclusion 'History *or* Theology', arguing that intelligent historiography is never merely the throwing together of raw, bare, 'facts', isolated from *interpretation*.[53] Without 'facts' or 'events' there is nothing to interpret (other than a world of sheer social construction); without 'interpretation' raw facts remain devoid of meaning and order. Luke, however, explicitly aims to present an account that is both 'accurate' (ἀκριβῶς) and 'ordered' (καθεξῆς).[54]

The central body of this study expounds Luke's 'Theology of Salvation' while offering critiques of Käsemann, Conzelmann and Haenchen on Luke-Acts.[55] Marshall provides a balanced account of the place of eschatology in Luke.[56] Since he contributes a chapter to the present volume, we need not develop this further. The importance of this work for this volume as a whole is his relation to respective claims of Wenham and Spencer. Spencer offers a critique that some might take to imply that Wenham's concern is with history in the 'neutral observer' sense of the term that Marshall repudiates – both in *Luke: Historian and Theologian* and in his commentary (1978).

Charles H. Talbert (1974, 1978, 1983–84)

Charles Talbert places Luke in the literary and socio-historical setting of the Mediterranean world. His major hermeneutical agenda is to ask how Luke would be heard, read, interpreted and understood by a hearer or reader in the first-century world of Greco-Roman society.[57] In an earlier work (1966) Talbert had argued that Luke's emphasis upon the public world and public tradition embodied a defence against gnostic appeals to 'secret' traditions.[58] Luke is anti-docetic. He emphasizes the public testimony of eyewitnesses, and he is concerned with apostolic tradition and the right interpretation of the Old Testament (cf. Lk. 24:32–48).

In his more recent work Talbert stresses the dual role of Luke as *both theological writer and literary artist*. The structural organization of his narrative exhibits literary 'architecture', often a binary and symmetrical architectural

---

[52] Marshall, *Luke* and *Gospel of Luke*.

[53] Marshall, *Luke*, 21–52.

[54] Marshall, *Luke*, 39–40.

[55] Marshall, *Luke*, 77–115.

[56] Marshall, *Luke*, 128–36.

[57] Talbert, *Perspective*; *Literary Patterns*; and *Luke-Acts*.

[58] Talbert, *Gnostics*.

scheme. Thus in Acts we find symmetry between Acts 1–12 and Acts 13–18, while in Luke's Gospel Luke 9:1–48 offers an aesthetic or symmetrical balance to Luke 22:7–23. *Chiastic* balance in binary forms and antithetical parallelism play a role. Talbert insists, however, that this architectural structure characterizes no less the literary production of Roman and Hellenistic authors. In Roman contexts he cites Virgil's *Aeneid*. Talbert also finds parallels with his concerns about traditions and succession. Luke-Acts confirms the legitimacy of a 'succession' of elders who follow Paul as leaders. He finds a parallel with Diogenes Laërtius, *The Lives, Teaching and Sayings of Famous Philosophers,* which takes up an earlier proposal suggested by Hans von Soden. The dedication to 'Theophilus' features in this context.

Talbert's general approach found favour in the research-discussions of the Luke-Acts Group of the Society of Biblical Literature in the late 1970s and early 1980s. Also, in general terms the points of departure in David Moessner's chapter in the present volume share much with Talbert's starting points. Moessner begins his chapter by appealing to the phenomenon of ancient narrative performance as reflected in Aristotle's *Poetics* and practised in the Hellenistic period in the *Literary Treatises* of Dionysius of Halicarnassus and Lucian of Samosata's *How to Write History*. He moves on to Polybius and to Diodorus of Sicily to explore their narrative devices with a view to comparing Luke as a composer of Hellenistic narrative poetics. Such an approach has clear implications for hermeneutics. Paul Ricœur, again, has demonstrated this in his magisterial three-volume *Time and Narrative*, of which the second chapter, as we have noted, explores Aristotle's *Poetics*.[59] In his *Lord of the Banquet,* Moessner approaches Luke's narrative composition on a broader base with reference to Deuteronomic traditions in the Old Testament, as we shall note when we come to consider this work briefly, below.[60]

More recent works relevant to this volume: Literary narrative theory (with a postscript on 'social world')

For reasons of space we cannot offer a survey even of all major recent Lukan studies as such, but we will continue to restrict our attention to those studies that are most relevant to hermeneutics and to the chapters in this volume.

Robert C. Tannehill (1986)
Robert Tannehill approaches Luke's Gospel as a literary and theological text that exhibits narrative unity.[61] Luke-Acts, he argues, is the work of a single

[59] Ricœur, *Time,* I, 31–51.
[60] Moessner, *Lord of the Banquet,* 45–284.
[61] Tannehill, *Narrative Unity,* I.

author who offers a coherent theological perspective, namely, that of the *controlling purpose of God*. Anticipating several chapters in this volume he views Luke-Acts as a unified narrative plan within which smaller scenes and particular characters serve. Mission, ministry and salvation belong together as a part of this coherent narrative. The emphasis is textual, literary and internal, rather than providing a 'source' or window through which to perceive external events.

This approach invites hermeneutical dynamics of interpretation and formation that cohere with those of chapters in this volume. In addition to clear affinities with Goheen and Hahn, Charles Scobie shares with Tannehill the hermeneutical principle that *only within their broader and wider hermeneutical horizon* do certain elements or literary components make full sense. Stephen Wright also underlines this with reference to the axiom of the hermeneutical circle in Schleiermacher.

D.B. Gowler (1991)

D.B. Gowler selects one particular aspect of narrative theory in his study *Host, Guest, Enemy and Friend*. This work originated as a doctoral dissertation supervised by Alan Culpepper, whose *Anatomy of the Fourth Gospel: A Study in Literary Design* (1983) also draws heavily upon literary theory. Gowler explores Luke's presentation of the Pharisees largely through the narrative category of *characterization*. Therefore it stands further from the main interests in the present volume than Tannehill, but shares with it a common utilization of literary theory. Here and there John Nolland also engages with characterization in his chapter on the parables, although not with explicit reference to Gowler.

In *New Horizons in Hermeneutics* I have surveyed the impact of narrative theory in hermeneutics.[62] In the context of biblical interpretation I traced this against the background of such writers as Vladimir Propp, Alexander Greimas, Gérard Genette, Tzvetan Todorov, Seymour Chatman, Roland Barthes and Paul Ricœur. Among biblical scholars, a very early study is Edwin M. Good's work on Jonah as a narrative satire (1965), and narrative perspectives reached a classic form in Robert Alter's *The Art of Biblical Narrative* (1981). One writer who specifically included biblical work on characterization is Wesley Kort (1975, 1988) who, like Ricœur, approaches this material within a temporal framework.[63]

David P. Moessner (1989)

David P. Moessner provided a milestone study with his *Lord of the Banquet: The Literary and Theological Significance of the Lukan Travel Narrative*. Here he takes the Deuteronomic traditions of the Old Testament as a point of departure,

---

[62] Thiselton, *New Horizons*, 471–514

[63] Kort, *Narrative Elements*; and *Story, Text and Scripture*.

rather than, as in his chapter in this volume, placing more emphasis on Hellenistic historiography. In his Foreword to the 1998 reprint, Richard Hays underlines the importance of this work, citing the verdicts of two Lukan specialists. Luke Timothy Johnson regards Moessner's work as 'the point of departure for any further discussion', while Robert Sloan declares that this 'creative proposal has offered Lukan scholarship a new way forward'.[64] Hays observes that Moessner offers readers a thoroughgoing exercise in comparative criticism, in which he reads Luke's Gospel as a unified narrative. 'At the same time Moessner's method, unlike some literary approaches, never abandoned historical questions.'[65] This makes Moessner's contribution to the present volume all the more valuable in two respects: it both demonstrates the value of narrative theory for hermeneutics in this volume, and it sheds further light on Spencer's critique of Wenham in Part II.

Perhaps predictably in view of his particular concern with the framework of the Old Testament for understanding, Hays also commends Moessner's utilization of the Deuteronomic view of Israel's prophetic history as a pattern of narrative performance attested in Second Temple Judaism. We can hardly exaggerate the importance of this as a way of understanding and actualizing the reader's role as a *participant in the action of the narrative history of Israel and the church.* This perspective plays an increasingly prominent role in N.T. Wright's hermeneutics of the Pauline Epistles.[66] We may note that Stephen Moore expresses reservations over James Dawsey's *The Lukan Voice* (1986) precisely because Dawsey fails to take account of *the temporal flow of narrative plot* that Tannehill, Moessner, Green and others underline.[67] Narrative approaches to the four gospels are too numerous to cite here.[68]

Luke Timothy Johnson (1977, 1991)

In his earlier work, *The Literary Function of Possessions in Luke-Acts*, Johnson argued that Luke transposed other modes of discourse, including the prophetic, into a literary method.[69] He places 'prophetic statements' at key junctures in the narrative to indicate a particular dynamic and narrative structure. 'The general category ... is that of story.'[70] His major conclusion coheres with

---

[64] Hays 'Foreword', in *Lord of the Banquet*, xi.

[65] Hays 'Foreword', xii.

[66] Most recently in Tom Wright's lectures, 'Paul for a New Millennium: Creation and Covenant', delivered as the *Firth Lectures* in the University of Nottingham, 2–3 March 2005, to be published in due course as part of a longer work.

[67] Dawsey, *The Lukan Voice*; cf. Moore, *Literary Criticism*, xviii.

[68] See, e.g., Powell, *Narrative Criticism?*; Kelber, *Mark's Story*; Grant, *Reading*; and Thiselton, *New Horizons*, 471–555.

[69] Johnson, *Literary Function*, 15.

[70] Johnson, *Literary Function*, 21.

that of Tannehill, Moessner, Stephen Wright and other contributors to this
volume in one particular respect: 'To understand the past, we must have some
grasp of the whole.'[71]

In his more recent commentary Johnson continues to underline the role of
'narrative' (*diegesis*, Lk. 1:1), and the unfolding of a narrative structure or narrative 'in sequence' (*kathexes*, Lk. 1:3). From his use of this last term elsewhere it
appears that Luke considers that the narration of events 'in order' has a distinctively *convincing* quality (see, e.g., Acts 9:27; 11:4; 15:12–14). 'The development of the plot itself has a persuasive force ... *Narratio* ("narration") is critical
to historical argument or personal defence ... (Acts 22:3–21; 24:10–21; 26:2–
23).'[72] 'We must seek Luke's meaning through the movement of the story', and
it is of critical importance *where* an episode comes in this *temporal sequence*.[73] As
we have already noted, Paul Ricœur among others expounds the profound significance of this for *hermeneutics*, where what is at issue is the *'temporal logic'* of
emplotment. Luke's 'sustained and sequential narrative' becomes *formative* in its
actualization.[74]

Joel B. Green (1995, 1997)
Since Joel Green has provided the next chapter of this collection, largely on
how Luke presents his material in terms of 'his narrative representation of
history', it is unnecessary to do more than note the directions of his contributions to recent Lukan studies. In his 1993 (1995) study he observes, 'The third
gospel presents its message in the form of a *narrative*. Its mode of persuasion is
perhaps more subtle (i.e., than didactic material) but no less *theological*.'[75] Following the basic axioms of narrative theory, Green attributes to Luke not a mere
'copying' of external reality, but a *configured, interpreted, reality*. In terms of Nicholas Wolterstorff's philosophy of art and speech acts, we might say that Luke *projects* a 'world' *into* which readers are drawn to enter, and *within* which they are
addressed and re-formed.[76] Luke *actualizes* his projected 'world' *formatively*.

Green also commences the introduction to his commentary by presenting
'The Gospel of Luke' as 'Narrative' (διήγησις). Luke himself categorizes his
work as 'narrative', and thereby invites *a mode of reading appropriate to narrative*.[77]

[71] Johnson, *Literary Function*, 220.
[72] Johnson, *Gospel*, 4.
[73] Johnson, *Gospel*, 4.
[74] Johnson, *Gospel*, 5–10. Like Moessner and Talbert, Johnson also appeals to parallels
in Hellenistic historiography.
[75] Green, *Theology*, 3.
[76] See Green, *Theology*, 4–6. Cf. Wolterstorff, *Works and Worlds*, esp. 222–31, and *Art
in Action*, esp. 122–55. On 'worldhood' in Heidegger see Heidegger, *Being and
Time*, 73–128; *Poetry*; and Thiselton, *Two Horizons*, 154–61 and 335–42.
[77] Green, *Gospel*, 1–4.

This opens up a reservoir of hermeneutical resources. We may recall Paul
Ricœur's work on temporal anticipation, memory and attention; on configuration and re-configuration. With this we may compare 'worldhood' in
Heidegger, Gadamer and Ricœur, and their notions of projected worlds in art
or in narrative. This leads on to the work of literary theorists on narrative time,
in which Gérard Genette (with Paul Ricœur, Seymour Chatman and others)
explores the temporal devices of order or sequence; duration, speed and
tempo; periodicity and frequency; flashbacks and premature disclosures;
devices to facilitate movement, direction, suspense, surprise, imagination and
reader-engagement; the projection of symbolic universes; the unfolding of
communal and individual identity; and dimensions of responsibility and
agency, often as comedy or tragedy.[78] All of these resources become acutely
relevant for the hermeneutical dynamics of reading narrative. In Green's commentary many of these remain implicit rather than explicit, but his emphasis
upon participatory involvement in the forward-moving momentum of narrative and narrative theology often presupposes them.

Three specific features mark Green's approach. First, like Tannehill and
Moessner, he emphasizes the *continuity and unity of Luke-Acts as an overarching
frame* within which specific episodes or texts are to be integrated.[79] Second,
Green opposes narrative *neither against 'history' nor against 'theology'*.[80] Narrative
is theology in Luke, but it is not an abstract system of timeless propositions.
This emerges strongly in his chapter below, on which we comment further.
Third, the intertextual relations and intratextual relations between Luke's narrative and other biblical and canonical material in the Old and New Testaments
must be taken seriously in the process of interpretation.[81] Many of Green's concerns find expression elsewhere also in this volume.

Postscript on 'social world' approaches to Luke
Since hermeneutics pays careful attention to *context* at every level, we cannot
leave this brief assessment of recent Lukan studies without noting the impact of
approaches from the standpoint of sociology and the 'social world'. We select
two studies worthy of particular note as samples.

- *Philip F. Esler* (1987) pays particular attention to social and political influences in Luke's theology.[82] These include issues about Jews and Gentiles
  in Luke's community; questions about table fellowship; the situations and
  economic status of poor and rich; and not least Luke's perceptions of, and

---

[78] See discussions in Thiselton, *New Horizons*, esp. 479–94; and in *The Promise of Hermeneutics*, 183–200.
[79] Green, *Gospel*, 6–10.
[80] Green, *Gospel*, 21–25.
[81] Green, *Gospel*, 11–20.
[82] Esler, *Community and Gospel in Luke-Acts*.

attitudes towards, Rome and imperial power. Although earlier writers had considered these areas, Esler draws upon a wealth of more recent historical and archaeological knowledge and social research and relates his conclusions more closely to an understanding of Luke's community and his theology.

- *J.H. Neyrey* (1991) edited a volume of essays on the social world of Luke-Acts which examines the social structure and conventions of the society of Luke's day with a view to interpreting their meaning. J.H. Neyrey and Bruce Malina explore honour and shame in relation to human personality (including social categorization and deviance); J.H. Elliott examines temple as against household; J.P. Pilch considers sickness and healing; and Neyrey, again, discusses meals and table fellowship. The thirteen essays also consider other topics of this kind.

These topics may not feature as prominently in this present volume as other literary and hermeneutical issues do, but they serve to remind us of a dimension of *contextual* enquiry that remains essential to hermeneutics. However, issues relating to context in the extra-linguistic world have received particular attention in earlier volumes in the Scripture and Hermeneutics series, notably in volume 4, *'Behind' the Text: History and Biblical Interpretation*.[83]

History, Narrative and Theology

Volume 4 of the Scripture and Hermeneutics series, to which we have just alluded, shares many of the concerns that emerge from within the four chapters that together constitute Part II of this volume. Many of the chapters in that volume, including those by Craig Bartholomew as a biblical specialist and by Alvin Plantinga as a philosopher of epistemology and logic, rightly distinguish between varieties of historical biblical criticism.[84] Yet while most participants in the Scripture and Hermeneutics project recognize the value of constructive historical enquiry, all within this project recognize that historical enquiry alone is not enough for genuine *understanding (Verstehen)* of the text in the fullest sense.

Christian theists seek transforming engagement with the active word of God. To this end we not only seek to *listen* to the biblical text with openness and expectancy, but we also seek to understand at ever deeper levels what it is *to interpret* Scripture, to *reflect* both upon Scripture and on our own processes of engaging with it, and to be *transformed* by the *formative* impact of Scripture in thought, life and identity.

---

[83] Bartholomew et al., *'Behind' the Text*.

[84] Bartholomew et al., *'Behind' the Text*, 1–16, 19–57, and elsewhere in that volume.

Volume 4 began to ask what 'more' is needed beside and beyond historical enquiry. The four chapters that constitute Part II of the present volume wrestle further with this issue. In particular, Chapter 2 (by Joel Green) and Chapter 5 (by David Moessner) explore *narrative*, both as narrative theology and narrative performance, as a textual vehicle and resource characteristic of, and integral to, Luke's communication of the gospel message and the theology of Luke-Acts. Chapters 3 and 4 (by Wenham and Spencer, respectively) pursue a particular debate about the status of historical enquiry as part of the task of interpreting, hearing and understanding the text of Luke-Acts, not least as divine address.

Joel Green, 'learning theological interpretation from Luke'

Joel Green is rightly concerned to underline the role and significance of Luke's narrative as *theology*. Luke seeks 'to reform the theological imagination' of his target audience, or 'model readers'. In this process 'the historiographical and theological tasks are indistinguishable'. The hermeneutical task can be assimilated and monopolized, however, at one end of the spectrum by *'hyper-concern with historical validation'*; while at the other end of the spectrum others seek to imperialize biblical interpretation under the flag of *'theological claims with reference to propositional statements'*.[85] This unacceptable division was inherited from the eighteenth and nineteenth centuries.

To my mind, the undue dominance of this disastrous polarization owes a great deal to a particular piece of history, which is insufficiently taken into account. The attitudes of both nineteenth-century conservatives and their nineteenth-century liberal counterparts owed more than was healthy to their two respective flag-bearers Charles Hodge and Horace Bushnell. Horace Bushnell (1802–76) was highly sensitive to the *literary* and *metaphorical* dimensions of biblical language.[86] He admired the emphasis of Samuel Taylor Coleridge on creative imagination, and he associated 'religion' with poetry, metaphor and symbol. Revelation fires the imagination rather than simply conveying information. By contrast, Charles Hodge declares, 'The Bible is to the theologian what nature is to the man of science. It is his storehouse of facts.'[87] Theology concerns 'facts' rather than ideas. William Baird cites a quotation from Hodge: 'I am not afraid to say that a new idea never originated in the Seminary.'[88]

---

[85]   Green, 'Learning Theological Interpretation from Luke', 56, 561 (italics mine).
[86]   Cf. Bushnell Chency, *Life and Letters of Horace Bushnell*, and Adamson, *Bushnell Rediscovered*.
[87]   Cited by Baird, *History*, II, from Hodge, *Life*.
[88]   Cited by Baird, *History*, II, from Hodge, *Life*, and 521.

'This Seminary', of course, was conservative Princeton from 1840 to 1872, while Bushnell presided over Yale as the home at that time of liberal theology. To understand how and why Hodge got away with such an astonishing (to twenty-first-century ears) view of the Bible and theology, it is necessary to recall just *how* 'liberal' Bushnell was, and on what basis he claimed a biblical foundation for his liberalism. Bushnell expounded an exclusively exemplarist or 'moral influence' theology of the cross. He opposed the interpretation of the atonement as a sacrifice understood in the sense of the Old Testament sacrificial system, and he did so on the basis of the biblical use of *metaphor*. Christ is a sacrifice, he urged, in much the same metaphorical sense as Christ is a Lamb. Christ was not offered on any altar. Hebrews 9:22 exasperated Bushnell's patience, as a harsh and unloving demand for satisfaction through bloodshed.

It is entirely understandable that conservatives of the day attributed the roots of such liberal theology in general to a *metaphorical, literary, poetic, or 'non-literal' reading of biblical texts*, in opposition to viewing it as quarry from which to mine 'scientific' *facts*. The nineteenth century was the era of scientific advances. Facts and logical deduction seemed to offer a certainty compared with which Romanticist notions of 'literature' seemed like dilettante distractions. Indeed, one of the two greatest exponents of hermeneutical theory in the twentieth century, Hans-Georg Gadamer, looked back to such a bias in his father's expectations of him in his youth: 'My father was a researcher in the natural sciences … He was quite disappointed … that I liked those "chattering professors" (*Schwätzprofessoren)*' who taught literature, philosophy and hermeneutics.[89]

How can anyone rationally and responsibly regard the Bible as what Umberto Eco and Jurij Lotman would call 'an engineering handbook'? If it is *that*, all language becomes merely informational and didactic or instructional. Then what becomes of the Psalms, of Job, of other Wisdom literature, or of the parables?

Furthermore, the world of the biological sciences, genetics and sub-atomic physics has moved far beyond the nineteenth-century notion of the world of science as a closed system of observable 'facts' linked by a simple causal chain. Geneticists, physicists and life scientists find themselves increasingly resorting to the use of models and metaphors to try to explain what cannot readily be contained within flat cognitive 'propositions'.[90] After Einstein, Heisenberg and others, the *temporal* dimension of space-time reality becomes inseparable from the states of affairs that invite enquiry. One of my former research candidates, Janet Martin Soskice, has demonstrated the capacity of metaphor to convey

---

[89] Gadamer, 'Reflections', 3.
[90] See Polkinghorne, *Faith, Science and Understanding*; *The Way the World Is*; *Quarks, Chaos, and Christianity*; and also Peacock, *Creation and the World of Science*.

cognitive truth whether in religion or in the context of the philosophy of science.[91]

We cannot dispense with a full and unqualified recognition of the multi-layered texture of biblical texts. Indeed, in our second volume in the Scripture and Hermeneutics series this emerges in our work on *Language and Biblical Interpretation*.[92] Joel Green has performed an indispensable service for hermeneutics in encouraging us *to read Luke as a work of narrative structure and narrative depth*, which draws us in as *participants* in the unfolding story of God's providential purposes and actions in Jesus Christ for the salvation of the world, and as that which not only invites *interpretation* and *reflection* appropriate to this communicative medium, but also powerfully *actualizes the formation* of Christian identity and character.

In *New Horizons in Hermeneutics*, as I have noted above, I traced the impact of such writers as Seymour Chatman and Gérard Genette in our understanding of narrative. In particular, they identify the creative role of a restructuring and reconfiguration of narrative time.[93] In *The Promise of Hermeneutics* I compared the use of these techniques in fictional literature with the *fictive* power of such reconfiguration in biblical writings.[94] However, the most striking exposition of the *formative* power of narrative comes from Paul Ricœur, who together with Gadamer stands as the most creative and imaginative writer on hermeneutics over the second half of the twentieth century. Much of what he says gives added point and added power to the arguments of Joel Green.

Ricœur throughout his long career of writing emphasized the *creative* functions of texts, metaphors, symbols and narrative. Unlike mere 'reports' of past '*facts*', symbol, metaphor and narrative project *possibilities*. Thereby they provoke and stimulate *reflections*. 'The symbol *gives rise* to thought.'[95]

Ricœur's concept of *possibility* owes much to his early study of Heidegger during his confinement as a prisoner of war in the 1940s. Heidegger viewed 'possibility' as a primordial *existentiale* 'in which *Dasein* is characterized *ontologically*'.[96] In this context, interpretation and understanding consist not in 'seeing actual objects or situations as much as seeing their *possible* uses, *possible* contexts ... [their] "potentiality-for-Being" ... Interpretation is grounded in something

[91] Soskice, *Metaphor and Religious Language*.

[92] Bartholomew et al., *After Pentecost*, throughout, but not least 80–72 (D.R. Stiver); 73–90 (N. Wolterstorff); 97–120 (A.C. Thiselton); 131–70 (C.G. Bartholomew); 224–40 (S. Wright); 241–62 (B.D. Ingraffia and T.E. Pickett); and 387–402 (I. Paul).

[93] Thiselton, *New Horizons*, 354–68; 478–86; and 566–73.

[94] Thiselton, with Walhout and Lundin, *Promise of Hermeneutics*, 172–200 and throughout.

[95] Ricœur, *Conflict*, 288 (italics mine); cf. 287–354.

[96] Heidegger, *Being and Time*, 183.

we have in advance – in a *fore-having* (*Vorhabe*).'[97] In other words, creative interpretation and understanding occurs within a framework of *temporality* as the precondition for *time*.

Ricœur explores two further concerns that contribute to this creativity, especially in relation to metaphor and narrative. In his work *The Rule of Metaphor* he writes, 'Metaphor presents itself as a strategy of discourse that, while preserving and developing the creative powers of language, preserves and develops the *heuristic* power wielded by *fiction*.'[98] At the same time, metaphor 'says something about reality'.[99] It is more, but not less, than referential: it employs 'split reference' to two distinct 'worlds', seeing one through the lens of the other.[100] Metaphor is neither a mere ornament nor a mere illustration. Drawing upon the work of Max Black and other philosophers of language, Ricœur perceives its power as *interactive*: it brings two 'worlds' together, thereby projecting new possibilities of *interpretation, reflection* and *formative* understanding. Alluding to Aristotle*'s Poetics*, Ricœur perceives metaphor as *poiesis, making*, rather than merely an 'image' that *reflects*. This bears upon the notion of *fiction* or the *fictive* as 're-making' or 're-describing'. In *The Promise of Hermeneutics* I have explicitly explored the creative role of theological fiction.[101]

Narratives present possibilities of human (and/or divine) *action within the scheme of time.* Three key foci here are *temporality, plot* and *action*. In his *Time and Narrative* Ricœur declares, '*By means of the plot,* goals, causes, and chance are brought together *within the temporal unity of a whole and complete account*. It is this *synthesis of the heterogeneous* that brings narration close to metaphor.'[102]

In the first volume of *Time and Narrative* Ricœur draws from Aristotle the notion of the *temporal* logic of plot, where the movement is centripetal, towards the centre. However, side by side with this he draws from Augustine a centrifugal or 'discordant' dynamic derived from temporal separation and distance or 'distension'. This separates the past domain of memory, the present domain of attention, and the future domain of hope. 'The mind performs three functions, those of expectation … attention … and memory'.[103] On the other hand, within the temporal logic of emplotment 'the dialectic of expectations, memory and attention' no longer remains a series of isolated reflections but becomes creative and eventful 'in interaction with one another'.[104] All this

---

[97] Heidegger, *Being and Time*, 191.
[98] Ricœur, *Metaphor*, 6 (italics his).
[99] Ricœur, *Metaphor*, 6.
[100] Ricœur, *Metaphor*, 6.
[101] Thiselton, *Promise*, 172–83.
[102] Ricœur, *Time*, I, ix (italics mine).
[103] Ricœur, *Time*, I, 19.
[104] Ricœur, *Time*, I, 20.

constitutes 'the *poetic* act of *emplotment*'.[105] Ricœur repeats that narrative 'understanding (*Verstehen*) hangs on these three interactive aspects: 'making', 'coherence' and 'plot'.[106]

Ricœur has elucidated the linguistic and philosophical dynamics that empower and lie behind the claims that Joel Green puts forward for the distinctive effect of *narrative* as *formative* and as *formation theology*. The centripetal and centrifugal dynamics of emplotment within the narrative mode yield formative powers of 'making' that surpass those of mere 'flat' report alone, while at the same time retaining the power to convey 'reality'. Ricœur shows us the theoretical foundation, or 'engine', that powers the claims for narrative effects put forward by Joel Green in his chapter below.

'Narratology' is no mere fad of the period between the end of the twentieth century and the beginning of the twenty-first. An appreciation of the wholeness of narrative, together with its temporal character and the dynamics of emplotment, assist our *interpretation, reflection* and personal and communal *formation* in reading Luke. No less Luke's very way of re-presenting the events of the gospel, and of interweaving them with the overarching frame of the Old Testament and other intertextual material, portrays Luke himself as a model interpreter of theological truth. Richard Palmer, in his volume on philosophical hermeneutics, partly anticipates Joel Green's observations about Luke 24:25–27, 32, 45: Luke presents *both* Jesus as *interpreting* the Scriptures, and the Scriptures as *interpreting* Jesus.[107]

David Wenham on the purpose of Luke-Acts, and Scott Spencer's critical response

David Wenham advances the hermeneutical axiom 'history matters a great deal. Christians believe that God has spoken to us in history'.[108] This coheres fully with major traditions among exponents of hermeneutical theory. First, hermeneutics takes seriously the *contingent* particularities of persons, events and situations as against the claims of generalizing, abstract, ideas. Second, a consistent emphasis within a developing pedigree of hermeneutical thinkers may be traced from Hegel and Dilthey through to Gadamer and Pannenberg on history and historical understanding. Third, the attempt of Bultmann and the Bultmann school to revive the fruitless *either/or* of the 'history *versus* faith' debate which dominated New Testament debates in Christology from Lessing through Strauss and Kähler to Bultmann has proved to be sterile. Karl-Josef

---

[105] Ricœur, *Time*, I, 21–22 (italics mine).
[106] Ricœur, *Time,* I, 41.
[107] Palmer, *Hermeneutics*, 23–26.
[108] Wenham, 'Purpose of Luke-Acts', 79.

Kuschel describes these Lessing-to-Bultmann debates as 'Failed Conversations of Yesterday'.[109] Moreover, a considerable part of Volume 1 in the Scripture and Hermeneutics series, *Renewing Biblical Interpretation*, including Karl Möller's contribution 'Renewing Historical Criticism' and Colin Greene's '"In the Arms of the Angels": Biblical Interpretation, Christology, and Philosophy of History', urges the importance of 'both ... and ...', not either/or.[110]

Wenham convincingly shows that historical reconstruction plays an essential part in hermeneutics for interpreting and understanding, for example, the text of 1 Corinthians. But does this apply equally to Luke-Acts? Like many other writers before him, Wenham turns to Luke's prologue to shed light upon Luke's stated aims and concerns (Lk. 1:1–4), citing in particular the work of Loveday Alexander.[111] Further, Luke shows particular concern for what we might well call 'the public domain': the public manifestation of Christian discipleship and allegiance to Christ's lordship in living this out in terms of one's use of money and possessions; interpersonal relations in the public domain; the role of time and 'place' in the story of salvation; and citizenship and public conduct in relation to Rome. The hermeneutical aim here for Wenham is to try to ascertain whether our *interpretation* of Luke-Acts accords with Luke's *overall purpose*. With Kümmel, we may note, he finds a further clue to Luke's purpose in Acts 28:31, namely, that the expansion of the gospel proceeded to Rome 'without hindrance'. Kümmel also notes (with others in this volume) that Jesus' journey to Jerusalem finds a parallel in Paul's arrival 'without hindrance' in Rome.[112]

All of this traditionally constitutes an initial move in biblical hermeneutics, namely, that of seeking to interpret texts within appropriate historical contexts and in accord with the writer's purpose. Scott Spencer, however, questions whether this kind of approach constitutes a sufficient account of Luke-Acts as a *confessional* text. He criticizes the kind of approach to the text found in most 'New Testament Introductions' as directing our attention to the wrong thing. Hypotheses such as Wenham's about Luke's purpose constitute 'a *possible* and *interesting* theory', but pay too much attention to what is 'outside' the text.[113] 'Interesting', most would agree, is not good enough for readers who seek *engagement* with, and *transformation* by, the text.

Nevertheless, is all this as it seems? The founder of modern hermeneutical theory, Friedrich Schleiermacher, first initiated hermeneutics as an independent multi-disciplinary area of study in the context of a dual ministry *both* as professor of theology in the then newly-founded University of Berlin *and* as

---

[109] Kuschel, *Born*, 35; cf. 35–175.
[110] Bartholomew et al., *Renewing*, 145–71, 198–239, and throughout.
[111] Alexander, *Preface*.
[112] Kümmel, *Introduction*, 99
[113] Spencer, 'Preparing the Way of the Lord', 119 (italics his).

preacher and expositor Sunday by Sunday in Trinity Church. Thirty volumes of his writings include ten volumes on theology, ten on philosophy and ten on preaching. In spite of their huge theological differences, Karl Barth expresses his admiration for Schleiermacher as one who regarded preaching as his 'proper vocation'.[114] Barth writes: 'Preaching to the congregation to awaken faith was by far the sweetest desire of his life.'[115] Schleiermacher writes that preaching is not a matter of imposing 'thoughts' upon the congregation, but of 'striking up the music', 'moving' the hearers, and awaking 'the slumbering spark'.[116] But to this very end Schleiermacher insisted that any living, transforming interpretation of the New Testament must include the new (at that time) discipline of 'Introduction to the New Testament', since this places us '(by gathering historical knowledge) in the position of the original readers for whom the New Testament authors wrote ... These writings could not be properly understood in the future' without regard to how 'these first readers could understand them'.[117] This historical aspect remains part of preparing to hear the voice of the Holy Spirit.[118]

As Stephen Wright reminds us (below), Schleiermacher never suggested that this task was the be-all and end-all of interpretation. We need critical assessment and comparison, but equally the more 'feminine' quality of the 'divinatory'. He writes, 'The divinatory (*divinatorische*) method seeks to gain an "immediate" understanding ... Divinatory knowledge is the feminine strength in knowing people; comparative, the masculine.'[119] To 'divine' creatively in openness but *without the critical and comparative* is to court *the way of the 'nebulist'*. To remain in the 'masculine' world of critical study without divination, however, is to court *the way of the 'pedant'*.[120]

Further, to urge the importance of traditional questions about history, language, context and genre, is *not* thereby to imply that we should divide the hermeneutical task into that of *first* exploring 'what the text *meant*' and *then* exploring 'what the text *means*'. The essayists in this volume tend to disclaim this notion. Nicholas Lash convincingly criticizes the model as presupposing a naïve stage-by-stage 'relay-race' model of the hermeneutical task.[121] The tasks remain *inseparable*. The interpreter constantly moves from one to the other, and

---

[114] See Thiselton, 'Schleiermacher's Hermeneutics'. The verdicts from Barth come in *Protestant Theology*, 425–73; and in *Theology of Schleiermacher*.

[115] Barth, *Theology of Schleiermacher*, xviii.

[116] Schleiermacher, *On Religion*, 119–20.

[117] Schleiermacher, *Hermeneutics*, 38 and 107; cf. also 115.

[118] Schleiermacher, *Hermeneutics*, 107; cf. 108–15.

[119] Schleiermacher, *Hermeneutics*, 150 (German, *Werke*, IV [1967], 153).

[120] Schleiermacher, *Hermeneutics*, 205 (italics mine).

[121] Lash, *Theology*, 79; cf. his devastating criticism of the model in 38–46, 75–80, and throughout.

if there is a distinction of strategic purpose, historical and genre enquiries constitute a 'checking' process in relation to 'divinatory' insights. Without Wenham's
emphasis on history and context, the possibility of 'nebulism' becomes more
acute, since such a checking process would have been lost from view.

When Lessing postulated the 'broad ugly ditch' between faith and history,
those who sought to take a stand on one side or the other of Lessing's ditch
gained nothing. The *impasse* began to be softened in the direction of resolution
when Wolfhart Pannenberg and others explored more carefully how 'event'
and 'interpretation' were intertwined. As Volume 2 of the Scripture and Hermeneutics Series suggests, language is too multi-layered and multi-dimensional
to permit any such dualist scheme as that between, for example, 'the language
of description' and 'the language of confession'. Confession in the sense of nail-
ing one's colours to the mast and staking one's life on faith or truth usually
involves *both* 'belief *in*' and 'belief *that*'. Luke-Acts brings these closely
together. Otherwise it is difficult to see why Luke makes so much of his
research into '*sources*', his appeal to *eyewitness* and his presentation of *states of
affairs that have kerygmatic significance and narrative form*. Finally, Luke's emphasis
on the public domain goes hand in hand with a Christology that carries no hint
of Docetism. In the language of a different debate, Luke's anchorage in the
everyday world is 'incarnational'.

David P. Moessner on Luke as Hellenistic narrative embodying the narrative plot of divine purpose and the suffering Messiah

1. Moessner underlines the three dimensions of hermeneutics that we
explored in Volume 2 of the Scripture and Hermeneutics Series, under the
rubrics 'Behind the Text', 'In the Text' and 'In Front of the Text'.[122] However,
he also emphasizes that ancient writers were explicitly aware of writing in
terms of these three models. In Aristotle, Dionysius of Halicarnassus, Lucian of
Samosata and others, 'narrative–performance' (διήγησις) embraced: (i)
authorial intent or purpose; (ii) narrative structure (*poetics*); and (iii) audience-
impact (comprehension). Together with other writers in the Hellenistic tradition, notably Polybius and Diodorus Siculus, Luke–Acts reflects this explicit,
structured, hermeneutical approach as integral to its purpose, structure and
composition.

What is important for hermeneutical theory is the balanced and comprehensive understanding that Luke-Acts shares with other ancient writers in
terms of what we should nowadays call full communicative action.[123] The

---

[122] Bartholomew et al., *After Pentecost*, esp. 97–120 (Thiselton), 284–311 (Van
Leeuwen), and elsewhere.

[123] On the communicative act as a major hermeneutical concept see Thiselton,
'Communicative Action'.

church in Corinth, I have argued elsewhere, was all-too-aware, even obsessed, with audience-orientated, audience-pleasing, rhetoric, and wished that Paul would weight his preaching and communicative strategy wholly in this direction.[124] However, Paul, like Luke, employs a balanced model which accords due weight to all three dimensions. Stephen Pogoloff and John Moores are among a number of writers who expose the seriousness of a one-sided preoccupation with 'rhetoric' and 'audience' as implying and forming 'a major shift in world-view. This (in post-modern terms) post-positivist or anti-foundational world-view can lead us to reformulate interpretation itself as a *rhetorical* enterprise.'[125] Stanley Fish also allows that 'what is at stake is a difference in worldviews' – namely, between '*homo rhetoricus*', for whom rhetoric is *both* form *and* content, and '*homo seriosus*'.[126] The Corinthians wanted a gospel shaped by the wishes, interests, aspirations and expectations of the audience; Paul keeps a sensitive eye on the audience (1 Cor. 9:20–25), but he insists on the *givenness* of the gospel in the purpose of God. The proclamation of the cross is not merely a human social construct, whether or not the audience finds it 'foolishness' (1 Cor. 1:18); the purpose of its communication is 'salvation' (1:18).

Moessner's emphasis on Luke's use of this rounded triadic model, therefore, has huge consequences for the very nature of *interpretation*. What is interpreted is not simply 'a text'; not simply the situation 'behind' the text; not simply the expectations of the audience; but *comprehensive communicative action* explicitly owned as such by writers in the ancient world. Their explicit unfolding of this reveals the importance of self-conscious *reflection* on the nature of the task by authors (ancient and modern) and readers (ancient and modern). The transformative *effects* of engagement with such communicative action on the part of readers becomes *formative:* formative for understanding, for belief, for thought, for life and for action. In the case of Luke–Acts, this formation extends to the formation of Christian identity as those who 'follow' the Jesus of Luke-Acts. The hermeneutical dynamics are transparently those of *interpretation, reflection and formation*.

2. Moessner makes it clear that, as we observed in Joel Green's chapter, *narrative plot* plays a crucial role in shaping that into which *those who participate within the continuing narrative in the post-resurrection are formed*. There is no need to repeat here the powerful and convincing *dynamics* of this process unfolded at the hands of Ricœur. Ricœur's hermeneutics remains the most forceful and

---

[124] Thiselton, *First Corinthians*, 12–17, 41–52, 147–75, 204–13, 1103–105, and throughout.
[125] Pogoloff, *Logos and Sophia*, 8. See also Moores, *Wrestling*, 1–32 and 132–60.
[126] Fish, *Doing*, 483.

incisive exposition of how *narrative* within the *temporal logic of emplotment* yields *identity formation* and the 'making' (*poiesis*) of belief systems and action-in-life.

We observed above that Charles Talbert and the Luke-Acts Seminars of the Society of Biblical Literature (1979–83) placed Luke-Acts within the milieu of literary parallels in the Mediterranean world. Talbert, we noted, found parallels between literary patterns within Luke-Acts and the 'architecture' of several Greco-Roman authors. He makes particular appeal to parallels with Diogenes Laërtius, *The Lives, Teachings and Sayings of Famous Philosophers*. Luke's Gospel and Acts correspond respectively with a life of Jesus (the founder) and the acts and preaching of his followers who became the apostles. Moessner appeals to parallel patterns with Polybius, Diodorus Siculus and Dionysius of Halicarnassus.[127] This represents an extension and development from his more specific emphasis upon parallels between Luke-Acts and Deuteronomic traditions of 'journey' in his *Lord of the Banquet*.

Again this has considerable import for hermeneutics. For Moessner focuses on these parallels not for the sake of mere description and comparison, but to expose and identify the 'narrative organization as an "arrangement" (οἰκονομία) ... designed to lead [the] audience to the proper (sc., authorially intended!) understanding of the events which he [the author] recounts'.[128] This closely matches Ricœur's account of the formative effects achieved by the interactive dynamics of the 'discordant' direction of a coherent temporal plot. Yet these effects are not constructed or controlled by the audience. Rather, the *narrative itself,* together with *how the emplotment* of the narrative has been *designed, composed and presented*, gives rise to *interpretation, reflection and formation* on the part of readers.

3. Moessner traces the narrative framework and narrative plot of Luke-Acts in terms of 'God's plan', which brings about 'release of sins' through the rejection and suffering of Israel's Messiah. This coheres well with Luke's own explicit description of this work as 'ordered' (καθεξῆς): that is, 'pertinent to being in sequence in time, space, or logic, in order' (Lk. 1:3).[129] The narrative plot has a beginning (ἀρχή) and both an end and a purpose (τέλος). The *continuity* of narrative through 'discordance' of time and distinct events presents a *coherent* forward-moving *dynamic*. Moessner's essay shows in detail how these principles are instantiated in Luke-Acts.

This incisive chapter, which draws upon *both historical* research and extrabiblical 'sources' *and* narrative or *literary content*, also contributes to our theological understanding of Luke-Acts. Many writers have disparaged and

---

[127]   Moessner, 'Reading Luke's Gospel', 128–132.
[128]   Moessner, 'Reading Luke's Gospel', 128.
[129]   BDAG, 490 col. Ii.

underplayed the role of the atoning and suffering work of Christ in Luke-Acts in such a way as to add to the supposed disjunction between research into Acts and Paul. Here, however, convincing multi-disciplinary research into the interaction between narrative theory, the history of ancient literature, theology and hermeneutics, provides fresh resources for 'Reading Luke' theologically and at several levels of reading.

Language, Parables and Levels of Reading

Howard Marshall on political and eschatological language in Luke

With Wenham, Marshall sees Luke 'as a historian', not least in the light of his prologue, but as a historian who writes a continuing narrative in which readers are involved, and for whom choices of style and language have considerable significance. For example, the Septuagint style of the 'Song of Mary' (Lk. 1:46–55) places it theologically as an extension of the mighty acts of God in the Old Testament, with which it stands in narrative continuity.

Marshall pays particular attention to the functions and dynamics of *metaphor* as ways of expressing certain political and eschatological realities. 'Language used in the songs in Luke 1–2 is not to be taken literally but is metaphorical'.[130] The apocalyptic or eschatological language of Luke 17:22–37 is not 'a literal account of what is going to happen'.[131] The language indicates the *cosmic* significance and importance of the events concerned and of the gospel. Marshall is cautious about such a sweeping formula as 'Luke has "de-apocalypticized" the language' as if it retained no eschatological significance whatever, but equally, he suggests, to identify sketches of Luke's language as apocalyptic 'is not helpful'.[132] The book of Acts relativizes eschatology, but also places it in the context of mission as a window of opportunity for the gospel.

The dynamics of metaphor remain a crucial area for the task of *interpretation*. Marshall alludes to the work of George Caird in this respect. Caird argued with conviction that theories that assumed that Jesus was 'mistaken' concerning a supposed imminent end of the world were based on a failure to appreciate the role of metaphor in the eschatological discourses.[133] Here, as in Marshall's

[130] Marshall, 'Political and Eschatological Language in Luke', 161.
[131] Marshall, 'Political and Eschatological Language in Luke', 166.
[132] Marshall, 'Political and Eschatological Language in Luke', 175.
[133] Caird, *Language and Imagery*, esp. 242–71. This material was based on lectures on the language of the Bible delivered in Mansfield College, Oxford, some twelve years earlier, which I was privileged to attend. Caird conveyed very forcefully his sense of exasperation at the failure of many New Testament colleagues to reassess the notion

chapter, recognition that 'end of the world' *language may* not be used to describe an 'end of the world' *event* has significant consequences for both meaning and theology. This has been a recurring concern in the Scripture and Hermeneutics project. Several chapters in Volume 2, *After Pentecost* (2001), address the role of metaphor, including Ian Paul's 'Metaphor and Exegesis'.[134] Ian Paul rightly points out that Ricœur drew on Max Black's *interactive* theory of metaphor. Metaphor thereby becomes creative, rather than merely illustrative, allowing one thing to be perceived through the lens of another.

Eschatology in Luke-Acts, in this sense, becomes like a lens *through* which to perceive the cosmic significance of the coming and proclamation of salvation through the person and work of Christ rather than a telescope to view future events as such. Hence, like Luke's political language also, it invites responsible *interpretation*. Given due hermeneutical *reflection,* the dynamics of this vehicle of language enhance the *formative* effects of the narrative plot of Luke-Acts.

John Nolland on parables and their ethical teaching and Stephen Wright's response on hermeneutics

John Nolland's chapter reflects a tradition within New Testament studies that works largely, although not exclusively, at the 'micro' level of details and particularities. At one level this is appropriately 'hermeneutical', for hermeneutics above all takes account of particularities and does not operate primarily with the abstract and general. Hans-Georg Gadamer constantly resists preoccupations with 'abstraction', 'method' (i.e., of science or rationalism), and 'generality', which seek to package and to categorize 'the other' in terms of some prior system of predetermined concepts, rather than 'listening' to, and respecting, what transcends such prior categorization.[135] Such sciences as statistics, he writes, impose a 'methodological abstraction' that appears to produce, as it were, 'objective' facts, but has already placed a prior frame of interpretation around them in its very approach.[136]

Yet, in a different sense, Stephen Wright's chapter implies that of the two hermeneutical axes that were fundamental to Schleiermacher, namely: (i) the *'comparative', 'critical'* and *'masculine'* pole of *'knowing'*; and (ii) the *'divinatory'* (*divinatorische*), the first (rather than both equally) characterizes Nolland's

---

of Jesus' 'mistake' in the light of metaphor and semantics. N.T. Wright follows Caird in *The New Testament and the People of God*, 280–99, and in *Jesus and the Victory of God*, 320–68, as Marshall notes.

[134] Paul, 'Metaphor and Exegesis'.

[135] Gadamer, *Truth and Method*, 19–30, 64–70, 89–110 and esp. 265–379, cf. also Gadamer, 'Reflections', 3–57, and *Philosophical Hermeneutics*, 3–42.

[136] Gadamer, *Philosophical Hermeneutics*, 11.

approach. But this pole alone cannot rise from 'philology' to 'hermeneutics' without what Schleiermacher calls the 'feminine' dimension of *understanding (Verstehen)*.[137] *Erklärung* (explanation) and *Verstehen* (understanding) permeate hermeneutics as the two essential paradigmatic and complementary approaches from Schleiermacher, Dilthey and Droysen to Ricœur, Habermas and Apel. Indeed, Karl–Otto Apel produced a volume on hermeneutical enquiry under the explicit title *Understanding and Explanation*, and throughout it writes simply of the 'E – V' debate, namely, that of the respective roles of *Erklärung* and *Verstehen*. He traces this polarity through the social sciences, the *Geisteswissenschaften*, philosophy, Wittgenstein, G.H. von Wright and Habermas.[138]

The problem goes still deeper than this when the texts under consideration are *parables*. For the hermeneutical functions of the parables of Jesus transcend the merely didactic or cognitive, even if some contest this. It may be contested, for example, if we consider parables exclusively within their canonical context as Lukan literature that looks back to the past, and it may also be contested if we follow the tradition of scholarship found in Jülicher and in part also in Jeremias. Partly in reaction against earlier 'allegorical' interpretation, and partly because it accorded with his liberal theology that regarded Jesus as a *teacher of simple truths*, Adolf Jülicher portrayed parable as a simple 'simile' (*Vergleichung*) used to illustrate and to convey a general truth. Parables function *not as creative, enticing, seductive, metaphors* but as straightforward *didactic, cognitive* similes.[139]

Jülicher used the term *eigentliche Rede* to denote direct speech that was not only 'literal' but also authentic, and *uneigentliche Rede* to denote indirect speech that was not only metaphorical but also, in one sense, inauthentic. As simple similes, parables taught truths about God and about *ethics*. Thereby they retain none of the multi-level metaphorical or reconfiguring *formative* power that constitutes a powerful dynamic in the work of Joel Green and David Moessner. If parables were metaphorical, puzzling or multi-layered, Jülicher attributed them to editorial processes in the early church. Genuine parables from Jesus himself, he assumed, performed the simple hermeneutical function of didactic explanation (cf. *Erklärung* in hermeneutical theory).[140]

To be sure, J. Jeremias adopted a similarly 'reconstructive' approach to the parables. The parables were treated as 'sources' of didactic themes for a reconstruction of 'the teaching of Jesus'.[141] This is not illegitimate, but it has little

---

[137] See Schleiermacher, *Hermeneutics*, 150 [German, *Sämtlicher Werke*, IV, 153].

[138] Apel, *Understanding*, throughout.

[139] Jülicher, *Die Gleichnisreden Jesu*, esp. 1–148.

[140] For an exposition and critique of Jülicher, see Thiselton (with R. Lundin and C. Walhout), 'Parables'. Cf. also Thiselton, *Two Horizons*, 347–52.

[141] Jeremias, *Parables*.

direct bearing on the *hermeneutics* of the parables of Jesus in the sense of their capacity to transform, to subvert and to produce formative effects. Their main role is to invite *reflection* on an explicit comparison between a conceptual content (*Sachhälfte*) and an illustrative picture-part (*Bildhälfte*). By contrast, for C.H. Dodd parables *arrest* the hearer, sometimes by a contrastive 'strangeness', but 'leaving the mind in sufficient doubt about its precise application *to tease it* into *active* thought'.[142]

Robert Funk takes up and develops this point. Parables are often provocative metaphors, *not* simply similes. Their hermeneutical function is often to entice the hearer into a narrative world by some literary strategy of seduction, and then by an act of reversal, unexpectedly to reshape this 'world' by the invasion of a transcendent dimension, with the effect of *subverting* or *shattering* and then *re-forming* the original 'world' of the hearer.[143]

Funk observes that the parable 'induces a vision of that which cannot be conveyed by prosaic or discursive speech'.[144] Simile would be merely 'illustrative' (or what C.S. Lewis called a 'pupil' metaphor). But in metaphor the parable 'is creative ... the point is *discovered*' (through what C.S. Lewis called a 'master' metaphor).[145] Funk is not alone in expounding this approach to the parables. Ernst Fuchs draws on Heidegger's notion of 'world' to trace similar hermeneutical dynamics.[146] Equally, John Dominic Crossan insists, 'Parable subverts world'.[147] Madeleine Boucher and P.S. Hawkins argue, contrary to Jülicher, that parables do not convey 'information'; indeed they hide as much as they reveal, conveying meaning to those who respond with transformative effects.

Precedent for such an account of the hermeneutical dynamics of parables comes in 2 Samuel 12:1–4. The prophet Nathan has the unenviable and tricky task of exposing all the evil that was involved in David's adultery to his king's very face. Rather than deliver an unwise rebuke or a bland ethical homily, Nathan tells the story of the rich man who took advantage of his position to sin against his poor neighbour by taking away the only precious thing he had. David is drawn into the narrative world; it seduces him unwarily to exclaim, 'This is an outrage'. Only then does Nathan subvert the world, to declare, '*You* are he!'

All the same, can we say nothing in defence of John Nolland's approach? Three points tell in favour of it in appropriate contexts. First, clearly different

---

[142] Dodd, *Parables*, 16 (italics mine).

[143] Funk, *Language*, 133–222.

[144] Funk, *Language*, 136.

[145] Funk, *Language*, 132 (italics mine). Cf. Lewis, 'Bluspels'.

[146] Fuchs, *Hermeneutik*, esp. 211–30. See my exposition and critique of Fuchs in *Two Horizons*, 327–56.

[147] Crossan, *Dark Interval*, 59.

parables function in different ways. As different sub-genres, they invite different hermeneutical strategies of interpretation. Second, the functions of parables may not only be multiform but may also *overlap*. Third, and most decisive,
like certain other chapters in this volume, Nolland's claims hardly address the
impact of the words of *Jesus* upon their *first hearers,* but relate more clearly to the
performance of parables as they have become embedded in *Luke's later canonical
context.* The question, then, remains: do these texts become more 'didactic' as
possible 'sources' of theology or ethics once they have become assimilated into
Luke's larger narrative frame? If so, a dual hermeneutical dynamic may now
operate, depending on whether we interpret specific parables as words of Jesus,
or as words of Jesus reconfigured within a larger canonical frame.

H.R. Jauss's reception theory may assist us here. Jauss enquires about the
effects of texts upon succeeding generations.[148] On one side, he suggests,
whether a text retains 'formative' effects will depend upon whether subsequent
generations respond to it in self-involving ways. On the other side, *the horizons
of expectation* of later readers will be different from those of the first hearers or
readers, and the 'formation' may then take a different shape.

If Luke presents a narrative of events that is *also* a history of Jesus and of the
apostolic church, then it is reasonable to imagine that Christian readers of
Luke-Acts will read Luke not only to experience its initial formative impact
but *also* to answer questions about the teaching and ethical axioms of Jesus.
Graham Stanton made this reasonable case as a response to Bultmann's
assumption that the earliest Christians had little or no interest in knowing
about Jesus of Nazareth, only in confessing him as Lord.[149] Stanton insisted that
these are not exclusive alternatives. Indeed, part of Volume 1 in the Scripture
and Hermeneutics Series develops this point. As we earlier noted, Colin
Greene argued there for the importance of a theological view of history that
avoided both 'positivist' historiography and imposing ideologies alien to the
biblical text.[150]

Arguably, Nolland's chapter does not explore the hermeneutical dynamics
of parables *as parables*. Thus his comments on why a 'dishonest' manager might
be a hero (Lk. 16:1–8) may apply to the canonical level of enquiry, but strictly
as *parable*-dynamics stem arguably from 'defamiliarization'. 'Defamiliarization'
in literary criticism, as this derives from V. Shklovsky, presents what might otherwise have been familiar or predictable in fiction or parable in a sufficiently
surprising light or context to make the hearers sit up or to shock them. At this
level, the 'ethics' of the manager is a device of literary fiction and need not have
ethical significance.

---

[148] Jauss, *Toward an Aesthetic*, 22, and throughout.
[149] Stanton, *Jesus of Nazareth*.
[150] Greene, 'In the Arms of the Angels'.

Nolland's particular choice of the parable of the Prodigal Son (Lk. 15:11–32) also invites interpretation in terms of parable 'world'. Funk traces how the first hearers of Jesus are drawn into a *pre-cognitive, lived-through world* (in Heidegger's sense of 'world'). Some in the audience feel delight that the remorseful son receives a loving and generous welcome from the father, while others in the audience share the loyal elder son's sense of outrage and resentment that he has never had the fuss made of him that the rebellious son now receives. Funk explains the hermeneutical dynamic: 'The word of grace and deed of grace divide the audience into younger sons and elder sons – into sinners and Pharisees … They either rejoice because as sinners they are glad to be dependent on grace, or they are offended because they want justice on top of grace.'[151] Funk alludes to Ernst Fuchs' aphorism: it is not simply that readers interpret texts; here *the text interprets the readers*.

Nolland's legitimate concern is for Luke's canonical context and Luke's theology, as this volume has as its theme. But he leaves us to answer the question for ourselves: how much does the original hermeneutic of parables spoken by Jesus remain in the later canonical context?

Stephen Wright's response complements Nolland's approach in several ways. First and foremost, as we have noted, he calls attention to the irreducible 'divinatory' dimension in Schleiermacher's hermeneutics, which persists in all serious hermeneutical enquiry as part of 'understanding' (*Verstehen*) in contrast to explanation (*Erklärung*) alone. Second, his emphasis on the dialectic between the parts and the whole within the hermeneutical enterprise supports Nolland's careful attention to the level of fine detail and his concern (also found regularly in this volume) to take account of the wider horizon of the canonical narrative of Luke-Acts. Third, Wright incisively diagnoses the hermeneutical problem exposed by Nolland of a 'double' voice when a parable spoken by Jesus is incorporated at another level into a Lukan framework. He perceptively identifies Schleiermacher's awareness of a 'double voice' problem. Fourth, he calls attention to the interwoven fabric of texts and 'life' in relation to the parables of Jesus. In the hermeneutics of W. Dilthey, 'life' (*Leben*) became a key theme, replacing Hegel's emphasis on mere 'idea' or 'spirit' (*Geist*). Dilthey observed that in the veins of the knowing subject in Locke, no real blood flowed.

Stephen Wright brings Nolland's discussion firmly back into the domain of hermeneutics in the wider sense of the term, even if Nolland explores more traditional contextual aspects of hermeneutics. Wright calls upon some of the multiform resources of hermeneutical enquiry in the major tradition that stems from Schleiermacher through Dilthey to Gadamer, Ricœur and others.

---

[151] Funk, *Language*, 16.

Michael Goheen on a 'missional' reading of Luke

Michael Goheen offers a judicious response (much as Moessner does also) to
those who seek to stress one narrower aspect of the hermeneutical task only.
'Various levels of criticism are necessary to hear what God is saying'.[152] He does
not disparage the role of lexicography, syntax, literary analysis and historical or
redemptive-historical analysis. These are 'prerequisites for hearing God speak'.
Yet, as contributors to this volume would agree, other levels of interpretation
are also involved. Goheen rejects the naïve compartmentalization between a
supposedly objective description of 'what the text meant' and 'what the text
means'. Appropriately, he cites the forceful and convincing critique of this
notion put forward by Nicholas Lash.[153] The former task is *part of*, and *integral
with*, the latter; it is not to be performed as a separate endeavour.

Goheen accepts an axiom of philosophical hermeneutics (following 'historical understanding' in Dilthey and its flowering in Gadamer) that *both* the
ancient text *and* modern readers are *historically-conditioned*. The transformative
engagement between 'the two horizons' of the text and the reader or interpreter takes place between two contingent historical situations, both of which
are to some degree shaped by the 'givenness' of their own respective place
within history and culture. Goheen observes that on one side some biblical
scholars pay insufficient attention to the '"*historical conditioning*" of the biblical
text', while on the other side 'missiologists, seeking contemporary relevance,
frequently fail to respect the cultural distance between text and context, and
read their own concerns back into the biblical text'.[154]

Bosch extends the term 'critical hermeneutics' (usually used to denote the
social and sociological hermeneutics of Habermas and Apel) to the need for
critical discrimination and awareness in addressing this problem. Even the very
concept of 'mission' must not be assumed to carry precisely the same linguistic
or logical currency in Luke-Acts as it often carries today. Hence Goheen offers
a fresh hermeneutical assessment of this issue, among others. He follows Bosch
in viewing Luke 4:16–30 as performing a significant indication of Luke's concept of mission in Luke-Acts. Further, in Luke's dynamic narration, the role of
Jerusalem is also pivotal. In theological terms, Jerusalem is the centre. Much of
the Gospel of Luke is devoted to Jesus' journey *to* Jerusalem; Acts portrays a
mission that reaches out *from* Jerusalem. Christian Gentiles are not 'new' Israel;
'the Gentiles are incorporated into Israel'.[155] Israel's mission, Jesus' mission and

---

[152] Goheen, 'Missional Reading', 230.
[153] Lash, 'What Might Martyrdom Mean?' reprinted in *Theology on the Way to Emmaus*,
75–94.
[154] Goheen, 'Missional Reading', 234 (italics his).
[155] Goheen, 'Missional Reading', 244.

the church's mission are 'part of one story of God's mission'.[156] Hence those who take up the unfinished story today are commissioned by God to take up the mission of the Servant.

The *language* of Luke-Acts, therefore, functions as part of a larger *narrative plot*. However, the narrative emplotment goes even wider than Luke-Acts as a self-contained narration. It stretches back into the Old Testament, notably to the mission of Israel and the Servant in Israel, and stretches forward to embrace the possibility of finding future actors and participants who will 'take up' the narrative when it reaches them. This profoundly reflects the very nature of narrative and narrative participation as it was understood in Second Temple Judaism – as Richard Hays, N.T. Wright and others have elucidated it, as we have noted above.

We need not repeat all that we have said above about narrative, plot and self-involvement with reference in particular to Ricœur, Genette, Joel Green, Moessner and other narrative theorists. This theme runs as a major hermeneutical thread through this volume. It appeals to a *'wider frame'* for *interpretation*; it does not exclude various levels of reading for *reflection*; and it draws upon the dynamic of *narrative* for the *formation* of missional consciousness and missional action.

Finally, Goheen's approach takes up some emphases in Lukan studies noted above. W.C. Robinson (whom Goheen does not appear to mention) portrays Luke-Acts as a dynamic, onward-moving narrative, motivated by implicit continuity with Isaiah 40:3 and other Old Testament material. Robinson also sees the journey to Jerusalem similarly as a motif for mission and also assigns a similar role to the inclusion of the Gentiles.[157] Jacob Jervell also anticipates Goheen (or Bosch) in insisting that the church includes the Gentiles not as a 'replacement' Israel, but by incorporating them within the true Israel in continuity with God's promises and purposes initiated in the Old Testament.[158] Jervell, too, includes a chapter on the Samaritans – although, again, Goheen does not appear to cite Jervell's work explicitly.[159]

Goheen places in clear profile some of the hermeneutical dynamics involved in: (1) reading Luke *at various levels*; (2) appreciating the *historical-conditionedness* of the two horizons of text and interpreter; (3) taking full account of the character of Luke-Acts as *dynamic temporal plot and narrative*; and (4) placing individual or smaller units in Luke within the *larger frame* not only of Luke-Acts but also of the ongoing narrative of God's dealings with his people and the world from the Old Testament and Isaianic roots, through the

---

[156]   Goheen, 'Missional Reading', 256.

[157]   Robinson, *Der Weg des Herrn*, 34–39.

[158]   Jervell, *People of God*, 41–74.

[159]   Jervell, *People of God*, 113–32.

distinctive episodes of Luke and Acts, to the continuing story today. Those who have a role within the 'grand narrative' are active participants within it. Further: (5) missional hermeneutics understands proclamation and narrative as *incarnating* the gospel in time.

This coheres very well with Richard Bauckham's recent book on hermeneutics and mission.[160] In response to Jean-François Lyotard's definition of postmodernity as 'incredulity towards metanarratives', Bauckham dissociates the 'metanarrative' of Scripture from the different kind of metanarratives of high modernity constructed by Freudianism, Darwinianism and Marxism, which seek to impose their valuating criteria on the world as a whole.[161] The Bible, Bauckham argues, is in part a dynamic metanarrative, but it is *not* a 'totalizing' system. The biblical writings bubble with numerous 'little' narratives that are embedded in particularities, sometimes with surprising twists and turns that nevertheless find a place within the grand narrative. The Bible *both* speaks of God's universal purposes *and* addresses 'my' situation. Hermeneutics operates as dialectic between the universal and the particular. This coheres well with Goheen's points. The Bible conveys information and *address*, and biblical mission involves *'incarnating the Gospel in time'*.[162]

Biblical Theological Readings and Distinctive Theological Themes

Parts III and IV require less detailed discussion, since 'theological reading' and biblical theology in the context of hermeneutics provided the main themes of Volume 5 of the Scripture and Hermeneutics series, *Out of Egypt: Biblical Theology and Biblical Interpretation*.[163] Karl Möller, for example, discusses Charles Scobie on biblical theology; Christopher Wright explores biblical theology, hermeneutics and mission; while R.R. Reno explores biblical theology and theological exegesis. These contributions and others prepare some of the ground for Part IV of the present volume. Hence our discussion here focuses more briefly than above on specific aspects of the area only.

Max Turner on Luke and the Holy Spirit

Max Turner, like David Wenham, provides a more traditional approach to *hermeneutics*, although his interpretation of Luke's theology of the Holy Spirit is

---

[160] Bauckham, *Bible and Mission*.
[161] Bauckham, *Bible and Mission*, 87–89.
[162] Goheen, 'Missional Reading', 252, citing Bosch (italics mine).
[163] Bartholomew et al., *Out of Egypt*.

distinctive. Whereas Wenham majors especially on historical contexts, however, Turner explores the *theological* contexts that shape the responsible exegetical judgements that form the basis of *interpreting* Luke's theology of the Holy Spirit. Thus contextual and exegetical features remain the most prominent, but these also engage with the narrative structure of Luke-Acts as a whole, and, in turn, with debates in today's world concerning the relation between Luke's theology of the Spirit and understandings of the work of the Spirit today. In addition, Turner includes some distinctively hermeneutical observations about the *questions* (or pre-understandings) that interpreters may most fruitfully bring to the text in the light of *what questions Luke* actually sought to address. As one example, it is important to see 'why Luke shows no concern to describe *how* Jesus experienced the Spirit', even if such 'how' questions spring to our lips readily in responding to issues of our day.[164]

Turner, then, provides an interpretative engagement between Luke-Acts and a number of questions that arise within today's horizons of expectation and understanding. Thus: (1) Was the Spirit given sacramentally in baptism, in confirmation, or in a more open-ended 'confession-initiation package'? (2) Was the Spirit given primarily as part of the experience of salvation and holiness, or as empowerment for mission and service? (3) Was baptism with the Holy Spirit and fire (Lk. 3:16) integral to all Christian discipleship, or to be understood as a *donum superadditum* of prophetic empowerment?

Turner begins his account of Luke-Acts with the framework of the Old Testament, the birth narrative and preparation for the gospel. Like other contributors to this volume he underlines continuities with the Old Testament, including that of the new exodus and the messianic restoration of Israel. He then examines sayings that explicate Jesus' own relation to the Spirit from conception to resurrection. The conception of Jesus 'represents a quite remarkable *novum*' in which a child who is to exercise Davidic eschatological rule (1:32–33) is to be 'generated ... *by* the Holy Spirit'.[165] Luke depicts Jesus' very being as bearing 'essentially the *impress* of this Spirit', which 'marks him as Israel's holy one, the messianic Son of God'.[166]

Is Jesus' Jordan experience of the Spirit: (1) *paradigmatic* as a *donum superadditum* of empowering for service; or is it (2) *paradigmatic* of Christian baptismal reception of the Spirit; or is it (3) *not paradigmatic*, but unique? Turner concludes that the Spirit is the power 'on the Messiah' that enables him to effect the saving liberation and reign of God that he proclaims. Luke understands the Spirit of prophecy as 'community-forming power'. The Spirit profoundly *shapes* the life of the individual and the community, and we may therefore infer

---

[164]   Turner, 'Luke and the Spirit', 273.
[165]   Turner, 'Luke and the Spirit', 272.
[166]   Turner, 'Luke and the Spirit', 273.

that what the Spirit speaks is *formative*. Turner also emphasizes the role of the *canonical context*: 'It is only with Acts that true light dawns.'[167] Much of our interpretation of the theology of the Spirit hinges on how we read Luke-Acts in relation to Paul and John. Turner concedes certain differences of emphases, but he sees a fundamental theological unity between them. The Holy Spirit is given *both* for Christian *formation, and* as empowerment for service, which presumably includes *interpretation* and *reflection*.

Scott Hahn on kingdom and church in Luke-Acts, and Charles Scobie on the journey motif as a hermeneutical key

Scott Hahn readily establishes the significant role of Davidic kingship Christology in Luke's Gospel, together with the importance of the covenant, on which David's kingship rested. Through Jesus such kingship will extend 'over all the nations'. Other christological categories emerge alongside that of kingship, especially that of prophet, and the one who brings together a united people. This leads to a discussion of the institution of the Lord's Supper. Luke's distinctive language becomes suggestive: Luke alone includes Jesus' command to repeat this meal in remembrance of him (Lk. 22:11; cf. Mk. 14:22; Mt. 26:26). The opening verses of Acts take up the theme of the kingdom of God, but after the experience of Pentecost (Acts 2:1–42) the promise of the restoration of Israel begins to be actualized in the apostles' being 'all together in one place' (2:1). Peter applies to Jesus the Davidic enthronement psalm (2:30; cf. Ps. 110), and through Jesus the *transformation* of the Davidic kingdom into the ecclesial community of the Spirit. This community shares in the breaking of bread.

What is the hermeneutical significance of this approach? In part it entails the role of *narrative continuity* between Luke-Acts and the Old Testament, and also in part the interpretative significance of the *larger horizon* that a 'biblical theology' reading brings to the text. We have discussed both of these issues in detail above. However, a third hermeneutical factor arises. Hahn provides an *interpretive* point of view (or hermeneutical *Sehe-Punkt* in Chladenius). From this viewpoint the restoration of Israel, covenant, Davidic kingship, the Lord's Supper and the nature of the church, all appear to come together as a seamless whole. Schleiermacher, Dilthey, Gadamer and Pannenberg all place weight upon the dialectic between particularity on one side and coherence or wholeness on the other. In Pauline studies, J. Christiaan Beker approaches the interpretation of Paul in this way. He writes, 'Hermeneutic consists in the constant interaction between the coherent center of the gospel and its contingent interpretation'.[168] One distinctive hermeneutical contribution of Hahn's chapter is

---

[167] Turner, 'Luke and the Spirit', 282.
[168] Beker, *Paul the Apostle*, 13.

to illustrate this approach with reference to Luke-Acts by his proposed 'theological' reading.

Charles Scobie also takes up hermeneutical resources and strategies that we have discussed above. We have noted the importance of the journey motif in Luke's Gospel and its prominence as a dynamic theological narrative in W.C. Robinson, Moessner, Goheen and others. We also underlined the hermeneutical validity of interpreting smaller units in Luke within a larger canonical narrative frame. This emerged in our discussions of Joel Green, Moessner, Goheen and Hahn.

Scobie strengthens this thesis in a number of ways. His investigation of chiastic structure in Luke-Acts suggests chiastic correspondences between Luke 1–2 and Luke 24, which place the journey motif at the literary centre of a larger chiasmus. Parallels between the travel narrative, the new exodus and Christian discipleship as a pilgrim journey contribute further to this theological reading of Luke. All of this underlines the *temporal logic of narrative plot*, which we explored in the hermeneutics of Ricœur. As Oscar Cullmann reminded us half a century ago, the New Testament often places more weight on the horizon of *time* than on metaphors of space. He declares, 'Primitive Christian faith and thinking do not start from the spatial contrast between the Here and Beyond, but from the time distinction between Formerly and Now and Then'.[169] The 'journey' appears to be a narrative of place, but becomes within its canonical context the unfolding of larger divine purposes and a paradigm of the temporal journey of discipleship. It explicates 'a salvation history perspective that views the church as the people of God journeying forward in faith'.[170]

Craig Bartholomew and Robby Holt on prayer in Luke and exegetical performance

Bartholomew and Holt readily demonstrate the widely accepted principle that Luke emphasizes the role of prayer more fully and more explicitly than Mark and Matthew, and that Luke highlights the role of prayer at critical points in his narrative. They also argue more distinctively that prayer in Luke 1:8–13 and in 24:50–53 forms an *inclusio* within which the narrative events of the gospel take place. Significant events occur in the context of prayer. In Acts, the disciples of Jesus practice regular prayer in continuity with the example of Jesus. The writers explore these features in relation to issues of hermeneutics, and in particular to the stance and way of approach with which modern biblical interpreters come to the text.

---

[169] Cullmann, *Christ and Time*, 37.

[170] Scobie, 'A Canonical Approach to Interpreting Luke', 345.

The heart of the argument emerges in the second half of this chapter: 'Prayer is a fitting way for disciples *to participate in* God's kingdom'. Prayer involves 'alignment with the will of God'.[171] Most precisely: 'In Luke's narrative, prayer is inseparable from ... understanding/participating in the divine drama.'[172] To appreciate the meaning and force of these words we need to recall all that has been said about narrative, narrative plot and narrative formation, as well as the incorporation of the Luke-Acts narrative within the larger narrative frame of God's purposive action as this emerges within the Old Testament and reaches a focus in Jesus Christ. This narrative, we saw, continues through the unfolding narrative history of the church in Acts, and moves onward into the 'unfinished story' where readers today *join this story as actors and participants*. This accords with how 'narrative story' was understood in Second Temple Judaism, and, further, with *participatory* 'narrative-worlds' in Gadamer and Ricœur.

Philosophical discussions of the logic of prayer have clarified this point and added force to it. The biblical interpreter who approaches the text prayerfully is not merely '*asking* for' better skills or even for a better understanding of the biblical text. As Vincent Brummer rightly observes in his philosophical exploration of prayer, *prayer is above all a co-sharing with God* in seeking the good of the world and the realization on earth of God's will, because prayer co-shares with God *God's desires and yearnings for his people and for the world.*[173]

In prayer, light begins to dawn on one of the dilemmas that runs through this and other volumes in this series. Do we read Scripture as information/history/statement or as address/challenge/call? If prayer is *entering into* God's love for the world and God's will for God's people, prayer will entail understanding that certain states of affairs are the case, and will require interpretation and reflection. But as a process of 'entering in' and co-sharing the desires and yearnings of God's heart, prayer involves finding ourselves addressed, challenged and called. Hence, for the biblical interpreter prayer involves: (1) being open *to see with the eyes of God* 'what is the case', and this requires *interpretation* and *reflection*; and also (2) being open *to love with the heart of God,* and this requires holiness and *formation.*

This process depends not on merely 'asking' in accordance with our own hopes or aims, but upon articulating those *desires and longings that God's Holy Spirit has placed within the heart* as 'sighs' (NRSV) or (more accurately) as 'an involuntary expression of great concern' (Rom. 8:26, Greek στεναγμός).[174] As

[171] Bartholomew and Holt, 'Prayer in/and the Drama of Redemption in Luke', 361(italics mine).
[172] Bartholomew and Holt, 'Prayer in/and the Drama of Redemption in Luke', 362.
[173] Brummer, *What Are We Doing When We Pray?*, esp. 74–98.
[174] BDAG, 942.

a group of us wrote together in 1987: Prayer, 'which at first seems all one's own doing is actually the activity of another. It is the experience of being "prayed in", the discovery that "we do not know how to pray as we ought" (Rom. 8:26), but are graciously caught up in a divine conversation.'[175] This is a 'divine conversation' because God-as-Trinity is the articulation of the experience of praying *to* the Father *through* Christ *by* the Holy Spirit. In all of this, 'the one who prays is caught up and thereby transformed'.[176] God thereby takes up believers as *participants* in the drama of redemption.

If openness to God and openness to the Scriptures are inseparable, this has profound hermeneutical consequences. For, as Gadamer insists, in contrast to this 'the goal of preserving one's "position"' constitutes the utter reverse of 'hermeneutics'.[177] The very thing that Gadamer, Betti and Ricœur have striven to exclude in all their writings is the imposition of the interpreters' own interests onto the text. Gadamer declares, 'Hermeneutics is above all ... the art of *understanding* ... In it what one has to exercise *above all is the ear* ...'.[178] Emilio Betti likewise stresses the role of listening and openness.[179] Hermeneutics, like prayer, involves *participation* and *formation*. Hence Gadamer makes much of *Bildung*, as a notion that combines nuances of culture, education and formation. Through *Bildung* may emerge 'a receptivity to the "otherness"' of that which addresses and re-forms us.[180] In Christian participation in the drama of redemption, this includes prayer inseparably alongside interpretation, reflection and formation.

Issues in Reception History and Reception Theory

The history of the reception of the texts came into prominence relatively recently, mainly in the twenty-first century. Brevard Childs was one of the first to include within his substantial commentary on Exodus regular sections on 'History of Exegesis'. This appeared as far back as in 1974.[181] He comments in his introduction: 'The history of exegesis is of special interest in illuminating the text by showing how the questions which are brought to bear by subsequent generations of interpreters influenced the answers which they

---

[175] The Doctrine Commission of the Church of England, *We Believe in God*, 108; cf. 104–21. (I use 'us' as a member of the Commission, then and since.)

[176] Doctrine Commission, *We Believe in God*, 108.

[177] Gadamer, 'Reflections', 36.

[178] Gadamer, 'Reflections', 17 (italics mine).

[179] Betti, *Die Hermeneutik*.

[180] Gadamer, *Truth and Method*, 17; cf. 9–19.

[181] Childs, *Exodus*.

received.'[182] He added that these also serve as 'historical controls' in relation to
how the present generation *is influenced* by exegetical traditions of the day.

In the interpretation of the New Testament, several contributions to the
commentary series *Evangelisch-Katholischer Kommentar zum Neuen Testament*
contain substantial material on 'Auslegungs und Wirkungsgeschichte', variously translated, 'history of interpretation and history of effects', or 'effective
history', 'post-history of the text' or 'history of influence'. The 'influence' is
two-sided, denoting both that of the text on successive generations of readers,
and that of successive generations of readers on the understanding of the text.
In particular we may single out three outstanding examples: Ulrich Wilckens
on Romans; Ulrich Luz on Matthew and Wolfgang Schrage on 1 Corinthians.[183] In the New International Greek Testament Commentary series I
sought to provide sections on 'the Posthistory, Influence (*Wirkungsgeschichte*)
and Reception' of a number of chapters or passages.[184] Most recently, a new
series published by Blackwell attempts to focus on the history of exegesis, but
the earliest volumes do not fully reflect concerns that genuine reception theory
identifies, at least in the sense associated with Jauss, Luz and others, as explained
below.[185] Reception history is not simply a description of any or every example
drawn from a history of interpretation.

In his commentary on Matthew, Luz states that the term *Wirkungsgeschichte*
(or his translators' approved equivalent *history of influences*) denotes 'history,
reception and actualizing of a text in media other than a commentary, e.g. in
sermons, canonical law, hymnody, art and in the actions and sufferings of the
church'.[186] In this respect, the three chapters below fit well into these categories, including that of Heidi Hornik and Mikeal Parsons on visual art. Meanwhile, H.R. Jauss brings to the subject a literary and aesthetic tradition distinct
from that of *Wirkungsgeschichte* in Gadamer's philosophical hermeneutics,
although related to Gadamer's thought as his former teacher. For Jauss,
Rezeptionsgeschichte primarily emerges in the context not only of Gadamer but
also of the reader-response theory of Wolfgang Iser, for whom textual meaning remains a *potentiality* until its effects are 'completed' in a succession of
performances.

Where both traditions of enquiry merge together is in their common
emphasis upon a chain of successive *horizons of expectation* which give rise to a
series of ongoing question-and-answer processes. Effects and traditions 'arise'
or 'emerge' as new formulations, modifications, reappraisals and
reformulations establish and identify continuities and disruptive discontinuities

---

[182] Childs, *Exodus*, xv.
[183] Wilckens, *Römer*; Luz, *Matthäus*; and Schrage, *Korinther*.
[184] Thiselton, *First Corinthians*.
[185] Cf. to date, Edwards, *John* and Kovacs and Rowland, *Revelation*.
[186] Luz, *Matthew 1 – 7*, 95.

in the historical process. To ask, further, *how* the text addresses (or sometimes fails to address) successive agenda then also tells us something further about the text. I discuss this more fully elsewhere.[187]

François Bovon and Andrew Gregory on the reception of Luke in the second century

François Bovon's chapter raises a number of hermeneutical issues. In summary it throws into prominence two diverse ways in which reading Luke became actualized, and contributed to a tradition of influence, in the second century. Some sources and writers appear to approach Luke *instrumentally* as a gospel to be 'used' to serve prior interests or as a basis upon which to weave new or additional stories of their own. These may offer unduly 'free' readings of Luke. On the other hand, some read Luke as a normative text for *preservation and comment*. Yet, even in this latter case, some still seek to manipulate the text to legitimate their prior interests. Arguably, Marcion's use of Luke constitutes a striking case in point.[188] Further, others within this second category tend to ignore the distinctive interests and literary or theological features of Luke but flatten the particularities of the three synoptic gospels into a 'harmony' of the gospels.

Some gnostic sources and readers transpose Luke's concern with time and narrative, with public world and history, into a source for 'ideas'.[189] Docetism is prominent, in spite of Luke's concerns about history and the public domain.

Such a picture might seem to say more about disruptions and discontinuities in a succession of reception or history of influences than continuity, and more about manipulative interpretation than hearing the text in its own right. However this does not yet convey the whole picture. The gnostic transpositions of meaning provoked Irenaeus to commence serious hermeneutical reflection on context and coherence in interpretation, together with the status of the rule of faith of apostolic tradition.[190] Although in recent years some have argued that gnostic exegesis was no less 'rational' or responsible than that of the church fathers within the terms of their own gnostic systems of thought, Samuel Laeuchli's work still stands as a demonstration of the 'semantic breakdown' or linguistic violence that gnostic exegesis often involved, not least in putting biblical *vocabulary* to linguistic or semantic *uses* that were alien to their context within the biblical writings.[191]

---

[187] Thiselton, 'The Holy Spirit in 1 Corinthians', esp. 211–16; also Lundin, Walhout and Thiselton, *The Promise*, 183–209.

[188] Bovon, 'Reception', 389.

[189] Bovon, 'Reception' 391–92, nn. 54–58.

[190] Irenaeus, *Haer*. 1.8.1; 1.9.1–2; 4.26.1; cf. also 1.3.1–4; and 1.17.1 – 19.2.

[191] Laeuchli, *Language of Faith*, throughout.

Readers will appreciate the complexities, difficulties and subtleties of this meticulous investigation, together with the surprises that Bovon identifies and notes. However, perhaps the most challenging inference for readers of Luke today is the ease with which even those who at one level regard Luke as 'normative' may nevertheless interpret it often in manipulative ways. This drives us to exercise a hermeneutic of suspicion, as Ricœur describes it, but without loss of what he also calls a 'post-critical naïvety'. Here we seek to be *addressed by* the text, but after due critical *reflection*, and at the same time to allow the text to exercise its *formative* effects upon us.

Andrew Gregory, who has produced his own study of these issues, agrees with Bovon about the difficulties and complexities involved in seeking to establish which second-century authors knew Luke.[192] Indeed, he is particularly cautious about data which, he believes, may point in more than one direction and remain inconclusive. He explores further how far some second-century authors have a primary interest in Luke's *text*, and how far their concern is with the world '*behind*' Luke's text. This hermeneutical issue raises its head even in the second century. In the third place, Gregory considers whether the steady assimilation of Luke into a fourfold gospel pattern, together with the church's insistence (or, at the very least, Irenaeus' insistence) that the gospels should be interpreted in accordance with the 'rule of faith', has the effect of facilitating the voice of Luke to be heard, or whether it imposes constraints upon 'reading Luke' and also upon using Luke as a source for historical enquiries.

Gregory rightly perceives that some of these questions impinge on how we regard the formation of the canon. We cannot explore these complex debates here. It is worth recalling, however, F.F. Bruce's judicious comment that the formation of the canon was not contingent upon actions of later church authorities in '*deciding*' these matters at a later date, but rather upon perceiving where and how God encountered God's people through Scripture. His comment may be controversial, but it remains worthy of reflection: 'We are ... dealing ... with the formation of ... writings which had *already* the stamp of authority upon them'.[193]

Heidi Hornik and Mikeal Parsons, '*Illuminating Luke*': Luke in Italian Renaissance and Baroque painting

We have noted already the observation of Ulrich Luz that visual art constitutes a prime area for the history of the reception of texts and their influence.

---

[192] Gregory, *Reception of Luke*. See esp. the first section of Gregory's chapter in the present volume.

[193] Bruce, *The Books*, 95 (italics his).

Appropriately, Hornik and Parsons trace the two-way 'influence' of Lukan texts upon works of visual art, and the influence of artists within their given social, cultural and artistic milieu upon traditions of interpreting Luke. This study thus belongs properly to the exploration of textual effects in hermeneutics and to the reception history of Luke.

In a perceptive study of the importance of *visual* media in hermeneutics, Martin Jay argues that there is a distinctively close connection between sight and language. He writes, 'Unlike the other senses of smell, touch or taste, there seems to be a close, if complicated, relationship between sight and hearing ... "The ability to visualize something internally is closely linked with the ability to describe it verbally ... The link between vision, visual memory, and verbalization, can be quite startling"'.[194] The power of the optical in religion, Jay continues, has strong and critical significance, even if in some circles the suspicion of humanly constructed images has also given rise to a distrust of the optical and visual, amounting to 'iconophobia'.[195]

Hornik and Parsons offer some brief introductory comments on reception theory and allude to legendary traditions concerning Luke as a painter. They then introduce Leonardo's Uffizi *Annunciation* in terms of two contexts: that of the High Renaissance in Florence; and that of the history of reception of Luke 1:26–38. Leonardo, however, brings to bear on his work more than a single tradition. He draws on a complexity of allusions and typifications. Most of all, his *Annunciation* serves 'as a powerful visual reminder of the humble astonishment that we, no less than Mary, should experience when we hear ... "*Dominus vobiscum*"'.[196]

The second example cited in this chapter is Caravaggio's London *Supper at Emmaus,* from within the dual contexts of a seventeenth-century Baroque style of art and Luke 24:29–32. The objects portrayed in the painting project a double meaning: eucharistic grapes; wine and water; and apples symbolic of the fall of humankind. The dynamic action includes a moment of recognition, although the recognition is not granted to all. Symbols and gestures depend upon interpretative 'competency', much in the sense in which John Searle and Jonathan Culler employ this term in semiotic and literary hermeneutics. The painting in this way actualizes a communicative act of comprehension through the visual medium.

Certain aspects of the first example, the *Annunciation*, might lead some to suggest that what H.R. Jauss would identify as *discontinuities* within an exegetical tradition emerge alongside continuities. Is the application of Eve

---

[194] Jay, *Downcast Eyes*, 8 (quoting from R. Rivlin and K. Gravelle, *Deciphering the Senses* [Simon & Schuster: New York, 1984] 88–89).

[195] Jay, *Downcast Eyes*, 12–13.

[196] Hornik and Parsons 'Illuminating Luke', 424.

typology to Mary, for example, part of a major exegetical tradition, or even an instance of a *sensus plenior* of the text, or does it risk imposing onto exegesis an extraneous tradition on the basis of a specific tradition of mediaeval piety? How much depends on Van Unnik's not yet fully established understanding of *Dominus vobiscum?*[197] Or does the text convey this assurance of divine presence irrespective of particular interpretation of the Latin translation of the Greek? Whatever answers we suggest to these open questions, Leonardo's presentation of Mary's astonishment and humble, glad obedience (cf. Lk. 1:46–55, the Magnificat) reveals a stable continuity of a major tradition of interpretation that draws us in as obedient participants. Similarly, the multiple meanings of aspects of the *Supper at Emmaus* cohere both with stable exegetical traditions and with 'double meaning' or multiple meaning in Ricœur and others as part of the participatory power of visual and semiotic metaphor.

The 'projected world' of painting or other visual art has close affinities with 'world' and 'world-of-art' in Gadamer and in the later Heidegger.[198] Parallel hermeneutical models occur in the hermeneutics and philosophy of art that Nicholas Wolterstorff expounds, explicating also their epistemological status.[199] All of this calls attention to the capacity of visual art not only to present 'worlds' with creative power, but also to shape *formation*. Ricœur attributes this kind of creative formation especially to metaphor and temporal narrative plot; Umberto Eco ascribes it to 'open' texts (in contrast to 'closed' or 'engineering' texts).[200] Works on philosophical and literary hermeneutics today tend to take account of the formative power of art to actualize worlds of meaning.

This last chapter presents visual media of art at first-hand rather than only as part of a theoretical discourse about reception. In the same vein, in one of his latest works Heidegger draws a contrast between 'speaking merely *about* language' and 'letting language, *from within* language, speak to us'.[201] Almost every chapter seeks to address interpreters as *participants* in the narrative that they seek to interpret.

---

[197] Van Unnik, '*Dominus Vobiscum*'.

[198] Gadamer, *Truth and Method*, 84–95, 100–64; and Heidegger, *Poetry*, including 'The Origin of the Work of Art', 15–87, esp. 32–37. Heidegger alludes to Van Gogh's painting of the peasant's boots, on which cf. Thiselton, *Two Horizons,* 307–42.

[199] Wolterstorff, *Works and Worlds* and *Art in Action*.

[200] Ricœur, esp. *Metaphor* and *Time*; and Eco, *Role of the Reader*, 4–11.

[201] Heidegger, *On the Way to Language*, 85.

Bibliography

Adamson, W.R., *Bushnell Rediscovered* (Philadelphia: United Church Press, 1966)

Alexander, L., *The Preface to Luke's Gospel* (Cambridge: Cambridge University Press, 1993)

Alter, R., *The Art of Biblical Narrative* (New York: Basic Books, 1981)

Apel, K.-O., *Understanding and Explanation: A Transcendental-Pragmatic Perspective* (trans. G. Warnke;Cambridge, MA: MIT Press, 1984)

Baird, W., *History of New Testament Research*, II (3 vols.; Minneapolis: Fortress Press, 2003)

Barrett, C.K., *Luke the Historian in Recent Study* (London: Epworth Press, 1961)

Barth, K., *Protestant Theology in the Nineteenth Century* (trans. Die protestantische Theologie im 19. Jahrhundert; London: SCM Press, 1972)

—, *The Theology of Schleiermacher: Lectures at Göttingen 1923–24* (ed. D. Ritschl; trans. G.W. Bromiley; Edinburgh: T&T Clark; Grand Rapids: Eerdmans, 1982)

Bartholomew, C., C. Greene and K. Möller (eds.), *Renewing Biblical Interpretation* (SHS 1; Carlisle: Paternoster; Grand Rapids: Zondervan, 2000)

Bartholomew, C., C. Greene and K. Möller (eds.), *After Pentecost: Language and Interpretation* (SHS 2; Carlisle: Paternoster; Grand Rapids: Zondervan, 2001)

Bartholomew, C., C.S. Evans, M. Healy and M. Rae (eds.), *'Behind' the Text: History and Biblical Interpretation* (SHS 4; Carlisle: Paternoster; Grand Rapids: Zondervan, 2003)

Bartholomew, C., M. Healy, K. Möller and R. Perry (eds.), *Out Of Egypt: Biblical Theology and Biblical Interpretation* (SHS 5; Carlisle: Paternoster; Grand Rapids: Zondervan, 2004)

Bauckham, R.J., *Bible and Mission: Christian Witness in a Postmodern World* (Carlisle: Paternoster Press, 2003)

Beker, J.C., *Paul the Apostle: The Triumph of God in Life and Thought* (Edinburgh: Fortress Press; Philadelphia: James Clarke, 1980)

Betti, E., *Die Hermeneutik als Allgemeine Methodik der Geisteswissenschaften* (Tübingen: Mohr Siebeck, 2nd edn, 1972)

Bornkamm, G., *Early Christian Experience* (trans. P.L. Hammer; London: SCM Press, 1969)

Bovon, F., *Luke the Theologian: Thirty-three Years of Research (1950–1983)* (trans. K. McKinney; Allison Park, PA: Pickwick Publications, 1987)

—, Luke 1: *A Commentary on the Gospel of Luke 1:1 – 9:50* (trans. C.M. Thomas; Minneapolis: Fortress Press, 2002)

Brown, S., 'The Role of the Prologue in Detecting the Purpose of Luke-Acts' in *Perspectives in Luke-Acts* (ed. C.H. Talbert; Danville, VA: Association of Baptist Professors of Religion, 1978), 99–107

Bruce, F.F., *The Books and the Parchments* (Exeter: Paternoster, 1953)

Brummer, V., *What Are We Doing When We Pray? A Philosophical Enquiry* (London: SCM Press, 1984)

Bushnell Chency, M., *Life and Letters of Horace Bushnell* (New York: Harper, 1880)

Cadbury, H.J., *The Making of Luke-Acts* (London: SPCK, 1961)

Caird, G.B., *The Language and Imagery of the Bible* (London: Duckworth, 1980)

Childs, B.S., *Exodus: A Commentary* (London: SCM Press, 1974)

Conzelmann, H., *The Theology of St Luke* (trans. G. Buswell; London: Faber & Faber, 1960)

—, 'Luke's Place in the Development of Early Christianity,' in *Studies in Luke-Acts* (ed. L.E. Keck and J.L. Martyn; London: SPCK, 1968), 298–309

Crossan, J.D., *The Dark Interval: Towards a Theology of Story* (Niles, IL: Argus, 1975)

Cullmann, O., *Christ and Time* (trans. F.V. Filson; London: SCM Press, 1951)

Dawsey, J., *The Lukan Voice: Confession and Irony in the Gospel of Luke* (Macon: Mercer University Press, 1986)

The Doctrine Commission of the Church of England, *We Believe in God* (London: Church House Publishing, 1987)

Dodd, C.H., *Parables of the Kingdom* (London: Nisbet, 1935)

Eco, U., *The Role of the Reader: Explorations in Semiotics* (London: Hutchinson, 1981)

Edwards, M., *John* (Oxford: Basil Blackwell, 2004)

Esler, P.F., *Community and Gospel in Luke-Acts: The Social and Political Motivations of Lucan Theology* (Cambridge: Cambridge University Press, 1987)

Fish, S., *Doing What Comes Naturally: Change, Rhetoric and the Practice of Theory in Literary and Legal Studies* (Oxford: Clarendon Press, 1989)

Flender, H., *St. Luke, Theologian of Redemptive History* (trans. R.H. Fuller and I. Fuller; London: SPCK, 1967)

Fuchs, E., *Hermeneutik* (Tübingen: Mohr Siebeck, 4th edn, 1970)

Funk, R.W., *Language, Hermeneutic, and the Word of God* (New York: Harper & Row, 1966)

Gadamer, H.-G., *Philosophical Hermeneutics* (trans. and ed. D.E. Linge; Berkeley: University of California Press; 1976)

—, *Truth and Method* (trans. rev. J. Weinsheimer and D.G. Marshall; London: Sheed & Ward, 2nd edn, 1989)

—, 'Reflections on my Philosophical Journey' in *The Philosophy of Hans-Georg Gadamer* (ed. L. Hahn; Chicago: Open Court, 1997), 3–63

Gowler, D.B., *Host, Guest, Enemy and Friend: Portraits of the Pharisees in Luke and Acts* (New York/Bern: Lang, 1991)

Grant, P., *Reading the New Testament* (London: Macmillan, 1989)

Green, J.B., *The Theology of the Gospel of Luke* (Cambridge: Cambridge University Press, 1993, 1995)

—, *The Gospel of Luke* (NICNT; Grand Rapids: Eerdmans, 1997)

Greene, C., '"In the Arms of the Angels": Biblical Interpretation, Christology, and the Philosophy of History' in *Renewing Biblical Interpretation* (ed. C. Bartholomew, C. Greene, K. Möller; SHS 1; Carlisle: Paternoster; Grand Rapids: Zondervan, 2000), 198–239

Gregory, A., *The Reception of Luke and Acts in the Period before Irenaeus: Looking for Luke in the Second Century* (Tübingen: Mohr Siebeck, 2003)

Heidegger, M., *Being and Time* (trans. J. Macquarrie and E. Robinson; Oxford: Basil Blackwell, 1962)

—, *On the Way to Language* (trans. P.D. Hertz; New York: Harper & Row, 1971)

—, *Poetry, Language and Thought* (trans. and intro. A. Hofstadter; New York: Harper & Row, 1971)

Hodge, A.A., *The Life of Charles Hodge* (New York: Arno, 1969)

Jauss, H.R., *Toward an Aesthetic of Reception* (Minneapolis: University of Minnesota Press, 1982)

Jay, M., *Downcast Eyes: The Denigration of Vision in Twentieth-Century French Thought* (Berkley: University of California Press, 1993)

Jeremias, J., *The Parables of Jesus* (trans. S.H. Hooke; London: SCM Press, 2nd edn, 1963)

Jervell, J., *Luke and the People of God: A New Look at Luke-Acts* (Minneapolis: Augsburg, 1972)

Johnson, L.T., *The Literary Function of Possessions in Luke-Acts* (Missoula: Scholars Press, 1977)

—, *The Gospel of Luke* (SP 3; Collegeville, MN: Glazier, 1991)

Jülicher, A., *Die Gleichnisreden Jesu* (Freiburg: Mohr, 2nd edn, 1899)

Käsemann, E., *Essays in New Testament Themes* (London: SCM Press, 1964)

Kelber, W., *Mark's Story of Jesus* (Philadelphia: Fortress Press, 1979)

Kort, W.A., *Narrative Elements and Religious Meanings* (Philadelphia: Westminster Press, 1975)

—, *Story, Text and Scripture* (Literary Interests in Biblical Narrative; University Park/London: Pennsylvania State University Press, 1988)

Kovacs, J., and C. Rowland, *Revelation* (Oxford: Basil Blackwell, 2004)

Kümmel, W.G., *Introduction to the New Testament* (trans. of 14th rev. edn [1965] by A.J. Mattill, Jr; London: SCM Press, 1966)

Kuschel, K.-J., *Born before All Time? The Dispute over Christ's Origin* (trans. J. Bowden; London: SCM Press, 1992)

Laeuchli, S., *The Language of Faith: An Introduction to the Semantic Dilemma of the Early Church* (London: Epworth, 1962)

Lash, N., *Theology on the Way to Emmaus* (London: SCM Press, 1986)

Lewis, C.S., 'Bluspels and Flalansferes' in *The Importance of Language* (ed. M. Black; Englewood Cliffs, NJ: Prentice-Hall, 1962), 36–50

Luck, U., 'Kerygma, Tradition und Geschichte bei Lukas', *ZTK* 57 (1960), 51–66

Lundin, R., C. Walhout and A.C. Thiselton, *The Promise of Hermeneutics* (Grand Rapids: Eerdmans; Carlisle: Paternoster, 1999)

Luz, U., *Das Evangelium nach Matthäus* (4 vols.; Düsseldorf: Benziger; Neukirchen-Vluyn: Neukirchener Verlag, 1994–2002; part translated into English, Matthew 1 – 7; Minneapolis: Fortress Press, 1992)

Marshall, I.H., *Luke: Historian and Theologian* (Exeter: Paternoster, 1970)

—, *The Gospel of Luke: A Commentary on the Greek Text* (Grand Rapids: Eerdmans; Carlisle: Paternoster, 1978)

Moessner, D.P., *Lord of the Banquet: The Literary and Theological Significance of the Lukan Travel Narrative* (Harrisburg: Trinity Press International, 1989)

Moore, S., *Literary Criticism and the Gospels* (New Haven: York University Press, 1989)

Moores, J.D., *Wrestling with Rationality in Paul* (Cambridge: Cambridge University Press, 1995)

Neyrey, J.H. (ed.), *The Social World of Luke-Acts: Models for Interpretation* (Peabody, MA: Hendrickson, 1991)

Palmer, R.E., *Hermeneutics: Interpretation Theory in Schleiermacher, Dilthey, Heidegger and Gadamer* (Evanston: Northwestern University Press, 1969)

Paul, I., 'Metaphor and Exegesis', in *After Pentecost: Language and Biblical Interpretation* (ed. C. Bartholomew, C. Greene and K. Möller; SHS 2; Carlisle: Paternoster; Grand Rapids: Zondervan, 2001), 387–402

Peacock, A.R., *Creation and the World of Science* (Oxford: Clarendon Press, 1979)

Pogoloff, S.M., *Logos and Sophia: The Rhetorical Situations of 1 Corinthians* (SBLDS 134; Atlanta: Scholars Press, 1992)

Polkinghorne, J., *The Way the World Is* (London: Triangle; Grand Rapids: Eerdmans, 1984)

—, *Quarks, Chaos, and Christianity: Questions to Science and Religion* (New York: Crossroad, 1995)

—, *Faith, Science and Understanding* (New Haven: Yale University Press, 2000)

Powell, M.A., *What Is Narrative Criticism?* (Minneapolis: Fortress Press, 1990)

Ricœur, P., *The Conflict of Interpretations: Essays in Hermeneutics* (Evanston: Northwestern University Press, 1974)

—, *The Rule of Metaphor: Multi-Disciplinary Studies in the Creation and Meaning in Language* (trans. R. Czerny, with K. McLaughlin and J. Costello; London: Routledge & Kegan Paul, 1978)

—, *Time and Narrative* (3 vols.; trans. K. McLaughlin and D. Pellauer; Chicago/London: Chicago University Press, 1984–88)

Robinson, W.C., 'The Theological Context for Interpreting Luke's Travel Narrative (9: 51 ff.)', *JBL* 79 (1960), 20–31

—, *The Way of the Lord: A Study of History and Eschatology in the Gospel of Luke* (Basel, 1962)

—, *Der Weg des Herrn – Studien zur Geschichte und Eschatologie im Lukas-Evangelium* (Hamburg-Bergstedt, 1964)

Schleiermacher, F.D.E., *On Religion: Speeches to its Cultured Despisers* (trans. J. Oman; intro. by R. Otto; New York: Harper, 1958)

—, *Hermeneutics: The Handwritten Manuscripts* (ed. H. Kimmerle; trans. J. Duke and J. Forstman; Missoula: Scholars Press, 1977)

Schrage, W., *Der Erste Brief an die Korinther* (4 vols.; Düsseldorf: Benziger; Neukirchen-Vluyn: Neukirchener Verlag, 1991–2001)

Soskice, J.M., *Metaphor and Religious Language* (Oxford: Clarendon Press, 1987)

Stanton, G.N., *Jesus of Nazareth in New Testament Preaching* (Cambridge: Cambridge University Press, 1974)

Stowers, S.K., 'Paul on the Use and Abuse of Reason', in *Greeks, Romans and Christians: Essays in Honor of J. Malherbe* (ed. D.L. Balch, E. Ferguson and W.A. Meeks; Minneapolis: Augsburg, 1990), 253–86

Talbert, C.H., *Luke and the Gnostics: An Examination of the Lucan Purpose* (Nashville: Abingdon, 1966)

—, 'The Redactional Quest for Luke the Theologian', in *Jesus and Man's Hope* (ed. C.H. Talbert; Pittsburgh: Pittsburgh Theological Seminary, 1970), 171–222

—, *Literary Patterns, Theological Themes and the Genre of Luke-Acts* (Missoula: Scholars Press, 1974)

—, *Luke-Acts: New Perspectives from the SBL Seminar, 1983* (New York: Crossroad, 1984)

– (ed.), *Perspective on Luke-Acts* (Danville, VA: Association of Baptist Professors of Religion, 1978)

Tannehill, R.C., *The Narrative Unity of Luke-Acts: A Literary Interpretation, I: The Gospel According to Luke* (Philadelphia: Fortress Press, 1986)

Thiselton, A.C., *The Two Horizons: New Testament Hermeneutics and Philosophical Description with Special Reference to Heidegger, Bultmann, Gadamer, and Wittgenstein* (Grand Rapids: Eerdmans, 1980)

–, *New Horizons in Hermeneutics* (Grand Rapids: Zondervan; Carlisle: Paternoster; London: Harper Collins, 1992)

—, 'Schleiermacher's Hermeneutics of Understanding', in *New Horizons in Hermeneutics* (Grand Rapids: Zondervan; Carlisle: Paternoster; London: Harper Collins, 1992), 204–36

—, 'Communicative Action and Promise in Interdisciplinary, Biblical and Theological Hermeneutics', in R. Lundin, C. Walhout and A.C. Thiselton, *The Promise of Hermeneutics* (Grand Rapids: Eerdmans; Carlisle: Paternoster, 1999), 133–240

—, *The First Epistle to the Corinthians* (Grand Rapids: Eerdmans; Carlisle: Paternoster, 2000)

—, '"Behind" and "In Front of" the Text: Language, Reference, and Indeterminacy', in *After Pentecost: Language and Biblical Interpretation* (ed. C.

Bartholomew, C. Greene and K. Möller; SHS 2; Carlisle: Paternoster; Grand Rapids: Zondervan, 2001), 97–120

—, 'The Holy Spirit in 1 Corinthians: Exegesis and Reception History in the Patristic Era', in *The Holy Spirit and Christian Origins: Essays in Honour of James D.G. Dunn* (ed. G.N. Stanton, B.W. Longenecker and S.C. Barton; Grand Rapids: Eerdmans, 2004), 207–28

Thiselton, A.C., with R. Lundin and C. Walhout, 'The Parables of Jesus', in *The Responsibility of Hermeneutics* (Grand Rapids: Eerdmans; Exeter: Paternoster, 1985), 83–90

van Unnik, W.C., '"Dominus Vobiscum": The Background of a Liturgical Formulae', in *New Testament Essays: Studies in Memory of T.W. Manson* (ed. A.B.J. Higgins; Manchester: Manchester University Press, 1959), 270–305

—, 'Luke-Acts, a Storm Centre in Contemporary Scholarship', in *Studies in Luke-Acts* (ed. L.E. Keck and J.L. Martyn; London: SPCK, 1968), 15–32

Vielhauer, P., 'On the "Paulinism" of Acts', in *Studies in Luke-Acts* (ed. L.E. Keck and J.L. Martyn; London: SPCK, 1968), 33–50

Werner, M., *The Formation of Christian Dogma* (London: Black 1957)

Wilckens, U., *Der Brief an die Römer* (3 vols.; Düsseldorf: Benziger; Neukirchen-Vluyn: Neukirchener Verlag, 1978–1982)

Wilson, S.G., 'Lukan Eschatology', *NTS* 16 (1969–70), 330–47

—, *The Gentiles and the Gentile Mission in Luke-Acts* (Cambridge: Cambridge University Press, 1973)

Wolterstorff, N., *Art in Action* (Grand Rapids: Eerdmans, 1980)

—, *Works and Worlds of Art* (Oxford: Clarendon Press, 1980)

Wright, N.T., *The New Testament and the People of God* (London: SPCK, 1992)

—, *Jesus and the Victory of God* (London: SPCK, 1996)

Narrative, History and Theology

2

Learning Theological Interpretation from Luke

Joel B. Green

That I would suggest that we learn theological interpretation from Luke will strike some as strange. Within the New Testament, we sometimes more typically have turned to other writers, Paul for example, for theological formulations. Consider, for example, those classical and contemporary contributions to 'New Testament theology' or 'New Testament ethics' which draw especially, if not exclusively, on John and Paul as the theological giants of the New Testament.[1] Even so sensitive a theological exegete as John Calvin did nothing to disabuse us of the common sense that the Gospel of Luke was something other than theological narrative. Writing a series of commentaries on each of the biblical books, he commented on the Gospels of Matthew, Mark, and Luke as a composite, not with regard to the discrete witness each has to the life of Jesus, but with reference to a synthetic picture of Jesus Calvin was able to produce from the synoptic gospels.

Those engaged today in the quest of the historical Jesus similarly bypass the narrative-theological contribution of the individual gospels, preferring instead to recreate, often from quite distinct databases of material, their own purportedly historical accounts of Jesus. The writings of Luke, accordingly, might attract attention for their historical value in reconstructing the story of Jesus and Christian origins, or for differing opinions regarding its historical veracity. Indeed, one of the unresolved problems in biblical studies is located here, in disparate valuations of the historicity of Luke's writings, especially the Acts of the Apostles. Some have taken a more positive view, but most have looked askance at the book of Acts as a historical source and have preferred to examine the narrative for its theological and/or ideological content.[2]

---

[1] E.g., Bultmann, *Theology of the New Testament*; Kümmel, *Theology of the New Testament*; Matera, *New Testament Ethics*.

[2] For favorable assessments, see, e.g., Bruce, 'Acts of the Apostles'; Hemer, *Book of Acts*; Gasque, *History of the Criticism of the Acts of the Apostles*. For less-than-favorable

Moreover, in some parts of the church, particularly in evangelical circles, the common assumption has been that narrative is not a good source for theology, since narrative relates events from which one would be foolish to derive general 'principles' of theological currency.[3] The first major New Testament scholar to signal a different valuation of Luke's work was Joseph Fitzmyer. In his first of several volumes in the Anchor Bible a quarter-century ago, Fitzmyer signaled the coming of age of redaction-critical study of the gospels by devoting more than 125 pages to 'A Sketch of Lucan Theology,' a contribution that was pivotal for the newfound recognition of Luke as a theologian in his own right.[4] Only a decade ago, when writing of *The Theology of the Gospel of Luke*, I still found it necessary to defend the possibility of assessing the specifically *theological* contribution of the Third Evangelist.[5]

It is not difficult to find the basis of the dis-ease associated with thinking of the Gospel of Luke and the Acts of the Apostles in such pointedly theological terms. Long-held views bequeathed from one generation to the next since the eighteenth century presume and perpetuate a radical distinction between 'history' and 'theology,' while at the same time defining theological claims with reference to propositional statements. Practically devoid of such statements, Luke and Acts seemed to contribute little to 'theology,' so were analyzed with reference to their potential contribution to our historical portraits of the apostolic era. My aim is to urge a rather different way of configuring the relationships among narrative, theology, and history.

Against this backdrop, the thesis I want to put forward is straightforward – perhaps deceptively so. I want to argue that, in his narrative representation of history, Luke engages in interpretation of Israel's Scriptures in order to reform the theological imagination of his Model Readers. Apart from certain terms that require definition, a task to which I will turn momentarily, this proposal may seem rather pedestrian to some. However, I want to insist that this claim brings in tow several necessary, perhaps more controversial, corollaries – controversial in relation both to the state of play regarding how we correlate history, theology, and narrative, and to a handful of conclusions that have become typical in Lukan scholarship today. These corollaries include the following:

---

assessments, see Haenchen, *Acts of the Apostles*; Conzelmann, *Acts of the Apostles*. More programmatically, see the classic contributions of Dibelius, *Studies in the Acts of the Apostles*. For these problems more generally, see Bartholomew et al. (eds.), *'Behind' the Text*.

[3] Cf., e.g., the words of caution in Fee and Stuart, *How to Read the Bible for All Its Worth*, 73–78, 96–102.

[4] Fitzmyer, *Luke*, I, 43–270; see also his *Luke the Theologian*.

[5] J.B. Green, *The Theology of the Gospel of Luke*, 1–21.

- Luke's use of the Scriptures is at least inadequately, if not even inappropriately, understood as *apologetic* in character. He is not seeking to defend Jesus' status before God, for example; rather, he is forming Christian identity while at the same time demonstrating how to read the Scriptures.
- Hence, Luke's use of the Scriptures is primarily ecclesiological rather than christological in orientation.[6]
- With reference to Luke's narrative enterprise, the historiographical and theological tasks are indistinguishable. One does not 'do theology' on the basis of but rather *with* history – by which I refer to 'the employment of the materials of the past and the configurations in which we organize and comprehend them to orient ourselves in the living present.'[7]
- To learn theological interpretation from Luke, then, is to set aside the hyper-concern with historical validation that has occupied so much of biblical scholarship, even biblical theology, in the modern era, in favor of renewed attention to signification. That is, rather than concerning ourselves primarily with whether things happened in this way, we attend to what significance these events have when construed within this narrative. This is because we recognize that *theological interpretation* takes as its starting point the theological claim that the church has received as canon these particular narrative representations of those events that appear in Scripture (rather than the church's having declared canonical a particular set of historical facts).
- Although those discipled by Luke in the way of theological interpretation of Scripture will continue to concern themselves with 'validity in interpretation,' authorial intent and/or the meaning of a text at the time and place of its historical address are not the measures by which to determine a valid reading of Scripture. This entails that we put aside the linearity of what many today regard as biblical hermeneutics – from 'what it meant' to 'what it means.' This is because the chasm that separates the contemporary reader and Lukan narrative is, in theological interpretation, defined theologically rather than historically.[8]

The astute reader will recognize that I have situated myself over against several important lines of recent New Testament study in general, and Lukan

---

[6] The best case for a christological reading of Israel's Scriptures in Luke-Acts is Bock, *Proclamation*.

[7] Schorske, *Thinking with History*, 3.

[8] I have developed this in several related essays, including: J.B. Green, 'Scripture and Theology: Uniting the Two So Long Divided'; 'Modernity, History, and the Theological Interpretation of the Bible'; 'Scripture and Theology: Failed Experiments, Fresh Perspectives'; and 'Practicing the Gospel in a Post-Critical World.'

scholarship in particular. These would include the widely held view that Luke's use of the Scriptures of Israel is christological in aim; the persistent claim among some that 'biblical theology' is fundamentally a historical enterprise; and the presumption that historical data provide the basis for theological interpretation. This is not because these procedures and perspectives are inherently wrong, but because they are out of place in particularly theological interpretation. My counter-argument will proceed along the following lines. First, I need to define several terms that function as shorthand throughout this chapter. Second, I want to discuss the task of history/writing, with attention to how this might inform our understanding of theological interpretation in Luke-Acts. As will become clear, my comments are pertinent irrespective of whether scholars agree that Luke-Acts should be understood within the generic category of historiography; the terms would change, but the basic challenges would remain the same if, for example, one thinks of Luke as biography. Third, I will show that Luke's dexterity with the Scriptures is disciplined as an exercise in theological formation. This will include discussion, largely at an implicit level, of the aims, assumptions, and criteria of validity in Luke's use of the Scriptures. In a concluding remark, I will urge, with appropriate caveats, that Luke is a master to whom we may apprentice ourselves as readers of Scripture.

Some Definitions

I need first to explain my use of three terms which may not be immediately transparent. First, I use the term '*Scripture*' in contrast to the term 'Bible' or 'biblical materials.' At stake is a category difference in assumptions and aims, making it entirely possible, nowadays perhaps even probable, that a reading of the Bible will not be a reading of Christian Scripture. Robert Morgan has observed at length the competing interests that occupy those who engage in biblical interpretation, concluding that 'the interpretation chosen does not depend on the nature of the texts alone ... Interpretation depends more on the interests of the interpreters.' He goes on to claim that 'the aims of biblical historians seem quite remote from those of Jews and Christians who interpret the Bible in the expectation of religious insight.'[9] Approaching the matter quite differently, David Kelsey has nevertheless observed similarly: 'To take the biblical writings simply as "texts" is, notoriously, not necessarily to take them as "Christian scripture."' To take biblical texts as Scripture has to do with the aim of Scripture, which, he writes, is to 'shape persons' identities so decisively as to transform them.'[10]

---

[9] Morgan with Barton, *Biblical Interpretation*, 15; see 1–43.

[10] Kelsey, *Uses of Scripture*, 90.

In short, 'the Bible is Scripture' is a theological statement. It draws attention, first, to the origin, role, and aim of these texts in God's self-
communication.[11] Second, it locates persons and a people, those who read the
Bible as Scripture, on a particular textual map, a location possessing its own
assumptions, values, and norms for guiding and animating particular beliefs,
dispositions, and practices constitutive of that people. Because of its priority in
the generation and sustenance of the world it supports, Scripture also holds the
potential for confirming or for reconfiguring the beliefs and commitments that
orient our lives in the world.[12]

'*Imagination*,' the second term I want to explain, refers to 'the power of
taking something as something by means of meaningful forms, which are
rooted in our history and have the power to disclose truths about life in the
world.'[13] 'Imagination' may seem too romanticist a term for some, who may
prefer 'conceptual scheme,' an ordered and ordering pattern that is at once *conceptual* (a way of seeing things), *conative* (a set of beliefs and values to which a
group and its members are deeply attached), and *action-guiding* (our lives proceed according to its terms).[14] My perception of the world is based in a network
of ever-forming assumptions about my environment, and in a series of well-
tested assumptions, shared by others with whom I associate, about 'the way the
world works.' Given that incoming sensory data are generally inadequate to
substantiate an unambiguous interpretation and response on our part, we can
immediately see the importance of these schemes; my mind disambiguates that
data according to what I have learned to expect to see, according to what I can
imagine to be the case.[15]

By way of preparing for my emphasis on narrativity in what follows, I
should add that, in the formation of imagination, narrative is pivotal. This is
because embodied human life performs like a cultural, neuro-hermeneutic
system, locating (and, thus, making sense of) current realities in relation to
our grasp of the past and expectations of the future,[16] and to speak thus of past,
present, and future is already to frame meaning in narrative terms. Indeed, sci-
entist-theologian Anne Foeret refers to humans as '*Homo Narrans Narrandus* –
the storytelling person whose story has to be told,' who tells stories to make
sense of the world and to form personal identity and community; and this perspective has been ratified again and again in recent interdisciplinary study.[17]

---

[11] See Webster, *Holy Scripture*, 5.

[12] Cf. Kort, *Take, Read*, 2–3.

[13] Bryant, *Faith and the Play of Imagination*, 5.

[14] See Flanagan, *The Problem of the Soul*, 27–55; cf. G. Green, *Theology, Hermeneutics,
    and Imagination*.

[15] Cf. Koch, *Quest for Consciousness*.

[16] Cf. Reyna, *Connections*; Siegel, *Developing Mind*.

[17] Reported in Leat, 'Artificial Intelligence Researcher Seeks Silicon Soul,' 7. See
    more fully, e.g., Feinberg, *Altered Egos*; Ashbrook and Albright, *Humanizing Brain*.

From neurobiology and its interactions with cultural anthropology and philosophy, then, we have a heightened interest in and recognition of *narrativity* as a human-forming, meaning-making enterprise. This is not first and foremost a statement about exegetical method, though the narrative form of Luke-Acts invites narrative-critical interests, but rather about narrativity as an essential aspect of our grasp of the nature of the world and of human identity and comportment in it. 'To raise the question of narrative,' presaged Hayden White, 'is to invite reflection on the very nature of culture and, possibly, even on the nature of humanity itself.'[18] Accordingly, it is crucial to inquire: What stories are shaping the worlds we indwell? What stories are we embodying? And, consequently: With respect to what narrative do we, will we, interpret?

Finally, I need to discuss my use of the category '*Model Reader.*' Other readers might have impressed themselves upon me – implied, competent, authorial, informed, and real, for example.[19] Apart from the hard work of tracing the reception history of a work like Luke,[20] however, I find these other kinds of readers less helpful for theological interpretation. Umberto Eco speaks of good reading as the practice of those who are able to deal with texts in the act of interpreting in the same way as the author dealt with them in the act of writing.[21] Such a reader – a Model Reader, to use Eco's term – is the precondition for actualizing the potential of a text to engage and transform us, for it is this reader whom the text not only presupposes but also produces. This requires that readers enter cooperatively into the discursive dance with the text, while leaving open the possibility that the text is hospitable to multiple interpretations. Whether Luke's *intended* readers or his *first, flesh-and-blood* readers in fact played the role of the Model Reader is an altogether different question, and one that we can hardly begin to answer. And in any case, specifically theological interpretation of Scripture moves beyond a narrow interest in the voice of the human author(s) to accord privilege to the role of this text in divine self-disclosure. Accordingly, such dispositions and practices as recognition, acceptance, devotion, attention, and trust characterize the Model Reader.[22] The consequence of this concern with the Model Reader in the context of theological interpretation is a concern with the formation of

For interdisciplinary work, see Fireman et al., *Narrative and Consciousness*; Hinchman and Hinchman, *Memory, Identity, Community*.

[18] White, *Content of the Form*, 1.

[19] See Rabinowitz, 'Reader-Response Theory and Criticism.'

[20] In this volume, see Bovon, 'The Reception and Use of the Gospel of Luke in the Second Century'; Gregory, 'Looking for Luke in the Second Century'; and Hornick and Parsons, 'Illuminating Luke: The Third Gospel in Italian Renaissance and Baroque Painting'.

[21] E.g., Eco, *Role of the Reader*, 7–11.

[22] See Webster, *Holy Scripture*, 68–106.

persons and communities who embody and put into play, who perform, the narrative of Scripture.

Use of the category of Model Reader does not allow us to slide into apathy concerning historical questions, since Eco's model attends to what he calls 'world structures.' To put it differently, the text is present to us as a cultural product, which draws on, actualizes, propagates, and/or undermines the context within which it was generated. The Model Reader supported by this text protects the text from colonization or objectification by the Reader by allowing the text its own voice from within its own socio-cultural horizons. However, we are able to embrace the role of Model Reader the more easily because (1) so much of our humanity is shared with the world within which this text found its origins; and (2) the text itself, when read closely and with respect for its difference, as in intercultural exchange more generally, unveils much of its own socio-cultural horizons. More challenging is our developing the habits of life that make us receptive to the vision of God, God's character and God's project, textualized in and broadcast through these pages. In this case, the Model Reader must not only learn to recognize the importance of address forms or genealogies (for example) in the Lukan narrative, but must come to the text with a disposition of openness to a reordering of the world, repentance for attitudes of defiance of the grace of God's self-revelation and a conversion of the imagination. This is why I say that the primary gulf separating Lukan narrative and the contemporary reader is more theological than historical.

History/Writing

Contemporary study of historical narrative is characterized by obvious truisms, the theological significance of which has not been adequately developed. Let me mention three of these. (1) The writing of history provides us with both less and more than the past. It is less than the past since the sum of events that could be recounted is practically infinite, so that one of the primary contributions of any historiographer is the selection of events to be included in the telling. The historian's work is partial, then, in that only a minute segment of the past can be chosen, but partial also in the sense that the historian's work is inevitably subjective. This subjectivity expresses itself in the simple reality that the historian knows the future of the past being narrated, and writes with that outcome in view. Of course, in selecting and arranging events, the historiographer exercises further judgment while ranking some events and their importance over others,[23] and this accounts for the claim that the writing of history provides more than the past. As Brian Stock notes, 'history, by becoming a text,

---

[23] See Lowenthal, *The Past Is a Foreign Country*, 214–19.

surpasses itself as a set of real events and is realized as a structure of meaning, thereby acquiring the capacity to be interpreted.'[24] (2) Whatever else it does, historiography must somehow account for the present to which the past has led. *Continuity* is therefore integral to the historian's craft, as the historian demonstrates through narrative representation how the present grows organically out of sequences of past events. The result is a powerful implement of community *legitimation, identity formation,* and *instruction.*[25] (3) In history/writing, events (which we experience serially as occurrences and situations) acquire narrative form (arranging what has happened in a web of causation and meaning), and narratives, in the classic sense, require a beginning, middle, and end.[26] Together, these seemingly mundane observations help to move us forward in our understanding of Luke's theological accomplishment, since they press the question of the teleology of Luke's narrative.

It may be helpful to think analogically. Inspired by a map he had drawn with his stepson, Robert Louis Stevenson set out to write the novel that took its name from what he had drawn: 'Treasure Island.' He began well, writing a chapter a day, and even prior to its completion the work began to appear serially in *Young Folks.* When his inspiration dried up, however, he had composed less than half of what would become a book of thirty-four chapters. Later, wintering in Switzerland, when he was able again to put pen to paper, the plot for his story had already been set and, indeed, was well-known to those who had begun to read the story, chapter by chapter, as it had developed and was published. Without suggesting that Stevenson would have liked to take the novel in a divergent direction, we can nonetheless appreciate the fact that he was not free to do so, if he was going to remain true to the story as it had already come to life in its first chapters. He was constrained by what went before.

Similarly, having set out to continue the story of Israel, Luke was constrained by what went before, and, so to speak, by what had already been published of that story in the form of the LXX. The Scriptures of Israel divulge no completed narrative, but point beyond themselves to the need for, and indeed the promise of, Israel's restoration, and it is not too much to say that the various

---

[24] Stock, *Listening for the Text*, 108. Some scholars find it easy to move from this line of thought to the idea that, therefore, patterns or frameworks are imposed upon events; this appears to be the perspective White adopts (see his *Content of the Form*, 1–25). Recent work in the philosophy of history, however, has made room for the *recognition* of thematic and causal ties among events in the real world (e.g., Carter, 'Telling Times').

[25] For this reason, Phelan rightly claims that 'the best weapon or best defense of the powerless is narrative' (*Narrative as Rhetoric*, 13).

[26] 'For all the body of history is simply a long narrative (διήγησις μακρά)' (Lucian, *De Hist. Conscrib.* §55).

Judaisms we encounter in the first century C.E. regarded themselves in some significant sense as the heirs of the as-yet open-ended Israel-story. Luke's account of the Way is no exception.

As they write their openings, narrators encounter the problem of a beginning. How does one indicate the logic whereby the initial events are shown to be the product of forces within the discourse itself rather than a given reported by the narrative?[27] This is especially true of historiography, since the particular challenge facing the historian is to weave events, even initial ones, into a web of significance by indicating causal relationships. To put it differently, narratives are constructed through a reversal of cause-effect relations. Knowing how things turned out, historians go back in time, in search of explanations, of causes.[28] In the case of the gospels and Acts, the problem of a beginning is the quest for a point of initiation capable of supporting, even funding, the significance allocated to Jesus and the mission of his followers. Each of the evangelists resolves this quandary in a different way.

The ongoing story within which the Gospel of Mark is located, which helps to give the story of Jesus' ministry its significance, and which is itself shaped by Mark's presentation of Jesus, has its roots in the divine promise of liberation for Israel from the bondage of exile as this is related by the prophet Isaiah (Mk. 1:1–3). In the opening of Matthew's Gospel, the evangelist refers to 'the book of origins,' a parallel to Genesis 2:4; 5:1, thus pointing to the consummation in Jesus' advent of the purpose of God in creation. The depths of meaning of the story of Jesus cannot be plumbed without engagement with the very beginning, or without reference to Abraham and David, Jesus' ancestors (Mt. 1:1). As for the fourth gospel, John expands the horizons even further. For him, the story of Jesus cannot be appreciated fully without reference to the beginning of the cosmos – indeed, to the primordial being of God: 'In the beginning was the Word, and the Word was with God, and the Word was God' (John 1:1). Each in its own way, the gospels and Acts self-consciously pick up the story in midstream and write the next chapter of the ongoing work of God. What of the beginning of Luke-Acts? Just as the story of the early mission-church (Acts) is inscribed into the story of Jesus (Luke), so the story of Jesus is written into the story of Israel's Scriptures, and especially the story of Abraham. In Luke's birth narrative (1:5–2:52), strong and extensive echoes of the Abraham tradition can be heard, leading to the conclusion that Luke's narrative is a self-conscious continuation of the redemptive story, in which divine promises to Abraham, long latent, are

---

[27] See Aristotle, *Poetics* 23.1 §1459a.17–29; Said, *Beginnings*. More generally, cf. Smith, 'Narrative Beginnings in Ancient Literature and Theory'; Parsons, 'Reading a Beginning/Beginning a Reading.'

[28] Cf. White, *Content of the Form*, 26–57.

shown not to have escaped God's memory but indeed to be in the process of actualization in the present.[29]

Locating the beginning of the Israel-story in the Abraham-cycle constrains the ensuing narrative in some ways, but it also leaves a multitude of possible plot lines. That, today, Christians, Jews, and Muslims can refer to Abraham as 'our ancestor' is proof enough of this potential polysemy. In important ways, then, the 'battle for the Bible' that occupies the Judaisms of Luke's world revolves around how one reads that ensuing narrative, and how convincingly a community links its 'present' to the 'past' represented in God's promises to Abraham. Luke explicitly counters some narratives when he reports the words of John to the crowds of those wishing to be baptized:

> You brood of vipers! Who warned you to flee from the wrath to come? Bear fruits worthy of repentance. Do not begin to say to yourselves, 'We have Abraham as our ancestor'; for I tell you, God is able from these stones to raise up children to Abraham. Even now the ax is lying at the root of the trees; every tree therefore that does not bear good fruit is cut down and thrown into the fire.
>
> (Lk. 3:7–9, NRSV)

This reading is validated in the Zacchaeus episode where, having heard that Zacchaeus engages in the very practices John had identified as 'fruits worthy of repentance' (3:10–14), Jesus announces that Zacchaeus is a 'son of Abraham' (19:9). Apparently, the narrative that has its beginnings in Abraham is realized through those whose dispositions and practices model Abraham's, and not necessarily through those for whom a paternity test would reveal Abraham to be a biological antecedent.

If a beginning leaves to the imagination not an infinite but at least a plurality of possibilities for narrative development, these options are significantly curtailed by the projection of an end – even when, as in the case of Luke's narrative, that end is somewhat amorphous and can only be anticipated, not recounted. The eschatological outlook of Luke-Acts comes onto the stage at a number of points, but nowhere more pointedly than in Acts 3:20, with the juxtaposition of 'seasons of refreshment,' the sending of Messiah Jesus, and 'times of restoration.' The Christology developed thus far reveals that the salvific blessings of Yahweh are available through the agency of the exalted Jesus. Even if he is presently detained in heaven, the Messiah is not for this reason any less involved in his messianic work. In conjunction with the promised sending of the Messiah (1:20), then, 'seasons of refreshment' points to times of blessing prior to the end time. Nevertheless, Jesus is presently detained in heaven, where he will remain until the parousia (cf. 1:9–11).[30] Of

---

[29] I have developed this proposal in J.B. Green, 'The Problem of a Beginning.'

[30] Cf. Bayer, 'Christ-Centered Eschatology in Acts 3:17–26,' 236–50.

course, Jesus and his followers were not the only persons for whom the hope of
the restoration of all things was integral to the theological imagination. This
was shared by the Pharisees, for example, who anticipated the advent of God's
dominion (Lk. 17:20), and whose common belief in the 'hope of the resurrection of the dead' could result in an alignment between Paul and the Pharisees
on the Jewish Council (Acts 23:6–9).

A shared beginning and a common, projected narrative end do not guarantee a shared narrative, however, since many avenues might be taken from point
A to point C. What distinguishes the Lukan narrative from other contenders
(and aligns it with others in early Christian literature) is its unyielding designation of the advent of Jesus of Nazareth as the midpoint of the narrative of
Israel's story. That is, the story of the actualization of God's promises to Abraham must pass through, it cannot bypass, this 'middle' – the life, death, and resurrection of Jesus. To be sure, Luke develops this 'midpoint' in a way that
makes his gospel distinctive in relation to the other canonical gospels, just as the
other gospels develop this midpoint, but in the end he has left no doubt that the
story of the mission-church in the Acts of the Apostles is nothing more, nothing less than the continuation of the story of Jesus in the Gospel of Luke
(see Acts 1:1–11). In the same way, Luke left no doubt that the story of Jesus in
the Gospel of Luke is nothing more, nothing less than the (proper) continuation of the story of Israel as this is related in the LXX.

In the Acts of the Apostles, this judgment is represented above all in those
speeches where the story of Israel is told, and where that story's natural, apparently ineluctable next chapter has it that 'God has brought to Israel a Savior,
Jesus, as he promised' (13:23). In the gospel, this judgment is expressed in statements such as this one on the Emmaus Road: 'Then beginning with Moses and
all the prophets, he interpreted to them the things about himself in all the scriptures' (24:27). Much more could be said about how the salvific mission of Jesus
and his followers is woven out of and into the cloth of exodus and new
exodus,[31] for example, so as to endow the whole with a formal coherence
whose authority and truth could only be the authority and truth of the reality
thus textualized. The historical narrative Luke has generated thus interprets the
coming of Jesus as the continuation (and, indeed, the actualization) of the story
of Israel, while at the same constraining all interpretation of the story of Israel
by urging that its emplotment could make sense only as it leads to and proceeds
from (that is, is determined by) its midpoint in the advent of Jesus. The consequence is a narration whose aim entails the legitimation that results from a
demonstration of uninterrupted continuity with and actualization of the Abraham-story. But it is also an identity-forming narrative, for it insists that the heirs
of the Abraham story are none other than 'us,' Luke's Model Readers. What is

---

[31] Cf. Pao, *Acts and the Isaianic New Exodus.*

more, because the Gospel of Luke ends before the story is complete (i.e.,
before the parousia and concomitant restoration of all things), the book of Acts
is its continuation and, because the narrative of Acts ends before the story is
complete, the story continues to be written (or lived) – provided those who
carry it forward do so within the constraints of the beginning, middle, and end
identified by Luke. In other words, the Lukan narrative identifies for its Model
Readers the true narrative and, through its development of characters and the
mission-church, exemplifies what it means to inhabit that narrative so that it,
and not some other, decisively shapes the life of the faithful.

Before moving on to demonstrate more fully how Luke uses the Scriptures,
a few summary notes may be sounded. In narrative terms, how one parses the
'beginning,' 'middle,' and 'end' is critical, for this determines the character of
that narrative, including which events are to be identified over others as cruxes
in the development of the narrative. Although certain constraints are unavoid-
able, it is nonetheless possible to read the story of Israel in a variety of ways.
That not all of these would be 'Christian' is evident from the intramural disputes within the Jewish people in the first century, leading eventually to the
partings of the ways between Jews and Christians. For Luke, the beginning,
middle, and end are, respectively, the Abraham-story and especially God's
promise to Abraham that he would be the progenitor of many nations; the
salvific coming of Jesus of Nazareth; and the prospective restoration of all
things. The plot of Luke's narrative is thus theologically (not christologically)
determined. Its subject is God, whose beneficence comes to expression in Jesus
Christ, active powerfully and formatively through word and deed and Spirit.
Yahweh's purpose thus determines the shape of this narrative and calls upon its
readers to choose sides, since engaging with this narrative involves its audience
in a formative and decision-making process. Luke's Model Readers will
embrace this narrative as their own, and seek to continue it in their lives.
'Theological interpretation,' then, is less method and more an intrinsically self-
involving theological vision of God, church, Scripture, and world, bound
together within the economy of salvation, with the people of God cast as pilgrims on a journey whose destination is known and achieved only by embracing, indwelling, and embodying the divine story.

Luke and Israel's Scriptures

In Acts 1–2, even before Peter's Pentecost address, Jesus' followers appear as
accomplished interpreters of Scripture. In Acts 1:15–26, the reconstitution of
the twelve, for example, the scene Luke sketches is replete with scriptural quotations and echoes. Most obvious is the citation of Psalms 69:26 and 109:8 in
Acts 1:20, which together build an awareness of divine pre-understanding and

guidance as well as ecclesial self-understanding. Judas' apostasy did not cancel God's purpose but was actually anticipated by it, so that in this case the Scriptures of Israel have been read with an eye to grappling from a divine point of view with the statement and resolution of the problem of Judas' 'turning aside.' Both texts from the Psalms have become 'scripts,' so to speak, indicating ahead of time how Judas (that is, the godless hater of the righteous one [Jesus] – Ps. 69) would be cursed and replaced (Ps. 109).[32] A less obvious but nevertheless potent use of the Scriptures takes the form of echoes from the story of 'Judas' and Tamar. The Judas of Luke-Acts recalls the earlier Judas (Hebrew 'Judah') and the twelve sons of Israel. The earlier Judas sells his brother (Gn. 37:27), the later Judas sells Jesus (Lk. 22:5; Acts 1:18). The first separates from his twelve brothers and goes to his own place (Gn. 38:1), while the second separates from the twelve apostles. Moreover, both stories contain the seeds of the future: 'As the Judas of Acts turns aside from his heritage ... so also Jews in the remainder of Acts who reject God's salvation align themselves with Judas and turn aside from their heritage with the twelve tribes of Israel.'[33] Additionally, with the opening of 1:15 ('in these days ...'), Luke inscribes this account into the vernacular of the Septuagint.[34] This, together with the exercise in lot-casting at the end of the account, locates this narrative very much within the horizons of God's relations with ancient Israel. Through using Scriptures in such ways Luke has drawn roughly contemporary events into an interpretive nexus. Israel's Scriptures represent God's own voice, providing God's perspective on the present. They help to assert divine legitimation for the shape and self-understanding of the community of Jesus' followers.

Subsequently, in Acts 2:1–13, those who gathered after the outpouring of the Holy Spirit on the believers hear prophetic speech enabled by the Holy Spirit: 'We hear them speaking about the great things of God' (2:11). What Luke portrays is similar to what we read in the Lukan birth narratives: being filled with the Spirit leads to praise (see Lk. 1:49, 'The Mighty One has done great things for me!').[35] The phrase 'great things of God' seems to be borrowed from the Psalms, where it is found in the context of doxology (see Pss. 106:2; 145:4, 12); elsewhere, too, God's mighty acts figure prominently in praise

---

[32] See Steyn, *Septuagint Quotations*, 54, 63; Moessner, 'The "Script" of the Scriptures in Acts,' 223–24; Brawley, *Text to Text Pours Forth Speech*, 62–71.

[33] Brawley, *Centering on God*, 180–81 and *Text to Text*, 71–74.

[34] Luke's phrase ἐν ταῖς ἡμέραις ταύταις is peculiar to Luke in the Greek Bible; however, ἐν ταῖς ἡμέραις occurs 122 times in the LXX, of which fifty-five appear in the phrase ἐν ταῖς ἡμέραις ἐκειναί.

[35] The exception is Lk. 1:41–45 (Elizabeth, filled with the Spirit, blesses Mary), but this provides no analog to the present scene. See Lk. 1:46–55, 67–79; 2:25–32; O'Reilly, *Word and Sign in the Acts of the Apostles*, 54–57.

(e.g., Ex. 15; Judg. 5; 1 Sam. 2). This evidence of intertextuality in 2:11 is of special interest since, in other episodes of 'inspired speech' (ἀποφθέγγομαι) in Acts, such speech is plainly comprehensible speech concerned with scriptural interpretation (2:14; 26:25). Peter's Pentecostal address (2:14–41) is identified as Spirit-inspired speech,[36] consisting above all of scriptural citation and explication (especially Joel 3:1–5; Pss. 15:8–11; 109:1 LXX, but also 1 Kgs. 2:10; Ps. 132:11; Is. 32:15; 57:19; Dt. 32:5; etc.), with the scriptural message comprehended in terms of its actualization in the ministry, death, resurrection, and exaltation of Jesus. We also find the verb in the context of Paul's speech before Herod Agrippa II and Porcius Festus, where Festus' outburst, 'You have lost your mind!' is countered by Paul's claim to inspired, sober speech (26:24–25). The basis of Festus' interruption is not ecstatic speech (which one might expect, given Festus' characterization of Paul), but rather Paul's exposition of Scripture as witness to Jesus. As Joseph Fitzmyer observes, 'Festus protests first over Paul's erudition, his strange way of arguing, and his allusions to Moses and the prophets. Festus has difficulty in following all this argumentation and especially in admitting such a thing as resurrection.'[37] Read in relation to these other texts where the verb ἀποφθέγγομαι is found in Acts, Luke's reference to inspired speech concerning 'the great things of God' in 2:11 is best understood as charismatic interpretation of Scripture.[38] It is not surprising, then, that in both Acts 2 and Acts 26, the consequence of Spirit-inspired speech is a charge against the speakers that they had lost their mental capacities. In neither case would this be due to maniacal or ecstatic behavior, but rather to the strangeness of their proclamation, writing as it would have the death and resurrection of Jesus into the story of Israel as that story's culmination. 'The great things of God,' accordingly, would find their center and meaning in the exaltation of Jesus of Nazareth.

I draw attention to these two occasions of scriptural interpretation early in the book of Acts not simply to celebrate the hermeneutical wisdom of the disciples, but especially to highlight what might easily be forgotten – namely, the obtuseness of the disciples when it comes to understanding Jesus' work within the purpose of God narrated in the gospel. This obtuseness comes into focus, above all, in two parallel texts:

'Let these words sink into your ears: The Son of Man is going to be betrayed into human hands.' But they did not understand this saying; its meaning was concealed

36 Cf. Jervell, *Apostelgeschichte*, 141–42.
37 Fitzmyer, *Acts of the Apostles*, 763.
38 The role of the Spirit in inspired interpretation of Scripture is well known in the literature of Second Temple Judaism (e.g., Josephus, at Qumran, in Sirach, in Philo). Cf. Levison, 'Holy Spirit,' 512–13 and *The Spirit in First Century Judaism*, 254–59.

from them, so that they could not perceive it. And they were afraid to ask him about this saying.

(Lk. 9:44–45)

Then he took the twelve aside and said to them, 'See, we are going up to Jerusalem, and everything that is written about the Son of Man by the prophets will be accomplished. For he will be handed over to the Gentiles; and he will be mocked and insulted and spat upon. After they have flogged him, they will kill him, and on the third day he will rise again.' But they understood nothing about all these things; in fact, what he said was hidden from them, and they did not grasp what was said.

(Lk. 18:31–34)

What is perplexing about these texts is precisely that there are two of them. We might not be surprised by the first, located as it is at the end of the Galilean section of the Gospel of Luke, and before the long journey that will occupy Jesus and his disciples from Luke 9 to 19. It is in the journey that Jesus engages especially in disciple-formation; this section comprises instruction for the most part, and this teaching is principally aimed, both directly and indirectly, at the disciples. Having begun in such a disappointing way, surely, as the journey draws to its close, the disciples will comprehend Jesus' words and the significance of his mission in the overarching purpose of God. Luke 18:31–34 is adamant on this point, however: 'they did not grasp what was said.'

Why are the disciples so slow to comprehend? One might suppose that God has concealed the meaning of Jesus' words.[39] However, in the context of revelatory prayer, 'turning to the disciples, Jesus said to them privately, "Blessed are the eyes that see what you see!"' (10:23), and the disciples are those to whom the secrets of the kingdom are revealed (8:10); moreover, Jesus' injunction in 9:44 ('Let these words sink into your ears') presumes that they should be able to understand. Nevertheless, Luke's wording in 18:34 is emphatic: they lacked understanding, the meaning was hidden, they lacked perception, and they avoided discussing it further on account of their fear. What is more, their failure continues through the entire Gospel of Luke, until the concluding moments of Luke's narrative, when the impasse is broken, with Luke reporting that Jesus 'opened their minds to understand the scriptures' (24:45). Prior to this, they lack the categories of thought, they lack an imagination adequate to correlate what Jesus holds together in his passion predictions: his exalted status and his impending dishonor.[40] They are unable to integrate in a seamless

---

[39] Cf., e.g., Schürmann, *Lukasevangelium*, I, 573; Fitzmyer, *Luke*, I, 814. Bovon thinks in terms of both predestination and the disciples' 'blindness to salvation history' (*Luke*, 393). Nolland (*Luke*, II, 514) thinks the failure of insight is satanic.

[40] 'It is in fact the very revelation of God's "secrets" (8:10) that leaves them perplexed before the incomprehensible way of God' (Schweizer, *The Good News according to*

way how Jesus' messiahship could be defined with respect to both his elevated status before God and his rejection by human beings. Their horizons of perception are too narrowly circumscribed, patterned as they are according to a conceptual scheme more conventional in Roman Palestine. Theirs are ill-formed imaginations, misshaped conceptual schemes, leading them to mouth the words, 'What can this mean?'

The disciples' hermeneutical quandary finds its resolution in three related actions, noted in Luke 24–Acts 2. First, the disciples have Jesus himself as their teacher, 'opening the Scriptures' to them (Lk. 24:32). Second, Jesus 'opened their minds to understand the Scriptures' (24:45). Third, they are the recipients of the Holy Spirit, who, as we have seen, enables inspired interpretation of the Scriptures. How Jesus 'opened the Scriptures' is not transparent from the Lukan narrative, which relates only that it was 'necessary that the Messiah should suffer these things and then enter into his glory,' and that, 'beginning with Moses and all the prophets, he interpreted to them the things about himself in all the scriptures' (24:25–27). Which Scriptures? We are not told, nor can we find in Israel's Scriptures plain and direct precedent for the divine necessity of messianic suffering. In fact, within the Lukan narrative, we have heard that the prophets or the Son of Man (and not the Messiah) 'must suffer.' Here, though, is where we find Jesus' hermeneutical lesson. By correlating the persecution of the prophets with messiahship, he is able to assert that the Scriptures provide a script for the eschatological king who would suffer before entering into glory.[41] Thus, in God's economy (that is, as an expression of God's βουλή), the high status of God's anointed one is not contradicted by humility or humiliation. Instead, in his passion and exaltation, Jesus embodied the status-reversal comprising salvation; his death was the focal point of the divine-human struggle over how life is to be lived, whether in humility or in self-elevation. Though righteous before God, though anointed by God, he is put to death. Rejected by people, he is raised up and vindicated by God – and all of this is subsumed under the one divine purpose. God's purpose embraces both rejection by humans and divine exaltation, and recognition of this fabula, this story behind the story – embraced so deliberately, embodied so fully by Jesus, the charismatic, authorized hermeneut – serves as the theological pattern by which to order the scriptural witness. Our understanding of Jesus' career is guided by the Scriptures, but so is our understanding of the Scriptures shaped by Jesus' career; the two are mutually informing.[42]

We can verify some of our thinking so far by inquiring the following: Who engages the Scriptures aright in the Gospel of Luke? There is the example of

---

Luke, 163). For ἵνα as a 'marker serving as substitute for the inf. of result, *so that*,' see BDAG, 477.

41 See Strauss, *Davidic Messiah*, 257.

42 See further J.B. Green, *Luke*, 848–49, 857.

Jesus, of course, explicit in such texts as Luke 2:42–52 and 4:1–13. There is the narrator himself, but he provides little by way of self-characterization and does not speak directly regarding his interpretive habits. Other exemplars are Mary, Simeon, Zechariah, and Hannah, all within the Lukan birth narrative. Each interprets God's restorative work by deploying scriptural language and images now understood in relation to the advent of Jesus. Like Jesus, Simeon and Zechariah engage in interpreting Scripture as persons on whom the Spirit rests, who are filled with the Spirit. Luke has characterized each as responsive to God's salvific work in the world. And each engages in this messianic reading of the Scriptures by way of setting out the nature of God's people – their identity and vocation.

The ensuing narrative of Acts is an extensive exercise in hermeneutics, in world-shaping. Who grasps the significance of the outpouring of the Spirit at Pentecost? Who reads the Scriptures aright – that is, in conformity with the will of God? Crucially, the primary obstacle that must be overcome as God restores his people, and as both Jews and Gentiles are called to transfer their allegiances over to him, is 'ignorance.'[43] This reality was observed by J.-W. Taeger, who saw that the human situation in Lukan thought was one characterized by ignorance needing correcting rather than sin needing forgiveness.[44] Aside from the enigma Taeger thus introduces into Lukan studies concerning the heightened interest one finds in Luke-Acts specifically on forgiveness of sins,[45] Taeger's view also suffers from an anemic understanding of 'knowledge' and 'ignorance.' We should understand Luke's notion of 'ignorance' less as the state of 'lacking information,' and more in terms of 'possessing a faulty imagination.' Thus, ignorance for Luke is actually misunderstanding – a failure at the most profound level to grasp adequately the purpose of God. Even when obeying God, people within the Lukan narrative obey him as they have come to perceive him, and the extent of their misperception is so grand that their attempts at obedience actually run counter to the divine will. That is, so long as they were committed to their former way of construing the nature of God and life before God, they were blinded to what God was doing. What is needed is a theological transformation: a deep-seated conversion in their conception of God and, thus, in their commitments, attitudes, and everyday practices. Consequently, the resolution of 'ignorance' is not simply 'the amassing of facts,' but a realignment with God's ancient purpose, now coming to fruition (that is,

---

[43] This is true of Jew and Gentile alike – see esp. Acts 3:17; 17:30.

[44] Taeger, *Der Mensch und sein Heil* see p. 37: '*Der Mensch ist kein salvandus, sondern ein corrigendus*'.

[45] Lk. 1:77; 3:3; 5:20–21, 23–24; 7:47–49; 11:4; 12:10; 17:3–4; 23:34; 24:47; Acts 2:38; 3:19; 5:31; 10:43; 13:38; 15:9; 22:16; 26:18; cf. J.B. Green, 'Salvation to the End of the Earth.'

'repentance') and divine forgiveness.[46] Luke's work is thus a narrative of enlightenment, so that prior understandings might be razed and the now-reconstructed understanding of the purpose and promises of God, an understanding that arises from the story of the Scriptures as Luke narrates it, might be welcomed.

According to Peter's address at Pentecost, the exaltation of Jesus and the consequent outpouring of the Holy Spirit have signaled a dramatic transformation in history, so the message of Jesus' witnesses calls for a radically different understanding of the world than that held previously. Within the speeches of Acts, Jewish people might hear the familiar stories borrowed from their Scriptures, but these stories have been cast in ways that advocate a reading of that history that underscores the fundamental continuity between the ancient story of Israel, the story of Jesus, and the story of the Way. Israel's past (and present) is understood accurately and embraced fully only in relation to the redemptive purpose (βουλή) of God, but this divine purpose can be understood only in light of Jesus' ministry, crucifixion, and exaltation, and through exegetes operating in the sphere of the Holy Spirit. The coming of Jesus as Savior may signal the fresh offer of repentance and forgiveness of sins to Israel (Acts 5:31; 13:38–39), but the acceptance of this offer by Jewish people is dependent on their embracing *this interpretation* of God's salvific activity. Greek audiences, too, are asked to adopt a new way of viewing the world. Note how, at Athens, Paul distinguishes between how God worked in the past (17:30a; cp. 14:16) and how he will now operate (17:30b) – a distinction that is marked by Jesus' resurrection and that calls for conversion. And what is conversion, but transformation of the theological imagination, which includes incorporation into the community of believers and concomitant practices?[47]

Epilogue

At the close of an otherwise perceptive essay on the theology of the cross in Acts, C.K. Barrett claims that Luke 'is not sufficiently interested in theology (beyond basic Christian convictions) to be called a [theologian] of any colour.'[48] Whether one agrees with this assessment of the Third Evangelist will depend almost entirely on how one defines 'theology.' If 'theology' is known by its propositions, then excluding Luke from the company of theologians would be well-justified. If, on the other hand, 'theology' is critical reflection

---

[46] Cf. Pokorný, *Theologie der lukanischen Schriften*, 62–63, 66–67.

[47] See J.B. Green, 'The Nature of Conversion in the Acts of the Apostles'; and, more generally, Meeks, *Origins of Christian Morality*, 18–36.

[48] Barrett, 'Theologia Crucis – in Acts?', 84.

on the practices of the church in the world,[49] then such a negative judgment would be mistaken. Nor, on this definition, would it be problematic to 'do theology' by means of narrative. In fact, I have urged that Luke the narrator is Luke the theologian.

Luke engages in history/writing as an essentially theological enterprise, one who works not on the basis of, but with, history to 'do theology.' His theological agenda prioritizes the Scriptures as witness to the divine purpose but recognizes that the Scriptures can be read in ways that are incoherent with God's purpose and program. Orienting a reading of Scripture christologically, Luke demonstrates how to read the Scriptures aright and, in doing so, brings 'the events that have been fulfilled among us' in a relationship of mutual interpretation. The christological center point of the biblical narrative is important, since this interpretive mutuality is not apropos 'experience' in general, as though the Scriptures ought generally to stand under or be interpreted by personal or communal experience. Rather, 'the events' to which Luke points are particularly those which manifest the beneficence of God in the salvific work of Christ, including his outpouring of the Holy Spirit. Luke's theological enterprise is ordered around a world-transforming narrative rather than a series of truth claims, a theological vision that Luke's Model Readers embrace as their own. It is for this reason that I have insisted that Luke's theological hermeneutic has an ecclesiological aim.

If theology is critical reflection on the church's practices, then the way is open to ask how Luke the theologian might direct us in our own theological formation. This is because, following in these footsteps, the theological enterprise would be less the amassing of encyclopedic knowledge of theology's content, more the exercise of a 'craft.' As Alasdair MacIntyre, puts it, a craft might involve procedures and steps, and might build on a history of performance, but it is ultimately defined by complexity and innovation that break out of those procedures and help to constitute evolving rules.

> The authority of a master within a craft is both more and other than a matter of exemplifying the best standards so far. It is also and most importantly a matter of knowing how to go further and especially how to direct others towards going further, using what can be learned from the tradition afforded by the past to move towards the *telos* of full perfected work. It is thus knowing how to link past and future that those with authority are able to draw upon tradition, to interpret and reinterpret it, so that its directedness towards the *telos* of that particular craft becomes apparent in new and characteristically unexpected ways.[50]

---

[49] See Wood, *Formation of Christian Understanding*. My sense is that 'theology' is often confused with 'doctrine,' and that this accounts for negative valuations of Luke's theological contribution. On the necessary distinction between these two, see McGrath, *The Genesis of Doctrine*, 37.

[50] MacIntyre, *Three Rival Versions of Moral Inquiry*, 65–66.

Mastering a craft thus entails standing in a tradition and engagement with the present, but it is especially about developing particular intuitions, forming particular dispositions, becoming a particular kind of person whose commitments and predilections have been shaped in relation to the activity in question. To learn the craft of theological interpretation from Luke, then, would be at least to stand within his tradition of reading Scripture according to the beginning, middle, and end he has identified, and doing so from a self-conscious location within the Christian narrative thus identified.

Theological interpretation has much to learn from the narrative approach Luke has exhibited, not least about the role of scriptural reading as a community-forming activity – a reading, then, that would accord privilege to our locating ourselves within the great story of God and his people as this is articulated in Luke-Acts, rather than to a particular exegetical technique or method. Of course, we must also take into account that this narrative was stalled neither by the completion of Luke's writing nor by the process of determining the shape and content of the Christian Scriptures. Our reading of Scripture is constrained in a way that Luke's was not, however, by the theological decisions around the selection and formation of the canon, which provides the context within which to come to terms with Luke's witness. Our reading is also constrained by the articulation of the 'rule of faith' and subsequent ecumenical creeds of the Great Church, by which particularly Christian readings of the Scriptures are measured. We must account for canon and creed, then, in our reading of the Bible as Christian Scripture. Likewise, the subsequent-and-still-unfolding story of God's people, especially as it has sought and seeks faithfully to indwell and perform this narrative, is present as our guide.

Bibliography

Ashbrook, J.B., and C.R. Albright, *The Humanizing Brain: Where Religion and Neuroscience Meet* (Cleveland, OH: Pilgrim, 1997)

Barrett, C.K., 'Theologia Crucis – in Acts?' In *Theologia Crucis – Signum Crucis: Festschrift für Erich Dinkler* (ed. C. Andresen and G. Klein; Tübingen: Mohr Siebeck, 1979), 73–84

Bartholomew, C., C.S. Evans, M. Healy, and M. Rae (eds.), *'Behind' the Text: History and Biblical Interpretation* (SHS 4; Carlisle: Paternoster; Grand Rapids: Zondervan, 2003)

Bayer, H.F., 'Christ-Centered Eschatology in Acts 3:17–26,' in *Jesus of Nazareth: Lord and Christ: Essays on the Historical Jesus and New Testament Christology* (ed. J.B. Green and M. Turner; Grand Rapids: Eerdmans, 1994), 236–50

Bock, D.L., *Proclamation from Prophecy and Pattern: Lucan Old Testament Christology* (JSNTSup 12; Sheffield: JSOT Press, 1987)

Bovon, F., *Luke 1: A Commentary on the Gospel of Luke 1:1–9:50* (Hermeneia; Minneapolis: Fortress Press, 2002)

Brawley, R.L., *Centering on God: Method and Message in Luke-Acts* (LCBI; Louisville: Westminster John Knox, 1990)

—, *Text to Text Pours Forth Speech: Voices of Scripture in Luke-Acts* (ISBL; Bloomington, IN: University of Indiana Press, 1995)

Bruce, F.F., 'The Acts of the Apostles: Historical Record or Theological Reconstruction?', in *ANRW* 2.25.3:2569–603

Bryant, D.J., *Faith and the Play of Imagination: On the Role of Imagination in Religion* (StABH 5; Macon, GA: Mercer University Press, 1989)

Bultmann, R., *Theology of the New Testament* (New York: Charles Scribner's Sons, 1951, 1953)

Carter, J.A., 'Telling Times: History, Emplotment, and Truth.' *History and Theory* 42 (2003), 1–27

Conzelmann, H., *Acts of the Apostles: A Commentary on the Acts of the Apostles* (Hermeneia; Philadelphia: Fortress Press, 1987)

Dibelius, M., *Studies in the Acts of the Apostles* (London: SCM Press, 1956); repr. *The Book of Acts: Form, Style, and Theology* (ed. K.C. Hanson; Fortress Classics in Biblical Studies; Minneapolis: Fortress Press, 2004)

Eco, U., *The Role of the Reader: Explorations in the Semiotics of Texts* (Advances in Semiotics; Bloomington, IN: Indiana University Press, 1979)

Fee, G.D., and D. Stuart, *How to Read the Bible for All Its Worth: A Guide to Understanding the Bible* (Grand Rapids: Zondervan, 1981)

Feinberg, T.E., *Altered Egos: How the Brain Creates the Self* (Oxford: Oxford University Press, 2001)

Fireman, G.D., et al. (eds.), *Narrative and Consciousness: Literature, Psychology, and the Brain* (Oxford: Oxford University Press, 2003)

Fitzmyer, J.A., *The Acts of the Apostles* (AB 31; New York: Doubleday, 1998)

—, *The Gospel according to Luke* (2 vols.; AB 28–28A; Garden City, NY: Doubleday, 1981, 1985)

—, *Luke the Theologian: Aspects of His Teaching* (New York: Paulist Press, 1989)

Flanagan, O., *The Problem of the Soul: Two Visions of Mind and How to Reconcile Them* (New York: Basic Books, 2002)

Gasque, W.W., *A History of the Criticism of the Acts of the Apostles* (BGBE 17; Tübingen: Mohr Siebeck, 1975)

Green, G., *Theology, Hermeneutics, and Imagination: The Crisis of Interpretation at the End of Modernity* (Cambridge: Cambridge University Press, 2000)

Green, J.B., *The Gospel of Luke* (NICNT; Grand Rapids: Eerdmans, 1997)

—, 'Modernity, History, and the Theological Interpretation of the Bible,' *SJT* 54 (2001), 308–29

—, 'The Nature of Conversion in the Acts of the Apostles,' in *San Luca Evangelista Testimone Della Fede Che Unisce Atti Del Congresso Internazionale (Padova, 16–21 Ottobre 2000)*, I: *L'Unità Letteraria e Teologica Dell'opera di Luca* (ed. G. Leonardi and F.G.B. Trolese; Padova: Istituto Per La Storia Ecclesiastica Padovana, 2002), 327–34

—, 'Practicing the Gospel in a Post-Critical World: The Promise of Theological Exegesis,' *JETS* 47 (2004), 387–97

—, 'The Problem of a Beginning: Israel's Scriptures in Luke 1–2,' *BBR* 4 (1994), 61–86

—, '"Salvation to the End of the Earth" (Acts 13:47): God as Saviour in the Acts of the Apostles,' in *Witness to the Gospel: Theology of Acts* (ed. I.H. Marshall and D. Peterson; Grand Rapids: Eerdmans, 1998), 83–106

—, 'Scripture and Theology: Failed Experiments, Fresh Perspectives,' *Int* 56 (2002), 5–20

—, 'Scripture and Theology: Uniting the Two So Long Divided,' in *Between Two Horizons: Spanning Biblical Studies and Systematic Theology* (ed. J.B. Green and M. Turner; Grand Rapids: Eerdmans, 2000), 23–43

—, *The Theology of the Gospel of Luke* (NTT; Cambridge: Cambridge University Press, 1995)

Haenchen, E., *The Acts of the Apostles: A Commentary* (Oxford: Basil Blackwell, 1971)

Hemer, C.J., *The Book of Acts in the Setting of Hellenistic History* (ed. C.H. Gempf; WUNT 49; Tübingen: Mohr Siebeck, 1989)

Hinchman, L.P., and S.K. Hinchman (eds.), *Memory, Identity, Community: The Idea of Narrative in the Human Sciences* (Albany: State University of New York Press, 2001)

Jervell, J., *Die Apostelgeschichte: Übersetzt und erklärt* (KEK 3; Göttingen: Vandenhoeck & Ruprecht, 1998)

Kelsey, D., *The Uses of Scripture in Recent Theology* (Philadelphia: Fortress Press, 1975)

Koch, C., *The Quest for Consciousness: A Neurobiological Approach* (Englewood, CO: Roberts, 2004)

Kort, W.A., *'Take, Read': Scripture, Textuality, and Cultural Practice* (University Park: Pennsylvania State University Press, 1996)

Kümmel, W.G., *The Theology of the New Testament According to Its Major Witnesses: Jesus – Paul – John* (London: SCM Press, 1973)

Leat, S.J., 'Artificial Intelligence Researcher Seeks Silicon Soul,' *Research News and Opportunities in Science and Theology* 3 (4 Dec. 2002) 7, 26

Levison, J.R., 'Holy Spirit,' in *Dictionary of New Testament Background* (ed. C.A. Evans and S.E. Porter; Downers Grove, IL: InterVarsity Press, 2000), 507–15

—, *The Spirit in First Century Judaism* (AGJU 29; Leiden: E.J. Brill, 1997)

Lowenthal, D., *The Past Is a Foreign Country* (Cambridge: Cambridge University Press, 1985)

MacIntyre, A., *Three Rival Versions of Moral Inquiry: Encyclopaedia, Geneaology and Tradition* (Notre Dame, IN: University of Notre Dame Press, 1990)

Matera, F.J., *New Testament Ethics: The Legacies of Jesus and Paul* (Louisville: Westminster/John Knox Press, 1996)

McGrath, A.E., *The Genesis of Doctrine: A Study in the Foundation of Doctrinal Criticism* (Grand Rapids: Eerdmans, 1990)

Meeks, W.A., *The Origins of Christian Morality: The First Two Centuries* (New Haven/London: Yale University Press, 1993)

Moessner, D.P., 'The "Script" of the Scriptures in Acts: Suffering as God's "Plan" (βουλή) for the World for the "Release of Sins,"' in *History, Literature and Society in the Book of Acts* (ed. B. Witherington, III; Cambridge: Cambridge University Press, 1996), 218–50

Morgan, R., with J. Barton, *Biblical Interpretation* (Oxford: Oxford University Press, 1988)

Nolland, J., *Luke* (3 vols.; WBC 35A-C; Dallas: Word, 1989–93)

O'Reilly, L., *Word and Sign in the Acts of the Apostles: A Study in Lucan Theology* (AnGr 243; Rome: Pontifical Biblical Institute, 1987)

Pao, D.W., *Acts and the Isaianic New Exodus* (WUNT 2.130; Tübingen: Mohr Siebeck, 2000)

Parsons, M.C., 'Reading a Beginning/Beginning a Reading: Tracing Literary Theory on Narrative Openings,' *Semeia* 22 (1991), 11–31

Phelan, J., *Narrative as Rhetoric: Technique, Audiences, Ethics, Ideology* (Columbus: Ohio State University Press, 1996)

Pokorný, P., *Theologie der lukanischen Schriften* (FRLANT 174; Göttingen: Vandenhoeck & Ruprecht, 1998)

Rabinowitz, P.J., 'Reader-Response Theory and Criticism,' in *The Johns Hopkins Guide to Literary Theory and Criticism* (ed. M. Groden and M. Kreiswirth; Baltimore: Johns Hopkins University Press, 1994), 606–609

Reyna, S.P., *Connections: Brain, Mind, and Culture in a Social Anthropology* (London: Routledge, 2002)

Said, E.W., *Beginnings: Intention and Method* (New York: Basic Books, 1975)

Schorske, C.E., *Thinking with History: Explorations in the Passage to Modernism* (Princeton: Princeton University Press, 1998)

Schürmann, H., *Das Lukasevangelium* (2 vols.; HTKNT 3; Freiburg: Herder, 1984, 1994)

Schweizer, E., *The Good News according to Luke* (Atlanta: John Knox Press, 1984)

Siegel, D.J., *The Developing Mind: How Relationships and the Brain Interact to Shape Who We Are* (New York: Guilford, 1999)

Smith, D.E., 'Narrative Beginnings in Ancient Literature and Theory,' *Semeia* 22 (1991), 1–9

Steyn, G.J., *Septuagint Quotations in the Context of the Petrine and Pauline Speeches of the Acta Apostolorum* (CBET 12; Kampen: Kok Publishers, 1995)

Stock, B., *Listening for the Text: On the Uses of the Past* (Parallax: Re-Visions of Culture and Society; Baltimore: Johns Hopkins University Press, 1990)

Strauss, M.L., *The Davidic Messiah in Luke-Acts: The Promise and Its Fulfillment in Lukan Christology* (JSNTSup 110; Sheffield: Sheffield Academic Press, 1995)

Taeger, J.-W., *Der Mensch und sein Heil: Studien zum Bild des Menschen und zur Sicht der Bekehrung bei Lukas* (SNT 14; Gütersloh: Gerd Mohn, 1982)

Webster, J., *Holy Scripture: A Dogmatic Sketch* (Current Issues in Theology; Cambridge: Cambridge University Press, 2003)

White, H., *The Content of the Form: Narrative Discourse and Historical Representation* (Baltimore: Johns Hopkins University Press, 1987)

Wood, C.M., *The Formation of Christian Understanding: An Essay in Theological Hermeneutics* (Philadelphia: Westminster Press, 1981)

3

The Purpose of Luke–Acts

Israel's Story in the Context of the Roman Empire

David Wenham

Although in some forms of postmodern thinking history may not matter, for the Christian interpreter of the Old and New Testaments history matters a great deal. Christians believe that God has spoken to us in history, supremely through Jesus. The Christian belief is that God spoke to us not in some timeless supra-cultural language, but in the context, the idioms, the culture and the language of a particular time and place. The particularity of the Christian religion is one of the strangest things about it, but it is also one of its glories, testifying to God's concern with the particular realities of human life: Jesus was concerned for particular people with particular names and particular problems and needs.

To interpret the historical word of God involves historical understanding, though it involves much more than that. To understand Jesus and his teaching, we need to understand something of his first-century Palestinian context, with its Pharisees, Samaritans, Romans, its temple and synagogues, its political and social and religious tensions, its modes of executing and burying people, and so on.

Of course, our understanding of Jesus comes almost entirely through the New Testament writings, and they too are divine communication (in the Christian view) spoken into and coming out of particular historical contexts. And to begin to understand them involves seeking to understand them in that context. Apart from anything else the writings are written in ancient Greek, and without some understanding of Greek we would not understand them at all.

But, though few people would deny the need to understand the ancient languages of the Bible, there is in some circles a tendency to downplay the importance of historical understanding, with theological and literary interpretations of various sorts being preferred. This is partly because historical approaches to the Bible have so often seemed speculative, contradictory to one another, and unhelpful for faith. However, this chapter is written in the conviction that historical understanding is both possible, and also a theologically necessary and helpful ingredient in the process of interpreting the Bible.

The possibility and the value of understanding the context of the biblical books are most easily illustrated from one of the New Testament letters, such as Paul's first letter to the Corinthians. It is hugely helpful to know: (a) who the author of the letter is (i.e., Paul) and to know something of his founding of the Corinthian church; (b) to know something about first-century Corinth and the Greco-Roman world; and (c) to have some clues about the problems in the Corinthian church. For example, seeing Paul's controversial teaching on marriage in 1 Corinthians 7 as a response to the other-worldly Greek-influenced super-spirituality of some of the Corinthian Christians puts his teaching in a very different and much more positive light than a superficial reading might suggest. It is very helpful to see that God's word through Paul was incarnated in a particular Greek context, just as God's word through Jesus was incarnated in a Palestinian context.

It is not always easy to recognize, however, the context of a New Testament book like 1 Corinthians. Sometimes there is extrabiblical evidence that is relevant (for example, about the city of Corinth), sometimes there is evidence from other biblical books (such as Acts), sometimes it is a matter of 'mirror-reading' the text. The process has been compared to listening to one end of a phone conversation and trying to reconstruct what is being said at the other end of the line – that's not always easy, and yet it can sometimes be done very successfully and fruitfully.

The process is more complicated in the case of a gospel than with a letter, because a letter is really one end of a conversation, whereas a gospel is not.

But, although I am well aware that many attempts to suggest a historical *Sitz im Leben* for the gospels are wildly improbable, I still believe that it is possible to make sensible and useful historical observations about the gospels.

The purpose of this chapter is to seek to do this with Luke and Acts. I take Luke and Acts to be a two-volume work by one author, and I intend to offer suggestions about the historical context in which it was written and about the author's intentions in writing the two volume work.[1] My case is based largely on some quite simple observations about the contents of Luke-Acts, but also on some evidence from other New Testament books and extrabiblical sources.

---

[1] The purpose of Luke-Acts has, of course, been endlessly discussed, and I will not attempt in this chapter to summarize the literature or the variety of scholarly views, nor to annotate fully the points I am making. For more detail see commentaries and introductions, and note esp. Maddox, *The Purpose of Luke-Acts*.

The Author of Luke-Acts

Paul's letters claim to be written by Paul; Luke-Acts does not make any direct claims about authorship.[2] However, the author does seem to imply that he was a companion of Paul, since in 16:10 he begins to use the first person in the narrative – the so-called 'we' passages – and he continues to do so, off and on, until the end of Acts. External evidence points in the same direction, since the unequivocal testimony of the early church is that Luke, the companion of Paul, was the author of the two volumes.[3]

Easily the most obvious explanation of the use of the first person is that the writer is speaking about himself and letting us know that he was present with Paul in his journeys, as described. Modern scholars have offered alternative explanations, suggesting that the author of Acts may have been drawing on someone else's diary or that the use of the first person may be a literary device. But I doubt if either of these alternative explanations would be seriously considered, were it not for the fact that some scholars are convinced that the author cannot have been a companion of Paul.[4] They are convinced that Acts presents a historically misleading picture of Paul, and so they cannot conceive of it being written by a companion of Paul.

The arguments for Acts being historically inaccurate are mainly based on a comparison of Acts with the Pauline letters. The historical narrative of Acts is thought to be incompatible with the narrative hints that Paul gives in Galatians especially; and the portrait of Paul given in Acts is thought to be a sanitized picture of the hero of the narrative: the Paul of Acts is said to be far less radical and angular, and far more irenic (e.g., towards Jewish Christianity) and far more sophisticated as a teacher than the real Paul revealed in his letters. These arguments have a grain of truth in them: of course, Paul's admiring follower and companion has a different perspective on Paul than Paul's own view of himself. But I have argued elsewhere that close investigation of the relationship between Acts and Paul's letters shows Acts to be remarkably well-informed

---

[2] But see Hengel's arguments about the antiquity of the titles 'according to Mark', 'according to Luke', etc. in his *Four Gospels*.

[3] E.g., Irenaeus, *Haer* 3.1.2. Of course, the early church tradition could simply be an inference from the 'we' passages, but there is no reason to suppose that that is all it is. If it were simply such an inference, it is still evidence that this is how the early church understood the 'we' passages.

[4] But for a different view see Porter, 'The "We" Passages'. The theological truthfulness and Scriptural authority of Luke-Acts do not depend on my view of the 'we' passages or on the Lukan authorship of Luke-Acts; but; if we are told (indirectly, through the 'we' passages) who the author is and something of his movements, then this may well be informative and useful in assessing the purpose of the two-volume work (the focus of this article) and in interpreting it.

about Paul (including about the events following his conversion in chapters 9–15), so that the common-sense reading of the 'we' passages remains the most likely reading.[5] The case for Lukan authorship of Acts, and so of Luke-Acts, is very strong (though my later conclusions are not mainly dependent on this conclusion).

Before leaving the 'we' passages and their significance, it is worth noting, by way of anticipating some of our later argument, that they cover chapters in Acts that describe Paul coming into conflict with all sorts of people and being brought before the Roman authorities on various occasions; Acts concludes with Paul being tried in the Roman courts of Felix and Festus and with him finally awaiting trial in Rome. Luke is apparently with Paul during the period of the trials and with him finally in Rome (27:1; 28:16). It is this that led some earlier scholars to suggest that Luke wrote Acts, or indeed Luke-Acts, as a sort of defence document for Paul. I will argue in this chapter that the scholars arguing that view were going in the right direction, even if Luke-Acts is much more than a defence document for Paul.

Significant Features of Luke–Acts

The identification of Luke as the author of Luke-Acts is by no means the most important consideration in identifying the context and purpose of the two-volume work. More significant are observations about six key features of Luke and Acts.

The prologue of the Gospel

A good place to start is with Luke's own statement of his purpose in the opening of his gospel:

> Since many have undertaken to put together an account of the things fulfilled among us, as the eyewitnesses from the beginning and ministers of the word handed them down to us, it seemed good to me also, having followed everything accurately from the beginning, to write for you in an orderly way, most excellent Theophilus, so that you may know the reliability of the words you have been taught (1:1–4).

---

[5] I have argued this most recently in my book *Paul and Jesus: The True Story*, where, among many other things, I contend that the 'famine relief' visit in Acts 11:27–30, seen in its context in Acts 11, is bound to have included discussion of what has been going on in the Antioch church, including Paul's part in it. It thus corresponds with the visit of Paul and Barnabas to Jerusalem described in Galatians 2 far better than with the Jerusalem Council of Acts 15. For more detail see also my 'Acts and the Pauline Corpus II'.

These verses raise a whole host of intriguing and important issues; they have been most fully discussed by Loveday Alexander in her book *The Preface to Luke's Gospel*. She explores in particular the genre of the prologue and finds that Luke is writing not in the high historical style of someone like Thucydides, but still in the style of intelligent 'scientific' writing. We cannot explore that question further here but will simply make a few passing comments.

First, Luke attests to a lively interest in the traditions of Jesus – with eyewitnesses handing things down, many people putting together accounts (as Luke is now doing), and Theophilus himself having been taught things.

Second, Luke puts himself in this company of passers-on-of-tradition and specifically speaks of his interest in providing a reliable account. The term 're-liable' could mean more than one thing: it could mean historically reliable, but it could also mean theologically or spiritually reliable. In the context of Luke's prologue with its references to 'eyewitnesses', 'having followed things', 'accurately', and 'from the beginning' it is hard to avoid the implication that Luke is expressing a strong concern for historical reliability, and that Luke does have such a concern may be confirmed by the way he continually relates the narrative of events in Luke and Acts to the secular historical context of his day, referring repeatedly to Roman emperors, governors and officials (e.g., 3:1–2; 8:3; 13:31; 23:6–12; Acts 12:1; 18:12; 24:27; 26:32).

But that interest does not exclude theological concerns, and it may be that the reference to things 'fulfilled' among us is significant, though the Greek verb might just mean 'accomplished'. We shall discuss fulfilment in due course.

The third thing to notice is the reference to Theophilus: we don't know who he was (or even whether the name could be a pseudonym), but it sounds as though Luke is addressing his work to a patron or to someone well-placed in society.

Jesus

The prologue is intriguing and important, even if it does not answer many questions definitely. Most of the remainder of this chapter will come at the question of Luke's purpose through a study of the themes found in the gospel.

Luke's first and foremost theme is Jesus. This may be stating the obvious, but it is still worth stating. From the announcement of Jesus' birth in chapters 1 and 2 of the gospel to the resurrection narratives, the exciting and important good news is of 'the Saviour, who is Christ the Lord' (2:11). The beginning of the book of Acts refers back to the gospel, and Luke comments on how in his first volume 'I have dealt with all that Jesus began to do and teach' (1:2). This is the theme of the first volume.

Luke's words about what 'Jesus began to do and teach' could be taken to imply that Acts is the story of what Jesus continued to do and teach after his

death and resurrection, through the Holy Spirit. But that interpretation probably does insufficient justice to the fact that Luke does write two volumes: one
leading up to the ascension of Jesus, and the second taking us forward from the
ascension. Acts is therefore not directly about what Jesus did and taught, but
rather about what the followers of Jesus did and taught.

However, what the church taught was 'Jesus and the resurrection' (Acts
17:18). Acts ends with the description of Paul preaching in Rome and 'teaching about the Lord Jesus Christ with all boldness and without hindrance'
(28:31).

In both volumes, then, the good news of Jesus is central: Luke's first
volume describes it; then Acts describes how the good news of Jesus and the
movement that he started spread through the world.

We are left in little doubt that Luke's purpose is primarily to explain in a
reliable way the story of Jesus and of his movement. Luke is clearly a great
enthusiast for Jesus, and there can be little doubt that he (like the apostles and
others whom he describes in Acts) wants his readers to believe in Jesus and to
follow him. But that is a rather general statement. Can we be more precise?

Wealth and poverty

One of the more satisfactory critical methods used by biblical scholars has been
redaction criticism. Redaction critics have been concerned to identify the particular theological concerns that have guided the authors' 'redaction' of the traditions that they have been using. In gospel studies this has often meant
reflecting on how Matthew and Luke have used and changed Mark and 'Q',
since the two-source hypothesis has been seen as an established result of criticism. The trouble with that approach is that the two-source hypothesis is nothing like as surely established as scholars once believed: it is quite uncertain if Q
existed; and even if Matthew and Luke did know and use Mark, as I am
inclined to think, they will also have had lots of other oral traditions (as Luke's
prologue suggests), so that neat conclusions about the theological/redactional
changes that they have made to Mark are often tenuously based.[6]

However, this does not mean that it is impossible to examine each of the
gospels and to reflect on what their particular concerns are. And, even if we
cannot be sure that Luke, for example, has changed Mark at this or that point
for theological or redactional purposes, we may sometimes think that likely,
and in any case a comparison of the different gospels may be illuminating for
our understanding of each.

---

[6] For scholars questioning traditional views of Q see, among others, Goodacre, *The
Synoptic Problem* and Hengel, *Four Gospels.* Goodacre refers to the importance of oral
tradition, as does Dunn in his *Jesus Remembered.*

Such a comparison makes clear Luke's interest in wealth and poverty. He has a whole stack of stories and sayings of Jesus which are unique to his gospel that bear on the themes of wealth and poverty. There are positive things said about the poor – notably in the first beatitude, where Luke has 'blessed are the poor' (and 'woe to the rich' 6:20, 24; contrast Matthew's 'blessed are the poor in spirit', 5:3) and in Jesus' programmatic sermon in Nazareth, which starts with Jesus reading Isaiah 61: 'The Spirit of the Lord is upon me; he has appointed me to preach good news to the poor.' (4:18). Luke is extremely interested in the Holy Spirit, but also in Jesus' ministry to the poor and marginalized. As well as the positive things said to the poor, there are serious warnings to the rich – for example, the parables of the rich fool and the rich man and Lazarus (12:13–21; 16:19–31).

Luke goes out of his way to show that repentance includes practical sharing of possessions; so John the Baptist explains repentance in concrete financial terms in 3:10–14 (also see 19:8, 9). Luke makes it clear that discipleship includes giving away money and wealth to those in need: Luke 12:32–34 sounds almost like Luke's attempt to preclude the view that only the rich young ruler was called to give up his wealth and to ward off 'spiritualizing' interpretations of 'laying up treasure in heaven' (see also 14:12–14; 16:1–13).[7] Luke also shows that Christian community involves sharing with Christian brothers and sisters: this comes out most clearly in the portrayal of the church in Acts 2–5.

Some people have tried to downplay the importance of the practical *koinonia* portrayed by Luke, noting that it is not repeated in later contexts in Acts and even arguing that it was a failed experiment which left the Jerusalem church in financial trouble. That judgment about the troubles of the Jerusalem church is historically implausible,[8] but – much more important from our point of view – it is quite clearly not what Luke wishes us to think. Luke sees the generosity and common life of the early church as a wonderful work of the Holy

---

[7] It has often been said that the rich young ruler had a particular problem with love of money which Jesus challenged but which may not be other people's problem, and that Jesus is interested in the heart and people's attitudes, not in whether they are rich or poor. There is surely some grain of truth in these points, but it is doubtful if Matthew and Mark see the call to 'sell your possessions' as only relevant to the rich young ruler (cf. Mt. 19:21 with 19:23–27, and Mk. 10:21 with 10:28, 29), and it is doubtful if Matthew understood 'laying up treasure' to be spiritual and not also financial (see 6:19, 20, 24). Luke 12:32–34, which is often seen (rightly or wrongly) as Luke's redaction of the traditions attested in Matthew and Mark, eliminates any ambiguity in regard to the financial dimensions of Christian discipleship.

[8] The later troubles – to judge from a passage like Acts 11:28–30 and from ch. 12 – had more to do with famine and persecution than with any mismanagement of the economy of the Christian community!

Spirit, which he undoubtedly wants us to admire. It is true that such communal life is not specifically mentioned later in Acts, but sharing between rich and poor continues in the collection sent from Antioch to Jerusalem described in Acts 11 and 12. And, for what it is worth, it is notable that Luke's hero Paul speaks of the importance of sharing and equality in the Christian church (2 Cor. 8; 9; Rom. 15), and there may be hints of financial sharing within Pauline churches, for example, in Thessalonica where some of the Christians seem to have been living off the generosity of others instead of earning their own living (2 Thess. 2:6–12, cf. also 1 Tim. 4:9–16 on widows being supported by the church).

Luke's interest in Christian spirituality being practical, including financial, is hardly to be doubted. It seems possible at least that Luke was moving in what we might call more 'middle-class' circles than was typical of the first Christian churches, and certainly in more moneyed circles, which presumably included people like Theophilus. The temptation for Christians in such circles, as we know in Western Christianity today, is to serve God and mammon, and to disassociate spirituality from renunciation of wealth. The temptation for some of us today when reading Luke is to talk about the theme of 'reversal' in general or about Jesus' ministry to the marginalized and those of low status, both of which are very important in Luke; but we must be careful not to evade the financial and material challenge of the gospel. It seems likely that Luke wanted to show that Jesus challenged affluent spirituality and saw the kingdom of God in a holistic way, with practical sharing being just as important as spiritual gifts and experience.[9]

Judaism and Christianity

If practical material discipleship was one of Luke's interests and purposes in his portrayal of Jesus and the Christian movement, it was not the only or probably even the most important one. Howard Marshall, in his useful article on Luke's

---

[9] Chapters 14 and 16 of the gospel make excellent sense in this context: in Lk. 14 Jesus is in a relatively affluent context and challenges it forcefully (e.g., 14:8, 12, 15–21, 28, 33; 16:9, etc.). Note also the relevant story of Zacchaeus, which is unique to Luke, in 19:1–9: the comment is sometimes made that Zacchaeus only promised to give away half his goods, as though this justifies something less radical than 'sell all your possessions'; but Luke's focus is on what he promised to give away, not on what he may have retained! On the other hand, it is worth observing that the Zacchaeus story is a positive story about a rich man finding salvation (note the key Lukan ideas of salvation and finding the lost in 19:10, also the almost Johannine idea of Jesus 'staying in the house' of Zacchaeus, cf. Jn. 14:23). If Luke was writing with wealthy people in mind, it is not surprising that he has something positive and hopeful to say to the rich, not just condemnation.

purpose, made the obvious but important point that biblical writers such as Luke typically had a variety of concerns that come out in their writings.[10] The old view that parables have one simple point has rightly been discarded; gospels also have more than one point!

The infancy narratives

A significant clue to one of Luke's primary goals in writing his gospel lies in the way he starts and ends his narrative of Jesus. The narrative begins in the Jerusalem temple, with John the Baptist's father Zechariah doing his stint of duty as a priest. Luke's Gospel ends after Jesus' resurrection and ascension with the disciples, not back up in the upper room, but 'in the temple praising God' (24:53). This might be accidental and of no significance, but it is probably of very great significance for Luke.

So far as the beginning is concerned, all of the Lukan infancy narratives move very strongly and almost entirely in the world of Jewish piety (focussed in the temple) and in the world of Jewish hope. We may traditionally think of Luke being the one evangelist who was probably a Gentile, but interestingly it is Matthew's infancy narratives that have the Gentile magi coming to visit Jesus and the holy family going from the holy land to Egypt (Mt. 2). Luke's narrative has the baby Jesus brought to the temple in Jerusalem 'to do for him according to the custom of the law' (2:27, cf. v. 39 '... they completed all the requirements of the law of the Lord'). There is a great stress on: (a) doing what the law of Moses required at childbirth (e.g., vv. 22, 23); and (b) the temple and events in the temple. In the temple Jesus is greeted by two elderly saints, Simeon and Anna (2:22–38). Luke, of course, is the only gospel that tells us anything about Jesus' childhood, and that is the story of Jesus coming up to the temple and being in the temple at the age of twelve (2:41–51).

The importance of this for Luke is suggested by what he says about Simeon and about Anna: Simeon is someone who was 'waiting for the consolation of Israel' and who had been told that he would see the Lord's 'Christ' (2:25, 26). When he sees Jesus he says that his eyes have seen God's salvation – a light for revelation to the Gentiles and for 'glory to your people Israel'. Anna, after seeing Jesus, gave thanks to God and began to speak of Jesus 'to all who were looking for the redemption of Jerusalem' (2:39). The point is clear: Jesus is one who is bringing the consolation of Israel, the redemption of Jerusalem. The background to this is the prophetic hope for God's redemption of Israel: both Simeon and Anna echo the promises of Isaiah 52 about God bringing Israel out from exile (cf. Lk. 2:31 with Is. 52:10, and Lk. 2:38 with Is. 52:9).

Nor is it just Simeon and Anna who identify Jesus as the one who is fulfilling God's promises to Israel. Throughout the infancy narratives in Luke this is the

---

[10] 'Luke and his "Gospel"'.

theme that comes back again and again: God is fulfilling his promises for salvation – through John the Baptist in a preparatory way (1:16, 17), but specifically through Jesus – as the promised Messiah and Son of David (so the angel in 1:32, 33; also 2:11), as the one remembering his mercy to Israel 'as he spoke to our fathers, to Abraham' (so Mary in 1:54, 55). Most explicit is Zechariah's prophetic hymn in 2:68–73, where Jesus is related to David, to the prophets and to Abraham.

Critics of Tom Wright have questioned his key idea that Jesus is seen in the New Testament as the one who is bringing Israel out of exile (e.g., in his *Jesus and the Victory of God*). It may be that the subtle concept of Israel still being in exile when Jesus came was not as widespread as Wright suggests, but there is no doubt at all that Luke sees Jesus precisely as the one who fulfils the hopes and aspirations of Israel, as expressed especially in the prophetic writings of the Old Testament.

The Nazareth manifesto
That conclusion is reinforced by Luke's description of Jesus preaching in the Nazareth synagogue in 4:16–29. This has often been recognized as a key passage for Luke, and rightly so.

The equivalent passage in Mark is in Mark 6:1–6. Mark's story of Jesus in the Nazareth synagogue comes in the middle of Jesus' Galilean ministry, and it is much briefer than Luke's account. In Luke it is the first incident from Jesus' ministry that is described (though there is a brief summary of Jesus' ministry in vv. 14, 15). And in Luke there is highly significant material not found in Mark, notably: (a) the description of Jesus reading from Isaiah 61 and then claiming that he himself was fulfilling it; and (b) Jesus' comments about Elijah and Elisha ministering to Gentiles and the violently hostile response of those in the synagogue, from whom Jesus escapes.

The positioning of the narrative and its contents suggests that Luke intends the passage as programmatic. Even if he did not know or use Mark, he does know that the incident described was not the first thing to happen in Jesus' ministry (see v. 23, 'What we have heard you did in Capernaum do here'), but he chooses to put it first. As for the contents, the Isaianic quotation itself seems to highlight key Lukan themes, such as the Holy Spirit and the poor, and the concluding story about Elijah and Elisha ministering to Gentiles and about the hostility shown by those in the synagogue towards Jesus seems at least in some way to anticipate the story in Acts where Paul and others regularly go to synagogues, fall out with them, and go to the Gentiles.

But it is the fulfilment theme that is perhaps most important. It is interesting and surely significant that Luke begins his account of Jesus' public ministry in his home town, and specifically in the synagogue. Luke comments that Jesus' going to the synagogue was 'as his custom was'. Jesus is a law-abiding

Jew, and he comes from the context of pious Judaism, as we saw in the infancy narratives.[11]

Then Jesus takes the scroll, reads from Isaiah 61, and says 'Today this Scripture is fulfilled in your hearing'. People are impressed with his reading and with his gracious explanation of it (4:20, 21).

The point both of the synagogue setting and of Jesus' preaching is to emphasize that Jesus is the fulfilment of God's promises to Israel in Scripture and in particular of the prophetic hope for God's salvation to Israel. Luke wants us to know that.

The journey to Jerusalem

If the synagogue in Nazareth is the starting point for Luke's story of Jesus, the central section of his gospel is sometimes called his 'travel narrative'. From 9:51 through into chapter 18 we have a major section of Luke's Gospel that has no parallel in Mark (though some parallels in Matthew, i.e., 'Q' material, according to the two-source hypothesis). If Mark is Luke's basic source then this is a very striking chunk of non-Markan material, and it is in any case interesting because it looks at first sight as though it is describing Jesus' last journey to Jerusalem – leaving Galilee in 9:51 and coming to Jericho and up to Jerusalem in chapters 18 and 19. But if the impression gained is of a steady progression from Galilee to Jerusalem, a closer examination of the section dispels that impression, since Jesus seems to be leaving Galilee and going south in 9:51, 52; back in Galilee in 10:13–15; in Bethany (perhaps, to judge from John) in 10:38; back between Samaria and Galilee in 17:11; and then on his way to Jerusalem via Transjordan, not Samaria, in chapter 18. This is puzzling, and scholars have wrestled to explain the section.

As plausible as any is the view that Luke has gathered in this section a variety of non-Markan traditions, using the last journey to Jerusalem as a convenient framework within which to put them. Scholars have offered various explanations of Luke's arrangement of the section. For the purpose of this chapter we do not need to decide on that issue, but simply to notice the strong sense of purposive movement towards Jerusalem in the section (13:22; 17:11). Jesus sets his face to go there (9:53). When he is told of Herod wanting to kill him, Jesus comments significantly: 'I must go on my way today and tomorrow and the following day, for it cannot be that a prophet should perish away from Jerusalem' (13:33).

From Jesus' death to Pentecost

This last text makes it clear that Jesus' death is significant. He is going up to Jerusalem to die. Why must Jesus die in Jerusalem? A possible hint is given in

---

[11] Cf. 4:15 and the portrayal of Paul as an observant synagogue-going Jew in the book of Acts (e.g., 13:5; 13:14; 14:1; 16:3; 21:22–26).

Luke's version of the transfiguration, where Jesus is described as discussing with
Moses and Elijah 'his exodus, which he was about to fulfil in Jerusalem' (9:31).
The word 'exodus' could simply be understood to mean departure, but used in
conjunction with the verb 'fulfil' it must mean more than that, especially as
Luke is as clear as the other gospels that Jesus dies at Passover time. Jesus' death
is a Passover-Exodus event, bringing salvation. This must take place in
Jerusalem.

Scholars sometimes argue that Luke does not understand or emphasize
Jesus' death as a saving event, but they are surely mistaken.[12] Luke may not have
the ransom saying of Mark 10:45, but strikingly he has the description of Jesus
as a servant right in the context of the passion and the Last Supper, and very
shortly before the arrest of Jesus where Luke explicitly and specifically cites
Isaiah 53:12: 'he was numbered with the transgressors' (Lk. 22:24–27, 37).[13]
Through this conjunction of texts, Luke must be pointing us to Isaiah 53 as a
key to understanding Jesus' death. He sees Jesus' death as an exodus event, such
as is described in Isaiah 52, and it is the death of the Lord's servant as described
in Isaiah 53 that brings forgiveness and freedom to the people in captivity.

Luke's distinctive description of Jesus' passion and death points in the same
direction. The atoning significance of Jesus' death is not spelled out explicitly,
but Jesus' prayer for the forgiveness of his enemies who are crucifying him is
full of implicit significance,[14] and so is his promise of paradise to the robber who
confesses his sins and calls on the dying Jesus to remember him (23:34, 40–
43).[15] Jesus is especially the friend of sinners in Luke, and he dies to bring them
to paradise.[16]

---

[12] It is true that in Acts and particularly in the preaching of the church the focus is on the
resurrection more than on the death of Jesus, but this probably relates to the evange-
listic nature of most of the preaching. Interestingly, in the speech to the Ephesian
elders Paul does refer to the saving death of Jesus (Acts 20:17–35). In the early chapters of Acts there is a stress on the horror of killing God's Messiah (rather than on the
atonement; e.g., Acts 2:36, 38); that message with its accompanying call for repentance makes sense historically and evangelistically in the Jerusalem context.

[13] Scholars tend to seize on the absence of Mk. 10:45 as evidence that Luke is playing
down the atoning significance of Jesus' death (and any link to the suffering servant of
Isaiah), but this is arguably an example of a source critical theory having a distorting
effect on interpretation. This is not to say that we may not learn anything from a
comparison of the Markan and the Lukan passion narratives: it is striking, for example, how Luke emphasizes Jesus' compassion for those around him and shows us how
Jesus died loving his Father and his neighbour.

[14] See Marshall, *Luke: Historian and Theologian*, 172, on the possible echo of Is. 53:12.

[15] On the textual uncertainty surrounding 23:34 see Marshall, *The Gospel of Luke*,
867–68.

[16] This is not to read Pauline theology into Luke, but to read Luke's remarkable
account in its own right. On the other hand, if the author of Luke's Gospel was a

So Jesus' death is a highly significant saving event, fulfilling Old Testament promises, and it must happen in Jerusalem. Jesus' resurrection also happens in Jerusalem, and so do the resurrection appearances. In Luke there is no instruction to the disciples to 'go to Galilee' as in Matthew and Mark (Mt. 28:10; Mk. 16:7), but all of the recorded appearances of the risen Jesus are in the Jerusalem area (Lk. 24). Why does Luke have this emphasis? It fits with what we have seen already about his emphasis on Jesus the saviour being the one who fulfils the Jews' religious aspirations and hopes.

Luke's favourite resurrection story is presumably the story of the two on the road to Emmaus, judging by the amount of space he gives it. It is a vivid and touching story. From our point of view, the notable thing is the emphasis in the story on the fulfilment of the Scriptures: the unrecognized Jesus interprets the Scriptures to the two disciples, explaining his fulfilment of them, and their hearts burn within them (24:25–27, 32); the risen Jesus makes the same point about his fulfilment of all the Scriptures when he appears to all the disciples in the upper room (24:44, in words reminiscent of Mt. 5:17).

From the resurrection Luke moves to the ascension, which only he among the New Testament authors describes and which again is in the Jerusalem area. Luke probably looks forward to the ascension right back at the start of the 'travel narrative' in 9:51, where he speaks of 'the days drawing near for Jesus to be received up'. Scholars have recognized in those words an allusion to the assumption of Elijah, described in the Old Testament (2 Kgs. 12:17).[17] Jesus seems again to fulfil the Old Testament, in Jerusalem.

The ascension of Elijah led to the Spirit falling on Elisha, and in Acts Pentecost follows the ascension. The disciples are quite specifically instructed 'not to depart from Jerusalem, but to wait for the promise' of the Spirit (1:4). The momentous importance of the coming of the Spirit at Pentecost is clear for Luke: it too is the fulfilment of Old Testament prophecy, and it is the last event that 'must' happen in Jerusalem. It is the signal for the gospel to begin to go out to the world.[18]

It is impossible to miss the importance of Jerusalem and the fulfilment of the Old Testament for Luke. All of the major saving events of Jesus happen in Jerusalem. Luke wants to make it unmistakably clear that Jesus is the fulfilment of Judaism and Jewish hope.

---

companion of Paul who admired him and worked with him over long periods of time, it only makes sense to find similar thinking in Paul and Luke (as also in Lk. 18:9–14).

[17] Luke associates Jesus with Elijah more than once (4:25, 26; 8:30) and sees Jesus as the prophet par excellence (e.g., 24:19).

[18] The gift of the Spirit is specifically a gift empowering the disciples for worldwide witness (Acts 1:8), and the gift of tongues in Acts 2 is specifically a gift that communicates with those gathered in Jerusalem 'from every nation under heaven' (2:5).

The ongoing story of Acts

In Acts the gospel goes out from Jerusalem, but the importance of Jerusalem does not suddenly cease. It is interesting that, in describing the gospel going out to Samaria and then to Cornelius, Luke describes Peter (and in Samaria John, as well) coming down from Jerusalem and being involved (Acts 8; 10). The extending mission is firmly linked to the Jerusalem starting point.

Paul then takes the leading role in the story, but interestingly he has to make a journey to Jerusalem, rather like Jesus' journey, before his final journey to Rome (20:22).[19]

The point that must now be obvious is that Luke wants to stress the Jewish/ Old Testament rootedness of Jesus and the Christian gospel. That indeed comes out in the various defences of himself that Paul makes in the last chapters of Acts. In chapter 22 he begins by explaining to the Jewish crowd in the temple that he is a Jew brought up in Jerusalem at the feet of Gamaliel according to the strict manner of the law (22:3). In chapter 23 he says to the Sanhedrin that he is a Pharisee, a son of Pharisees (23:6). In chapter 24, before the governor Felix, he comments that 'I worship the God of our fathers, believing everything laid down by the law and written in the prophets' (24:14). In chapter 26, before Festus and Agrippa, he refers to his Jerusalem upbringing, to his upbringing as a strict Pharisee, and he comments that he is on trial 'because of my hope in the promise made by God to our fathers, to which our twelve tribes hope to attain' (vv. 6, 7). At the end he says that he has been 'saying nothing but what the prophets and Moses said would come to pass' (v. 22).

When Paul eventually comes to Rome in the very last chapter of Acts, he specially calls together the local leaders of the Jews and tells them that he has done nothing against the Jewish people or the customs of our fathers, and he tries to convince them 'about Jesus both from the law of Moses and the prophets' (28:23). They don't all believe him, and Paul speaks to them of divine judgment and of the gospel going to the Gentiles, but it is striking that, though we are now in the capital of the pagan Gentile world, Paul is still shown to be making links with the Jews. And even their unbelief is seen as the fulfilment of Isaiah's prophecy (vv. 26, 27).

---

[19] Paul's whole ministry and mission start in Jerusalem, in the most orthodox and pious of circles. He starts as a persecutor of the church and then, when he confronts the risen Jesus near Damascus, his anti-Christian mission is converted into a Christian mission to Damascus and the world. See Riesner, *Paul's Early Period*, 237–41.

Whereas in Paul's own account of his conversion in Gal. 1 he does not return from Damascus to Jerusalem for three years, in Acts 9 the account of Paul's conversion is followed almost immediately by his return to Jerusalem, where he is introduced to the apostles by Barnabas (vv. 26–30). It may be that Luke wants to show Paul being integrated into the Jerusalem church before he describes Paul's evolving Gentile mission.

So, from the infancy narratives at the start of the gospel to the last scene in the book of Acts, Luke goes out of his way to connect Jesus and the Christian movement with Jerusalem, Jewish piety and the Old Testament.[20] But why does Luke have this emphasis? Unlike Matthew, Luke does not seem to be strongly Jewish himself, nor does he use fulfilment proof texts in the way that Matthew does. Furthermore, Luke is extremely interested in the Gentile mission and devotes much of Acts to describing the gospel going out from Jerusalem to Judea, Samaria and thence to the ends of the earth. So why is Luke so interested in the Jewish origins of Christianity? That may become clear through briefly noting two further aspects of Luke's portrayal of Christianity and Judaism.

The controversial Gentile mission

As we have just observed, Luke was very interested in the Gentile mission. It is anticipated in Luke's Gospel: for example, in the infancy narratives in Simeon's comment about Jesus being a light to the Gentiles (2:32); in the 'Nazareth manifesto' when Jesus refers to Elijah and Elisha going to Gentiles (4:25–27); and probably in the sending out of the seventy (or seventy-two), if the number seventy relates to the nations of the world (10:1).[21] It is also anticipated in the very strong emphasis in the gospel on Jesus' ministry to sinners, Samaritans and other sorts of outsiders: a chapter like Luke 15 speaks of Jesus ministering to sinners and being criticized by the Pharisees and Jewish leaders. Gentiles were regarded typically as sinners, and, although the Prodigal Son is not a Gentile, he goes to a Gentile country and is certainly a sinner, whom the father warmly welcomes, to the elder brother's chagrin. It is not hard to see that there may be anticipation of the controversial Gentile mission of the church here.[22] But it is, of course, in Acts that Luke's absorbing interest in the Gentile mission becomes clear. He takes us deliberately out from Jerusalem, to Judea and Samaria, and then on to the Gentile world.

Luke was an enthusiast for Gentile mission, but he was aware of how controversial it was. It was controversial among Jews (see the reactions to Jesus in

---

[20] For more detailed and more expertly presented evidence on this see the contributions of David Moessner and Scott Hahn to this volume.

[21] The sending out of the seventy is unique to Luke. Luke has no parallel to Mk. 6:45 – 8:22, where Mark describes Jesus' ministry in Gentile areas, including to the Syro-Phoenician woman. Possibly he wants to keep the Gentile mission for the book of Acts, though his 'great omission' may be for other reasons.

A different possible hint of Luke's interest in Jesus' universal relevance is his tracing of Jesus' genealogy back to Adam (Lk. 3:38; cf. Matthew's genealogy, that goes back only to Abraham).

[22] This is a somewhat different take on the parable from N.T. Wright's interpretation of the parable in terms of exile and return from exile, *Victory*, 125–31.

Lk. 4:28 [cf. 15:2] and to Paul in Acts 21:28 and passim). It was also controversial in the early church. In particular, the policy pursued by Paul and others of not requiring Gentile converts to be circumcised and keep the Old Testament law was objectionable to Jewish Christians, especially in Jerusalem. What was perhaps even more objectionable was what was seen as the contamination of Jewish Christians when they had fellowship with 'unclean' Gentiles (e.g., Acts 11:2, 3; 15:1; 21:21).

Luke refers to the sharp controversy over these issues and makes it very clear that it was Jesus himself and the Holy Spirit who were the instigators of mission to sinners, outsiders and Gentiles (e.g., Acts 1:8; 15:28, etc.) and that it was the unambiguous guidance of the Holy Spirit that the Gentiles did not need to be circumcised and become Jews (e.g., Acts 10; 11). He also makes it very clear that, although it was a difficult issue, the 'liberal' leading of the Holy Spirit was recognized and accepted by the apostles and leaders of the Jerusalem church (e.g., 11:18; 15:19). He also makes it very clear, as we noted at length above, that Christianity came out of pious Judaism and is to be seen as the fulfilment of the Old Testament.

Christians innocent of trouble-making

One of the notable features of Acts especially is the frequent description of conflict between Jesus' followers and the people who opposed them, particularly the synagogue and temple authorities.[23] In describing that conflict Luke makes it very clear that Jesus and the Christians are not to blame.

That comes out in the accounts of Paul before the authorities in the later chapters of Acts (chapters 21–26). It is clear that the riot which led to Paul's arrest was not his fault, and that the various Roman authorities and Herod Agrippa can find nothing wrong with him at all. The opponents of Paul accuse Paul of being 'a plague, one who stirs up riots among all the Jews throughout the world' (24:4, 5), but the narrative of Acts makes it clear that the violent troublemakers are the Christians' opponents (notably, though not exclusively, Jews), and Agrippa sums it up when he comments that 'This man could have been set free if he had not appealed to Caesar' (26:32).

Conflict between the Jews on the one side and Paul and his missionary colleagues on the other recurs throughout the book of Acts. Acts portrays Paul as regularly starting his missions to places within the synagogue and the Jewish community (which is congruent with what we saw above); but then things go wrong, and the Jews take action, often violent action, against Paul and he is thrown out as the Jews accuse the Christians of upsetting the world and acting against Caesar (17:6). Acts makes it clear that Paul is in no way the instigator of

---

[23] There is also conflict with non-Jews (e.g., Acts 16:19; 19:23–27). In these cases, as in the case of conflict with Jews, the Christians are seen to be the innocent party.

the violence, and that the authorities consistently recognize or come to recognize the innocence of Paul and his colleagues. For example, Gallio the governor of Achaia dismisses the case brought against Paul, on the grounds that it is not a case of wrongdoing or crime, but of interpretation of the Jewish law (18:14, 15).

This theme of Christians being unjustly accused of being troublemakers is anticipated in Jesus' trial, where he is accused by the Jewish leaders of misleading the nation and rebelling against Caesar. The verdict of both Pilate and Herod Antipas is that Jesus is guiltless (Lk. 23:4, 15).[24] The theme is anticipated also in the programmatic story of Jesus in the Nazareth synagogue, where the people turn on Jesus and try violently to get rid of him when he speaks of Elijah and Elisha going to the Gentiles (4:25–29).

The story of Jesus in the Nazareth synagogue brings together the theme of Jesus being a loyal Jew fulfilling Old Testament expectation and the theme of Gentile mission (Elijah and Elisha) and the theme of violent opposition to the Jesus movement. That combination of themes is found in different shapes and sizes elsewhere in Luke and especially Acts. Paul's final visit to the Jerusalem temple in Acts 21 is a deliberate act of Jewish piety and Paul showing his loyalty to the law, but it leads to a riot instigated by his Jewish opponents, who accuse him of flouting the law and of having brought a Gentile into the temple (21:28). This incident in the temple leads to Roman intervention on behalf of Paul, and ultimately leads Paul to Rome. The incident in the Nazareth synagogue does not involve Romans, though Luke began his narrative of Jesus' ministry by specifically locating it in the secular context of the Roman Empire (3:1–3).

Conclusions: A Context and Purpose for Acts

The observations we have made about Luke-Acts point us in certain directions as we try to identify a likely context and purpose for Luke-Acts. Luke, we proposed, may well have been written with a relatively wealthy readership particularly (though not exclusively) in mind, hence his focus on radical discipleship and spirituality. The name 'Theophilus', if he was Luke's patron, could point in that direction.[25] The name may also point in the direction of a predominantly Gentile readership, as may Luke's sustained interest in the

---

[24] The repentant thief recognizes Jesus as innocent (23:41), and the centurion in Luke describes Jesus as a 'righteous man' (23:47; cf. 'Son of God' in Mt. 27:54; Mk. 15:39). It is worth noting in passing that Luke's centurions and other Roman officials are often portrayed sympathetically and as well disposed towards Jesus and his followers (Lk. 7:4, 5; Acts 10; 23:19–22; 27:43). But there are some indifferent or rotten Roman eggs (e.g., Acts 24:26, 27)!

[25] So might the high-rhetorical style of the prologue.

mission to the Gentiles.[26] Maybe Theophilus lived in Rome, or had strong Roman connections. So Luke brings his Christian story to Rome.

But Luke is selective in his telling of the Christian story, and he focuses in the second half of Acts on Paul. This makes sense if Luke was a companion of Paul who was very interested in Paul and his ministry, but it may well also be because Paul was a controversial character, accused by his opponents of being a trouble-maker. To see Luke-Acts as a defence brief of Paul himself is probably too restrictive: it is a much bigger account of Jesus and the origins of the Christian church. But what seems plausible is that Luke is writing for a well-placed Roman or Romans with questions about the Christian movement and espe-cially about its relationship to Judaism. If Acts is to be believed, there had been all sorts of tensions and troubles between Jews and Christians in the Roman Empire.

At this point some evidence external to Luke-Acts contributes to the argu-ment, because there is plenty of evidence of such tensions and troubles, includ-ing in Rome itself.

The most interesting evidence in this respect is the Roman historian Suetonius's description of Claudius expelling all the Jews from Rome 'because they were rioting at the instigation of Chrestus' (*Divus Claudius* 25.4). This expulsion, which may be dated to 49 C.E. and which is referred to in Acts 18:2, is most probably to be seen as a response to serious troubles within the Jewish community in Rome over the question of Christ and Christianity.[27]

It has plausibly been argued that Paul's letters allude to and/or reflect these troubles. Thus, his first letter to the Thessalonians was written around 49 C.E., probably from Corinth, where according to Acts Paul had met up with Aquila and Priscilla, victims of Claudius's expulsion (Acts 18:2). In that historical con-text Paul refers mysteriously to 'wrath' having come on the Jews (1 Thess. 2:16), which may well be a reference to the expulsion, as well as to a massacre of Jews in Jerusalem at the hands of the Roman authorities.[28]

---

[26] Luke is interested in the universality of the gospel: Jesus is good news not just for Gentiles, but also for other 'outsiders', such as the poor, women, tax collectors and Samaritans. To say that Luke may have interested Gentiles in mind is not to say that he may not also have wanted to address people from a Jewish background, showing them the Jewish credentials of Jesus and the Christian church.

[27] On the expulsion, see Riesner, *Paul's Early Period,* 157–201. Luke does not tell us that the expulsion had anything to do with Christians. But he refers to Aquila and Priscilla being among those expelled, and they may already have been Jewish-Christian leaders. Why he does not explain more about the disturbance if it was a Jewish-Christian conflict is hard to say: perhaps it is just that it would not be very rel-evant to the narrative of Acts 18, and/or that Luke can and does presuppose knowl-edge of the incident in his readers.

[28] Josephus, *J.W.* XI.223–31. The context of 1 Thess. 2:16 is a reference to the Jews opposing the Christian mission and 'hindering us from speaking to the Gentiles',

Paul's letter to the Romans has also been thought to reflect a post-expulsion situation.[29] The plausible suggestion has been made that the Christian community in Rome originally had a Jewish-Christian leadership, with people like Aquila and Priscilla being leaders, but then the expulsion of the Jews from Rome changed things radically and left Gentile Christians in charge. However, after the death of Claudius in 54 C.E. the Jews and the Jewish Christians were able to return to Rome, and this may very well have produced tensions within the church between the old Jewish-Christian leaders and the new Gentile-Christian leaders. Paul's letter to the Romans may be seen as responding to such tensions, with Paul explaining both the Jewish roots of the gospel and the new universalism that had come through Jesus, as well as encouraging Jewish-Christians and Gentile-Christians to 'welcome one another' (15:7).

Whether these particular hypotheses about 1 Thessalonians and Romans are accepted or not, both letters (and other letters of Paul) testify to: (a) acute tensions between Jews and Christians; (b) Christian concerns about Jewish unbelief and the relationship of Judaism and Christianity; and (c) strained relations within the Christian community between Jewish-Christians and Gentile-Christians. The fact that Paul is addressing such issues in his letter to the Romans suggests that he sees the issues as relevant to Christians in Rome at the time he is writing his letter (probably about 56 C.E.).

This evidence from outside Luke-Acts suggests a plausible context for the two-volume work. The troubles between Christians and Jews will have raised all sorts of questions for people in Rome (and indeed elsewhere in the Roman Empire), especially for educated Romans who may have been attracted to both Judaism and Christianity. They will have wondered, among other things: how do these two related but different movements relate? Why has there been trouble all over the place? Is the accusation that the Christian upstarts have caused the trouble justified? Are the Christian claims to theological legitimacy sustainable?[30] The difficulties between Jewish-Christians and Gentile-Christians will have raised related questions, as well as practical questions about keeping the law or not keeping it and about table fellowship.[31]

---

which may be an oblique hint that the trouble in Rome was to do with the Christian mission to Jews and to Gentiles (see my *Paul and Jesus*, 87–90).

[29] See, among others, Wedderburn, *The Reasons for Romans*, 54–59.

[30] Note Maddox's conclusions in his *Purpose of Luke-Acts*, 184, 85. He pertinently quotes Acts 28:22, where the Jews speak of 'this sect we know that everywhere it is spoken against'.

[31] Arguably Paul's letter to the Romans is addressing just that issue in response to Jewish-Christians who see Christianity as a form of Judaism and want all Christians to respect the forms of Judaism (e.g., Sabbath keeping and circumcision), but also in response to Gentile Christians who are inclined to say 'good riddance' to Judaism (7:4–6; 11:17, 18, etc.). Paul, like his admirer Luke, insists that Jesus is the fulfilment

Luke answers these questions by showing that:

(a) neither Jesus nor the Christian movement nor Paul in particular were starting a new religion; they all started in Jerusalem and were fulfilling the Old
Testament. Whereas Matthew emphasizes fulfilment of the Old Testament
in a way that addresses Jews and/or Jewish Christians and portrays Jesus in
the light of their questions, Luke emphasizes fulfilment in the wider context of questions about Judaism and Christianity.[32] Luke also shows how the
development of the Gentile mission – with the gospel going out from Jerusalem to the world (including Rome) and with Gentile Christians not being required to keep the law – was a legitimate Spirit-led continuation of
God's Old Testament purpose.[33]

(b) the troubles that there have been have not been provoked by the Christians. They have been provoked by others who have been threatened by
the new movement, notably by the Jews who have seen the new movement with its outreach to Gentiles as an attack on the Jewish community
and its purity and its temple.

(c) that the Roman authorities, though not all very admirable characters, consistently recognized the innocence of the Christians from all accusations of
criminal or disruptive activity.

We suggested that Luke's defence of the Christians makes sense in the light of
events such as the expulsion of Jews from Rome in 49 C.E. Christians were
again in the imperial spotlight in 64 C.E., when the Emperor Nero accused
them of starting the fire of Rome and attacked them ferociously. Luke might
be thought to be defending the Christians with that context and accusation in
mind, but there is no very obvious evidence of this. The Christians' problems
in Acts are with Jews, and the Romans are mostly portrayed in a positive or
neutral light. Paul appeals hopefully to 'Caesar', that is to Nero, and Nero does
not seem to be an antichrist.

This could favour an early date for Luke-Acts, in the early 60s. Such a date
has been defended by scholars, who have suggested that Luke ends with Paul
under house arrest in Rome – slightly anticlimactically – because this is as far as
the story has got. Other scholars, however, have been convinced that Luke is

---

of the OT promises and law, but that the Gentiles have now been brought into the
people of God and that Christians are not 'under' the law.

[32] Judaism was a '*religio licita*' in the Roman world with special privileges; in that context the question of whether Christianity was the same or different from Judaism was
a particularly significant question.

[33] Luke has a particular interest in the Holy Spirit and shows how the anointing of
Jesus and the charismatic experience of the early church are part of God's promise to
his people and of his missionary purpose for the world (Lk. 4:18; Acts 2, etc.).

writing after the destruction of Jerusalem in 70 C.E. The strongest argument for this view is probably the Lukan version of the eschatological discourse in chapter 21: where Mark in chapter 13 refers mysteriously to the desolating sacrilege, Luke refers unambiguously to armies surrounding and conquering Jerusalem. It looks as though Luke has 'redacted' Mark in the light of the events of 70 C.E. That argument is, however, quite uncertain, and may be another case of jumping to conclusions too quickly from assumptions about Luke's sources. There is in fact a good case to be made for the view that Luke had a non-Markan source or sources in chapter 21, and that some of Luke's non-Markan traditions were known to Paul well before 70 C.E.[34]

Apart from Luke 21, the destruction of Jerusalem does not feature very prominently in Luke's writings. It is something predicted by Jesus, but in Acts in particular there seems to be little interest in it. Luke's interest in Jerusalem is undoubted, but he is interested in the historical and theological journey from Jerusalem to Rome and in Jews, Gentiles and Christians, rather than in the city of Jerusalem itself.

This might again fit in with an early date of Luke-Acts. If Luke were writing in the early 60s in Rome (where the 'we' passages take him), having previously spent some prolonged time in Caesarea, he would have known that the political situation in Judea was precarious and that Jesus' predictions of the destruction of the temple were only too likely to be fulfilled, and this would have been one ingredient in his thinking about Christianity and Judaism. But he has come with Paul to Rome and it is this, more than the fate and future of Jerusalem, that is at the heart of his concerns.

There is arguably striking parallelism with Paul's letter to the Romans.[35]

---

[34] See my discussion of Lk. 21:23, 24, 34–36 in *Paul: Follower of Jesus or Founder of Christianity?*, 289–333. What is intriguing about Lk. 21:20–24 is that, where Matthew and Mark specifically refer to the defilement of the temple ('the abomination of desolation'), Luke speaks of the desolation of Jerusalem. This failure to mention the temple can hardly be seen as evidence that Luke is writing post-70 C.E., since the destruction and ransacking of the temple was the awful climax of the conquest of the city. It might possibly be connected with Luke's positive references to the temple which we noted (e.g., in the infancy narratives and at the end of the gospel), and those references may be a further argument against a post-70 C.E. date for Luke. Would Luke have linked Jesus and the early Christians so closely with the temple, often portraying it as a place of true piety, if it had recently and famously been destroyed by Titus and his armies?

[35] It is important not to read Paul into Luke, but if Luke was a companion of Paul who worked closely with him, then parallel ideas come as no surprise. We would expect to find Pauline ideas in Luke and Lukan traditions in Paul, and we do.

The possible connections between Luke-Acts and Romans in particular are intriguing: Romans was written just before Paul's fateful final journey to Jerusalem

Paul is writing in the late 50s after the Claudian expulsion of Jews and its aftermath, offering a theological explanation of how the Christian gospel fits in with the Old Testament, with Judaism, with Jewish unbelief. Luke is writing a little later, a gospel not a letter, but addressing some of the same issues. Tom Wright has suggested that Paul wanted to prepare the Roman Christians for the destruction of Jerusalem, which he could foresee and which would very likely change the Christian centre of gravity from Jerusalem to Rome; he wanted Jewish-Christians and Gentile-Christians to hold together, theologically and in fellowship.[36] Luke could be in a similar position, foreseeing the 'times of the Gentiles' and showing in his two-volume work how God's Old Testament Jewish-focussed purpose has led from Jerusalem to Rome.[37]

---

and Rome (with the author of Luke-Acts present with Paul, to judge from Acts 20:5); Acts ends with Paul (and the author of Luke-Acts) in Rome following the journey, and could have been written at that point. (It is striking to compare the reference to Paul's final journey in Acts 19–21 with Romans 15.)

Both Romans and Luke-Acts could have been addressed to people in Rome. The overlapping of theological interests and perspectives in Romans and Luke-Acts would make sense if they came out of the same period and the same Pauline circle. Furthermore, the 'we' passages suggest that the author of Luke-Acts was with Paul during his very long imprisonment in Caesarea (21:17; 27:1). It is not silly to suggest that this could have been the time when Luke wrote his gospel and most of Acts. Among other things this could explain the relatively detailed coverage of Paul's last visit to Jerusalem and of his trials and journey to Rome. Although we argued against the view that Luke-Acts as a whole could be seen as a defence brief of Paul, the issues that Luke-Acts discusses (e.g., Jews and Christians, the Jewish heritage and law, the troubles involving Christians and Jews, the apostle Paul) are precisely the matters that were on the agenda in the trials of Paul described in Acts (chs. 21–26), and it only makes sense that Luke would have reflected a lot on them in his time in Caesarea. He was not writing for the corrupt governor 'most excellent Felix' (Acts 24:3), but for 'most excellent Theophilus' (Lk. 1:3), presumably a more sympathetic person but another person of note, who may have heard similar rumours and had some similar questions.

For scholars, the biggest difficulty with dating Luke-Acts to the early 60s is probably the consensus that Luke used Mark and that Mark was not written until the late 60s. But the scholarly consensus, especially on the dating of Mark, is a very uncertainly based inference, not at all 'an assured result of criticism'.

[36] See Wright, 'Jerusalem in the New Testament'; also Walker, *Jesus and the Holy City*, ch. 4.

[37] Both Paul and Luke are tantalizingly ambiguous about what they expected eventually for Jerusalem and the Jewish nation, but both hint that beyond the present time of 'wrath' there will be redemption (Lk. 21:24; Acts 1:6; Rom. 11:25, 26).

Luke's two-volume work may be seen as explaining in narrative form Paul's phrase 'the Jew first, and then the Greek' and what Paul expresses in Rom. 15:8, 9

But, if there are similarities, there are also differences, with Paul having a strong pastoral concern for the unity of the church and Luke a strong apologetic concern, not least about the accusation that Christians were troublemakers.[38]

Some of the specific suggestions I have made, particularly with regard to the dating of Luke-Acts, are speculative, but my main argument about Luke's apologetic purpose does not depend on all the particulars. Luke was writing to answer questions that were provoked by historical events and his historical context. His apologetic for Christ and Christianity had the following elements. (a) A firm historical component: he was writing about recent history and about events that people had experienced or heard about. He wanted to correct historical misperceptions. (b) A clear theological component: he wanted to show that Christianity was not a novel religion, but that Jesus was the fulfilment of the Old Testament and of God's purposes for Israel and the world.[39] Luke wanted to clarify these issues for his readership and so to establish or encourage faith in Jesus.

This understanding of Luke is by no means brand new,[40] and it is important to say that the apologetic purpose we have suggested was only one of Luke's interests and goals. He had other concerns and interests, as, for example, his desire to challenge his readers to generously practical discipleship

---

where he speaks about Christ being a servant to the circumcised and fulfilling the promises to the patriarchs, and then of God's mercy reaching the Gentiles. Paul and Luke trace the story of salvation from Adam via Abraham via Jesus to the Gentiles.

[38] Not that this distinction is total: Luke has often been seen as having an irenic purpose in relation to the tensions between Jewish-Christians and Gentile-Christians. And Paul has been seen as having an apologetic purpose in Romans – explaining himself and 'his gospel', not least in face of some hostility to his message (e.g., 15:31).

[39] Luke explains that God did 'visit' his people through Jesus, but they did not acknowledge the time of his visitation, and they have accordingly come under judgment (e.g., 1:68; 19:44). The Jewish rejection of Jesus and so of their own heritage is made clear in Luke-Acts, as are the consequences in terms of judgement. But the picture is not all negative in Luke-Acts: as we have seen, he portrays pious Jews sympathetically, and there are a significant number of Jews, including Pharisees, who believe or who are open-minded (e.g., Acts 5:33–39; 17:4, 11; 23:6–9.) In Matthew the picture is arguably more consistently negative, with the hypocrisy of the religion of the scribes and Pharisees being emphasized. Luke's more positive picture could partly reflect his context – he is not writing within a Jewish-Christian context in conflict with the synagogue, as Matthew probably is; it could also reflect his association with Paul as an ex-Pharisee, who has not forgotten his Pharisaism (Acts 23:6; Phil. 3:5).

[40] It is not a million miles away from John Nolland's proposal that Luke was written for a God-fearer considering the Christian faith (*Luke*, xxxii).

within the Christian community,[41] and also his evident interest in the practice of prayer.[42] But the observations we have made contribute to making historical and so hermeneutical sense of Luke's immensely valuable two-volume work, and hopefully show the value of reading New Testament texts with an eye to their historical context.

---

[41] Dr Jeremy Duff, to whom I am indebted for useful comments on this chapter, wonders if the emphasis on Jesus' ministry to the poor may have had an apologetic purpose. In a world where so many religious leaders were known to be mercenary and 'on the make' for themselves, Luke wants to make it clear that the Christian religion was the antithesis of this and was (centrally) about the uplift of the poor and the marginalized and about the building of community, not the advancing of individual status. Compare Paul's policy of working with his own hands and his commitment to service, e.g., in 1 Cor. 9.

[42] Luke emphasizes the importance of personal and corporate prayer for Jesus and the church (e.g., Lk. 11:1–13; 18:1–14; Acts 2:42; 3:1; 4:24, etc.).

Bibliography

Alexander, L., *The Preface to Luke's Gospel* (Cambridge:Cambridge University Press, 1993)

Dunn, J.D.G., *Jesus Remembered* (Grand Rapids: Eerdmans, 2003)

Goodacre, M., *The Synoptic Problem* (London: Continuum, 2001)

Hengel, M., *The Four Gospels and the One Gospel of Jesus Christ* (London: SCM Press, 2000)

Maddox, R., *The Purpose of Luke-Acts* (Edinburgh: T&T Clark, 1982)

Marshall, I.H., *Luke: Historian and Theologian* (Exeter: Paternoster, 1970)

—, *The Gospel of Luke* (Exeter: Paternoster, 1978)

—, 'Luke and his "Gospel"', in P. Stuhlmacher*Das Evangelium und die Evangelien* (Tübingen: Mohr, 1983), 289–308

Nolland, J., *Luke* (WBC; Dallas: Word, 1989)

Porter, S.E., 'The We Passages', in *The Book of Acts in its First-Century Setting*, II (ed. D.W.J. Gill and C. Gempf; Grand Rapids: Eerdmans; Carlisle: Paternoster, 1994), 545–74

Riesner, R., *Paul's Early Period* (Grand Rapids: Eerdmans, 1998)

Walker, P.W.L., *Jesus and the Holy City* (Grand Rapids: Eerdmans, 1996)

Wedderburn, A.J.M., *The Reasons for Romans* (Edinburgh: T&T Clark, 1988)

Wenham, D., *Paul: Follower of Jesus or Founder of Christianity?* (Grand Rapids: Eerdmans, 1995)

—, *Paul and Jesus: The True Story* (London: SPCK; Grand Rapids: Eerdmans, 2002)

—, 'Acts and the Pauline Corpus II: The Evidence of Parallels', in B.W. Winter and A.D. Clarke, *The Book of Acts in its First-Century Setting*, I (Grand Rapids: Eerdmans; Carlisle: Paternoster, 1993), 215–58

Wright, N.T., 'Jerusalem in the New Testament', in *Jerusalem Past and Present in the Purposes of God* (ed. P.W.L. Walker; Carlisle: Paternoster; Grand Rapids: Baker Books, 1994), 53–77

—, *Jesus and the Victory of God* (London: SPCK, 1996)

4

Preparing the Way of the Lord

Introducing and Interpreting Luke's Narrative:
A Response to David Wenham

F. Scott Spencer

No one would mistake John the Baptist for a modern New Testament scholar
or Christian pastor charged with interpreting the Scriptures for her congregation. John preferred the desert over the study and fiery heralding and 'crying
out in the wilderness' over more decorous lecturing and sermonizing in class-
room and pulpit. He had no time or inclination for writing commentaries or
homilies, and his peculiar dress and diet bear little resemblance to academic
regalia and church suppers. Yet, for all his idiosyncrasies, John's mission of
'preparing the way of the Lord' (Lk. 3:3–6, fulfilling Is. 40:3–5) exemplifies a
vital component of the Christian scholar's and minister's task: *to prepare auditors
and readers of scriptural narratives (like Luke-Acts) to encounter the Lord's presence, to
'hear God's voice,' to receive the good news (gospel) of divine revelation.* There are, of
course, other possible motivations for New Testament study ranging from
intellectual curiosity to polemical animosity. But since the books of the New
Testament were all written as confessional documents, by believers for believers ('from faith to faith'), and have been preserved and proclaimed through the
centuries in communities of faith, interpreting the New Testament as sacred
Scripture, as revealed 'word of God' (by whatever means and to whatever
extent), remains a necessary aim of New Testament scholarship.[1]

But how best to accomplish this task? How best to introduce New Testament writings, to 'prepare the way' for apprehending God's wisdom through
them? How best (to switch from John's vocation to Jesus' parable) to cultivate

---

[1] See the helpful discussion of the New Testament as 'Word of God' and 'the
Church's Book' in Schneiders, *Revelatory Text*, 27–93 (chs. 2–3).

the ground, to prepare the heart, to receive the 'seed' of God's word in such a way as to 'bear fruit' (Lk. 8:4–15)? Hefty *Introductions* have long been a staple of New Testament scholarship, putatively providing students with the foundational knowledge they need to maximize their understanding of this strange collection of ancient writings that testify to Jesus Christ. Traditionally, 'matters of introduction' have focused on historical-critical concerns pertaining to original authors and audiences, sources and traditions, dates and provenances, textual authenticity and scientific veracity. Accordingly, matters of religious faith and experience are often bracketed out from introductory textbooks (*Theologies of the New Testament* are a separate cottage industry), although their theological orientations are usually clear enough: 'conservative' *Introductions* defend historical reliability and ecclesiastical tradition; 'liberal' texts highlight ideological diversity and modern criticism; and 'centrist' studies slot somewhere in the middle.[2] Still, whatever their underlying presuppositions and whatever label we attach to them, *New Testament Introductions* by and large have not engaged in any substantive way with the thoroughgoing *theological milieu and message*, of the respective New Testament books. And, consequently, it has not been at all transparent how such *Introductions* actually prepare students to interpret the New Testament with any degree of skill and sophistication, especially to navigate its deep theological waters.

But over the past several years, the *Introduction* business in New Testament study has received some new theological life, evidenced in three significant publications by American authors, both Catholic and Protestant. Although distinctive from each other in many respects, the comprehensive *Introductions* of individual Catholic scholars, Raymond Brown and Luke Timothy Johnson, and the collaborative project of Protestant scholars Paul Achtemeier, Joel Green, and Marianne Meye Thompson, share a fundamental commitment to 'preparing the way' for careful and fruitful encounter with the text and theology, literature and religion of the New Testament – on its own terms.[3] While continuing to affirm the value of historical analysis, each of these works (in its

---

[2] Standard representatives of the respective positions include: Guthrie, *New Testament*, on the 'conservative' side; Kümmel, *Introduction*, on the 'liberal' end, and Brown, *Introduction*, in the 'centrist' category (by self-admission, pp. xi–xiii). The first two focus almost exclusively on conventional 'background' topics, at the expense of content analysis. Brown also covers traditional introductory issues at some length, but further devotes considerable, primary attention to commentary and exposition (see below).

[3] Brown, *Introduction*; Johnson, *Writings*; Achtemeier, Green, and Thompson, *Introducing*. For a major, recent introduction to the Old Testament that reflects similar canonical and theological priorities ('to mediate and make available fresh learnings of Old Testament studies that will be of peculiar force for pastors and Christian congregations'), see Brueggemann, *Introduction* (citation, p. xi).

own ways) places a prior emphasis on literary and theological approaches to interpreting the New Testament as the church's Scripture. While the least innovative of the bunch, Brown clearly lays out his agenda in contradistinction to previous introductory texts:

> [T]he primary goal [of this Introduction] is to get people to read the NT books, not simply to read about them ... If I were teaching an introductory course, my first assignment in every instance would be for the students to read the respective NT writing. Many *Introductions* assume that the audience is eager or even required to read the NT; I assume that often the audience needs to be shown how engaging the NT books are and how they speak to people's lives and concerns. Accordingly I shall regularly leave the (often disputed) issues of sources, authorship, dating, etc., to the latter part of each Chapter and begin with a *General Analysis of the Message* designed to accompany the reading of the respective NT book. It will point out the flow of thought, elements that are characteristic of the author, and what is significant and interesting. At times this *Analysis* will be almost a minicommentary that should help make the NT intelligible and enjoyable ...
>
> [R]eligious, spiritual, and ecclesiastical issues raised by the NT will receive ample attention throughout this book ... Although it is certainly possible to study the NT from a secular or noninvolved standpoint or from that of comparative religion, the majority of readers will be interested in it because it is supposed to be important for them religiously.[4]

Observe the similar perspectives of Johnson and Achtemeier, Green, and Thompson:

> [H]owever important the prehistory of texts may be, however helpful the distinctions between tradition and redaction, the complete and finished literary form of the writing is what demands interpretation within the canon ... The writings of the NT are first and foremost religious writings ... Their subject matter concerns what it means to be human in the light of faith, specifically in light of the experience of the Holy that the first Christians claimed to have had in Jesus.
>
> The NT writings approach us as witnesses to and interpretations of specifically religious claims having to do with the experience of God as mediated through Jesus.[5]

> The documents of the NT are documents written 'from faith for faith.' Not only are they written by individuals who believe, and believe passionately, in the truth to which they bear witness, but they also hope to persuade their readers to join in sharing their convictions about the significance of Jesus and orienting their lives to serve faithfully the God of Jesus Christ. While historical and literary studies can greatly illumine the NT, the primary importance of the NT lies neither in the historical information it provides nor in its literary and stylistic artistry but rather in its

---

[4] Brown, *Introduction*, x–xi (emphasis his).

[5] Johnson, *Writings*, 6–7.

function within the church as Scripture, as those writings that uniquely and ulti-mately guide, nourish, and shape our faith and life with God.[6]

While this last citation from Achtemeier, Green, and Thompson elevates theo-logical concerns over both historical and literary matters in New Testament interpretation, the 'literary angle' concentrated on the final form of each writ-ing (*pace* Johnson) also receives special attention in the volume's subtitle (*Its Lit-erature and Theology*) and in the extensive narrative analyses that form the heart of chapters on the gospels and Acts (at the expense of issues of author, date, set-ting, purpose, etc. treated briefly, if at all, at the end [*pace* Brown]).

In his chapter on 'The Purpose of Luke-Acts' in the present volume, David Wenham unequivocally affirms the need to interpret the Bible and Luke's two-volume work in particular as 'divine communication' and 'word of God.' His overarching hermeneutical goal is thus aligned with the *Introduction* schol-ars just mentioned (though he never cites them). However, Wenham's assess-ment of the place of 'introductory matters' in this interpretive enterprise differs from that of Brown, Johnson, and Green,[7] as he argues *against* 'a tendency [in some circles] to downplay the importance of historical understanding, with theological and literary interpretations of various sorts being preferred' and *for* 'the conviction that historical understanding is ... a theologically necessary and helpful ingredient in the process of interpreting the Bible.'[8] 'History matters a great deal' for Wenham as a primary path to 'interpret[ing] the historical word of God.' To make his case, which in large measure is a defense of classic concerns of *New Testament Introduction*, Wenham revisits matters of: (1) author-ship and authenticity; (2) special features and themes; and (3) historical context and purpose. In what follows, I aim to evaluate Wenham's historical approach as a vehicle for 'hearing God's voice' in Luke-Acts in conversation with the recent introductory texts of a more literary-theological bent mentioned above as well as newer historically-driven *Introductions* by Bart Ehrman and L. Michael White explicitly *unconcerned* with faith-based, theological interpretation.[9]

Authorship and Authenticity

While indicating parenthetically that 'my later conclusions are not mainly dependent' upon judgements regarding who wrote Luke-Acts, Wenham

---

[6] Achtemeier, Green, and Thompson, *Introducing*, 12.

[7] For convenience sake, I will cite Green as the representative of the text by Achtemeier et al., since he is the primary Lukan scholar among the three authors and, I assume, had principal responsibility for the chapters on Luke and Acts.

[8] Wenham, 'Purpose of Luke-Acts,' 80.

[9] Ehrman, *New Testament*; White, *From Jesus*.

nonetheless follows the more traditional pattern of starting with the issue of authorship. On the basis of the 'we' passages in Pauline sections of Acts, internally, and 'the unequivocal testimony of the early church,' externally, Wenham argues for the 'common-sense' conclusion that a travel companion and missionary partner of Paul – named Luke – composed both the third gospel and the book of Acts. Those scholars who dissent from such a view are primarily constrained, in Wenham's opinion, by a priori assessments of historical divergences, if not contradictions, between Luke's narrative and Paul's letters – hence, they 'cannot conceive' of Acts' composition by one of Paul's partners. By contrast, since Wenham believes 'that close investigation of the relationship of Acts and Paul's letters shows Acts to be remarkably well-informed about Paul,' he has no bias against, and good reason for, accepting Lukan authorship of Acts (and, consequently, Luke's Gospel as well).[10]

But Wenham seems to have his own presumptive bias (as we all do) affecting his approach to biblical authorship and interpretation. In his historical model, Wenham appears to link closely authorship with authenticity, writer with reliability. A companion of Paul, while allowed his own slant on Paul's career, would not and did not, in Wenham's view, distort or challenge Paul's personal testimony in any radical way. As a Pauline devotee and eyewitness to at least some events in Paul's life, Luke can thus be counted upon as a trustworthy transmitter of the gospel. And, though Wenham does not say this explicitly, the thrust of his chapter suggests that the historical accuracy of Luke-Acts, certified by a scrupulous historian-author, assures readers of its iconic status as 'word of God' and prepares them to accept this historically grounded 'word' with greater understanding and commitment.

While I appreciate Wenham's careful comparative investigations of Acts and the Pauline letters as a necessary corrective to sweeping judgements about Acts' supposed counter-Pauline 'tendencies,'[11] I have certain reservations about his conclusions regarding authorship and their implications for theological interpretation.

First, with respect to Luke-Acts, opinions of authorship and authenticity come up against the primary evidence of *anonymity*. As Wenham well knows,

---

[10] Wenham, 'Purpose of Luke-Acts,' 81–82.

[11] Wenham's studies referenced in n. 5 of his chapter merit special attention; see also his more extensive *Paul: Follower of Jesus or Founder of Christianity?* Wenham's emphasis on the complementary connection between Acts and Paul's letters balances recent historical 'biographies' of Paul by Murphy-O'Connor (*Paul*) and Crossan and Reed (*In Search of Paul*) that continue to drive a sharp wedge between the two writings, to the detriment of Acts. Chilton (*Rabbi Paul*), however, while maintaining a critical stance toward Acts, still regards this work as 'an extremely valuable resource in any attempt at biography'; 'what Acts says should be assessed, not simply rejected' (xv).

the Lukan author never identifies himself[12] as 'Luke' or by any other name. All we get are personal pronouns 'I/me' (in the prologues of each volume) and 'we' (in the Pauline half of Acts). The fact that the author has these (few) self-conscious moments *without* interjecting his name or any other autobiographical tidbit suggests that he regards his own identity as insignificant to his message (contrast the apostle Paul on this point, especially in a letter like Galatians). I think the author of Luke-Acts would be happy if his readers responded to him like the evil spirit responded to Sceva's sons: 'Jesus, I know, and Paul I know; but who are you?' (Acts 19:15). In turn, the writer might reply, 'Nobody important; don't worry about me – knowing Jesus and Paul is what matters'. As for the 'we' passages in particular, embedding himself in a plural company only further neutralizes the author's personality and encourages readers' identification (audience participation) with him in the narrative (*'we'* are in this together). As Green, who otherwise accepts traditional Lukan authorship as the most plausible theory, comments:

> Interestingly ... the 'we-passages' do nothing to alter the initial anonymity of the author of Acts. Even when involved in first-person narration, the narrator of Acts identifies himself not as an individual with a name, but as one of a group. He may at times be present as a participant-observer, but his focus in not on his individual identity. Rather, the 'we' of his narration contributes to the vividness of his account and invites his audience to read themselves into the narrative.[13]

Second, granting that the author of Luke-Acts was an erstwhile companion of Paul or at least 'a follower of the Pauline tradition' (which White regards as an 'undisputed' datum in New Testament scholarship)[14] does not certify historical veracity (in the positivist-empirical sense) or theological harmony with Paul throughout the two volumes. As any courtroom can attest, eyewitness reports of the same events do not always mesh. Even if the Lukan writer was an eyewitness on the scene with Paul, that is no guarantee he saw eye to eye with Paul or interpreted events in the same way, particularly some years removed from the experience. (And, by the way, there is no *necessary* reason to privilege Paul's

---

[12] I assume that the author of Luke-Acts was male or at least adopts a masculine persona in writing the narrative because of the self-referential masculine participle (παρηκολουθηκότι) in the prologue (Lk. 1:3); cf. D'Angelo, 'Knowing,' 285; Gaventa, *Acts*, 50.

[13] Achtemeier, Green, and Thompson, *Introducing*, 268–69.

[14] White, *From Jesus*, 247–48. While beginning his analysis of Luke and Acts with the authorship question and placing the writer in the Pauline orbit, White does not regard the Pauline link as a certification of historical accuracy. Of course, 'a follower of the Pauline tradition' might not have been one of Paul's missionary partners but rather a later adherent of Paul's teaching, a generation or more after the apostle's death.

self-testimony over Luke's reportage or to demand that Luke capitulate to Paul's authority – autobiography is just as subject, if not more so, to selective memory and tendentious portraiture).[15] Undoubtedly, the author of Acts was a big fan of Paul, bordering on hero worship, and would not have deliberately contravened his hero or undermined his reputation, but again, a supportive admirer is not a guarantor of 'objective' information. (If we really wanted the scoop on the U.S. president, would we depend on his chief of staff for the 'bare facts'? Maybe, maybe not.)

Further, the famous 'we' references, that bear much of the load in the case of Wenham and others for traditional Lukan authorship, remain problematic by virtue of their sporadic deployment at only a few places in the second half of Acts. At best, they affirm the author's identity as 'a *sometime* companion of Paul'[16] or '*peripheral* participant' in the Pauline mission.[17] What does this say about questions of authenticity? Is Luke somehow more reliable at those isolated segments in the narrative where he asserts himself as part of 'we'? What does that say about the rest of his work (most of it) where 'we' does not appear? In the prologue the writer claims to have done his homework and built his account on the eyewitness reports of *others* (Lk. 1:1–4), but is that a kind of special pleading to compensate for his otherwise limited personal involvement in the story? I raise these questions not to cast aspersions on the Lukan project or to undermine its truthfulness (I think 'Luke' was a diligent, faithful, even brilliant writer according to the historiographical canons of his day), but simply to challenge the supposed nexus between authorship and authenticity in Lukan hermeneutics. To anticipate my main argument below, if we want to know the truth of Luke-Acts, to 'hear God's voice' through this literature – knowing who the author was does not get us very far and may even trip us up. Better to know and wrestle with the text – the unfolding narrative in all its literary and theological profundity and complexity – and leave the historical author in the background (which is what he seems to want his readers to do).[18] As Johnson puts it, cutting sharply to the chase: 'In any case, the question of authorship does not help us greatly in interpreting the [Lukan] work. We have ... a two-volume work by an otherwise unknown Christian to an otherwise unknown

---

[15] Cf. Chilton, *Rabbi Paul*, xv: 'Sometimes there is good reason to infer that Paul keeps a self-interested silence that Acts breaks.'

[16] Fitzmyer, *Gospel*, 49 (emphasis mine); see also his 'Authorship.'

[17] Kurz, *Reading*, 123 (emphasis mine); cf. Spencer, 'Acts,' 406–408.

[18] I have kept the focus, as Wenham does, on the 'real,' historical author. Narrative and rhetorical critics, however, also consider the constructed roles of 'implied' authors and 'narrators' *within* literary texts, which may correspond in varying degrees to the actual producers of the texts. For example, Paul's famous 'I' confession in Rom. 7:7–25 may reflect more a rhetorical presentation of 'everyone's' viewpoint than a personal autobiographical reminiscence.

patron [Theophilus] … we have only the text itself to guide our investigation into its destination and intentions.'[19]

Features and Themes

After giving primary attention to the authorship issue and implying its relevance to the integrity of Luke's Gospel, Wenham admits that 'the identification of Luke as the author of Luke-Acts is by no means the most important consideration in identifying the context and purpose of the two-volume work.'[20] To his credit, he then proceeds, in the largest section of his chapter, to deal with six features, or themes, of Luke's narrative: prologue, Jesus, wealth/poverty, Judaism/Christianity, Gentile mission, and conflict/innocence. By any reckoning, these are major matters meriting careful consideration. Without debating the fine points of each topic (on the whole, Wenham's summaries are clear, straightforward, and uncontroversial, 'based largely,' in his own words, 'on some quite simple observations about the contents of Luke-Acts'[21]), I offer some assessment of the *analytical methods* he employs and a few suggestions regarding *additional matters* pertinent to theological interpretation of Luke's narrative.

Analytical methods

Investigating the distinctive features of Luke-Acts, Wenham begins, appropriately, at the beginning – the gospel prologue – alert to the popular narrative strategy of introducing key patterns and themes early in the story. [22] In the

---

and 'narrators' *within* literary texts, which may correspond in varying degrees to the actual producers of the texts. For example, Paul's famous 'I' confession in Rom. 7:7–25 may reflect more a rhetorical presentation of 'everyone's' viewpoint than a personal autobiographical reminiscence.

[19] Johnson, *Writings*, 214. Among the three newer literary-theological *Introductions* being considered, only Johnson takes up the authorship question first in his treatment of Luke-Acts; but he only does so in order to dismiss its interpretive relevance. Interestingly, coming from a very different, rigorously historical-critical perspective, Ehrman agrees with Johnson's assessment. Regarding the writer of Acts, Ehrman concludes: 'Knowing the name of the author of this book, or even knowing that he was a companion of one of its main characters, does not help us very much in trying to understand what he wanted to emphasize about the history of the early Christian church' (*New Testament*, 139).

[20] Wenham, 'Purpose of Luke-Acts,' 82.

[21] Wenham, 'Purpose of Luke-Acts,' 80.

[22] Ehrman, *New Testament*, 60–161 (chs. 5 – 10), devotes special attention to the prefaces, prologues, and opening segments of the gospels and Acts as keys to understanding these narratives' main emphases.

prologue, Wenham focuses particularly on its claim to present a 'reliable' or 'accurate' (ἀκριβῶς, Lk. 1:3) account of 'the things fulfilled among us' (1:1). Acknowledging that such a program 'does not exclude' theological or spiritual truthfulness, Wenham nonetheless accentuates the prologue's 'strong concern for *historical* reliability,'[23] buttressed by repeated appeals to 'secular historical' Roman authorities. While granting this key historical component of Luke's project, I would also highlight a major *narrative* dimension, stressed in the pro-logue, concerning the 'orderly' (καθεξῆς) development of the gospel story, not necessarily in strict chronological sequence, but, above all, according to an overarching theological plot – God's unfolding plan (βουλή) of salvation.[24] The two adverbs, 'accurately' (ἀκριβῶς) and 'orderly' (καθεξῆς) appear next to each other in 1:3, with the former, however, more closely linked to the earlier participle, 'having followed' (παρηκολουθηκότι), and the latter more directly tied to the subsequent infinitive, 'to write' (γράψαι). Thus, while 'accurately' characterizes Luke's preparatory research, 'orderly' aptly describes the *produced writing*. This balances nicely, as Green has observed, with the prologue's pri-mary designation of the ensuing work as διήγησις (1:1),[25] an 'orderly account' or a 'narrative' designed to 'lead [the reader] through' (διά + ἄγειν) a carefully orchestrated plot, 'step by step' (cf. Acts 11:4).[26] The goal of such a work is not reportage for its own sake, a chronicling of data for the record – but, rather, proclamation, persuasion, even propaganda. As Green puts it,

---

[23] Wenham, 'Purpose of Luke-Acts,' 83 (emphasis mine).

[24] Key references to the 'purpose/plan of God' (βουλὴ τοῦ θεοῦ) emerge in Lk. 7:30; Acts 2:23; 4:28; 5:38–39; 13:36; 20:27. On the basis of this motif and the nature of Luke's narrative, Tannehill, *Narrative Unity*, 2, concludes: 'The author of Luke-Acts consciously understands the story as unified by the controlling purpose of God and wants readers to understand it in the same way … Luke-Acts has a unified plot because there is a unifying purpose of God behind the events which are narrated, and the mission of Jesus and his witnesses represents that purpose being carried out through human action.' Further on 'God's purpose' as the organizing principle of Luke's narrative, see Squires, *Plan*.

[25] Green, *Gospel*, 36, delineates five sets of balanced phrases structuring the Lukan prologue, including 'to set down an orderly account' paired with 'to write an orderly account.'

[26] The prologue's term for 'orderly' (καθεξῆς) appears again in Acts 11:4 to describe Peter's 'step by step' report to the Jerusalem church concerning his recent encounter with Cornelius in Caesarea. What follows is Peter's *retelling* of events previously nar-rated in 10:1–48 from his 'own' perspective, in the 'order' he chooses for maximum emphasis on God's control of what happened ('who was I that I could hinder God'? [11:17]). Narrative 'order' in Luke-Acts thus has more to do with the theological significance of events than their historical sequence. See Tannehill, *Narrative Unity*, 9–12.

For Luke 'narrative' is proclamation. Luke has in mind the use of history to preach, to set forth a persuasive interpretation of God's work in Jesus and the early church, and the medium of that proclamation is the narrative account whose 'order' is crucial for our understanding of that interpretation.[27]

Establishing, detailed and deliberate 'orderly' reading as an interpretive fundament of Luke's two-volume narrative calls into question thematic approaches that merely assemble a gaggle of (proof) texts which happen to cohere around a particular topic. Although Wenham does not trumpet 'orderly' reading as a main feature of Lukan interpretation, he does practice it to good effect in his longest thematic section, where he carefully traces the development of 'Judaism and Christianity'[28] from the gospel 'infancy narratives' to the 'ongoing story in Acts.'

Wenham also discusses redaction criticism, specifically in his investigation of the 'wealth and poverty' theme. As applied to Lukan studies, this approach, while appreciating the evangelist's compositional techniques, usually focuses more upon editorial (redactional) alterations to putative sources, Mark and 'Q' (sayings tradition common to Matthew and Luke). Brown makes heavy use of redaction-critical analysis in his introduction to Luke's Gospel (albeit still concerned to explicate the entire narrative), Johnson less so, and Green hardly at all. Here Wenham tilts more toward Johnson and Green, wary of making too much theological hay out of selected adjustments Luke might have made to a supposed Markan template, largely because Luke's bibliographic appropriation of Mark is not as widely accepted by scholars as it once was and because, if we take the prologue seriously, Luke's repertoire of sources (oral and written) was more extensive than we are able to track. Wenham might have also added redaction criticism's Achilles heel of ignoring or downplaying the significance of Lukan overlaps with Mark (where Luke *agrees* with Mark is potentially just as revealing of Lukan thought as where he differs) as well as the fact that

---

[27] Green, *Gospel*, 38. As Acts 11:4 illustrates the meaning of καθεξῆς (see previous note), Acts 9:27 uses a cognate form of διήγησις, as Green further observes, in recounting how Barnabas 'described/narrated' (διηγήσατο) Saul's recent Damascus-road christophany (cf. 9:1–18) in order to expound the significance of Saul's experience to the Jerusalem apostles and persuade them to believe his testimony. These elements of exposition and persuasion are central to Luke's 'narrative' agenda.

[28] Without belaboring the point in this brief response, I simply note Wenham's anachronistic use of the terms 'Judaism' and 'Christianity.' Luke-Acts does not yet envision a parting of the ways into two discrete faiths. The term 'Christian' appears only twice in Luke's writing, both from outsiders' viewpoints (Acts 11:26; 26:28), 'to designate not a separate religion over against Judaism but rather a messianic sect (cf. 5:17; 15:5; 24:14; 26:5; 28:22) or reform movement wholly within Judaism' (Spencer, *Journeying*, 29).

editorial changes (if that's what they are) may be motivated by stylistic or rhetorical conventions instead of intrinsic or theological concerns.[29] Still,
Wenham continues to value comparative analysis of Luke with other gospels,
irrespective of source theories, as a means of discerning distinctive Lukan
themes (a method also effectively employed in Ehrman's investigation of
Luke).[30] For example, juxtaposing Luke's interest in the poor *simpliciter* (6:20)
with Matthew's consideration of 'the poor *in spirit*' (5:3) reinforces Luke's preoccupation with social and economic issues surrounding those materially, not
just spiritually, disadvantaged in contrast to wealthy elites, who are repeatedly
featured – and challenged – in Luke's narrative.

While basically affirming Wenham's handling of redaction criticism and the
wealth/poverty theme, I offer two caveats. First, though acknowledging the
limitations of this method focused on *inter-gospel* emendations, I still think it
can be theologically illuminating to study Lukan appropriation – and in some
cases, alteration – of an undisputed source, the LXX (Septuagint) or Greek Old
Testament, that Luke frequently cites. Such study is complicated by the knotty
textual history of the LXX (and the Hebrew Bible, too), but it remains worth
pursuing. Observing how Luke handles Scripture – how Luke heard the 'word
of God' for his day – provides suggestive clues as to how we might respond to
Luke's narrative as divine revelation for us today. As a simple example, Luke's
addition of 'in the last days, God says' to Peter's introduction of Joel 2:28–32
(3:1–5 LXX) in the Pentecost scene (Acts 2:17) and repetition of 'and they
will prophesy' (2:18) indicate a willingness to bring Scripture up to date, to
hear God's urgent message in the eschatological 'now' ('the last days'), and also
to look to Scripture to shape the mission of God's people ('they will prophesy').

A second caveat relates to Wenham's questionable move from detecting
Luke's narrative emphasis on wealth/poverty to reconstructing Luke's socio-
historical identity and community: 'Luke was moving in what we might call
more "middle-class" circles than was typical of the first Christian churches, and
certainly in more moneyed circles, which presumably included people like
Theophilus.'[31] Apart from the anachronistic reference to 'middle-class' (putting the term in inverted commas doesn't help much, since ancient Mediterranean society operated under a different social and economic system than

---

[29] See the helpful critique of redaction criticism (in the introductory chapter on Luke's
       Gospel) in Ehrman, *New Testament*, 103–105.
[30] Ehrman, *New Testament*, 103–21. Though Tannehill (*Narrative Unity*) engages in a
       rigorous narrative-critical analysis of Luke, focused on the internal dynamics of
       Luke's story, he recognizes: 'Brief comparisons of Luke with Matthew and Mark are
       useful where there are parallel texts, for these comparisons help us to recognize the
       distinctiveness of the Lukan version' (p. 6).
[31] Wenham, 'Purpose of Luke-Acts,' 86.

modern Western capitalism), it does not follow that themes and characters in a narrative's, internal world necessarily reflect *real* (not just realistic) issues and people in the author's and readers', external environment. For example, while it can be insightful, as Tannehill has shown, to read Luke's Gospel imaginatively as figures in Acts – like the Jewish woman (widow?) Tabitha or the Roman officer Cornelius – *might have responded* to a story populated by characters like them,[32] we cannot be certain that Luke was writing especially, still less exclusively, *for* such people or *within* such a community (full of women/widows and soldiers/officials). Luke's universal emphasis upon 'all flesh' subverts any narrow profile of his community drawn from his narrative.[33] Moreover, 'most excellent' Theophilus – the only hard clue we have to Luke's 'real' reader or audience – either matches only a small remnant of Luke's dramatis personae (Roman officials, perhaps, but certainly not women, widows, lepers, shepherds, et al.) or represents no particular 'real' individual but rather any 'lover of God.' In any case, for the goal of hearing God's word through the Scriptures of the church – the *whole* church – I worry that speculative historical judgements, such as that concerning Luke's and the Lukan community's hobnobbing in 'moneyed circles,' might tend to disenfranchise various reader-seekers. If I do not happen to run in wealthy circles and, in fact, have been snubbed by those who do, why should I care what an ancient aristocratic author says about anything, even one who seems favorably disposed (annoyingly patronizing?) toward the poor?

Additional matters

When a scholar ably covers six main features or themes of a New Testament writing in a space-constrained chapter, it is a bit unfair to charge that he did not do enough. So what is the magic number? Eight topics? Ten? Twenty? Clearly, biblical interpretation is not a game of scoring the most points. But it does having something to do with emphasizing the most salient points. While (again) I commend Wenham for selecting six central (not peripheral) Lukan themes and handling them well in a brief compass, I'm a little surprised – especially given the hermeneutical concerns of the present volume – at two critical omissions. As well as exposing these two items that I think should be included, front and center, in any introductory list of key Lukan themes, I propose one further topic of particular relevance to 'hearing God's voice' through Luke's narrative.

After discussing the prologue, Wenham turns to *Jesus*, 'Luke's first and foremost theme,' even at the risk of 'stating the obvious, but it is still worth

---

[32] Tannehill, '"Cornelius" and "Tabitha."'
[33] See Spencer, *Journeying*, 20–21.

stating.'[34] However, while Jesus is undeniably a prominent Lukan figure, it in fact is not so obvious to some recent interpreters that he ranks 'first and foremost', at least not before *God* and the *Holy Spirit*. Such opinions proceed, deductively, neither from a systematic theological impulse to promote Trinitarian orthodoxy, on the one end, nor from an eccentric polemical aim to demote Jesus' Christology, on the other. Fully recognizing Jesus' consistently honored position, from the Lukan narrator's viewpoint, as Lord and Christ, Savior and Redeemer, Son of God and Son of Man, scholars such as Joel Green and Beverly Roberts Gaventa nonetheless dare to read Luke's account on its own terms as an affirmation of Israel's *God* as the prime mover of the gospel story. Mary is not just caught up in the moment and theologically naïve when she exults in the marvelous action of 'God my Savior' (Lk. 1:47) to her and her people; rather, she announces at the outset of Luke's narrative its principal to reveal *God's salvific purpose*, to recount 'the grace of God' (Acts 11:23; 14:26) – through Jesus, intimately and climactically, yes – but ultimately, to the 'glory of God' (Luke 2:12, 20; Acts 7:2, 55). Green makes the point succinctly with respect to Luke's first volume: 'To a degree not fully appreciated in many earlier studies of the Third Gospel, Luke's narrative is *theo*logical in substance and focus; that is, it is centered on God.'[35] And Gaventa vigorously presses the same case with respect to Luke's sequel:

> Readers who set aside the expectation that Acts is an institutional history, shaped and reshaped by human leaders, will instead see God at work from the beginning until well past the end. God is the one who glorifies Jesus and raises him from the dead, who rescues the apostles from prison, who directs Ananias to baptize Saul, and who insists upon the inclusion of the Gentiles. God sends Paul and his co-workers into Macedonia, heals people through the hands of Peter and Paul, and finally directs Paul safely to Rome. If readers of Acts find themselves in a journey, the major sights are not those created by human hands; they result from the actions of God alone.[36]

Closely aligned with the work of God and Jesus, the *Holy Spirit* – also known as the Spirit of the Lord (Lk. 4:18; Acts 5:9), 'my [i.e., God's] Spirit' (Acts 2:17–

---

[34]   Wenham, 'Purpose of Luke-Acts,' 83.

[35]   Green, *Gospel*, 22 (emphasis his). Green also interprets 'the purpose of Luke-Acts … [to] be primarily ecclesiological – concerned with the practices that define and the criteria for legitimating the community of God's people, and centered on the invitation to participate in God's project' (*Gospel*, 22). But the 'ecclesiological' and 'theological' impulses obviously cohere closely around 'God's people' and 'God's project.'

[36]   Gaventa, *Acts*, 26. Gaventa pioneers a trenchant theocentric analysis of Acts throughout her commentary.

18), and the Spirit of Jesus (Acts 16:7) in Luke-Acts – emerges 'at the center of the story,' as White observes, with special prominence 'in directing key moments in the narrative.'[37] If God is the prime mover behind Luke's story of salvation and Jesus its prime mediator, the Spirit functions as the prime motivator and manager – empowering and directing Jesus and the early church from the beginning (witness Jesus' baptism and Nazareth sermon in Luke and the church's pentecostal experiences in Acts)[38] to fulfill God's purpose. And, apropos to our concerns in this volume, the Spirit's guidance in Luke's narrative is not simply functional – mobilizing God's agents to accomplish God's work – but also *hermeneutical* – enabling perplexed seekers to apprehend God's word. As the God-fearing Ethiopian eunuch stumbles over the meaning of Isaiah 53 and pleads for someone to guide him, *the Spirit* dispatches Philip the evangelist to the scene (8:28) – in the middle of the desert! – and arranges for a revelatory rendezvous at the precise moment the eunuch was reading the troubling text (8:26–39).[39] To be sure, the 'good news about Jesus' (8:35), Philip explains, provides the hermeneutical principle for understanding Isaiah's suffering servant; but it is the Spirit who provides the hermeneutical opportunity for understanding to take place (leading to faith and baptism).[40]

Although he does not give separate headings to 'God' and 'the Holy Spirit' in his treatment of major Lukan themes, I do not think for a second that Wenham would deny their importance in Luke's narrative or that he is touting some sort of 'Christomonism' at the expense of classic Trinitarian commitment to God and the Spirit in divine communion with Christ (any more than I am mounting some 'subordinationist' slam against Jesus by emphasizing God and the Spirit). But, still, my interest in God-centered and Spirit-directed readings of Luke-Acts is not purely pedantic (I hope). As Wenham regards it important 'to state the obvious' about Jesus' centrality in Luke's story – presumably because the obvious can so easily become the oblivious by being taken for granted – so I think that not-so-subtle reminders of the *theological* and *pneumatological* thrust of Luke's narrative may profitably support our hermeneutical project.

Likewise, I briefly suggest that a third feature of Luke's narrative may spark greater attention to and more acute apprehension of God's word in and

---

[37] White, *From Jesus*, 254. On the strategic role of the Holy Spirit in Luke-Acts, see Shepherd, *Narrative Function* and, in this volume, Turner, 'Luke and the Spirit: Renewing Theological Interpretation of Biblical Pneumatology.'

[38] Lk. 3:21–22; 4:18–19; Acts 2:1–13; 4:31; 8:14–17; 10:44–48; 11:15–17; 19:1–7.

[39] The Spirit ultimately snatches Philip away to continue his mission up the coast to Caesarea (8:39–40). The direct guidance of the Spirit thus frames Philip's encounter with the eunuch (8:29, 39). See Spencer, *Portrait of Philip*, 154–58.

[40] The Spirit also plays a key role in directing Peter and helping him to understand his perplexing sheet-vision (see Acts 10:19–20; 11:12).

through the story. This is not as grand a theme as those involving God, Jesus, and the Spirit, but focusing, as it does, on human response to the gospel, it speaks directly to our hermeneutical vocation as interpreters of Scripture. The theme of *hearing and accepting God's word* developed *within* Luke's work is surely designed to impact the responses of external hearers/readers *to* the narrative. A story that begins with the nine-month muting of a venerable, 'righteous' priest for failing to accept a heavenly announcement of 'good news' from 'the presence of God' (Lk. 1:19) can hardly help but snap the hearer/reader to sharp attention. If you do not listen and believe what God is revealing, then you may find yourself, literally, with nothing to say – certainly nothing of theological value. This point is further punctuated by Jesus' parable of the Sower, which is all about faithful reception of God's word leading to fruitful action (Lk. 8:4–15); by direct exhortations to 'listen up' ('pay attention to how you listen,' 8:18; 'This is my Son, my Chosen; listen to him!' 9:35); by select examples of devoted listeners, such as Mary of Bethany (10:38–42) and Lydia of Philippi ('the Lord opened her heart to listen eagerly to what was said by Paul,' Acts 16:14); and by the preponderance of speech-material in the travel segment of Luke's Gospel and throughout Acts before a wide range of audiences. Closer analysis of this strong *acoustic* (ἀκούω) accent in Luke-Acts – probing how and why some people get the point and some do not – promises to yield additional interpretive insights to contemporary hearers/readers of Luke's story.

Context and Purpose

Wenham's final section, to which the title and substance of his chapter build, seeks to identify a plausible historical context and purpose for Luke-Acts that make the best 'hermeneutical sense' of the two volumes. Operating from the premise that 'Luke was writing to answer questions that were provoked by historical events and his historical context,'[41] Wenham attempts to find an interpretive nexus between internal features in Luke's narrative, discussed in the previous section, and external events in first-century Roman and Jewish history detected in Paul's letters, like 1 Thessalonians and Romans, and contemporary historians, such as Suetonius and Josephus. The puzzle comes together most neatly for Wenham in the *Lukan portraits* of (a) Jewish-Christian conflict (especially over the place of Gentiles in the messianic community) (b) Christian innocence (especially Paul's) of political rabble-rousing, interlocking with the *Roman policies* (c) expelling Jews from Rome (because of the incendiary 'Chrestus') in 49 C.E. and (d) other violent opposition to Jewish and/or Christian adherents through Nero's reign. Thus,

---

[41] Wenham, 'Purpose of Luke-Acts,' 101.

Wenham infers a major 'apologetic purpose' behind Luke's writing with both a 'firm historical component' – to address 'recent history and ... events that people had experienced or heard about' – and a 'clear theological component' – to demonstrate that 'Christianity' was not a suspicious, new-fangled religion, but a legitimate fulfillment of Israel's ancient faith.[42]

This conclusion offers a *possible* and *interesting* theory of Luke's purpose and context. Others have advanced similar proposals, as Wenham acknowledges, and he also underscores that apologetic vindication 'was only one of Luke's interests and goals' (discipleship instruction and spiritual formation being other examples). But as a *primary* and *introductory* foundation to interpreting Luke-Acts, as Wenham's chapter implies, his historical hypothesis remains problematic, suffering from being both too presumptive and too reductive.

First, while Luke's narrative is a product of its originating historical and cultural milieu, as all writings are, we cannot presume that it directly aims to explain and interpret some *particular event* in 'recent history,' even a momentous action like Claudius' edict against Roman Jews, to which it alludes (albeit in passing [Acts 18:2]). An epic narrative like Luke-Acts – recounting a panoramic story of God's people from the birth of Jesus (long anticipated in prophecy) to the expansion of the church (to the ends of the earth) – while reflecting the concerns of its own immediate situation, is not a transparently *occasional* document in the sense of a Pauline letter (and even here determining the precise occasion[s] is no easy task).[43] Luke-Acts refers to scores of historical events spread over six decades, any number of which (events) may have affected both author and readers, but perhaps none in any unique, catalytic fashion that propelled the writer, at some specific date and time (which we cannot now pinpoint – no publication data or ISBN number on the earliest manuscripts) to put stylus to papyrus. As much or more than the Claudian expulsion act, the cataclysmic destruction of Jerusalem in 70 C.E. – either as anticipated (near future) or accomplished (recent past) disaster – likely cast its ominous shadow over Luke's work (as the terrible events of 9/11 hover over the current generation of American writers). *But in what way and to what degree?* The Lukan drama has a bright spotlight trained on Jerusalem[44] and drops a few hints about the city's destruction, but the script nowhere signals this or any

---

[42] Wenham, 'Purpose of Luke-Acts,' 101.

[43] Wenham's case for the effect of the Claudian edict on Luke's writing is partly based on theories that the same edict also occasioned (to some degree) the composition of 1 Thessalonians and Romans. Such theories, however, do not enjoy consensus in New Testament scholarship, especially since these letters never mention Claudius or his infamous ban.

[44] Along with 'the role of the Holy Spirit' (see above), White (*From Jesus*, 254) underscores 'the role of Jerusalem' as 'the two themes at the center of the [Lukan] story.'

other secular event as the *primary cause* for its writing. The only 'events' or 'things' announced in the prologues as focal points of Luke's two-volume narrative are the broad complex of matters 'concerning' (περί) 'all that Jesus did and taught from the beginning' (Acts 1:1) in 'fulfillment' of God's plan (Lk. 1:1).[45]

Therefore, in interpreting Luke-Acts, to privilege the influence of any external event instigated by Rome over the narrated Christ-event(s) ordained by God presumes more than Luke's story authorizes and runs the risk of muffling, even distorting, Luke's theological message. A story that trumpets the advancement of God's just, rule through the work of the crucified Jesus, whom 'God has made both Lord and Messiah' (Acts 2:36), has profound political implications in the context of Roman imperial hegemony. But from Luke's perspective, that story is shaped by God's eternal will, not by Rome's historical whim, and has transcendent, cosmic repercussions above and beyond the exigencies of Roman politics.

This caution against isolating (supposed) precipitant events behind Luke's production does not spring from some anti-historical, de-contextual bias. I think it remains incumbent on any New Testament interpreter, no less one with a theological aim, to give all due and honest attention to the original context of a narrative like Luke-Acts before attempting to bridge the hermeneutical gap (more like a chasm after two millennia) to the current horizon. But I envision *context* in a much broader, 'thicker' (as in Geertz's classic 'thick description') way than Wenham suggests in the present chapter – hence my second concern that his proposal regarding Luke's context is too reductive. Beyond tracking key historical-political events making headlines in Luke's era, it is vital to understand the pervasive *social-cultural environments* and *symbolic-ideological universes* in which Luke-Acts is embedded and from which it emerges – all the more so since this work is a 'high context' document that largely assumes (without explanation) readers' shared understanding of conventional customs and values governing ancient Mediterranean society.[46] The groundbreaking collection of essays edited by Jerome Neyrey on *The Social World of Luke-Acts: Models for Interpretation* discusses several core cultural

---

[45] The notion of 'events,' 'things,' or 'matters' in the prologues to Luke and Acts is conveyed in three περί clauses followed by genitive *plural* terms denoting a whole complex of occurrences: περὶ τῶν πεπληροφορημένων ('concerning the things which have been fulfilled,' Lk. 1:1); περὶ ὧν κατηχήθης λόγων ('concerning the events/matters of which you were instructed,' Lk. 1:4); and περὶ πάντων ('about/concerning all things,' Acts 1:1). No *specific event* is pinpointed, certainly not one from Roman secular history. The focus starts and stays big – on the overarching network of God-ordained, Christ-related events.

[46] See Malina, 'Reading Theory,' 19–20.

'scenarios' — such as those surrounding honor-shame codes, kinship ties, patron-client relations, purity-pollution boundaries, and ritual-ceremonial acts — reflected in Luke's narrative world. Green's *Introduction* focuses on 'environmental conditions' and 'institutional contexts' that comprise the New Testament's 'many worlds.'[47]

While such social and cultural analysis of the New Testament can be undertaken for purely academic reasons (as one might investigate ancient China, for example), it can also shed considerable light on theological matters. Two quick cases in point: (a) for those seeking to encounter God in scriptural narratives like Luke-Acts, imaging a benevolent, fatherly, holy God in the context of ancient patronage, kinship, and purity systems (God as Heavenly Patron, Honored Patriarch, and Holy of Holies), can be an eye-opening and life-transforming experience;[48] and (b) likewise, understanding the christological significance of the 'shorn,' shamed servant of Isaiah 53, whom Philip ('starting with this scripture') identifies with Jesus in Acts 8:35, is enhanced by exploring this figure's socio-cultural resonance with the Ethiopian eunuch (Philip's interlocutor), a man stigmatized by his own humiliating status (as a eunuch), 'cut off' from normal community and family relations ('who can describe his generation'? Is. 53:8/Acts 8:33).[49]

Conclusion

In considering 'matters of introduction' as a foundation for interpreting Luke's two-volume work, Wenham proves most helpful in exposing key features or themes that build up over the course of the narrative. From the start, such exposure puts the student of Luke-Acts on alert: here are major emphases not to be missed in hearing/reading this story; 'pay attention to how you listen' (Lk. 8:18) to these matters and to how they carry the narrative's 'good news.' My main quibble with Wenham at this point concerns two seminal thematic 'matters' that I think deserve attention (in addition to those Wenham stresses) in any introduction to Lukan study: the protagonist roles of *God* and the *Holy Spirit*.

Less persuasive, as an introductory desideratum, is Wenham's focus on historical author and events external to (behind) the Lukan narrative. Apart from the presumptive, reductive, and speculative pitfalls of such investigation that I have suggested, I also remain wary of that oft-exposed (but still oft-ignored) trap of *circular reasoning*. Which comes first — probing the internal world *of* the

---

[47] Achtemeier, Green, and Thompson, *Introducing*, 15–51 (ch. 2).

[48] See, e.g., Neyrey, *Render to God*, 82–106.

[49] See Spencer, 'Ethiopian Eunuch.'

story or external events *behind* the story?[50] Ideally, readers would do both at the same time, holding inner and outer dimensions of the narrative in dialectic tension. But that is difficult to do, especially for the introductory student, and potentially misleading. By locking in too early in the interpretive process on an event or other piece of evidence outside a narrative that happen to correspond with some feature(s) within the story, and then hypothesizing that external matter as a *primary, precipitant cause* for writing the story, the reader's vision may become skewed in one direction, to the neglect of other dynamic vectors in the story. The problem with interpretive circles – going round and round between selected external and internal reference points – is that they are too tight, too closed to alternative readings, and too self-fulfilling.

The classic example in Lukan study revolves around the tradition of authorship by Dr Luke, a practicing physician. Starting with this datum, the hunt was on for medical language in Luke-Acts suggesting a doctor's touch, which was not hard to find given the narrative's interest in healing episodes (of course, the same interest is patent in Matthew, Mark, and John). The circle was quickly joined, and Lukan hermeneutics assumed the posture of a medical investigation. In the wake of Cadbury's devastating critique,[51] few scholars today, even those who hold to Lukan authorship read the narrative this way (as a kind of medical journal) or place much stock in Luke's occupation as a determinative factor in his work. Wenham certainly does not adopt this approach, but I am afraid that his introductory emphasis on the Claudian edict and other 'current events' as catalytic occasions for Luke's writing runs in a similar, delimiting hermeneutical 'circle.'

As a briefly stated counter-proposal (needing much more elaboration), I think that we best prepare our students and congregants to 'hear God's voice' in Luke's Gospel by *first* (remember, this chapter has been about *introduction*) guiding them through a close, 'orderly' reading of the canonical Lukan story, informed by the principal symbolic 'scenarios' structuring Lukan society. By 'immersion' in such deep, teeming literary and cultural waters – to reprise the Baptist image we started with – perhaps we, with Jesus, can break through to sense the Spirit's presence and to hear the heavenly voice anew (Lk. 3:21–22).

---

[50] Although beyond the limited scope of this response to Wenham, the vital realm of today's reader *before* (or *in front of*) the text must also be considered (see, e.g., Schneiders, *Revelatory Text*, 157–79). We inevitably bring a whole set of presuppositions and agendas to the reading process that also contribute to circular interpretations. We find what we look for (imagine that!) and wonder why others can't seem to see things our way. A healthy dose of self-awareness – and self-criticism – cracks a few openings in the circle.

[51] Cadbury, *Style*.

Bibliography

Achtemeier, P.J., J.B. Green, and M.M. Thompson, *Introducing the New Testament: Its Literature and Theology* (Grand Rapids: Eerdmans, 2001)

Brown, R.E., *An Introduction to the New Testament* (ABRL; New York: Doubleday, 1997)

Brueggemann, W., *An Introduction to the Old Testament: The Canon and Christian Imagination* (Louisville: Westminster/John Knox Press, 2003)

Cadbury, H.J., *The Style and Literary Method of Luke* (2 vols.; HTS 6; Cambridge, MA: Harvard University Press, 1919–20)

Chilton, B.D., *Rabbi Paul: An Intellectual Biography* (New York: Doubleday, 2004)

Crossan, J.D., and J.L. Reed, *In Search of Paul: How Jesus' Apostle Opposed Rome's Empire with God's Kingdom* (New York: HarperCollins, 2004)

D'Angelo, M.R., '"Knowing How to Preside over His Own Household": Imperial Masculinity and Christian Asceticism in the Pastorals, *Hermas*, and Luke-Acts,' in *New Testament Masculinities* (SemeiaSt 45; ed. S. D. Moore and J. C. Anderson; Atlanta: Society of Biblical Literature, 2003), 265–95

Ehrman, B.D., *The New Testament: A Historical Introduction to the Early Christian Writings* (Oxford: Oxford University Press, 2nd edn, 2000)

Fitzmyer, J.A., *The Gospel According to Luke, I–IX* (AB 28; New York: Doubleday, 1981)

—, 'The Authorship of Luke-Acts Reconsidered,' in *Luke the Theologian: Aspects of His Teaching* (New York: Paulist Press, 1989), 1–26

Gaventa, B.R., *The Acts of the Apostles* (ANTC; Nashville: Abingdon, 2003)

Green, J.B., *The Gospel of Luke* (NICNT; Grand Rapids: Eerdmans, 1997)

Guthrie, D., *New Testament Introduction* (Downers Grove, IL: InterVarsity Press, 1970)

Kümmel, W.G., *Introduction to the New Testament* (NTL; London: SCM Press, rev. edn, 1975)

Kurz, W.S., *Reading Luke-Acts: Dynamics of Biblical Narrative* (Louisville: Westminster/John Knox Press, 1993)

Johnson, L.T., *The Writings of the New Testament: An Interpretation* (Minneapolis: Fortress Press, rev. edn, 1999)

Malina, B.J., 'Reading Theory Perspective: Reading Luke-Acts,' in *The Social World of Luke-Acts: Models for Interpretation* (ed. J.H. Neyrey; Peabody, MA: Hendrickson, 1991), 3–23

Murphy-O'Connor, J., *Paul: His Story* (Oxford: Oxford University Press, 2004)

Neyrey, J.H., *Render to God: New Testament Understandings of the Divine* (Minneapolis: Fortress Press, 2004)

—, (ed.), *The Social World of Luke-Acts: Models for Interpretation* (Peabody, MA: Hendrickson, 1991)

Schneiders, S.M., *The Revelatory Text: Interpreting the New Testament as Sacred Scripture* (New York: HarperCollins, 1991)

Shepherd, W.H., Jr., *The Narrative Function of the Holy Spirit as a Character in Luke-Acts* (SBLDS 147; Atlanta: Scholars Press, 1994)

Spencer, F.S., 'Acts and Modern Literary Approaches,' in *The Book of Acts in its First Century Setting*, I: *Ancient Literary Setting* (ed. B.W. Winter and A.D. Clarke; Grand Rapids: Eerdmans, 1993), 381–414

—, 'The Ethiopian Eunuch and His Bible: A Social-Science Analysis,' *BTB* 22 (1992), 155–65

—, *Journeying Through Acts: A Literary-Cultural Reading* (Peabody, MA: Hendrickson, 2004)

—, *The Portrait of Philip in Acts: A Study of Roles and Relations* (JSNTSup 67; Sheffield: Sheffield Academic Press, 1992)

Squires, J.T., *The Plan of God in Luke-Acts* (SNTSMS 76: Cambridge: Cambridge University Press, 1993)

Tannehill, R.C., '"Cornelius" and "Tabitha" Encounter Luke's Jesus,' *Int* 48 (1994), 347–56

—, *The Narrative Unity of Luke-Acts: A Literary Interpretation*, I: *The Gospel According to Luke* (Philadelphia: Fortress Press, 1986)

Wenham, D., *Paul: Follower of Jesus or Founder of Christianity?* (Grand Rapids: Eerdmans, 1995)

White, L.M., *From Jesus to Christianity: How Four Generations of Visionaries and Storytellers Created the New Testament and Christian Faith* (New York: HarperCollins, 2004)

5

Reading Luke's Gospel as Ancient Hellenistic Narrative

Luke's Narrative Plan of Israel's Suffering Messiah as God's Saving 'Plan' for the World

David P. Moessner

This Gospel is represented fittingly by the calf, because it begins with priests and ends with the Calf who, having taken upon himself the sins of all, was sacrificed for the life of the whole world.

(Ambrose, *Exposition of the Gospel of Luke* 1.4.7)[1]

They alter the scriptural context and connection, and dismember the truth ... with their specious adaptations of the oracles of the Lord. It is just as if there was a beautiful representation of a king made in a mosaic by a skilled artist, and one altered the arrangement of the pieces of stone into the shape of a dog or fox, and then should assert that this was the original representation of a king.

(Irenaeus, *Against Heresies* I.7.5, 9.3)

Introduction: The Thesis Stated

(i) Ancient narrative (διήγησις) performance was conducted in the Hellenistic period through a standard, though highly developed, poetics. As posited in Aristotle's *Poetics* and reflected in the rhetorical school debates of the Hellenistic period (e.g., Dionysius of Halicarnassus' *Literary Treatises*;[2] Lucian of

---

[1] Ambrose, *Exposition of the Gospel of Luke,* 1.4.7, in Just (ed.), *Luke*, 2.
[2] For the development of the standard poetics into a system of *oikonomia* by the time of Dionysius of Halicarnassus (Augustan period), see, e.g., Moessner, 'Arrangement,' 149–64, esp. 151–53.

Samosata's, *How to Write History*[3]), ancient narrative theory integrated a trialectic hermeneutics of authorial intent (purpose) ↔ narrative structure (poetics) ↔ audience impact (comprehension). All three components are dynamically interdependent such that no single component can operate without the concurrent enabling engagement of the other two. These three dimensions formed narrative's distinctive epistemology; their trialectic interaction rendered the truth claims of a text.[4]

When the gospel writers set pen to papyrus, therefore, they were utilizing a genre with norms and expectations of its epistemology and social function widely shared by authors and 'literate' audiences alike throughout the Greco-Roman world. According to Aristotle, every proper, complete narrative plots a 'single action' with a unique sequence of *beginning, middle, and end*, whether that action be the mimesis of the poet or the actions of peoples configured for a 'single period of time' of the historian.[5] Isolated from the distinctive plotting of a particular gospel, a 'lectionary' passage could become an abstraction, a non-'event,' or even fabricated 'saying' of Jesus. This standard narrative hermeneutics thus helps explain the outrage of the early church when their own gospels were dissected, passages 're-arranged,' and their one Christ 'dismembered.'[6]

(ii) The (post)modern hermeneutical approaches to narrative of both redaction criticism and reader-oriented criticisms have disabled this finely synchronized, ancient narrative hermeneutic by disengaging the dynamic 'components' from each other. In neither approach have the three narrative horizons[7] of author, formal poetics, and audience impact been properly blended and coordinated as one interpretive enterprise. We shall limit our attention to *redaction criticism's* construal of a discrete but highly significant

---

[3] Cf. Avenarius, *Lukians*, esp. 165–78; Homeyer, *Lukian*, esp. 239–81.

[4] For a fuller treatment, see Moessner, 'Ministers,' 308–11.

[5] Cf. e.g., Halliwell, *Poetics*; Cooper, *Poetics,* esp. 15–62; Butcher, *Theory*, esp. 121–27; Fuhrmann, *Poetik*, esp. 25–31; Grube, *Critics,* 70–92; Russell, *Criticism*, 99–113; Eden, *Fiction,* 69–75; Trimpi, *Muses*, 50–63; Heath, *Unity,* 38–55; Ricœur, *Time*, I, 31–51; cf. n. 12, below.

[6] The Gospel of Thomas is a good example of a collection of the sayings of Jesus whose utterances have been dislodged or left unconnected with the historical deeds or settings of his public career, i.e., a proper narrative construal. For instance, the words of Jesus that find parallels in the canonical gospels take on a wholly different import in the sayings context of Thomas.

For an example of different narrative contextual meanings for a unit of tradition based on Luke's alleged use of Q as a written source, see, e.g., Bovon, 'Trajectory,' 285–94.

[7] I am indebted to Anthony Thiselton for his provocative explication and development of this term in his groundbreaking synthesis of NT and philosophical hermeneutics, *Horizons*, esp. 293–326.

event within Jesus' public career, namely, *the crucifixion*, as depicted primarily within the first of the Third Evangelist's two volumes, the Gospel of Luke.

From the poetics to the church's gospels: The thesis expanded

Long before the fourth century, the composed orality of Homeric epic had pervaded the earliest attempts at writing – from the pioneering historical accounts of the Ionic logographers to the later written versions of sophistic oratorical performance so creatively eschewed in Plato's prose 'dialogue.'[8] Precisely because the earliest traces of Greek oral literature cannot possibly be explained apart from their preoccupation with 'audience impact,' suasive forms of expression for all sorts of communication had been developing centuries before Aristotle.

Thus through the burgeoning discipline of oratory in the fourth century, rhetorical techniques were already being codified and applied to a variety of forms and genres of both oral and written performance. As R.L. Enos has documented so well, 'Democracy provided the context that made rhetoric a source of social power. This force of rhetoric prompted a blossoming of attention to discourse that moved from the poetic to the practical ... Rhapsodes, historians, orators and logographers demonstrated a compatible and correlative relationship between oral and written composition long before systems of rhetoric were formalized.'[9] This means, then – to employ Aristotle's wider notion of 'thought' (διάνοια)[10] – that an author's overall purpose for impacting an audience and the selection of a written genre appropriate to that impact had become the basis for the coherence of a text rather than Aristotle's more rarefied notion of the 'unity of causality' of the poets.[11] Later composers and literary critics, for instance, did not follow Aristotle's rather idiosyncratic privileging of the poet's 'one action plot' over against the 'looser' unity of the single 'period of time' of the historians, and so on.[12] In fact, it is not long after

---

[8] The extent to which writing was primarily an aide to persuasive speech is striking in Plato's dialogue *Phaedrus*, where Socrates casually refers to a taxonomy of 'souls and corresponding discourses' (271d, e).

[9] Enos, *Rhetoric*, 136, 139.

[10] See Moessner, 'Audience,' 63–66.

[11] Cf. Aristotle *Poetics*, 9.25–29, 'The poet (ποιητής) must be a "maker" (ποιητής) not of verses but of plots/stories (μῦθοι), since he/she is a poet by virtue of [his/her] "representation" (μίμησις), and what he/she represents (μιμεῖται) are actions/events (πράξεις)' (translation mine; numbering according to LCL *Aristotle*, vol. 23, 2nd rev. edn, 1995). See also n. 13, below, for the relation of the poet to the historian.

[12] Cf. Russell, *Criticism*, 17: 'the Aristotelian insight that imaginative literature uses discourse in a fundamentally different ("mimetic") way from oratory is either forgotten or set aside as not relevant to the business of reading, judging and reproducing the classical texts'; see esp. 114–47 on the influence of rhetoric.

the time of Aristotle before writers of history like Polybius (ca. 202–120 B.C.E.), Diodorus Siculus (f l. Julian period) or Dionysius of Halicarnassus (f l. Augustan period) – each thoroughly immersed in the culture of suasive speech – will conceive their own narrative histories as persuasive, *diegetic poiēsis*.[13]

Polybius of Megalopolis

Polybius' *Histories* provides a crucial link in tracing the trialectic hermeneutic of composed orality from the *Poetics* of Aristotle to the unabashedly rhetorically charged history-narratives of the first century B.C.E.

To be sure, Polybius does not refer to his narrative composing as poetic mimesis à la Aristotle, but rather he is the first (extant) composer of multi-volume narrative (διήγησις) to appeal to his narrative organization as an 'arrangement' (οἰκονομία) specifically designed to lead his audience to the proper (sc., authorially intended!) understanding of the events which he recounts. Similar, then, to Aristotle's formulation, the historian should portray events of a specific time period as they are known to have occurred in order to provide a reliable picture of 'all the events in their contiguous relationships that happened to one or more persons' (ὅσα ἐν τούτῳ συνέβη περὶ ἕνα ἢ πλείους, ὧν ἕκαστον ὡς ἔτυχεν ἔχει πρὸς ἄλληλα, *Poetics* 23.22–23). Yet contrary to Aristotle, Polybius will compose his narrative history like Aristotle's well-constructed epic, as 'converging to the same goal' (*History* I.3.4 [πρὸς ἕν γίνεσθαι τέλος τὴν ἀναφορὰν ἁπάντων]; cf. *Poetics* 23.26 [πρὸς τὸ αὐτὸ συντείνουσαι τέλος]). For it is his bold assertion that never before in the history of the world had events coalesced in this most unusual way to link the world as one and thus produce a 'common history' (καθόλου πραγμάτων, I.4.2[14]). Polybius must, he contends, construct a narrative

---

[13]   See, e.g., Dionysius of Halicarnassus, *Pompeius*, §3; cf., e.g., Heath, *Unity*, 151: 'Aristotle seems to have regarded chronological closure as the equivalent in history to the unified action of epic and drama, the structural *sine qua non* of good order. Later rhetorical theory does not follow him in this.'

[14]   See Scafuro, 'History,' 102–15; Polybius refers to his work as τὰ καθόλου, in contrast to historians who concentrate on limited geographical areas of (a) specific nation(s), who thus write κατὰ μέρος (e.g., *Histories,* I.4.2; III.23.3; V.31.3; VII.7.6; VIII.2.11; XVI.14.1; XXIX.12). Scafuro contends that Polybius' critique of Ephorus, Theopompus, Kallisthenes, and especially Timaeus as 'universal histori-ans' (Bk. 12) extends only to the events that are contemporary with the time of their own writing; only on that basis can he attack their own lack of 'autopsy' or shoddy interrogation of other *autoptai*. In essence, then, Polybius is redefining the categori-zation of their 'universal histories' (from the beginnings of recorded civilization to their own day) to the status of 'monographs' of limited scope, whereas his own work, though concentrating on one period of history, is the true *universal* history since it weaves together the events that for the first time were truly 'common' to the

that reflects this unity through its own 'economy' or 'arrangement' (οἰκονομία[15]):

> I.3.3–4 Previously the doings of the world had been, so to say, dispersed, as they were held together by no unity of initiative, results or locality; but ever since this date history has been an organic whole (σωματοειδῆ συμβαίνει γίνεσθαι τὴν ἱστορίαν), and the affairs of Italy and Africa have been interlinked (συμπλέκεσθαί τε τὰς ... πράξεις) with those of Greece and Asia, all leading up to one end (τέλος).

This great unifying act of Fortune must be represented by a narrative 'continuity' (τὸ συνεχές; cf. esp. I.5.5[16]) which reflects this unprecedented interweaving of events. Even through 40 long volumes, Polybius must create a narrative 'road' that will lead all those who take the journey to comprehend this unparalleled convergence of peoples and affairs. Rather than the tightly-knit 'necessary or probable causality' of the one-action plot of tragedy or epic, the unity of Polybius' composition will be established through a *continuity* of narrative performance (τὸ συνεχές[17]) which leads the audience to this 'one result' (τέλος). Again, our trialectic hermeneutic undergirds and ensconces Polybius' enterprise: Polybius' goal (authorial intent) to reflect for his audience the harmonious workings of Fortune will be represented through a continuity of narrative poetics (form of-/formal text) through which the audience will comprehend Fortune's one result (audience impact/understanding).

Diodorus of Sicily

By the first century B.C.E. rhetoric had become an all-encompassing heuristic for compositional performance, for both speaking and writing.[18] Curiously, it is a non-Greek historian composing in Koine, Diodorus Siculus, who provides some of the most detailed descriptions of how a *single plot* for a multi-volume work is properly carried out through its 'narrative continuity' (τὸ συνεχές).

---

peoples of the whole (known) world. Cf. Scafuro, 'History,' 111: 'Rather than invent a new name – one that represented the fact that its universality was 'horizontal' (synchronic) rather than 'vertical' (diachronic) – he kept the old names of *koinē historia* and *hē katholou.'*

[15] See esp. *History*, I.13.9. All translations of Polybius' *The Histories* from W. R. Paton unless otherwise identified as my own or as slight modifications.

[16] ὁ συνεχὴς λόγος, ('the message/text that continues on ...' i.e., to its overall goal (τέλος).

[17] Cf., e.g., *Histories*, IV.1.8; VI.2.1.

[18] See esp. Enos, *Rhetoric*, 91–140.

1. The plotting of narrative 'arrangement' (οἰκονομία): Audience comprehension through 'managed interpretation'

Sounding much like Polybius a century earlier, Diodorus praises historiography as the grandest of all human composing because, when rightly conceived and executed, the universal history narrative mirrors forth the moral patterns that Providence, together with Fate, has bestowed to human life. Indeed, Diodorus conceives of himself as a mouthpiece for 'history's divine voice' (διαβοώμεναι τῷ θειοτάτῳ τῆς ἱστορίας στόματι, 1.2.3) and a 'minister of Divine Providence' (ὑπουργοὶ τῆς θείας προνοίας, I.1.3) in her interweavings with 'Fate,' which united the whole of the inhabited world 'as though [they were] the affairs of one city/state' (ὥσπερ τινὸς μιᾶς πόλεως, I.3.6).[19] Diodorus in fact climaxes his own decision to write by summarizing the greater benefit his new narrative configuration will grant:

> I.3.5,8 We decided to compose a history according to a plan which would reward its readers with the greatest of benefits but, at the same time, inconvenience them the least (μὲν ὠφελῆσαι δυναμένην, ἐλάχιστα δὲ τοὺς ἀναγινώσκοντας ἐνοχλήσουσαν .... The account which keeps within the limits of a single narrative (ἡ δ' ἐν μιᾶς συντάξεως περιγραφῇ πραγματεία) and contains a connected account of events (τὸ τῶν πράξεων εἰρόμενον ἔχουσα) facilitates the reading and contains such recovery of the past (τὴν μὲν ἀνάγνωσιν ἑτοίμην παρέχεται) in a form that is perfectly easy to follow (τὴν δ' ἀνάληψιν ἔχει παντελῶς εὐπαρακολούθητον).[20]

Thus Diodorus envisions a narrative path mimetic of Providence's grand orchestrations.[21]

---

[19] For fuller treatment, see Moessner, 'Ministers,' 304–18.

[20] Diodorus, *Library of History*, I.3.2.

[21] For the role of τάξις in a more theoretically developed system of 'arrangement' (οἰκονομία) in the younger contemporary Dionysius of Halicarnassus, which includes 'division'/'partitioning' (διαίρεσις), 'order'/'sequence' (τάξις), and 'method or effectiveness of development' (ἐξεργασία), see Reid, 'Oratory,' 63–90, esp. 67–83; Moessner, 'Arrangement,' 149–64, esp. 151–53. Diodorus appears to be working with a very similar formal poetics, emphasizing the 'effectiveness of development' in engaging the reader by making sure that the 'order' (τάξις) has a well-balanced emplotment or entanglement of both linear and lateral connectors in promoting the 'continuity of the narrative.' 'Most' of his predecessors in writing universal history, he contends, have 'not developed their narrative presentations as effectively as possible for the greatest benefit [to the reader] (οὐ μὴν ἐξειργάσθαι πρὸς τὸ συμφέρον κατὰ τὸ δυνατὸν τὰς πραγματείας αὐτῶν)' (I.3.1). This 'arrangement' is, in turn, much like Dionysius', wholly contingent also upon the proper 'beginning' and 'ending' points of major sections, referred to as 'division' by the Halicarnassan; see esp. Dionysius of Halicarnassus, *Thucydides*, 9–20.

2. The plotting of narrative 'arrangement': 'Managed interpretation' (οἰκονομία) through 'fully completed' (αὐτοτελεῖς) sequences of events

Diodorus describes his method for 'balanced' 'arrangement' to be the same as that of the fourth-century historian, Ephorus of Cyme – namely, composing volumes 'complete in themselves' (αὐτοτελης). [22] 'Complete' volumes appear to consist of the full scope of the nexuses of cause and effect of important events of a given period surrounding a ruler or actions of a city/state, which in turn are related to other key movements and developments within the larger work. The rationale for composing in this way is *based upon the audience's ability to comprehend the knowledge intended by the author.* A book 'complete in itself' enables readers to 'remember' what is presented because the chains of earlier causes developed through medial influences and leading to specific outcomes are 'clear' (σαφῆ) and uninterrupted for the readers (τὴν ἱστορίαν εὐμνημόνευτον καὶ σαφῆ γενέσθαι τοῖς ἀναγινώσκουσι) (XVI.1.1):

> XVI.1.2. For incomplete accounts of actions (ἡμιτελεῖς πράξεις) in which the culminating events exhibit no continuity with the beginning events (οὐκ ἔχουσαι συνεχὲς ταῖς ἀρχαῖς τὸ πέρας) interrupt the interest even of avid readers (μεσολαβοῦσι τὴν ἐπιθυμίαν τῶν φιλαναγνωστούντων), whereas those accounts which do exhibit the continuity of the narrative (τὸ τῆς διηγήσεως συνεχές) up to the very conclusion of the events (μέχρι τῆς τελευτῆς) produce a narrative account which is well-roundedly complete (ἀπηρτισμένην τὴν τῶν πράξεων ἔχουσιν ἀπαγγελίαν).

We note the same conception as in Aristotle's *Poetics* of a complete and balanced narrative that shows how *beginning* points develop through a *middle* series of connections to the causally effected *end* events to impact the audience in *prescribed* fashion! [23] 'Half-completed' (ἡμιτελεῖς) sequences simply do not supply the proper emplotment of significance (τὸ συνεχές) *for the reader.* Parallel, then, to Aristotle's depiction of a discrete plot as embedded with specific meaning and responses for its targeted audiences, Diodorus appeals to the same trialectic hermeneutic of: (a) authorial intent, (b) ensconced in a

---

[22] The referent here is not to be confused with the referent in Book I.3; in Book XVI 'self-completed' refers to individual volumes or books of the larger work, whereas Diodorus' criticism in Book I is directed against history writers who confine their entire scope to one nation or war (cf., e.g., Thucydides). Such description thus results in 'isolated' or 'independent' events, unrelated to the larger workings of Providence and Fate.

[23] See, e.g., Aristotle, *Poetics,* 8.30–35: 'the various components of the events should be so structured that if any is displaced or removed, the sense of the whole is disturbed and dislocated.'

plotted narrative, to produce (c) a realized interpretation on the part of the audience.[24]

The thesis illustrated: The 'rejection of Messiah' as the climax of 'God's plan' for the 'release of sins' in the Gospel of Luke

Luke as a composer of the Hellenistic trialectic narrative poetics
In his two short *prooimia*, Luke divulges his familiarity with the standard of '*oikonomia*'[25] of the Hellenistic trialectic narrative hermeneutic that we sketched above.[26] Luke's mention of his:

(i) 'Scope' (ἀνατάξασθαι, Luke 1:1; cf. σύνταξις) [27] – 'all' (πάντα) the 'matters/events' (Lk. 1:1, 3) – *all* (πάντα) ... until the day he was taken up' (Acts 1:2);[28]

(ii) 'Beginning point' (ἀρχή)[29] for the narrative ordering – 'those from the beginning eyewitnesses' (Lk. 1:2) – 'all that Jesus *began* (ἄρχομαι) to do and to teach' (Acts 1:2);

---

[24] Only once (*Library of History*, XXVI.1.1) does Diodorus admit that certain individual auditors are incorrigible solipsists who will never be satisfied with the content that the author wishes to convey. Yet even here it is not a question of the audience not understanding what the author has structured his/her narrative to mean, but rather a refusal to be satisfied with the conveyed content. For Luke's 'management' of his intention to stress the divinely scripted mission to 'all the nations' as integral to Israel's 'calling,' see Moessner, 'Audience,' 61–66, 75–80; for the 'end' (both τέλος and τελευτή) of the Luke-Acts narrative accomplished with Paul's fulfillment of Isa. 45:22 ('all the nations at the end of the earth') and Acts 1:8 ('witness [of the servant] to the "end" of the earth') through his proclamation in Rome, that great 'pagan' power that controls all those nations, see Moessner, '"End(s)ings",' 203–21.

[25] The 'economics' of narrative 'arrangement' and/or 'management' of meaning *for the audience*. See esp. Polybius, *The Histories*, I.1–15; Diodorus, *Library of History*, I.3.1– 8; V.1.1–4; XV.95.4; XVI.1.1–3; Dionysius of Halicarnassus, *Thucydides*, esp. 9–20, and *Pompeius*, 3; Lucian, *How to Write History*, §§49–50, 55.

[26] See also Meijering, *Theories*, 171–225; Reid, 'Theory,' 46–64, and 'Oratory,' 63– 90; Moessner, 'Arrangement,' 149–64.

[27] Cf. Papias (citing John 'the Presbyter') on Mark and Matthew as cited by Eusebius, *Ecclesiastical History*, III.39.14–16: Although Mark did not produce a literarily acceptable narrative account (σύνταξις) as Matthew had done (τὰ λόγια συνετάξατο), Mark still resonates with the authoritative voice of Peter (cf. §15: Mark wrote *not* in τάξει but nevertheless ἀκριβῶς! [cf. Lk. 1:3]).

[28] All translations of biblical texts are my own.

[29] Cf. Polybius, *Histories*, I.5.1: 'The starting-point must be an era generally agreed upon and recognized, and one self-apparent from the events, even if this involves my going back a little in point of date and giving a summary of intervening occurrences.'

(iii) Main 'divisions' (ἄνωθεν ... καθεξῆς), Luke 1:3; cf. διαίρεσις[30] – "in the first volume, all that Jesus *began* ... until ... he was taken up ... power from the Holy Spirit shall come ... and be (my) witnesses (to me) in Jerusalem ... all of Judea and Samaria, and to the end of the earth" (Acts 1:1–2, 8);

(iv) General 'purpose' of 'clear(er) certainty' (ἀσφάλεια, cf. τέλος,[31] σαφή/-νεια) for composing yet another version of a 'narrative' already 'at hand' (Lk. 1:1a, 4) 'of the traditions in which you have been taught' – all indicate Luke's intent to write proper Hellenistic narrative, inclusive of Hellenistic auditors' expectations cultivated in the atmosphere of Greco-Roman rhetoric.

Luke's 'plan of God' as the epistemological configuration for the crucifixion of Jesus

Consequently, not unlike Polybius or Diodorus, Luke also wants to compose a narrative about a 'plan of God'[32] that will better illumine his audience vis-à-vis 'events come to fruition' in his *and* their own day. And though Luke does not employ a term for his 'narrative plan,'[33] 'the plan of God' (Lk. 7:30; Acts 2:23; 4:28; [5:38]; 13:36; 20:27; [27:42–43]) functions as a pithy moniker for the main 'subject' of his multi-volume narrative, while his *prooimia* suggest *mutatis mutandis,* like Polybius or Diodorus, that the grand sweep of God's 'plan' for the salvation of the world needs to be more fully and cogently laid out so that the church and world may have a deeper appreciation of this totally unprecedented, unrivalled action of the one Divine Reality. Luke's address to his audience comes alive when we see that a more pervasive, underlying 'trialectic' Hellenistic poetics sounds the peculiar combination of terms and claims of

---

For if readers are ignorant or indeed in any doubt as to what are the facts *from which the work opens* (τῆς γὰρ ἀρχῆς ἀγνοουμένης), it is impossible that what follows should meet with acceptance or credence; but once we produce in them a general agreement on this point they will give ear to the whole of the *continuous message* of the narrative (πᾶς ὁ συνεχὴς λόγος,. 1.5.5 [emphasis mine]).

[30] Cf. the threefold taxonomy of narrative 'arrangement,' n. 21, above; for Dionysius (*Thucydides,* 9–20), as well as for Diodorus, without the proper 'beginning' and 'ending' points in the 'division,' 'effectiveness of development' of the plot through speeches, dramatic scenes, synchronisms, etc. to produce the intended audience comprehension is impossible.

[31] Cf. esp. Diodorus, *Library of History,* XVI.1.1–2 (see above).

[32] For this notion in Diodorus, Dionysius of Halicarnassus, Josephus, Luke, et al., see Squires, *Plan,* esp. 15–52, who compares the formulations of providence and divine control over history in the various writers but does not treat the narrative epistemology which shapes the more comprehensive narrative configurations and hence significances of those formulations.

[33] E.g., Diodorus employs ἐπιβολή (*Library of History,* I.3.2).

Luke's hermeneutically revealing *prooimia*. By such direct appeal Luke stakes a claim with his readers, offering his narrative as a worthy and authentic recon-figuration of the 'many' other attempts (cf. Lk. 1:1).[34]

The significance of the 'absence' of Mark 10:45 in Luke-Acts
(Post)modern exegetes, especially those 'at home' within the redaction-critical method, find it difficult to explain why Luke, if he really views Jesus' death as atoning, would commit the 'unforgivable sin' of 'omitting' Mark 10:45! Apart from the assumptions of how Luke utilizes his sources in configuring his own narrative, the absence of Mark 10:45, with its direct attribution of Jesus' death as a 'ransom' of redemption (λύτρον), is interpreted as telling for Luke's 'thought.' The operative assumption now is that if Luke had explicit atoning statements elsewhere, then the aporia revealed by Mark 10:45 (or Matt. 20:28) would not be so determinative. Moreover, because the longer reading of the 'words of institution' was for many years disputed, and because Acts 20:28 appears to some as an erratic block within the many speeches of Acts where such specificity of atonement seems to be lacking, the reasonable conclusion is that Luke himself lacks or avoids such an understanding, or, at the least, mutes such significance to a marginal note.[35]

But we have seen that in Hellenistic poetics the meaning of any incident or event (πρᾶξις/πρᾶγμα) is conferred by the movement of the plot; any event is 'figured' by its relation to all the other events and characters and their causally configured interactions according to the 'thought' of the author. The signifi-cance that the author wants his readers to comprehend *may* be directly stated through the narrator, who functions as a managerial guide through the plot, or through any one or more of the other plotted characters. Yet there is no 'point' for direct speech when the plot itself makes the significance of an event clear (*Poetics*, 19.7–8). Direct-speech commentary is at best a secondary means of emplotment, configured for rhetorical emphasis and entertainment. Thus in asking whether Luke signifies the death of Jesus as atoning for sin, we will have to read/hear the plot of Luke-Acts within its plotted 'continuity'; speeches of main characters as well as narratorial comments will be an important place to look, but they will not be the primary media of significance.

---

[34] For a fuller presentation, see Moessner, 'Appeal,' 84–123, esp. 85–97.
[35] E.g., Conzelmann, *Theology*, 201; Wilckens, *Missionsreden*, 216; Haenchen, *Acts*, 91–92; Kümmel, 'Accusations,' 134, 138; Marshall, *Luke*, 172; Käsemann, *Essays*, 92; Green, *Theology*, 124–25; Buckwalter, *Character*, 231–72; Doble, *Paradox*, 235–37. Some notable exceptions to this 'reading' include: Fitzmyer, *Theologian*, 212; Neyrey, *Passion*, 184–92; Karris, 'Luke 23:47,' 65–74; Ford, 'Reconciliation,' 80–98; Moessner, 'Christ,' 165–83.

Hints concerning the significance of Jesus' death from the 'continuity of the narrative'

Does Luke attribute to Jesus' death an atonement for sin? Limits of space allow only summary observations and suggestions regarding the role that Jesus' crucifixion plays within the 'complications' of the Luke-Acts 'arrangement.' But it is our contention that the *dynamis* of the building plot points primarily to the *rejection* of Jesus' public career as forming the dynamic center of God's saving events of release/forgiveness/atonement of sin, and the crucifixion as the 'turning point' (μετάβασις) and thus climax of that rejection. The resurrection/ascension/enthronement/glorification of Jesus the Christ begins the 'resolution'/'new equilibrium' (λύσις) of 'release' that constitutes the church's witness and anticipates the consummation of 'all things' when the Christ 'returns.'

1. 'Beginnings' defined by the central thrust of 'all the Scriptures': 'The Christ must suffer'

Luke emphasizes the unparalleled significance of Jesus' death by his extensive synchronic overlapping of the 'end' of the gospel volume and the opening of the sequel volume, which, similar to Polybius or Diodorus, starts with events before the new 'beginning' of Pentecost in order to elucidate its broader perspective for the whole plot. With such a 'linking'[36] passage, Luke reconfigures *chronologically* one day of resurrection (Lk. 24:1–51) into forty days of teaching and appearances of the resurrected Christ (Acts 1:3–14). Specifically, Luke 3:21–24:53 corresponds to (≈) Acts 1:1–2; Luke 24:13–43 ≈ Acts 1:3; Luke 24:36–49 ≈ Acts 1:4–5; Luke 24:50–51 ≈ Acts 1:6–11; and Luke 24:52–53 ≈ Acts 1:12–14. Such synchronic entanglement enables Luke to forge his second volume with the first to create one overarching plot.[37] Acts 1:3–5 're-arrange' the resurrection appearances of Emmaus (Lk. 24:13–35) and the Upper Room[38] (24:36–49) to highlight the suffering Messiah as the hermeneutical key to all of Scripture and therefore to the significance of Jesus' role as Israel's rejected 'Christ' within that scriptural plot.

---

[36] Diodorus introduces 'linking' passages toward the beginning of each new book that summarize the main content of the volume just completed and relate that material to what will be accomplished in 'the continuity' of the new volume. Such rhetorical-poetic devices are designed to 'manage' the readers' comprehension and steer it along the appropriate lines of interpretation for both part and whole: *Library of History*, II.1.1–3; III.1.1–3; IV.1.5–7; V.2.1; VI.1.1–3; [VII–X]; XI.1.1; XII.2.2–3; XIII.1.1–3; XIV.2.4; XV.1.6; XVI.1.3–6 [cf. XV.95.4!]; XVII.1.1–2; XVIII.1.5–6; XIX.1.9–10; XX.2.3; [XXI–XL] ([] indicate fragmentary books without extant linking passages).

[37] Contra Parsons and Pervo, *Unity*.

[38] Cf. Acts 1:12.

The ongoing 'continuity' of the two-volume narrative is thus defined by the 'beginning' points of 'witness' to the whole plot of the Christ, 'beginning with the baptism of John,' and the empowerment of witness by the 'baptism of the Holy Spirit.' Both 'beginning' points imply the whole plot of Scripture, since witness to Jesus' baptism 'by' John is to witness to Jesus' anointing by the Holy Spirit to be the 'beloved Son' and 'Servant' of the Scriptures (Gn. 22:2; Isa. 42:1 in Luke 3:22; Acts 10:38) who 'must suffer, rise from the dead, and through his name a release of sins be proffered into all the nations' (Lk. 24:46–47). Moreover, what is to be proclaimed to all the nations, beginning (ἀρξάμενοι) from Jerusalem (24:47), is this new comprehension, this sweeping hermeneutic of Moses, the prophets, and the Psalms that finds its τέλος in Jesus as the *suffering* Christ (cf. Isa. 53:12 in Luke 22:37b: τὸ περὶ ἐμοῦ τέλος ἔχει). To be 'my [Jesus'] witness' in the 'power of the Holy Spirit' (Acts 1:8) encompasses the risen, *crucified* Christ's 'opening' of and fulfilled presence in the kingdom of God through his authoritative opening of the Scriptures (τοῦ συνιέναι τὰς γραφάς ... οὕτως γέγραπται ... ὑμεῖς μάρτυρις τούτων (Luke 24:45, 46, 48).[39]

The 'suffering' of the Christ, however, does not necessarily indicate an atoning death. Yet the plot of the Christ must include his suffering death. The question thus becomes this: what role in the plot does this death play? Is it only a formal requirement (a person must be dead before he/she can be raised up from death!)? Or is the death integral materially to a cause-effect nexus such that the resurrection functions as the conclusion of the 'turn about' (περιπέτεια) and thus simultaneously also the beginning of the new state of affairs, namely, the reality of an eschatological 'release of sins'? Does the release of sins result as a direct consequence of the cause (*propter hoc*) which is the death of the Christ, or does this release simply follow sequentially (*post hoc*) as a component of a larger chain of events whose 'turning point' (μετάβασις) lies somewhere else, perhaps in the resurrection itself? Whichever point it may be, Luke has connected his 'beginnings' in such a way that the Messiah who 'suffers' – who is Jesus – remains central to the apostolic 'witness' of the church.

2. The 'today' of salvation motivates 'the continuity' of the narrative

While it is certainly true that one can point to the entire Christ event within the larger 'plan of God' for all time and space as the critical 'saving act' of God, it does not follow that this saving event is not itself arranged in the epistemological structure of διήγησις which moves to a momentous 'turn of events'/'change of fortune'/'climax' (μετάβασις) in 'the continuity' of the plot. Rather than see Jesus as, in principle, a time-free, unrestricted epiphany of

---

[39] The οὕτως is epexegetic for the infinitive συνιέναι and summarized as a whole by 'these things' (τούτων, 24:48) "concerning me" (περὶ ἐμοῦ, 24:44). For a fuller treatment see Moessner, 'Ministers,' 304–23, esp. 318–23.

God's salvation, Luke sees the 'today' of salvation as the coming to fruition of the long history of God's dealings with Israel and the world since 'before the foundation of the earth ... Yes, I tell you, it shall be required of this generation' (Lk. 11:50–51; cf. 1:1!). This 'today' fulfills 'all that stands written' in God's dealings with Israel as the Jewish peoples consummate their long legacy of rejecting the prophets and the emissaries of redemption sent to Israel by putting to death the 'Christ' of those same Scriptures (cf. Lk. 13:31–35).

2.1 Luke 4:16–30 – Jesus, 'son of Adam, son of God' (3:23–38), has refused to let the 'slanderer' (διάβολος) redefine his lineage for his unprecedented calling (4:1–13) – including the 'scriptural' privilege of the 'righteous' to invoke God's special protection in times of need (Ps. 91:11 in Luke 4:9–12) – as he begins his 'teaching' 'in the power of the Spirit' in the synagogues of Galilee (4:14–15).

When Jesus declares to his hometown synagogue worshippers that the 'good news' to the poor and the release for the blind and crushed enacted by the anointed prophet of Isaiah 61 has become reality 'today' in their very gathering, their reaction follows the stereotypical pattern. They refuse to accept God's messengers on God's terms and demand a sign of proof, 'Physician, heal yourself ... do here also in your home town' (Lk. 4:23). Jesus, in turn, follows Israel's long line of prophets by announcing God's judgement upon an unbending, recalcitrant folk, 'And Elijah was sent to none of them [widows in Israel] ... not one of them [lepers in Israel] was cleansed [by Elisha].' God's judgement of Israel turns them away in favor of the Gentiles.[40]

But the patterned responses of both the congregants and Jesus are dramatically altered by the 'arrangement' of this passage with the rest of the plot.

(a) Luke entwines this experience of rejection with the subsequent material of Jesus' public ministry in a cause-effect nexus. The attempt of the synagogue, from their 'hill' 'outside the city,' to 'stone' him as a false prophet or 'rebellious son of Israel' (Dt. 21) issues in a host of the 'poor,' handicapped, oppressed, 'widows,' 'blind,' and so on receiving 'salvation' 'today' as Jesus passes through their towns and proclaims the 'good news' of God's reign (Lk. 4:31–37, 38–39, 40–41 [42–43]; 5:1–11, 12–16, 17–26, 27–32; 6:6–11; 18–19; 7:1–10, 11–17, 18–23 [v. 35 – 'Wisdom's children'], 36–50; 8:1–3, 26–39, 40–56 [43–48!] 9:1–6, 10–11, 37–43 [49–50]). The larger crowds as a whole, however, especially as they react with enthusiasm to Jesus' unusual authority and power to teach and to heal, are in turn castigated for their stubborn refusal to 'change their mind'/'repent' and to accept Jesus as God's anointed of the Scriptures (6:24–26, 46–49; 7:24–30, 31–35; 9:37–43 [44–45]; cf. 10:13–15 [retrospect]). This chain of action, reaction, and pronouncements of judgement crescendos all the way from Galilee to Jerusalem (Lk. 19:41–44) to the temple (21:5–24) to the climax of 'the place called the Skull' (23:26–31).

---

[40] See, e.g., Moessner, *Lord*, esp. 114–207.

(b) The 'continuity of the narrative' is set, as a Hellenistic auditor would expect, by the opening scenes of 'the beginning' through the cause-effect chain of events. The fame which already precedes Jesus' arrival in his home country (4:14–16) is thus placed in a negative or, at best, an ambiguous light. 'Being praised by all' (4:15) 'and all were speaking well of him and marveling' (4:22!) is the first major complication or entanglement that defines the movement of the plot and would appear to determine its outcome in the 'turning point' and 'resolution.' Already by the end of 4:30, it *sounds* as if the Nazareth 'turning upon' (cf. περιπέτεια) Jesus points – like the opening synchronisms – directly, unequivocally to the rejection of Jesus as the decisive fulfillment of 'good news' (4:21; cf. 4:15, 22, 36–37; 5:15–16, 26; 6:19 [including crowds from Tyre and Sidon]; 7:11, 16–17; 8:4, 19, 40, 42b; 9:11, 18–19, 37, 43).

(c) Toward the end of the Galilean phase when Peter declares for 'the disciples' that Jesus is 'the Christ of God' (Lk. 9:18–22), Jesus turns to all the crowds and declares that if any of them wish to be aligned with him, each one must pick up his or her own cross and follow him in a path of suffering. 'For whoever wishes to save one's life will lose it; but whoever loses one's life for my sake, that person will save it!' (9:22–24). Death, even crucifixion, results in *life* – provided a person *follows* Jesus the Son of humankind into that destiny. But there is something even more mysterious about this life through death. After the acclamation that he is 'the Christ of God,' Jesus fills out the plot of this Christ, the Son of humankind, who through his many sufferings and rejection by the Sanhedrin and execution will 'rise up on the third day' (9:22). Moreover, whoever of his audience is 'ashamed' of these words by Jesus about 'life for his disciples only through death' will be shamed by this Christ 'when he comes into his glory with the Father and the holy angels' (9:24–26). The new life which comes through death is depicted as the glorified life of the Christ, Son of humankind! (Cf. Acts 7:54–60; Stephen already 'envisions' this new life of 'glory *as he dies*'; cf. the persecuted 'saints of the Most High' in Dan. 7:13.) These exhortations of Jesus not only square with Jesus' words throughout Galilee, but they also continue to establish the 'continuity of the narrative' as moving toward *Jesus' rejection* as the eschatological pivot into life. The 'today' of salvation occurs only through the 'suffering' of the Christ which, straining toward a showdown with death, will *secure* life for eternity (cf. Lk. 18:30).

2.2 Luke 9:51–19:44 [The Great Journey] – In Luke 9:51, re-sounding the resolve of Ezekiel – priest, 'son of humankind'[41] – to declare God's judgement against an idol-sated Jerusalem, and the flint-like purpose of the prophet-

---

[41] See esp. Ezek. 21:2 LXX. Cf. the 'setting of the face' or unbending resolve of Ezekiel, 'son of humankind/mortal,' to declare judgement in Ezek. 6:2; 13:17; 20:46; 25:2; 28:21; 29:2; 38:2. Cf. God's 'face' in 14:8; 15:7.

'servant' (παῖς) of Isaiah 50:4–11[42] to accept humiliation from his own people as he announces good news, Jesus himself exhibits 'unbending determination' to complete his journey of 'taking up' by moving resolutely towards Jerusalem. This journey of 'ascension'[43] has already been described as progression to his 'exodus'/'death'/'departure,' discussed by Moses and Elijah and Jesus on a mountain with lightning and cloud and voice from heaven (Lk. 9:31 in 9:28–36). Though Luke provides neither itinerary nor map of Jesus' subsequent movements,[44] he scatters a number of 'notices of travel' which reinforce this new continuity of resolve. In fact, passages like 13:31–35 imbue the whole of the journey with the certitude that Jerusalem is the most fitting, indeed, God-ordained, scripturally-intended destination for Jesus,[45] since he journeys as a prophet who must be pressed with the fate of the long line of prophets sent, rejected, and even killed by their own people in Israel's central place (cf. 10:38;[46] 11:53–54 [following vv. 47–51]; 13:22, 31–35; 14:25; 17:11; 18:31; 19:11, 28, 37, 41–44). Is this 'continuity' of destiny sustained by any other cause-effect nexuses such that this great 'medial' section builds upon the 'complications' of the first part so as to 'thicken' to a key 'turning point' at the 'end' in a way which enables auditors 'to follow' (cf. Diodorus, *Library of History*, XVI.1.2!)?[47]

(a) As Jesus progresses toward his goal, more and more of the throngs of Israel press upon him and join him in his journey (Lk. 11:29; 12:1; 13:34; 14:25). Accordingly Jesus intensifies his warnings to a people (λαός) he perceives to be an increasingly 'faithless generation' who, like the synagogue congregation of his hometown, Nazareth (4:16–30), demand 'a sign' of his authority ('evil generation,' 11:29; 'killers of the prophets,' 11:49–51; 'hypocrites,' 12:56; 13:15; 'workers of iniquity' who patronize Jesus' 'eating and drinking and teaching in their streets,' 13:26–27). These prophetic rebukes are laced with pronouncements of judgement upon a 'hardened,' intractable folk

---

[42] Isa. 50:4: 'set the face as a solid rock.'

[43] Cf. Elijah in 4 Kgdms. 2:1, 11 (2:1–14).

[44] In Lk. 17:11 Jesus is 'passing along corresponding to the middle of Samaria and Galilee'; it is not clear whether this is through the middle of the land between Samaria and Galilee, or along the boundary of the two regions outside of the two in the Decapolis. Commentators are likewise divided whether from 9:51 Jesus is presented primarily in Galilee, Samaria, or in the Transjordan (the Decapolis and Perea).

[45] See esp. 13:35 with Ps. 117:26 LXX and Jer. 12:7; 22:5.

[46] For the emphasis upon πορεύομαι and cognates as the linking vocabulary of 'the journey notices,' see, e.g., Gill, 'Observations,' 200–205.

[47] Jesus' journey to death and rising up 'fulfills Moses and all the prophets'; see esp. Lk. 16:29, 31; 18:31; 24:27, 44; cf. Lk. 1:70: 4:24; 6:23; 9:8, 19; 10:24; 11:47, 49, 50; 13:28, 33, 34; 16:16; 24:25; Acts 3:18, 21, 24, 25; 7:42, 52; 10:43; 13:15, 27, 40; 15:15; 24:14; 26:22, 27; 28:23; see also Moessner, *Lord*, 47–56.

(10:12, 14–15; 11:31–32, 42–52; 12:45–48, 57–59; 13:3–5, 24–30, 35; 14:24; 16:27–31; 17:26–30, 19:27, 41–44), 'on account of whom,' like Moses in Deuteronomy,[48] Jesus *must die*.[49] Indeed, as Jesus presses on toward the city that stones the prophets, his anointed consciousness of the 'divine necessity'[50] of God's plan to be delivered over to death (3:22; cf. already 5:35) comes more and more to expression (12:49–50; 13:33–35; 14:27; 17:25; 18:31–33; 19:42; cf. 9:22, 23–24, 44). Gazing down from the Mount of Olives upon the city of Israel's destiny, Jesus weeps for a nation that has failed to recognize its 'exodus visitation of deliverance' from God (ἐπισκοπή, 19:44; Ex. 3:16!; 13:19; cf. Gn. 50:24). Thus, Luke's great journey plots Jesus' journey to receive the 'prophet's reward.'[51]

(b) Yet, similar to the end of the Galilean section, Jesus' consciousness that he must die 'because of' a people who refuse to 'change their mind' about him as the Christ of Scripture is laced also with the God-initiated, intended means to bring a definitive, unrepeatable 'release of sins' precisely *through* Israel's rejection of him. In Jesus' great journey, Luke plots the same paradox of 'life through death' as *release to Israel, not in spite of, but because of their rejection.* Through Jesus' 'predictions' of his suffering, both sides of this paradox are expressed as the one will or plan of God.

In Luke 14:25–27, Jesus warns the 'many crowds' pressing about him of the journey of discipleship that demands their total allegiance, even placing his commands above family and parental duties. Whoever does not carry his or her own cross in this journey to death cannot be Jesus' disciple. But the converse is also true. Whoever bears Jesus' cross and shame as faithful to the end will be rewarded with the life of heaven. Indeed, all who follow the road of discipleship now are already tasting the banquet of the 'kingdom of God,' being 'saved' in wholeness of body in a new relation to God, and so on. What is characteristic of all these children of Wisdom is that they are submitting to God's reign 'in their midst' by submitting to Jesus' authority to declare and enact directly what God demands for life. In short, their posture is tantamount to 'repenting'/

---

[48] Dt. 1:37; 3:26–27; 4:21–22.

[49] Moses 'is completed'/'dies' 'through the word of the Lord,' Dt. 34:5; cf. 'this word' in Dt. 1:37; 3:26–27; 4:21–22!

[50] Cf. the impersonal verb δεῖ, 'it is necessary,' as expressing a divine point of view or plan that Jesus must die, in 9:22; 13:33; 17:25; cf. 9:22; 22:37; 24:7, 26, 44.

[51] Conzelmann, *Theology,* 60–73, stresses that Luke's 'journey' was a portrayal of Jesus' 'consciousness' that he must suffer. Because Conzelmann's development of 'redaction criticism,' however, relied too heavily upon modern conceptions of an individual author, working with discrete written sources and with Mark as a definitive template, Luke's 'own' emphases resemble more the 'Gospel according to the changes of Mark' rather than the plot of a Hellenistic narrative *oikonomia*.

'changing their mind' about how God's decisive 'release of sin' is taking place in Jesus' presence and, therefore, about what God's eschatological presence is 'like' (e.g., Luke 12:35–38; 13:1–5, 6–9, 18–19, 20–21; 14:28–30, 31–33, 34–35; 16:19–31, etc.).

In Luke 18:31–34, 35–43, Jesus' demands to follow him on the path of suffering are poignantly illustrated by the 'blind beggar' who 'sees' Jesus and begins to 'follow him' to Jerusalem. Jesus has previously announced in revealing detail to the 'twelve': '*We* are going up to Jerusalem where all that stands written through the prophets about the Son of humankind will be consummated, for he will be handed over to the Gentiles and be mocked and treated contemptuously and spat upon, and when they have scourged him, they will put him to death and on the third day he will rise up' (18:32–33).

The shroud of mystery over Jesus' premonition of death and rising still engulfs the twelve representatives of Israel as they remain 'clueless' to the meaning of anything Jesus has told them. Similar to 9:44–45, there is a divine 'covering' of their understandings that prevents them from grasping the significance of Jesus' words. It is as though their persistent ignorance and consequent opposition to God's plan of salvation are integral to the plan itself.[52] They are both responsible for their ignorance and opposition and yet are unwittingly being led to follow their own mindset regarding God's saving act. The 'little ones' on the margins of society, however, do not seem to place their own desires and goals for 'self' as centrally as the twelve and others like the Pharisees who not only do not 'change their minds' but also try actively to hinder others from 'seeing.' Already as early as the opening sequences which establish 'the beginning' of the plot (Lk. 1:5–3:20), the pious worthy Simeon had prophesied of significant 'fallings' as well as 'risings' through the intentions of God when 'the Christ' exposes the heart of Israel (Lk. 2:25–35). It is certainly true that Jesus' overwhelming desire to 'divide' Israel down the middle, as he is constrained by his 'baptism of fire,' is in fact moving toward its fulfillment (12:49–53; 13:31–35; 17:25).

To sum up: in both passages and their immediate contexts a paradox pervades Jesus' journey. On the one hand, the demand for faithful following to Jesus' death as the 'way of the cross' is indispensable to their receiving the salvation that already 'today' participates in the 'life to come' when 'the Christ comes in his glory' (cf. 9:26). For as Jesus presses toward Jerusalem, 'whoever seeks to purchase security for his or her life will forfeit it, but whoever forfeits one's life will gain it' (17:33). On the other hand, Jesus' passion predictions subvert a straightforward *quid pro quo* of judgement to Israel for their refusal to repent, for these words are pregnant with a 'change of fortune' for life precisely

---

[52] Cf. Rom 5:6, 8, 10: 'While we were still – too weak/sinners/enemies of God – Christ died for us' (ὑπέρ ἡμῶν; cf. Lk. 22:19–20).

for those who 'today' would follow Jesus toward his death. The 'outcome'/ 'resolution' in Jerusalem would seem to decide, ultimately, who will or will not receive 'life.'

Luke 22:1–24:53: The 'Today' of the Passion and Resurrection 'Narratives'

The 'passion meal' and the Mount of Olives (Lk. 22:1–53)

One of the remarkable 'events' of all four gospels is that one of Jesus' own twelve disciples/apostles 'delivers Jesus over' to death. In Luke's 'Last Supper' before his crucifixion, Jesus celebrates the Passover as the 'passion meal' of God's plan of salvation.

The passion meal (Lk. 22:14–38)

At table, the 'hands of sinful humanity' (Lk. 9:44; 24:7) clasp together finally to reject the Christ of Scripture. 'One of the number of the twelve' had already joined company with the 'Satan' (cf. 4:13!) to arrange with 'the chief priests and the Temple guard how he might deliver him [Jesus] over to them' (22:5 in 22:1–6). Now at the 'upper room' Jesus tells all twelve apostles, 'Look, the hand of the one who is about to deliver me over is with me at table. For the Son of humankind goes (πορεύομαι) as it has been ordained; but woe to that man through whom he is delivered over!' (22:21–22).

But Jesus has just eaten the Passover with them all, including his taking of bread, breaking it and declaring, 'This is my body which is about to be given for your sake. Keep doing this to recall me to your presence' (τοῦτό ἐστιν τὸ σῶμά μου τὸ ὑπὲρ ὑμῶν διδόμενον· τοῦτο ποιεῖτε εἰς τὴν ἐμὴν ἀνάμνησιν). He also took a second cup, 'This cup is the new covenant [enacted] through my blood which is about to be poured out on your behalf' (ἐν τῷ αἵματί μου τὸ ὑπὲρ ὑμῶν ἐκχυννόμενον) (22:19–20). Here again we have a promise of life in tandem with the warning of final judgement; but now this life is tied directly to Jesus' impending, imminent giving of his own life on a Roman cross after he is handed over by his own of 'this generation.' Even as they try to take control of each other and strive for rank in their midst (22:23–24), Jesus maintains that he is now, as he has been all along, one who serves (ὁ διακονῶν) rather than one who lords it over them (cf. Isa. 53:11 – δικαιῶσαι δίκαιον εὖ δουλεύοντα πολλοῖς). In fact, as they argue over which of them is the greatest, Jesus is already bequeathing his Father's kingdom to them. For they had in fact up to this point endured with him through all of his trials and now can expect to rule with him and 'eat and drink at my table in my Kingdom … while judging the twelve tribes of Israel' (22:28–30).

But is Jesus' bequeathing (διατίθεμαι) a kingdom based on their 'faithful' discipleship or upon something else, such as his death which will establish 'the new covenant' (ἡ καινὴ διαθήκη, 22:20), ushering in a new 'fulfillment of the Kingdom of God' when he, again, will eat the Passover meal with them (22:15–18)? The answer issues from the unequivocal 'but now!' (ἀλλὰ νῦν, 22:36a). 'But now' their period of remaining with Jesus during the whole public ministry of 'trials' (22:28; cf. 18:28!) is radically reconstrued by Jesus as the time when he himself had vouchsafed their protection and provisions as he sent them out. 'But now' (22:36) circumstances will be very different; there will be in fact a radical reversal, a περιπέτεια of their 'following.' For between Jesus' bequeathing the kingdom to the apostles (22:28–30) and warning of their imminent trials (22:35–38), Jesus reveals that 'Simon' will lead them all in their 'falling' before he 'turns around' (ἐπιστρέφω) to lead their subsequent 'rising' (22:31–34).

Peter's vow to follow his 'Lord' in the 'plan' of God, even to death, is rendered hollow and pathetic by Jesus' sarcastic exhortations which immediately follow (22:33–37 [cf. 'and they were all speaking well of him … Doubtless you will say, "physician, heal yourself!"']). 'Now' they will have to fend for themselves and brandish the sword, 'for I say to you, that which stands written must come to its intended purpose with respect to me, namely, "And he was reckoned as one of the lawless" (Isa. 53:12). For indeed, that which [is written] concerning me is now coming to its goal!' (22:37). So now 'the twelve' representatives of Israel will join hands with 'this generation' in numbering Jesus as 'one without the law.' As if on cue, they cry out, 'Lord, here are two swords!' – to which Jesus can only retort, 'Enough of this!' (ἱκανόν ἐστιν)[53] (22:38). Jesus has just summed up the nature and goal of his entire 'sending' with the climax of the fourth Servant Song (καὶ ἐν τοῖς ἀνόμοις ἐλογίσθη … καὶ διὰ τὰς ἁμαρτίας αὐτῶν παρεδόθη, Isa. 53:12). The 'faithless generation' of Israel led by their 'twelve apostles' is 'delivering Jesus over' 'just as it stands written' (ἐὰν δῶτε περὶ ἁμαρτίας, ἡ ψυχὴ ὑμῶν ὄψεται σπέρμα μακρόβιον – τὸ σῶμά μου τὸ ὑπὲρ ὑμῶν διδόμενον τοῦτο ποιεῖτε εἰς τὴν ἐμὴν ἀνάμνησιν, Isa. 53:10 – Luke 22:19)! The prophecies of Simeon and Hannah, of the sword that divides Israel *through* God's 'saving act,'[54] have come true for the *twelve* who will become 'witnesses of these things to all the nations' (Lk. 24:46–48).

---

[53] See esp. Dt. 3:26 LXX (ἱκανούσθω σοι; Moses does *not* want to die outside the land); 3 Kgdms. 19:4 (ἱκανούσθω νῦν; Elijah *does* want to die outside the land!).

[54] Lk. 2:29–35, 38.

The Mount of Olives (Lk. 22:39–53)

Jesus 'goes' (πορεύομαι)[55] as it has been ordained to the mountain (22:39; cf.
22:22) and prays, 'one of the twelve' leads the 'crowd' to seize Jesus and 'delivers
over the Son of humankind' to the authority of the high priest, while
another of 'the twelve' follows Jesus' script and strikes with the sword (22:49–
50; cf. 22:36–37). The 'hour' of 'trial/temptation' is coming to its final
moments of fulfillment (22:53; cf. 4:13; 12:39, 40, 46). Is this 'hour' 'of the
authority of darkness' of Jesus' final rejection the decisive 'breaking point' or
'turning of events' (μετάβασις) of the whole plot? If so, does this 'change of
fortune' (μεταβολή) consist in the eschatological 'release of sins'? Does the
author provide any signal to the audience that the beginning of a 'turn around'
(περιπέτεια) of the status quo of Israel and the nations has in fact arrived?

The 'council of the people (λαός)' (Lk. 22:54–71) and Pilate (23:1–25; cf.
3:1; 13:1)

As Jesus is led into the council chamber Peter 'follows' (at a distance!), falls
prey to the 'hour of temptation,' and is ashamed of the Son of humankind and
of his words (22:31–32, 40, 46, 60–62). At that very moment 'the Lord *turns*' to
'gaze up at Peter' who then 'remembered (ὑπεμνήσθη) the word of the Lord,
how he had said to him that "before the cock crows – *today* (σήμερον) – you
will deny me three times!" And going outside [of the courtyard], he wept bitterly'
(22:54–62). Peter *remembers* and sees the rejected, humiliated Jesus in his
presence as he calls to mind the very words that had prophesied his own 'falling.'
Luke's audience themselves will *remember* Jesus' words about 'remembering'
him in their presence when they break the bread and pour the cup. For
Peter has just sealed this generation's rejection of the Christ of the Scriptures.
Their leader, Peter, will have no thought, no memory of such a one who is
about to be reviled, *today*, as a false 'Christ,' a 'king' (!) and led to execution.
Such association with humiliation and lawlessness is for him unthinkable. His
faithfulness in following has failed (ἐκλίπῃ ἡ πίστις σου, 22:32). Jesus' burning
desire to divide the very households of Israel has certainly come true for his
own (22:7–38; cf. 12:49–53). But as Jesus *turns* to him (22:61), does Peter
already begin to 'change his mind,' has Peter already started the process of leading
the twelve to 'turn around' (σύ ποτε ἐπιστρέψας στήρισον τοὺς ἀδελφούς
σου, 22:32b)?

When the council of the people demands to know whether Jesus is 'the
Christ,' he responds by declaring that 'from now on, the Son of humankind
will be sitting at the right hand of the power of God' (22:67–69). Their *rejection*
of the Christ of the Scriptures (cf. Ps. 110:1 in 20:42–43) heralds the enthronement
of Jesus the Son of humankind. Their *final denial* of his calling as God's
Son, Israel's elect servant, itself precipitates Jesus' exaltation as the Son whose

---

[55] See n. 46, above.

investiture consummates God's saving act. Jesus' announcement 'from now on' reverberates the completion from the middle of the narrative of his 'passion predictions' when he 'will be raised' (9:22; 18:33) or when he as Son of humankind 'comes in his glory and of the Father and the holy angels' (9:26). More than that, the chief priests and the scribes echo the 'voice' from heaven (Lk. 3:22; cf. 9:35) but in the sarcastic taunts of the 'slanderer': 'You, then, are the Son of God?!' (22:70a; 4:3, 9). The 'end' recalls the 'beginning,' as well as the 'middle.' We are reminded of Diodorus' advice for 'remembering' 'clearly' (εὐμνημόνευτον καὶ σαφῆ) what is important in the 'continuity' of the narrative by 'following' chains of earlier causes 'complicated' through medial developments that lead to a specific outcome or result (τέλος/συντέλεια) of a 'completed' (αὐτοτελής) plot (*Library of History*, XVI.1.2). It sounds as though Jesus' earlier words about his own death issuing in life have now become the hermeneutical key to the climax of the 'plot of the Christ' (cf. 9:44; 18:31–34 with 23:8–12).

Before Pilate, the 'people' (λαός) of Israel join their leaders in demanding that he be crucified. Though they had 'hung on his every word' when Jesus had taught them day after day in the temple (19:47–48; 21:38), now, again like the Nazareth synagogue worshippers, these Passover pilgrims 'turn on' (περιπέτεια) Jesus and demand to have *released, in his place,* Barrabas the murderer and insurrectionist (23:13–25).

The crucifixion (Lk. 23:26–56)

The taunting words of Psalm 21:8 [LXX] reverberate throughout Jesus' crucifixion between 'two other evil doers' (cf. 23:32). First, the 'rulers' of the people (23:35), then 'the soldiers' (23:36–37), and even one of the 'evildoers' mock Jesus' kingship, 'let him save himself!' (σωσάτω ἑαυτόν)/'save yourself'! But the other 'evil doer' sounds the confession of the 'we' of Isaiah 53:3–6 [LXX] ('he was dishonored and was not reckoned as human. But this one was bearing *our* sins and *for our sake* was being abused! And yet *we* had reckoned him as one in trouble, in suffering, and [deserving of] ill treatment. But he himself was wounded because of *our* sins and mutilated because of *our* lawlessness!'). '"Do *you* not fear God, seeing that you are under the same sentence of judgement!? And yet *we ourselves* are sentenced justly, for *we* are receiving back due retribution for the things *we* have done. But this one, he has done nothing wrong!" And he said to him, "Jesus, *remember* (μνήσθητι) me when you come into your kingdom!"' (23:40–42). This second malefactor is not ashamed of Jesus and of his words when he comes in his glory. He has become the quintessential disciple who, in forfeiting his own life for Jesus' sake, will gain it – who sees that life flows from Jesus' death – for him! Fitting then, that Jesus answers, '*Today,* you will be with me in Paradise!' (cf. Isa. 51:3). Jesus' death pours forth life. His body *is* being given for him! The 'today' of salvation has come to its climax.

Nor should we be surprised that this 'hour of darkness' 'over the whole earth/ land' immediately yields forth the 'end' of presence for the sacrifice in the holy place as 'the veil of the sanctuary was split down the middle' (23:44–45). And it is most fitting again that Jesus should quote Scripture as he expends his last gasp, 'Father, into your hands I am giving over my spirit' (Ps. 30:16 [LXX] in 23:46). Jesus, the suffering righteous one, has submitted fully to God's plan. Thus Luke has woven together the 'turning point,' the 'change of fortune' for the 'lawless,' both in the dynamic configuration of events *and* in direct-speech interpretation to proclaim, 'Today, this Scripture [of final salvation] is fulfilled in your hearing!'

The Burial and Resurrection: Calls to Remembrance (Lk. 23:47–24:49)

The three larger sections that constitute the 'resurrection narrative' are tightly woven to interpret 'the Christ of Scripture' who 'must suffer and be raised.' The tomb becomes a 'sign of remembrance,' while the presence of the resurrected crucified one in the midst of the women's 'remembrance' indicates that the 'release of sins' and the resultant new life have already been in place before any belief in the resurrection of the Christ is evidenced; the 'resolving' dénouement is already well in motion:

The burial and 'recalling to their presence' of the women (Lk. 23:47–24:12)

Once Jesus expires, Luke shows, again, how it is the 'little ones' and despised of Jewish society, the women from Galilee and a Roman officer, who first express their 'change of thinking' about the suffering Messiah. While the onlookers as a whole had sensed that a grave injustice was taking place (Lk. 23:28), it is a Roman centurion (cf. 7:1–10; 19:1–10) who 'glorifies God' by changing his way of thinking and declaring Jesus a 'righteous/just man' (23:47). Coupled with the 'evil doer's' confession from the cross, the linkage for Luke's auditors with the suffering righteous of the Psalms and *the* righteous servant of Isaiah 40–55 could hardly be missed. Another 'righteous' man, who now also, unwittingly, is serving God's plan of salvation by 'welcoming the kingdom of God' (cf. 23:42), places the *body of Jesus* (τὸ σῶμα τοῦ Ἰησοῦ) in a tomb, the 'place of remembrance' (0/μνημεῖον).[56] Moreover, this tomb is new; it has served no other as a 'place of remembrance' (23:53). It is all the more interesting that the women from Galilee 'following' the *body*, 'observed

---

[56] Cf. Bauer, *Lexicon*, 'lit. a "sign of remembrance", esp. for the dead (Hom. +).'

the place of the tomb and *how his body was placed!*' (ὡς ἐτέθη τὸ σῶμα αὐτοῦ, 23:55).

On the day after the Sabbath rest, when the women go to the tomb to place spices and ointments on the body (24:1), 'they did not find the body' (τὸ σῶμα) of the Lord Jesus but encounter instead two men who exhort them to '*remember* (μνήσθητε) how he had spoken to you while he was still in Galilee, when he said, "The son of humankind must be delivered over into the hands of sinful human beings and be crucified and on the third day rise up"' (24:6b–7). Like Peter in the high priest's courtyard, 'they remembered his words' (ἐμνήσθησαν τῶν ῥημάτων αὐτοῦ, 24:8). But these are very different words! By remembering, they 'recall him to their presence' in a way that contrasts rather baldly with the apostles' lack of 'faith' (cf. 22:32). The women's 're-membering' opens up for them the significance of Christ's rejection as a death 'for them' that ushers them into the fulfilled kingdom of eschatological life as they embrace the risen Christ's presence. That the women's 'remembering' is tantamount to comprehending the plot of the Christ of the Scriptures becomes 'certain' (ἀσφαλής) from the 'unraveling' emplotment.

The group of women (three named, 'and all the rest'), who return and pro-claim that the plot of the Christ has come true, contrasts with the group of 'the eleven (males) and all the rest' who consider the women's announcement 'an idle tale' 'and were refusing [iterative imperfect] to believe them' (ἠπίστουν αὐταῖς, 24:9–11).

Nonetheless, Peter is not content simply to disbelieve and runs to the 'place of remembrance' and 'starts marveling to himself what had taken place' (24:12). Is the 'place of remembrance' beginning to function as a 'sign of remembrance' of the plot of the Christ (i.e., a μνημεῖον a σημεῖον; cf. 'and all began to marvel, "Is this not Joseph's son?,"' Luke 4:22).

And he was remembered 'in the breaking of the bread' (Lk. 24:13–35)

On that very same day, two disciples 'on the way' to Emmaus, who have heard the women's report, become entangled in what unfolds like an anti-plot but which 'turns' out actually to 'unravel' the 'turning point' of the whole plot as the 'resolution' of the new state of affairs.

Instead of Jesus journeying to Jerusalem, they journey away from Jerusalem (24:13). Instead of disciples joining Jesus to journey there with him, two disci-ples are joined by Jesus who begins to accompany them (24:14–15). Now, rather than Jesus admonishing those in his party for not knowing the 'signs' of the events taking place in their midst, the 'two' admonish Jesus for 'alone not knowing the things that have taken place' in Jerusalem (24:17–18). Moreover, instead of Jesus uttering predictions about his passion and raising up when the disciples do not 'know' the meaning of his words, now the two disciples sum-marize the career of Jesus, a 'mighty prophet,' by echoing his own passion predictions – right when the living Jesus appears not to know 'what things' they are talking about (24:19–20). But when they express their own shattered hope ('he was going to redeem Israel' [αὐτός ἐστιν ὁ μέλλων λυτροῦσθαι τὸν Ἰσραήλ, 24:21a]), they go on to 'report' that the women could not find his *body* (τὸ σῶμα αὐτοῦ) but saw and heard two 'angels'/'messengers' declare that he was alive (24:21b–23). And when they add that 'some of them,' although going to the tomb and finding it to be 'just as the women had said, yet did not *see* him' [Jesus] (24:24), Jesus has had enough (cf. 22:38!). 'You foolish folk, stubborn of heart to believe all that the prophets have spoken! Was it not divinely scripted that the Christ was to suffer these things and so enter into his glory?!' (24:25–26). Nor does he stop there. As they continue 'on their way,' he gives them a 'Bible study' like no other, 'beginning from Moses and from all the prophets, interpret[ing] to them those things concerning himself in all the Scriptures' (24:27).

With the resurrected Jesus in their very midst – even with scriptural evidence from the glorified Christ himself to the events that have just transpired to the one who is 'on the way' with them – these two do not comprehend the plot of the Christ. What is it, then, that they do not understand about a suffering, rejected Christ that does not, will not, open 'their mind' to comprehend the Christ in their very midst? Like Peter, they have rejected the 'suffering Christ' and apparently refuse to entertain such thoughts, even when – in stark contrast to the women – they cannot 'remember' words that Jesus had uttered to them before and has just rehearsed for them again. How, then, is this 'counter-plot' broken?

Similar to Peter, the two cannot let matters drop once Jesus acts as though he is going to part company and continue on when they approach Emmaus. They urge him to 'stay' with them (Lk. 24:28–29). But their eyes are not opened until they see and hear again the sign at table that Jesus had enacted in order that they may recall him to their presence, 'breaking the bread and giving it to *and* for them!' (τὸν ἄρτον … καὶ κλάσας ἐπεδίδου αὐτοῖς, 24:30). Only as they understand that the body of the Christ was broken for them do they comprehend and behold the Christ of the Scriptures. Already 'on the way' their sluggish 'hearts' were being 'fired' by Jesus' 'opening up' to them the central thrust of all Scripture in the suffering, glorified Christ (24:32). But it was not until they heard and saw Jesus within this scriptural panorama '*break* and *give* the bread' that they 'remembered him.' Thus it makes perfectly good sense that once they 'recall him to their presence' as the broken Christ who has already redeemed them, there is no reason for the visible resurrected-crucified one to 'lodge/stay with them.' 'And so he became invisible to them'[57] (24:31b). The

---

[57] Note: The text does not indicate that Jesus departed from them or evacuated their space, but 'became invisible/vanished from them' (i.e., 'not appearing' *from* their 'point of viewing,' Lk. 24:31b).

presence of the living crucified one has completely *turned them around* and they return to Jerusalem with 'the good news' – 'how he was made known to them in the breaking of the bread' (ὡς ἐγνώσθη αὐτοῖς ἐν τῇ κλάσει τοῦ ἄρτου, 24:33–35)!

(iii) 'And while they looked on, he began to eat ... and opened their mind to comprehend the Scriptures' (Lk. 24:36–49)
Right when the Emmaus disciples utter the phrase 'in the breaking of the bread,' Jesus himself is prompted to break into the conversation of the larger group of disciples in Jerusalem (Lk. 24:36).[58] Now instead of feigning his presence as an 'unknown guest' (24:14–30), he 'showed to them his hands and his feet' as their crucified host (24:40). Now instead of fear (24:37–38), joy overwhelms them, yet they continue to be in disbelief (ἀπιστούντων αὐτῶν ἀπὸ τῆς χαρᾶς, 24:41; cf. 22:45 – ἀπὸ τῆς λύπης!). Again, it is not until he opens up for them the Scriptures while eating in their presence that they finally embrace the plot of the Christ and become qualified to receive the empowerment of the Holy Spirit in their mission as 'witnesses to all of these things' (24:45–49). As we have already seen, the plan of God necessarily involves the sending of the apostles as witnesses to Israel and the nations simply because this universal 'saving act' represents the very heart of the scriptural plot of the plot of the Christ (hence the book of Acts). The Scriptures not only must 'open the mind' of the marveling disciples, but also the Scriptures in turn are themselves 'opened' by the living crucified one who is 'recalled to the disciples' presence' 'in the breaking of the bread.'

Conclusions

(i) The significance of the entire rejection and suffering that culminates in Jesus' death 'for you' is the key that unlocks and 'opens up' the divine perspective on the whole plot of the Christ from the Scriptures. Rather than pull a resurrected Jesus down as a 'god in a crane' – to invoke Aristotle's *deus ex machina*[59] – in order to reverse and retrieve some meaning to the 'tragedy' of Jesus' death, Luke releases the dénouement, the unraveling, directly as a 'result' or 'consequence' of the tightening events of Jesus' rejection that come to an eschatological 'turning' in his death. Indeed, we have seen that throughout the whole of Luke's Gospel, it is the cross-bearing of the Christ that points to and issues in 'the one result' of the release of sins into new life. Israel's and the nations' 'conspiring together' to crucify the Christ (Psalm 2 in Acts 4) no longer has any

---

[58] ταῦτα δὲ αὐτῶν λαλούντων αὐτὸς ἔστη (Lk. 24:36a).
[59] *Poetics*, 15[1454b].1–5.

power or force precisely because such twisted disobedience has been 'turned around' (περιπέτεια) in the death itself that releases forgiveness and ushers in a new opportunity to join the eschatological 'people' of God in solidarity with the resurrected-suffering Christ. In this 'continuity of the narrative,' the 'body' (σῶμα) of Jesus becomes a metonymic prompt for the audience – as it was for the women – of Jesus' death 'given for you,' while, 'in the breaking of the bread' serves as a metaleptic prompt of the whole plot of the Christ – as it was for the Emmaus disciples – in which Jesus' promise of his presence in the broken bread is 'given for you' (cf. Acts 2:42).

(ii) Luke's 'unraveling' the plot of the 'suffering Christ' combines both 'discovery' (ἀναγνώρισις) and 'reversal' (περιπέτεια) for the disciples, and thus constitutes what Aristotle prescribed as the preferred entanglement (συμπλοκή) and release (λύσις) of 'complex plots.'[60] The disciples' discovery of the unknown guest 'in the breaking of the bread' coincides with their complete reversal in comprehending the Christ of the Scriptures in their midst. The rest of their enlightened 'turning around' constitutes the beginnings of the church in the mission of witness to Israel and through Israel to all the nations as filled out in the 'continuity of the narrative' of the 'plan of God' of volume two, the Acts of the Apostles. Consequently, the Gospel of Luke can be read like no other. There is no indication that 'what' Luke wrote, according to his *prooimion* to both volumes[61] (Lk. 1:1–4), was to be anything other than what the church would eventually entitle 'the Gospel according to …' Notwithstanding the canonical separation of the two, the third gospel points inescapably to its sequel in which the Christ of volume one remains instrumental through the second: the church exists and thrives only from the 'witness' of the risen-crucified One, empowered by the Holy Spirit. Church and Christ are inseparable; thus Acts is the only book of the New Testament that 'narrates' the ongoing presence of Christ in God's church and world.

(iii) Redaction criticism as typically applied to the Gospel of Luke confuses 'the continuity' of the Markan narrative with the Lukan. By rendering judgements upon Luke's motivation and historical situation for individual pericopes of his narrative through comparisons with Mark's sequence and diction in alleged 'parallel passages,' the continuity of Luke's cause-effect nexuses, which configure the 'continuity' of his narrative in the first instance, is broken up. In effect, redaction criticism's treatment of individual units in Luke render Luke's

---

[60] Aristotle, *Poetics*, 18.

[61] It is pure speculation whether Lk. 1:1–4 was 'originally' written as the preface only to volume one or to both volumes; as it stands, the beginning preface functions de facto – by convention – as the *prooimion* to all the following volumes; cf. the multi-volume Hellenistic historians and esp. Diodorus' 'linking passages' following the secondary *prooimia*; see n. 36, above.

διήγησις as a whole 'incomplete' (ἀτελής) and 'half-completed' (ἡμιτελής) as it disengages from each other the three interdependent components of authorial thought/intent↔formal poetics↔reader comprehension of the standard Hellenistic narrative epistemology. Consequently, the 'death of Jesus' has often been reconfigured according to a newly fabricated 'continuity of the narrative' which Luke never intended and perhaps even countered through his own diegetic enterprise (Lk. 1:1–4). In short, redaction criticism's conclusion that Luke attributes no atoning significance to Jesus' rejection and death has bypassed the Hellenistic epistemology of narrative 'arrangement' and, thereby, also severed the intricate lacing of Jewish Scripture that binds added witness to Luke's fundamental portrayal of Jesus, the suffering, righteous, and raised up 'Christ of God.'

To sum up: in the opening of the third gospel, Jesus is presented to the Lord with a sacrifice of redemption as the firstborn of Israel;[62] in the 'end,' Jesus presents himself to the Lord as a sacrifice for the redemption of Israel and all the nations.

---

[62] Lk. 2:22–23; to fulfill Ex. 13:2!

Bibliography

Aristotle, *Poetics* (ed. and trans. S. Halliwell; LCL 199; Cambridge, MA: Harvard University Press, 2ⁿᵈ edn, 1995)

Avenarius, G., *Lukians Schrift zur Geschichtsschreibung* (Meisenheim/Glan: Hain, 1956)

Bauer, W., *A Greek-English Lexicon of the New Testament and other Early Christian Literature* (ed. F.W. Danker; Chicago: University of Chicago Press, 3ʳᵈ rev. edn, 2000).

Bovon, F., 'Tracing the Trajectory of Luke 13,22–30 back to Q: A Study in Lukan Redaction,' in *From Quest to Q: Festschrift James M. Robinson* (ed. J.M. Asgeirsson, K. de Troyer, M.W. Meyer; BETL 146; Leuven: Leuven University Press/Peeters, 2000) 285–94

Buckwalter, H.D., *The Character and Purpose of Luke's Christology* (SNTSMS 89; Cambridge: Cambridge University Press, 1996)

Butcher, S.H., *Aristotle's Theory of Poetry and Fine Art* (New York: Dover Publications, 1951)

Conzelmann, H., *The Theology of St. Luke* (New York: Harper & Row, 1960)

Cooper, L., *The Poetics of Aristotle: Its Meaning and Influence* (New York: Longman, Green and Co., 1927)

Diodorus Siculus, *Library of History* (12 vols.; trans. C.H. Oldfather, C.B. Welles, R.M. Geer; LCL; Cambridge: Harvard University Press; London: Heinemann, 1946–1967)

Dionysius of Halicarnassus, *Letter to Gnaeus Pompeius*, II (trans. S. Usher; LCL 466; Cambridge, MA: Harvard University Press; London: Heinemann, 1985), 347–99

—, *On Thucydides*, I (trans. S. Usher; LCL 466; Cambridge, MA: Harvard University Press; London: Heinemann, 1974)

Doble, P., *The Paradox of Salvation: Luke's Theology of the Cross* (SNTSMS 87; Cambridge: Cambridge University Press, 1996)

Eden, K., *Poetic and Legal Fiction in the Aristotelian Tradition* (Princeton: Princeton University Press, 1986)

Enos, R.L., *Greek Rhetoric before Aristotle* (Prospect Heights, IL: Waveland Press, 1993)

Eusebius, *Ecclesiastical History*, I (trans. K. Lake; LCL 153; Cambridge, MA: Harvard University Press; London: Heinemann, 1975)

Fitzmyer, J.A., *Luke the Theologian: Aspects of His Teaching* (New York: Paulist Press, 1989)

Ford, J.M., 'Reconciliation and Forgiveness in Luke's Gospel,' in *Political Issues in Luke-Acts* (ed. R.J. Cassidy and P.J. Scharper; Maryknoll: Orbis Books, 1983), 80–98

Fuhrmann, M., *Aristoteles Poetik* (Munich: Heimeran, 1976)

Gill, D., 'Observations on the Lukan Travel Narrative and Some Related Passages,' *HTR* 63 (1970), 200–205

Green, J.B., *Theology of Luke* (Cambridge: Cambridge University Press, 1995)

Grube, G.M.A., *The Greek and Roman Critics* (London: Methuen, 1965)

Haenchen, E., *The Acts of the Apostles* (Philadelphia: Westminster Press, 1971)

Halliwell, S., *The Poetics of Aristotle: Translation and Commentary* (London: Duckworth, 1987)

Heath, M., *Unity in Greek Poetics* (Oxford: Clarendon Press, 1989)

Homeyer, H., *Lukian. Wie man Geschichte schreiben soll. Griechisch und Deutsch* (Munich: W. Fink, 1965)

Just, A. (ed.), *Luke* (ACCS, NT III; Downers Grove, IL: InterVarsity Press, 2003)

Karris, R.J., 'Luke 23:47 and the Lucan View of Jesus' Death,' *JBL* 105 (1986), 65–74

Käsemann, E., *Essays on New Testament Themes* (SBT 41; London: SCM Press, 1964)

Kümmel, W.G., 'Current Theological Accusations Against Luke,' *ANQ* 16 (1975), 134–38

Lucian (of Samosata), *How to Write History*, VI (trans. K. Kilburn; LCL; Cambridge, MA: Harvard University Press; London: Heinemann, 1959)

Marshall, I.H., *Luke: Historian and Theologian* (Grand Rapids: Zondervan, 1970)

Meijering, R., *Literary and Rhetorical Theories in Greek Scholia* (Groningen: E. Forsten, 1987)

Moessner, D.P., 'The Appeal and Power of Poetics (Lk. 1:1–4): Luke's Superior Credentials (παρηκολουθηκότι), Narrative Sequence (καθεξῆς), and Firmness of Understanding (ἀσφάλεια) for the Reader,' in *Jesus and the Heritage of Israel* (ed. D.P. Moessner; vol. 1 of Luke the Interpreter of Israel; Harrisburg: Trinity Press International, 1999), 84–123

—, '"The Christ Must Suffer," the Church Must Suffer: Rethinking the Theology of the Cross in Luke-Acts,' in *Society of Biblical Literature 1990 Seminar Papers* (ed. D.J. Lull; Atlanta: Scholars Press, 1990), 165–83

—, '"Completed End(s)ings" of Historiographical Narrative: Diodorus Siculus and the End(ing) of Acts,' in *Die Apostelgeschichte und hellenistische Geschichtsschreibung. Festschrift für Dr. Plümacher* (ed. C. Breytenbach and J. Schröter; AGJU 57; Leiden: E.J. Brill, 2004), 193–221

—, 'Dionysius' Narrative "Arrangement" (*oikonomia*) as the Hermeneutical Key to Luke's Re-vision of the "Many,"' in *Paul, Luke and the Graeco-Roman World: Essays in Honour of Alexander J. M. Wedderburn* (ed. A. Christophersen, C. Claussen, J. Frey and B. Longenecker; JSNTSup. 217; Sheffield: Sheffield Academic Press, 2002)

—, '"Managing" the Audience: Diodorus Siculus and Luke the Evangelist on Designing Authorial Intent,' in *Luke and His Readers: Festschrift A. Denaux* (ed.

R. Bieringer, G. Van Belle, J. Verheyden; BETL 182; Leuven: Leuven University Press/Peeters, 2005), 61–80

—, '"Ministers of Divine Providence": Diodorus Siculus and Luke the Evangelist on the Rhetorical Significance of the Audience in Narrative "Arrangement,"' in *Literary Encounters with the Reign of God* [Studies in Honor of R.C. Tannehill] (ed. S.H. Ringe, H.C. Paul Kim; New York: T&T Clark, 2004), 304–23

—, *Lord of the Banquet: The Literary and Theological Significance of the Lukan Travel Narrative* (Philadelphia: Fortress Press; Harrisburg: Trinity Press International, 1998)

Neyrey, J., *The Passion According to Luke. A Redaction Study of Luke's Soteriology* (New York: Paulist Press, 1985)

Parsons, M.C., and R.I. Pervo, *Rethinking the Unity of Luke and Acts* (Minneapolis: Fortress Press, 1993)

Plato, *Phaedrus,* in *The Collected Dialogues of Plato, including the Letters* (trans. R. Hackforth; ed. E. Hamilton and H. Cairns; Bollingen Series 71; Princeton: Princeton University Press, 1961), 475–525

Polybius, *The Histories,* I–VI (trans. W.R. Paton; LCL; London: Heinemann; New York: Putnam's, 1922–27)

Reid, R.S., '"Neither Oratory nor Dialogue": Dionysius of Harlicarnassus and the Genre of Plato's Apology,' *RSQ* 27 (1997), 63–90

—, 'Dionysius of Halicarnassus' Theory of Compositional Style and the Theory of Literate Consciousness,' *Rhetoric Review* 15 (1996), 46–64

Ricœur, P., *Time and Narrative,* I (Chicago: University of Chicago Press, 1984)

Russell, D.A., *Criticism in Antiquity* (Berkeley and Los Angeles: University of California Press, 1981)

Scafuro, A.C., 'Universal History and the Genres of Greek Historiography' (unpublished Ph.D. dissertation; Yale University, 1983)

Squires, J.T., *The Plan of God in Luke-Acts* (SNTSMS 76; Cambridge: Cambridge University Press, 1993)

Thiselton, A.C., *The Two Horizons: New Testament Hermeneutics and Philosophical Description* (Grand Rapids: Eerdmans, 1980).

Trimpi, W., *Muses of One Mind: The Literary Analysis of Experience and Its Continuity* (Princeton: Princeton University Press, 1983)

Wilckens, U., *Die Missionsreden der Apostelgeschichte* (WMANT 5; Neukirchen-Vluyn: Neukirchener Verlag, 1974)

Language, Parables, and Ways or Levels of Reading Luke

6

Political and Eschatological Language in Luke

I. Howard Marshall

Luke is certainly one of the more cultivated writers of Greek in the New Testament, and one way in which this is seen is in his variety of styles of writing.[1] Every reader is aware of the complex periodic sentence which forms the prologue to his gospel. It is couched in a literary style which aligns the book with the scientific treatises and the historical works of the time and establishes at the outset that Luke is writing as a historian.[2] It is immediately followed by a narrative extending over two chapters and characterized by the diction of the Septuagint, almost as if Luke realized that he was carrying on the story that began there by adding on a new episode, rather like the way in which people sometimes say that the New Testament contains the initial chapters of the story of the church and we are writing further chapters of the unfinished story, or rather (to be more accurate) we are saying and doing the things that could form part of such a record. Failure to observe the variation in literary styles may lead to misunderstanding of what Luke is trying to convey to the readers. We shall look at two examples of passages where careful attention to the use of language is called for.

The Hymns and the Mission of Jesus: Political and Military Language

Within the two opening chapters a notable element is the inclusion of various poetic pieces, in particular the songs traditionally known from their respective opening words in Latin as the Magnificat and the Benedictus.[3] What is

---

[1] The substance of this article was delivered as the International Centre for Biblical Interpretation Annual Lecture at the University of Gloucestershire in June 2005.
[2] Alexander, *Preface to Luke's Gospel.*
[3] For what follows see the fuller treatment in Marshall, 'The Interpretation of the Magnificat: Luke 1:46–55'.

of particular interest in them for our present purpose is the reference to the mighty acts of God in language expressive of historical political acts:

> He has performed mighty deeds with his arm;
> he has scattered those who are proud in their inmost thoughts.
> He has brought down rulers from their thrones
> but has lifted up the humble.
> He has filled the hungry with good things
> but has sent the rich empty away (Lk. 1:51–53)

> He has come to his people and redeemed them.
> He has raised up a horn of salvation for us
> in the house of his servant David ...
> salvation from our enemies
> and from the hand of all who hate us ...
> to rescue us from the hand of our enemies,
> and to enable us to serve him without fear. (Lk. 1:68–70, 71, 74)

These sentiments are expressed by verbs in the aorist, and they can be understood as describing what God has done in the past but also what he is presently doing or is about to be doing in the imminent future, actions that will be of a piece with what he has done for his people in earlier generations. The language is the language of political and military deliverance, the kind of things that might be done by a mighty king who carries out the twofold task described, for example, in *Psalms of Solomon* 17. Here the deliverer sets the people of Israel free from their external enemies and enables them to live in peace and security without fear. But he also carries out an internal revolution which brings down the proud and mighty who have gained their positions, partly at least, by oppressing the poor. This internal revolution also provides dignity and wealth for those who were downtrodden. Political deliverance is understood to be a manifestation of the power of God acting for the good of his people (*Pss. Sol.* 17:23–46).

The surrounding narrative in Luke 1–2 indicates that these hopes are tied to the coming of John and Jesus, the former as a prophet and the latter as a ruler over the house of Jacob, standing in the line of David. The hope, of course, is not exclusively political. Inevitably it is tied up with more religious and spiritual aspects, the forgiveness of the sins of the people who turn to God and the spread of holiness and righteousness.

The political language can include metaphorical language: Zechariah envisages that 'the rising sun will come to us from heaven to shine on those living in darkness and in the shadow of death' (Lk. 1:78–79), and his hearers or readers would not be expected to take his words literally. But there is also the more important question of whether the 'straight' language is meant to be understood in its ostensible political and material significance or in some other way. Compare how Jesus declares that he has been anointed 'to proclaim good news to the poor ... to proclaim freedom for the prisoners and recovery of sight for the blind, to see the oppressed free, to proclaim the year of the Lord's favour' (Lk. 4:18–19). Is he referring to the actual healing of blind people like Bartimaeus (Lk. 18:35–43) or to the setting free of literal prisoners (conceivably those held in prison because of monetary debts that they were unable to pay, or disciples suffering persecution, like Peter and others in the book of Acts)? Or is he using metaphorical language for the spiritual deliverance that Jesus brings to people who are blind to the reality of God and held in the grip of sin? The either/or may be inappropriate, because a case might be made that the mission of Jesus includes all of these things.

When the story of the mission of Jesus does get under way, however, it quickly becomes apparent that despite all the fanfare in Luke 1–2 the realities are not going to be massive acts of political deliverance (although that is not to say that the mission of Jesus has no political concern or relevance). Instead we have a wandering prophet going around the country areas of Galilee and Judea, certainly with healing powers that he exercises, but equally certainly with no indication of starting a political revolution by raising an army and fighting the enemies of the people, still less of calling on supernatural power to zap his opponents (Lk. 9:51–56). In the end he is put to death charged with being, or rather claiming to be, a king, and Pilate regards even that claim as being without substance. The situation is no different in Acts where a wider group (that Luke continues to refer to as 'disciples') carry on essentially the same kind of activities as those of Jesus and his disciples.

We thus have a problem of interpretation. How are we to relate the language of Luke 1–2 to the actual events that followed? There are various possible solutions. At the outset we should beware of thinking that there will be a simple one. We are, after all, dealing with open-textured language and the complex realities it expresses. Nevertheless, we can try to isolate different types of answers to our problem.

One possibility is that the prophetic material in the opening chapters is concerned with the distant future, with the ultimate triumph of the Messiah that we traditionally associate with divine judgement, carried out with destructive power to establish the rule of God over the world. Mary and Zechariah speak like the prophets of old who look forward to the last day when there will be some kind of divine intervention that exceeds all human hopes and possibilities. So the reference is not to the earthly mission of Jesus, but rather jumps over it to the powerful parousia of the Son of Man, although there may be some anticipation of the final act of deliverance in the earthly activities of Jesus.[4]

---

[4] For this kind of view see Talbert, *Reading Luke*, 24–26.

The merit of this solution is that it recognizes that there must be some continuity and identity between the earthly mission of Jesus and the final dénouement. Yet it remains implausible. It is not at all likely that the words that begin the gospel have only limited, minimal reference to the story that immediately follows, so that the whole of the rest of the gospel and the book of Acts must be regarded as a gigantic parenthesis before these prophecies find their fulfilment. The natural expectation is that we shall see these prophecies being fulfilled, at least in substantial part, as we read further into the story.

A second type of solution is to say that the songs express mistaken hopes.[5] They depict human longings for a particular kind of salvation, political salvation brought about by the mighty actions of God, whereas what God was going to do was something radically different, through the mission of the humble, poor, rejected Jesus. The effect of the ensuing story is to show us that these human expectations are decisively exposed as inadequate and misleading. God acts in other ways, and the gospel is meant to convert us from false ideas of deliverance and the means by which it is achieved to the divine way, which is rather different. Thus again the language of the songs is not directly applicable to Jesus.

Again, this kind of approach is unconvincing. It is out of tune with the way in which the actors in Luke 1–2 are depicted as devout, godly people who are guided and directed by the Holy Spirit. It is inconceivable that a narrator who describes Zechariah as a Spirit-inspired prophet and Mary as one upon whom the Holy Spirit has come should present them as unreliable guides. Moreover, as with the previous solution, this one does not adequately take into account the material in the songs that does correspond rather well with the later story.[6]

A third and more promising type of solution is to claim that the songs express, in the language of military rhetoric, the realities of the spiritual mission of Jesus. They use a different kind of language to bring out the significance of what is happening. We have a parallel to this in the comment Jesus made when the seventy-two returned from their mission and described how the demons had been subject to them when they used the name of Jesus to exorcise people (cf. Acts 3:6; 16:18). He said, 'I saw Satan falling like lightning from heaven' (Lk. 10:18). The precise interpretation of this statement is disputed. Many scholars understand it to be a report of a vision of Satan's fall, whether past or future, while others suggest that Jesus is using the language of myth to express

---

[5] Ford, *My Enemy Is My Guest*, 13–36; cf. Tannehill, *The Narrative Unity of Luke-Acts*, I, 35, n. 46, who speaks of Zechariah as to some extent 'an unreliable interpreter of the story'.

[6] Perhaps one might compare the suggestion that the Christology in Acts is a corrective of that in the gospel. This is not at all likely, and the differences between them reflect, rather, Luke's depiction of the natural development in Christology from the period before the resurrection to that afterwards.

the significance of what is really happening when his disciples cast out demons.[7] Either way, the language expresses the cosmic significance of what is happening – what might be regarded as comparatively low-key events are part of a larger whole. Thus the language of the myth of Lucifer is used to bring out the significance of the mission. In the same way, then, the language of political rhetoric is one way of expressing the realities of the mission of Jesus.

There are in fact quite a lot of ways in which what is to come in the narrative of the mission is anticipated in the songs. The rejoicing of Mary is parallel to that of Jesus at what God is doing (Lk. 1:47//10:21). The motif of God as Saviour comes to effect in the change in the life of Zacchaeus (Lk. 1:47//19:10). The message of Jesus is for the humble and lowly (Lk. 1:48//6:20). Mary is confirmed as the object of God's favour – but with an important corrective regarding spiritual kinship (Lk. 1:48b//11:27, with the corrective in 11:28). God acts mightily through Jesus in visiting his people (Lk. 1:49a, 68//7:16). God's name will be holy (Lk. 1:49b//11:2). His mercy is displayed (Lk. 1:50//18:39). There will be a reversal of status (Lk. 1:51–52//10:21; 14:11) with different treatment of the poor and the rich (Lk. 1:51//6:21 and 24). God's concern for Israel, the offspring of Abraham, is seen (Lk. 1:54, 68//13:16; 19:9; 24:21). His ancient covenant is remembered and renewed (Lk. 1:72//22:20).

The effects of doing this are twofold. First, the mission of Jesus is of such a kind that the metaphor of politics can be used to interpret it. Its deeper meaning and overall significance is brought out. It is 'political' but, to appropriate a well-known catch phrase, 'not as we know it'. Politics is concerned with the security of the realm, the maintenance of law and order within it, and the development of its communal life and its material prosperity. Here we have the establishment of a kingdom that is significantly different and, for want of a better term, is spiritual in that it is concerned with the inward allegiance of people to God as a result of which they live in new ways. The power by which it is established is also spiritual; it can be expressed in mighty works of healing but lacks the armed force of the typical worldly ruler. What the language does is to bring out the important fact that what was going on was not just a prophet preaching to people and healing the sick, and suffering at the hands of the people who could not tolerate his message. This is the divine equivalent to a military campaign in which the ultimate forces are the supernatural powers of God and Satan. Or, rather, what Luke does is to show that a different route will achieve the ideals expressed in political language.

Second we are now able to see that the language used in the songs in Luke 1–2 is not to be taken literally but is metaphorical. We have become used to this sort of thing in Christian hymnody. We recognize that songs like 'Onward, Christian soldiers' and 'Fight the good fight', based as they are on Scripture, use

---

[7] Gathercole, 'Jesus' Eschatological Vision'.

a military metaphor, and we automatically spiritualize them without difficulty. Similarly, we use the language of athletics, again based on scriptural usage, with metaphors drawn from footraces and wrestling. Regardless, then, of the origin of the language used in the Lukan songs, which have been thought to reflect the Maccabean struggles for independence,[8] the effect of the gospel is to demonstrate clearly enough that these songs must be understood in the light of what follows, namely, as metaphorical expressions of the inner meaning of the mission of Jesus and the disciples.

Here, then, is the first instance in which we need to pay attention to Luke's use of language. He can use political language metaphorically to refer to the spiritual changes brought about by the mission of Jesus. Or, more precisely, what appear to be military actions to bring about change are seen to be metaphorical of the work of the One who went about teaching and doing good. It is, however, only as the story proceeds that we find ourselves forced to revise our interpretation of the opening songs. We might compare how, similarly, the recognition of Jesus as Messiah in the first parts of all three of the synoptic gospels is followed by the elucidation in the second part that he is a suffering Messiah.

Eschatological Language and the Mission

In the light of this, I hope, fairly uncontroversial example of Luke's use of language, we can now turn to a second area of interest. This is the presence and nature of what is loosely called apocalyptic language, but which, in the light of what follows, may be more appropriately termed eschatological language. The problem arises from a consideration of what will happen in the sequel to the gospel. Our twofold problem, accordingly, is the correct identification of the language and the relation of what is said in it to Luke's story and purpose as a whole.

The story of the mission of Jesus is followed in Luke's second volume by an account of the work of Jesus' followers after his physical departure from the scene. Recent study has drawn attention to the way in which parallelisms can be traced between various threads in the story. Two things may cause some surprise, however. The first is that the followers of Jesus do not simply repeat the kind of things that he said in the way that followers of a philosopher might repeat his teaching while developing it in various ways. The familiar cliché that the proclaimer becomes the proclaimed is doubtless an over-simplification, but it is reasonably accurate. And if the accent of Jesus was on the kingdom of God, it is not surprising if the missionaries lay the stress on the King himself. The two

---

[8] Winter, 'Magnificat and Benedictus'.

terms 'kingdom' and 'king' are, of course, complementary. In the ancient world, at any rate, a kingdom presupposes a king and vice versa. But to shift the focus from the kingdom to the King does nuance the message in a different way. The significant factor, of course, is that although the kingdom is the kingdom of God, rule over it is entrusted to his agent, the Messiah.

The second surprising thing is that the actual language of kingdom and kingship retreats from the centre of attention. It is central in the gospel but marginal in Acts. There is only one reference to Jesus as king in Acts (Acts 17:7) and the term 'kingdom' is found only eight times, compared with the very much larger number of occurrences in the gospel. Moreover, in Acts 'kingdom' is generally used by the narrator rather than by the preachers or other speakers. Admittedly the identity of Jesus as 'the Christ' and 'Lord' comes to the fore, and these are terms that have much the same significance as 'king'. Perhaps we should not underemphasize the extent to which 'Christ' was a special Jewish word for a king, reflecting the fact that he is 'the Lord's anointed'.

What happens in Acts is that the concept of salvation becomes rather more significant. It is already present in Luke, specifically in the infancy narratives, as if already in the gospel Luke was majoring on the benefits that come to human beings with the advent of the kingdom of God and stressing that Jesus and the kingdom are the vehicles of God's blessing for people. Thus a new language for describing the content of the message and the role of the divine messenger is being developed. It is not, of course, peculiar to Luke, being widely attested in the epistles as well, but its comparative rarity in Matthew and Mark is noteworthy.

Furthermore, the central theme of Acts becomes the mission of the followers of Jesus from Jerusalem to Rome, set in the context of the struggles regarding the place of Gentiles in the church and the outside opposition to the church.

To the careful reader of the gospel, however, this historical development may have seemed somewhat puzzling. Was this what was to be expected in the future after the events in the gospel had run their course? Hence our two problems arise. The first is the interpretation of the teaching about the future in the gospel, and the second is the relation of this teaching to the actual story that is told in Acts.

The nature of Luke's eschatological language

Throughout the gospel there is considerable stress on future events, and the gospel treats them thematically in a number of places. After the references to future judgement by John the Baptist (Lk. 3:9, 17) there is teaching in Luke 9:23–27 that the future of people is related to their response to Jesus: the Son of

Man will come and will be ashamed of those who rejected Jesus. Some of those present will not die before they see the kingdom of God. The fact of future divine judgement is repeatedly mentioned (Lk. 10:13–16; 11:29–32; 12:4–5, 8–9; 13:22–30; 14:14; 16:19–31). The disciples are to be like servants awaiting the return of an absent master who will come unexpectedly or, rather, at an unpredictable time (Lk. 12:35–48; cf. 19:11–27).

In the first of the two main eschatological passages (Lk. 17:20–37), a question is asked about the coming of the kingdom of God, and Jesus dismisses the question as wrongly conceived. Regardless of the interpretation of his answer, he goes on immediately to talk about longing for the days of the Son of Man and refers to an event like a gigantic flash of lightning. He compares the situation with that in the time of Noah when people were living their ordinary lives, ignorant of or ignoring the warnings given by Noah about impending destruction. Similarly, people ignored the warnings of Lot and the heavenly messengers about the impending destruction of Sodom and Gomorrah. In both cases total destruction ensued. So, said Jesus, it will be when the Son of Man is revealed. People should hasten to escape before it is too late; some will succeed in doing so, while others will perish (Lk. 17:22–37; cf. 18:8). We may note in passing that such language makes sense only if it refers to something that could happen within the lifetime of the hearers. We might compare how hard it is to get people to take seriously warnings about the dangers that lie some time ahead as a result of global warming and associated climatic changes which could seriously affect this planet in what is for us the distant future. The statements by Jesus are concerned, rather, with something that was in his mind a real threat to his hearers.

In the second main passage (Lk. 21:5–36) there is a further account of what lies ahead. There will be false messiahs and wars and revolutions, which are not to be confused with the end. Alongside these wars there will be natural disasters, together with 'fearful events and great signs from heaven'. Before all this, however, there will be hostility to the followers of Jesus, leading in some cases to imprisonment, betrayal and even martyrdom.[9] One specific event will be the razing of Jerusalem to the ground by hostile armies and the carrying off of its people as captives. There will be signs in the sky and in the ocean; at that time people will see the coming of the Son of Man in a cloud. These things will be signs that the redemption of the hearers and the kingdom of God are near. They will affect the whole world, and again the warning is given that people may be caught up in human pleasures and cares and not be aware of their dire situation.

These two thematic pieces of teaching in Luke 17 and 21 occupy a major part of the gospel and stand alongside the other similar teaching about the

---

[9] It is not altogether clear where the 'flashback' comes to an end. Most probably the description of the events that are to take place 'before all this' runs to v. 19.

coming of the Son of Man. They are couched in solemn terms. What do we do with them and how are we to understand them?

It is not uncommon to refer to these passages and to their language as 'apocalyptic'. Part of our problem arises from the well-known slipperiness of the term 'apocalyptic'.[10] Scholars have not found it easy to define what is meant by the term, and questions arise regarding its applicability to this teaching. Such standard features of apocalyptic as revelation by a figure caught up to heaven or admitted to heavenly secrets and a strong dualism between good and evil, light and darkness, God and the supernatural powers of evil are muted or absent. However, the mood of pessimism regarding the immediate future and the concentration of attention on the end events, involving divine victory over the forces of evil (and the human beings who have succumbed to them) and final judgement upon them are present.

One key point in apocalyptic material is sometimes thought to be the use of language that cannot be taken as a literal description of what is to happen. One might think of apocalyptic language as a sort of mythological description of the world to come in terms of this world.[11] So far as the material in Luke is concerned, this deep-rooted notion needs some correction.[12]

(1) Apocalyptic and the Old Testament.

A preliminary point is that some of the 'apocalyptic' language is in reality nothing more than material drawn from the Old Testament and is used to indicate that a particular event is to be seen as fulfilling the Old Testament prophecy or fitting the pattern of some typology. This is clearly the case with the 'abomination of desolation' in Mark and Matthew, where the parenthetical note 'let the reader understand' makes the point that there is something here to be decoded. Luke (or perhaps his source) has done the decoding for his readers but still retains the term 'desolation' (Lk. 21:20), although this makes the allusion to Daniel 9:27; 12:11 almost undetectable. The biblical imagery of the flood and the destruction of Sodom and Gomorrah is used to indicate how unexpected the coming of the Son of Man will be as a judgement on the ungodly (Lk. 17). Here the language of comparison, rather than prophecy, is

---

[10] Barker, 'Slippery Words'.

[11] Morris comments on vv. 25–26: 'in vivid apocalyptic imagery Jesus speaks of heavenly portents. It is not easy to see how literally the words are meant to be taken' (*Luke: An Introduction and Commentary*, 327). Cf. the list of features of apocalyptic given by Koch, which includes 'mythical images rich in symbolism' (*The Rediscovery of Apocalyptic*), as cited by Allison in *DJG*, 17, though Allison himself notes that in the teaching of Jesus there are 'no allegories and no involved symbolism' (*DJG*, 18). According to Geddert, the gospel writers 'use apocalyptic imagery to refer to events predicted for the future' (*DJG*, 21).

[12] The proposal made here could also be applied to Matthew and Mark.

used. But the language is also used in the actual framing of the warning. The need to flee as quickly as possible is expressed by using the term 'going back', reminiscent of the picture of Lot's wife turning back (Lk. 17:31), and a note is included to ensure that the readers pick up the allusion in the wording. We also find use of Old Testament language in the description of the natural disasters and heavenly portents (Lk. 21:25–26; Ps. 65:7; Is. 34:4), showing that the words of Jesus are of a piece with what the prophets have always said. And, of course, there is the Danielic picture of the Son of Man coming in a cloud (Lk. 21:27; Dan. 7:13).

(2) Language of comparison
Some of the language is obviously meant to be understood as comparison and not as a literal account of what is going to happen. But what is the envisaged picture? Just as the people of Sodom had to run before the advancing stream of destruction (like a volcanic stream of lava), so the readers must seek to escape from judgement – but presumably by doing whatever is necessary spiritually (repentance) to escape from it. This could be the point of Luke 17:33, especially in the light of the more obviously spiritual requirement in Luke 9:24. Then there is the vivid picture of two people asleep or working together, where one escapes and the other is taken. Clearly this is a separate piece of imagery, since one envisages daytime while the other surely refers to night time.[13] The picture this time could be of a raid in which the raiders haphazardly carry off one member of a family but not another.[14] Again, it is surely metaphorical of the need to be prepared for judgement, recognizing the point made elsewhere that the lines of judgement can run through families and each person must be individually in the right with God (Lk. 12:52–53).

(3) Wars and natural disasters
There is nothing unusual about the prophecies of wars and natural disasters that should make us see a special 'apocalyptic' kind of phraseology or imagery here. They foretell events of a kind which would be entirely credible to people in the ancient world who experienced the events of 66–70 C.E. in Judea (and other natural disasters listed in contemporary historians). The boundary between the kind of natural disasters and other events that are known in human experience and the horrendous pictures painted by the apocalyptic writers is a thin one. The story of Noah's flood would have been

---

[13] Rengstorf, *Das Evangelium nach Lukas*, 197, held that grinding the flour for the day's fresh baking of bread was done just before dawn, as was still the practice in the twentieth century. Cf. Schweizer, *Good News*, 275.

[14] This seems more likely than the idea that the reference is to the believers being snatched away to safety and the unbelievers being left behind.

taken as literal fact by first-century people and provided a precedent for 'the roaring and tossing of the sea' (Lk. 21:25). Is there, indeed, anything here that goes beyond what can be imagined by people who have experienced a really bad storm (Ps. 107:23–32)? Likewise, the ancient world knew of eclipses of the sun and moon, the conjunctions of planets and the occasional comet. Even the destruction of Sodom and Gomorrah would be seen as entirely credible in the light of the eruption of Vesuvius which took place in the first century (79 C.E., admittedly rather late for Jesus and the author of the gospel, but not for its later first-century readers), and the problem is more that such an eschatological outpouring is envisaged as being of wider extent than an area known to be prone to the risk (cf. how Noah's flood is described as worldwide). Thus the natural portents and disasters would have been entirely within the range of actual and conceivable events for the readers. It is only the stupendous coming of the Son of Man and the winding up of history that go significantly beyond what people have experienced.

The same observation holds true for people in the present world who have experienced the Holocaust and the genocide in Rwanda, the Balkans, Sudan and elsewhere; the wars and rumours of wars on a gigantic scale are things that we have sadly grown used to. They are scarcely 'apocalyptic' in the sense of being 'out of this world'. Maybe when we read of events like the Son of Man coming like lightning or the comparisons with the flood and the fiery storm over Sodom and Gomorrah, the signs in the heavens and the tidal waves at sea, we feel that we are in the realm of the supernatural. Not after recent events, however! The horrendous tsunami, with the attendant disasters in India, Sri Lanka, Thailand, and many other places; the prophecies of the effects of global warming; and the whole phenomenon of poverty in the majority world caused by floods and famines make us realize that the kind of events which are prophesied in the gospel and would not have appeared 'out of this world' in the first century are by no means inconceivable in the twenty-first.

So the evidence accumulates that the problems of apocalyptic language must not be exaggerated.

(4) Divine intervention

Perhaps, then, the apocalyptic element is the divine intervention in history in the coming of the Son of Man, which will be for those who are not ready like the disaster of the flood or the destruction of Sodom and Gomorrah in Genesis – events that would have been seen as 'acts of God' for first-century people. It is the interruption of human life not by natural or manmade disaster but by a divine act.

Clearly this possibility would have seemed perfectly credible to people in the first century. We tend to think that, due to our scientific knowledge, we are in a different position. But let us be consistent with ourselves. If, as seems to be the generally accepted current theory, the universe began with an inconceivable event that scientists popularly refer to as 'the big bang', who are we to deny that it may end with something similar?[15] But I would not want to press this argument. The timescale of the scientists for the collapse of the universe is immensely long, and any such event is so remote in time that comparison with an expected parousia in the lifetime of Jesus' or Luke's hearers is inappropriate. Nevertheless, lesser disasters, like a holocaust if some terrorist got hold of a nuclear device and used it, or the spread of bacteriological infection, cannot be ruled out as impossible.

(5) De-apocalyptized language?

How far is it the case, if at all, that Luke has 'de-apocalypticized' the language? It is sometimes suggested that he has historicized it by comparison with Mark.[16] But the evidence for this is not convincing. Certainly Luke has substituted for the passage in Mark 13 about the abomination of desolation the more explicit threat of the siege of Jerusalem. This might be regarded as a de-apocalypticizing of Mark's language, but in fact the threat in Mark would have been understood by his readers as a repetition of what happened historically with Antiochus Epiphanes (1 Macc. 1:54), so that Luke is only spelling out more clearly what is already there in Mark.[17] And in fact what has happened is the replacement of one set of prophetic allusions from the Old Testament with another set, so that the event is still seen as the fulfilment of prophecy. What Luke apparently omits is the gathering of the elect by the Son of Man after his coming. But this is effectively replaced by the reference to the redemption that is at hand (Lk. 21:28). The coming of the Son of Man is understood as a judgement affecting the whole earth, and somehow it affects the people who are spending their lives dissolutely while those who are 'awake' will be spared. There is no significant difference in style from Mark here.

---

[15] I recognize that 'not with a bang but a whimper' may be more in accord with how some scientists see things.

[16] Conzelmann, *Die Mitte der Zeit*, 104–27, argued that Luke historicized the apocalyptic material, by which he meant that Luke separated off the fall of Jerusalem from its connection with the end events (104) and 'dehistoricised' the eschatology by distancing it from all events within history (119). Our claim is that the material always had the characteristics of referring to historical events that were understood as divine acts of judgement. Cf. Schweizer's verdict that Luke has attempted to show that what has already happened (the fall of Jerusalem) is not (just) secular history 'but a part of God's eschatological action' with 'a material connection with the events of the eschaton proper' (*Good News*, 324).

[17] Perhaps Luke has Gentile readers in view and makes things clearer for them, but he is not consistent in explaining obscure Jewish points.

(6) Cosmic imagery to denote political events?

G.B. Caird and N.T. Wright have argued that the language of cosmic events may be a way of referring to political events.[18] They and other writers want to argue that the coming of the Son of Man may be a way of speaking of the historical judgement on Jerusalem, seen as a human action which was at the same time a divine intervention. The other cosmic signs are likewise thought to symbolize political events.

The hypothesis is not a simple one to establish, partly because the to- and fro-ing in Luke 21 (and its parallels) sometimes makes it difficult to identify the temporal sequences, and the parallels between the judgement on Jerusalem and the coming of the Son of Man (in both cases should people be ready and prepared to move?) make it difficult to decide whether these are parallel references to the one event or genuinely two different events. Nevertheless, there are good reasons to dispute the suggestion:

(a) We have seen good evidence that both the natural and manmade disasters can be understood literally and are of a piece with the clearly historical disaster of the siege of Jerusalem.

(b) The early church undoubtedly took the language about the coming of the Son of Man to refer to a divine, supernatural intervention. Note that very little (if any) explanation is given of it. And if this teaching of Jesus does not lie at the root of the early church's expectation of the coming of the Son of Man, then no good alternative presents itself.[19]

(c) The flow of Luke 21 suggests that the siege of Jerusalem is followed by a period of time (the times of the Gentiles), and only after that does something happen, namely the coming of the Son of Man. It does not make sense to see the fall of Jerusalem as 'your redemption drawing near'; something less destructive is needed! The common suggestion that part of the purpose of the so-called apocalyptic chapters is to teach believers that there is a distinction to be drawn between the siege of Jerusalem and the (final) coming of the Son of Man and that the occurrence of the former is not necessarily a sign of the imminence of the latter makes good sense. Just as the captivity of the Jews lasted traditionally seventy years, so a similar time span for 'the times of the Gentiles' could have been realistic.[20] But it is unlikely that a long period was envisaged that would make nonsense of addressing the hearers with 'your redemption is drawing near'.

---

[18] Caird, *Language and Imagery*, 242–71; Wright, *The New Testament and the People of God*, 280–99, and *Jesus and the Victory of God*, 320–68.

[19] Cf. Adams, 'Historical Crisis'.

[20] What did Christians think ca. 140 C.E.? Did the Bar Kokhba revolt arouse any messianic excitement among Christians, or was it so confined to a Judea where Christians were few on the ground that it would easily have passed without notice?

(d) The evangelist who has explained the abomination of desolation so that its historical referent is quite clear has not done anything similar with the Son of Man's coming. He did not need to do so.

(e) The passage about the siege of Jerusalem in Luke 21 which is already 'literal' contains the advice to flee before destruction finally takes place and makes sense. But in Luke 17, when the language is used of the appearance of the Son of Man, flight is probably not an option; there is nothing in verses 34–35 to suggest that one can flee. The flight motif earlier (vv. 31–32) seems to be more of a warning to be spiritually prepared.[21]

(f) In Luke 21 we have military events and persecution listed along with natural disasters (vv. 10 and 11, 12), then military events in verses 20–24, followed by heavenly portents and earthly disasters. The 'obvious' way to interpret this account is surely to see these as different items: nothing in the text suggests that the disasters and portents are coding for military events.

(g) Consequently the question arises whether the coming of the Son of Man can be encoding for the judgement on Jerusalem. This will not work for Luke 21:28–37, for here redemption and deliverance is in mind, the kingdom of God is near, and standing before the Son of Man is a positive experience, whereas the fall of Jerusalem is entirely negative and not to be interpreted in this positive kind of way. Whatever be the case in the other gospels, the times of the Gentiles have to be fulfilled first. Nor will it work for Luke 17 in what is surely meant to be ultimately a message of hope for the disciples.

The conclusion to be drawn from this discussion is that the so-called 'apocalyptic' language would have been understood literally and that there are no problems in understanding it as such with the only 'other-worldly' element being the coming of the Son of Man and the winding up of history. To describe such a chapter as Mark 13 (and parallels) as 'the apocalyptic discourse' is to muddy the waters, unless we mean nothing more by this term than a prophecy of things to come like other biblical prophecy. Symbolical and mythological language is largely absent. The passages are eschatological rather than apocalyptic.

Eschatology and the book of Acts

Nevertheless, there remains a problem. The eschatological prophecies are there, and they occupy a significant amount of space and a key position in the gospel. The gospel devotes a considerable amount of attention to the coming

---

[21] This may seem to beg the question whether the coming of the Son of Man in Lk. 17 is coding for the divine judgement on Jerusalem. Certainly the prospect is fairly uniformly negative, but by the time we get to v. 33 the thought seems to be of a

of the Son of Man and the associated events. This was a 'given' for Luke, as we can see by the source criticism that indicates that Jesus' teaching on this theme was remembered and incorporated in the Gospels of Matthew and Mark. He could not well avoid it.

However, when we move over into the book of Acts we find little or no mention of these cataclysmic events (just as we could not find the political elements in Luke 1–2 in the rest of the work and had to conclude that the political language was to be taken metaphorically). The fate of Jerusalem, which is also alluded to in Luke 13:34–35 and 23:27–31, is nowhere mentioned in Acts. It is surely extraordinary that there is no mention of it (whether as a prophesied event or as an actual occurrence in a book that many scholars would date after 70 C.E.) in the preaching in Acts or in the story itself, although of course the story does come to an end somewhere in the early sixties before the revolt by the Jews against Rome had begun.[22]

The coming of the Son of Man is likewise ignored. A couple of references are made to the role of Jesus as the judge (Acts 10:42; 17:31), but that is as far as it goes. The significance of the future role of Jesus for believers plays no part in the teaching. There is, however, one exception: Stephen identifies Jesus as the Son of Man who is standing in heaven, but, instead of the Son of Man coming to earth for his people, Stephen dies and his future is in the safe hands of the Son of Man.[23] Luke has depicted how the heavenly Son of Man does have a relevance for believers here and now that might be thought to be much greater than the hope of a distant coming: he will faithfully welcome them to the presence of God here and now at the point of their death.

Instead we have a story of mission with a new programme, in which the witness to Jesus is to be taken to the ends of the earth, and an account of how the gospel spreads along one arc from Jerusalem to Rome. The one element that corresponds to the prophecies in Luke 21 and elsewhere is the threatened hostility to Christian believers. Arrest, persecution, being handed over to synagogues and prisons, being brought before kings (including emperors) and governors and even being put to death (Stephen, James, the attempt on Peter, the attempt on Paul) are frequent motifs in the story, and the only element that is absent is betrayal by family and friends.

Concern about the future is put on one side. Prominently placed at the beginning of Acts there is the question by the eleven whether this is the time when the kingdom will be restored to Israel together with an authoritative answer by the risen Jesus. The question may well have arisen out of the

---

judgement for which people can prepare themselves by spiritual attitude, and this does not fit the circumstances of the siege of Jerusalem but rather of being in the right relationship to the Son of Man.

22 The point may be significant for the date of Acts and suggest a pre-70 publication.

23 We are not told that Stephen actually ascends to heaven. Is it implied?

reference in the gospel to Jerusalem being trodden down by the Gentiles until the times of the Gentiles are fulfilled. The end of the times of Gentile occupation and domination of Jerusalem would have been understood as being brought about by the restoration of sovereignty to the Jews themselves. The twelve's question was 'When?' and the answer given is 'I'm not telling you something that is determined by the Father', which may well imply that the Father himself has not yet set a time.[24] But the implication of the conversation is that this is not a matter which should concern the disciples: they have something to occupy their attention: they are to be witnesses to Jesus in a worldwide task, which will presumably take quite some time to carry through.[25]

One way of understanding what is happening is to see things in the light of what we have observed between the prologue and the story of the mission.

The suggestion (not a new one)[26] is that the gospel tradition received by Luke could be understood as concentrating attention on the future of the kingdom of God and the Son of Man. That is to say, the gospel is understood to focus on a futurist eschatology. But whereas with the military language in Luke 1–2 it can be argued that Luke was able to show that it should be reinterpreted in terms of the spiritual mission of Jesus and the growth of a spiritual kingdom, it is not quite the same to say that the eschatological language in the teaching of Jesus is to be understood in the light of what actually happened in Acts as somehow related to or describing mission. It does not make sense to regard the eschatological language in the gospel as being metaphorical of anything. It is meant quite literally. There is nothing to demythologize, since the material expressed in eschatological language is not mythological. The difference is that the military language could be translated into a different idiom. But the eschatological language describes one particular series of events in a fairly literal manner. Luke picks out one strand in the series, the attacks on believers, but he ignores the others, and while retaining the element of judgement in the culminating event, he shows how the parousia as the final redemption of believers can be anticipated in the post-mortem welcome into heaven for believers.[27]

What is perhaps more surprising is the lack of any reference to the mission of the witnesses in Luke 17 and 21. There is nothing corresponding to Mark

---

[24] Thus this conversation has the same function as the statement in Mk. 13:32, which has no parallel in Lk. 21.

[25] But there is no indication that it would be endless! The expectation of the parousia is not dead in Acts.

[26] Cf. Schweizer, *Good News*, 323–29.

[27] True, it is a martyr who receives the special welcome, but it may be assumed that the same will be true for all believers, since it is broadly true for all that 'we must go through many hardships [not 'persecutions', as in NRSV] to enter the kingdom of God' (Acts 14:22, TNIV).

13:10 (Mt. 24:14), and the saying in Mark 14:9 is a casualty of the replacement of that story with the similar one in Luke 7.

In approaching this puzzle we may begin by observing that the amount of explicit material in Mark on mission is not great. Although Mark has the mission of the twelve (Mk. 6:1–6, 30) nothing is said about it continuing into the future or setting a pattern for similar work. However, the reference to leaving one's family 'for my sake and the sake of the good news' (Mk. 10:29) must be understood in terms of going out on mission and Mark 14:9 assumes ongoing mission. There may be mission symbolism in the notoriously obscure Mark 14:28 (one can do no more than speculate that the fulfilment of the command was accompanied by a commission, as in Mt.). Matthew, however, has behaved differently by gathering together systematically the instructions for mission by the disciples into a long-term instruction in Matthew 10 and giving it an eschatological setting (Mt. 10:23; cf. Mt. 10:17–22 with the summary in Mt. 24:9). No end to the mission marked by the return of the disciples to be with Jesus is recorded, but this may be the result of Matthew's general reordering of his Markan material. Going to Galilee becomes the occasion for the great commission.

In Luke 9, the mission of the twelve is limited in time (Lk. 9:10) as in Mark, and similarly in Luke 10, although there the enormous scope of the need is stressed, and it is most likely that the number of seventy-two engaged in mission is seen as prefiguring the mission to the Gentiles. Luke has lost Mark 14:9, along with the rest of the pericope. In fact, it is only really in Luke 24:47–49 that there is a clear summons to mission. However, Luke's practice is to drop material that he found in Mark and either place it somewhere else or replace it with something comparable. It is thus possible that he saw the extended teaching in Luke 24:44–49 as the substitute for Mark 13:10. Another factor is quite simply the book of Acts itself understood as an integral part of the two-volume work. The inclusion of the second volume saved him from having to say all that he wanted to say within the narrow confines of the gospel.

Be this as it may, the total effect is that the eschatological elements in the teaching of Jesus are placed in a different perspective by the pericope in Acts 1 and by the way in which the story that Luke goes on to develop is a story of mission rather than anything else. Needless to say, Luke's story was constrained by the fact that the early church was a missionary movement, but working under this constraint he has shown how the church was not to sit and wait for the restoration of the kingdom to Israel but to discover that the word of God was spreading throughout the world.

Thus the attention of the disciples is directed away from the future and speculation about it to the need for mission, and the one major element that is retained from the eschatological prophecies is the fact of persecution. Well, not quite. The return of Jesus is highlighted right up front (Acts 1:11). The element of future judgement remains. The preaching to the Jews implies that judgement faces the Jewish people as 'this corrupt generation' from which people can escape by repentance (Acts 2:40). The threat of being 'completely cut off from their people' is placed before those who refuse to heed the words of Jesus (Acts 3:23), and the fact that Jesus alone can save indicates that people will continue to be part of the doomed generation unless they respond positively to him (Acts 4:12). Clearly those who do receive repentance and forgiveness (Acts 5:31) are assumed to be still heading for destruction rather than salvation; they are opponents of God (Acts 7:51–52). Jews who reject Jesus are unworthy of eternal life (Acts 13:46). And there is a final implied threat of judgement in Acts 28:26–27 for those who will not turn to God to be healed. The Son of Man who will judge the world is implicitly identified with the man, Jesus. The motif of judgement and of future blessing (Acts 3:20f.) is thus clearly present, but the pictorial language is absent. So this element is not overlooked.[28] It might be better to say that, as far as the disciples are concerned, it is eclipsed: it is still there but other things, as it were, get in front of it and put it in the shadow.

Luke, then, turns out to have a considerable element of eschatological language and teaching (rather than apocalyptic language) in the gospel, which is largely absent from Acts, where the story is of the mission of the church and its progress through many tribulations rather than of the disasters and judgements prophesied in the gospel. Just as the political language of Luke 1–2 has been overtaken by the story of the prophet mighty in word and deed in the body of the gospel, so the eschatological forecasts of Luke 17 and 21 have been overtaken by the story of the mission of the followers of Jesus without thereby losing their validity. It becomes clear that Luke-Acts must be read as a whole, lest we ascribe a false meaning or overemphasis to certain individual parts of the story.

There may be something parallel in the Johannine tradition. If we grant the likelihood that the Gospel of John and Revelation emerged from the same Johannine circle, then it is striking that we have alongside each other the eschatological, apocalyptic Revelation, with its catalogue of disasters and call to readiness for martyrdom, and the gospel, with its strong encouragement to the

---

[28] The omission of any reference to the fall of Jerusalem in Acts is puzzling. Possible considerations include: (1) The preaching of the apostles did not in fact contain any reference to it. They did not threaten their Jewish audiences with it to induce them to repentance. (2) Chronologically, it occurred later than the end of Luke's story which terminates somewhere in the early 60s, i.e., before the outbreak of the war. It may even have been after Luke had completed the composition of Acts. (3) It is part of the general fact that the apostles did not repeat the teaching of Jesus but preached about Jesus. Acts is virtually silent on the teaching of Jesus.

disciples to be Jesus' witnesses in the world despite persecution. The same stretch of future history is being presented from different angles, and where Revelation concentrates more on the need for spiritual readiness for the conflict (while not ignoring the task of witness), the gospel concentrates more on the task of mission. The two perspectives complement each other despite their very different idioms.[29]

Conclusion

We have looked at two examples of language in Luke that could be problematic if their nature is not properly understood. On the one hand, we identified the material in Luke 1–2 that could be construed in terms of political possibilities and saw that the ensuing story requires us to interpret it in a metaphorical sense of the spiritual coming of the kingdom of God and the Messiah. In the light of Luke 3–24 we can see how a metaphorical significance can be ascribed to it. Although the opening prologue of the gospel significantly throws light on the story that follows, it is also the case that the prologue can be understood fully only in the context of what follows.

On the other hand, we have considered the material in the gospel, especially in Luke 17 and 21, that deals with future events. In order to understand it properly we argued that to identify it as 'apocalyptic' is not helpful, since this inclines us to accept as metaphorical or mythological what is meant to be understood, for the most part, literally. Rather, it deals with the future and, in terms of its content rather than its style, it is better called eschatological (using that term to refer to teaching about the future, understood as the time leading up to the end and including the end itself). We then faced the problem that when Luke comes to tell the story of what was future from the standpoint of the gospel he tells the story of the church's mission. The story is not what we might have expected. A change of perspective is brought about by the conversation in Acts 1 which has the effect of relativizing the place of the eschatological events. Already in the gospel the importance of the mission is emphasized by the symbolism of the seventy-two and by the stress on the divinely ordained and prophesied mission to preach repentance and forgiveness. The place allotted to both elements, the eschatological teaching and the story of mission, is determined by the fact that they are both 'givens' for Luke.

To speak in such terms is not to embrace the view of Conzelmann that in Acts the Holy Spirit and the mission of the church are in effe0ct a substitute for knowledge of the time of the parousia.[30] There is nothing in any of the gospels

[29] Marshall, *New Testament Theology*, 590–92.
[30] Conzelmann, *Die Mitte der Zeit*, 127.

to suggest that the early Christians spent their time passively waiting for the parousia.

Properly understood, what do the eschatological teachings convey? Luke 21 is a prophecy of the destruction of the temple, and the disciples ask when it is going to happen. Nevertheless, the discourse is concerned with when the end will come, and the repeated point is 'not yet' (Lk. 21:8, 9, 12, 24). This does not take away from the imminence of an event that could occur within the life-time of the disciples and for which they must always be ready. But, to some extent at least, the effect is to create a period of time during which the disciples are persecuted but have an occasion for testimony (Lk. 21:12–19). The escha-tological discourse thus provides a window of opportunity, but the way in which it is to be filled does not emerge until Acts. Likewise, it foretells the inci-dence of persecution, and we should not forget that fully one quarter of Acts is devoted to Paul as a prisoner and there are attacks on Christian witnesses as early as chapter 4.

Luke, then, is consistent in his emphasis on the mission of Jesus and the disciples in the here and now, expressed metaphorically in political terms in the prologue to the gospel and placed in the context of the expectation of the future coming of the Son of Man in the eschatological passages – but in such a way that the present task of mission receives its proper emphasis. The language of politics illuminates the nature of Jesus' mission but is not to be misunderstood as pointing to a political, military Messiah; and the language of eschatology provides the context for the life of the disciples but is not to be misunderstood as directing their attention away from the opportunities for witness and mission. As with the material in the prologue, so too the eschatological passages must not be read in isolation but rather in the context of Luke-Acts as a whole. Even on a first reading of the material, the reader is able to move to and fro mentally and gain a fresh understanding of the earlier parts in the light of the whole.[31]

---

[31] The fact that in our canon Luke has been appropriately grouped with the other synoptic gospels and separated from Acts by John does not affect the character of the gospel and Acts as two parts of one work, nor does it forbid us from reading them connectedly.

Bibliography

Adams, E., 'Historical Crisis and Cosmic Crisis in Mark 13 and Lucan's *Civil War*', *TynBul* 48.2 (1997), 329–44

Alexander, L., *The Preface to Luke's Gospel: Literary Convention and Social Context in Luke 1.1–4 and Acts 1.1* (Cambridge: Cambridge University Press, 1993)

Barker, M., 'Slippery Words: III. Apocalyptic', *ExpTim* 89 (1977–78), 324–29

Caird, G.B., *The Language and Imagery of the Bible* (London: Duckworth, 1980)

Conzelmann, H., *Die Mitte der Zeit: Studien zur Theologie des Lukas* (Tübingen: Mohr Siebeck, 5th edn, 1964)

Ford, M., *My Enemy Is My Guest: Jesus and Violence in Luke* (Maryknoll: Orbis Books, 1984)

Gathercole, S.J., 'Jesus' Eschatological Vision of the Fall of Satan: Luke 10,18 Reconsidered', *ZNW* 94 (2003), 143–63

Koch, K., *The Rediscovery of Apocalyptic* (London: SPCK, 1972)

Marshall, I.H., 'The Interpretation of the Magnificat: Luke 1:46–55', in *Der Treue Gottes trauen: Beiträge zum Werk des Lukas Für Gerhard Schneider* (ed. C. Bussmann and W. Radl; Freiburg: Herder, 1991), 181–96

—, *New Testament Theology: Many Witnesses, One Gospel* (Downers Grove, IL: InterVarsity Press, 2004)

Morris, L., *Luke: An Introduction and Commentary* (Leicester: InterVarsity Press, 2nd edn, 1988)

Rengstorf, K.H., *Das Evangelium nach Lukas* (Göttingen: Vandenhoeck & Ruprecht, 1937)

Schweizer, E., *The Good News according to Luke* (London: SPCK, 1984)

Talbert, C.H., *Reading Luke: A Literary and Theological Commentary on the Third Gospel* (New York: Crossroad, 1982)

Tannehill, R.C., *The Narrative Unity of Luke-Acts: A Literary Interpretation* (Philadelphia: Fortress Press, 1986)

Winter, P., 'Magnificat and Benedictus – Maccabean Psalms?', *BJRL* 37 (1954), 328–47

Wright, N.T., *The New Testament and the People of God* (London: SPCK, 1992)

—, *Jesus and the Victory of God* (London: SPCK, 1996), 320–68.

7

The Role of Money and Possessions in the Parable of the Prodigal Son (Luke 15:11–32)

A Test Case

John Nolland

The parables of Jesus frequently make use of elements drawn from social, political and economic life. Sometimes the assumptions that lie behind the imagery are quite troubling to our moral sensibilities, for example: the implicit devaluing of the life of the slave of all work in Luke 17:7–10, who must prepare the evening meal for his master after working all day in the fields; or the nobleman who becomes king in Luke 19:11–27, on the basis of a client relationship he establishes with a foreign power.

Sometimes scholars have sought to 'liberate' parables from a traditional reading which has been deemed to entail morally repugnant assumptions, for example a rereading of the parable of the man who built a vineyard and rented it out (Lk. 20:1–19 and parallels) in which the tenants who lay claim to the vineyard become the heroes, or if not the heroes, at least people whose response bears reflecting on, pointing, as it is claimed, to their oppressed state.[1] Inasmuch as we can treat the social, political and economic elements as belonging only to the imagery they can, perhaps, be seen as incidental and dispensable in relation to the intention of the parable. But even where a parable is not judged to be primarily ethical in its focus, if God is figured in the parable[2] then it is not likely to be possible to avoid entirely implicating him in the

---

[1] See, e.g., Hester, 'Socio-Rhetorical Criticism'; Herzog, *Parables,* 98–113.
[2] By 'God is figured in a parable' I do not mean that some figure in the parable is simply a cipher for God. Figures in parables are first and foremost the figures they are

ethical stance of the one who takes his place in the imagery of the parable. Even where there is nothing of particular ethical difficulty, it has at times proved difficult to determine whether the focus of a particular parable is ethical or not. We may ask, for instance, whether the parable of the Good Samaritan in Luke 10:29–37 is to be seen as an example story, or whether its investments are elsewhere.

David Holgate has offered an interpretation of Luke 15:11–32 in which he claims that this parable is to be read against the background of the *topos* 'on covetousness' in Greco-Roman moral philosophy.[3] According to Holgate, the parable is designed to encourage a particular set of attitudes to possessions. A parable that has been read, almost universally, in a theological manner, as being about repentance and restoration to God,[4] is now being read ethically, with no specific reference to God. With Holgate's work as my point of reference I intend to use Luke 15:11–32 as a focus text for exploring a set of linked questions about how values in relation to money and/or possessions should be seen as functioning in the Lukan parables.[5]

People everywhere commend ethical values by telling stories. They tell stories in which the appropriateness of action in accord with the particular ethical value being advocated seems especially evident. The parable of the

---

in the parables. By 'God is figured' I mean to point in a shorthand manner to the intention of the parable to illuminate something about God and/or his action, and in particular to do so in connection with one specific character in the parable.

[3] Holgate, *Prodigality*. Other recent studies on the parable (listed chronologically) include Bailey, *Finding*; Pöhlmann, *Verlorene Sohn*; Hendrickx, 'Man'; LaHurd, 'Rediscovering'; Geddert, 'Parable'; Parsons, 'Hand in Hand'; Borghi, 'Lc 15,11–32'; Harrill, 'Indentured Labor'; Parsons, 'Elder Brother'; Wendland, 'Finding'; Bailey, 'Jacob'; Batton, 'Dishonour'; Ford, *Parables*, 90–121; Rohrbaugh, 'Dysfunctional Family'; Bonar, 'Two Sons'; Brown, 'Parable'; O'Meara, 'Luring'; Rau, 'Auseinandersetzung'; Reinstorf and van Aarde, 'Kingdom Parables'; Forbes, 'Repentance'; Barton, 'God's Love'; Forbes, *God*, 109–51; Landmesser, 'Rückkehr'; Hultgren, *Parables*, 70–91; and Bailey, *Jacob*. For earlier bibliography see Nolland, *Luke*, II, 777–79; Bovon, *Lukas*, III, 37–40.

[4] There is some looseness of language involved in speaking of the parable as being 'about repentance and restoration to God'. This language might be taken to suggest an interest in an allegorical decoding of the parable or at least a Jülicher-like 'one-point' approach, but is only intended as a shorthand way of identifying the general realm that the parable is concerned to illuminate.

[5] If I were simply addressing Holgate's interpretation of 'the Prodigal', then careful attention to Luke's structuring of the material in ch. 15 would deserve pride of place in the discussion (see Nolland, *Luke*, II, 769, 771–72, 775, 780–81, 788–89), but the concern here is to offer something that is programmatic in relation to the evaluation of proposals about the significance of material on wealth and possessions in any of the Lukan parables.

Good Samaritan (10:30–37), as I understand it, is one such story.[6] When we
are needy enough, neighbour help from anybody at all is very welcome. It is
from down in the ditch that we need to contemplate the question of who our
neighbour is. Our capacity to recognize, at least at this level, what our need is
provides a foundation for commending an ethic in which anyone we encounter who is in need qualifies as one to whom we are called to be a loving neighbour. The man in the ditch found a neighbour in the Samaritan that he did not
find in either the Jewish priest or Levite. From the perspective of the ditch it
can only look mean and cruel to limit the scope of neighbour assistance. Our
question is, at one level, whether the parable of the Prodigal Son (hereafter
'the Prodigal') functions in a manner that is analogous to this.

A central assumption of this study is that, at least for their Lukan significance, it is fitting to consider the whole set of parables in Luke together as offering significant hermeneutical keys as to how any one of the parables is to be
understood. So a significant part of the study is devoted to a survey of the whole
set of Lukan parables, in search of perspectives that can be appealed to in the
consideration of any particular parable.

Holgate's contention immediately throws up two questions (among
others): (1) Does the set of parables as a whole set up for us *expectations as to
whether and, if so, in what way, God is likely to feature in any particular parable* (for
Holgate, God does not turn up in any major way in 'the Prodigal')? (2) *How
large a role does use or attitude to money or possessions play in the Lukan parables?* If we
are, however, to look at the parables as a set, we need first to consider what
constitutes the set.

What Should Be Counted as a Parable?

We cannot establish any clear boundary between parables and figurative language in Luke. It is, however, clear that Luke is happy to apply the word parable to quite brief items: for Luke, 'Doctor, cure yourself!' is a parable (4:23), as
are the brief pieces about not spoiling a new garment to patch an old and not
putting new wine into old skins (5:36–38). The piece on a blind person acting
as guide for another person (6:39) is also labelled as a parable. So I will be generous in what I gather into the scope of the Lukan parables and will feel free to
include, without further defence, smaller figurative pieces as parables where
they have a contribution to make to creating perspective on the Lukan parables. It will be important, however, to be cautious about generalizing from the
very small items on the edge of Luke's parables category to the parables that

[6] See Nolland, *Luke*, II, 586–98.

involve a more developed narrative. We turn now to the question of whether and how God turns up in the parables.[7]

Whether and How Does God Feature in Lukan Parables?[8]

Parables in which God plays no role

God does not feature at any level in 'Doctor, cure yourself!' (4:23), but this is not actually one of *Jesus'* parables. 'Those who are healthy do not have need of a doctor, but those who are sick do' might count as a mini-parable of Jesus (5:31) in which God, again, does not feature at any level. God is no more present in the material about the blind guide (6:39), the speck and the log (6:41–42), the good and bad trees (6:43) or the match between fruit and tree (6:44). God is nowhere in sight in the image of the children calling to one another in the marketplace (7:31–32). There is no place for God in the image of the lamp covered with a vessel or placed under the bed (8:16). God has no part in the parable of the Good Samaritan (10:29–37), unless we take either the Samaritan or the man in the ditch as a Christ figure, and neither of these suggestions has, I think, much to commend it.[9] If we want to include it in the list of parables, the image of a cup cleaned on the outside, but very different inside (11:39) has no God referent. There is probably no place for God in the image of salt that has lost its saltiness and become useless (14:34–35), unless we treat the throwing away of the salt as an image of judgement, which is unlikely as only failure seems to be in view.

There is perhaps some room for God in the parables about patching clothing and about storing wine (5:36–38): God could be seen as the one who is behind the anticipated outcomes. But in the parable narratives as such the outcomes involve no outside intervention; they are simply the later effects of the initial action. If God is present here, it is as the one who stands behind processes

---

[7] In the various surveys that follow it has not generally been possible to document the relevant scholarly literature. I have, however, sought to do so, at least minimally, where significant controversy is involved. Otherwise my work in Nolland, *Luke*, provides grounding for the judgements offered.

[8] There is a similar looseness of language here, and indeed throughout the present study, to that pointed out in n. 4, above. The task of surveying a large number of parables efficiently does not allow for nuance. The concern here is with whether an appropriate application of the parables involves reference to God and, if so, in what way. A brief statement of my overall approach to the parables may be found in Nolland, *Luke*, I, xliii–xlvii.

[9] For details of my approach to this parable see Nolland, *Luke*, II, 586–98.

that are imminent within the structure of that reality within which humanity lives. Perhaps it is best not to try to find God in these parables.

Parables in which God's action is presented figuratively

God is likely to be directly in mind in the material on building on a foundation of rock versus building without a foundation (6:47–49). At least this is so if the crisis anticipated in the imagery of the flood is – as I am confident it is – the judgement of God and not simply times of difficulty and danger in life.[10] God is imaged in a how-much-more manner in the parable about getting help from a friend at midnight (11:5–8). And he is imaged again in the father who will not give a snake or scorpion to his child who asks for a fish or an egg (11:11–13). God turns up in the image of the judge in the exhortation to make things right with one's accuser before one stands before the judge (12:57–59). God will be the man who has an unfruitful fig tree planted in his vineyard, which he threatens to have rooted out (13:6–9). The advice to take the lowest place at wedding banquets is on the face of it a piece of prudential advice (14:7–11), but it is likely to be labelled a parable by Luke because there is a correlation between how we might be inclined to behave in promoting ourselves before others and in promoting ourselves before God. Indeed, the practical form that promoting ourselves before God is likely to take is that of promoting ourselves in the eyes of other people. In the parabolic application of the prudential advice God is figuratively present as the host who invites the humble guest to move up higher.[11] God appears in the image of the slave-owner in the parable of the slave of all work (17:7–10). Our efforts are no favour to him, simply what belongs to our station. God is compared in a how-much-more comparison with the unrighteous judge bothered into action by the widow's request (18:1–7).[12]

God is imaged in the man who planted a vineyard in the parable of the man who did so and let it out to tenants (20:9–16).[13] The sending of the son is clearly to be correlated with the ministry of Jesus and thus represents a decisive moment in God's dealings with his people.

God is also the inviting host in the parable of those who offer their excuses and are replaced (14:16–24), but it is important here that now is the time when the invitations are being given out: that is the significance of Jesus' ministry. There is a connection here with the parables discussed below in which Jesus'

---

[10] Against, e.g., Rengstorf, *Lukas*, 93; cf. Duplacy, 'Véritable Disciple', 84.
[11] See discussion in Nolland, *Luke*, II, 748–49.
[12] See Nolland, *Luke*, II, 868.
[13] But see Hester, 'Socio-Rhetorical Criticism'; Herzog, *Parables*. Neither of these studies, however, offers their rendering of the parable as a reading of the parable in its present gospel contexts.

role in the kingdom comes into focus. Again, God is imaged in the rich man who calls to account his dishonest steward (16:1–8): the challenge is to grab the window of opportunity that remains between the summons and the encounter. However, inasmuch as God is to be understood as issuing the summons through the ministry of Jesus, there is again a connection with the parables below in which Jesus' role in the kingdom comes into focus. The time of the telling of the parable is of significance here – because it is the time of Jesus' ministry.

The traditional understanding offers something similar in the case of 'the Prodigal' (15:11–32). The father's compassion is God's compassion, but it is being exercised in and through the ministry of Jesus.

Parables in which Jesus is present figuratively as one who acts in the place of God

A place for Jesus in connection with the action of God has already become evident in the parables surveyed in the previous paragraph. But in those parables Jesus is the agent of God, implicitly or explicitly identified separately from the God for whom he acts. The parables now to be considered go a step further.

Inasmuch as Jesus acts for God, and to some degree in Luke stands in the place of God, God is directly visible as the creditor in the parable of the two forgiven debtors (7:40–43). The situation is similar in the case of the servants waiting for their master's return (12:35–38). Whatever might have been the case earlier, in the present Lukan text it is Jesus' coming as Son of Man which is being waited for in 12:40. The same applies to the image of the unexpected time of the thief's arrival (12:39), and again to the parable of the servant put in charge during the master's absence (12:42–48). We have Jesus in the place of God again in the parable about the householder who closes up for the night and will not admit latecomers (13:24–30).

The parables of the lost sheep and of the lost coin (15:3–10) defend and commend the kind of activity that is going on in the ministry of Jesus. But Dupont drew attention to the parabolic assumption of ownership, which introduces a God function into the parable (in the case of the shepherd and the sheep, cf. Ezek. 34:11–16).[14] The implication is that in some sense Jesus takes the place of God and performs the acts of God: 'the conduct of Jesus is the concrete form taken by the salvific intervention of God'.[15] Jesus is not so directly a God-figure in the parable of the well-born man who goes off to a distant country to get royal power (19:11–27), but he is the one who is to rule as king in the kingdom of God (cf. v. 11).

---

[14]   Dupont, 'Brebis Perdue', 282.
[15]   Dupont, 'Implications', 9.

Parables in which God/Jesus is present figuratively in connection with the kingdom of God

In a rather more indirect manner we can find a place for God in the parable of the Sower (8:4–8, cf. vv. 11–15). Or perhaps it might be better to say that we can find a place here for the coming of the kingdom of God. This is a parable that has inspired many different interpretations, and they cannot be rehearsed here. As I understand it, the dynamic of the parable revolves around the potency of the seed available to this particular sower: he seems to act like a fool-hardy farmer, but he knows something that others do not; he knows the potential of his seed and has no need to act with conservative care and caution. The gospel interpretation takes up the question of the reception accorded the seed, and that has its own importance, but the parable, though it has room for this, is focussed on the inevitability of the abundant crop that will crown the efforts of this farmer. Here we are being asked to contemplate the forces being set loose in the ministry of Jesus and, beyond that and derivatively, in the ongoing mission of the Christian church.[16]

The parables of the growth of the mustard seed (13:18–19) and of the yeast that makes its way through three measures of flour (13:20–21) include God in the same way: in connection with the impact of the present and coming kingdom.

There is something similar about the way that the overpowering of the strong man functions (11:21–22). In the ministry of Jesus, one who is stronger is overcoming the strong man. Again, it is the coming of the kingdom that is in view.

The perspective is likely to be the same in the story of the unclean spirit who leaves behind his residence for a time, only to return after a while with seven even worse companions (11:24–26). The story seems to be about the deceptiveness of apparent improvement in one's lot, so long as the 'powerful man' (v. 21) is still firmly in control. In the Lukan context, it is a warning against false hope – hope that is not firmly anchored in the present coming of the kingdom of God, in the person and activity of Jesus himself (v. 20). The difficulty with this story of the departing and returning demon is that the parable itself deals only with the negative case. The kingdom of God, and therefore God himself, are only present because we may surmise that the reason for telling this negative story is that a positive alternative is being indirectly commended.

At first God may seem to be nowhere in sight in the twin parables of the building of the tower and the decision whether, as a king, to fight or sue for

---

[16] For something of the range of views and a defence of my own see Nolland, *Luke*, I, 368–76.

terms of peace with the opposing army coming against him (14:28–32). But these parables are probably somewhat similar to the Matthean parables of the treasure in the field and the pearl of great value (Mt. 14:44–45): the point is the need to act appropriately in a critical moment. In the Matthean parables the critical moment is seen as offering great reward; in the Lukan parables the focus is on the negative effect of getting it wrong. But both sets of parables have an aspect of the coming of the kingdom in view.[17]

We have been dealing with a series of parables in which the impact of the kingdom of God through the ministry of Jesus is in focus, and in which God himself, therefore, is also, if indirectly, in focus. The same kind of thing is the case with the final Lukan parable: the sprouting of the leaves as an indication that summer is on the way (21:29–31). But now the application is to the future eschatological coming of the kingdom (v. 31) with the coming of the Son of Man in glory (cf. vv. 27, 36).

Parables in which God plays a direct role

While we have seen God imaged in some way in several of the parables, he turns up directly in the story of the rich man and his yet bigger storage barns (12:16–21). Since Luke labels the call to choose the lowest place as a parable (14:7–11), he is likely to consider the material following, on inviting to your banquet only those who cannot invite you in return (14:12–14), as a parable also. God does not quite turn up directly here, but the idea of being 'repaid at the resurrection of the righteous' (v. 14) gives God a clear role in the action of the story. The situation is similar in the parable of the rich man with poor Lazarus at his gate (16:19–31). It is the angels and Abraham who are the visible actors, but they act for God; and God stands behind the passive verb in 'a great chasm has been fixed' (v. 26). God plays both a direct role and an off-stage role in the parable of the Pharisee and the tax collector praying in the temple (18:9–14): he is both the one prayed to and the one in whose eyes the tax collector, rather than the Pharisee, achieves a standing as upright.

God makes an appearance in two ways in the parable of the unrighteous judge and the woman who bothered him with her appeals (18:1–7). The parable gets into this list because the judge says 'I neither fear God nor care about human beings' (v. 4), but this is fairly incidental to the main thrust of the

---

[17] It is possible, however, that these parables earlier expressed God's commitment to seeing through what he had begun in the ministry of Jesus. Hunzinger ('Unbekannte Gleichnisse', 213–16) offers an attractive case for seeing these parables as originally designed to make a comparison with God (as with the other 'which of you' parables in Lk. 11:5, 11; 15:4, 8; 17:7; but see 14:5), who, having made the beginning he has with Jesus' ministry, will surely bring the kingdom to its fruition.

parable. There is also a how-much-more comparison between God and the unrighteous judge, so the parable has its primary place above in '*Parables in which God's action is present figuratively*'. Something quite similar is the case with 'the Prodigal': God features implicitly or indirectly but nevertheless as himself, rather than under some secondary image or in the euphemism 'against heaven' (vv. 18, 21). In the traditional understanding God is present in a much more important manner under the image of the father.

Summary

We can readily divide the parables, then, into those in which God plays no role, those in which God's action is presented figuratively, those in which Jesus is present figuratively as one who acts in the place of God, those in which God/Jesus is present figuratively in connection with the kingdom of God, and those in which God plays a direct role in the narrative. Some overlap of categories is evident, but this is not sufficiently marked as to place in doubt the usefulness of these categories.

- With the notable exception of the parable of the Good Samaritan, parables in which God plays no role are all very brief parables, and there might be some question about whether they belong in the set of Lukan parables.
- God is imaged in Lukan parables as a friend, a father (twice if we count 'the Prodigal'), a rich man let down by a dishonest steward and a slave owner, and twice each as a judge, a vineyard owner and a banquet host. God is also presented more indirectly as the bringer of judgement under the imagery of the coming of a flood.
- Jesus, as one who acts in the place of God, is imaged as a creditor who forgives debts, an absent master, a thief coming at an unexpected time, a householder who closes up at night, the owner of the lost coin and of the lost sheep and a nobleman who goes away to gain kingly power.
- The activity of God/Jesus in terms of the coming of the kingdom is imaged as fertile seed, mustard seed, yeast and fresh growth as the harbinger of summer. The coming of one who is stronger than a strong man is more complicated, with its role as a positive counterpart to the unclean spirit who temporarily leaves. There is also here the prospect of the negative effect of getting things wrong in connection with the coming of the kingdom. This is imaged in the failed attempt to build a tower and the folly of attacking an opposing army with too few troops.
- Finally, there are quite a number of parables in which God turns up directly – for the most part as the one who deals with people beyond the present life, but also, implicitly, as the one in whose eyes the penitent tax

collector is justified. God plays a minor role as himself in a parable in which he is primarily represented figuratively; indirectly he plays a minor role as himself in 'the Prodigal'.

From the place of God we turn now to the place of money and possessions in the Lukan parables.

The Place of Money and Possessions in Lukan Parables

Parables in which money or possessions play an explicit or implicit role

Since issues of wealth and poverty are of considerable importance in Luke,[18] we might expect matters relating to money and possessions to feature significantly in the Lukan parables. While they do feature, we shall see in the following section there is not actually the kind of focus on issues of wealth that we might have expected.

The parable of the two forgiven debtors (7:40–43) is about debt and its forgiveness. The question of whether one has enough money to finish a job arises in the parable about building a tower (14:28–30). The Good Samaritan (10:29–37) spends two denarii on care for the injured man and promises more as needed. Management of wealth is of central importance in the parable of the dishonest steward (16:1–8). Here the trouble into which the steward gets himself and the way forward he finds beyond the loss of his stewardship both involve the manipulation of resources. The parable of the rich man and Lazarus (16:19–31) clearly focus on wealth and poverty. It is a failure to give the owner his share of the produce that sets up the central dynamic of the parable of the tenants in the vineyard (20:9–16). Ten slaves get a mina each to do business on their master's behalf in the parable of the well-born man who goes off to a distant country to get royal power (19:11–27). What one does with one's wealth is clearly in focus in the story of the rich man and his yet bigger storage barns (12:16–21). That one gets 'repaid at the resurrection of the righteous' (14:14) introduces an economic note into the parable about inviting the disadvantaged to your parties (vv. 12–14). Further, if one does not settle the case with one's accuser on the way to the magistrate, then one will not get out of debtors' prison until one has paid the last denarius (12:57–59). Two of the three excuses are economic in focus in the parable in which those who offer their excuses are replaced (14:16–24).

The Prodigal (15:11–32) asks for, and receives, his share of the inheritance, but he squanders it and gets a poor paying job. In the end he hopes for a better

---

[18] See, e.g., Johnson, *Literary Function*; Pilgrim, *Good News*; Seccombe, *Possessions*; Horne, *Glaube*; Kiyoshi, *Besitzverzicht*.

job as a servant at home and is extravagantly restored. His elder brother has been constantly on the job but has never had the resources released to celebrate with his friends. Indeed he is offended that his father kills the fatted calf in his brother's honour. He points out that his younger brother has consumed the father's estate, in spite of being assured that all that the father has is his (i.e., the elder son's). In the parable of the unrighteous judge and the woman who bothered him with her appeals (18:1–7), we may probably presume that the justice sought has economic significance.

We may also cast the net wider here and include parables that refer more indirectly to economic expenditure, or loss or gain. The prospect of waste motivates action in the background of the parables about patching clothing and storing wine (5:36–38). Generosity with one's resources is involved in giving help to a friend at midnight (11:5–8). The father who would give a snake or a scorpion to his child who asks for a fish or an egg (11:11–13) would be giving something worthless. The unfruitful fig tree (13:6–9) is using the land resource and giving no return. The dynamic of the short parable concerning the unexpected time of the thief's arrival (12:39) centres around the prospect of losing one's goods to a thief. The same is true in the parable about the overpowering of the strong man (11:21–22). The dynamic of the parables of the lost sheep and of the lost coin (15:3–10) is provided by the value one naturally sets on what is one's own. In the parable of the sower (8:4–8), the fruitfulness of the seed represents the farmer's livelihood, his economic survival. An important component of the parable of the Pharisee and the tax collector praying in the temple (18:9–14) is the negative image of the tax collector, based at least in part on the dubious nature of the tax collector's financial dealings with the public.

It is clearly right to cast the net more widely, but once we have done so it is hard to know where to stop. In some way or other, almost every situation in life involves economic resources. The one who takes care to build only on secure foundations spends more on the house than the one who does not bother with good foundations (6:47–49). Salt that has lost its saltiness and become useless (14:34–35) involves an economic loss. We would need to reach just too far to include some parables, however, in a list of parables that involve money or possessions. For example, the parables of the growth of the mustard seed (13:18–19) and of the yeast that makes its way through three measures of flour (13:20–21) seem to me to be quite free of economic interest.

Parables which are told to communicate something about money or possessions

It is one thing to have money or possessions play an explicit or implicit role in the story; it is another thing to make the judgement that attitudes to wealth, or practices in the handling of wealth, have a central role in the purpose of the story. We also need to distinguish between parables that speak about material resources as one means of implementing the approach that the parable commends and parables that have attitudes to, or use of, material resources as their main concern.

I take up the latter first. However we finally decide to understand the parable, there is clearly something exemplary in the way that the Good Samaritan spent money on the man who had been hurt. But the expenditure of money is but one of a string of actions on the part of the Samaritan that demonstrate his compassion. Similarly, in the parable of those who offer their excuses for not being prepared to come to the dinner, the higher priority placed on trying out the newly bought oxen or viewing the newly bought land over coming to the dinner is clearly being frowned upon. But the third excuse is about having just been married. So it is clear that while possessions-based excuses have a high profile here, they ultimately belong alongside other kinds of excuses that might have been offered. While not just any kind of excuse would work in the specific narrative shape used in the story, the excuses included are only examples and should be understood to stand for any kind of excuse that might be offered for refusing to come to the banquet that is the kingdom of God.

We turn now to the issue of whether money or possessions only play an explicit or implicit role in the story or whether the parable directly concerns attitudes or practices that relate to the handling of money or possessions. It is unlikely that the parable of the two forgiven debtors (7:40–43) mainly addresses financial indebtedness as such. For the central dynamic of the parable is created by the difference in scale of the indebtedness of the two debtors. The parable offers no comment on debt. Because of this focus on the scale of debt, neither does the parable offer any comment on the forgiveness of financial debt. This is confirmed when we see that nothing further about the release from debt is offered besides the fact that neither debtor could pay, and yet again when we see that the focus of the story has to do with how the respective debtors might be expected to respond to their release from debt – not how they should respond, not how they did respond, but how they might reasonably be expected to respond. If one knows oneself to have been released from a large debt, then one will be extremely grateful! It is nice to be released from even a small debt, but there is not a lot to stir the passions in release from what is perceived to be a modest debt.

By contrast, the parable of the rich man and Lazarus (16:19–31) does seem to be about wealth. The rich man is defined first in terms of his extravagant lifestyle, and second in terms of the poor man who lay at his gate but who gained nothing at all from his proximity to the rich man. Lazarus is defined in terms of his poverty, his suffering and his longing for something better – specifically his longing for some scraps from the rich man's table. The two figures experience radically contrasting fates beyond death. And the difference is explained in terms of reversal (v. 25): Lazarus has now what the rich man denied him earlier; the rich man suffers now after 'having it all' in his lifetime. Verse 30 introduces the idea of repentance into the story. It is clear that the rich man should have acted differently, and that 'differently' can, within the story, be related to what he did with his wealth.

In the story of the rich man who builds bigger barns (12:16–21) it is also clear that we have a parable about the use of wealth. We again have a key figure who is rich, and after a very good harvest he becomes even richer. The action of the story revolve around what should be done about this increased wealth. The rich man's solution is to build bigger barns to store it all, so that he might draw upon it to sustain a leisured and extravagant lifestyle on into the indefinite future. God's intervention reveals the limited framework within which the rich man operates. As he faces death, he has no good answer to God's question about who will benefit from what he (the rich man) has stockpiled.

The clear focus on wealth in these two parables would not necessarily rule out a wider application. We might want to suggest that there are other kinds of wealth, besides the material, that also need to be used appropriately. We might want to suggest that even those who are not wealthy have resources and are responsible for how they use them. But in these cases we are consciously, though not necessarily inappropriately, generalizing.

The consideration of these five parables generates for us a small matrix into which we might be able to fit the various parables that explicitly or implicitly involve money or possessions (I will assume without demonstration that none of the parables where economic expenditure or loss or gain is present in a more indirect or less focussed manner are about attitudes to or utilization of wealth). There are parables that use imagery from the world of money and possessions that: (1) are concerned in a focussed way with matters of money or possessions; (2) are concerned about money or possessions, but only as an example in relation to a larger concern; and (3) are not actually concerned about money or possessions at all. We have also begun the task of identifying what kind of features in the stories might help us to allocate them to the appropriate category. As we seek to assign the rest of the parables explicitly or implicitly involving money or possessions to their places in this matrix, there will be opportunity to ponder further the question of what features act as signals to enable appropriate allocation.

Besides the parable of the rich man and Lazarus and the rich man who builds bigger barns, it is in the parable of the dishonest steward (16:1–8) that economic matters are the most prominent. We even have an explicit application of the parable to the realm of the economic in verse 9. But is the parable really concerned about the handling of money? If it is, it would have to be about the handling of money of people who have already got themselves in trouble through their handling of money; and this seems to be an altogether too narrow focus for the parable. We can hardly take the generous writing down of debts as an economic act without recognizing that the abuse of stewardship also involves economics. Writing down the debts due to the master is, in any case, a rather odd image for any kind of economic activity that might be encouraged. It would be better to treat the parable as operating at a higher level of generality. As I have suggested elsewhere, 'the challenge is to have the shrewdness to recognize and seize the opportunity that exists in the midst of threat'.[19] In a Lukan setting such shrewdness must take into account how one relates to one's economic resources. Nevertheless the parable must lose its economic connection (by being construed in relation to a higher level category) before it can regain it (one's shrewdness will be displayed in what one does with one's wealth, as in other areas). The parable seems to fit best into category 3, although because of the secondary application to the economic sphere it might just (improbably and doubtfully) be squeezed into category 2.

The parable about inviting the disadvantaged to your parties (14:12–14) may advance our argument more clearly. As we noted above, repayment at the resurrection of the righteous belongs to the realm of the economic. The telling is in terms of the immediately economic and the material works well with an immediately economic application. All the same, is the narrow focus literally intended? Or is it not more likely that the narrow focus provides an instance of an approach that has a much more general applicability? The concern is to break away from patterns in which reciprocity of benefit is the controlling feature, and to replace them with patterns of generosity to the needy. Yet even allowing for a concern for a wider application, the focus on the utilization of wealth remains. This is most likely a category 1 parable, but some might possibly place it in category 2.

The parable about settling the case with one's accuser on the way to the magistrate (12:57–59) only brings money into the picture in the case of failure to follow the advice. So it is not a parable with any concern about how one uses money. This is a category 3 parable.

The parable of the unrighteous judge and the woman who bothered him with her appeals (18:1–7) certainly does not focus on money. Inasmuch as money might be involved it is money for the widow to receive, not to give. This, too, is a category 3 parable.

The Lukan parable about building a tower (14:28–30) surely involves a secondary application: the resources for building the tower that Luke has in mind

---

[19] Nolland, *Luke*, II, 802. Loader's suggestion ('Rogue'), that Jesus is the rogue figure of the parable is not without its attractions: judged by the owner (the Jewish leadership) as not exercising faithful stewardship, Jesus meets the attempt to displace him from stewardship by handing out blessings from God. Finally, however, the parable is too much about the steward looking after himself for Loader's suggestion to be convincing.

are hating one's family and taking up a cross. Originally the parable may well have made the point that God, having made a beginning with Jesus' ministry, will surely bring the kingdom to its fruition.[20] Either way, this would remain a category 3 parable.

The two remaining parables, apart from 'the Prodigal', both focus much more obviously on wealth in their content. In the parable of the tenants of the vineyard (20:9–16) the tenants are meant to hand an agreed share of the produce over to the representative of the owner; in the parable of the well-born man who goes off to a distant country to get royal power (19:11–27), the chosen slaves are to engage in business on their master's behalf, using the capital he has handed out to them. As these parables are normally understood, however, they have no special focus on money.[21] In both parables it is answerability to God that is considered to be at stake. With the tenants in the vineyard it is hard to keep any real money focus without keeping a literal vineyard focus; in the case of the one who goes off to get royal power and return, there is in Luke such an obvious allegorical connection with Jesus' exaltation to heaven and return that it becomes impossible to retain any real focus on money. In both parables it would be in line with the Lukan intent to see that one's attitude towards and use of possessions is one of the areas in which answerability to God finds appropriate expression. But the resource imagery in the parables does not make any such connection. The situation seems to be the same as that for the parable of the dishonest steward (16:1–8). These two parables are category 3 parables, but because of possible secondary application to the economic they might just be squeezed into category 2 – but probably should not be.

Summary: Possible additions to, or modifications of, our three categories outlined above

Only one other parable merits inclusion within our category 1 (parables about the use of money or possessions) in addition to the parables of the rich man and Lazarus (16:19–31) and the rich man who builds bigger barns (12:16–21). This single addition is the parable about inviting the disadvantaged to your parties (14:12–14). On the other hand, we allowed for the possibility that it should be

---

[20] See n. 17, above.

[21] In the case of the parable of the tenants of the vineyard it has been proposed, as we have already briefly noted, that this parable might be read, in the context of the experience of oppressive absentee landlords, as identifying the vineyard owner as a villain, and as opening up the question of whether throwing him over might not be a proper response to his annual demands (see n. 1, above). But this is not possible in the Lukan frame and is placed in question by the 'value added' emphasis suggested by the report of the planting, the digging of the pit for the winepress and the building of a watchtower.

allocated to category 2. We noted that Holgate allocates 'the Prodigal' to category 1.

Our original entries in category 2 (parables in which the use of money serves as an example) included the parable of the Good Samaritan (10:29–37) and the parable of those who offer their excuses and are replaced (14:16–24). To this category we have not made any definite additions, although there was just a possibility that a couple of parables allocated to other categories might belong here.

Our initial example of a category 3 parable (not about the use of money or possessions) was the parable of the two forgiven debtors (7:40–43). To this we have been able to add the parable of the dishonest steward (16:1–8), but with the caveat that it might just be squeezed into category 2; the parable about settling the case with one's accuser on the way to the magistrate (12:57–59); the parable about building a tower (14:28–30); and the parable of the unrighteous judge and the woman who bothered him with her appeals (18:1–7). 'The Prodigal' has traditionally been allocated in this category.

Leaving 'the Prodigal' out of the count, of the parables in Luke in which money or possessions are explicitly or implicitly involved in the story, fully half (five parables) have been allocated to category 3: despite their imagery, these parables are not actually concerned about wealth or money. Another two belong to category 2: they are concerned with wealth or money, but only as an example in relation to a larger concern. There seem to be just three parables (or possibly only two) out of ten that belong to category 1, focussing explicitly on the use of or attitude to money or possessions.

In the Lukan parables, *imagery of economic activity does not normally imply a concern in the parable about money and its use*. It is for the most part *an image* of something else. It does on occasion signal a concern about a person's relationship to money. But, in the entire corpus of Lukan parables *of more than forty there are just two or three which are concerned with the use of or attitude to money or possessions as such*, and another two or three that exhibit a concern about money or possessions, but only as *an example in relation to a larger concern*.

There can, therefore, be no presumption that, in Luke, imagery concerning the use of or attitude to money or possessions signals that the parable is actually concerned about such matters. As we have surveyed the parables we have been able to observe various kinds of features within the stories that have enabled us to decide what the actual focus of each particular parable is. Two notable common features of all three parables that have been identified as being concerned with the use of or attitude to wealth or money emerge: first, in each case the story reaches its goal beyond this present life; and, secondly and closely related, in each case God, or that which represents the action of God (resurrection, angels, Abraham and the torment of Hades), is found directly within the story world.

Locating 'the Prodigal' in relation to the surveys above

While nothing can replace detailed attention to the parable itself, our surveys above, probing for whether and how God turns up in Lukan parables and for the significance given to wealth and possessions in these parables, establish a lens for looking at 'the Prodigal'.

God almost always turns up (except in some of the very brief parables) in a significant role in the Lukan parables, the one exception to this being the parable of the Good Samaritan. The general presumption, therefore, is that God should be somehow figured in 'the Prodigal'. But the parable of the Good Samaritan sets another precedent: it is a major Lukan parable in which God plays no role. To compare this parable with that of the Prodigal will be important for evaluating the claims of a Holgate-like approach.

In the Lukan parables, as we have seen, imagery of economic activity does not normally mean that the parable is concerned about money and its use. Only two or three of more than forty Lukan parables are actually about the use of, or attitudes to, wealth. Even where the imagery is clearly about money and its uses, only two or three of ten parables are about wealth. In these three, the story reaches its goal beyond this present life, and ultimate answerability for what one has done in one's life is either to God himself or to something that indirectly represents the action of God. Though 'the Prodigal' is heavily concerned with the use of wealth, as we saw above, the parable does not match in these two noted respects the other three parables that are concerned about use of wealth. There is also the category of Lukan parables which are concerned about wealth or money, but only use wealth as an example in relation to a larger concern: the parable of the Good Samaritan (10:29–37) and the parable of those who offer their excuses and are replaced (14:16–24). Could 'the Prodigal' fit here in this category? Note that the parable of the Good Samaritan turns up again here. Allocating 'the Prodigal' to this set would retain something of the focus of Holgate's investments but would also call for the focus on attitudes to and the use of wealth to be set within some bigger frame. The linguistic and thematic emphases of 'the Prodigal' on family offer us 'family relations' as a possible category into which the concern with the economic can be subsumed.

Values, Attitudes and Priorities Presumed for Hearers of the Lukan Parables

A third kind of survey of the Lukan parables may help us further forward here. 'The Prodigal' can only work as a story if a typical hearer can warmly approve of the actions of the father in the story and can hope at the end that the elder brother will relent and join the celebration.[22] If a hearer is, instead, embarrassed by the father's actions, feeling that these actions are demeaning to him as a father of adult children, or if the hearer reacts with incredulity at the injustice of the father, then the parable will have failed. To that degree the parable appeals to, or even depends upon, values and attitudes assumed to be present in the hearers. This third survey, therefore, would focus on identifying the values, attitudes and priorities that the stories assume of their hearers.

There is, unfortunately, not the space available here to present this third survey in full. It must instead suffice to report and, where possible, to support briefly what is most immediately pertinent to our quest. Because of its particular importance for comparison with 'the Prodigal', however, the following discussion considers the value assumptions involved in the parable of the Pharisee and the tax collector in the temple at prayer (18:9–14).

Does it matter whether parables share or conflict with readers' attitudes and values?

There is no scholarly agreement about exactly what is going on in the parable of the Pharisee and the tax collector. In particular, the range of scholarly views about how the Pharisee's prayer should make the listener think of this Pharisee range all the way from an image of the ideal pious man[23] to an overdrawn caricature of a figure of pride and hypocrisy who promotes himself before God in a quite blatant manner.[24] My own view is that what we have here is something much more subtle. Our Pharisee is meant to create a good impression initially, but there are just enough hints to unsettle: we are not warmed by the love of God when we are in the presence of this upright and apparently godly man, and his apparent love for God does not translate into a heart of compassion for his fellows.[25] The clear assumption is that the hearer appreciates the piety of the

---

[22] There are dissenting voices here, e.g., Breech, *Silence*. Breech considers that the father is insecure and that he favours the younger son over the elder. Breech also considers that the younger son is not improved by his experience (he remains motivated by greed to the end), and that it is the elder son who sees things as they really are. See Breech, 184–214. Breech has not been found persuasive. In any case his view is not possible in a Lukan framework, or even within the framework provided by the juxtaposition of the three parables found in Lk. 15. For scholars who offer views related to that of Breech see nn. 36–38, below.

[23] E.g., Linnemann, *Parables*, 58.

[24] Schottroff, 'Erzählung', 448–52.

[25] What is behind the juxtaposition of the Pharisee's own achievements and reference to their lack in the tax collector and others? His kind of righteousness does not encourage him to reach out to others but rather separates him from them. See discussion in Nolland, *Luke*, II, 874–89.

Pharisee and shares in the commonly held bad opinion of tax collectors. But our hearer is also meant to be disturbed by the fact that the Pharisee erects a pedestal for himself, and to be impressed by the humble and heartfelt confession of the tax collector. It is assumed that the listeners have value resources available that, at least with the pointer provided by 18:14a, will enable them to work their way beyond their initial impressions. The hearer's need here to determine priorities in values has relevance to 'the Prodigal'.

What emerges from a survey of reader value assumptions in the Lukan parables? First, the range of values that emerges in the Lukan parables looks rather bourgeois. There is certainly much that is reminiscent of the kind of wisdom perspective found in Proverbs. But what are perhaps most evident are the perspectives of ordinary people of the first-century world, who had a clear and secure place, however modest, in their own communities, and whose main schooling had been in the school of life. It will be reasonable to expect the reader values anticipated in 'the Prodigal' to fall within this range.

Further, it is clear in the Lukan parables that to assume a value is, for the most part, also to commend or to reinforce it, but the degree to which commendation is evident is varied. Various parables that deal with having a long-term perspective or a big enough frame of reference (11:24–26; 12:16–21; 14:28–32) are urging people to take account of the big picture and are, therefore, commending and not just reflecting the importance of putting things within a comprehensive frame. By contrast, we find in the parables that assume that people will want to avoid disaster (6:39, 48–49; 12:58–59; 16:19–31) no particular commendation of the idea that people should do so, and the same may be said for perhaps most of the values and assumptions that function as assumed hearer values (reinforcement, yes; but not commendation). Even when there is strong commendation of, say, the importance of consistency (6:41–42) or of taking a big enough view, the commendation is for the purpose of reinforcing the need for a *particular* kind of consistency (in connection with identifying fault) or for reckoning on *particular* factors (mostly that of how God will respond) in the larger frame. Though commendation or reinforcement of various existing hearer perspectives does take place, in no case is the parable *about* commending that value. If this pattern holds in relation to 'the Prodigal', then, regardless of the hearer values that the story appeals to, the parable will not be *about* these values.

Commending values that are not necessarily already the values of the hearers

Our attention has been on hearer values, but parables can commend values that are not necessarily already the values of the hearers. The parable of the Good Samaritan commends a perspective on neighbour that the listeners are not yet likely to have. The parable of the Pharisee and tax collector at prayer invites a fresh evaluation of existing cultural stereotypes. Both the parable of the rich man and his barns and of the rich man and poor Lazarus are designed to unsettle a standard set of unreflective assumptions about wealth and poverty. In fact, inasmuch as parables are designed to produce change they will always be, no matter what appeal they first make to pre-existing hearer values, concerned to take the hearer on to some new place. With notable exceptions (mostly the parables listed in this paragraph), however, that which the parables are designed to achieve, and therefore the perspectives being commended, are not directly available within the story world of the parable, but depend upon drawing a connection between the story world and something quite other. Obviously, this is because most of the parables are not actually *about* their literal story content.

Locating 'the Prodigal' in relation to the discussion of values

The time has come now to locate 'the Prodigal' in relation to the above discussion of values, attitudes and priorities. An important distinction that has emerged is between perspectives or values that a parable assumes and even commends, and the parable being *about* some perspective or value. Paradoxically, parables are *about* some perspective or value only in cases where that perspective or value is not 'present' as an assumed reader value in the actual story (though in some cases hearer values are appealed to in order to build towards the perspective or value that the parable is *about*).[26]

I claimed above that the parable could only work as a story if a typical hearer could warmly approve of the actions of the father and could hope at the end that the elder brother will relent and join in the celebration. But this was only to tell part of the story. While the desire of the parable is for us to side with the father, within the story itself there are two kinds of reaction to the father's actions: negative and positive. The elder son forcefully articulates the negative reaction; the positive reaction is only implicit. Those who join in the music and dancing of 15:25 are positive about, or at least accepting of, the father's actions. The same is true of the servants who explain to the elder brother what has been going on (v. 27): their version of developments reflects the naturalness of the father's response, and to that degree provides support for the father over against the negative reaction of the elder son, which is about to be reported (vv. 28–30). Alongside the implicit representation of the positive reactions of others we may set the father's own explanation in verses 31–32.

---

[26] I have in mind, e.g., the way in which hearer values are involved in exploring the story of the Pharisee and the tax collector (18:9–14) for clues as to why it is the latter (as one who is upright in the sight of God) and not the former who leaves the temple.

The desire of the parable is clearly for us to side with the father.[27] But it is important for the story that the elder brother's perspective not be lightly swept aside.[28] There is a clash between two opinions here, and if the second opinion were to be no more than caricatured then the parable is not likely to prove persuasive. The opposition needs to be argued out of its opinion – and not just insulted about its opinion. The story must therefore lend at least an initial credibility to the point of view of the elder brother. There must be a world of thought and attitude to which the elder brother's perspective can be related, in the context of which the view seems credible. A justice framework is the one that immediately suggests itself. The values of the elder brother are not being appealed to, but they are being acknowledged and taken seriously.

The only other Lukan parable that in any way matches this level of moral complexity is that of the Pharisee and the tax collector. Both parables make use of perspectives that stand in tension one with another. In both cases it proves necessary to establish a hierarchy of values in relation to the matter at hand. In the one case the hearer must decide whether it is the Pharisee or the tax collector who is in the right; in the other the choice is between whether the father or the elder son is in the right.[29] And in both cases the story is weighted in order to guide the hearer to the correct choice. Holgate treats 'the Prodigal' as an example story, and in this respect there is an important likeness here between this parable and one of the other parables that has been regularly assigned to this category.

The Relationship between 'the Prodigal' and the Good Samaritan

In two lines of earlier exploration, we identified the need to examine the relationship between the parables of the Prodigal Son and of the Good Samaritan. First, the Good Samaritan is the only (other?) substantial Lukan parable in which God does not feature. Secondly, a significant likeness between the two parables might encourage the allocation of 'the Prodigal' to the category of Lukan parables which have a concern about wealth or money, but only as an example in relation to a larger concern.

There are some genuine likenesses between the two parables. Both are introduced with ἄνθρωπος ('a certain man/person') + an imperfect tense verb (10:30; 15:11);[30] both have ἐσπλαγχνίσθη ('he had compassion') at the key

---

[27] But see n. 22 and the studies identified in nn. 36–38, below.

[28] See n. 22. That Breech can take the parable as he does suggests that the storyteller has not been guilty of caricature.

[29] The younger son, as the one who changes, has a quite different role.

[30] In Luke the same pattern is found in other parables in 14:16; 16:1 (and in 19:12 without the verb in the imperfect), and elsewhere only in 14:2.

turning point in the story; and both of the parables have three main characters (the priest and the Levite for these purposes function as one character). The second of these points must guarantee some relationship between the parables, and to the link created by the shared use of ἐσπλαγχνίσθη we shall need to return.[31] But the difference between the two parables is more striking.

Each parable may have three main characters, but the configuration created by the three characters is quite different in each parable. In 'the Prodigal' all three characters play a vital active role. And the story focuses in turn on each of the three characters (son, then father, then elder brother). In the Good Samaritan one of the characters is quite passive, and it is this passive character who is the central character, the one from whose place of need the whole story is to be viewed. In the Good Samaritan there is a contrast between the priest and the Levite on the one hand and the Samaritan on the other hand, but the scale of treatment of the two cases is quite unbalanced, with the great bulk of the parable given over to the actions of the Samaritan. In 'the Prodigal' contrast is also important, but here we have two major contrasts: that between the two brothers, but also that between the father and the elder brother.[32] We cannot look to the Good Samaritan for support for allocating 'the Prodigal' to that category of parables in which God plays no role, or to the set of parables in which there is a concern about money or possession as an example in relation to a larger concern.[33]

The Role of God, Money and Possessions in 'the Prodigal'

Thus far our concern has been to locate 'the Prodigal' within the frame created by the whole set of Lukan parables. Now we need to turn our attention in a more focussed way to the parable itself. We have seen the following: first, that

---

[31] Beyond these two verses this verb is used elsewhere in Luke only in connection with Jesus' compassion for the widow of Nain (7:13).

[32] In addition, the attention given to each of the main characters in 'the Prodigal' is much more even. Also strikingly different is the younger son's double movement: away from the father and back to the father. Finally, the open-endedness of 'the Prodigal' as to how the elder son will respond to his father's entreaty represents a major difference between these two parables. The question with which Jesus finishes in 10:36 offers no real parallel, as the answer is intended to be quite clear.

[33] The parable of those who offer their excuses and are replaced (14:16–24) is the other parable in which there is a concern about wealth or money as an example in relation to a larger concern. Although there are three main characters in this parable as well (the man giving the dinner, those who excuse themselves and the replacement guests), there is nothing further to link this parable with that of the Prodigal son.

God plays an important role in all of the extended parables except the Good Samaritan, and that the links between this parable and 'the Prodigal' are not such as to enable us to look to the Good Samaritan for support for allocating 'the Prodigal' to the category of parables in which God plays no role. Further, we have discovered that in the Lukan parables imagery of economic activity does not normally imply a concern in the parable about money and its use. We have noted other features as well.[34]

We observed that although Lukan parables generally affirm or even commend the hearer values or perspectives they draw upon, the parables are never *about* these hearer values or perspectives. Parables are, instead, about values and perspectives that are not directly present in the stories themselves. We noted that in the case of 'the Prodigal' there is a complex interplay between hearer values and perspectives and the values and perspectives of the characters in the story, and that this complexity is matched only in the parable of the Pharisee and tax-collector in the temple, a parable which is also similar in other ways to 'the Prodigal'.

The role of God

Holgate is not the only scholar who has proposed an interpretation for 'the Prodigal' that makes no link between the father and God. I have already drawn attention to Breech's views (see note 22, above): both the father and the younger son are at fault; it is the elder brother who sees things as they are. But we should note that Breech freely admits that in Luke's hands the father is a figure for God and his action points to what is taking place in the ministry of Jesus.[35] Ford finds in Breech's work his starting point for interpreting the parable, but Ford's advance on Breech is to argue that each of the three figures gets it wrong.[36] But Ford interprets the parable entirely in isolation from the Lukan context; in this also he has followed Breech's lead. Rohrbaugh is another scholar who avoids giving God a place in the parable. While Rohrbaugh does not visibly depend on Breech, he does evidence the same disregard of the Lukan frame. Rohrbaugh draws on the resources of cultural anthropology to

---

[34] There are two or three Lukan parables that are about money or possessions, but 'the Prodigal' lacks the shared features that characterize this set. There is another category of Lukan parables that have a concern about wealth or money, but only as an example in relation to a larger concern. 'The Prodigal' does not lack any specific shared feature that would preclude it from this set, but neither does it have the kinds of links to parables in this category that would specifically encourage allocation there.

[35] Breech, *Silence*, 184–86.

[36] Ford, *Parables*, 90–121. While he does not ignore biblical studies concerns, Ford's study is primarily informed by psychological considerations.

argue that we have a picture of a dysfunctional family. All three key figures contribute to the dysfunction, but this family is portrayed as making some important progress and as offering hope of making more.[37] Batton seems to want to break the link between the father and God as well.[38] Also drawing on cultural anthropology, but with a feminist agenda and a focus on issues of honour and shame, she reads the parable as a challenge to the patriarchal values held by the dominant males in ancient Palestine and, in advocating the importance of family reconciliation, as even offering a gynocentric point of view. But, like the others, Batton distances herself from the Lukan use of the parable.

Where Holgate, so far as I have been able to discover, stands totally alone is in suggesting that in the Lukan use of the parable there is no link between the father and God. Curiously, his monograph seems to offer no specific arguments for denying that God is figured by means of the father. Instead there is an analysis of the parable that emphasizes: the liberality and compassion of the father (suggesting that the father functions in a central way as a positive example); the negative consequences of the prodigality of the younger son; and what Holgate sees as the meanness of the elder son.[39] Holgate also mounts a case for preferring the other distinctly Lukan parables to the materials of Luke 15 as the primary context within which to interpret 15:11–32.[40] Both of these efforts are designed to bring into sharper focus the elements in the parable that have to do with money and possessions, and specifically with attitudes to and use of them.

Given the lack of any argument for breaking the link between the father and God, the otherwise complete scholarly consensus that there is such a link, as well as the pattern of likelihood of such a link established by examining the whole body of Lukan parables, it seems unnecessary to offer fresh argument here for the link between the father and God.[41] The link is secure.

The role of money and possessions

If the link between the father and God is secure, as I have maintained, then it follows that the parable cannot be *about* attitudes to and the use of money or possessions. But whether the parable is *about* attitudes to and the use of money

---

[37] Rohrbaugh, 'Dysfunctional Family'. Rohrbaugh also considers that the family has elements of dysfunction in its relationship to its village.

[38] Batton, 'Dishonour'.

[39] Holgate, *Prodigality*, 39–68.

[40] Holgate, *Prodigality*, 69–88.

[41] Bailey's caveat (*Poet and Peasant*, 159) that 'the father is not God *incognito*' remains valid: the father is first and foremost a father in a human family; his actions point to the activity of God in and through their identity as actions of a particular human father. Bailey has continued to develop his insights into 'the Prodigal' in *Finding*, 'Jacob' and *Jacob*.

or possessions or not, we have already noted the strong emphasis on possessions and their use in 'the Prodigal', and there remains the double question of the perspectives in this area which are exhibited by characters in the narrative, and the hearer perspectives in this realm which are implicitly being related to by the teller of the parable.

Holgate correlates this with a *topos* from Greco-Roman moral philosophy, 'On injustice and covetousness and greed'[42] and is able to link many features of the parable to elements he finds in texts which depend on this *topos*. According to Holgate, the younger son manifests a covetousness that is concerned to gain in order to indulge in spendthrift self-indulgence. He violates the ideal of shared possessions; with a misguided excess of liberality he lives beyond his means and squanders his share of the family assets and is caught in a downward cycle that must end in disaster. By contrast, the father exhibits the balanced liberality that, in the *topos*, is the golden mean between the extremes of the excessive liberality of the younger son and what will be seen as the meanness of the elder son.[43] The father shows his liberality in his use of possessions, his good management of his resources and his readiness to risk and to trust. He shows liberality by example in his compassion, in the celebration he arranges and also in his words of moral exhortation. While the younger son dissipates the family resources in a misguided excess of liberality, the elder son is just plain mean. Keen to secure his own hold on the family estate, he makes no protest about the division precipitated by the younger son. With the estate in hand he fails to enjoy its resources or share them with his friends. He complains about his father's liberality to the younger son.

Though Holgate does not address the matter, one must assume that the way he sees the parable working is by appealing to and thereby reinforcing, but probably also by adding nuance to, the existing values of the listeners. The parable is seen to embody values that will be visible to those who inhabit a world in which these values are discussed. There are various exegetical moves made by Holgate that I would want to question, but it will be sufficient here to raise the question of whether the elder son is quite so obviously the negative figure that Holgate takes him to be. I have already indicated that I think differently. It is not hard to see that the elder son has a point in his complaint about his father's actions. There is no justice here! All the fuss is being made over the one who has done all the wrong. There is a problem here, and at some level the father addresses the problem, rather than denying the problem.

---

[42] Holgate, *Prodigality*, 90–130, describes the *topos*, and it is then explored in relation to the prodigality of the younger son (132–67), the father (168–91), the younger son after he 'comes to himself' (192–226) and the elder son (217–46).

[43] Holgate also devotes a chapter (*Prodigality*, 192–226) to the restoration of the younger son, which he entitles 'The Younger Son Learns Liberality', but the connections between what happens with the younger son and liberality are quite tenuous.

Holgate is not the only one who is impressed by the prominence in the parable of the economic. W. Pöhlmann is also concerned to identify the narrative world of the parable against the background of Greek assumptions of the period (and, in Pöhlmann's case, Jewish assumptions as well).[44] He explores Greek sapiential and economic traditions about the household and about agricultural economy, as well as the Jewish sapiential ethos of the household as found in Proverbs and related materials. He also examines parallels to the two contrasted brothers, and to the role of the young spendthrift in ancient writings. Pöhlmann finds in the parable the collision of two worlds. One world consists of the following: the wisdom perspective that sets the general background for the parable; perspectives evident in materials on sons who are very different from each other; and materials on the young spendthrift which give the background to specific features of the parable. The other world is the world of the kingdom of God that Jesus is bringing to visibility in his parables. According to Pöhlmann, the wisdom perspective of this first world is initially visible in the father, is violated by the younger son, and then continues in the elder son from the point in the story where the father clearly abandons it as he welcomes the returning younger son. The restoration of the younger son is not just an undeserved act of grace that leaves the wisdom perspective fundamentally intact; it is instead a legal act which breaks through and contradicts the order and justice of the household. This is how things are in the kingdom of God.

Pöhlmann does a very fine job of setting the parable into the rural and agrarian culture to which it belongs, and he gives a good account of how the various features of the parable would be seen by anyone coming to it with the sapiential ethos which he has explored. There is no doubt that he has found the right home for the parable. People in the parable act against a background of these perspectives, and the parable is most intelligible to people who belong in this same world of values. But should the father's action come as quite the shock that it does to Pöhlmann? Though methodological control is difficult, fresh light has been thrown on various elements of the New Testament by drawing on the peasant and Middle Eastern culture. K.E. Bailey pioneered work along these lines in relation to the Lukan parables.[45] C.S. LaHurd has recently pointed out that it was Arab *men* who considered the father's unconditional acceptance as unexpected. She canvassed the opinions of Arab *women* about whether the father's behaviour was unexpected in light of their experience of the Middle Eastern family. They did not find it at all abnormal and spoke of the son as being

---

[44] Pöhlmann, *Verlorene Sohn*. See also Hendrickx, 'Man', who works on a narrower front and focuses attention on the ethos of the agricultural household in Hesiod, in order to illuminate the world of the parable.

[45] On the father's welcome of the returning son see Bailey, *Poet and Peasant*, 181–82, 206.

'his own blood' and suggested that the 'loving heart of the father' forgets the wrong and the lost money and thinks only about getting his son back. 'The son is his fortune', said one.[46] There is a rabbinic story preserved in Deut. Rabbah 2:24 in which a king sends for his son who has fallen into evil ways, calling on him to repent and return. The son sends a message to the effect that he is ashamed to appear before his father, to which the reply comes, 'Can a son be ashamed to return to his father?'. Application is then made to returning to God as Father: 'is it not to your Father that you return?'. Paternal affection and commitment are understood as opening up the way back and as making it possible for the son to leave behind the shame of the past.[47] It is surely a transcultural human experience to long for the restoration of an estranged child.

It will be much truer to life to think here of a tension between competing human values. What the parable explores is not the collision between a classic wisdom perspective and the values of the kingdom of God. Rather, it explores the tension between the concerns of justice, which are part of the classic wisdom perspective, and the importance and desirability of family reconciliation. The younger son has, no doubt, lost all right to a place in the family and its resources. The whole episode has been a blot upon the family. But what loving father could be happy about or entirely reconciled with such a state of affairs? The question is, has a window of opportunity for changing things been opened up by the return of the younger son? It will be quite understandable in any culture or time that some will answer with a resounding no. But it is also quite evident that others will immediately applaud the action of the father. Which perspectives or set of concerns should have the upper hand here?

The story acknowledges the significance of both sets of concerns but then makes its investment in encouraging the listener to favour the father's compassion and desire to restore the family over the elder brother's insistence upon justice. It does this first by its sympathetic portrayal of the excitement of the father (15:20–24). Then it portrays the elder son's complaint in somewhat

---

[46] LaHurd, 'Rediscovering', 67. Some of the language here is LaHurd's, with the language of her informants set off in quotation marks.

[47] Scott, *Hear*, 122–25, claims that the parable makes use of and subverts the mytheme of the father with two sons, who favours the younger over the elder. But while the OT certainly has God favouring the younger son on various occasions (Gn. 4:4–5; 21:12; 28:13–15; Ex. 3–4; Mal. 1:2–3), the mytheme as he describes it is not demonstrated. Rebekah favours her younger son, but Isaac favours the elder son (Gn. 25:28); Jacob favours his youngest sons, but they are the sons of his favourite wife, and the youngest is yet more favoured because Jacob believed that his brother had been killed, and falls into a special category as the son of his old age and as a child whose mother died in childbirth (Gn. 29–45). Scott's citation of a piece from *Midrash on Psalms* Ps. 9:1, in which a king favours a dirty juvenile son over a well-scrubbed grown-up son, brings in an extra dynamic and is not really relevant.

negative tones: he is not just pointing out the justice of things; he is whining (vv. 28–30).[48] Finally, it gives the father the last word as it lets him make his own case to the elder son (v. 31).

For the story to do its work, listeners must feel that they have been addressed where they are – that their perspectives have been acknowledged and built from – but they must also be persuaded that, all things considered, the father made the right choice. On the basis of his choice there was something to celebrate extravagantly – death has given way to life, the lost has been found. The family will be complete if only the elder son can accept the development and come on in and celebrate.

I began this section by maintaining that, if the link between the father and God is secure, then it follows that the parable cannot be *about* attitudes to and the use of money or possessions. It is beyond the scope of this chapter to address in any fully developed manner what the parable is *about*. But we will not have finished our task if we do not say something about how the imagery of money and possessions contributes to the overall meaning of the parable. By this stage it is evident that, in terms of the categories in the section 'The place of money and possessions in Lukan parables' above, our parable belongs in category 3: it is a parable that is not actually concerned about wealth or money. The most immediately available comparison point is the parable of the two forgiven debtors (7:41–43), where remission of debt functions as an image for forgiveness by God. As Jesus welcomes sinners and eats with them he is functioning as the father does in the story (15:2). Here is the compassion of God for his wayward children. Here, as in James 2:3, 'mercy triumphs over judgement'. The same people who were expected to recognize the authenticity of the perspective on neighbour created by the Samaritan's compassion (10:30–37) are now being asked to recognize the authenticity of what Jesus is claiming as God's action in himself (Jesus) of extending his compassion to his wayward but returning children.

Conclusion

One's attitude to money and possessions is of considerable importance for Luke, but this is not a matter he pursues in many of the parables. Money and possessions figure prominently in about a quarter of the Lukan parables, but in only two or three cases is the parable *about* the use of money or possessions (in a few others there is a concern about the use of money or possessions as an example in relation to a larger concern).

---

[48] Also, he acts in anger, he does not address his father respectfully, he represents his own faithful work for the father in negative terms and he goes beyond what is actually known, with his claim that his brother spent his money on prostitutes.

The question of whether 'the Prodigal' is about the use of money or possessions turns in part on whether God is figured in the parable. He does appear in almost all of the more developed Lukan parables. The exception is the Good Samaritan, and the links between 'the Prodigal' and the Good Samaritan are not such as to align the two in this respect. In the scholarly debate, Holgate stands alone in denying a link between the father and God in the Lukan use of the parable, and he offers no argument. The link between the father and God is to be affirmed.

Parables work in part by making use of existing hearer values. The Lukan parables draw upon quite a range of the kinds of perspectives that are likely to have characterized ordinary people in the first-century world. In appealing to existing values the parables typically affirm and often clearly commend such values. But the parables are never actually *about* the perspectives that are being drawn upon.

Distinctly in the Lukan parable corpus, in the parable of the Pharisee and the tax-collector and in 'the Prodigal', use is made of listener values that in their application to the stories stand in tension with one another. One set of values must be chosen over the other. In both cases, features in the parable and the context help to guide the hearer's choice.

By means of the parable the assertion is being made that God, in connection with the ministry of Jesus, is doing something that is rather like what the father in the story is doing. Only the hearer who can be brought to see that the human father is acting in a commendable manner will be in a position to appreciate what is being asserted about God's action. God's action is made intelligible by being mirrored in the father's action.

But what commends the father's action is not some value in relation to money or possessions, except in a negative sense: for the father there is something here that transcends the wisdom values of prudence and justice and is more important to him than wise stewardship of the family assets; here there is an opportunity to restore a lost son to the family.

There is, however, one loose end that yet remains. Earlier I signalled the need to return to the shared use of ἐσπλαγχνίσθη ('he had compassion') which, I suggested, guaranteed some kind of connection between the parables of the Good Samaritan and 'the Prodigal'. The father has compassion and the Good Samaritan has compassion. What links these two figures? It is, I think, the elder son, who is challenged in the story to emulate the compassion of his father. If the action of the father points to the compassion of God, it does so in part in order to challenge people to emulate that compassion. What for the father is a restoration of a son to the family is for the elder brother, if he will but see it, a restoration of a brother to the family. The Good Samaritan may not be a Christ figure, but in his actions he is mirroring precisely that compassion of God that was being freshly experienced by the needy in the ministry of Jesus. And Luke would have us see the connection.

Bibliography

Bailey, K.E., *Poet and Peasant: A Literary-Cultural Approach to the Parables in Luke* (Grand Rapids: Eerdmans, 1976)
—, *Finding the Lost: Cultural Keys to Luke 15* (Concordia Scholarship Today; St Louis, MO: Concordia, 1992)
—, 'Jacob and the Prodigal Son: A New Identity Story: A Comparison between the Parable of the Prodigal Son and Gen. 27 – 35', *NETR* 18 (1997), 54–72
—, *Jacob and the Prodigal: How Jesus Retold Israel's Story* (Downers Grove, IL: InterVarsity Press, 2003)
Barton, S.C., 'Parables on God's Love and Forgiveness (Luke 15:1–32)', in *The Challenge of Jesus' Parables* (McMaster New Testament Studies; Grand Rapids: Eerdmans, 2000), 199–216
Batton, A., 'Dishonour, Gender and the Parable of the Prodigal Son', *TJT* 13 (1997), 187–200
Bonar, C.A., 'Two Sons – Seven Deadly Sins', *HPR* 98 (1998), 17–24
Borghi, E., 'Lc 15,11–32: Linee Esegetiche Globali', *RivBib* 44 (1996), 279–308
Bovon, F., *Das Evangelium nach Lukas 3: Teilband: Lukas 15,1–19,27* (EKKNT 3.3; Düsseldorf/Zürich: Neukirchen-Vluyn, 2001)
Breech, J.E., *The Silence of Jesus: The Authentic Voice of the Historical Man* (Philadelphia: Fortress Press, 1983)
Brown, C., 'The Parable of the Rebellious Son(s)', *SJT* 51 (1998), 391–405
Duplacy, J., 'Le Véritable Disciple: Un Essai d'Analyse Sémitique de Luc 6, 43–49', *RSR* 69 (1981), 71–86
Dupont, J., 'La Parabole de la Brebis Perdue (Matthieu 18, 12–14; Luc 15, 4–7)', *Greg* 49 (1968), 265–87
—, 'Les Implications Christologiques de la Parabole de la Brebis Perdue', in *Jésus aux Origines de la Christologie* (BETL 40; Gembloux: Duculot; Leuven: Leuven University Press, 1975), 331–50
Forbes, G.W., 'Repentance and Conflict in the Parable of the Lost Son (Luke 15:11–32)', *JETS* 42 (1999), 211–29
—, *The God of Old: The Role of the Lukan Parables in the Purpose of Luke's Gospel* (JSNTSup 198; Sheffield: Sheffield Academic Press, 2000), 109–51
Ford, R.Q., *The Parables of Jesus: Recovering the Art of Listening* (Minneapolis: Fortress Press, 1997), 90–121
Geddert, T., 'The Parable of the Prodigal: Priorities (Luke 15:11–32)', *Direction* 24 (1995), 28–36
Harrill, J.A., 'The Indentured Labor of the Prodigal Son (Luke 15:15)', *JBL* 115 (1996), 714–17
Hendrickx, H., 'A Man Had Two Sons: Luke 15:11–32 in Light of the Ancient Mediterranean Values of Farming and Household', *EAPR* 31 (1994), 46–66

Herzog, W.R., *Parables as Subversive Speech: Jesus as Pedagogue of the Oppressed* (Louisville: Westminster John Knox, 1994), 98–113

Hester, J.D., 'Socio-Rhetorical Criticism and the Parable of the Tenants', *JSNT* 45 (1992), 27–57

Holgate, D.A., Prodigality, Liberality and Meanness in the Parable of the Prodigal Son: A Greco-Roman Perspective on Luke 15:11–32 (JSNTSup 187; Sheffield: Sheffield Academic Press, 1999)

Horne, F.W., *Glaube und Handeln in der Theologie des Lukas* (GTA 26; Göttingen: Vandenhoeck & Ruprecht, 2nd edn, 1986)

Hultgren, A.J., *The Parables of Jesus: A Commentary* (BIW; Grand Rapids: Eerdmans, 2000), 70–91

Hunzinger, C.H., 'Unbekannte Gleichnisse Jesu aus dem Thomas-Evangelium', in *Judentum-Urchristentum-Kirche* (ed. W. Eltester; BZNW 26; Berlin: Töpelmann, 1960), 209–20

Johnson, L.T., *The Literary Function of Possessions in Luke-Acts* (SBLDS 39; Missoula: Scholars Press, 1977)

Kiyoshi, M., *Besitzverzicht und Almosen bei Lukas* (WUNT 2.163; Tübingen: Mohr Siebeck, 2003)

LaHurd, C.S., 'Rediscovering the Lost Women in Luke 15', *BTB* 24 (1994), 66–76

Landmesser, C., 'Die Rückkehr ins Leben nach dem Gleichnis vom verlorenen Sohn (Lukas 15,11–32)', *ZTK* 99 (2002), 239–61

Linnemann, E., *Parables of Jesus: Introduction and Exposition* (trans. J. Sturdy; London: SPCK, 1966)

Loader, W., 'Jesus and the Rogue in Luke 16:1–8a: The Parable of the Unjust Steward', *RB* 96 (1989), 518–22

Nolland, J., *Luke* (3 vols.; WBC 35; Dallas: Word, 1989–93)

O'Meara, R., '"Luring the Crocus through the Snow": The Parable of the Man Who Had Two Sons (Luke 15:11–32)', *ABR* 46 (1998), 17–35

Parsons, M.C., 'Hand in Hand: Autobiographical Reflections on Luke 15', *Semeia* 72 (1995), 125–52

—, 'The Prodigal's Elder Brother: The History and Ethics of Reading Luke 15:25–32', *PRSt* 23 (1996), 147–74

Pilgrim, W.E., *Good News to the Poor: Wealth and Poverty in Luke-Acts* (Minneapolis: Augsburg Press, 1981)

Pöhlmann, W., *Der verlorenen Sohn und das Haus: Studien zu Lukas 15,11–32 im Horizont der antiken Lehre von Haus, Erziehung und Ackerbau* (WUNT 68; Tübingen: Mohr Siebeck, 1993)

Rau, E., 'Jesu Auseinandersetzung mit Pharisäern über seine Zuwendung zu Sünderinnen und Sündern: Lk 15,11–32 und Lk 18,10–14a als Worte des historischen Jesus', *ZNW* 89 (1998), 5–29

Reinstorf, D., and A. van Aarde, 'Jesus' Kingdom Parables as Metaphorical Stories: A Challenge to Conventional Worldview', *HvTSt* 54 (1998), 603–22

Rengstorf, K.H., *Das Evangelium nach Lukas* (NTD 3; Göttingen: Vandenhoeck & Ruprecht, 1962)

Rohrbaugh, R.L., 'A Dysfunctional Family and Its Neighbours (Luke 15:11b–32): The Parable of the Prodigal Son', in *Jesus and his Parables: Interpreting the Parables of Jesus Today* (ed. V.G. Shillington; Edinburgh: T. & T. Clark, 1997), 141–64

Schottroff, L., 'Die Erzählung vom Pharisäer und Zöllner als Beispiel für die theologische Kunst des Überredens', in *Neuen Testament und christliche Existenz* (Festschrift H. Braun; ed. H.D. Betz and L. Schottroff; Tübingen: Mohr Siebeck, 1973), 439–61

Scott, B.B., *Hear then the Parables of Jesus: A Commentary on the Parables of Jesus* (Minneapolis: Fortress, 1989)

Seccombe, D.P., *Possessions and the Poor in Luke-Acts* (SNTSU B/6; Linz, 1982)

Wendland, E.R., 'Finding Some Lost Aspects of Meaning in Christ's Parables of the Lost – and Found (Luke 15)', *TJ* 17 (1996), 19–65

8

Reading Luke, Hearing Jesus and Understanding God

Reflections on Some Hermeneutical Issues:
A Response to John Nolland

Stephen I. Wright

Introduction

John Nolland's chapter explicitly raises many fascinating questions about the interpretation of Jesus' parables in Luke, especially one of his most famous ones. It also implicitly raises many equally fascinating questions about hermeneutics. The prime purpose of this response is to bring some of these implicit hermeneutical questions to the surface. However, a few of the explicit issues to do with the texts will be addressed along the way, although with no pretence of bringing them to closure.

As the renewal of biblical hermeneutics is central to the purposes of the Scripture and Hermeneutics Seminar, in these volumes we remain rooted both in the practical business of reading texts (which Nolland's chapter exemplifies) and in reflection on the theory behind the practice. This will be my main focus here. It may seem a little unfair to John Nolland to subject his chapter to this kind of metacritical treatment when such could equally be applied to any other chapter in the book (including, of course, this one). But it might be argued that the parables of Jesus bring central issues in biblical hermeneutics to the fore in a uniquely acute fashion.[1] Thus John Nolland's discussion of Luke 15 opens up

---

[1] Thus it is no coincidence that the movement known as the 'New Hermeneutic', exemplified by the scholarship of Gerhard Ebeling, Ernst Fuchs and Eberhard Jüngel in Germany, showed particular interest in the parables: see, for instance,

with special clarity a cluster of matters which may, and should, be related, *mutatis mutandis*, to our reading not only of Luke's Gospel more generally, but also of the Bible as a whole.

The focus of this volume and of Nolland's contribution is the literary text of Luke. The questions associated with the attempt to decide what Luke reveals or conceals about Jesus as a historical figure are not, by and large, at issue (though as I shall argue below, I do not believe we are at liberty simply to ignore this dimension entirely). The business of reading a text as rich as Luke offers, indeed, matter enough for many volumes, even apart from those distinct historical concerns.

Thus Nolland's positive argument deals with a wide range of parable texts found in canonical Luke, with just occasional and incidental reference to a parable's possible prehistory.[2] Equally, it is on the grounds of their lack of coherence with the overall picture given by Luke that Nolland discounts certain possible readings, or at least their relevance for his own case.[3] The prospect of coming together around the canonical text as it presents itself is certainly an attractive one. Such an approach may appeal both to scholarship that is suspicious of overmuch speculation and to faith that is concerned with the received text rather than conceivable *ur*-texts. However, it has surely been amply demonstrated over the last two centuries that what may appear initially as an innocent and simple process of reading a text is far from either innocent or simple. The richer the perceived figurative and suggestive quality of the text, the more complex and interesting the process becomes.

Given that Jesus' parables fall into this category of richly suggestive texts, it becomes especially relevant to attend to what is going on as we read them. For a language to do this with reference to Nolland's reading I will draw primarily on the classic work of Schleiermacher.

Schleiermacher's Hermeneutics

Schleiermacher's lectures on hermeneutics[4] no doubt strike us today as outdated in their optimism. They are imbued with that confidence in a

---

Fuchs, *Hermeneutik*, 211–30, and Jüngel, *Paulus*, 139–74. This movement exercised influence on a number of those who were to become influential parable scholars in America, such as Robert Funk, Amos Wilder and John Dominic Crossan: see Funk, *Language*; Wilder, *Rhetoric*; Crossan, *Parables*.

[2] E.g., n. 17.

[3] E.g., n. 13; and p. 200–201 on the readings of Ford and Rohrbaugh.

[4] Delivered in Berlin between 1810 and 1834. See the extracts in Mueller-Vollmer, *Reader*, 72–97. On Schleiermacher's hermeneutical approach see Ricœur, 'Schleiermacher's Hermeneutics' and *Theory*, 22f., 71–79, 92f.; Thiselton, *New Horizons*, 204–36; Wolterstorff, 'Promise', 73–75.

combination of human learning and the possibility of imaginatively grasping the 'genius' of texts, even ancient ones, which so characterized the Romantic mood. More recent intellectual currents have taught us to be suspicious of both our learning and our insight. But this may cause us to overlook the extent to which Schleiermacher penetrates to the core of the process of interpretation and describes the challenge in which (whether it is fully articulated or not) thorough interpreters of texts still find themselves engaged.

Central to Schleiermacher's construal of the hermeneutical task is the distinction between 'grammatical' and 'technical' interpretation.[5] Both are necessary in every act of interpretation. The 'grammatical' kind considers the words as a part of the system of language; the 'technical' considers the words as a manifestation of the life of a writer. The 'technical', in turn, requires a perpetual spiralling of 'divination', or 'immediate comprehension of the author as an individual', and 'comparison', that is 'subsuming the author under an individual type'.[6]

Thus to 'understand' a text in the fullest sense entails not merely being able to decode the words according to their signification as a part of a linguistic system, but also being able to grasp their unique purport as a particular user has deployed them. Interpretation therefore requires not only linguistic competence, but also personal insight. Clearly, the more the text concerned bears the hallmarks of inventiveness and originality, the more insight will be required: the Bible and Shakespeare need (and deserve) our acts of 'divination' in a way that the *Yellow Pages* never will. This divination is never a purely intersubjective act in which a reader glimpses in a flash the nature and purpose of the writer, because processes of critical 'comparison', which set the writer alongside others, always offer a balance.

Yet as Schleiermacher points out, even such comparison cannot be undertaken without 'divination'.[7] As a part of this double axis of interpretation, a crucial manoeuvre, says Schleiermacher, is a reading of the part in the light of the whole and vice versa, on several levels. Thus 'grammatical' interpretation requires that one read the words of the text in the light of the language and history of its era as a whole – but also that one take note of the way in which the language is enriched or enlarged by this specific text.[8] 'Technical' interpretation requires that one let the style of the writer as it is known from his wider work, as well as the 'state of the genre' at the time of writing, inform one's

---

[5] 'Psychological' is another word Schleiermacher uses for 'technical'. Although 'technical' has connotations in modern English of 'scientific', in Schleiermacher's context it underlines his emphasis that interpretation is an *art* or skill (cf. Greek *technē*). On the background of this word in Aristotle see Ricœur, *Theory*, 76f.

[6] Mueller-Vollmer, *Reader*, 96.

[7] Mueller-Vollmer, *Reader*, 96.

[8] Mueller-Vollmer, *Reader*, 84.

reading of the text at hand.[9] And in both 'grammatical' and 'psychological' senses, one part of the text is to be illuminated by the whole, and vice versa.[10]

Part-Whole Hermeneutical Circles and Reading Luke 15:11–32

Nolland's argument about the interpretation of Luke 15:11–32 deploys the version of the hermeneutical circle that reflects a dialectical process of understanding between perceiving the parts and divining the whole. This emerges in vigorous fashion. Nolland argues, in effect, that to read the parable with Holgate on the basis of a Hellenistic *topos* is to bring to bear the 'whole' of the language current in the first century upon the 'part' of this particular text, but in an inadmissible manner. It is inadmissible, Nolland believes, because it appears to ignore on one side the more immediate 'whole' of Luke's Gospel, which suggests the probability of a Godward reference in the parable together with the absence of economic matters as a prime concern in it; and at the same time on the other side it arguably ignores the 'part' of the parable itself, whose *prima facie* subject is family division and reconciliation, not wealth and poverty.

In this fundamental structure and thrust of his argument I find Nolland very convincing. He would no doubt agree with Schleiermacher that the task of part-whole comparison on the various levels is infinite, since a complete knowledge of the language and authors of a period remains unattainable. Anything, therefore, approaching a full appraisal of this text in its various contexts would demand a far more comprehensive marshalling of material than is possible in a short chapter. Yet Nolland has alerted us implicitly to the importance of maintaining a hierarchy in our part-whole comparisons: the immediate literary *co-text* is more important than the wider literary *context* (especially when the 'wider one' is represented by such a small *exemplum* as the one offered by Holgate). Such a hierarchy commends itself on both literary and theological-canonical grounds: it respects the unity of the text as we find it.

However, in another respect I should like to probe Nolland's deployment of this part-whole circle more critically. One might ask whether Nolland has been *too selective in setting Luke 15:11–32 within the wider 'whole' of Lukan parables, rather than within the 'whole' of the entire gospel.* Does this not tend to predetermine the outcome of the argument too much in the directions that he

---

[9] Mueller-Vollmer, *Reader*, 95. In this case Schleiermacher does not go on explicitly to outline the opposite arc of the circle, viz. that the text at hand should contribute to our understanding of the author's own style and the 'state of the genre' at the time, but this may be assumed as a logical corollary in the light of his wider argument.

[10] Mueller-Vollmer, *Reader*, 85, 94.

favours, namely, that of excluding a direct concern with wealth and poverty from the Prodigal parable?

If parables are indeed suggestive, figurative texts which mean more than they explicitly say, which Nolland everywhere assumes, then one must draw that 'something more' from another source; and the natural source to look to is the co-text of the rest of the gospel, *especially in its less obviously 'figurative' parts*. Since Luke's concern with matters of wealth and poverty is well documented, would it not be reasonable to be at least inclined to read this *into* parables rather than to exclude it from them? I have argued elsewhere in more detail that the longer narrative parables peculiar to Luke are tightly woven into his surrounding narrative in ways that make them mutually interpretative in rich, even luxuriant fashion.[11] It may suffice here to note the economic connotation in Luke of *bios*, 'life', 'living', 'property', which occurs in Luke 15:12, 30 with reference to the younger son's first demanding, then squandering, the family fortune. See also 8:43 (the haemorrhaging woman had spent all her 'living' on physicians) and 21:4 (the widow put all her 'living' into the treasury).[12] This does not mean that I would want to see the encouragement of a balanced economic generosity as the main purpose of the parable along the lines proposed by Holgate. I will return to this later in outlining my own understanding of the parable more fully. But the atmosphere of the gospel is more permeated with economic realities than Nolland seems to allow.

In fact, to bring the whole of the gospel into play as the matrix for interpreting this parable would *strengthen* the other aspect of Nolland's case, which is to point to the father in the parable as a figure for God. Luke 6:36 ('Be merciful, just as your Father is merciful') and 11:2 ('When you pray, say, "Father ..."') are key texts in which Jesus is depicted as portraying God as a gracious father, and if one is looking for the overall thrust of Luke's portrayal of Jesus, it would be natural to interpret the implicit language of the parable in light of the explicit language of these other sayings.

We now turn to examine Nolland's approach in the light of a more fundamental part of Schleiermacher's construal of the task, the necessity of 'divination'.

---

[11] See Wright, *Voice*, 30–61.

[12] Cf. Wright, *Voice*, 39. Even if we limit the field of comparison, with Nolland, to parables, I think more should be made of the wealth theme. The use of the same word (*diaskorpizō*) for the younger son's 'squandering' (15:13) and for that of the steward in the following parable (16:1) is highly suggestive. On links between these two parables see Donahue, *Gospel*, 167ff.

'Divination' in the Reading of Luke 15:11–32

Nolland's argument reveals the inevitable part played by *'insight'* or *'divination'* in reading texts such as the parables.[13] As 'figurative' language of a very distinctive kind, they exemplify very clearly the need not only for 'grammatical' interpretation, but also for what Schleiermacher usually terms 'psychological' interpretation. For figurative language is defined as language that is somehow out of the ordinary, or bears the stamp of individual usage as opposed to a mere dictionary-defined function. It is thus language that explicitly draws attention to the need for divination, as well as straightforward linguistic competence. We need to get a sense of how the individual writer is *using* a word or set of words. Some figurative language, of course, does make it into the dictionary; but the more widespread the usage, the less 'figurative' it is in any useful sense of that term.

As relatively lengthy 'figures', these particular configurations of words that we call the parables of Jesus, especially those couched in narrative form, say far more than a mere knowledge of the Greek language of the time, or even the Greek language of Luke's Gospel, can reveal to us. Without some insight into their distinctive individual quality our interpretation will be manifestly inadequate. They cannot be treated as mere products of a system of language. They beckon us to put into them, or to draw out of them, more than may be visible on the surface. Where that 'something else' should come from has been disputed. The danger of modern parable interpretation since Jülicher's ground-breaking work[14] has been the tendency to think in too nearly positivist ways about the task, as if one could simply read this further meaning off the surface, or bring data to bear from the wider text or cultural and literary milieu to reach 'the real meaning'. In other words, it seems that many scholars have been very happy to undertake Schleiermacher's 'grammatical' and 'comparative' programmes, but they have been uneasy about acknowledging the inevitability of the acts of 'divination' entailed along the way. One reason for this is fairly clear.[15] Jülicher's reading was bound up with a vehement rejection of 'pre-critical' readings that he saw as tainted precisely with the supposed 'insights' of their practitioners.[16] In consequence, he left himself no theoretical space for 'insight' at all, though of course in his portrayal of Jesus as a teacher of universal moral truths he was in fact exercising it vigorously.

---

[13] I have explored this issue at some length in Wright, *Voice*, passim, but esp. 1–29.
[14] *Gleichnisreden.*
[15] Other reasons may simply be lack of knowledge of Schleiermacher's work, reluctance to be associated with his wider theological agenda, or desire to keep the task of biblical interpretation within a (supposedly) more strictly 'scientific' framework. I cannot here comment on the extent to which these might be factors in the case of the influential parable commentators of the twentieth century.
[16] On this see Wright, *Voice*, 127–41.

All of this leads me to be uneasy with the manner in which Nolland asserts that the link between the father in Luke 15 and God is 'secure'.[17] For on the surface of his argument he appears to employ only what Schleiermacher called a 'comparative' method, but in fact, by necessity, he is simultaneously employing a 'divinatory' one which sees in this particular parable (and others) more than is there on the surface. He is, of course, in very good company in his specific conclusions, but to what extent is the assertion that the link between the father and God in Luke 15 is 'secure' simply the report of a majority 'insight', rather than something which can be concluded on the basis of a comparison with the other parables?

The point may be developed with reference to Nolland's comments on the parable of the Pounds in Luke 19:11–27. Nolland writes that in this parable, Jesus 'is the one who is to rule as king in the kingdom of God (cf. v. 11)'[18] and 'there is in Luke such an obvious allegorical connection with Jesus' exaltation to heaven and return that it becomes impossible to retain any real focus on money'.[19] Leaving aside for the moment the question of the focus (or lack of focus) on money, it is worth asking why this allegorical equation between Jesus and the man of noble birth appears 'obvious', at least to many interpreters. We should first note that it is the *interpreters* who are making the link, by an act of 'divination' that reads between Luke's lines.

Such 'reading between the lines' is a natural, normal, and often unreflective part of the reading process, as twentieth-century studies of narratology and reader response have surely demonstrated. However, the question is whether this is the only conceivable way of seeing the parable in Luke's context. I have argued in some detail with reference to the six uniquely Lukan narrative parables,[20] and in broader terms with reference to the narrative parables generally (including that of the Pounds),[21] that instead of the construal of these figurative texts revolving around an immediate quasi-allegorical decoding of the individual characters, we should see the stories *as a whole* as reflecting an entire 'slice of life' from a particular cultural milieu of the day. (I argue that it is Jesus' milieu, not the evangelist's, but that distinction can be left aside for the moment.) Through their shape that invites a fresh perspective upon it, I argue further that *one should not let wider, perhaps explicitly theological, ramifications obscure this thrust.*[22]

---

[17]   Nolland, 'Role', 201.

[18]   Nolland, 'Role', 183.

[19]   Nolland, 'Role', 192.

[20]   Wright, *Voice*.

[21]   *Tales*; on the Pounds, see 147–53.

[22]   I do not, of course, claim complete originality here and owe much to the framework of Via, *Parables*, and Herzog, *Parables*, though I diverge quite widely from their specific interpretations.

In the case of the Pounds parable, one could certainly draw the link between the king and Jesus in view of the 'whole' of the Lukan co-text (cf. 1:32f.; 19:38, which comes soon after the parable; 23:2f., 38, 42). But if one takes the *parable* as a 'whole' into account, we find a picture of a wealthy man who is self-confessedly 'hard' (v. 22), entrusting subordinates with money with which to trade, rewarding risk-taking investment and dealing ruthlessly with the third servant's cautious attitude, and finally, on his accession to his throne, dealing brutally with rebels in a manner worthy of a victorious Roman general: 'bring them here and kill them in front of me' (v. 27). Especially in view of the probable reminder of the accession of Archelaus in 4 C.E., it seems to me at least as likely that the parable functions (even as part of Luke's reportage) as a warning to Jesus' hearers not to be beguiled by his approach to Jerusalem into thinking that he was starting a bandwagon of violent revolt, as that it speaks of Jesus' own departure and return. The latter may fit in nicely with an overall Christian theology, but it depends upon a high degree of disregard for the details of the parable (the other 'parts', if you like, or the smaller 'whole'), or at least a considerable allegorization/spiritualization of them.

If one is committed at least to a semi-allegorical reading in which Jesus is the nobleman, then the more seriously one takes the details of the parable, the more, surely, one is compelled to admit that the picture the nobleman affords is far more *unlike* the picture of Jesus' kingship than it is *like* it. One need look no further than 22:24–30 to corroborate this point. Jesus confers on his disciples a kingdom as his Father has conferred one on him, but it is about as unlike the style of the 'Gentile' kings as one could imagine. It would still be possible to read the parable with the nobleman as a figure for Jesus, but that would mean that the focus is entirely on the pattern of departure and return: the character of the 'king' and the nature of his transactions with his subordinates fall out of view as being (embarrassingly?) irrelevant. This marginalizing of details is, of course, in line with the 'one-point' approach to parable interpretation that Jülicher inaugurated, and which Dodd and Jeremias made so influential.

My main point here is not to establish the 'right' reading of this or of any other parable, but rather *to expose the complexity of what is involved* in such a quest. The history of parable interpretation down to the present surely reveals quite plainly that the interpreter needs to exercise 'divination', simply because of the perceived figurative nature of the texts. Such 'divination' takes the form of a wager about the *kind* of figure that is operative here.[23] For much of Christian history, readers took the wager that what we had was a kind of veiling, metaphorical speech, under which were concealed all sorts of rich nuggets of

---

[23] If one prefers, one could take Ricœur's language of the necessary 'guess' of the interpreter instead of Schleiermacher's 'divination' (Ricœur, *Theory*, 75–79).

truth.[24] Jülicher's wager was that the parables in their essential nature were *similes* — that is, on the lips of Jesus they would all have taken the form of an *explicit* comparison. For him there was no veiling, but rather an exposure: Jesus clearly stated what he was comparing to what.[25] Later interpreters have brought other categories to bear as a way of divining what is going on in this figurative language. For Via, the parables were 'aesthetic objects'.[26] For others, the *story* form of many parables is crucial, together with the social world they evoke. These interpreters explore the way in which the narrative *as a whole* might function as a metaphor for (say) the kingdom.[27] Bailey, while taking the cultural milieu and literary structure of the parables extremely seriously, presupposes a fundamentally theological intention and thus returns to a modified form of metaphorical-allegorical interpretation.[28] Etchells suggests that we find in the parables a *crossing* of metaphor (in which this-worldly reality refers to other-worldly) and metonymy (in which an aspect of this world evokes a wider this-worldly reality).[29] And so, no doubt, this story of interpretation will continue.

Before I clarify further my own preferred framework, let me underline the point. Interpreters have always found it necessary to bring some sort of overarching interpretative framework to bear on this parabolic language we find in the gospels. In modern times, this has been conditioned more by historical and literary concerns than by theological ones, but *it remains no less a framework brought by the interpreter for that*. The parables are being understood through a *wager* as to the *kind of text Luke would have written* and/or the *kind of speech Jesus would have uttered*. Further, in serious parable scholarship, the interpreter (or a predecessor) decides upon a particular wager, it appears, through precisely the process outlined by Schleiermacher: a process in which acts of insight into the overall purpose of the speaker/writer alternate with acts of comparison with the rest of their *oeuvre*, in an unending spiral of growing understanding. Sometimes, however, a dominant framework reveals manifest inadequacies and there is a need to challenge it, as has happened increasingly to the framework of Jülicher over the last three or more decades. When this happens, arguments about interpretation cannot be continued merely on the level of what might be

---

[24] The rather imprecise term 'allegorical' is often used as a shorthand to designate these early readings. I discuss this rich tradition in *Voice*, 62–112.

[25] Jülicher still had to face the problem of the *tertium comparationis*, the precise point at which (say) the kingdom was 'like' something else, which remains unstated in so many of the parable texts as we have them.

[26] *Parables*.

[27] See, e.g., Ricœur, 'Biblical Hermeneutics'; Scott, *Hear*.

[28] Bailey, *Poet* and *Eyes*. Cf. also Blomberg's 'several-point' approach, set out in *Interpreting*.

[29] Etchells, *Reading*.

the 'correct' understanding of individual texts: we can properly speak of a paradigm shift. A fresh wager or wagers are made and must be tested out on the more fundamental level of our grasp of the writer's or speaker's overall style or purpose.

The Hermeneutical Challenge of Double Authorship

The complexity of the process is increased considerably by the fact that we are dealing here with *both* 'writer' and 'speaker': with an author (Luke) reporting the words of another (Jesus). Schleiermacher was alert to the dynamics at work in such a case. He recognized that in our use of grammatical aids to help us understand a text, we are in fact making use of 'another author, and so all of the rules of interpretation apply here as well'.[30] The reader has to go through the hermeneutical process twice. How much more must this be the case when dealing not with mere grammatical aids, but with the writer of a gospel. In this respect, I wonder if Nolland's argument regarding the parable of the Prodigal Son falls between two stools.

On the one hand, although he is arguing overtly on the level of Luke's work rather than Jesus', the case he advances is based, as we have seen, not on the gospel as a whole but on reported parables of Jesus from the gospel. There is no explicit insight offered as to the overall purpose of Luke within which his reading (or any reading) might be validated. On the other hand, he offers no explicit framework within which we may make sense of such parabolic language itself, assumed to be that of Jesus (if indeed a single, simple framework would do for the variety of cases he assembles – which I doubt). One feels, in other words, that *some necessary act of 'divination' concerning the style, thrust and mode of Jesus' entire corpus of speech* (and therefore his life from which it emerges) *is missing too*. I am not suggesting in the least that no such insights into the overall purpose of Luke, or of the historical Jesus, *inform* Nolland's reading of the texts. Simply, they do not play the explicit part in this argument that I think they need to do.

Thus, for example, if we perceive that a concern with wealth and possessions plays a very important part in Luke's *oeuvre*, we will be more ready to see it, though not necessarily as the dominant theme, in a parable such as that of the Prodigal Son, as I have already suggested. If we perceive that Jesus tells stories which make sense as evoking a meaning and message through their entire configuration, without the necessity for (at least quasi-) allegorical decoding of individual figures within them, we may not be inclined to see a reference to God as Father as a primary function of a parable such as this, even though we may allow it as an echo.

---

[30] Mueller-Vollmer, *Reader*, 90.

Implicit in all of this is the desirability of interpreting such texts on a variety of levels, and of clearly stating which level we are addressing at any one time, insofar as they are distinguishable, or which combination we are addressing, insofar as they are not. Thus we may want to read the text as a part of Jesus' speaking, as a segment of Luke's writing, as a part of the canon of Scripture, as an expression of central themes in Christian theology, and so on. This again is why Nolland's conclusion about the 'security' of a particular reading leaves me dissatisfied.

Although he makes it reasonably clear that he is writing about Luke, not Jesus, one can argue that it is necessary to write of the original speaker even when one's main focus is the gospel writer. This is a case of difficulty in distinguishing between levels. In other words, one upshot of over two centuries of historical scholarship on the gospels is that we should be content *neither* with stripping away the supposed layers of accretion in the interests of finding the *ipsissima verba* (or even the *ipsissima vox*) of Jesus – an inevitably speculative and ultimately fruitless quest, *nor* with reading the text purely as the work of Luke (or one of the other evangelists) – an approach which oddly effaces the prime human impulse behind the gospels, that of Jesus himself. Whether one's pathway thereafter is a primarily historical one (as with J.D.G. Dunn's notion of the 'impact' of Jesus on his followers and hence on the gospel texts) or a more literary/deconstructive one (highlighting the ungraspable 'traces' of human authorship within the text, as with Derrida and those influenced by him) will depend on one's particular concerns and interests as an interpreter. Putting it more boldly, I believe we are at a point where the distinction between writer and prior speaker must, in practical terms, be deconstructed – however one chooses to proceed from that point onwards.

In fact I think Nolland's argument reflects this breakdown of distinction between Luke and Jesus. In his section on the assumed values of the recipients of the parables, in particular Luke 15:11–32 and 18:9–14, he writes interchangeably of 'hearers' and 'readers'. This may reflect the fact that the gospel would originally have been read out loud in the assemblies, but it seems also to reflect a sense that the way in which the parable seems to have 'worked' in Luke's context is essentially continuous with the way in which it 'worked' in Jesus' context. Certainly Nolland draws no distinction between a putative setting in Palestine during Jesus' ministry, and a Greco-Roman one further afield for Luke. I think, in fact, he is right to assume such continuity. One finds in Luke's parable texts such as the Prodigal Son a literary form that is clearly imaginable as a spoken rhetorical form on the lips of Jesus, as well as an integrated part of Luke's narrative rhetoric. Given that it is so imaginable, and without adopting any of the historical-critical apparatus for discerning the *ipsissima verba*, it would be odd to erase such a trace from one's interpretation in the interests of scholarly caution or rectitude, or faith-inspired commitment to a 'canonical' as opposed to a 'historical' Jesus.

Hearers and Readers

Nolland's account of the 'reader/hearer values' assumed by the Prodigal Son parable is subtle and persuasive. I especially welcome the balance he offers to readings that have overemphasized the 'subversive' quality of the parables. In stressing that for a parable to 'work' it must appeal to *something* in the recipients' value system, even if it then pushes them further than habits with which they have become over-comfortable, he offers a valuable corrective to the line of thought that sees the parables as fundamentally challenging their recipients' worldview, even dislocating all possible worldviews.[31] One of the special advantages of his reading is that he allows us to see the prodigal's elder brother (and the Pharisee in Luke 18:9–14) as a character who might arouse genuine sympathy, rather than as the stereotypical 'bad guy'. This helps us to see the story as realistic, maintains its tension and helps us to imagine it as genuinely persuasive in its original setting, although not necessarily to all of its hearers.

All the same, reading/hearing the story like this seems to work as well for a putative setting in the ministry of Jesus as it does for its co-text in Luke's Gospel – or even better. For it enables the parable to stand out, as it were, from the flatness of the page in its three-dimensional rhetoric. (Indeed, I wonder if this is what Nolland actually has in mind.) Given that this seems to be the case, I would wish to go a little further than Nolland and probe this uneasy distinction between Luke and Jesus a bit more. If we are to imagine the story being told on the lips of Jesus, why should we assume that he intended the father to represent God, and what place might the theme of money have in the story?

Here I must introduce a little more fully my own wager about Jesus' longer narrative parables: that they functioned, in their original form (still clearly discernible in their gospel settings) as synecdoche, namely, the figure of speech in which a part stands for the whole, or vice versa.[32] They offer 'slices of life' which make an implied suggestion about 'the way things might be' on a much broader canvas. In their *indicative* form they narrate the presence of God's kingdom in surprising, yet graspable, ways, with implied *imperative* corollaries, changes of attitude or action looked for in the hearers. In this sense, to see a metaphorical or allegorical reference in one or more of the characters may

---

[31] Exemplified in Crossan's statement that in the parables Jesus announces God as the one who 'shatters world, this one and any other before or after it' (*Parables*, 27). On this see Wright, *Voice*, 201f.

[32] See Wright, *Voice*, 182–226.

blunt our sense of the parable's rhetorical power, which depends on the parable's *realism* in depicting an aspect of the world in which Jesus and his hearers
lived. Nolland acknowledges this realism in the Prodigal Son parable, which as
he rightly says focuses on the tension between concerns of justice and family
reconciliation.[33] It seems to me to break up this realism if one assumes either in
the speaker or his hearers an immediate reference of the father to God. The
appeal is made precisely on the *human* grounds of 'do you not think, in the
end, this is the better way?'. It is similar in its own way to the large posters in a
war-torn West African state depicting two people embracing, as part of a campaign to encourage reconciliation. The extent to which the father's action in
the story might have been extraordinary or, conversely, conceivable, is disputed, but this does not affect this fundamental matter of the ground of appeal.
Jesus sets before his hearers a wonderful human example of overcoming rebel-
lion and alienation through compassion and forgiveness. In such a case, I have
no doubt, he would have seen the hand of God. Yet this does not mean that the
parable is told primarily to make a revelation about God.

Such a reading allows for the full ethical challenge of the parable – in a context such as that in which Luke has very plausibly placed it. The story is 'good
news', for it presents a possibility; but it is also challenge: can you not see (Jesus
seems to say) my welcoming of the 'sinners' as analogous to the family reconciliation sought by the father in the story? *And can you not 'go and do likewise'?*[34]
This is not, indeed, primarily a challenge 'about' wealth and possessions, narrowly considered.[35]

We should be cautious about inadvertently evacuating such a story of some
of its realistic force by overlooking the details which even quite a cursory reading with socially aware eyes can pick up.[36] Thus the story revolves around a son
demanding and then squandering his share of the family fortune, the destitu-
tion that drives him to his knees, and the father's willingness to write off this
gross mishandling of funds in the interests of restored relationship. One might

---

[33] Nolland, 'Role', 204.
[34] I would want to press the links between the two parables of the Prodigal Son and the
Good Samaritan further than Nolland: *both* are 'example stories', *both* are 'good news
stories', *both* express the kingdom of God without any character having to be a direct
representation of God.
[35] As an aside, I find Nolland's frequent use of the word 'about' in discussing parable
interpretation somewhat limiting: it tends to imply that the parables have a smaller
and less rich range of signification than I think they do; and it tends to imply that they
work only on the level of ideas, not that of speech-*acts*.
[36] Similarly, I wonder if one can discount 'economic associations' from the little parables of the mustard seed and yeast quite as readily as Nolland does ('Role', 188).
Anything entailing food entails the economy, and quite pressingly so in a society
such as that of Jesus.

say that the story concerns the priority of reconciliation over against not only strict justice, but also adherence to wealth and the rage and despair which can attend its loss. In its use as an analogy with Jesus' welcome of the sinners, one might think initially that this economic association would drop out of view, yet it does not: the tax collectors were those who sought to make themselves rich at the expense of the people of the land (giving away the family silver, as it were), and there is thus an economic dimension to Jesus' welcome of them. But in any case (as I know John Nolland would agree), the gospel parables can say more than their immediate co-text on its own requires or suggests: we would not have to put on one side as irrelevant any elements of the Prodigal Son story which did not seem directly to apply to the setting announced in Luke 15:1, 2.

This 'wager' about the narrative parables, and this one in particular, goes against the construal of Jülicher, who transmuted even stories like this into the rhetorical form of simile: 'As a father greets a contrite son ... so the way to the father-heart of God is always open'.[37] Jeremias followed essentially the same line of thought in emphasizing the defensive thrust of this parable and its accompanying pair in Luke 15:3–10: Jesus, in his view, was defending his own ministry on the grounds of an assertion about the character of God.[38] Undoubtedly Jesus is represented in the chapter as seeing that ministry as being in line with God's character, as the conclusions to the shorter parables make plain (vv. 7, 10).[39] But to turn the Prodigal Son parable into a simile, which is a danger of Nolland's position, though he does not go that far, is subtly but significantly to change its particular rhetorical character (and to smudge over the 'part' of a particular text in its angularity in the interests of a 'whole', neatly flattened view of the topics of Jesus' utterances). A story invites its hearers into an imagined world in which they must at least partly use their own imaginations to find their way around if they are to discover its treasures. It does not deal in bald assertions or syllogistic argument. It has impact on the emotions as well as the mind. It often (as here) leaves the conclusion at least partly open, teasing its hearers or readers into ongoing meditation.

To suggest that the primary way in which this parable works is by inviting its hearers into a realistic world so as to motivate and inspire a readjustment of their own vision of the world and behaviour within it, rather than by 'revealing' or 'arguing' something about God through the action of the father, should not entail that we set an arbitrary limitation on its resonance. Especially in an

---

[37] *Gleichnisreden,* II, 362. I give here only the core of Jülicher's long sentence.
[38] *Parables,* 128–36.
[39] We should note that, even in these shorter parables, the force of the rhetoric derives from something which takes place in human experience (the search of the shepherd and the woman); the 'just so' sayings testify to Jesus' own belief, but the images of the shepherd and the woman could do their work on the hearers, in support of Jesus' activity, without them.

oral context, stories and the words of which they are composed may trigger all kinds of associations, mundane and divine. That is the semiotic and social reality whose full implications would only be felt over a century after Schleiermacher: signs suggest other signs, potentially ad infinitum. No doubt there may have been plenty of such resonances, for both Jesus and his hearers, in the parable of the Prodigal. I simply propose that in our construal of the language purporting to come from Jesus, it is helpful to distinguish between the immediate thrust of a parable in the rhetorical shape which it possesses, and the wider echoes it might be presumed to have originally awakened, whether intentionally or not.

So much for my wager about how Jesus might have used the parable. When we consider it as a *written* figurative text within a surrounding co-text the wager will be different, although with the complexity we have noted: that the trace of another voice, the stamp of another author, keeps making its presence felt. For Luke, I have argued,[40] the longer parables appear to function as *metonymies* in relation to the gospel, which is a more technical way of saying that they act as 'the gospel in miniature'. With their narrative structure suggesting both hope and judgement, and their implied demands, they express and evoke in concrete form the good news of God's acts of salvation which for Luke embraces the entire sequence of Jesus' life and work from before birth to beyond Pentecost. In this respect, too, we do well to retain a sense of the parable *as a whole*, rather than fastening purely on individual characters or details, for it is as a small story that it represents the bigger story. But as in the case of the parables' function in the ministry of Jesus, there will of course be echoes between words, concepts, figures and characters, reverberating around the gospel, which cannot and should not be tied down or contained, but which will naturally carry less weight the more distant or strained they seem.

The Infinite Task

What do we conclude? According to Schleiermacher, the interpreter is not to rest until he or she has understood a text not only as well as, but 'even better than its author'.[41] Might we say that, in some respects, Luke indeed may have understood the parable of the Prodigal Son better than its original speaker, insofar as he is in a position to look back on the entire career of the earthly Jesus, and place it carefully within his story of that career? Thus the echoes of the action of God-in-Christ may be heard in the parable, even though its this-worldly rhetoric still makes itself felt. And when we set Luke in his entire canonical context, perhaps *we* are on the road to understanding this text even

---

[40] Wright, *Voice*, 30–61.
[41] Mueller-Vollmer, *Reader*, 83.

better than Luke, for the echo-chamber becomes suddenly vaster, and we are able to gain a sense of both the newness and the deep-rootedness of the glimpse of forgiveness it offers, and of the way in which it offers it.[42]

Therefore the question of the interpretation of a parable such as this cannot be decided *tout court* as *either single or final*. Readers who wish to plumb the depths of Scripture will be alert to the various levels we have identified, and the issue of whether and how God is figured in this parable (or wealth is at issue) will be decided partly according to which level we are talking about. For each level, individually and in combination, an act of 'divination' is required, a construal of the individuality of these parables, going hand in hand with 'comparison' in an endless spiral. As Schleiermacher observed:

> So formulated, the task is infinite, because in a statement we want to trace a past and a future which stretch into infinity. Consequently, inspiration is as much a part of this art as of any other. Inasmuch as a text does not evoke such inspiration, it is insignificant.[43]

The history of hermeneutics since Schleiermacher would offer many more categories with which to approach the task of interpreting a text like this parable, which we do not have space to explore here. The task no doubt also achieves greater nuance in some respects. For instance, Ricœur's discernment of the importance of attending to *discourse*, the actual events of speech and writing, rather than just the innate structures of language or the inner motivation of the author, would support my emphasis here on the need to 'read' Jesus and Luke in an insightful way which respects their text as a human product.[44] In criticism of Schleiermacher, his over-optimism about understanding an author through the written word is a dominant theme, and Ricœur's preference for the idea of the 'guess' as the initial act of the interpreter may seem preferable to Schleiermacher's 'divination', 'because the author's intention is beyond our reach'.[45] Nevertheless, figurative language, including parable, does seem to highlight the interpreter's need for sensitivity to the *human* trace within the text, and Ricœur himself does not wish to *exclude* the concept of intention from hermeneutics so much as to set it in dialectic with the 'exteriorization' of meaning which written discourse engenders.[46]

---

[42] I start to open up this dimension of interpretation, all too briefly, in Wright, *Voice*, 227–45.

[43] Mueller-Vollmer, *Reader*, 83.

[44] Ricœur, *Theory*.

[45] Ricœur, *Theory*, 75. But see the caveat in Wolterstorff, 'Promise', 73–75: Schleiermacher may not have been as interested in the 'psychology' of the author as has commonly been assumed.

[46] Ricœur, *Theory*, 22f.

Perhaps, however, the most important adjustment to Schleiermacher's vision of the task comes through Gadamer, with his rehabilitation of 'prejudice' and the frank recognition of the importance of tradition in our understanding. Schleiermacher recognized 'bias' as a *danger* for the interpreter,[47] taking a typically Enlightenment view of the importance of individual detachment and independence.[48] We now generally recognize not only the likelihood of some 'bias', but also our inevitable rootedness in traditions of knowledge and interpretation. That does not deprive us of all access to truth, but it does condition our approach to it. It is a long and honourable tradition within the Christian church to see the father of the Prodigal Son as an image of the Father of Jesus Christ, and for Christians that tradition, rather than an argument based on the supposed purpose of either Jesus or Luke in telling the story, or its supposed original reception, is the best grounds for doing so. As Jerome wisely said, doctrine should not be founded on the basis of a parable; but to find doctrine somehow reflected in a parable is a wholesome use of the treasure trove of Scripture. We should not be ashamed of our response to a text as Christian readers.

Yet we should not let a single response exhaust a parable's meaning. In Ricœur's words, 'The right of the reader and the right of the text converge in an important struggle that generates the whole dynamic of interpretation'.[49] Furthermore, attention to the rhetorical form in which the parable is found – in the case discussed here, the indirect story – may be particularly important as we seek a mode of *communicating* the gospel of God's kingdom today which does justice to Jesus' own methods and to the infinite richness of his words.

---

[47] Mueller-Vollmer, *Reader*, 83.
[48] See Mueller-Vollmer, *Reader*, 84: 'Various aids may be indispensable for a beginner's first steps, but an independent interpretation demands that the interpreter acquire his background knowledge through independent research'.
[49] Ricœur, *Theory*, 32.

Bibliography

Bailey, K.E., *Poet and Peasant* and *Through Peasant Eyes* (Grand Rapids: Eerdmans, combined edn, 1983)

Blomberg, C.L., *Interpreting the Parables* (Leicester: Apollos, 1990)

Crossan, J.D., *In Parables: The Challenge of the Historical Jesus* (San Francisco: Harper & Row, 1973)

Donahue, J.R., *The Gospel in Parable: Metaphor, Narrative and Theology in the Synoptic Gospels* (Philadelphia: Fortress Press, 1988)

Dodd, C.H., *The Parables of the Kingdom* (London: Nisbet, 1936)

Etchells, R., *A Reading of the Parables of Jesus* (London: Darton, Longman & Todd, 1998)

Fuchs, E., *Hermeneutik* (Tübingen: Mohr Siebeck, 4th edn, 1970)

Funk, R.W., *Language, Hermeneutic, and Word of God: The Problem of Language in the New Testament and Contemporary Theology* (New York/Evanston/London: Harper & Row, 1966)

Herzog II, W.R., *Parables as Subversive Speech: Jesus as Pedagogue of the Oppressed* (Louisville: Westminster John Knox, 1994)

Jeremias, J., *The Parables of Jesus* (trans. S.H. Hooke; London: SCM Press, rev. edn, 1963)

Jülicher, A., *Die Gleichnisreden Jesu* (2 vols.; Freiburg I.B./Leipzig/Tübingen: Mohr Siebeck, 2nd edn, 1899)

Jüngel, E., *Paulus und Jesus: Eine Untersuchung zur Präzisierung der Frage nach dem Ursprung der Christologie* (Tübingen: Mohr Siebeck, 1962)

Mueller-Vollmer, K. (ed.), *The Hermeneutics Reader: Texts of the German Tradition from the Enlightenment to the Present* (New York: Continuum, 1985)

Ricœur, P., 'Biblical Hermeneutics', *Semeia* 4 (1975), 29–145

—, *Interpretation Theory: Discourse and the Surplus of Meaning* (Fort Worth: Texas Christian University Press, 1976)

—, 'Schleiermacher's Hermeneutics', *Monist* 60.2 (1977), 181–97

Scott, B.B., *Hear then the Parable: A Commentary on the Parables of Jesus* (Minneapolis: Fortress Press, 1989)

Thiselton, A.C., *New Horizons in Hermeneutics: The Theory and Practice of Transforming Biblical Reading* (London: HarperCollins, 1992)

Via, D.O., *The Parables: Their Literary and Existential Dimension* (Philadelphia: Fortress Press, 1967)

Wilder, A.N., *Early Christian Rhetoric: The Language of the Gospel* (London: SCM Press, 1964)

Wolterstorff, N., 'The Promise of Speech-Act Theory for Biblical Interpretation', in *After Pentecost: Language and Biblical Interpretation* (ed. C. Bartholomew, C. Greene and K. Möller; SHS 2; Carlisle: Paternoster; Grand Rapids: Zondervan, 2001), 73–90

—, *Divine Discourse: Philosophical Reflections on the Claim that God Speaks* (Cambridge: Cambridge University Press, 1995), 37–129

Wright, S.I., *Tales Jesus Told: An Introduction to the Narrative Parables of Jesus* (Carlisle: Paternoster, 2002)

—, *The Voice of Jesus: Studies in the Interpretation of Six Gospel Parables* (Carlisle: Paternoster, 2000)

9

A Critical Examination of David Bosch's Missional Reading of Luke

Michael Goheen

Listening to God in the Text

The contention of this chapter is that if we want to hear what God is saying to his people when we read Luke we must employ a missional hermeneutic. Such a statement entails two bold claims that are certainly controversial within biblical studies. A faithful reading of the biblical text enables us to hear what God is saying to his people; that is, hermeneutics and God's address are two sides of the same coin. Moreover, mission is central to a faithful hermeneutic. Mission is not just one of the many things Luke talks about, but it undergirds and shapes the text so that to read Luke in a non-missional way is to misread Luke and misunderstand what God is saying.

On the first claim, Craig Bartholomew says, 'Hermeneutics is a sophisticated word for knowing better how to listen to the text so as to hear properly *what God is saying* to his people, at this time and in this place'.[1] Al Wolters has offered a helpful model that explores this claim. According to Wolters, one of the hallmarks of biblical scholarship in the last two centuries is the yawning chasm that has opened up between critical readings of Scripture and religiously committed readings. That is, scholarly attention to the historical, cultural and literary (and even theological) details of the text has been separated from hearing God speak today in the text. Like Bartholomew, Wolters wants to see God's speech and human interpretation as two sides of the same coin. He calls his approach 'confessional criticism'. 'Criticism' affirms that this is a scholarly analysis that recognizes all of the human dimensions of the text; 'confessional' means that Scripture is the word of God.

Wolters distinguishes nine levels of biblical interpretation: textual criticism which establishes the text; lexicography which determines the meaning of the

---

[1] Quoted by Wolfert, 'From Ivory Tower to Parish Ministry', 18 (emphasis mine).

words; syntax which resolves the syntactical relation between the words; diachronic literary analysis which traces the prehistory of the canonical text as it stands; synchronic literary analysis which deals with the final form of the text viewed as literature; historical analysis which examines the original historical context; ideological criticism which probes the significance of an author's social location; redemptive-historical analysis which looks at the text in light of the overarching story that binds the canon together and find its centre in Jesus Christ; and confessional discernment which 'has to do with the basic belief that God speaks in the Bible, that he conveys a message to believers of all ages by means of the Scriptures'.[2] The relationship between these levels moves in two directions: in a bottom-up relationship, the lower levels are foundational for the higher levels. I have given them in a bottom-up order. While these various levels of criticism are necessary to hear what God is saying, it would be reductionistic to limit biblical interpretation to them. In a top-down relationship, the upper levels will shape the lower levels. On the one hand, lexicography, syntax, diachronic and synchronic literary analysis, historical, ideological and redemptive-historical analysis are all prerequisites for hearing God speak. On the other hand, our theological assumptions will be formative for the levels below. For Wolters, good hermeneutics involves numerous levels, and it is precisely through good hermeneutics that we can hear what God is saying in the text.

Expanding on the level that Wolters calls 'redemptive-historical analysis' enables us to clarify the second claim: mission is central to biblical interpretation. Since the Bible is a 'grand narrative which climaxes in Jesus Christ', a redemptive-historical reading seeks to understand all the subordinate parts within the whole metanarrative and in relation to its centre.[3] Thus Wolters rightly calls for a christocentric reading of Scripture. Christopher Wright develops this: a redemptive-historical interpretation is not only messianic, but missional.[4] Referring to Luke 24:45–47,[5] Wright argues that Jesus himself articulates a hermeneutic that is both christocentric and missional when he elaborates 'what is written' in the Old Testament story in terms of its centre and climax in Jesus and the mission of the church to the world.

---

[2] Wolters, 'Confessional Criticism', 103.
[3] Wolters, 'Confessional Criticism', 102.
[4] 'Down through the centuries, it would be fair to say, Christians have been good at their messianic reading of the Old Testament, but inadequate (and sometimes utterly blind) in their missional reading of it … a messianic reading of the Old Testament has to flow onto a missional reading' (Wright, 'Mission as a Matrix', 108).
[5] Then he opened their minds so they could understand the Scriptures. He told them, 'This is what is written: The Christ will suffer and rise from the dead on the third day, and repentance and forgiveness of sins will be preached in his name to all nations, beginning at Jerusalem (Lk. 24:45–47).

He [Jesus] seems to be saying that the whole of the Scriptures (which we now know as the Old Testament), finds its focus and fulfilment *both* in the life and death and resurrection of Israel's Messiah *and* in the mission to all nations, which flows out from that event. Luke tells us that with these words Jesus "opened their minds so they could understand the Scriptures", or, as we might put it, he was setting their hermeneutical orientation and agenda. The proper way for disciples of the crucified and risen Jesus to read their Scriptures is from a perspective that is both *messianic* and *missional.*[6]

Since the term 'mission', and its more recent adjectival equivalent 'missional', carry so much mistaken semantic weight, we must briefly elaborate on their meaning. Mission is often understood to refer to something the church does to bring the gospel to other parts of the world or to unbelievers. While evangelism, service projects, church planting, cross-cultural missions and the like are certainly parts of the missional calling of the church, a missional hermeneutic assumes a much broader and deeper understanding of mission. Wright captures it in the following words: 'In short, a missional hermeneutic proceeds from the assumption that the whole Bible renders to us the story of God's mission through God's people in their engagement with God's world for the sake of the whole of God's creation.'[7]

This understanding of mission focuses attention on a number of assumptions that are important for a missional hermeneutic. First, the Bible tells one unfolding story of redemption. All characters and parts of this story must be understood in terms of this unified narrative plot line.[8] Thus to rightly understand God, his people and their relationship to the world one must see how each is rendered in this story. Second, this story is about God's mission to restore the creation from sin. Mission is used here in the general sense of a 'long-term purpose or goal that is to be achieved through proximate objective and planned actions'.[9] Mission is first of all about what God is doing for the renewal of his creation; God's mission is theologically prior to any talk about the mission of God's people. Third, God carries out his redemptive purposes by choosing a community to partner with him in his redemptive work. The mission of God's people must be understood in terms of participation, at God's calling and command, in God's own mission to the world. Fourth, the existence of God's people is for the sake of the world. The community God has chosen exists to bring God's saving love and power to a world under the sway of sin. This mission defines their identity and role in the world.

---

[6] Wright, 'Mission as a Matrix', 107.

[7] Wright, 'Mission as a Matrix', 122.

[8] This is not to say that the Bible gives us a tidy and simple plot or story. Cf. Bauckham, *Bible and Mission*, 92–93.

[9] Wright, 'Mission as a Matrix', 104.

Another way of saying this is to say that in the biblical story we see God's mission, Israel's mission, Jesus' mission and the church's mission closely connected. God's mission is to redeem the world from sin. God chooses Israel to be a light to the nations and a channel of God's redemption to the world. When Israel fails in her task, Jesus takes up and successfully accomplishes that mission. He gathers a renewed Israel and sends them to continue the mission he has begun. This mission defines the existence of the church until Christ returns. The Bible, then, is a product of and witness to this mission.[10] Thus a missional understanding becomes a 'central hermeneutical key' by which we interpret any part of Scripture.[11]

Yet, in biblical studies, mission has not been a central category for interpretation. Perhaps this highlights the distorting presuppositions that shape biblical scholarship. Our reading of texts is shaped by what Gadamer refers to as anticipatory fore-structures or 'prejudices' that orient our interpretation. These interpretive categories allow us to enter into dialogue and interpret the text, which is likewise engaged with the self-same matter at hand. As Lash puts it:

> If the questions to which ancient authors sought to respond in terms available to them within their cultural horizons are to be 'heard' today with something like their original force and urgency, they have first to be 'heard' as questions that challenge us with comparable seriousness. And if they are to be thus heard, they must first be articulated in terms available to us within *our* cultural horizons. There is thus a sense in which the articulation of what the text might 'mean' today, is a necessary condition of hearing what that text 'originally meant.'[12]

The problem is that our 'missional anticipatory structures' have been closed by a non-missionary self-understanding making us unaware of the centrality of mission in the Scriptures. In an article written almost thirty years ago Elisabeth Schüssler Fiorenza states this clearly:

> Exegetical inquiry often depends upon the theological and cultural presuppositions with which it approaches its texts. Historical scholarship therefore judges the past from the perspective of its own concepts and values. Since for various reasons religious propaganda, mission, and apologetics are not very fashionable topics in the

---

[10] Wright, 'Mission as a Matrix', 103, 120. Wright offers a helpful way of making the point that mission is central to the biblical story. We can speak of a biblical basis for mission but just as meaningfully speak of a missional basis for the Bible. We could not say that about work or marriage. For example, we can speak of a biblical basis for marriage but not of a marital basis for the Bible (106).

[11] Wright, 'Mission as a Matrix', 108. See the whole article by Wright for an excellent articulation of a missional hermeneutic.

[12] Lash, 'What Might Martyrdom Mean?', 17–18.

contemporary religious scene, these issues have also been widely neglected in New Testament scholarship.[13]

Today we are moving into a changed setting. Our culture is increasingly less influenced by the gospel; the church has lost its place of privilege and is pushed to the margins. Consequently, there is growing in the Western church a 'raised consciousness of mission'.[14] Can this new setting re-open our 'missional antici-patory structures'?[15] Can the work of contemporary missiology pose questions to the biblical text that will help recover our understanding of the essential mis-sionary thrust of Scripture? Specifically, what would a missional reading of Luke look like? We will consider answers to these questions, especially by examining David Bosch's reading of Luke.

A number of studies on the Bible and mission that also treat Luke have appeared in recent years,[16] but this essay engages David Bosch for several rea-sons. First, Bosch must be considered one of the leading missiologists of the latter part of the twentieth century. He taught missiology at the University of South Africa until his untimely death in 1992. His book *Transforming Mission* is widely considered to be the most important book published in mission studies in the last half of the twentieth century. Second, he was originally trained as a New Testament scholar and maintained his interest in biblical studies through-out his life. His doctoral work was completed under Oscar Cullman.[17] Of *Transforming Mission* New Testament scholar J.G. Du Plessis notes that his 'ex-tensive bibliography leaves the professional exegete somewhat astounded at the range of his biblical scholarship' and that he must be 'reckoned as a formida-ble exegete with a comprehensive and penetrating knowledge of trends in bib-lical scholarship'.[18] Third, throughout his career he maintained a vital interest

---

[13] Fiorenza, 'Miracles, Mission, and Apologetics', 1.

[14] LeGrand, *Unity and Plurality*, xiv.

[15] In his 2003 Epworth Institute lectures entitled 'Recovering Mission-Church: Reframing Ecclesiology in Luke-Acts', Joel Green speaks of a missional 'reframing': 'where we stand helps to direct our gaze and influences what we see in Scripture. With the image of "reframing" I want to call to our attention the way picture frames draw out different emphases in the pictures they hold. Similarly, even if the essential nature of the church has not changed, new frames bring to the forefront of our thinking and practices fresh emphases. If we take seriously the missional orientation of the work of Jesus and his followers as these are narrated in the Gospel of Luke and Acts of the Apostles, what do we see?'

[16] Senior and Stuhlmueller, *Biblical Foundations;* Larkin and Williams, *Mission in the New Testament;* Köstenberger and O'Brien, *Salvation to the Ends of the Earth;* Nissen, *New Testament and Mission.*

[17] Cf. Bosch, *Die Heidenmission in der Zukunftsschau Jesu.*

[18] Du Plessis, 'For Reasons of the Heart', 76.

in exploring the relationship between biblical studies and mission. In the process he has provided significant foundational hermeneutical reflection on the use of the Bible for mission. Besides a number of papers on the subject, the first section of his magnum opus treats New Testament models of mission. After reflecting on the New Testament as a missionary document he explicates the contributions of Matthew, Luke-Acts, and Paul to mission.[19] The remainder of this chapter will examine critically Bosch's missional reading of Luke.

Bosch's Missional and Critical Hermeneutic

Bosch's hermeneutical approach can be seen against the backdrop of several contrasts he observes between the way biblical and mission scholars approached Scripture during the 1980s and early 1990s. The first contrast concerns the *historical conditioning* of the biblical text: what is the relation between the ancient text and the contemporary situation? Biblical scholars oriented by the spirit of the Enlightenment insist on an uncommitted approach to Scripture and in turn produce a 'distancing effect' by which the text becomes a strange object to be examined and dissected rather than heard and obeyed.[20] Consequently, biblical scholars are reticent to draw any kind of direct connection between the text and our situation. Thus they 'frequently fail to show whether, and, if so, how, the Bible can be of significance to the church-in-mission and how, if at all, a connection between the biblical evidence and the contemporary missionary scene can be made'.[21] By contrast missiologists, seeking contemporary relevance, frequently fail to respect the cultural distance between text and context and thus read their own concerns back into the biblical text. Sometimes they are guilty of 'simplistic or obvious moves' from the New Testament to our missionary setting in an attempt to make a direct application of Scripture to the present situation.

Not only do biblical scholars emphasize the historical conditioning of the text, they also stress the tremendous literary, theological and semantic *diversity* of the New Testament record. Thus biblical scholarship has become a highly specialized science in which biblical scholars seldom look beyond their own fields of competence. Missiologists, on the other hand, tend to overlook this rich diversity and reduce their biblical foundation for mission to a single word, idea or text as the unifying hermeneutical framework for approaching Scripture.[22]

---

[19] Bosch, *Transforming Mission*, 15–178.
[20] Bosch, 'Toward a Hermeneutic', 72.
[21] Bosch, 'Mission in Biblical Perspective', 532; 'Toward a Hermeneutic', 66.
[22] Has Bosch characterized both biblical scholarship and missiology in ways that give the impression that they are more unified than they are? Does not biblical

To move beyond these problems Bosch takes his cue from a shift he sees taking place in biblical scholarship from the Enlightenment paradigm to a postmodern paradigm.[23] To understand the text one must be interested not only in its pre-history and *Sitz im Leben*, but also in its post-history – not only in what it originally meant, but also in what it means today. Bosch follows Gadamer, who argues that the application of a text is important for properly interpreting that text. Interpretation does not mean seeking to escape our historical horizon – this is both undesirable and impossible. Understanding occurs when our present horizon meets or fuses with the horizon of the text.

There is no simple direct line between the ancient text and our contemporary situation. To establish a direct relationship between the language of the text and our situation is to risk 'concordism', which 'equates the social groups and forces within first-century Palestine with those of our own time'.[24] The historical, cultural and social gaps are such that there can be no 'simplistic or obvious moves from the Bible to the contemporary missional practices'.[25] Rather, we bring our missionary context into dialogue with the original text and seek to shape practices that are 'consonant' but not identical with that text.[26] We hold simultaneously the constancy of the meaning of the text and the contingency of that meaning for various circumstances. The biblical text remains the firm point of orientation, but understanding it is a creative process. Biblical scholarship and the historical-critical method are essential in taking the 'pastness' of the biblical text seriously; one may not read the past anachronistically. Yet a faithful reading of the Bible cannot end there.

Bosch expresses this not only with the notion of 'consonance', but also in terms of a historical 'logic'. He is fond of quoting Hugo Echegaray:[27] 'Jesus did

---

scholarship present more of a 'diverse, if not hopelessly fragmented and feuding front' (Du Plessis, 'For Reasons of the Heart', 80)? Are there not a growing number of works from mission studies sensitive to the historically conditioned and diverse nature of the NT record?

[23] It is intriguing to note that Bosch's use of biblical scholarship does not seem to reflect this emphasis: 'it is striking that he exclusively uses exegetical material from the historical-critical tradition or related disciplines. The vast mass of material produced in recent years in NT studies which make use of the literary or textual communicative approaches (especially in the United States of America) is not taken into account at all' (Du Plessis, 'For Reasons of the Heart', 80).

[24] Guttierez, quoted in Bosch *Transforming Mission*, 22–23.

[25] Brueggeman, 'Bible and Mission', 408. Cf. Bosch, 'Toward a Hermeneutic', 77.

[26] Bosch, 'Toward a Hermeneutic', 75–76.

[27] Bosch references pp. xv–xvi of Echegaray's *Practice of Jesus*, which is in fact Guttierrez's quote of Echegaray. Echegaray's comment is found on page 94 of the same book. Bosch paraphrases Echegaray in various ways; I have provided the original quote.

not set up a rigid model for action but, rather, inspired his disciples to prolong the logic of his own action in a creative way amid the new and different historical circumstances in which the community would have to proclaim the gospel of the kingdom in word and deed'.[28] The New Testament authors carefully retained the traditions about Jesus but modified them to meet new historical circumstances and missionary settings. Likewise, our interpretation of the New Testament text is an attempt to read the past to speak to the present, to dialogue with the text in terms of our contemporary missional situation.

Bosch terms the approach he advocates 'critical hermeneutics'[29] – a term he borrows from D.T. Nel[30] but whose content is indebted to Ben Meyer.[31] The key concept for this hermeneutical approach is 'self-definition'.[32] Critical hermeneutics seeks a view from within the community by inquiring into the self-definition of that community. The approach 'requires an interaction between the self-definition of early Christian authors and actors and the self-definition of today's believers who wish to be inspired and guided by those early witnesses'.[33] How did the early church understand itself? How do we understand ourselves? How does the interaction between those self-definitions affect our view of mission?

According to Bosch, the early church's self-definition was thoroughly missionary.[34] The mission of the early church was prompted and motivated by a new self-definition. It was this *new* self-definition, arising from their understanding of the self-definition of Jesus, that compelled them to be involved in a missionary outreach to the world. This missionary self-understanding and involvement in mission on the part of the authors who gave birth to the New Testament means that approaching the Bible from the vantage point of mission will lead to the centre of its message. Thus Bosch follows those who believe that mission is central to the New Testament. Martin Hengel sees the history and theology of the early church as essentially mission history and mission theology.[35] Heinrich Kasting says that, in the early church, mission was 'a

---

[28] Bosch, 'Toward a Hermeneutic', 76; *Transforming Mission*, 21, 34; 'Reflections', 179.

[29] Bosch, *Transforming Mission*, 23.

[30] Nel, 'Kritiese Hermeneutiek'.

[31] Meyer, *Early Christians*.

[32] Meyer argues that it was a changing self-definition that led to launching the mission to the Gentiles. Self-definition, according to Meyer, has three moments: horizons, self-understanding and self-shaping. One's self-understanding is shaped within a certain field of vision or historical horizon and leads to self-shaping, the intentional drive to live in harmony with that self-understanding (*Early Christians*, 26–28).

[33] Bosch, *Transforming Mission*, 23.

[34] Bosch, *Transforming Mission*, 41.

[35] Hengel, 'Origins of the Christian Mission', 53.

fundamental expression of the life of the church'.[36] Martin Kähler avers that mission is 'the mother of theology': the New Testament record is the product of a missionary encounter between the early church and the world.[37] It is from within this missional self-understanding that the New Testament authors interpret the ministry of Jesus to give direction to their own missionary calling. Understanding our missionary calling from the standpoint of the gospels will mean a dialogue between our self-definition and this missionary self-definition of the early church, testing continually whether our self-definition corresponds to, or is consonant with, that of the first witnesses.

There are a diversity of understandings of mission among the first witnesses of the New Testament: 'the New Testament does not reflect a uniform view of mission but, rather, a variety of "theologies of mission"'.[38] No single overarching term for mission can be found in the New Testament. Each author interprets the mission of Jesus from within the situation of his own missionary setting. Yet Bosch speaks of a single paradigm of the early church that underlies these various theologies of mission. Within each book we find different expressions, 'sub-paradigms', of this one paradigm. Luke, Matthew and Paul all interpret mission in different ways in their particular contexts according to differing historical circumstances and self-definitions, but they all share fundamental assumptions about mission that are rooted in their understanding of Jesus and his mission. Before looking at Luke's unique contribution to the early church paradigm of mission, we need to consider what it is that he shares with the other gospels. More specifically, what is the missionary thrust of Jesus' life that shaped the early church's missionary existence?

Missionary Thrust of Jesus and the Missionary Paradigm of the Early Church

The missionary paradigm of the early church was rooted in the person and work of Jesus. If we explore what Bosch refers to as the self-definition of early Christians 'we will be forced to ask about the self-definition of *Jesus*', since the mission of the early church is 'moored to Jesus' person and ministry'.[39] Jesus is the primal missionary, and the ultimate basis for Christian mission lies in his person and work. Bosch explores five features of what he terms 'the missionary thrust' of Jesus' person and work that shape the early church paradigm of mission and thus are common to all gospels.

---

[36] Kasting, *Die Anfänge*, 127.
[37] Kähler, *Schriften zur Christologie*, 190.
[38] Bosch, *Transforming Mission*, 16.
[39] Bosch, *Transforming Mission*, 24.

The first feature is his all-inclusive mission to Israel. The ministry of Jesus must be understood in the context of a struggle for the true Israel. What distinguished Jesus was his resolute stance against sectarianism. His ministry was to *all* Israel: 'There undoubtedly is a difference between Jesus and the Jewish religious groups of his time, between his self-definition and theirs. All of them ... concern themselves with the salvation of only a *remnant* of Israel. Jesus' mission is to *all* Israel.' [40] Jesus consistently challenged all attitudes, practices and structures that restricted or excluded any from membership in the Israelite community. Jesus turns to people who have been marginalized from Israel on cultic, ritualistic, moral, religious and political grounds.

If Jesus restricted his mission to the reconstitution of Israel, why, asks Bosch, is there so much in the gospels that nourishes the idea that the covenant will reach beyond the Jews? The primary inspiration for this thrust 'could only have been the provocative, boundary-breaking nature of Jesus' own ministry'. [41] There is a natural logic that moves from this boundary-breaking mission within Israel to the mission to the Gentiles as the 'fundamental missionary dimension of Jesus' earthly ministry'. [42]

The second feature is Jesus' understanding of the reign of God. Central to his missionary self-understanding are two characteristics of Jesus' understanding of God's reign that fundamentally differ from that of his contemporaries. In the first place, God's reign is both future and already present. Since it is present, God's power to heal and save has flowed into history. Since it is future, the counter-forces remain a reality. And so, secondly, the conviction that God's reign has come impels Jesus to launch an all-out attack on evil in all its manifestations because 'God's reign arrives wherever Jesus overcomes the power of evil'. [43] Thus Jesus erects signs of healing and salvation that point to the presence of the kingdom. Again we see the missionary thrust of Jesus' ministry. His ministry inspires us to prolong the logic of his mission. Since God's reign has *already* come, it *will* come. God's reign is both gift and promise, celebration and anticipation. The church's mission is to live in the tension of the already-but-not-yet so that 'something of the "not yet" may take shape in the here and now'. [44] Thus the church, like Jesus, erects signs of God's reign; it commits itself to attack evil in its manifestations and 'to initiate, here and now, approximations and anticipations of God's reign', especially in the life of the church. [45] The church's communal life itself will be a sign to the coming kingdom, a people in whom

---

[40] Bosch, *Transforming Mission*, 26 (italics his). Here Bosch is dependant on the analysis of Senior and Stuhlmueller, *Biblical Foundations*, 154.

[41] Bosch, *Transforming Mission*, 30.

[42] Bosch, *Transforming Mission*, 30.

[43] Bosch, *Transforming Mission*, 32.

[44] Bosch, 'How My Mind Has Changed', 9.

[45] Bosch, *Transforming Mission*, 35.

something of the 'not yet' is in evidence.[46] As sign the church will embody new relationships that point to the love and justice of the kingdom. As such it will be a 'radically revolutionary movement' providing an attractive alternative.[47]

Jesus' attitude toward the *Torah* is the third feature of the missionary thrust of his work. For centuries the Torah marked off and distinguished the people of God. In contrast to his contemporaries, Jesus loosens the connection between God's people and the Torah. He attacks the hypocrisy of those who embrace the authority of the Torah yet do not obey it; he radicalizes the law in an unparalleled manner; and he abrogates certain aspects of the law.[48] Now the reign of God, and not the Torah, is the decisive centre for the people of God. The missionary thrust of this attitude to the Torah is found in the basis it provides for the outreach to Gentiles that issues in a 'Torah-free self-definition of Gentile Christianity'.[49] Now the covenant community can take root and embody salvation in all cultures.

A fourth feature is Jesus' relationship with his disciples. The announcement of the gospel leads to the calling of the first disciples. From the beginning there is an explicit missionary purpose in their call: 'The calling of the disciples is a call to follow Jesus and a being set aside for missionary activities. Calling, discipleship, and mission belong together.'[50] This missionary identity holds 'not only for those who would walk with Jesus but also for those who would respond to this call after Easter'.[51] Jesus' understanding of discipleship differed in fundamental ways from his contemporaries, but perhaps what stands out is what they were called to become disciples for. It was 'to be with him' and 'to be sent out to preach and have authority to cast out demons' (Mark 3:14f.). 'Following Jesus or being with him, and sharing in his mission thus belong together.'[52] Jesus gives the disciples the authority to do his work (Lk. 9:1–9). They become the vanguard of the messianic people of the end time. Those who would follow the original disciples also appropriated the term disciples to themselves, and so they took up that same calling and relationship to Jesus. Thus Jesus' ministry issued in a disciple-community marked by participation in his mission, and this carried forward into the early church.

Participation in the mission of Jesus is not merely a matter of specific activities that define the church. Mission is also the social embodiment of the good news of the kingdom in a community. Mission is the manifestation of salvation as seen in renewed relationships in a renewed community. Thus the attempt to

---

[46] Bosch, *Transforming Mission*, 374–76.

[47] Bosch, *Transforming Mission*, 47–49.

[48] Bosch, *Transforming Mission*, 35.

[49] Bosch, *Transforming Mission*, 44.

[50] Pesch, 'Berufung und Sendung', 15. Quoted in Bosch, *Transforming Mission*, 36.

[51] Bosch, *Transforming Mission*, 36.

[52] Bosch, *Transforming Mission*, 38.

comprehend various understandings of mission in the New Testament will involve an attempt to ascertain what kind of community the particular author is attempting to shape. For example, how are the communities to which Luke writes to embody the good news in their particular setting?

The missionary thrust of Jesus' resurrection is the fifth and final feature. The resurrection determines the early church's self-definition and identity. The gospels narrate the mission of Jesus from a post-Easter standpoint. The early church interprets the cross as the end of the old age and the resurrection as the beginning of the new. The missionary significance of the resurrection is threefold. The resurrection puts the seal of approval on the practice of Jesus. In fact, it is 'precisely the Easter faith that enables the early Christian community to see the practice of Jesus in a specific light – as the criterion for understanding their own situation and calling'.[53] Now their lives are to be characterized by Jesus' mission; their mission is to continue the mission of Jesus. Moreover, the resurrection and exaltation show the victory of the cross. Therefore, mission is 'the proclamation and manifestation of Jesus' all-embracing reign, which is not yet recognized and acknowledged by all but is nevertheless already a reality'.[54] Finally, the outpouring of the Spirit means that the forces of the future world are streaming into the present. Yet the counter-forces remain. Mission is a constitutive element of this eschatology: the power of God's reign is present and yet it has not arrived in full. This creative tension led the church to its missionary engagement with the world.

These five features form a paradigm of mission that the early church shared. Thus Luke holds these features in common with other New Testament writings. Luke's writing constitutes a 'sub-paradigm' of this broader understanding of mission.

Starting Points: Occasion, Acts and Luke 4:16–30

Bosch's reading of Luke begins with the occasion for the writing, Luke's connection to Acts and the fundamental significance of Luke 4:16–30.[55] Luke writes to a community in transition facing a crisis situation.[56] Following LaVerdiere and Thompson, Bosch believes that Luke wrote his gospel in the eighties for a number of Gentile communities.[57] Much water had gone under

---

[53] Bosch, *Transforming Mission*, 40

[54] Bosch, *Transforming Mission*, 40.

[55] See also Green, 'Proclaiming Repentance', who analyses Luke's understanding of mission from the standpoint of Luke 4:16–30 along with Acts 2:1–41. Green speaks of Luke 4:16–30 as the 'missionary programme' for Luke.

[56] Bosch, *Transforming Mission*, 85.

[57] LaVerdiere and Thompson, 'Communities in Transition', 582–83.

the bridge since the time of Jesus and even since the time of the missionary journeys of Paul. The church, which had begun as a renewal movement within Judaism, was by that time primarily a second-generation Gentile church. There were at least three elements that comprised their crisis: identity (Who were they? How did they relate to their Jewish roots? How did they relate to Jesus?[58]); stagnation (as a second-generation church they did not share the fervour of the first generation, and a flagging enthusiasm plagued the church); and hostility (from both Jews and pagans). In light of these new circumstances in which the community found itself, to challenge his contemporaries to form an identity and self-definition in continuity with Jesus' own, Luke returns to the tradition of Jesus. According to Bosch, Luke is concerned primarily with ecclesial formation that is rooted in, consistent with, and an extension of Jesus' mission.

Underlying Bosch's missional reading of Luke is the conviction that the 'principle manner in which Luke attempts to articulate his theology of mission is by writing not only one book, but two'.[59] Acts is not an afterthought – Luke intended from the beginning to write two books: 'the two volumes were, from the beginning, planned and written as a unity'.[60] The two books are unified in several ways that have missiological significance. In interaction with Conzelmann's seminal study on Luke,[61] Bosch articulates three connections.

First, Luke employs a *geographical* structure as a vehicle for conveying missiological meaning. In Luke, Jesus' ministry unfolds in three stages *to Jerusalem*: Galilee (4:14–9:50), journey from Galilee to Jerusalem (9:51–19:40) and final events in Jerusalem (19:41–24:53). In the tradition of the prophets, the Jews saw Jerusalem as a highly concentrated theological symbol, as the redemptive centre of the world, as the place where the Messiah would appear and where the nations would be gathered to praise God. Luke shares this view of Jerusalem with his contemporaries. Thus Luke highlights the fact that all the central events of the gospel – passion, death, resurrection, appearances, ascension – take place here. In Acts the church's mission also proceeds in three phases *from Jerusalem* (Acts 1:8) – beginning in Jerusalem (Lk. 24:47), into Samaria and the coastal plains and finally into the Roman Empire, ending with Paul's arrival at Rome. This geographical structure discloses the close 'relationship between the mission of Jesus and the mission of the church'.[62]

---

[58] '[T]he church which [Luke] represented confronted a set of conditions calling for a new formulation of Christian identity' (LaVerdiere and Thompson, 'Communities in Transition', 582).

[59] Bosch, *Transforming Mission*, 88.

[60] Bosch, *Transforming Mission*, 104.

[61] Conzelmann, *Theology of St. Luke*, 1960.

[62] Bosch, *Transforming Mission*, 89. The relationship between Jesus and the church is conceived in at least two ways for Bosch. (1) The mission of Jesus lays the *historical*

In the second place there is *redemptive-historical* significance. Conzelmann suggests that Luke introduces the idea of salvation history, which is comprised of three epochs: (1) the epoch of Israel, up to and including John the Baptist; (2) the epoch of Jesus' ministry as the middle of history (cf. the German title of his book – *Die Mitte der Zeit*); (3) the epoch of the church beginning at Pentecost. This theological interpretation of history highlights both the central significance of Christ's work as well as the close connection of the mission of the church to that work. The mission of the church continues the mission of Jesus. Or, perhaps more accurately, the exalted Christ continues his mission by the Spirit through the church (Acts 1:1). Bosch believes that Conzelmann has overstated his case and that these three periods cannot be subdivided so absolutely. While the era of the church during Luke's time differed in significant respects from the era of Jesus' ministry, they were also united in one era of the Spirit.

And this takes us to the final perspective – the *pneumatological*. In Luke, Jesus' mission begins with the coming of the Spirit (Lk. 3:21–22); in Acts the church's mission begins with the outpouring of the Spirit (Acts 2:1–13). The Spirit is prominent not only as the initiator, guide and power of the church's mission; he also empowers Jesus for his (cf. Luke 4:18; cf. Acts 10:38). The Spirit is the Spirit of mission and connects the two books. While the Spirit has only been marginally related to mission throughout the church's history, renewed study in Luke has enabled us to see the 'intrinsic missionary character of the Holy Spirit'.[63] This has implications also for the division of redemptive history: 'Luke unites the time of Jesus and the time of the church in one era of the Spirit'.[64] On the one hand, there is clearly a distinction between the epochs of Jesus and of the church. Luke realized more than any other New Testament author that he was living in a time that differed significantly from the time of Jesus' earthly mission. On the other hand, there is a close relationship between the eras. The church lives in historical continuity with the life and work of Jesus.

Various missional readings of Luke take different clues for their analysis. The text that functions as a significant clue for Bosch is Luke 4:16–30.

---

foundation for the church's mission. Luke treats Jesus' mission as 'universal in intent but incomplete in execution' while, in Acts, the church then takes up and completes that universal mission. (2) The mission of Jesus becomes a *criterion* for the church's mission. The church continues the mission of Jesus in his way.

[63] Bosch, *Transforming Mission*, 115. Likewise in *The Doctrine of the Holy Spirit,* Berkhof argues that to properly understand the Spirit, one must first see the Spirit in a mission context, not an ecclesiological or soteriological context. An older work that also highlights the connection between the Spirit and mission is von Baer, *Der Heilige Geist.*

[64] Bosch, *Transforming Mission*, 87.

Although Bosch does not derive his whole approach from this text, it is formative. One of the reasons Bosch is led to foreground this pericope is that it has replaced Matthew 28:16–20 in missiological discourse as the primary text for providing a foundation for the mission of the church. In these verses Jesus announces a 'unique and revolutionary missionary program'.[65]

The event narrated in this section takes place much later in Jesus' ministry in Mark and Matthew (Mark 6:1–6; Matt. 13:53–58), but Luke moves it up to the beginning. Further, the story is modified 'almost beyond recognition'.[66] This shows that, for Luke, the content of the story is exceptionally significant. The account is a 'preface to Jesus' entire public ministry',[67] 'a condensed version of the gospel story as a whole',[68] a 'programmatic discourse',[69] 'a sort of manifesto'[70] and 'the basis of Luke's entire gospel and a prelude to Acts'.[71]

Bosch notes three fundamental concerns of Luke's Gospel as a whole that are revealed in Jesus' inaugural sermon: the Gentile mission; the centrality of the poor in Jesus' mission; and the setting aside of vengeance.

Jew, Samaritan and Gentile

Luke is concerned to demonstrate how the Gentile mission has been motivated theologically. A number of features in Luke establish that the mission to the Gentiles is rooted in the mission of Christ. First, as we have seen, the fact that Luke writes two books and not one is significant. The connection between Luke and Acts shows that the church's mission flows from the ministry of Jesus. Specifically, while the mission of Jesus is universal in intent, it is incomplete in execution. Jesus confines himself to Israel. However, he explicitly commissions his disciple-community to move from Jerusalem to all nations. Acts narrates the disciples' mission as the historically logical continuation of Jesus' mission.

Further, within the Gospel of Luke there are three implicit references and one explicit reference to a mission beyond Israel. The infancy narratives seem to point to a mission beyond the bounds of Israel (e.g., 2:31–32; 3:6). Jesus' sermon in Nazareth also points in this direction (4:16–30). It is precisely the challenge of Jesus to their 'ethics of election' that so antagonizes the Nazareth congregation. God is not only the God of Israel but also of the Gentiles. He

[65] Harms, *Paradigms from Luke-Acts*, 49.
[66] Bosch, *Transforming Mission*, 89.
[67] Anderson, 'Broadening Horizons', 260.
[68] Dillon, 'Easter Revelation', 249.
[69] Dupont, *Salvation of the Gentiles*, 20–21.
[70] Bosch, *Transforming Mission*, 100.
[71] Bosch, *Transforming Mission*, 89, 112.

tells the story of God's grace to a Gentile woman through Elijah and to a Gentile man through Elisha (4:25–27). In fact, it appears he tells these stories to challenge the Jews with the fact that if God's offer to the Jews is refused, God's redemptive work will move to the Gentiles.

The final implicit reference to a mission that moves beyond Israel is the way Luke treats the Samaritans. Luke, unlike Mark and Matthew, narrates several stories that involve Samaritans, all of which are found in the journey section. The background for these stories is the hatred of the Jews for the Samaritans. Jesus prohibits calling down judgement on the Samaritans (9:51–56). He also speaks positively of Samaritans in his stories of the Good Samaritan (10:25–37) and the healing of the ten lepers (17:11–19).

There is also one explicit reference to the Gentile mission in Luke, and that is in Jesus' final words to his disciples (24:46–49). In this closing story of the gospel, there is no more ambiguity. The risen Christ meets his disciples and opens their minds to the redemptive-historical progression of Scripture, which will involve preaching repentance and forgiveness of sins to all nations.

Bosch is concerned that for a long time it has been 'customary among scholars to interpret Luke's two-volume work almost exclusively in terms of the Gentile mission only'.[72] However, he believes that is only part of Luke's message. In fact, Luke has an 'exceptionally positive attitude toward the Jewish people'.[73] Luke's concern, according to Bosch, is to provide a framework for the Gentile mission that shows its coordination with the Jewish mission.

Luke's 'beginning from Jerusalem' (24:47) is not just a matter of geographical fact; it carries theological substance. Jerusalem is the centre not only for the Gentile gathering, but also for a mission to Israel: 'Anyone who wanted to address all Israel had to do so in Jerusalem.'[74] The gospel is for the Jew first and then for the Gentile. This is not a matter of historical sequence or of communication strategy based on the idea that Jews were more likely to respond. Rather, the Jews have theological priority in redemptive history. The Jews must first be gathered before the Gentiles are incorporated into Israel. Further, the turn to the Gentiles is not on the basis of the rejection of the gospel by the Jews. To be sure, resistance and rejection are part of the story. However, Luke also highlights the great acceptance of the gospel by Jews (Acts 2:41; 4:4; 5:14; 6:7; 21:20). It is the combination of rejection and acceptance, more specifically the division within Israel (cf. Lk. 2:34), that leads to the Gentile mission.

[72] Bosch, *Transforming Mission*, 91.
[73] This positive attitude is seen in: (1) Luke's redaction of the tradition where he is more positive toward Israel than Matthew; (2) his use of two books to remind the Gentile Christians of their Jewish roots; and (3) his elaborating the theological significance of Israel in redemptive history.
[74] Hengel, 'Origins of the Christian Mission', 59. Quoted in Bosch, *Transforming Mission*, 94.

These issues can be properly seen when one recognizes that Luke is concerned with the restoration of the true Israel. This restoration is a matter of conversion, purification and incorporation: Many within Israel are converted to Jesus; many within Israel reject the gospel and are purged from Israel; then Gentiles are added and incorporated into the true Israel. The church is not a 'third race' but the true Israel, made up of those who are converted and now share in the Abrahamic covenant.[75]

Good News for the Poor and the Rich

Luke has an interest in the poor and other marginalized groups. Jesus opens his ministry with the words 'The Spirit of the Lord is on me, because he has anointed me to preach good news to the poor' (Lk. 4:18), and this concern continues throughout the gospel. Particular categories of people are prominent in Luke – the poor, women, tax collectors and Samaritans.[76] We have noted Luke's positive treatment of Samaritans. Likewise, Luke includes only positive references to tax collectors.[77] Jesus' association with women was a 'stunning crossing of a social and religious barrier in the patriarchal society of his day'.[78]

Closely related to his interest in the marginalized is Luke's attention to economic issues, like poverty and wealth, as seen: (1) in the material that is unique to Luke such as Mary's words in the Magnificat (1:53), Jesus' words of blessing on the poor and woe on the rich (6:20, 24), the parable of the rich fool (12:16–21), the story of the rich man and Lazarus (16:19–31) and the exemplary conduct of rich Zacchaeus (19:1–10); (2) in the way Luke edits the tradition handed on to him – for example, when John the Baptizer spells out the fruits of repentance in terms of economic relationships; and (3) in the language frequently employed by Luke to indicate need, such as πτωχός (poor), but also in the language of wealth such as πλούσιος (rich) and ὑπάρχοντα (possessions).

Bosch does not offer a novel contribution to the debate on the identity of the poor. He believes it to be primarily a social category, a 'collective term for all the disadvantaged' or 'all who experience misery'[79] like the captives, the maimed, the blind and the lepers. He sees this in the fact that Luke uses the word 'poor' to either head or conclude lists of the disadvantaged. The word describes those who have been deprived of dignity and selfhood, of sight, of voice, of health and of bread. It may also have a spiritual nuance, referring to

---

[75] Bosch, *Transforming Mission*, 96.

[76] Bosch, 'Mission in Jesus' Way', 5–7.

[77] Bosch, 'Mission in Jesus' Way', 16. Cf. Scheffler, 'Suffering in Luke's Gospel', 69.

[78] Bosch, *Transforming Mission*, 86. Cf. Senior and Stuhlmueller, *Biblical Foundations*, 261.

[79] Bosch, *Transforming Mission*, 99.

those who are devout and humble and live in utter dependence on God, but this is secondary. The term points to those on the margins – to those who have been excluded for various reasons.

Luke also spends a great deal of time talking about the rich. 'Rich' is to be understood in the context of the 'poor'. The rich are greedy, arrogant exploiters, whose life's entire orientation is the love of money. They are the insiders, the powerful in the community who are 'not rich toward God' (12:21). On such folk, Jesus pronounces his woe sayings (6:24–26). It is in light of this situation, where there are the insiders and outsiders, the poor and the rich, the marginalized and those who belonged, that Jesus announces a reversal that has come about in Jesus (1:51–53, 4:18; 6:20–26, 16:25).

Such themes are clear, but what is Luke's purpose? Two works on Luke shape Bosch's answer. A key phrase and idea he picks up from Senior and Stuhlmueller plays a significant role – 'the boundary-breaking ministry of Jesus'.[80] Jesus' ministry was inclusive, to all Israel. It is this boundary-breaking thrust of Jesus' ministry that is to be carried forward in the mission of the church. Luke is concerned for inclusion of the poor and marginalized, but also for the rich in the church. Bosch also leans heavily on the work of Schottroff and Stegemann. These authors ask about the significance of this theme in Luke. Some in church history have drawn a straight line from some texts in Luke to their own situations and have pursued poverty. Others have dismissed this theme as belonging to an age now long past. However, they argue, Luke had in view a particular situation in which there were tensions between the rich and poor. Luke tells the story of Jesus to address this tension and to foster 'solidarity between rich, respected Christians and poor, despised Christians'.[81] Jesus announces a 'reversal of the dismal fate of the dispossessed, the oppressed, and the sick by calling on the wealthy and healthy to share with those who are victims of exploitation and tragic circumstances'.[82] Luke 'wants the rich and respected to be reconciled to the message and way of life of Jesus and the disciples; he wants to motivate them to conversion that is in keeping with the social message of Jesus'.[83] Bosch develops this in a missiological way. The church is to embody eschatological salvation today so others might see. The church Luke writes to is to be a community that embodies economic justice, generosity, solidarity between rich and poor and economic repentance on the part of the rich.

Luke carries this out in a number of ways. He contrasts Zacchaeus (19:1–10) with the rich young ruler (18:18–30). The repentance of the disreputable Zacchaeus was demonstrated when he gave half of his possessions to the poor,

[80] Senior and Stuhlmueller, *Biblical Foundations*, 265, cf. 257, 259.
[81] Schottroff and Stegemann, *Jesus and the Hope of the Poor*, 67–120.
[82] Bosch, *Transforming Mission*, 118.
[83] Schottroff and Stegemann, *Jesus and the Hope of the Poor*, 91. Quoted in Bosch, *Transforming Mission*, 102.

while the upstanding young ruler refused Jesus' call to conversion because he was very rich. Further, Jesus includes material in his Sermon on the Plain that differs decisively from Matthew (6:30–35). This material 'is shot through with references to what the conduct of the rich ought to be toward the poor'.[84] The rich are to renounce large portions of their possessions and waive the recovery of debts. Finally, Luke speaks of almsgiving as an expression of the mercy and justice of God's inbreaking salvation.[85] In light of this, Bosch concludes, Luke cannot be called an evangelist of the poor but he is, more correctly, an evangelist of the rich.[86]

Bosch rejects an exclusive interpretation of a 'preferential option for the poor'. This is because the poor as well as the rich are called to repentance. Further, there is hope for the rich if they are willing to repent and live in solidarity with the poor and oppressed, to be converted to God and to each other. Luke's controlling motif is that God's salvation has broken into history in Jesus, and the communities to which Luke writes must embody that good news in their lives, in both economic and social dimensions.

Good News of Peace

Relying almost exclusively on the book of J. Massyngbaerde Ford, Bosch develops peace-making as a major theme in Luke. The communities to which Luke wrote lived 'in the wake of the devastation of the Jewish War, in which the political hopes of the Zealots were crushed; many of his readers lived in a war-torn country, occupied by foreign troops who often took advantage of the population; violence and banditry have been their meat and drink for many a year'.[87] In this situation Luke presents them with a challenge: rooted in the mission of Jesus, the church is to pursue a ministry of peace-making and non-violence, especially by loving one's enemy in word and deed. This embodied the peace of the kingdom and was a call to his enemies to repentance and

---

[84] Bosch, *Transforming Mission*, 102.

[85] ἐλεημοσύνη (almsgiving) is found ten times in the Lukan writings (Lk. 11:41; 12:33; Acts 3:2, 3, 10; 9:36; 10:2, 4, 31; 24:17) and is unique to Luke except for its appearance in Matthew 6:1–4.

[86] Willem Saayman is concerned that Bosch's words here can be misunderstood in two ways. (1) Since Luke's message is aimed at the rich, it is up to them to improve the plight of the poor. (2) Since Luke's Gospel is equally for the rich and poor, this implies that Christians should feel equal concern for both groups. Saayman disputes both of these misunderstandings ('South African Perspective', 42).

[87] Bosch, *Transforming Mission*, 112.

salvation: 'the preaching of love even to enemies in order that, if at all possible, such enemies may be won over'.[88]

Bosch's analysis hinges on a certain interpretation of Luke 4:16–30 that is dependent on Jeremias and Ford. Luke's account of Jesus' inaugural sermon comes in the context of the revolutionary messianism of the first chapters of Luke. According to Ford, Luke intentionally structures his first few chapters to highlight the 'seething cauldron' of Palestine rife with revolutionaries, apocalyptic thinking and messianic expectations.[89] Against this backdrop in Luke 4 Jesus announces the good news of peace: 'no more vengeance'.

The clue to understanding this message in Jesus' inaugural sermon is coming to terms with the dramatic shift that takes place in the story from acceptance (4:16–22) to murderous intent (4:23–30). Bosch finds this *volte-face* inexplicable, even impossible, as it is normally read. He finds the solution in pursuing the question of how Isaiah 61 would have been read by the Jews of that time.[90] To disheartened exiles living under foreign power, the prophet predicted the year of the Lord's favour – but also a day of vengeance on Israel's enemies (Is. 61:2). The further words of the prophet look forward to a day when foreigners would serve Israel (Is. 61:5–7). The original audience in Nazareth would hear these words as an announcement of liberation from Roman, not Babylonian, domination. Further, the Melchizedek scroll from Qumran interprets the Jubilee (which Jesus announces here) in terms of a day of vengeance on God's enemies. Thus Jesus' contemporaries would have interpreted Isaiah 61:1–2 in terms of violent political liberation.

When Jesus reads Isaiah 61:2, he stops in the middle of a Hebrew parallelism. He proclaims the favourable year of the Lord but refuses to announce the day of the vengeance. The eyes of the congregation are fastened on him in suspicion. To a congregation longing for retribution and judgement, Jesus' termination of the Isaiah quote sparks consternation. In light of this Jeremias takes a fresh look at what is normally interpreted as a positive response in verse 22.[91] He retranslates that verse: 'They protested with one voice and were furious, because he only spoke about (God's year of) mercy (and omitted the words about the messianic vengeance).' Jesus' further words serve only to fan the flame of astonishment and hostility, and so they attempt to assassinate him.

Luke introduces Jesus' ministry in this Nazareth pericope. It is a ministry in which vengeance has been superseded. This sets the stage for Jesus' entire ministry. Bosch finds this motif elsewhere in Luke: Jesus, in response to the question of John's disciples, again omits vengeance (7:22f.); when dealing with the

---

[88]   Bosch, *Transforming Mission*, 28.
[89]   Ford *My Enemy Is My Guest*, 1–52.
[90]   Ford, *My Enemy Is My Guest*, 53–64.
[91]   Jeremias, *Jesus' Promise*, 41–46.

Samaritans Jesus refuses to embrace the vengeance that his contemporaries would certainly have espoused in light of the defilement of the temple by Samaritans (C.E. 6–9) and the murder by Samaritans of a large company of pilgrims on their way to Jerusalem to celebrate the Passover (C.E. 48–52);[92] similarly he sees this motif in Jesus' unexpected response to the news of slaughtered Galileans (13:1–9);[93] and in Jesus' whole conduct through his arrest, trial and execution (e.g., 23:34; 23:43).[94]

Against the background of a vengeful and holy wrath against their enemies, Jesus exhibits forgiveness and healing. The call to the communities to which Luke writes is to continue Jesus' mission of peace-making so that perhaps those hostile to the gospel may repent and experience salvation. Bosch's appropriation of this peace-making is missiological in contrast to the way other Lukan scholars have adopted this theme. Peace-making is not motivated by self-interest for the sake of self-preservation in a hostile empire. Rather, peace-making is motivated by love for enemies so that they might be reconciled to Christ, be enfolded in the new community and enjoy eschatological salvation.[95]

Salvation, Repentance and Forgiveness of Sins

It is clear that the closely related themes of salvation, repentance and forgiveness are central to Luke's Gospel. Luke uses the words σωτηρία or σωτήριον (salvation) twelve times in Luke-Acts, compared to no occurrences in Matthew and Mark, and one in John. Further, among the synoptics only Luke calls Jesus σωτήρ (Saviour). Similarly, the terms for 'repentance' (both μετανοέω and ἐπιστρέφω) appear regularly throughout Luke and are often linked to 'sinner' (ἁμαρτωλός) and 'forgiveness' (ἄφεσις). Examples of repentance and forgiveness are found throughout Luke's Gospel (e.g.,

---

[92] Ford, *My Enemy Is My Guest*, 83–86.

[93] Cf. Ford, *My Enemy Is My Guest*, 89–101.

[94] Cf. Ford, *My Enemy Is My Guest*, 108–35.

[95] Commenting on Ford's theme of peace-making, Powell says: 'It is interesting to compare Ford's understanding of Luke's intention with that of Conzelmann and others. Like Conzelmann she believes that Luke wants to establish peaceful relations between the Christians of his day and their enemies in Roman society. She does not define this motivation, however, in terms of the Church's self-interest … Luke's concern for peace is grounded in the theological concept of love for enemies, rather than in some practical program for self-preservation and expansion' (*What Are They Saying*, 90–91). Ford stresses that the church is to follow the example of Jesus because it is the right thing to do. Bosch stresses the missional and ecclesial importance of this stance to win over enemies.

Zacchaeus, the Prodigal Son, the thief on the cross). The message the church is to carry to all nations is repentance and forgiveness of sins (24:47).

In the Lukan perspective, Bosch argues, salvation cannot be reduced to the vertical relationship between God and humankind. Rather, Luke stresses the comprehensive nature of salvation. Bosch cites Scheffler, who argues that salvation in Luke has six dimensions: economic, social, political, physical, psychological and spiritual.[96] 'Salvation involves the reversal of all the evil consequences of sin, against both God and neighbour.'[97] Evil takes many forms: pain, sickness, death, demon-possession, personal sin and immorality, the loveless self-righteousness of those who claim to know God, the maintaining of special class privileges, the brokenness of human relationships. The proclamation of salvation in Jesus responds: 'If human distress takes many forms, the power of God does likewise.'[98] Like σωτήριον, another favourite word group of Luke, usually translated 'forgiveness' (ἄφεσις/ἀφίημι), also has a wide range of meanings which include the freeing of slaves, the cancellation of monetary debts, eschatological liberation, healing, exorcism and forgiveness of sins.[99] This is an imprisonment metaphor: Jesus has been sent to release *all* those in bondage.

Jesus announces salvation with his words, demonstrates it with his deeds and embodies it in his solidarity with the marginalized. In a paper prepared for an ecumenical conference on world mission Bosch argues that mission in Jesus' way, according to Luke, includes these three closely-intertwined dimensions: empowering the weak and lowly, healing the sick and saving the lost.[100] Communal solidarity, deeds and proclamation all are part of Jesus' assault on evil.

Three other aspects of this salvation in Luke are significant for Bosch. First, it is the economic dimension of salvation that receives prominence. It is economic justice and a new relationship between rich and poor that are given attention in Luke.[101] Second, there is a strong emphasis on the social dimension of salvation. Salvation involves the breaking down of barriers that stand between people. Those on the margins find a place in God's kingdom. Finally, salvation is an assault on the demonic power of evil that lies behind all evil, especially seen in the exorcisms (e.g., Lk. 11:20).[102] Evil was something experienced in the ancient world as real and tangible. It was the demons and evil forces in first-century society which deprived men and women of health,

---

[96] Scheffler, 'Suffering in Luke's Gospel', 57–108.
[97] Bosch, *Transforming Mission*, 107.
[98] Bosch, *Transforming Mission*, 32–33.
[99] Bosch, 'Mission in Jesus' Way', 10, 16; *Transforming Mission*, 33.
[100] Bosch, 'Mission in Jesus' Way'.
[101] Bosch, *Transforming Mission*, 117.
[102] Bosch, *Transforming Mission*, 33.

dignity and fullness of life.[103] Luke uses the word 'salvation' to describe what Jesus did in the face of this sickness, demon possession and exploitation.

The missional thrust of this theme is evident. No doubt Bosch would agree with I. Howard Marshall that the missional importance of Luke's theme of salvation, repentance and forgiveness is that it gives content to the message the church must proclaim.[104] But it is more: Bosch's understanding of mission moves beyond evangelism. The wide scope of salvation means that the church not only proclaims it but embodies it in deeds and life. Since salvation is cosmic, the church's embodiment of this salvation will be cosmic. Mission will be the assault on evil in all its manifestations in its communal embodiment, its deeds and its proclamation.[105] Bosch's later missiology continues to work with these conclusions based on Luke's understanding of salvation challenging the many dualisms and ways salvation has been reduced in various Christian traditions.[106]

Summary: The Ecclesiological Shape of Mission

Differing views of mission will issue in differing missional readings of Scripture.[107] In fact, there is much debate on this fact among those who advocate a missional reading of Scripture. For Bosch, mission is as broad as the salvation of the kingdom.[108] His shortest definition of mission, repeated often, is: 'Mission is the totality of the task which *God* has *sent* his *Church* to do in the *world*'.[109] Another helpful definition that highlights the breadth of his understanding of mission is that mission is 'the proclamation and manifestation of Jesus' all-embracing reign, which is not yet recognized and acknowledged by all but is nevertheless already a reality'.[110] He says further:

---

[103] Bosch, *Transforming Mission*, 98.

[104] Marshall, *Luke*, 159–61. Cf. Powell, *What Are They Saying*, 118–19.

[105] Bosch does not use the language of word, deed and communal embodiment. Yet this threefold understanding of mission underlies much of what he says. Bosch was a theological broker who attempted to mediate opposing parties (Du Plessis, 'For Reasons of the Heart', 75–76). His stress on community, word and deed challenged reductionistic views of mission in both the ecumenical and the evangelical traditions.

[106] Bosch, *Transforming Mission,* 393–400.

[107] Cf. Köstenberger, 'The Place of Mission'.

[108] Kritzinger, 'Mission and Evangelism', 147–54.

[109] Bosch, 'Why and How', 36 (emphasis his). Cf. Bosch, 'Mission and Evangelism', 169.

[110] Bosch, *Transforming Mission*, 40.

The theology of mission is closely dependent on a theology of salvation. Therefore the scope of mission is as wide as the scope of salvation; the latter determines the former. According to Scripture salvation is cosmic ... It is, in a very real sense, re-creation, new creation ... One biblical word for this restoration is the *Kingdom of God*; it refers to the deliverance of humanity from sin, evil structures and brokenness ... Mission serves the Kingdom, proclaims it, and gives expression to it.[111]

A central feature of mission for Bosch is the way the church gives communal expression to the kingdom of God. Mission is not simply the discharge of certain tasks like preaching or showing mercy or doing justice. While these are all essential to a missionary church, all these things flow from the communal life of the church. Central to the missionary existence of the church is the embodiment of the all-embracing salvation of God's kingdom revealed and ushered in by Jesus Christ. Bosch often pictures the church in terms of an attractive alternative community,[112] which is also revolutionary as it challenges the powers of the culture that oppose God's kingdom.[113]

It is not surprising, then, that when Bosch unfolds Luke's paradigm of mission he is often drawn to New Testament scholars who take a compositional-critical[114] approach to the gospels.[115] These scholars read Luke in terms of ecclesial formation rooted in the historical ministry of Jesus. Bosch likewise reads Luke in these terms. Luke's presupposition is that central to the church's mission to continue what Jesus began is the call to embody his comprehensive salvation in their lives *for the sake of the world.*

Yet the embodiment of salvation means different things for various communities at different times and places. As Bosch puts it: 'Mission means "incarnating the Gospel in time." This means that mission is always contextual. In its mission the Church must always ascertain what the issues of the day are and address those ... The concrete expression of mission may therefore vary – and indeed does – from place to place, from situation to situation.'[116] Thus Luke and Matthew, while sharing similar foundational assumptions about mission, shape their gospels to speak to different issues. Luke addresses the questions of

---

[111] Bosch, 'Mission and Evangelism', 173.
[112] 'Perhaps it would be correct to say that, in the course of time, the essence of my thinking in this area has crystallised in the concept of the church as the "alternative community"' (Bosch, 'How My Mind Has Changed', 8).
[113] Bosch, *Church as Alternative Community*; 'How My Mind Has Changed'; *Transforming Mission*, 47–49. Livingston, 'David Bosch', 11–16.
[114] Holladay, 'Contemporary Methods of Reading the Bible', 134.
[115] E.g., LaVerdierre and Thompson, 'Communities in Transition', 570; Senior and Stuhlmueller, *Biblical Foundations*, 211–12; Schottroff and Stegemann, *Jesus and the Hope of the Poor*, 68.
[116] Bosch, 'Mission and Evangelism', 173.

identity, stagnation and hostility. We might summarize Luke's missional message, as Bosch understands it, as follows. Luke challenges the church to which he writes to be:

- A community where Jesus is present by his Spirit
- A community that, though living in a new situation, continues the mission of Jesus
- A community that embodies, demonstrates and announces a comprehensive salvation
- A community whose identity is defined by a witness to God's kingdom in life, word and deed
- A community whose faithful witness will bring suffering
- A community with roots in Israel and the Old Testament story with a mission to Jew and Gentile
- A community that practices and proclaims repentance and forgiveness
- A community that practices and proclaims solidarity with the marginalized
- A community which practices and proclaims a gospel of peace, especially toward their enemies

Bosch and a Missional Hermeneutic

Bosch has made an important contribution toward a missiological hermeneutic in general and a missional reading of Luke in particular. His reflection generally on hermeneutics, and specifically on Matthew, Luke and Paul is rich and repays careful study. His contribution is best assessed by placing it in the context of the historical development of a missiological hermeneutic, noting his important place but also noting how the move toward a more consistent missional hermeneutic has continued to progress.

During the nineteenth and early twentieth centuries, mission was understood rather narrowly as a geographical movement from a Christian nation to a mission field to win converts and plant churches. Mission advocates focussed on certain texts and detached incidents from Scripture that authenticated this view of mission. Toward the middle of the twentieth century, a broadening understanding of mission caused mission scholars to return to the Bible afresh. The division of the world into the Christian West and the pagan non-West, and the separation of mission and church as two different enterprises, began to break down. The International Missionary Council held in Willingen, Germany (1952) offered a new theological paradigm for mission – the *missio Dei*. The concept of the *missio Dei* emerged as an organizing structure that allowed numerous insights from the past twenty-five years to be coordinated. This coincided with the Biblical Theology Movement, which had shaped the ecumenical movement during the decades of the 1940s and 1950s.[117] Johannes Blauw was commissioned by the World Council of Churches to survey and appraise the work of biblical scholarship, and to bring those insights to bear on the mission of the church in light of this new understanding of mission. Blauw expressed a general consensus about the biblical foundation of mission.[118] Blauw's work served as the major work for Bible and mission until the mid-1970s. New developments in biblical studies and significant changes in the world church subsequently rendered Blauw's work inadequate. During the 1970s and 1980s mission scholars returned to the issue of the Bible and mission and produced a number of studies. Perhaps the book by Senior and Stuhlmueller is the most noteworthy work to have been produced during this period.

Bosch entered the conversation at this time. He produced a number of works in this area, but the arrival of *Transforming Mission* was a watershed. It gathered up the insights and steps taken toward a missional hermeneutic and gave sophisticated expression to a missional reading of Matthew, Luke and Paul.[119] A number of significant themes that advance a more consistent missional hermeneutic can be found in the corpus of Bosch's work: mission as a central thrust of Scripture's message; the centrality of the *missio Dei*; various mission theologies rooted in the mission of Jesus; the missionary identity of the church; the broad scope of mission centred in the comprehensive salvation of the kingdom of God; the communal dimension of mission; and a hermeneutic of 'consonance' or historical logic[120] that enables the ancient missionary paradigms to speak authentically to the present. All of these themes have contributed toward a missional reading of Luke, as the preceding analysis shows.

The development toward a missional hermeneutic has appropriated the insights of Bosch and has continued to move forward toward a more consistent expression of the centrality of mission in Scripture. Perhaps the most helpful articulation of a missional hermeneutic to date is Chris Wright's article soon to appear in book form.[121] Wright wants to move beyond a 'biblical foundations for mission' (the term used most often by Bosch), beyond multicultural hermeneutics, beyond use of the Bible to support the world mission of the church, beyond important themes in Scripture for mission, to a missional hermeneutic. For Wright, mission is what the biblical story is all about: God's mission, Israel's

---

[117] Cartwright, 'Hermeneutics', 454.

[118] Blauw, *The Missionary Nature of the Church*.

[119] A book that follows in the tradition of Bosch but moves beyond Matthew, Luke and Paul to most of the other books of the NT is Nissen's *New Testament and Mission*.

[120] Bosch's appropriation of Echegaray is especially helpful in this regard.

[121] Wright, 'Mission as a Matrix'.

mission, Jesus' mission and the church's mission. When we view Bosch through this lens, two things become clear: (1) Bosch has taken us a long way along the road toward a missional hermeneutic with his work; and (2) others have continued to travel along that road, developing his insights toward a more consistent missional hermeneutic.

The following makes this clear: Bosch rightly critiques a 'foundations of mission' approach that isolates texts important for mission, when mission is an enterprise that is already understood ahead of time. Rather, Bosch wants to attend to the missionary thrust of Scripture as a whole and the missionary thrust of whole literary units. A critical analysis of Bosch's treatment of Luke provides us with an opportunity to see how this can be done even more consistently.

Luke and God's Mission in the Metanarrative of Scripture

The first question is this: Does Bosch enable us to understand Luke in terms of the missionary thrust of Scripture as a whole? While Bosch employs the mission of God as the underlying structure for understanding Luke, this is seriously weakened by his failure to place Luke in the context of the broader metanarrative of Scripture which narrates the unfolding purpose of God. In *Transforming Mission* Bosch devotes 184 pages to developing a biblical foundation for mission. Only four pages are devoted to the Old Testament, and his approach is to elaborate themes important for mission to the nations. Bosch quotes Rzepkowski approvingly when he says: 'The decisive difference between the Old Testament and the New Testament is mission. The New Testament is essentially a book about mission.'[122] This is because there is 'in the Old Testament, no indication of the believers of the old covenant being sent by God to cross geographical, religious, and social frontiers in order to win others to faith in Yahweh'.[123]

---

[122] Rzepkowski, 'Theology of Mission', 80. Quoted in Bosch, *Transforming Mission*, 17. It seems to me that a recovery of the missionary nature of Israel would strengthen his concern for a communal-embodiment dimension of mission.

[123] Bosch, *Transforming Mission*, 17. This raises another issue that I will not address: the consistency of Bosch's definitions of mission. Throughout his copious writings one can find numerous 'mission is ...' statements. He is not always consistent in defining mission as broadly as we indicated earlier. Mission as crossing boundaries to do certain things lingers. His fear is that he may fall into the error termed 'panmissionism' by Freytag (*Reden und Aufsätze*, 94), and articulated by Stephen Neill (*Creative Tension*, 81): 'If everything is mission, nothing is mission' (Bosch, *Transforming Mission*, 511). In analysing Bosch's broad view of mission, Kritzinger raises similar questions about the boundary of mission ('Mission and Evangelism', 153–54). He fears that even Bosch's view is too comprehensive. Kritzinger already hints at the direction I

Köstenberger has called attention to this weakness in Bosch.[124] He rightly notes that 'a salvation-historical approach to Scripture is imperative for an accurate understanding of the Bible's own teaching on mission'.[125] LeGrand argues that to understand mission in the New Testament one must attend to the 'eschatological, centripetal universalism' in the Old Testament that is 'brought to complete expression in the New Testament'.[126] Put another way, Luke is part of a much bigger story that involves the mission of God and the mission of Israel. The mission of Jesus and the mission of the church cannot be understood apart from the Old Testament story of the mission of God and the mission of Israel.[127]

Precisely the Gospel of Luke makes this connection between Israel's mission, Jesus' mission and the church's mission as part of one story of God's mission. Joel Green helps us see this when he highlights the important theme of the purpose of God in Luke's Gospel.[128] According to Green, Luke uses a whole host of expressive terms to indicate that the story of Jesus must be read in the light of the overarching purpose of God as it has been narrated in the Old Testament – terms such as βουλή (purpose) βούλομαι (to want) δεῖ (it is necessary) θέλημα (will) θέλω (to will)ὁρίζω (to determine) πληρόω (to fulfil) προφήτης (prophet). Jesus' mission must be seen in the context of the whole biblical story as he serves the missional purpose of God. Speaking of both Jesus and John, Green says, 'The Scriptures supply the salvation-historical framework for understanding their respective missions and so root their activity in the ongoing story of God's redemptive work'.[129] The salvation framework, or missional purpose, of God includes the mission of Israel, the mission of Jesus and the mission of the church as part of one story. Jesus' story is the 'next step' in the God-Israel relationship. There is a 'oneness of God's

---

would want to move in to critique both Kritzinger and Bosch. One may distinguish between missionary dimension and missionary intention. If mission is seen as a dimension of all of life, Neill's criticism loses its force. Further, mission is not about something we do but about our committed participation in the purposes of God for the redemption of the whole creation (Wright, 'Mission as a Matrix', 137). Looked at in this way, mission is as broad as life.

[124] Köstenberger, 'The Place of Mission', 356–57.
[125] Köstenberger, 'The Place of Mission', 359.
[126] LeGrand, *Unity and Plurality*, 3. See also the importance of the OT for mission in Richard Bauckham's insightful book *Bible and Mission*.
[127] For the importance of making the connection between the biblical narrative, God's mission, Israel's mission, Jesus' mission and the church's mission for a missional hermeneutic see Wright, 'Mission as a Matrix'.
[128] Green, *The Theology of Luke*, 22–49.
[129] Green, *The Theology of Luke*, 25.

aim' wherein God's purpose is served first by Israel, then by Jesus, and finally by those who follow Jesus.[130] He says,

> The struggle to achieve the divine aim Luke recounts did not reach its resolution in the Third Gospel, but spilled over into the activity of the Jesus-movement in Acts. In an important sense, then, Acts is grounded in God's purpose as related in the Gospel of Luke, just as the Gospel is grounded in God's purpose as related in Israel's Scriptures.[131]

An example of this is the use that Luke makes of the Servant Songs of Isaiah. T.S. Moore argues that Luke depicts Jesus as the one who comes to fulfil the calling of the Servant in Isaiah.[132] He argues further that Luke also formulates his version of the concluding commission with the Servant of Isaiah in mind.[133] In this way the mission of Jesus is connected to the mission of the church: both discharge the ministry of the Isaianic Servant. Thus Luke 'used the Servant concept not only for his Christology, but also for his missiology'. Consequently, as 'followers of Christ, believers today are privileged to be commissioned by Him to take up the mission of the Servant'.[134]

But the connection can be made not only forward from Jesus' mission to the church's mission, but also back from Jesus' mission to Israel's mission. Not only does the church continue Jesus' mission, but Jesus fulfils Israel's mission. The Servant Songs of Isaiah must be put in the context of the broader Old Testament story of a people called to incarnate as a community the redemptive purposes of God in the midst of the world for the sake of the nations.[135] Isaiah's promise comes in the midst of Israel's failure to be the faithful servant and looks forward to one who will arise out of Israel to fulfil her mission to be a light to the nations. Jesus comes as 'one who fulfills Israel's destiny'. When 'Israel's role of world mission ... was forfeited through disobedience' that role pictured in the Servant is 'transferred in the Gospels to Jesus'.[136] The Servant will also gather a renewed Israel who will continue the Servant's mission. Thus we see a

---

[130] Green, *The Theology of Luke*, 26.
[131] Green, *The Theology of Luke,* 22.
[132] Moore, 'The Lucan Great Commission', 47–51.
[133] Moore, 'The Lucan Great Commission', 51–58.
[134] Moore, 'The Lucan Great Commission', 60.
[135] Gn. 12:1–3, Ex. 19:3–6. Cf. Dumbrell, *Covenant and Creation*, 66, 80, 90.
[136] Köstenberger and O'Brien, *Salvation to the Ends of the Earth*, 49–50. The role is not only transferred in the gospels but already in Isaiah. Commenting on Is. 49:1–6, Brevard Childs speaks of a servant that arises within Israel 'as a faithful embodiment of the nation Israel who has not performed its chosen role (48:1–2)' (*Isaiah*, 385).

missional connection between the roles of Israel, Jesus and the church as each participates in the missional purpose of God.[137]

It is this overarching missional purpose of God that must be grasped for a consistent missional hermeneutic. Wright puts it strongly,

> To read the whole Bible in the light of this overarching perspective of the mission of God, then, is to read 'with the grain' of this whole collection of texts that constitute our canon of Scripture. In my view this is the key assumption of a missional hermeneutic of the Bible. It is nothing more than to accept that the biblical worldview locates us in the midst of a narrative of the universe behind which stands the mission of the living God.[138]

Bosch believes that a biblical foundation of mission needs to take seriously the missional thrust of the biblical story as a whole. Our missional reading of Luke needs to be pushed in this direction in a more consistent way than that which Bosch provides.

A Narrative Missional Reading of Luke

The second question is this: Does Bosch enable us to understand the missionary thrust of Luke as a whole? If Luke narrates the story of Jesus who serves the missional purposes of God, then the *whole* of Luke is written to form a missional community. There are not just some important texts and themes in Luke that can give direction to the Christian mission; rather, the whole of Luke narrates the mission of Jesus, which becomes the basis for the mission of those who follow him. A missional hermeneutic will ask what Luke's view is on mission when Luke is read as a narrative whole. In other words, a missional hermeneutic is not only interested in the *whole* scriptural story, it is also interested in the *whole* of the author's work, which in this case includes Acts. It is questionable whether this comes through in Bosch; one could read Bosch – even contrary to what Bosch himself says – as providing a selection of important themes from Luke for mission.

A number of observations alert us to the problem. In the first place, important Lukan themes that need to be seen in their relation to mission are either absent or treated inadequately. For example, Bosch mentions prayer in a list of themes to which Luke returns again and again.[139] Surprisingly, Bosch does not return to treat the importance of prayer for Luke. Clearly prayer is a significant

---

[137] Links between the missional calling of Israel, Jesus and the church would greatly strengthen Bosch's concern for the communal dimension of mission.

[138] Wright, 'Mission as a Matrix', 134–35.

[139] Bosch, *Transforming Mission*, 86.

topic in Luke's Gospel[140] and central for the missional life of the church. Similarly, the important themes of witness, suffering,[141] table fellowship[142] and the Spirit find no or meagre treatment![143]

Closely related, in the second place, is the fact that important sections of Luke are either absent or treated inadequately. The large travel section in Luke and the important section dealing with the controversy between Jesus and the Jewish leaders are both loaded with missional significance, yet this is not mentioned.[144] Perhaps more important is the scant treatment of Luke 24:46–49. Bosch himself says of this text that 'Luke's entire understanding of the Christian mission' can be found here in a nutshell. The various elements found in this text constitute the 'fibers of Luke's mission theology running through both the gospel and Acts, binding this two-volume work together'.[145] Yet this is treated in a short section under the broader issue of Jew, Samaritan and Gentile.[146]

Third, there are Lukan themes that are treated well in a preliminary way when Bosch discusses the one paradigm of the early church. But, when Bosch deals with Luke, these themes are not integrated into the discussion on the Lukan sub-paradigm of mission. We do not see Luke's unique approach to these subjects, nor their relationship to other themes in Luke. Examples include the kingdom of God, the significance of the already-but-not-yet period of redemptive history and the gathering of disciples to participate in Jesus' mission.

Finally, there is the problematic structure of Bosch's chapter. The chapter is divided into two primary sections. After general comments about the significance of Luke for mission, the first section treats four missionary motifs – Gentile mission, gospel for poor and rich, salvation and peace-making. In Bosch's analysis, all of these motifs except for salvation explicitly arise out of Luke 4. In a much shorter second section entitled 'The Lukan Missionary Paradigm', he gathers in summary form eight major ingredients of Luke's paradigm – Spirit,

---

[140] Cf. Harris, 'Prayer in Luke-Acts'; Smalley, 'Spirit, Kingdom, and Prayer'. Cf. Bartholomew and Holt, 'Prayer in/and the Drama of Redemption in Luke: Prayer and Exegetical Performance' in this volume.

[141] 'The closeness of our missionary thinking to the New Testament may perhaps be in part judged by the place which we accord to suffering in our understanding of the calling of the Church' (Newbigin, *Trinitarian Faith*, 42).

[142] Luke mentions nineteen meals, and thirteen of these references are unique to Luke. In Luke, Jesus' life seems to revolve around meals (Karris, *Luke*, 47–48).

[143] Bosch includes brief summaries of Luke's pneumatology (*Transforming Mission*, 113–15), witness (116) and suffering (121–22) in a section he calls 'major ingredients of the Lukan paradigm' (113). Yet they are treated very briefly.

[144] On the importance of the travel section see Green, *Gospel of Luke*, 396–98.

[145] Bosch, *Transforming Mission*, 91.

[146] By comparison see the rich chapter by Senior and Stuhlmueller, who examine the missional message of Luke from the standpoint of Lk. 24:46–49.

correlation of Jewish and Gentile mission, witness, 'repentance, forgiveness and salvation', rich and poor, peace-making, ecclesiology and suffering – some of which do not arise out of Luke 4 or the earlier discussion. Questions arise: How do these two major sections fit together? Why does he choose and highlight the themes he does?[147] Why do some themes arise in the second section and not the first? Are the various motifs of Luke's understanding of mission sufficiently integrated and related to each other with this structure?

These four examples highlight problems with the compositional critical approach Bosch has adopted. Luke gives us an interpretation of Jesus' mission that is foundational for the church's mission in the form of a narrative. Recent Lukan studies have turned to a more narrative approach in studying the gospels, since this approach takes seriously the form in which the gospel has come to us. A more narrative approach to Luke that begins with the fundamental insight that Luke is seeking to form the community to which he writes in a missional way would avoid many of the problems we have articulated with Bosch's approach. Put another way, a more narrative approach would accomplish even more fully what Bosch wants to do – take seriously the missional thrust of Luke as a literary whole, a missional thrust which is concerned to form his intended audience into a more faithful missionary community.

Final Questions

Joel Green asks: 'What would happen if biblical studies took the Christian mission seriously?' and 'What would happen if the Christian mission took the (full) biblical witness seriously?'[148] The contention of this chapter is that the answer to the first question is that we would be able to hear more faithfully what God is saying in Luke. The answer to the second is that our mission would be much more faithful to what God intends for his people. It is this concern that led the Scripture and Hermeneutics Seminar to include a paper on missional hermeneutics when it kicked off with the theme 'renewing biblical interpretation'. Dan Beeby made a plea to consider a missional hermeneutic as one way toward that renewal.[149] This present chapter has presented a missional reading of Luke by one of the leading missiologists of the twentieth century as an illustration of that approach. Hopefully, a missional hermeneutic will become increasingly common, and committed participation in the missional purposes of God will grow.

---

[147] Du Plessis speaks of Bosch's exposition as 'burning with reasons of the heart', which are 'the hopes and fears of the poor, the lost and the powerless' (Du Plessis, 'For Reasons of the Heart', 83). Does this help us to see why he chooses themes of peace-making, and the poor and marginalized, for example, over prayer?

[148] Green, 'Proclaiming Repentance', 14.

[149] Beeby, 'A Missional Approach to Renewed Interpretation'.

Bibliography

Anderson, H., 'Broadening Horizons: The Rejection at Nazareth Pericope of Luke 4:16–30 in Light of Recent Critical Trends', *Int* 18 (1964), 259–75

von Baer, H., *Der Heilige Geist in den Lukasschriften* (Stuttgart: Kohlhammer, 1926)

Bauckham, R., *Bible and Mission: Christian Witness in a Postmodern World* (Grand Rapids: Baker Books, 2003).

Beeby, H.D., 'A Missional Approach to Renewed Interpretation', in *Renewing Biblical Interpretation* (ed. C. Bartholomew, C. Greene, K. Möller; SHS 1; Carlisle: Paternoster; Grand Rapids: Zondervan, 2000), 268–83

Berkhof, H., *The Doctrine of the Holy Spirit* (Richmond, VA: John Knox Press, 1964)

Blauw, J., *The Missionary Nature of the Church: A Survey of the Biblical Theology of Mission* (New York: McGraw-Hill, 1962)

Bosch, D., *Die Heidenmission in der Zukunftsschau Jesu: Ein Untersuchung zur Eschatologie der Synoptischen Evangelien* (Zürich: Zwingli, 1959)

—, 'The Why and How of a True Biblical Foundation for Mission', in *Zending op Weg Naar de Toekomst: Essays aangeboden aan prof. Dr.J. Verkuyl* (Kampen: Kok Publishers, 1978), 33–45

—, *Witness to the World: The Christian Mission in Theological Perspective* (Atlanta: John Knox Press, 1980)

—, *The Church as Alternative Community* (Potechefstroom: Institute for Reformational Studies, 1982)

—, 'How My Mind Has Changed: Mission and the Alternative Community', *JTSA* 41 (Dec. 1982), 6–10.

—, 'Mission and Evangelism: Clarifying the Concept', *ZMR* 68.3 (July 1984), 161–87

—, 'Mission in Biblical Perspective', *IRM* (Oct. 1985), 531–38

—, 'Toward a Hermeneutic for "Biblical Studies and Mission"', *MSt* III.2 (1986), 65–79

—, 'Mission in Jesus' Way: A Perspective from Luke's Gospel', *Missionalia* 17.1 (April 1989), 3–21

—, *Transforming Mission: Paradigm Shifts in Theology of Mission* (Maryknoll: Orbis Books, 1991)

—, 'Reflections on Biblical Models of Mission', in *Toward the 21ˢᵗ Century in Christian Mission* (ed. J.M. Phillips and R.T. Coote; Grand Rapids: Eerdmans, 1993)

Brueggemann, W., 'The Bible and Mission: Some Interdisciplinary Implications for Teaching', *Missiology* 10.4 (Oct. 1982), 397–412

Cartwright, M.G., 'Hermeneutics', in *Dictionary of the Ecumenical Movement* (ed. N. Lossky et al.; Grand Rapids: Eerdmans, 1991), 454–58

Childs, B., *Isaiah* (Louisville: Westminster John Knox, 2001)

Conzelmann, H., *The Theology of St. Luke* (New York: Harper, 1960)

Dillon, R.J., 'Easter Revelation and Mission Program in Luke 24:46–48', in *Sin, Salvation and the Spirit* (ed. D. Durken; Collegeville: The Liturgical Press, 1979)

Dumbrell, W., *Covenant and Creation: A Theology of Old Testament Covenants* (New York: Thomas Nelson, 1984)

Du Plessis, J.G., 'For Reasons of the Heart: A Critical Appraisal of David J. Bosch's Use of Scripture in the Foundation of Christian Mission', *Missionalia* 18.1 (April 1990), 75–85

Dupont, J., *The Salvation of the Gentiles: Essays in the Acts of the Apostles* (New York: Paulist Press, 1979)

Echegaray, H., *The Practice of Jesus* (Maryknoll: Orbis Books, 1980)

Fiorenza, E.S., 'Miracles, Mission, and Apologetics: An Introduction', in *Aspects of Religious Propaganda in Judaism and Early Christianity* (ed. E.S. Fiorenza; Notre Dame, IN: University of Notre Dame Press, 1976)

Ford, J. Massyngbaerde, *My Enemy Is My Guest: Jesus and Violence in Luke* (Maryknoll: Orbis Books, 1984)

Freytag, W., *Reden und Aufsätze*, II (Munich: Chr. Kaiser Verlag, 1961)

Green, J.B., '"Proclaiming Repentance and Forgiveness of Sins to All Nations": A Biblical Perspective on the Church's Mission', in *The World is My Parish: The Mission of the Church in Methodist Perspective* (ed. A.G. Padgett; SHM 10; Lewiston, NY: Edwin Mellen, 1992), 13–43

—, *The Theology of the Gospel of Luke* (Cambridge: Cambridge University Press, 1995)

—, *The Gospel of Luke* (NICNT; Grand Rapids: Eerdmans, 1997)

—, 'Recovering Mission-Church: Reframing Ecclesiology in Luke-Acts' (lectures given at the inaugural Epworth Institute Conference, 2003)

Harris, O.G., 'Prayer in Luke-Acts: A Theology of Luke' (PhD. Diss., 1966)

Harms, R.B., *Paradigms from Luke-Acts for Multicultural Communities* (New York: Peter Lang, 2001)

Hengel, M., 'The Origins of the Christian Mission', in Hengel, *Between Jesus and Paul: Studies in the Earliest History of Christianity* (London: SCM Press, 1983), 48–64

Holladay, C.R., 'Contemporary Methods of Reading the Bible', in *The New Interpreters Bible*, I (ed. L.E. Keck; Nashville: Abingdon Press, 1994)

Jeremias, J., *Jesus' Promise to the Nations* (London: SCM Press, 1958)

Kähler, M., *Schriften zur Christologie und Mission* (Munich: Chr. Kaiser Verlag, 1971)

Karris, R., *Luke: Artist and Theologian: Luke's Passion Account as Literature* (New York: Paulist Press, 1985)

Kasting, H., *Die Anfänge der Urchristlichen Mission* (Munich: Chr. Kaiser Verlag, 1969)

Köstenberger, A.J., 'The Place of Mission in New Testament Theology: An Attempt to Determine the Significance of Mission within the Scope of the New Testament's Message as a Whole', *Missiology* 27.3 (July 1999), 347–62

Köstenberger, A.J. and P.T. O'Brien, *Salvation to the Ends of the Earth: A Biblical Theology of Mission* (Downers Grove, IL: InterVarsity Press, 2001)

Kritzinger, J.J., 'Mission and Evangelism: A Critical Appraisal of David Bosch's Views', *Missionalia* 18.1 (April 1990), 140–55

Larkin, W.J., and J.F. Williams, *Mission in the New Testament: An Evangelical Approach* (Maryknoll: Orbis Books, 1998)

Lash, N., 'What Might Martyrdom Mean?', *ExAud* 1 (1985), 14–24

LaVerdiere, E.A., and W.G. Thompson, 'New Testament Communities in Transition: A Study of Matthew and Luke', *TS* 37 (1976), 567–97

LeGrand, L., *Unity and Plurality: Mission in the Bible* (Maryknoll: Orbis Books, 1990)

Livingston, K., 'David Bosch: An Interpretation of Some Main Themes in His Missiological Thought', *Missionalia* 18.1 (April 1990), 3–19

Meyer, B.F., *The Early Christians: Their World Mission and Self-Discovery* (Wilmington: Michael Glazier, 1986)

Marshall, I.H., *Luke: Historian and Theologian* (Grand Rapids: Zondervan, 1970)

Moore, T.S., 'The Lucan Great Commission and the Isaianic Servant', *BSac* 154 (1997), 47–60

Neill, S., *Creative Tension* (London: Edinburgh House Press, 1959)

Nel, D.T., 'Kritiese Hermeneutiek as Model vir Sendingwetenskaplike Navorsing' (unpublished doctoral dissertation; Pretoria: University of South Africa, 1988)

Newbigin, L., *Trinitarian Faith and Today's Mission* (Richmond: John Knox Press, 1964)

Nissen, J., *New Testament and Mission: Historical and Hermeneutical Perspectives* (Frankfurt am Main: Peter Lang, 3rd edn, 2004)

Pesch, R., 'Berufung und Sendung, Nachfolge und Mission: Eine Studie zu Mk. 1, 16–20', *ZKT* 91 (1969), 1–31

Powell, M.A., *What Are they Saying about Luke?* (New York: Paulist Press, 1989)

Rzepkowski, H., 'The Theology of Mission', *Verbum SVD* 15 (1974), 79–91

Saayman, W., 'A South African Perspective on Transforming Mission', in *Mission in Bold Humility: David Bosch's Work Reconsidered* (ed. W. Saayman and K. Kritzinger; Maryknoll: Orbis Books, 1996), 40–52

Scheffler, E.H., 'Suffering in Luke's Gospel' (unpublished doctoral dissertation; University of Pretoria, 1988)

Schottroff, L., and W. Stegemann, *Jesus and the Hope of the Poor* (Maryknoll: Orbis Books, 1986)

Senior, D., and C. Stuhlmueller, *The Biblical Foundations for Mission* (Maryknoll: Orbis Books, 1983)

Smalley, S., 'Spirit, Kingdom, and Prayer in Luke-Acts', *NovT* XV (Jan. 1973), 59–71

Wolfert, T., 'From Ivory Tower to Parish Ministry', *Images* (Redeemer University College, Fall 2004), 18–19

Wolters, A.M., 'Confessional Criticism and the Night Visions of Zechariah', in *Renewing Biblical Interpretation* (ed. C. Bartholomew, C. Greene, K. Möller; SHS 1; Carlisle: Paternoster; Grand Rapids: Zondervan, 2000), 90–117

Wright, C., 'Mission as a Matrix for Hermeneutics and Biblical Theology', in *Out of Egypt: Biblical Theology and Biblical Interpretation* (ed. C. Bartholomew, M. Healy, K. Möller, R. Parry; SHS 5; Carlisle: Paternoster; Grand Rapids: Zondervan, 2004), 102–43

Distinctive Theological Themes in Luke–Acts

10

Luke and the Spirit

Renewing Theological Interpretation of Biblical Pneumatology

Max Turner

The Scripture and Hermeneutics project has not only illustrated the relatively bankrupt status of a purely historical-critical approach to the biblical writings, it has also launched a cogent and multifaceted appeal for the renewal of biblical interpretation in a more canonical, hermeneutical and ecclesially motivated direction – while rightly emphasizing that such an approach must still remain rigorously critical.

Luke-Acts has undoubtedly received its fair share (if not more) of 'purely historical' studies, sometimes of arcane matters of little theological import. But, by and large, studies of Luke's presentation of *the Spirit* are not in the class of the arcane. A survey of scholarship on the Spirit in Luke-Acts throughout the last century confirms that the majority of studies had evident ecclesial, and often explicitly theological, orientation.[1] Many were sparked by the mid-century liturgical renewal debates in the main historic churches as to whether the Spirit was given sacramentally in baptism (most notably argued by Lampe and Beasley-Murray),[2] or in confirmation (argued most thoroughly by Dix, Thornton and Adler),[3] or in some more open-ended 'conversion-initiation' package that did not tie the Spirit to either sacrament (so Barth and Dunn).[4] Most of those studies engaged not merely with Luke-Acts, but also with the

---

[1] For such a survey, and for references to other similar surveys, see Turner, *Power*, 20–79.

[2] Lampe, *Seal of the Spirit*; Beasley-Murray, *Baptism*.

[3] Dix, *Theology of Confirmation*; Thornton, *Confirmation*; Adler, *Das erste christliche Pfingstfest* and *Taufe und Handauflegung*.

[4] Barth, *Die Taufe ein Sakrament?*; Dunn, *Baptism*.

rest of the New Testament, and some with the Fathers, and beyond. Significantly, yet others represented the first appearance of the vast pentecostal/charismatic movements on to the stage of academic theology, with primarily pentecostal readings of Luke-Acts from Stronstad, Shelton, Ervin, R.P. Menzies and Penney,[5] and more broadly charismatic ones from Schweizer, Dunn, Haya-Prats, Montague, Turner and Wenk.[6] In short, on this particular *topos* we do not lack examples of what the Scripture and Hermeneutics project wishes to encourage in readers of Luke: namely, ecclesial readings, intended to shape authentic Christian belief and praxis. In the same breath, however, we must note that the evident diversity in interpretation of the *significance* of the Spirit, and of the Spirit's relationship to conversion-initiation, needs to be addressed.

Beginning with areas of agreement, we may justifiably claim that since von Baer's magisterial study of the subject in 1926,[7] there has largely been consensus among Lukan scholars on the following points. (1) Of the synoptic writers, it is Luke who evinces the strongest redactional interest in the Spirit.[8] (2) The essential background for his pneumatological material is thoroughly Jewish, deeply rooted in the Old Testament. (3) The Spirit is the uniting motif and the driving force within the Lukan salvation history and legitimizes the mission to which this leads. (4) For Luke, the Spirit is largely the 'Spirit of prophecy', and in Acts especially as an 'empowering for mission'. (5) Correspondingly, Luke shows relatively little interest in the Spirit as the power for the spiritual, ethical and religious renewal of the individual. (6) Luke's pneumatology develops beyond Judaism in giving the Spirit christocentric functions: the Holy Spirit is now the 'Spirit of Jesus' too (Acts 16:6–7).[9] There is also almost consensus on a seventh point: that Luke expects the Spirit 'normally', or 'ideally', to be given at, or in close temporal proximity to, conversion-initiation. On this last point, even some prominent *pentecostal* Lukanists (e.g., R.P. Menzies and Penney) are prepared to agree.

[5] Stronstad, *Charismatic Theology of Saint Luke* and *Prophethood of All Believers*; Ervin, *Conversion-Initiation and the Baptism in the Holy Spirit*; Shelton, *Mighty in Word and Deed*; R.P. Menzies, *Development* and *Empowered for Witness*; Penney, *Missionary Emphasis*.

[6] Schweizer, *Holy Spirit*; Dunn, *Baptism* and *Jesus and the Spirit*; Haya-Prats, *L'Esprit, Force de l'Église*; Montague, *Holy Spirit*; Turner, *Power* and *Holy Spirit*; Wenk, *Community-Forming Power*.

[7] Von Baer, *Der heilige Geist*.

[8] Mark has six references to the Spirit; Matthew has twelve, while Luke has some twenty references in his 'former treatise', and no less than *sixty* in the book of Acts. What is more, the *language* he uses (especially that of people being 'filled with' the Spirit, or 'full of' the Spirit) is demonstrably his own editorial variation on septuagintal expressions for Spirit-endowment: cf. Turner, *Power*, ch. 6, esp. 165–69.

[9] For elaboration of the consensus, see Turner, *Spirit*, ch. 3.

Where the post-von Baer consensus breaks down most critically, however, is on the relationship of the Spirit to salvation. Is the Spirit, for Luke, *exclusively* a prophetic empowering for mission and service (as R.P. Menzies and Stronstad affirm), or is the Spirit also the source of a person's experience of eschatological sonship, new covenant 'life' and the transforming presence of God's reign (so von Baer, Dunn and Turner, albeit differently)?[10] In what follows we shall examine: (1) the Spirit in the preparation for the gospel (Lk. 1–2; 3:16–17); (2) Jesus and the Spirit (Lk. 1:35; 3:21–22; 4:1, 14, 16–21, etc.), in particular assessing the degree to which his experience of the Spirit may be presented as 'paradigmatic' for Christians; (3) the promise of the Spirit (Lk. 3:16; 11:13; 12:12 [21:15] and 24:49); (4) Luke's interpretation of the Spirit in Acts 1–2 and beyond; and (5) Luke and the Spirit in canonical context and in theology today. In the first four of these parts, we shall adopt a largely 'historical-critical' approach, one chiefly informed by redaction, composition-critical and more broadly narratival approaches. That is, we shall be asking how Luke's narrative about the Spirit might be expected to shape the symbolic universe of his readers – especially the world of their hopes and expectations concerning the Spirit.

The Spirit in the Preparation for the Gospel

Leaving the relatively elevated Greek style of the prologue (1:1–4) behind, Luke immediately plunges his readers into the linguistic and conceptual world of the Old Testament and intertestamental Judaism, and of their hopes for salvation. These hopes are crystallized in the *angelic* announcements to Zechariah (Lk. 1:13–17), to Mary (1:30–35) and to the Bethlehem shepherds (2:9–14). And they are correspondingly celebrated in the *Spirit*-prompted doxological, hymnic and prophetic utterances of prominent characters in the birth narratives (Elizabeth in 1:42–45; Mary in 1:46–55; Zechariah in 1:68–79 and Simeon in 2:28–35). The Model Reader (see below) is left in no doubt as to the essential 'content' of the salvation anticipated. It consists in that 'forgiveness of sins', announced programmatically in Isaiah 40:2 and spectacularly elucidated in the chapters of Deutero-Isaiah that follow. Which is to say that it is specifically a 'forgiveness' which ends God's historical chastisement of the nation for her disobedience, brings her back out of her spiritual 'exile' into the promised land and leads her to its very heart, Jerusalem/Zion, where God will take up his glorious reign and transform his servant Israel as a light to the nations – all this through a messianic servant and son of David. In other words, Luke's birth

---

[10] For the most recent discussion of the cardinal issues of disagreement between Menzies, Dunn and Turner, see Turner, 'Spirit and Salvation'.

narratives loudly trumpet the fulfilment of hopes for an Isaianic new exodus
and consequent messianic restoration of Israel.[11] The dense intertextuality with
the Isaianic hopes, and the christocentric and eschatological interpretation of
them, both here and in the rest of the gospel, imply an *ideal* readership which is
steeped in the LXX or Hebrew Scriptures and prepared to recognize Jesus as the
fulfilment of their essentially Jewish hopes for Israel. So 'Model Readers' are
most probably believers from a Jewish background (or erstwhile Gentile God-
fearers).

Within the two opening chapters of Luke we encounter nine references to
the Spirit (1:15, 17, 35, 41, 67, 80; 2:25, 26, 27) – almost *half* of the total in
Luke's Gospel.

A Jewish reader would immediately recognize three of the references as
very typical workings of what they regarded as the 'Spirit of prophecy'. Both
Elizabeth and her husband Zechariah are said to be 'filled with the Spirit' in
order to speak following a prophetic oracle (1:41, 67). Of Simeon, it is said that
it 'had been revealed to him' by the Spirit that he would not die before he saw
the promised Messiah (2:26). Such revelations and 'immediately-inspired'
speech would have been regarded as *quintessential* expressions of the Spirit of
prophecy.[12] There are two further references to Simeon as one upon whom the
Spirit permanently resided (2:25), and as one whose conduct in the temple (his
entry at the appropriate moment, and his recognition of and prophetic utterance concerning Jesus) manifested the Spirit (2:27: the dative here is one of
attendant circumstances). While the Judaism of Jesus' day regarded the presence and activity of the Spirit as rare – the blessing of the Spirit being thought of
as largely 'withdrawn' because of Israel's sin – these five occasions all cohere
with the Jewish understanding that the Spirit of prophecy could nevertheless
be expected: (a) to announce a salvation-historically significant birth; and (b) to
endow holy people in Israel's holiest place, the temple.[13]

The triplet of references in Luke 1:15, 17, 80 all pertain to John the Baptist
and mark him out as a unique figure on the stage of Israel's salvation history.
Like Simeon, he is permanently endowed with the Spirit: indeed, uniquely he
is even 'filled with the Spirit' right from his mother's womb (1:15). And as a
result he is to be enabled to act powerfully as the prophet in the tradition of
Elijah who prepares Israel for the Lord's coming (1:17). The Spirit upon him is
thus evidently a form of the 'Spirit of prophecy', although the fact that he

[11] For these themes, see esp. Strauss, *Davidic Messiah*, and Pao, *Acts*. On their presence
in Luke 1–2, and on related source and background questions, see also Turner,
Power, ch. 6.
[12] See Turner, *Power*, chs. 3–4.
[13] See Turner, *Power*, ch. 6. The common scholarly assumption that Jews considered
the Spirit to have been almost entirely withdrawn rests on a misunderstanding: see
Levison, 'Did the Spirit Withdraw?'.

receives this even before he is born, and becomes 'strong in (the) s/Spirit' in earliest childhood (1:80), long before he undertakes any public prophetic role, suggests that his endowment has as much to do with his own life before God as with the prophetic function he eventually serves for others. But other than to describe the Baptist's *in utero* leap of recognition of Jesus (1:41, 44), which his mother Elizabeth interprets through a prophetic recognition oracle granted by the same Spirit (1:42–45), Luke passes over the first thirty years or so of the Baptist's life in the Spirit in silence.

We next encounter John the Baptist, on Luke's chronology ca. 28–29 C.E. (cf. 3:1), as a fully-fledged prophet of Israel's impending Isaianic restoration (3:1–20).[14] He specifically identifies himself as the 'voice in the wilderness', preparing the new exodus 'way of the Lord', and so (as Luke adds to Mark) for the 'salvation' that will be seen by 'all flesh' (Is. 40:3–5; Lk. 3:4–6). Accordingly, he demands a radical repentance to be crystallized in a once-off water baptism in preparation for that 'forgiveness of sins' announced in Isaiah 40:2 (Lk. 3:2). All of this can be taken as spelling out the 'word of the Lord' that came to him (3:2), and it will naturally be understood as revealed to him *by the Spirit*, even if Luke does not say as much, because, as we have indicated, such charismatic revelation is *prototypical* of the 'Spirit of prophecy'.

If the Baptist sets the general Isaianic new exodus scene, he is also more specific in contrasting his own preparatory ministry of water baptism with the coming one's baptizing with 'Holy-Spirit-and-fire' (3:16). This contrast is clearly intended as *essential and programmatic*, as it is in the other three gospels (we may note that John's promise that the coming one would 'baptize in Holy Spirit' is remarkably the *only* saying in the tradition that is virtually repeated in all four gospels).[15] That is, the contrast aims to encapsulate the *main aspect* of John's messianic hopes, relevant to *all*, not merely something secondary and incidental to them (as, e.g., in much pentecostal exegesis which relegates Luke's concept of 'baptism in Holy Spirit' to a *donum superadditum* of prophetic empowerment for witness, important as empowerment is for Luke).

John the Baptist himself probably meant that the awaited Messiah would cleanse and restore Israel by acting in the great power of the Spirit with which the Messiah was to be anointed. That is what he would most probably have meant by the claim 'he will baptize (=cleanse/purify) with fiery Spirit'.[16] He regards his own baptismal ministry as having 'winnowed' Israel, separating the repentant wheat from the residual chaff: the Messiah is to complete the task of cleansing the nation and bringing judgment on those that resist (3:17). The Spirit would be expected to be on the Messiah as a 'spirit of judgment and

---

[14] On which see Turner, *Power*, ch. 7, and Green, *Luke*, 159–83.

[15] See Hooker, 'John's Baptism'.

[16] See Turner, *Power*, ch. 7.

of burning' (Is. 4:4), and especially as the Spirit announced in Isaiah 11:1–2 (summarized in Targum Jonathan as 'And a *king* shall come forth from the *sons* of Jesse, and *the Messiah* shall *be exalted* from *the sons of* his *sons*. [2] And *a* spirit *before* the LORD shall rest upon him, a spirit of wisdom and understanding, a spirit of counsel and might, a spirit of knowledge and the fear of the LORD').[17] But John may also have anticipated that the Spirit-anointed one would fulfil the new exodus hopes of Isaiah 61:1–3 (hence Jesus' pointed response to his doubts in Lk. 7:22), and thereafter bring justice to the nations, as in Isaiah 42:1–4. What he almost certainly could *not* have expected, however, is the kind of fulfilment of his words that Luke envisages in Acts 1–2, with Jesus as the heavenly Lord of the Spirit, bestowing the gift from God's right hand, now as the Spirit of Jesus, his own executive power.

Jesus and the Spirit in the Gospel of Luke

Some nine sayings explicate Jesus' own relation to the Spirit from conception to resurrection: Luke 1:35 (from his Semitic source for the birth narratives); 3:16 (from Q, see above); 3:22 (following Mark); 4:1 (twice – both redactional additions to Mark's summary); 4:14 (again redactional); 4:18–21 (probably from Luke's special source); 10:21 (redactional); 11:20 (from Q); and 12:10 (paralleled in both Mark and Q).[18] It is noticeable that most are redactional, that they cluster mainly around the programmatic beginnings of Jesus' ministry, and that they largely fit the profile of what Judaism was to call 'the Spirit of prophecy'.

The conception of Jesus by the Spirit

Of these nine, the first – Luke 1:35 – would have been the most likely to surprise many first-century readers: it represents a quite remarkable *novum*. A child, one destined to exercise Davidic eschatological rule (1:32–33), is to be born to (the co-textually 'virgin') Mary. This uniquely holy 'son of God' is to be generated, according to the angelic explanation to Mary, *by* the Holy Spirit (1:35). Judaism could (if rarely) refer all creation (and all resurrection-new-creations) to the Spirit,[19] but the special act of creation anticipated in Luke 1:32–35 comes as a mystery with no parallels (except, of course, the even more enigmatic Mt. 1:18). If we press Luke's language for its allusions, the references

[17] For the numerous texts illustrating such a Jewish view, see Turner, *Power*, chs. 4–5. The italics indicate targumic addition to – or interpretation of – the text.
[18] For the source allocations, see the respective parts of Turner, *Power*, chs. 6–9.
[19] Cf. Turner, *Power*, ch. 4.

to the Spirit as 'coming upon' Mary, and as the 'overshadowing' presence of 'the power of the Most High', point backward to Isaiah 32:15 (and Ex. 40:35), and forward to Luke 24:49 and Acts 1:8. The remarkably compressed annunciation thus portrays the Spirit as the power of Israel's new exodus restoration (for that is what Is. 32:15–18, and the related 44:3–5, are about), and it correspondingly depicts Jesus' very *being* as essentially the *impress* of this Spirit, and hence marks him as Israel's holy one, the messianic Son of God. In relation to the more general aims of this chapter, two points deserve attention.

First, against prominent interpreters from Schweizer to R.P. Menzies, Luke is clearly working with a very broad concept of the Spirit of prophecy: one which *includes* both marked ethical/soteriological influence and acts of creative power. While 1:32–35 takes these to a new level, Jewish interpreters were in fact regularly prepared to associate the 'Spirit of prophecy' with both religious/ethical enabling and works of power: most obviously so in the assortment of messianic traditions based on Isaiah 11:1–4, but also much more widely (indeed, soteriological/ethical transformative effects are *primary* characteristics of the Spirit of prophecy in some of the oldest layers of 1QH, in *Jos. Asen.*, and in Philo).[20] *Second,* no reader of Luke 1:32–35 is liable easily to conclude at this juncture that Luke attempts to portray Jesus' experience of the Spirit as essentially paradigmatic for that of later disciples! At this stage in his account the reader is much more likely to conclude that Luke wishes to demonstrate that Jesus not merely *matched* the Isaianic hopes for the Messiah of the Spirit, but even in some way *transcended* them. This may partially explain why Luke shows no concern to describe *how* Jesus experienced the Spirit between his conception and the Jordan event. He even leaves entirely unclear whether Jesus' youthful messianic wisdom and dedication to his Father (2:41–52) is simply the result of his Spirit-conception, or whether there is an ongoing, overshadowing 'presence' and 'strengthening in the Spirit' that matches and surpasses what is said of the Baptist in 1:15, 80. The regular step-parallelism between what is said of the Baptist and what is said of Jesus in these opening chapters, and the allusions to the figure in Isaiah 11:1–4, would suggest the latter explanation; but on this potentially intriguing question Luke is simply silent, leaving readers to fill in his gaps.

Jesus' Jordan experience of the Spirit

The reader next encounters a cluster of five closely interrelated sayings describing, and elucidating, Jesus' baptismal reception of the Spirit (3:22; 4:1 [twice], 14, 18). There is broad consensus on the following points:[21]

---

[20] See Turner, *Power*, chs. 4–5, and, more recently, Levison, *Spirit*.
[21] See R.P. Menzies, *Development*, chs. 8–9; Turner, *Power*, chs. 8–9.

(a) The baptismal narrative *separates* Jesus' water baptism *from* (but also loosely *joins* it *to*) a subsequent prayer experience involving a vision of the dove-like Spirit's descent, accompanied by a voice implicitly *interpreting* that Spirit-reception as a specifically messianic consecration and anointing (cf. the Davidic allusion to Ps. 2:7 in the words 'you are my beloved son') of God's Isaianic servant (cf. the additional 'in whom I am well pleased', echoing Is. 42:1) and bearer of 'good news' (hence the dove).

(b) The redactional connectives describing Jesus as 'full of the Spirit' (4:1), and as returning to Galilee 'in the power of the Spirit' (4:14), deliberately present Jesus' ongoing ministry as thenceforth fully exemplifying the Spirit's work.

(c) All of this is brought together in Jesus' seminal announcement in 4:16–21, which sums up and governs the picture of 'Jesus and the Spirit', right to the end of his public ministry, as an eschatological fulfilment of the hopes of Isaiah 61:1–2 (and 58:6): he is anointed with the Spirit to announce and effect eschatological 'good news' of release to 'the poor'. The latter term is primarily a metaphor for *Israel's* destitute condition (the benighted, humbled and forlorn estate from which she needs to be saved, according to the hymns of Luke 1–2), but Luke certainly means it to include especially the economically disadvantaged, as well as the broader category of those disenfranchised by disease and by other social criteria.[22]

Jesus' experience of the Spirit as paradigmatic?

There is little agreement between modern interpreters as to the precise import of Jesus' experience for Luke's understanding of *Christian* relationship to the Spirit. We may distinguish three positions:

(1) *Jesus' Jordan experience of the Spirit is a paradigmatic* donum superadditum *of empowering.* This position is held, albeit in different ways, by both confirmationist and pentecostal interpreters. It has obvious strengths.

---

[22] There is a minor disagreement as to whether the Spirit provides miraculous powers of healing and exorcism. According to R.P. Menzies, Luke cannot directly relate the Spirit to such events precisely because (in contrast to Matthew and Mark) for him the Spirit is the (Jewish) 'Spirit of prophecy'. But Judaism has no problem with attributing miraculous power to the Spirit of prophecy (see Turner, *Power*, ch. 4; and Levison), and Luke specifically identifies healings as cases of the 'good news' of release to the poor in 7:21–22 (cf. Acts 10:38) and understands them as effects of Jesus' Spirit-enabled commands (see *Power*, chs. 8–9 and 11). It is mildly ironic that Menzies tries to save Luke's 'Jewish' concept of the 'Spirit of prophecy' from including miracles by positing the very *un*-Jewish idea that the Spirit generates a mana-like 'power' that is responsible for them instead.

Given what has been said about Jesus and the Spirit in Luke 1:32–35, and the evident messianic wisdom and filial intimacy with God to which it leads (exemplified in 2:41–52), it is hard to see how the Jordan experience can be anything other than some kind of 'second blessing' empowering of Jesus for his mission. For Menzies (the most rigorous exponent of the position), it is clear that Jesus receives the gift precisely as the Spirit of prophecy, bringing him the revelation and inspired speech that characterize his messianic/prophetic ministry. Jesus' own use of Isaiah 61:1–2 is taken as decisive for such an understanding, and the remaining two clear references to the Spirit on Jesus conform to Jesus' use of Isaiah 61 (in 4:1 Jesus is 'led in the Spirit',[23] in his contest with Satan, and in 10:21 the Spirit affords Jesus charismatic revelation/wisdom and inspired doxological response: all prototypical gifts of the 'Spirit of prophecy'). The disciples are then to receive essentially the same gift at Pentecost.

(2) Jesus' Jordan experience of the Spirit is paradigmatic of Christian baptismal reception of sonship, God's reign, and new-covenant 'life'. For Dunn (the strongest advocate of this position), Jesus' baptism marks the beginning of a whole new epoch of salvation-history – that of the dawning kingdom of God. It is precisely the Spirit which brings this to Jesus, and enables its correlate experiences of eschatological sonship and new covenant life. In the period of the ministry this is limited to Jesus; only in Luke's third epoch – the age of the church – does the descent of the Spirit at Pentecost extend this to the disciples, and to those who come to faith through their witness.[24] Dunn does not deny that Luke thinks the Spirit also empowers Jesus, but for Luke this is merely as a corollary of the more theologically significant work of the Spirit, which brings Jesus his archetypal experience of the kingdom of God, and with it his programmatic experience of new-age sonship (3:22).[25]

(3) Jesus' experience of the Spirit is unique, even if important elements of it are carried over into the church after Pentecost. In the period covered by the gospel, Jesus 'receives' the Spirit twice: at conception and at his baptism. After Luke 1:35, it makes little sense to speak of Jesus (as Dunn did) as belonging to the old covenant, or to the epoch of Israel, and of his only receiving eschatological sonship with the gift of the Spirit at his baptism.

---

[23] Where Mark (1:12) and Q (Mt. 4:1) merely have the Spirit lead Jesus *into* the wilderness, Luke differs. For him, the period of the wilderness temptations is one *throughout which the Spirit guides Jesus* – presumably giving him the charismatic wisdom/insight he needs to withstand Satan's interpretation of Scripture, and the godly resolve to do so (cf. Turner, *Power*, 201–204).

[24] Dunn, *Baptism*, 26–43.

[25] Dunn, *Baptism*, 32. Cf. also Dunn, 'Spirit and Kingdom'.

And although the Jordan experience contains a significant note of sonship (3:22), Luke clearly understands the event primarily as a prophetic empowering of Jesus as the Isaianic Servant (cf. the use of Is. 42:1 at 3:22, and of Is. 61:1–2 in a paradigmatic way in 4:18–21), to bring into effect the promised Isaianic new exodus 'salvation'. Dunn has himself largely conceded these points.[26] But this probably means that Luke 1:35 and 3:21–22 denote unique and unrepeated actions of the Spirit, rather than being paradigmatic, and in any case the combination of the two is certainly not paradigmatic in any direct sense: Luke does not believe that disciples first receive eschatological sonship by the Spirit, and then (thirty years later?) receive the Spirit as empowering for mission. As we shall see, Luke knows of only one gift of the Spirit to believers.

Again, Dunn was right to see the Jordan event as pivotal, and to see the Spirit as the presence of the kingdom of God. But in his earlier writing he tended to reduce this to an experience for *Jesus alone*, in its own separate second epoch of salvation-history; an experience that would become paradigmatic for that of the disciples only when they enter Luke's *third* salvation-historical epoch at Pentecost.[27] Unfortunately, this was misleading on two cardinal issues, largely corrected by Dunn in his later writings.

In the *first* instance it gave too much emphasis to Jesus' ministry as a separate second 'epoch' of Lukan salvation history, with its own special conditions. It was, after all, somewhat precious to suggest that the two to three years of Jesus' ministry constituted a distinct 'epoch'. The fact is that Luke only recognizes *two* salvation-historical periods: for him there is just the ('Old Testament') period of *hope* for the kingdom of God, running up to John the Baptist's prophetic ministry, and then the time of *fulfilment* beginning with Jesus' ministry (7:28; 16:16), and extending into the ongoing period of the church.

The *second*, immediately related but more significant, mistake was Dunn's earlier failure sufficiently to recognize the *disciples'* experience of the presence

---

[26] Dunn, 'Baptism in the Spirit, esp. 16–17. Much earlier he had made the point that 'the Evangelists … understood the relation between Jesus and the Spirit in terms primarily of one inspired and empowered, a prophet like Moses' (*Christology in the Making*, 140, emphasis his). And elsewhere Dunn accuses Luke of a 'crude' and 'lop-sided' pneumatology, most notably in his '*complete disregard for the experience of sonship*' (*Jesus and the Spirit*, 190–91, emphasis his) – in which case, of course, 'sonship' can hardly be what Luke regards as the paradigmatic core of Jesus' Jordan experience of the Spirit! But Dunn's judgment is perhaps unfair to Luke: while it is true that he does not use the *word* 'sonship', he clearly thinks the disciples' experience is one of profound filial obedience to the Father, which is 'sonship' in all but name.

[27] For a description of his (changing) position, and its (differing) relation to both von Baer's and Conzelmann's tri-epochal view of Lukan salvation history, see Turner, *Power*, 48–53.

of the kingdom of God in Jesus' ministry. According to Dunn, in the period of the ministry the kingdom of God was limited to Jesus: 'the new age and covenant had come, but only in him; only he had begun to experience them'.[28] But that is not Luke's picture. For him, the ministry of Jesus makes the kingdom of God, or 'salvation', *present and available to those who accept Jesus' message*. The Isaianic good news of messianic release is made available in the 'today' of his announcement (Lk. 4:18–21; 19:9), and it is experienced as forgiveness of sins and restoration of the lost/outcasts into the community of God's inbreaking reign (Lk. 7:36–50; 14:15–24; 15:1–32; 16:16; 19:9–10), in celebratory table fellowship (7:34; 15:2, etc.), in liberating miracles of exorcism and healing (programmatically at 4:18–21; 7:21–23; 11:20; Acts 10:38; cf. 13:16), and in a new life of discipleship to Jesus' teaching, and faith in him as God's eschatological envoy.[29] In all of this the *Spirit is the power on the Messiah that enables him to effect the saving liberation and reign of God that he proclaims.*[30] And 'blasphemy against the Spirit' (Lk. 12:10) is probably continuing resolute opposition to this work of the Spirit.

The Promise of the Spirit to Disciples in Luke's Gospel (Lk. 3:16; 11:13; 12:12 [21:15] and 24:49)

Luke's first treatise has little to say about the relationship of disciples to the Spirit. Until the reader gets to Luke's *second* work, the Baptist's promise (3:16) would probably be taken as fulfilled in the totality of Jesus' Spirit-anointed ministry. On one occasion (Lk. 12:12//Mk. 13:11 and Mt. 10:19–20), the disciples are promised that they will receive the Spirit's aid when they are called on to defend themselves before courts. Some kind of inspired speech afforded by the Spirit of prophecy is clearly meant, but there is curiously no hint of any broader work of the Spirit inspiring the disciples.[31] A reader who had only

---

[28] Dunn, *Baptism*, 41.

[29] See Turner, *Power*, ch. 11, for detailed discussion of the different ways in which Luke regards salvation as made present in Jesus' ministry.

[30] Turner, *Power*, chs. 9, 11. In Lk. 11:20, miracles of exorcism are interpreted as concrete events of God's liberating reign, and they are attributed to the 'finger of God' rather than to the Spirit (as in Mt. 12:28). If it is Luke who has introduced the change to Q (which is uncertain), this is not because he is unable to attribute such works to the Spirit of prophecy (he probably regards the 'finger of God', like the 'hand' or 'arm' of the Lord, as co-referential terms for the Spirit), but to strengthen his Mosaic/new exodus motifs (cf. Ex. 8:19): see Turner, *Power*, 256–59; cf. Woods, 'Finger of God'.

[31] In Lk. 21:15 (//Mk. 13:11), a similar promise is made that Jesus himself will give the needed words and wisdom. But Luke knows that the risen Lord will only do this

Luke's Gospel could easily deduce that such inspired speech was expected to be very occasional, perhaps even exclusively for times of trial. Equally enigmatic is the saying in Luke 11:13 which promises disciples who ask a 'good s/Spirit',[32] rather than an evil or harmful look-alike. In the context of the following Beelzebub controversy, and the linguistic connections with 10:17–19, this appears to assure disciples that the power by which they exorcise is benign (some kind of sharing in the Spirit upon Jesus?), not magical or demonic, as Jesus' detractors imply.[33] Only with his very last words in the gospel does the Lukan Jesus raise the hope of a more comprehensive gift of the Spirit. In 24:49a he begins by saying, 'Behold, I am sending the promise of my Father upon you'. It is not clear whether this is a reference to the Spirit (proleptically reflecting the kind of teaching in Acts 1–2) or (more probably) is intentionally more general, and has in view the whole promise of salvation, of which the Spirit will only emerge as the key in Acts.[34] The closing words of the discourse, however, tell the disciples to 'stay in the city until you are clothed with power from on high' (Lk. 24:49b). These last four words (three words in Greek) refer to the Spirit with a description that identifies the gift with the hopes of Isaiah 32:15–18 – that is, as the Spirit poured out from on high which will restore Israel and make her a light to the nations. So the gospel finishes with a brief note of expectation which matches the opening flurry of promises in Luke 1–2, and an allusion to the wording of Isaiah 32 brings to the passage a teasing pneumatological perspective. But a reader will need Luke's second volume in order to understand clearly the precise import of the allusion.

Luke's Interpretation of the Spirit in Acts 1–2 and Beyond

We are left in no doubt at all by the opening chapters of Luke's second treatise that the promise of the Spirit is a Christian version of the Spirit of prophecy. Not only does Luke explain the Pentecost experience in terms of the quintessential promise of the Spirit of prophecy to all God's people (Joel 2:28–32), but he redactionally adds to the citation of Joel a repeat of the assertion 'and they shall prophesy' at Acts 2:18 (thereby creating an inclusio with 2:17), and has Peter promise precisely this gift to *all* God's people (2:38–39) – 'to all whom

---

through the Spirit – as becomes clear in the careful blending of the wording of the two promises in the case of Stephen in Acts 6:10.

[32] The reading πνεῦμα ἀγαθόν of p⁴⁵ L, etc., appears to be the original (Turner, *Power*, 340).

[33] See Turner, *Power*, 337–41.

[34] So Mainville, *L'Esprit dans l'Oeuvre de Luc*, 141–54, 315–16. Nothing in the gospel itself prepares for the designation of the Spirit as the 'promise of the Father' – not even 11:13.

the Lord calls to himself' (Acts 2:39b=Joel 2:32). What is more, in the rest of Acts the Spirit is consistently portrayed as the source of the very gifts Judaism regarded as prototypical to the 'Spirit of prophecy', thus:

(a) The Spirit is thus the author of *revelatory visions* and *dreams*: programmatically at 2:17, but also specifically at Acts 7:55–56 (and Luke would probably trace such vision/dream guidance as 9:10–18; 10:10–20; 16:9–10 and 18:9–10; 22:17–18, 21; 23:11 to the Spirit (cf. the specific mention of the Spirit in these contexts, 10:19; 16:6–7).
(b) The Spirit gives *revelatory words* or *instruction* or *guidance*: 1:2; 1:16 (=OT); 4:25 (=OT); 7:51 (=OT); 8:29; 10:19; 11:12, 28; 13:2, 4; 15:28; 16:6–7; 19:21; 20:22, 23; 21:4, 11 and 28:25 (=OT).
(c) The Spirit grants *charismatic wisdom* or *revelatory discernment*: Luke 21:15 and Acts 5:3; 6:3, 5, 10; 9:31; 13:9 and 16:18.
(d) The Spirit inspires *invasive charismatic praise* (e.g., the tongues on the day of Pentecost: 2:4; 10:46; 19:6).
(e) Finally, the Spirit inspires *charismatic preaching* or *witness* (Acts 1:4, 8; 4:8, 31; 5:32; 6:10; 9:17) or *charismatic teaching* (9:31; 13:52 and 18:25 [?] etc.) – this is not strictly anticipated in Judaism, but it is an obvious extension of the Jewish concept of the Spirit as the Spirit of prophecy (combining some of the above), and derives from pre-Lukan Jewish Christianity.[35] Along with the specific references to the Baptist's promise (1:5; 11:16) and references to believers receiving this gift of the Spirit (specified explicitly as Joel's gift at 2:17–18, 33, 38–39 and as 'the same Spirit' at 10:44, 45, 47, 11:15; 15:8),[36] *nearly all of the references to the Spirit in the book of Acts are included in the above examples.*[37] Luke, then, evidently regards 'the promise' made to believers to be a Christianized version of Joel's 'Spirit of prophecy'. In that sense Acts 2:14–39 is genuinely programmatic for the pneumatology of Acts as a whole.

---

[35] See Turner, 'The Spirit of Prophecy', esp. 68–72, 87–88. My position has been unfortunately misrepresented on this point by Woods, 'Finger of God', 255–61.
[36] Other references to believers receiving the Spirit are 8:15, 16, 17, 18, 19 and 19:2, 6.
[37] We are left with only eight references that do not immediately fit the categories of gifts we would regard as prototypical of the Spirit of prophecy: (1) Acts 5:3, 9 referring to Ananias and Sapphira 'lying to' and 'testing' the Holy Spirit by their deceit; (2) Acts 6:5 and 11:24, ascribing charismatic 'faith' to the Spirit, and 13:52 similarly charismatic 'joy'; (3) Acts 8:39, which speaks of the Spirit snatching Philip up and transporting him away; (4) Acts 10:38, referring to Jesus' own anointing with Spirit and power; and (5) Acts 20:28, where the Spirit is described as appointing overseers. These can all, nevertheless, be understood as pertaining to activities of the Spirit of prophecy (see Turner, *Power*, ch. 13, esp. §2.2).

But how does this gift relate to the *soteriology* of Acts? As is well known, pentecostal interpreters (most prominently Menzies and Stronstad) understand the gift of the Spirit purely as a prophetic *donum superadditum*, directing the mission of the church and empowering its witness. On their view, the disciples are clearly already 'saved' members of God's people *before* they receive the Spirit at Pentecost.

Unfortunately, this appears to involve a misunderstanding that reduces Lukan soteriology to no more than 'forgiveness of sins' (understood as initial justification), incorporation into the community of God's people and hope for the resurrection and final arrival of the kingdom of God. But Luke means much more than that.[38] Already in the ministry of Jesus he has depicted salvation as a multifaceted experience of release from harmful powers, and enjoyment of God's dynamic presence, in and through the Spirit-anointed ministry of Jesus. Indeed, what Luke means by salvation, or God's reign, seems to be so bound up with Jesus and the Spirit that the reader could only fear that his being withdrawn into the heavens through the ascension will bring all this to an end – at least until he returns.

Against such a reading, however, Luke sets the quite different expectation that *the kingdom of God would be intensified,* and consequently Israel would be significantly purified, restored and renewed, *in and through the death of Jesus* (22:16–20, 28–30; 23:43) *and his consequent resurrection and entry into glory* (24:25–26). These hopes are taken up in the prologue of Acts (1:1–11). The work Jesus began, centred on the kingdom of God, he is now to continue (1:1, 3); the Baptist's promise of the purification of Israel in fiery Spirit (Lk. 3:16) is now to be realized (Acts 1:5); the resulting Israel of fulfilment, to be restored around the apostolic rulers of the twelve tribes (Lk. 22:28–30; Acts 1:21–26), will be a light to the nations and 'witnesses' even 'to the end of the earth' (Acts 1:8, taking up the language of Is. 43:10–12 with the unusual wording of Is. 49:6). All this they will accomplish, the same verse tells us, when they are empowered by 'the Spirit from on high' – once more with the allusion to the restoration hopes of Isaiah 32:15–18; 44:3–4, already noted at Luke 24:49.[39]

It is not too difficult to piece together from such clues how Luke relates Joel's promise of the Spirit of prophecy to the hopes for an imminent intensification of God's reign and of the experience of 'salvation' in the community. If the Spirit of prophecy upon Jesus brought the presence of salvation in the ministry, so now Jesus' exaltation reception of the Spirit promised by Joel and Isaiah, and his pouring out of the same from the right hand of God (2:33), bring the intensification of God's reign and salvation which transforms the community in ways hoped for in Luke 1–2, but which are still largely unfulfilled at the

---

[38] See Turner, 'Spirit and Salvation', 106–109.

[39] Turner, 'Spirit and Salvation', 109–11.

close of the ministry. The same gift of the Spirit of prophecy bringing charismatic revelation, wisdom and various kinds of inspired speech provides *both* the empowering for mission *and* the renewed and transforming and saving immanent Lordship of Jesus in and to the community. It is no coincidence that with the arrival of the Spirit at Pentecost we begin to see (in Luke's summaries concerning the Jerusalem church in Acts 2:42–47; 4:32–35; 5:12–16, and elsewhere) the community of Jesus' followers living in ways that reflect the hopes of Israel's restoration. It is precisely because Luke understands the Spirit of prophecy as *essentially* what Wenk calls 'community-forming power'.[40] And the Spirit of prophecy experienced as God's self-revealing, empowering and transforming presence in the community would also naturally be expected *profoundly to shape the individual's life before God*. That is, the Spirit of prophecy is what brings that initial and ongoing experiential knowledge of God, and of the risen Lord, which constitutes each believer's own experience of cleansing of the heart (15:9), of baptizing with Holy Spirit (11:16), and all other subsequent experiences that are part and parcel of Lukan 'salvation'.[41] Recognition of this also helps explain why Luke considers the Spirit of prophecy normally to be given in the complex of conversion-initiation (2:38–39): when it is not (as at 8:16 and 19:2–5), this is both signalled as exceptional and immediately corrected.[42] This is not because Luke thinks all converts should immediately be endowed with power for mission (contra, e.g., Penney)[43] – but because he knows they need Joel's promise to shape their very existence and continued dynamic 'life' as members of the messianic restoration of Israel and its mission.

Luke and the Spirit in Canonical Context and in Theology Today

Reading Luke with Acts

The first three sections above highlight the deep ambiguity of Luke's Gospel, taken on its own, on such central themes as Israel's hope for restoring salvation, the kingdom of God and the relation of these issues to the Spirit. These hopes reach something of a cliff-hanging climax with Jesus' 'triumphal' entry into Jerusalem, but the puzzle of promises then almost seems to break into pieces at the feet of the crucified Messiah, tragically rejected by the chief priests and

---

[40] Cf. The full title of his monograph, in the Bibliography below.
[41] For a similar view of the soteriological force of the Spirit in Acts, see Turner, *Power*, chs. 10 and 13, 'Spirit and Salvation', 109–16, and 'Interpreting the Samaritans'.
[42] See Turner, *Power*, ch. 12.
[43] See Turner, 'Every Believer as a Witness?'.

rulers of Israel themselves (cf. Lk. 24:19–20). The resurrection-ascension scenes which close the gospel renew the hopes, and embed them again in the totality of Old Testament Scripture (24:27, 32, 44–47), but nevertheless leave so much of the vision allusive and unexplained. It is only with Acts that true light dawns. Or, to be more precise, almost any reading of Luke, informed by the general proclamation of the early church, would be able to glean much between the lines of his gospel. But it is *the pronounced intertextuality of wording and themes between Luke and Acts that affords the reader the keenest interpretive insight into both texts.* The interconnections clarify the movements in the grander story of how Israel's messianic hopes for her transforming salvation, and for God's reign amongst her, began to come to a surprising kind of fulfilment through the church. In respect of the 'story' of the Spirit, as we saw in section 4, above, Acts provides a startling, and challenging, interpretation both of John's promise that Jesus would baptize with Spirit (Lk. 3:16; Acts 1:5; 11:16–17) and the 'promise of the Father' of Isaianic 'power from on high' (Lk. 24:49; Acts 1:8). His narrative simply equates them in a christocentric fusion, which is simultaneously interpreted as Joel's promise that in the day of salvation *God* would 'pour out' the transforming Spirit of prophecy on his people – and, remarkably, it proves to be Jesus, as heavenly Lord, who pours out the divine Spirit instead (Acts 2:17, 33). And if Luke's Gospel could be read to suggest that the Spirit was an utterly unique empowering for Jesus, to be extended in an occasional way to his immediate circle of disciple-witnesses (see section 3, above), the creative fusion in Acts clarifies it as a vividly experiential gift given to *all* believers (cf. Acts 2:1–4, 33, 38–39 and confirmed time and again in the ensuing narrative). Similarly, while the promised Isaianic restorative spirit/power 'from on high' (Is. 32:15–18; 44:3–4) could be understood in sectors of Judaism as some restricted version of the Spirit of prophecy – merely a *donum superadditum* empowering for special service – the link between the allusions to these verses in Luke 24/Acts 1 and the allusion in Luke 1:35 suggests that the gift of the Spirit to believers is envisaged as *both* God's creative/transformative presence (producing the fruit of holiness and filial sonship) *and* his empowering for service. Thus significant *elements* of the two distinct 'moments' of the Spirit in the life of Jesus (those at conception and baptism) appear to be carried over into the *single* gift of the Spirit to disciples envisaged in Acts.

We need not draw out this part of the discussion further, other than to make a more methodological observation. We have noted that modern interpreters of the Spirit in Luke-Acts have reached consensus on a majority of points. The consensus is not due to agreement on critical method, for it embraces those who make heavy use of different 'behind the text' methods, combined with redaction-/composition-criticism, and those who rely on more 'in the text' approaches. The consensus is largely due, it seems, to the degree that the texts of Luke and Acts are transparently mutually interpretive (with Acts carrying the major hermeneutical freight on this subject). The crucial difference – the relation of the Spirit to salvation – rests on a far more complex, wide-ranging and subtle set of disagreements.[44] Ultimately the problem is how to 'hear' Luke's works on aspects of a question on which he is largely silent, or merely whispers: perhaps because he assumes common presuppositions with his intended hearers. 'Background' studies on the Spirit do not yet appear to provide a persuasive 'key' to agreement on what Luke and his readers might merely assume, for there is significant difference on how to read Jewish understandings of the eschatological 'Spirit of prophecy'. As we suggested above, perhaps even more significant is the measure of disagreement over what Luke *means* by 'salvation', and how that maps on to a constellation of related Lukan themes: forgiveness of sins, Jesus' messianic proclamation, the kingdom of God, the restoration of Israel, Isaianic 'power from on high', witness and so on. This may be a largely text-immanent issue, but none the easier to settle decisively for that. Other divisive factors hinge on how Luke is read alongside (especially) Paul and John (whether emphasizing distinctiveness and development, or unity and complementarity), and on judgements at the canonical and contemporary theological level about how Luke-Acts is to be read as Scripture, and which reading most effectively shapes and nurtures the spiritual life of the church today. It is to these latter aspects that we now turn.

Reading Luke–Acts amongst the other New Testament witnesses

What would change were we to read Luke's pneumatology in the broader context of the pluriform New Testament witness? Many of the kinds of study referred to above read Luke-Acts for the writer's characteristic and, more important, for his *distinctive,* emphases. So, for example, as we have noted, it is often maintained that Luke can attribute neither miracles of power nor immediate ethical effects to the Spirit, because that would allegedly be inconsistent with his view of the Spirit as essentially the Jewish Spirit of prophecy. I have argued, per contra, that this view misunderstands both Judaism and Luke and rests on a tissue of flimsy evidence and improbable argument. If Luke is read *alongside* Mark and Matthew, however, the view that he does not accept healings and exorcisms as the work of the Spirit becomes more difficult for the reader to hold, precisely because such a position would then be seen as a *contradiction* of Jesus' own teaching and of explicit redactional comments in Mark 3:29–30 and Matthew 12:15–18, 28. A contemporary of the evangelists just might have felt free to choose between what he considered conflicting witnesses. But any later *canonical* reader – one who has come to regard all the

44 For analysis of the major 'behind the text' and 'in the text' factors at the root of scholarly division, see Turner, 'Spirit and Salvation', passim.

gospels as *Scripture* – would be more likely simply to *accommodate* Luke to the others, taking the texts which *can* be read to connect Spirit and power of miraculous deeds (Lk. 1:35; 4:14, 18–21; Acts 10:38) as ample evidence of his essential harmony with Mark and Matthew.

Similar considerations apply to a canonical reading of baptism in the Spirit and reception of the Spirit. A pentecostal reading takes the promise of the Baptist in Luke 3:16; Acts 1:5 and 11:16 to refer to a *donum superadditum* of empowering for witness. I do not think it is a particularly plausible reading at any of those points, and a broader understanding of it as a promise of Israel's messianic cleansing, restoration and transformation seems more inviting in each case, even if Luke-Acts were read in isolation. But such a broader reading becomes all the more compelling when Luke is set alongside Matthew, Mark and John. In Matthew and Mark, the Baptist's contrast would most naturally be understood soteriologically (i.e., as another metaphor for the messianic enactment of God's reign).[45] Similarly, in John, the Baptist's opening promise (1:33) forms an inclusio with John 20:22–23 and is interpreted as the transforming impartation of the Spirit as the eschatological breath of life, with echoes of Genesis 2:7 and Ezekiel 37:9.[46] If the other three gospels take the Baptist's promise as fundamentally, or at least inclusively, soteriological in force, canonical readers are more likely to take Luke in that sense too – failing powerful arguments in the text leading in a different direction.

---

[45] See Hooker, 'John's Baptism'. Classical Pentecostals might simply reply with the reverse strategy, viz. that we should use Luke-Acts to 'clarify' Matthew and Mark. But while it is true that Luke has more to say on the issue than the other two, that does not mean his position is the clear one, demanding subsequence. The fact of the extensive scholarly debate about Luke's meaning is itself evidence of a considerable measure of ambiguity about the meaning of Luke-Acts on this issue.

[46] See Turner, *Holy Spirit*, ch. 6; Bennema, 'Giving of the Spirit' and 'Spirit-Baptism'; Thompson, 'Breath of Life'. I am aware of the sophisticated defence of a traditional pentecostal reading argued by R.P. Menzies, 'John's Place'. He advocates that Jn. 20:22 relates to the 'life-giving' function of the Spirit, and that this is quite separate from the post-ascension missiological empowering by the Spirit-Paraclete. He would then be free to identify Jn. 20:22–23 with 'birth of water and Spirit' (3:3, 5), and 1:33 with the promise of the gift of the Paraclete (given at Pentecost), though he does not make this identification explicit. The problems with this reading are: (i) Jn. 1:29 and 33 relate thematically more closely to 20:22–23 than to Jn. 14–16; (ii) both Jn. 20:22–23 and the Paraclete promises relate to experience of the Spirit as the Spirit of prophecy bringing charismatic revelation, wisdom and understanding which are *simultaneously* both life-giving and empower mission; (iii) John regards the functions of the Spirit granted in 20:22–23 as taken over by and enhanced by the gift of the Spirit-Paraclete, so 20:22–23 cannot be repeated after the Spirit-Paraclete is given. See Bennema, 'Giving of the Spirit', for detail.

Canonical reading will also inevitably affect understanding of the nature of the 'gift of the Spirit' in Luke-Acts. It raises the question of how Luke's pneumatology is to be integrated with that of John and Paul. For them, the Spirit of prophecy is clearly fundamentally *both* soteriological *and* (as a subset of that) empowers mission.[47] In attempting a canonically harmonious reading, several options for interpreting Luke's relationship to the other major New Testament witnesses have been canvassed. For perhaps the majority of Pentecostals, including scholars like Hunter, Ervin, Williams and Arrington, Luke works with a *two-stage* pneumatology.[48] In their opinion, Luke assumes that the Spirit brings a person to conversion and is then given to that person to cleanse their heart in regeneration and to impart salvation and life to them. Through this gift of the indwelling Spirit a person may grow in fellowship with God and the risen Lord, and bear the fruit of the Spirit in such virtues as are listed in Galatians 5:22. But this is to be distinguished from receiving the subsequent Pentecost gift. The former corresponds more to the *Easter* gift of the Spirit to the disciples (related in Jn. 20:22), than to Acts 2. The gift in Acts 2, by contrast, is purely the charismatic Spirit of prophecy, which empowers with miraculous gifts for service and mission.[49] It is a second-blessing 'baptism with Spirit', of 'filling with the Spirit', attended by such visible and striking phenomena that it makes even a ranking magician jealous (Acts 8:18–19). Expressing this clear two-stage pneumatology, Howard Ervin can thus assert that the Samaritans, roundly converted by Philip's ministry in the power of the Spirit, are Christians in the fullest sense and 'their baptism is in itself a witness that these ... converts had experienced the regenerative action of the Holy Spirit in their lives', but they had yet to receive the baptism in the Spirit.[50]

---

[47] For the argument that both John and Paul are still working with a Christian version of the Spirit of prophecy, see Turner, *Holy Spirit*, chs. 4–8; Bennema, *Power*; Fee, *God's Empowering Presence*. While Fee does not work with the category 'Spirit of prophecy' as such, he nevertheless emphasizes the Spirit's activity in the kinds of charismata that would normally be included in the extension of such an understanding of the Spirit.

[48] Hunter, *Spirit-Baptism*; Ervin, *Spirit-Baptism*; Williams, *Renewal Theology*, esp. II; Arrington, *Acts*. Arrington's view is clearest in his discussion of Acts 19:1–6, where he states that 'the disciples at Ephesus were believers in Christ and were indwelt by the Holy Spirit, but they had not received the fullness of the Spirit. Paul asked them not about the regenerating work of the Spirit that is realized at the time of belief but about their post-belief reception of the Spirit' – which he proceeds to describe as charismatic endowment equipping the disciples to proclaim the gospel (*Acts*, 193). But for Luke it is not a question of their knowing only of the regenerative Spirit; they know of no (gift of the?) Holy Spirit at all (19:2).

[49] Such a view can be found in Chrysostom and Calvin, and is given its most scholarly defence by Beasley-Murray, *Baptism*, 118–19.

[50] Ervin, *Spirit-Baptism*, 73.

However, Pentecostals who are also Lukan specialists, such as Stronstad, Shelton, Menzies and Penney, tend to recognize that this is almost certainly not actually what Luke said, or implied. Indeed, his text regularly *subverts* such a reading. Luke does not distinguish two stages, first receiving the soteriological gift of the Spirit and then, subsequently, pentecostal power. He knows of only one gift of the Spirit, which he *equates* with being baptized with the Spirit. Thus Jesus' words in Acts 1:5 about the disciples soon being baptized with Holy Spirit are spelled out subsequently as their being 'filled with' the Holy Spirit (2:4) and Joel's promise being 'poured out' upon them (2:17, 18, 33) or 'falling upon' them (11:15), *and these are all equated with 'receiving the gift of the Spirit'* in 2:39; 10:47; 11:15; 15:8. We get the same equation most clearly in the Cornelius incident. The Spirit is said to 'fall upon' his household in 10:44, and this is subsequently described as 'the *gift* of the Holy Spirit' being 'poured out' upon them (10:45); their 'receiving' the Spirit (10:47); their being 'baptized with the Spirit' (11:16), and their being 'given' the Spirit (15:8) – and to most of those expressions the speaker adds 'as on/to us at the beginning'. The Samaritan account has similar features. It equates the Spirit's 'falling upon' the Samaritans (8:16) with their 'receiving' or 'being given' the Spirit (8:15, 17, 18, 19). His editorial explanation in 8:16 virtually precludes the view that Luke thinks the Samaritans have already received some other 'gift of the Spirit', which brought salvation and life. In short, for Menzies 'the gift of the Spirit' in Luke-Acts denotes only a small *subset* of what *the same sort of language* means for John and Paul, albeit a highly *distinctive* one. Indeed, to be more precise, what Luke means by the essentially Jewish 'gift of the Spirit [of prophecy]' matches fairly well the grouping of prophetic gifts in 1 Corinthians 12:8–10, and Luke's canonical *contribution* is thereby to show that these are received as a distinct *donum superadditum* (initially evidenced by the gift of tongues), and one with a *profoundly missiological dynamic and purpose*.[51]

Ultimately I find this ingenious, but implausible, as a canonical or theological reading. A canonical reader might be more liable to assume that the writer of Acts was a fairly long-time co-worker of Paul (intimated in the 'we' sections of Acts; not to mention Col. 4:14; Phlm. 24), and so would have had a more than passing knowledge of his fundamentally soteriologically-orientated charismatic pneumatology. In that context, it is unlikely that Luke would be read to affirm a view of the gift of the 'Spirit of prophecy' that *excluded* such a soteriological dimension. Rather, it would naturally be read to *include* it,[52] not least because Paul's own *soteriological* view of the gift of the Spirit essentially depends on the same charismatic gifts of God's christocentric, self-manifesting,

---

[51] For Menzies' position in more detail, see *Empowered for Witness*, chs. 12 – 13; Menzies and Menzies, *Spirit and Power*, ch. 3.

[52] For more detailed consideration see Turner, *Holy Spirit*, ch. 10.

revelatory and transforming wisdom. Classical Pentecostals may suspect that those with this view read Luke-Acts through Pauline spectacles and, in some way, *against* the grain of Luke's text.[53] But other readers, including those of a more broadly charismatic stripe, will opine that Paul merely makes explicit what is nevertheless *implicit* in Luke-Acts: that the Spirit of prophecy is the transforming and empowering presence of God's messianic reign amongst his people. Similar considerations apply to the understanding of how the gift of the Spirit in Luke would be read in relation to the gift of the Spirit (of prophecy) in John.[54]

To conclude this section: canonical and theological readings are inevitably bound to highlight scriptural unities rather more strongly than possible authorial diversities, especially where the latter appear to imply a conflict. Where responsibly possible, the canonical and theological reader will inevitably seek harmony. Luke does not *explicitly* connect the Spirit with the broader soteriological functions which John and Paul elucidate. But his broad, dynamic, individual and corporate, highly experiential view of the 'salvation' of God accomplished in Acts *demands an explanation* as to what immanent power of God could achieve such a result. Almost certainly, for Judaism and for most of early Christianity, *an* answer was that the promised Spirit (of prophecy) could achieve it. Luke, who himself adamantly affirms the Spirit as the Spirit of prophecy, does not provide any *other* viable explanation of so vital a change. He knows of no *other* presence of God that might accomplish such fulfilment of Israel's eschatological hopes. And the most significant change occurs, according to him, with the outpouring of the Spirit at Pentecost. Paul, earlier than Luke's writing, and John after him, both explain new covenant experience of salvation, *including* all of its empowering for mission, in terms of the charismatic Spirit of prophecy. It is then difficult for the canonical reader to believe that Luke-Acts represents a different pneumatology which restricts the Spirit *exclusively* to missiological effects.

Reading Luke–Acts for scriptural norms

At the beginning of this chapter, we noted that most readings of the Spirit in Luke-Acts were, and are, 'ecclesial' readings, in that they were mainly undertaken in order to shape church belief and praxis. Many have been concerned primarily to elucidate the contribution of Luke-Acts (esp. Acts!) to the understanding of the sacraments of baptism and/or confirmation, and they have shown only minor concern to elucidate the broader *nature* and *function* of the

---

[53] Menzies and Menzies, *Spirit and Power*, 100, 102, 105–106, accuse me of just such a reading.

[54] See all the works of Bennema noted in nn. 46–47 above, esp. n. 46.

gift of the Spirit in Luke's works. But, since Wesley and Fletcher,[55] a whole stream of revivalist Christianity, leading up to the massive pentecostal movements of today, has looked to Acts for the key to the dynamic empowered life of the early church as described there, and has discovered the answer in a reading of Luke-Acts which understands 'baptism with Holy Spirit' as a 'subsequent', highly experiential, working of the Spirit.[56] For Wesley and Fletcher (as with earlier Puritans, notably Richard Baxter and John Goodwin), the primary focus of this subsequent 'baptism/filling with the Spirit' was a transforming and ongoing experience of being filled with God's love, sanctifying grace ('Christian perfection') and a full personal assurance of faith, boiling over into active witness. For classical Pentecostals, however, the focus of Spirit-baptism has shifted almost entirely to empowerment for mission,[57] and Luke-Acts, read for its most distinctive emphases, has become the canon-within-the-canon legitimating such a view. For pentecostal interpreters this is not merely a 'neutral exegetical' issue: pentecostal hermeneutics is deeply influenced by the dialectic between scriptural interpretation and corporate experience.[58] The explosive impact of the Spirit at Topeka and Azusa Street in the early 1900s seemed to confirm the exegetical expectation of a baptism with the Spirit that was subsequent to conversion, because it came to hungrily seeking *believers* of longstanding Christian faith and commitment. And Pentecostals would maintain that the same is experienced today. For them, Acts is not a different 'historical' world of the past, but a scripturally narrated world that we can and *should* step into, and own. And the gateway to that world of experience is Spirit-baptism. Classical Pentecostals regard 'subsequence' and 'separability'[59] as not merely the norm discernible in Acts, but also as pragmatically necessary for the life and nurture of the church. They suspect unitary accounts of the gift of the Spirit (ones such as advanced above, that combine soteriological and empowering

---

[55] For a nuanced analysis of Spirit-baptism in their teaching, and reclaiming its importance for them, see Wood, *Meaning of Pentecost*. Wesley traced his understanding of Spirit-baptism back at least to the (as he thought fourth-century) homilies of (Pseudo-) Makarios (see Wood, *Meaning of Pentecost*, 348–52).

[56] See the various forms of this as described by Synan, *Holiness-Pentecostal Movement*; Menzies, *Anointed to Serve*; Dayton, *Theological Roots*.

[57] For the most articulate pentecostal separation of the work of the Spirit in holiness/sanctification from that of Spirit-baptism as charismatic empowerment of the Spirit of prophecy for mission, see Menzies and Menzies, *Spirit and Power*, ch. 15.

[58] For an important pentecostal view of the relationship between exegesis and experience-related interpretation, see Thomas, 'Reading the Bible'.

[59] The first of these terms is used to make the point that the gift of the Spirit in Luke-Acts is normally given *after* the graces of conversion; the second is used to emphasize that Spirit-baptism is also *theologically distinct* from the work of God in conversion and the life of personal discipleship.

works of the Spirit)[60] of inevitably leading to the eclipse of prophetic and empowering charismata,[61] and/or to an expectation of the restriction of these to a relatively small number of specially endowed people, and to a passive approach to divine enabling. Menzies gently charges me with having failed 'to articulate a theology that provides a fully biblical sense of purpose and expectation with reference to the Spirit's empowering'.[62] But what appears to have been missed in these criticisms is that anyone who takes Luke-Acts as a norm for the church's life in the Spirit is liable to have a very high expectation of charismatic empowering indeed. Luke's writings throw down a fundamental challenge to the canonical and theological reader.[63] As both Dunn and Menzies have emphasized well, in their very different ways, the gift of the Spirit, for Luke, is a profoundly dynamic *experience* of God. For Luke, the Spirit is God revealing himself – accosting us, surprising us, giving us dreams and revelations, leading us in unexpected directions, manifesting himself in unexpected ways and places, making Christ almost palpably present to us, grasping us with profound and transformational understanding, bringing joy and praise to our lips and hearts, giving special wisdom in testing circumstances, on occasion 'filling us' with special prophetic words, and more generally empowering us to share the good news of our God and of his wondrous deeds accomplished in Christ. That is what Luke means when he talks of Jesus pouring out Joel's promised eschatological gift of the Spirit of prophecy in Acts 2. And it is clear that he does not think of this gift merely as one for the golden age of the church's beginnings. For him, as indeed Joel promised, the gift of the Spirit is *essentially* the Spirit of prophecy and it is for *all* God's people. And so, as the 'children's children' of the first post-Pentecost believers, and as those also called by the Lord, it is implicitly *for the present-day readers too* (cf. Acts 2:38–39). Luke-Acts is a challenge to reject the regular temptation to domesticate the Spirit and to reduce the gift to some merely theoretical immanence, the presence and activity of which is primarily an object of 'belief', rather than of more immediate experience. Luke invites his readers to become 'full' of the Spirit of prophecy, even a contemporary 'Philip' or 'Stephen'. And in that invitation, too, there is little doubt that he walks shoulder to shoulder with his canonical companions, Paul and John.

In the final analysis, what divides Wesleyan Holiness, classical pentecostal and integrative charismatic interpretations of the Spirit in Luke's writings is

[60] For a survey of such integrative accounts in the charismatic renewal movements see Lederle, *Treasures Old and New*, esp. chs. 4–5, and Turner, *Holy Spirit*, ch. 10.
[61] See Menzies and Menzies, *Spirit and Power*, ch. 6 (against Turner) and ch. 7 (against Fee) and cf. Chan, *Pentecostal Theology*, 89–94.
[62] Menzies and Menzies, *Spirit and Power*, 100–101.
[63] I have tried to elucidate this challenge much more fully than in what follows, and with more specific reference to the text of Luke-Acts, in *Power*, ch. 14.

probably less significant than what unites them. Together they represent a radical renewal of theological interpretation of biblical pneumatology – one which seeks to recover the dynamic of the Spirit in Acts (and elsewhere in the New Testament) for the life of the church today. The vigorous expansion of the pentecostal and charismatic movements, to an estimated five hundred million participants in just one century, attests the fecundity of such readings and has done much to restore pneumatology to its appropriate place in broader biblical and systematic ecclesiologies.

Bibliography

Adler, N., *Das erste christliche Pfingstfest: Sinn und Bedeutung des Pfingstberichtes Apg 2:1–13* (Münster: Aschendorffsche Verlag, 1938)

—, *Taufe und Handauflegung: Eine exegetisch-theologische Untersuchung von Apg 8:14–17* (Munster: Aschendorffsche Verlag, 1951)

Arrington, F.L., *The Acts of the Apostles* (Peabody, MA: Hendrickson, 1988)

Von Baer, H., *Der heilige Geist in den Lukasschriften* (Stuttgart: Kohlhammer, 1926)

Barth, M., *Die Taufe ein Sakrament?* (Zurich: EVZ Verlag, 1951)

Beasley-Murray, G.R., *Baptism in the New Testament* (London: Macmillan, 1962)

Bennema, C., 'The Giving of the Spirit in John's Gospel – A New Proposal?', *EvQ* 74 (2002), 195–213

—, *The Power of Saving Wisdom: An Investigation of Spirit and Wisdom in Relation to the Soteriology of the Fourth Gospel* (Tübingen: Mohr Siebeck, 2002)

—, 'Spirit-Baptism in the Fourth Gospel: A Messianic Reading of John 1,33', *Biblica* 84 (2003), 35–60

Chan, S., *Pentecostal Theology and the Christian Spiritual Tradition* (Sheffield: Sheffield Academic Press, 2000)

Dayton, D.W., *Theological Roots of Pentecostalism* (Peabody, MA: Hendrickson, 1987)

Dix, G., *The Theology of Confirmation in Relation to Baptism* (Westminster: Dacre, 1946)

Dunn, J.D.G., 'Baptism in the Spirit: A Response to Pentecostal Scholarship on Luke-Acts', *JPT* 3 (1993), 3–27

– *Baptism in the Holy Spirit: A Re-Examination of the New Testament Teaching on the Gift of the Spirit in Relation to Pentecostalism Today* (London: SCM Press, 1970)

—, *Christology in the Making* (London: SCM Press, 1980)

—, *Jesus and the Spirit* (London: SCM Press, 1975)

—, 'Spirit and Kingdom', *ExpTim* 82 (1970–71), 36–40

Ervin, H.M., *Conversion-Initiation and the Baptism in the Holy Spirit: A Critique of James D.G. Dunn, Baptism in the Holy Spirit* (Peabody, MA: Hendrickson, 1984.

—, *Spirit-Baptism: A Biblical Investigation* (Peabody, MA: Hendrickson, 1987)

Fee, G.D., *God's Empowering Presence: The Holy Spirit in the Letters of Paul* (Peabody, MA: Hendrickson, 1994)

Green, J.B., *The Gospel of Luke* (Grand Rapids: Eerdmans, 1997)

Haya-Prats, G., *L'Esprit, Force de l'Église* (Paris: Cerf, 1975)

Hooker, M., 'John's Baptism: A Prophetic Sign', in *The Holy Spirit and Christian Origins: Essays in Honor of James D.G. Dunn* (ed. G.N. Stanton, B.W. Longenecker, and S.C. Barton; Grand Rapids: Eerdmans, 2004), 22–40

Hunter, H.D., *Spirit-Baptism: A Pentecostal Alternative* (Lanham: University Press of America, 1983)

Lampe, G.W.H., *The Seal of the Spirit* (London: SPCK, 2nd edn, 1967)

292 *Max Turner*

Lederle, H.I., *Treasures Old and New: Interpretations of 'Spirit-Baptism' in the Charismatic Renewal Movement* (Peabody, MA: Hendrickson, 1988)

Levison, J.R., 'Did the Spirit Withdraw from Israel? An Evaluation of the Earliest Jewish Data', *NTS* 43 (1997), 35–57

—, *The Spirit in First Century Judaism* (Leiden: E.J. Brill, 1997)

Mainville, O., *L'Esprit dans l'Oeuvre de Luc* (Montreal: Fides, 1991)

Menzies, R.P., *The Development of Early Christian Pneumatology with Special Reference to Luke-Acts* (Sheffield: Sheffield Academic Press, 1991)

—, *Empowered for Witness: The Spirit in Luke-Acts* (Sheffield: Sheffield Academic Press, 1994)

—, 'John's Place in the Development of Early Christian Pneumatology', in *The Spirit and Spirituality: Essays in Honour of Russell P. Spittler* (ed. W. Ma and R.P. Menzies; London: T&T Clark, 2004), 41–52

Menzies, W.W., and R.P. Menzies, *Spirit and Power: Foundations of Pentecostal Experience* (Grand Rapids: Zondervan, 2000)

Menzies, W.W., *Anointed to Serve: The Story of the Assemblies of God* (Springfield, MO: Gospel Publishing House, 1971)

Montague, G.T., *The Holy Spirit: Growth of a Biblical Tradition* (New York: Paulist Press, 1976)

Pao, D.W., *Acts and the Isaianic New Exodus* (Tübingen: Mohr Siebeck, 2000)

Penney, J.M., *The Missionary Emphasis of Lukan Pneumatology* (Sheffield: Sheffield Academic Press, 1997)

Schweizer, E., *The Holy Spirit* (London: SCM Press, 1981)

Shelton, J.B., *Mighty in Word and Deed: The Role of the Holy Spirit in Luke-Acts* (Peabody, MA: Hendrickson, 1991)

Strauss, M.L., *The Davidic Messiah in Luke-Acts: The Promise and its Fulfillment in Lukan Christology* (Sheffield: Sheffield Academic Press, 1995)

Stronstad, R., *The Charismatic Theology of Saint Luke* (Peabody, MA: Hendrickson, 1984)

—, *The Prophethood of All Believers: A Study in Luke's Charismatic Theology* (Sheffield: Sheffield Academic Press, 1999)

Synan, V., *The Holiness-Pentecostal Movement in the United States* (Grand Rapids: Eerdmans, 1970)

Thomas, J.C., 'Reading the Bible from Within Our Traditions: A Pentecostal Hermeneutic as Test Case', in *Between Two Horizons: Spanning New Testament Studies and Systematic Theology* (ed. J.B. Green and M. Turner; Grand Rapids: Eerdmans, 2000), 108–22

Thompson, M.M., 'The Breath of Life: John 20:22–23 Once More', in *The Holy Spirit and Christian Origins: Essays in Honor of James D.G. Dunn* (ed. G.N. Stanton, B.W. Longenecker and S.C. Barton; Grand Rapids: Eerdmans, 2004), 69–78

Thornton, L.S., *Confirmation: Its Place in the Baptismal Mystery* (Westminster: Dacre, 1954)

Turner, M., 'Every Believer as a Witness in Acts? – in Dialogue with John Michael Penney', *Ashland Theological Journal* 30 (1998), 57–71

—, *The Holy Spirit and Spiritual Gifts: Then and Now* (Carlisle: Paternoster, 1999)

—, 'Interpreting the Samaritans of Acts 8: The Waterloo of Pentecostal Soteriology and Pneumatology?', *PNEUMA* 23 (2001), 265–86

—, *Power from on High: The Spirit in Israel's Restoration and Witness in Luke-Acts* (Sheffield: Sheffield Academic Press, 1996)

—, 'The Spirit and Salvation in Luke–Acts', in *The Holy Spirit and Christian Origins: Essays in Honor of James D.G. Dunn* (ed. G.N. Stanton, B.W. Longenecker and S.C. Barton; Grand Rapids: Eerdmans, 2004), 103–16

—, 'The Spirit of Prophecy and the Power of Authoritative Preaching in Luke-Acts: A Question of Origins', *NTS* 38 (1992), 66–88

Wenk, M., *Community-Forming Power: The Socio-Ethical Role of the Spirit in Luke-Acts* (Sheffield: Sheffield Academic Press, 2000)

Williams, J.R., *Renewal Theology, I–III* (Grand Rapids: Zondervan, 1990)

Wood, L.W., *The Meaning of Pentecost in Early Methodism: Rediscovering John Fletcher as John Wesley's Vindicator and Designated Successor* (Lanham/Oxford: Scarecrow Press, 2002)

Woods, E.J., *The 'Finger of God' and Pneumatology in Luke-Acts* (Sheffield: Sheffield Academic Press, 2001)

11

Kingdom and Church in Luke-Acts

From Davidic Christology to Kingdom Ecclesiology

Scott W. Hahn

The past two decades have seen a flowering of scholarship on the use and significance of the Scriptures of Israel in the third gospel.[1] The premise of much of this scholarship has been succinctly expressed by Augustín del Agua: 'the OT tradition ... is the hermeneutic reference of meaning sought by Luke in his narration'[2] and 'the source par excellence for the narrative elaboration of his theological project.'[3] Among the many works on Luke and the Old Testament are some excellent studies of Luke's treatment of Israelite covenantal traditions.[4] However, not all of these traditions have received equal attention: the Abrahamic and Mosaic covenants have been emphasized at the expense of the Davidic.[5] Moreover, despite the fact that, as Joel Green notes, 'Luke's use of the Scriptures is primarily ecclesiological rather than christological,'[6] the few studies written on Davidic covenant motifs in Luke-Acts – for example, Mark Strauss' monograph *The Davidic Messiah in Luke-Acts* – have focused on Christology.[7] The influence of the Davidic covenant traditions on Luke's

---

[1] Important works on the OT background of Luke's theological project include Moessner, *Lord*; Evans and Sanders, *Luke*; Kimball, *Exposition*; Brawley, *Text*; Denova, *Things*; Bock, *Proclamation*; and Evans and Stegner, *Gospels*.

[2] Del Agua, 'Narrative,' 643.

[3] Del Agua, 'Narrative,' 641.

[4] On the Abrahamic covenant in Luke, see Brawley, *Text*, and 'Covenant,' 109–32.

[5] For example, Brawley (*Text* and 'Covenant') makes astute observations concerning the Davidic covenant in Luke, but he foregrounds and emphasizes the Abrahamic, as does Van Den Eynde, 'Children.'

[6] Green, 'Learning Theological Interpretation,' 57.

[7] See also Bock, *Proclamation*, esp. 55–90. An earlier piece is Bruce, 'Messiah.'

ecclesiology remains largely unexplored.[8] This chapter will attempt to address that lacuna.

The work of Strauss and others has won some support for the view that royal Davidic messianism is a major christological category for Luke's Gospel.[9] Nonetheless, the conclusion has yet to be drawn that if Jesus is the Davidic king proclaiming a coming kingdom, that coming kingdom must be, in some sense, the *Davidic kingdom*. Perhaps the connection is not made because Luke calls the coming kingdom 'the kingdom *of God*' and not 'of David'; indeed, the precise phrase 'kingdom of God' is not found in the Old Testament. However, it is notable that the Chronicler twice employs a virtually synonymous phrase – 'the kingdom of Yahweh' – to describe the Davidic monarchy (1 Chr. 28:5; 2 Chr. 13:8; cf. 1 Chr. 17:14; 29:11–22). The Chronicler understood that the reign of the house of David was based on a divine covenant in which the son of David was also declared to be son of God (2 Sam. 7:14; Pss. 2:7; 89:27). Therefore, the kingdom of David was the manifestation of God's rule over the earth – that is, God's kingdom for Israel and the nations.[10]

Raymond Brown saw quite clearly the close relationship (indeed, identification) of the kingdom of God and the kingdom of David:

> The story of David brings out all the strengths and weaknesses of the beginnings of the religious institution of the kingdom for the people of God ... The kingdom established by David was a political institution to be sure, but one with enormous religious attachments (priesthood, temple, sacrifice, prophecy) ... *It is the closest Old Testament parallel to the church* ... To help Christians make up their mind on how the Bible speaks to [whether the church is related to the kingdom of God], it would help if they knew about David and his kingdom, *which was also God's kingdom*.[11]

Building on Brown's insight into the relationship of the kingdom of God, the kingdom of David, and the church, this chapter will advance the thesis that the kingdom of David informs Luke's presentation of Jesus' kingship and kingdom, providing much of the content and meaning of these terms. Specifically,

---

[8] Pao notes: 'Strong emphasis on christological uses ... tends to overshadow concerns for the ecclesiological function ... of scriptural traditions in the Lukan writings' (*Acts*, 17).

[9] See Juel, 'Review' (of Strauss, *Messiah*); and Bock, 'Proclamation,' 293–94: 'the fundamental category of Lukan Old Testament christology is a regal one.'

[10] The Chronicler describes the worshipping assembly of this kingdom, most often led by the Davidic king himself, with the term קָהָל, or, in the LXX, ἐκκλησία (e.g., 1 Chr. 13:2–4; 28:2–8; 29:1, 10, 20; 2 Chr. 1:3–5; 6:3–13; 7:8; 10:3; 20:5–14; 23:3; 29:23–30:25). Chronicles uses this term more frequently than any other part of the LXX and may provide the background for understanding Luke's deployment of ἐκκλησία in Acts.

[11] Brown, 'Communicating,' 5–6 (emphasis mine). Cf. Levenson, *Sinai*, 155–56.

the Davidic royal Christology of Luke's Gospel sets the stage for his development of a *Davidic kingdom ecclesiology* in Acts.[12] Inasmuch as Christians believe
themselves still to be participating in the ecclesial reality whose birth is portrayed in Acts, my thesis implies that a Davidic kingdom-ecclesiology is still
relevant for contemporary Christian theology.[13]

The argument will unfold as follows: first, the textual evidence for the
growing recognition that Luke's Christology is fundamentally both *royal* and
specifically *Davidic* will be reviewed. Second, in order to shed light on Luke's
use of royal Davidic imagery, the canonical portrayal of the kingdom of David
in the Old Testament will be explored. Third, it will be seen how all eight
major characteristics of the Davidic kingdom in the Old Testament are present

---

[12] McKnight notes that 'the God of Jesus was the God of Israel, and the kingdom of
Jesus was a kingdom for Israel' (*Vision*, 83). One may go further and say that the
kingdom of Jesus is the kingdom of Israel, and the kingdom of Israel is the kingdom
of *David*.

[13] While this study is not methodologically explicit, the attentive reader will recognize
a strong affinity between the hermeneutic at work in what follows and the
hermeneutical principles advocated by several contributors to the five previous volumes of this ongoing Scripture and Hermeneutics Series. I am engaged in a canonical analysis of the Bible's 'grand narrative,' within a confessional framework that is
Catholic yet ecumenical, informed by speech-act theory as a means to grasp both
God's covenantal declarations to his people in the Old and New Testaments and the
perpetuation of those declarations in the church's eucharistic liturgy. The 'canonical' approach to biblical theology originated with Childs, *Biblical Theology in Crisis*,
and is discussed recently by Bartholomew, 'Biblical Theology.' My approach is not
identical to that of Childs, however. I understand 'canonical' as applied to biblical
theology in three senses: (1) the subject of study is the *final,* or *canonical,* form of the
text; (2) the texts are understood in light of their *canonical* context, as books within a
bi-covenantal corpus; and (3) an underlying unity of the canon is presumed, such
that all the texts of the canon are allowed to speak synchronically on a given subject.
For advocacy of a 'narrative' or 'story' approach to biblical theology, see
Bartholomew and Goheen, 'Story.' Such an approach is not limited to literary analysis of narrative texts, but rather seeks to situate the interpretation of all biblical texts
within the larger biblical 'story' or 'metanarrative.' The criteria for specifically Catholic biblical exegesis are set forth by Vatican II (*Dei Verbum* 12; CCC §112–114):
(1) the *content* and *unity* of Scripture; (2) the *living tradition* of the church (expressed
primarily in the liturgy); and (3) the *analogy of faith* (for elaboration see Martin, 'Directions'). On speech-act theory, see Vanhoozer, 'Speech Acts.' I find Vanhoozer's
treatment of 'discourse of the covenant' useful in describing the speech-acts by
which God establishes relationships with humankind. Ultimately, three divine
speech-acts are the focus of this chapter: the establishment of the covenant between
God and David (2 Sam. 7); between Christ and the Apostles (Lk. 22:14–30); and
between God and the church in the eucharistic 'breaking of the bread' (Acts 2:42;
20:7; 1 Cor. 11:23–26).

in Luke's portrayal of Jesus' person and mission. Fourth, in order to trace the connection between the Christology of Luke and the ecclesiology of Acts, Jesus' conferral of his Davidic kingdom upon the apostles in the Lukan Institution Narrative will be examined. Fifth, the promise of vice-regency over the Davidic kingdom given to the apostles in the Institution Narrative will be seen as fulfilled in their rule over the nascent ἐκκλησία in Acts. Thus, the ἐκκλησία of Acts is the restored kingdom of David, spreading to 'the ends of the earth.'

Royal Davidic Christology in Luke

We have mentioned the significance of Strauss' recent work on Luke's royal Davidic messianism. Against scholars who assert that Luke's dominant christological category is Prophet, Lord, or Isaianic Servant, Strauss argues that Luke's royal Davidic Christology is primary and capable of integrating other messianic types – like that of Prophet – within it. The following are the key texts in Luke from which Strauss and others have argued the importance of royal Davidic messianism:[14]

- Luke emphasizes that Jesus' legal father Joseph was 'of the house of David' (Lk. 1:27).[15]
- At the annunciation, Gabriel describes Jesus to Mary (Lk. 1:32–33) in a thoroughly Davidic way, adapting the key Davidic covenant text (2 Sam. 7:1–17).[16]
- In the *Benedictus*, Zechariah begins by praising God for having 'raised up a horn of salvation for us *in the house of his servant David*' (Lk. 1:69), a reference to a royal Davidic psalm (Ps. 132:17).[17]
- Jesus' birthplace is Bethlehem, called 'the City of David' by both the narrator (2:4) and the angels (2:11). At the same time, Joseph's Davidic lineage is repeated for emphasis (2:4).
- Appropriately, the first witnesses to the birth of the Son of David, the great 'shepherd king' of Israel's memory, are shepherds (Lk. 2:8–20), possibly alluding to Micah 5:1–3.[18]

---

[14] See Bock, *Luke*, 115; Brawley, *Text*, 85–86; Lane, *Luke*, 157–63; Ravens, *Luke*, 24–49, esp. 34.

[15] Cf. Green, *Luke*, 84–85.

[16] As demonstrated by Green, *Luke*, 85, 88; likewise Fitzmyer, *Luke*, 338.

[17] An allusion to Ps. 132:17, where a horn sprouts up from David, is probably intended (Green, *Luke*, 116). Cf. Bock, *Luke*, 20, 180. On other, more subtle, Davidic allusions in the *Benedictus*, see Farris, *Hymns*, 95–96.

[18] Cf. Green, *Luke*, 130; Ravens, *Luke*, 42–43.

- At Jesus' baptism, the divine voice utters over him, 'Thou art my beloved Son,' an adaptation of words from Psalm 2, the royal coronation hymn of the Davidic kings (Ps. 2:7).[19]
- In Luke 3:23–28, Luke traces Jesus' genealogy through David.[20]
- In Luke 6:1–5, Jesus compares himself and his disciples to David and his band of men, and he claims the same apparent freedom from cultic regulations that David enjoyed.[21]
- At the transfiguration, the divine voice again reiterates the royal coronation hymn (Ps. 2:7): 'This is my Son, my Chosen.'[22] The title 'chosen,' or 'chosen one,' is also an epithet of David (Ps. 89:3).[23]
- Jesus' statement in Luke 10:22, 'All things have been delivered to me by my Father' seems to recall the covenantal father-son relationship of God to the Davidic monarch (see Pss. 2:7–8; 8:4–8; 72:8; 89:25–27).
- On entry into Jericho, Jesus is hailed twice by a blind man as 'Son of David' (Lk. 18:35–43), foreshadowing his royal entrance to Jerusalem.[24]
- Luke intentionally describes Jesus' triumphal entry (19:28–48) so as to correspond to Zechariah 9:9–10, which in turn uses images of Solomon's coronation procession to describe the coming of an eschatological king, almost certainly a Davidide (cf. Zech. 12:7–13:1).[25]
- At the Last Supper, Jesus speaks of a 'new covenant,' evoking Jeremiah 31:31 and the broader context (Jer. 30–33), which foresees a 'new covenant' uniting Israel and Judah under the Davidic monarchy.[26]
- The end of the Institution Narrative (Lk. 22:29–30) evokes several Davidic images: the conferring of a kingdom by covenant (Ps. 89:3–4); eating at the king's own table (2 Sam. 9:9–13); and ruling from thrones over the tribes of Israel (Ps. 122:3–5).
- In the Passion Narratives Davidic titles are used of Jesus with contempt, but nonetheless accurately: 'King of the Jews' (Lk. 23:37–38; cf. 2 Sam. 2:11) and 'Chosen One' (Lk. 23:35; cf. Ps. 89:3–4).
- At least three key passages in Acts also press Jesus' claims as the Davidic Messiah: (1) *Peter's* first recorded sermon, at Pentecost (Acts 2:14–36, esp. vv. 25–36); (2) *Paul's* first recorded sermon, at Pisidian Antioch (13:16–

[19] Cf. Green, *Luke*, 186; Bock, *Luke*, 341–43.
[20] On David in Lk. 3:23–28 see Bock, *Luke,* 357. The following temptation sequence features a Davidic allusion in its second scene. See Brawley, *Text*, 20.
[21] See Bock, *Luke*, 527; and Johnson, *Luke*, 101.
[22] Bock, *Luke*, 873–74.
[23] Strauss, *Messiah*, 265–67.
[24] Green, *Luke*, 663–65; Bock, *Luke*, 1507–12; Fitzmyer, *Luke*, 1214.
[25] See Green, *Luke*, 683–88; and Bock, *Luke*, 1556–58, who point out the connections with Zech. 9:9 and 1 Kgs. 1:33 (the coronation of Solomon).
[26] Cf. Bock, 'Reign,' 43, 48–49.

41, esp. vv. 22–23, 33–37); and *James'* first and only recorded speech, at the Jerusalem council (15:13–21).[27]

It is not only the number, but also the placement, of these Davidic references that point to their significance. The heaviest concentrations of Davidic christological imagery occur in two places: (1) in the infancy narratives, which set the theological agenda for Luke's two-volume work and define terms used throughout – like 'Christ' and 'Son of God' – in explicitly Davidic categories; and (2) in the apostolic speeches of Acts, whose importance in explicating Luke's theology is widely recognized. Thus, the number and position of Davidic royal motifs make a *prima facie* case for the primacy in Luke of a royal Davidic Christology.

Yet it is not enough to make this observation without also ascertaining its significance: what exactly did it *mean* to Luke and his first-century audience – composed presumably of both Jews and Gentile converts familiar with the Scriptures of Israel – that Jesus was the messianic king of David's line? What features characterized the Davidic monarchy? What connotations did the Davidic monarchy carry for first-century believers steeped in Second Temple Judaism? To answer these questions, we must return to Luke's 'hermeneutic reference of meaning' – the Old Testament. For, as del Agua shows, 'Luke has elaborated his Christology and ecclesiology in the light of the Old Testament tradition of the *basileia*.'[28]

The Shape of the Davidic Monarchy in the Old Testament

A first-century reader of Israel's Scriptures like Luke would have read all of them (the Law, Prophets, and Psalms; cf. Lk. 24:44) synchronically, as if speaking at the same time to the same reality. What is the shape of the Davidic kingdom that would appear from these Scriptures to such a reader? When the texts are read together, an entire constellation of concepts, locations, and institutions that were intimately related to David, his legacy, and one another appears.[29] At

---

[27] See Strauss, *Messiah*, 130–95.

[28] Del Agua, 'Narrative,' 645.

[29] It is here that our canonical methodology is quite evident. Traditional source-critical biblical scholarship would insist on seeing a variety of incompatible perspectives on the Davidic kingdom in the various biblical documents. To allow all of these documents to speak as with a common voice on a certain subject – i.e., the Davidic kingdom – is a quintessentially *canonical* move, presuming an underlying unity to the canon attributable to divine inspiration, human redaction, and/or the selectivity of the process of tradition.

the center of the constellation is David and/or the Son of David. Within the constellation, the following eight characteristics or elements have a claim to being the brightest stars:

(1) The Davidic monarchy was *founded upon a divine covenant* (ברית MT, διαθήκη LXX), the only human kingdom of the Old Testament to enjoy such a privilege.[30]

(2) The Davidic monarch was *the Son of God*. The filial relationship of the Davidide to God is expressed already in the foundational text of the Davidic covenant (2 Sam. 7:14), but it is also found in other Davidic texts.[31]

(3) The Davidic monarch was *the 'Christ,' that is, the 'Messiah' or 'Anointed One.'* The anointed status of the Davidic king was so integral to his identity that he is frequently referred to simply as 'the anointed one,' or 'the Lord's anointed.'[32]

(4) The Davidic monarchy was inextricably bound to *Jerusalem, particularly Mt. Zion*, which was the personal possession of David and his heirs (2 Sam. 5:9), and would have had no significant role in Israelite history had not David made it his capital (cf. Josh. 15:63; Judg. 1:21; 19:10–12; 2 Sam. 5:6–12).[33]

(5) The Davidic monarchy was inextricably bound to *the temple*. The building of the temple was central to the terms of the Davidic covenant from the very beginning, as can be seen from the wordplay on 'house' ('temple' or 'dynasty') in 2 Samuel 7:11–13.[34] Even after its destruction, the prophets remained firm in their conviction that YHWH would restore his temple to its former glory as an international place of worship.[35]

(6) The Davidic monarch ruled over *all twelve tribes*. It was only under David and the son of David, Solomon, that both Judah and all the northern tribes

---

[30] The key text outlining the conditions and promises of this covenant is 2 Sam. 7:8–16 (see Gordon, *Samuel*, 71; Laato, 'Psalm 132,' 56), although the term 'covenant' only occurs elsewhere: e.g., 2 Sam. 23:5; 1 Kgs. 8:23–24; Ps. 89:3; 2 Chr. 13:5; 21:7; Sir. 45:25; Is. 55:3; Ezek. 34:25 LXX.

[31] E.g., Pss. 2:7; 89:26; 1 Chr. 17:13; 28:6. 'The individual most often designated as "the son of God" in the Hebrew Bible is undoubtedly the Davidic king, or his eschatological counterpart' (Collins, *Scepter*, 163).

[32] See 1 Sam. 16:13; 2 Sam. 19:21, 22:51; 23:1; 1 Kgs. 1:38–39; 2 Kgs. 11:12; 23:30; 2 Chr. 6:42; 23:11; Pss. 2:2; 18:50; 20:6; 28:8; 84:9; 89:20, 38, 51; 132:10, 17.

[33] See Japhet, 'Sanctuary,' 6; and Ishida, *Dynasties*, 118–19.

[34] Cf. Kruse, 'Covenant,' 149. On the significance of Solomon's temple building efforts, see Hurowitz, *House*; Mason, 'Messiah,' esp. 348, 362; Ishida, *Dynasties*, 145–47; and Swartley, *Traditions*, 154.

[35] Is. 2:1–4; 56:6–8; 60:3–16; 66:18–21; Jer. 33:11; Ezek. 40–44; Dan. 9:24–27; Joel 3:18; Hag. 2:1–9; Mic. 4:1–4; Zech. 6:12–14; 8:20–23; 14:16.

were united as one kingdom and freed from foreign oppression (2 Sam. 5:1–5; 1 Kgs. 4:1–19).[36] For this reason the Prophets associate the reunification of the northern tribes of Israel ('Ephraim') and the southern tribes of Judah with the restoration of the Davidic monarchy.[37]

(7) The Davidic monarch ruled over an *international empire*. David and Solomon ruled not only over Israel but also the surrounding nations.[38] The Psalms theologically justify and celebrate this state of affairs,[39] and the Prophets envision its restoration.[40]

(8) The Davidic monarchy was to be *everlasting*. One of the most prevalent emphases in the Psalms and Deuteronomic history is that the Davidic dynasty will be eternal (2 Sam. 7:16; 23:5; Ps. 89:35–36). Not only the dynasty, but also the lifespan of the reigning monarch himself, was described as everlasting (Pss. 21:4; 72:5, 110:4).[41]

Thus, when read synchronically, the Old Testament – in the Prophets (both Former and Latter) and the Psalms – gives a composite picture of the Davidic monarchy in which the Son of David, anointed as Son of God by divine covenant, rules eternally from Jerusalem over all Israel and the nations, gathering them to worship at the temple. For theological interpretation, it is important to see each element of this composite picture not in isolation but in its relationship to the entire Davidic 'constellation.'

Excursus: The Davidic Kingdom between Old and New Testaments

This constellation of characteristics of the Davidic kingdom was not forgotten, and the hope of its restoration was not abandoned, in the years between the end of the exile and the coming of Christ.[42] Especially from the mid-second century B.C.E. to the late first century C.E., there is substantial witness to a general

---

[36] Abimelech's reign in Shechem was certainly only local (Judg. 9:1–57), and Saul never liberated Israel from Philistine vassalage (1 Sam. 14:52; 31:1–7).

[37] Is. 11:1–16; Jer. 30:1–9; Ezek. 37:15–28, etc.

[38] 2 Sam. 8:11–12; 10:19; 12:30; 1 Kgs. 3:1; 4:20–21; 10:15. See Meyers, 'Empire,' 181–97.

[39] Cf. Pss. 2:8; 18:43, 47; 22:27; 47:1, 9; 72:8, 11; 66:8; 67:2–5; 86:9; 89:27; 96:7, 99:1, etc.

[40] Is. 2:3–4; 42:1–6; 49:1–7, 22–26; 51:4–6; 55:3–5; 56:3–8; 60:1–16; 66:18–19; Amos 9:11–12; Mic. 4:2–3; Zech. 14:16–19.

[41] For a discussion of the tension between these texts and others which imply that the Davidic covenant can be or has been broken, see Waltke, 'Phenomenon,' 123–40.

[42] It is true that between ca. 500 B.C.E. and ca. 200 B.C.E. extant witnesses to an expectation of the restoration of the kingdom of David are sparse, though not wholly lacking. However, there is very little documentation for *any* aspect of Israelite/Jewish

Jewish expectation of the restoration of the Davidic kingdom in the Pseud-
epigrapha and the Dead Sea Scrolls.[43] Many of these texts – especially *4 Ezra*,
the *Psalms of Solomon*, and 4Q *Florilegium* (4Q174) – foresee the coming of an
eschatological figure who is the Son of David,[44] and:

(1) the recipient of the covenant of 2 Samuel 7,[45]
(2) the Son of God,[46]
(3) the 'Messiah' or 'Anointed One,'[47]
(4) who will reign in Zion,[48]
(5) restore the temple,[49]
(6) reunite the twelve tribes,[50]
(7) and rule over all nations,[51]
(8) for eternity.[52]

Thus, even without the witness of the New Testament, it would be possible to
establish that among Jews of the first century C.E. there was a general expectation of the future restoration of the kingdom of David by a messianic figure.[53]
The anticipated restoration, however, was more of a *transformation* than a mere

---

history or religion in this time frame. For an assessment of the evidence see Laato,
Star, 208–316; Horbury, *Jewish Messianism*, 36–63 and *Messianism among Jews and
Christians*, 35–64; Collins, *Scepter*, 33.

[43] See Collins, *Scepter*, 12, 57, 67, 95, 209. The Dead Sea scrolls cited below may be
found in García Martínez and Tigchelaar, *Scrolls*.

[44] *4 Ezra* 12:32, *Pss. Sol.* 17:4, 21; 4Q161 (4QpIsaᵃ) 8 X, 17; 4Q252 (4QCommGen
A) V, 1–3. Arguably, the 'Son of God' in 4Q246 (4QapocrDan ar), the 'Son of Man'
in *1 Enoch*, and the 'Messiah' in *2 Baruch* are Davidic, since Davidic prophecies and
characteristics are attributed to them. On 4Q246 see Collins, *Scepter*, 154–65, esp.
163–65. On Davidic messianic interpretations of the Son of Man in 4Q246, *4 Ezra*,
and the NT, see Gese, *Essays*, 158.

[45] *Pss. Sol.* 17:4; 4Q174 (4QFlor) 1 I, 7–13; 4Q252 V, 1–5; cf. Sir. 45:25; 47:11;
4Q504 (4QDibHamᵃ) 1–2 IV, 6–8; *T. Jud.* 22:3.

[46] *4 Ezra* 13:32, 52; 4Q246 (4QapocrDan ar) II, 1; 4Q369 (4QPrayer of Enosh) 1 II, 6;
4Q174 1 I, 11.

[47] *4 Ezra* 7:28; 12:32; *Pss. Sol.* 17:32; *2 Bar.* 70:10; 72:2; 4Q252 V, 3.

[48] *4 Ezra* 13:35–36; *Pss. Sol.* 17:22, 30; 4Q174 1 I, 12; 4Q504 1–2 IV, 3.

[49] *4 Ezra* 12:48 [implied]; 4Q504 1–2 IV, 12; *Sib. Or.* 5:420–27; *1 En.* 53:6.

[50] *4 Ezra* 13:39–48; *Pss. Sol.* 17:26–28; 31; 43–44; 4Q174 1 I, 13 ('save *Israel*'); cf. *T.
Jud.* 24:1–25:3; *1 QM* V, 1; Sir. 36:11.

[51] *4 Ezra* 13:33, 37–38; *Pss. Sol.* 17:29–34; *Sib. Or.* 5:425–28; 4Q161 8–10 III, 21–22;
4Q246 II, 5–7.

[52] *Pss. Sol.* 17:35–38; 4Q174 1 I, 1–5, 11; 4Q246 II, 5–9; 4Q252 V, 4; *2 Bar.* 73:1; *1
En.* 49:1–2; cf. 1 Macc. 2:57.

[53] See Collins, *Scepter*, 209; Ravens, *Luke*, 112; and Strauss, *Messiah*, 38–53.

reimplementation. That is, the restored kingdom was expected to exceed what was actually realized under David and Solomon. Thus, descriptions of the coming kingdom often include supernatural elements. To cite just one example, the messianic king of the *Psalms of Solomon* is immortal (17:35), sinless (17:36), and capable of repelling enemies without the use of military force (17:33), but by his words alone (17:36). The transcendent and supernatural elements of the kingdom here and in the rest of the Second Temple and Qumran literature have their roots in the ideal descriptions of the kingdom in the Psalms (Pss. 2:7–11; 72:5–8; 89:19–37) and Prophets, especially Isaiah (e.g., Is. 2:1–4; 11:4–9).

Jesus and the Restoration of the Davidic Monarchy in Luke

Having examined the eight major characteristics of the Davidic monarchy in Israel's scriptural traditions, it is now possible to return to Luke and ask: Does the shape of Jesus' kingship as portrayed by Luke resemble that of David? It is possible to answer in the affirmative, since each of the eight characteristics also describes Jesus and his ministry:

(1) God's *covenant* with David, as described in Nathan's oracle (2 Sam. 7:9–16), provides all the content of the angelic description of Jesus in Luke 1:32–33.[54] Later, Jesus associates his kingship with a 'new covenant' (22:20) and says that a kingdom has been 'covenanted' to him by the Father (22:29).[55]

(2) Jesus is the *natural* (not merely adopted) *Son of God* (1:35), and the title is used of him throughout the gospel.[56]

(3) It is abundantly clear that Jesus is the *Christ* (2:11, 4:41, etc.),[57] indeed, he is the 'Lord's Christ' (2:26), a title only applied to kings in the Old Testament (cf. 1 Sam. 16:6; 24:6 LXX, etc.), and the 'Christ of God' (Lk. 9:20), a title only applied to David (2 Sam. 23:1).[58]

(4) Luke, more than any other gospel, emphasizes the priority of *Jerusalem*.[59] For Luke, it is theologically important that the word of God go forth *from Jerusalem* to the ends of the earth (Lk. 24:47; Acts 1:8; cf. Is. 2:3). The gospel begins in Jerusalem (1:5–23), the only two narratives from Jesus' childhood find him in Jerusalem (2:22–52), for most of the narrative he is

---

[54] As demonstrated by Green, *Luke*, 85, 88; likewise Fitzmyer, *Luke*, 338.

[55] On the 'covenanting' of the kingdom, see the discussion of διατίθημι in Lk. 22:29, below.

[56] See Tannehill, *Unity*, 25.

[57] See Tannehill, *Unity*, 38.

[58] The title 'Christ' is probably always intended in a Davidic sense in Luke. Cf. Tuckett 'Christology,' 133–64, esp. 147–48; Nolan, *Son*, 173; and Tannehill, *Unity*, 58.

[59] Fitzmyer, *Luke*, 164–65; Bechard, 'Significance,' 675–91.

traveling to Jerusalem (9:51–19:27), and the gospel climaxes in Jerusalem (19:28–24:49), wherein the disciples are told to 'remain' (24:49).

(5) What is true of Luke and Jerusalem is also true with regard to the *temple*. The gospel begins there (1:5–23), Jesus 'childhood' is set there (2:22–52),[60] for most of the gospel he is traveling there (9:51–19:27), and the climax is reached when Jesus is teaching *from the temple in Jerusalem* (19:45–21:38). In Acts, the temple remains the focus of the early Christian community (Acts 2:46).[61]

(6) Luke's Jesus shows by many signs that he intends to restore the *unity of the twelve tribes of Israel*. The appointing of twelve apostles is the most prominent sign of this intention (6:12–16), and he explicitly promises that they will judge 'the twelve tribes of Israel' (22:30). But there are many other more subtle signs of Jesus' intent to reunify the kingdom, including the use of the terms 'Israel' and 'sons of Israel' – evoking the entire nation – rather than 'Judea' or 'Jews';[62] the words of the angel that the good news of Jesus' birth is 'for the entire people' (2:10), that is the whole nation of Israel; the presence of Anna, a representative descendant of the northern tribes (Asher), at the presentation (2:36);[63] and the inclusion of the Samaritans in Jesus' mission as representatives of the ten northern tribes.[64]

(7) The extension of Jesus' kingship *over all the nations* is anticipated throughout Luke. Already in the infancy narratives, Simeon speaks of Jesus as 'a light of revelation to the nations' (2:32). Luke traces his genealogy back to Adam, the father of all humankind (3:38). As precedent for his ministry Jesus cites Elijah and Elisha's healings of Gentiles (4:25–27), and he himself heals the servant of a Roman (7:1–10), while praising his faith above that of Israel (7:9). He predicts that 'men will come from east and west, and from north and south' to sit at table in the kingdom of God (13:29), and finally and most explicitly, Jesus teaches the disciples that 'forgiveness of sins should be preached in his name *to all nations*, beginning from Jerusalem' (24:47).

(8) The angel Gabriel promises to Mary that Jesus 'will reign over the house of Jacob *forever*, and of his kingdom there will be *no end*.'[65] The everlasting reign of Christ is presumed in the rest of the gospel, especially in passages where Jesus is the mediator of eternal life (18:18–30).

---

[60] On the importance of the temple in Lk. 1–2, see Green, *Luke*, 61–62 and Taylor, 'Luke-Acts,' 709.

[61] On the importance of the temple in Luke-Acts generally, see Chance, *Jerusalem*; and Clark, 'Role,' esp. 175–76.

[62] See Ravens, *Luke*, 25.

[63] See Bauckham, 'Anna.'

[64] Ravens, *Luke*, 105–106.

[65] See Bock, *Luke*, 116–17.

Thus it can be seen that all eight major characteristics of the Davidic monarchy are manifested in Jesus and his ministry. There is a coherence to the titles and attributes – for example, 'King,' 'Christ,' 'Son of God,' eternal reign – that Luke predicates of Jesus and his ministry: the common factor in all of these is their typological origin in the figure of *David*. Indeed, more of Jesus' identity and role could be integrated into this Davidic typology. Jesus in Luke is clearly a *prophet*, for example, and Luke considers David to have been a 'prophet' (Acts 2:30a) through whom the Holy Spirit spoke (Acts 1:16). Luke's Christology, therefore, is not so composite as is sometimes imagined: the unifying factor is royal Davidic typology.[66]

Moreover, Jesus' career as presented in the gospel may be interpreted as a systematic effort to restore the kingdom of David.[67] The significance of the choice of twelve apostles has been mentioned above. It is also significant that, as Fitzmyer notes, 'Once the ministry proper begins, the areas of Jesus' activity are defined as Galilee (4:14–9:50), Samaria (9:51–17:11), and Judea/Jerusalem (17:11–21:38).'[68] Jesus' ministry follows the geographical progression of the dissolution of the kingdom of Israel: the northern tribes in the region of Galilee were taken by Assyria in 733 B.C.E., Samaria itself fell in 722 B.C.E., and Judah and Jerusalem in 587 B.C.E. During his roughly north-to-south itinerary in Luke, Jesus gathers disciples from all of these territories until, by the triumphal entry, they have become a 'multitude' (19:37) forming the reunited kingdom of David *in nuce*.

Jesus' activity in Samaria, which Luke alone among the synoptics records (cf. Lk. 9:51–10:37; 17:11–19), is vital to Jesus' mission of reunification. Luke has Jesus minister in Samaria (9:51–56; 17:11–19), and there is reason to believe that the seventy were sent into this region (10:1–12) and that other parts of the travel narrative took place there.[69] Luke apparently accepted the Samaritans' claim to be the remnant of the ten northern tribes, and their reunification with Judah was necessary to restore the Davidic kingdom.[70]

---

[66] Cf. Bock, *Proclamation*, 262. It may be possible to integrate the Royal-Davidic and Isaianic-Servant Christologies in Luke. See Block, 'Servant,' esp. 49–56, and Strauss, *Messiah*, 292–98, who argue for the Davidic character of the 'Servant' of Is. 40–66.

[67] Cf. Ravens, *Luke*, 20.

[68] Fitzmyer, *Luke*, 165–66. See also Lane, *Luke*, 98, cf. 99–103; cf. Johnson, *Luke*, 170, 175.

[69] See Ravens, *Luke*, 76–87. For example, the injunction 'eat what they set before you' (Lk. 10:8) may be meant to assuage scruples over food cleanliness in Samaritan territory (82–83; cf. Neyrey, *Passion*, 8).

[70] Ravens, *Luke*, 47, 70, 72–87, 99. Cf. Jervell, *Luke*, 113–32; and Pao, *Acts*, 127–29. In addition to the Samaritan ministry, three other Lukan pericopes may reinforce the view that his mission was, in part, an effort to heal the divisions of Israel. First, in Lk. 6, Jesus heals a man with a withered hand (6:6–11). In the OT only Jeroboam I

In sum, we have seen that Jesus' *kingship* in Luke has the salient characteristics of the Davidic monarchy as portrayed in the canonical texts. Moreover, Jesus' ministry can be interpreted as a mission to reunite the northern and southern tribes into one *kingdom* under the Davidic heir. In Luke, Jesus is the royal Son of David who journeys to the city of David to restore the kingdom of David. This much is clear. It remains to be seen, however, what relationship exists between this Lukan Davidic Christology and the ecclesiology of Acts. The key figures in this relationship are the apostles, who in their persons and ministry form the link between the person and ministry of Jesus and the age of the church.[71] It is now necessary to examine key texts at the end of Luke's Gospel and the beginning of Acts which show how the Davidic-messianic identity and mission of Luke's Jesus flow into and shape the identity and mission of the twelve and the community they establish, the ἐκκλησία.

The Institution Narrative (Luke 22:14–30)

The Institution Narrative (*IN*) is a key transitional text for linking the royal Davidic identity and mission of Christ with the early apostolic church as the restored Davidic kingdom. The *IN* serves to establish the apostles as vice-regents of the Davidic kingdom (as we shall see below), empowering them in the opening chapters of Acts to rule over the church.

(1 Kgs. 13:1–6) suffered a withered hand – he who made the division of the kingdom of David permanent by establishing a rival heterodox cult (1 Kgs. 12:25–33). Luke notes that it was the man's *right hand*, thus making a clear allusion to Ps. 137:5: 'If I forget you, O Jerusalem, let my right hand wither!' Jeroboam had 'forgotten' Jerusalem (1 Kgs. 12:25–33). Jesus' healing of the Jeroboam-like man of Lk. 6:6–11 manifests his power to overcome the division of David's kingdom. Second, in Lk. 10:30–37, Jesus tells a parable of a Samaritan recognizing a Jew as 'neighbor' (πλησίον) or 'kinsman' (so in the LXX, cf. Lev. 19:18; Ex. 2:13, 32:27). The Jew/Samaritan division represents a divided kingdom, a topic Jesus addresses in Lk. 11:14–23, asserting that 'every kingdom divided against itself is laid waste, and a divided house falls' (11:17). The division of the *kingdom of David* and the *house of David* – still painfully evident in Jesus' day – is in view, which was not merely a political issue but also a spiritual issue (1 Kgs. 12:25–33). Fulfilling prophecy, Jesus will heal the division by a ministry of 'gathering' (Lk. 11:23). Third, the parable of the Prodigal Son (15:11–32) can also be understood as referring, in one sense, to the division of the kingdom of David (Bailey, *Jacob*, 156–201). The older son would represent Judah and the younger son Ephraim, head of the northern tribes. The younger son goes to a far-off country – i.e., exile – and wastes his inheritance on harlotry, the very sin the prophets accused Ephraim/Israel of committing (Jer. 3:6; Hos. 4:15; 5:3). Significantly, the father in the story is determined to reconcile *both* sons to himself and to each other.

[71] See Clark, 'Role,' 169 et passim.

The full significance of the *IN* will be better grasped if two initial observations are made. First, in Luke, the *IN* is preceded by four pericopes highlighting Jesus' royal and specifically Davidic identity (18:35–39; 19:11–27; 19:28–40; 20:1–40), which serve to reassert the royal Davidic Christology, so clearly enunciated in the infancy narratives, as an introduction to the dramatic events of the passion week.[72] The royal Davidic themes will be taken up and advanced particularly in the *IN*, as will be seen below.

Second, the *IN* is not the first, nor is it the last, Lukan narrative which weds the imagery of *kingdom* with *table fellowship*. The motif of eating and drinking is more prominent in Luke than in the other gospels, and an organizational scheme of ten meal narratives may be discerned in the gospel – seven preceding the passion and two following it, with the *IN* at the strategic juncture.[73] The Last Supper is a literary Janus, culminating the sequence of Jesus' earthly meals but already strongly anticipating the table fellowship in his resurrected state (Lk. 24:30, 43).[74]

All ten Lukan meals may be read as foretastes or proleptic experiences of the messianic kingdom banquet (cf. Is. 25:6–8; Zech. 8:7–8, 19–23), since the Messiah is present at them. This is particularly evident in the meals that the Messiah himself hosts: the feeding of the five thousand (9:10–17), the Last Supper (22:7–38), and the meal at Emmaus (24:13–35). In only these three meals in Luke is bread (ἄρτον) said to be 'broken' (κλάω or κατακλάω); the same expression will be used in Acts 2:42, 46; 20:7, 11; 27:35. Kingdom motifs distinguish these three meals:

- all five thousand are 'satisfied' and twelve basketfuls remain (9:17), bespeaking the fullness of the twelve tribes of Israel under the Son of David (cf. 1 Kgs. 4:20; 8:65–66);
- the Last Supper is characterized by the imminent coming of the kingdom (as will be seen below);
- and the Emmaus sequence is initiated with the disciples' remark 'We had hoped he was the one *to redeem Israel*,' that is, to restore the Davidic kingdom, as the infancy narratives make clear (esp. 1:68–69).

---

[72] See Strauss, *Messiah*, 306–17.

[73] Cf. Lk. 6:20; 9:10–17; 11:2; 13:28; 15:11–32; 22:18. On the significance of meals in Luke see Koenig, *Feast*, esp. 15, 181; LaVerdiere, *Dining*; *Eucharist*; and *Breaking*; and Neyrey, *Passion*, 8–11. The ten meals in Luke are Levi's banquet (5:27–39); the feast at Simon the Pharisee's house (7:36–50); the feeding of the 5,000 at Bethsaida (9:10–17); the meal at the home of Martha (10:38–42); dinner at the Pharisee's house (11:37–54); Sabbath dinner at yet another Pharisee's home (14:1–24); supper at the house of Zacchaeus (19:1–10); the Last Supper (22:7–38); breaking of bread at Emmaus (24:13–35); and eating in the presence of the apostles (24:41–43). See LaVerdiere, *Dining*, 12; and *Eucharist*, 82–83.

[74] See the discussion in Nelson, *Leadership*, 66–69, 73.

Jesus' displays of table fellowship were a Davidic trait. David extended *hesed* (covenant loyalty) through table fellowship (2 Sam. 9:7, 10, 13; 1 Kgs. 2:7). The generous meals for all Israel hosted by David and his royal sons (Solomon, Hezekiah, and Josiah) were treasured memories of Israelite tradition.[75] The Davidic Psalms employ images of eating and drinking to celebrate God's provision and the joy of communion with him,[76] and the prophets describe the restoration of David's city (i.e., Zion; cf. Is. 25:6–8; Jer. 31:12–14) and David's covenant (Is. 55:1–5) with images of feasting. Strikingly, in Ezekiel the primary role of the eschatological Davidic 'shepherd' is to 'feed' Israel (Ezek. 34:23).

While some see the first seven meals in Luke as anticipations of the Eucharist,[77] specifically eucharistic themes seem to be clearest only with respect to the meals mentioned above – the feeding of the five thousand, the Last Supper, and Emmaus – where Jesus 'breaks bread.' Obviously the Last Supper is the most important in this regard.

Luke's account of the Last Supper includes several unique features vis-à-vis Matthew and Mark,[78] including the following: (1) the repetition of Jesus' statement that he 'will not eat until the kingdom of God comes' and its placement at the beginning of the pericope rather than in the body;[79] (2) the command 'do this in remembrance of me' (v. 19); (3) the specification of the cup as the *'new'* covenant;[80] (4) the placement of the discussion of precedence among the disciples here rather than earlier in Jesus' career;[81] and (5) the inclusion of unique features in the promise of 'thrones' for the apostles and its location at the end of the IN (22:28–29; cf. Mt. 19:28). It is significant that *kingdom motifs* mark four of these five uniquely Lukan elements of the IN, and elements in the third and fifth have a strongly *Davidic* resonance. Luke, more than any other evangelist, wishes to stress the relationship between the Last Supper and the kingdom of God. Each of these unique elements deserves consideration:

(1) Whereas in Matthew and Mark Jesus makes the statement 'I shall not drink again of the fruit of the vine until I drink it new in the kingdom of God' after the distribution of the eucharistic elements (Mt. 19:29; Mk. 14:25), Luke records this statement before the supper (Lk. 22:18) and adds the similar statement 'I shall not eat it until it is fulfilled in the kingdom of God'

---

[75] See 2 Sam. 6:19 (David); 1 Kgs. 8:65–66 (Solomon); 1 Chr. 29:20–22 (David); 2 Chr. 30:21–26 (Hezekiah); 35:7–19 (Josiah).

[76] Pss. 16:5; 22:26; 23:5; 34:8, 10; 36:8; 63:5; 65:4; 132:15.

[77] See discussion in LaVerdiere, *Eucharist*, 79–95; and the measured, appreciative critique by Koenig, *Feast*, 184–85.

[78] Jervell, *Luke*, 79.

[79] Lk. 22:16, 18, cf. Mt. 36:29; Mk. 14:25.

[80] Lk. 22:20, cf. Mt. 26:28; Mk. 14:24.

[81] Lk. 22:24–30; cf. Mt. 20:24–28; Mk. 10:41–45.

among Jesus' introductory words before the meal (22:16). The placement of the prophecy at the beginning of the supper account and its repetition: (1) emphasize that the following meal is somehow related to the kingdom and its arrival; (2) imply that the arrival of the kingdom is imminent; and (3) link the kingdom with both 'eating' and 'drinking.'[82] 'Eating' and 'drinking' in the kingdom will be mentioned again in verse 30, where the disciples are assured that they will 'eat and drink ... in my kingdom.' Thus the statements in verses 16 and 18 form an *inclusio* with verse 30 around the narrative of the Last Supper. Eating and drinking are prominent manifestations of the kingdom's presence. When later the risen Christ eats with the disciples, it indicates that the kingdom has indeed come.[83] Durrwell comments:

> St. Luke puts this text ... before the institution of the Eucharist ... Luke realized that the meal in the joy of the Kingdom was beginning in the Last Supper. That is why he modified the text from Mark ... to make it a prophecy of an immediate reality ... His Kingdom of God 'at once suggests the sphere in which the new paschal rite was to unfold, that is, the church' [Benoit, 'Recit,' 388]. In giving us to understand that our Lord would eat and drink again in the Kingdom, he must have had in mind the meals of the risen Christ which he, alone of the Evangelists, lays such stress upon.[84]

(2) Luke's account of Jesus' words over the bread has both common and unique features. First, Luke shares the tradition of the radical identification of the messianic king with the eucharistic bread: 'This is my body.' The same point is made over the cup: 'this cup ... is the new covenant *in my blood*,' that is, consisting of my blood. Second, Luke alone includes Jesus' command to repeat this meal 'in remembrance' of him. It is this command which makes the pericope an *institution narrative*. Without it, nothing is being instituted: it is only the account of Jesus' last meal before his death. But with the command to repeat the meal when Jesus is no longer visibly present, the pericope becomes the foundational story and theological explanation for the early church's continuing practice of 'breaking bread' as recorded in Acts.[85]

The meaning of Jesus' radical self-identification with the bread and wine was, and is, a mystery that can only be accepted based on faith in the

---

[82] Cf. Neyrey, *Passion*, 12–15.

[83] Cf. Lk. 24:30, 42–43; Acts 1:4, 10:41, and discussion below. St. Bonaventure notes, 'The Glossa observes: "I will no longer celebrate the Mosaic Passover, until it is completed in the church, which is the kingdom of God, spiritually understood"' (Karris, *Works*, 2045).

[84] Durrwell, *Resurrection*, 323.

[85] Acts 2:42, 46; 20:7, 11; 27:35.

veracity of the speaker.[86] Various dogmatic formulations throughout church history have at times obscured as much as explicated this mystery. Nonetheless, certainly in Luke 22:19–20 Jesus is not using the bread and wine as illustrations which make clear his coming sacrifice – that is, as an object lesson or visual parable – since 'far from helping of themselves to explain the death of the body and the shedding of blood, it is precisely the bread and wine which need explaining by means of the former.'[87] Jesus' words are not so much an explanation or a teaching as a 'speech-act', a declaration that brings about what it expresses. Long before the formal development of speech-act theory, Benoit observed 'He [Christ] does not merely state that the bread is his body; he decrees that this must come to pass, and that it has come to pass. His speech does not come after the event, it brings the event to pass.'[88] What is implicit here at the Last Supper, Luke makes explicit in the Emmaus account, in which the visible presence of the Lord vanishes during the distribution of the pieces (23:31), since, in light of 22:19, his presence is now identified with the bread. Thus the messianic king is 'made known' to the disciples 'in the breaking of bread' (24:35). Later, Luke links his and his reader's liturgical experience to Jesus' Last Supper by including himself among those who gather on the first day of the week to 'break bread' (Acts 20:7). Through the *IN* and the Emmaus account, Luke's readers are to understand that the risen Christ is truly present in the bread they break together. Thus, where the Eucharist is, there is the king; and it follows – where the king is, there is the kingdom. (Thus the writers of the *Didascalia Apostolorum* described the Eucharist as 'the likeness of the body of the kingdom of Christ.')[89]

(3) Luke alone of the synoptics specifies the cup as the '*new* covenant in my blood' (22:20), which changes the most immediate Old Testament reference from Exodus 24:6–8 (the Sinaitic covenant) to Jeremiah 31:31.[90] The 'new covenant' of Jeremiah 31:31 is explicitly said to be *unlike* the broken covenant of Sinai (Jer. 31:32). In the wider context of Jeremiah 30–33, it is clear that this 'new covenant' involves not only a new level of intimacy with God (31:33–34) and the reunification of the divided (Davidic) kingdom (31:31, cf. 30:4 et passim), but *also the restoration of the Davidic monarchy* (30:9; 33:14–26) and *covenant* (33:19–21). Thus, the declaration

---

[86] Cf. Jn. 6:66–69. Thus Benoit remarks, 'How can bread and wine become the body and blood of the Lord? It is a mystery of faith; we believe it because we believe in the Word of the Lord' (*Jesus*, 116). Benoit's entire discussion (pp. 112–17) is helpful.

[87] Benoit, *Jesus*, 113.

[88] Benoit, *Jesus*, 116.

[89] See Vööbus, *Didascalia*, 243–44.

[90] On the reference to the 'new covenant' in Jeremiah, see Bock, 'Reign,' 43. On the relationship of covenant and kingdom, cf. Ossom-Batsa, *Institution*, 159.

of the 'new' covenant in Luke 22:20 points to the restored Davidic kingdom-covenant constellation as promised in the Prophets, rather than merely to the memory of Sinai.[91] In fact, the 'new' covenant *is not a complete novum, it is the renewal of the Davidic covenant.*[92] Moreover, by identifying the cup with the 'new' covenant, Jesus marks this meal – the eucharistic 'breaking of bread' that is to be continued 'in remembrance' of him – as a covenant-renewal meal for the new covenant, just as the Passover was the covenant-renewal meal par excellence of the Mosaic covenant. Luke's readers should understand that when they participate in the eucharistic cup, they reaffirm their place within the promised 'new covenant,' which is in essence the renewed and transformed Davidic covenant.

(4) Luke places the discussion of precedence among the disciples in the context of the Last Supper (22:24–27) rather than elsewhere in the gospel narrative (cf. Mt. 20:24–28; Mk. 10:41–45) because the kingdom is about to be conferred upon them (vv. 28–29), and therefore they must understand the proper way to exercise its authority. In their parallels, Matthew and Mark speak of 'rulers' (οἱ ἄρχοντες, οἱ δοκοῦντες ἄρχειν), but Luke highlights the kingdom motif by speaking of Gentile 'kings' (οἱ βασιλεῖς) who 'exercise lordship' (κυριεύουσιν). Jesus is both King (βασιλεύς) and Lord (κύριος) – more truly and with greater legitimacy than the Gentile kings – but his mode of exercising authority is radically different. The hierarchy of domination and pride characteristic of the kingdoms of this world will be replaced in the kingdom of God by a hierarchy of service (22:26–27). Significantly, the word used here for service, διακονία, frequently connotes waiting at table,[93] and verse 27 immediately confirms this sense. Jesus exercises his royal authority through *table service*, and the disciples will as well (v. 27). This re-emphasizes the connection throughout this passage between the concepts of royal authority/kingdom and those of eating/drinking, and forms another link with verse 30a below, where the disciples 'will eat and drink at my table.'

(5) After correcting the disciples' misguided notions of the meaning of authority in his kingdom, Jesus assures them of their vice-regency in verses 28–30. To the apostles, who have shared with Jesus in his trials, he says, κἀγὼ διατίθεμαι ὑμῖν καθὼς διέθετό μοι ὁ πατήρ μου βασιλείαν ('I *assign* to you, as my Father *assigned* to me, a kingdom', v. 29b, RSV). The usual English translations of the verb διατίθημι – 'assign' in RSV, 'confer' in NRSV – do not quite capture the sense of the word for Luke. Luke's style, as all ac-

---

[91] Cf. Bock, 'Reign,' 43.

[92] The Davidic context is immediately confirmed in the next verse (v. 21) when Jesus alludes to a psalm of David (Ps. 41:9).

[93] Cf. BAGD, 184a def. 2.

knowledge, is heavily dependent on the LXX, in which the phrase
διατίθεσθαι διαθήκην is used almost 80 times as the equivalent of the Hebrew כרת ברית, 'to make a covenant' – in fact, διατίθημι even without the
noun διαθήκην can denote covenant-making.[94] Since the nominal form
διαθήκη with the meaning 'covenant' has just been employed in verse 20
above, the sense of 'covenant-making' would seem to accrue to the verb
διατίθημι here.[95] A more precise, if awkward, translation of verse 29b
would thus be 'I covenant to you a kingdom, as my Father covenanted one
to me.'[96]

The only kingdom established on the basis of a covenant in Scripture is the
kingdom of David (cf. Ps. 89:3–4, 28–37). Moreover, the use of father-son terminology in verse 29b evokes the father-son relationship of the Lord with the
Son of David as reflected in 2 Samuel 7:14, Psalm 2:7, and Psalm 89:26–27.
Significantly, in each of these three passages, father-son terminology is
employed in the context of *God granting a kingdom to the Davidide* (cf. 2 Sam.
7:13; Ps. 2:6, 8; 89:25, 27). The meaning of Luke 22:29b becomes clear: God
has 'covenanted' a kingdom to Jesus, since Jesus is the Son of David, the legal
heir to David's covenant and throne (cf. 1:32–33). Now Jesus, through the
'new covenant in [his] blood' (v. 20), is 'covenanting' to the disciples that same
kingdom of David. This is not the promise of a conferral (future tense), but the
declaration of a conferral (present tense).[97] This *present conferral* of the kingdom mil-
itates against those scholars who acknowledge a present kingdom in Luke-Acts
but limit it to the person and ministry of Christ. As Darrel Bock comments
with respect to an earlier passage (Lk. 11:20), 'An appeal only to the presence of
God's kingly power in the person and message of Jesus misses the significance
of this transfer of power to others and ignores the kingdom associations Jesus
makes in explaining these activities.'[98]

---

[94] Cf. 1 Chr. 19:19; 2 Chr. 5:10; 7:18; Ezek. 16:30; and the discussion in Nelson, *Leadership*, 204.

[95] Διατίθημι and διαθήκη often bear the sense 'to make a testament' and 'testament/
will' respectively in secular Greek literature (BAGD, 189b def. 3; 183a def. 1), but
not here (contra Jervell, *Luke*, 105, n. 24; and Nelson, *Leadership*, 204). As Nolland
points out: 'Though the verb can bear such a sense [i.e., 'bequeath'], its parallel use
in connection with God here hardly encourages us to move in such a direction'
(*Luke*, 1066). See the discussion in L&N, §34.43; Marshall, *Luke*, 814–15; Priest,
'Banquet,' 222–38.

[96] Cf. Becker, 'Covenant,' 369: 'In Lk. 22:29 in the phrase *diatithemai ... basileian*,
appoint a kingdom, ... exactly expresses the formula *diatithemai diathēkēn*. The new
covenant and the kingdom of God are correlated concepts.'

[97] Bock, *Luke*, 1740. Cf. Pao, *Acts*, 124–27; Neyrey, *Passion*, 27–28.

[98] Bock, 'Reign,' 41.

The purpose of the 'covenanting' of the kingdom to the disciples is that they 'may eat and drink at my table in my kingdom.' Here it is apparent that the kingdom has not been removed *from* Jesus *to* the apostles, because the kingdom remains 'my [Jesus'] kingdom.'[99] Rather, the exercise of authority in the kingdom is being shared.[100]

In Luke 22:30, Jesus follows the example of his forefathers David and Solomon (cf. 1 Kgs. 2:7): having received the kingdom by covenant, he shows covenant loyalty to those who continued with him in his trials (v. 28) by extending to them the filial, covenantal, and royal privilege of table fellowship.[101] Thus, the promise of eating and drinking at Jesus' table confirms the previous statement of 'covenanting' the kingdom to the disciples.

Yet one cannot fail to note that the disciples are now – at the Last Supper – 'eating and drinking at my [Jesus'] table.' The conclusion is inescapable that there exists some intentional correspondence between the eucharistic eating and drinking in the narrative present of Luke 22 and the eschatological eating and drinking promised in verse 30a.[102] As we shall see below, in Acts the kingdom is portrayed as already present in the ministry of the apostles and the growing ἐκκλησία. When the apostles 'break bread' in 'remembrance' of Jesus in the post-Pentecost community (the church), it is an experience of the messianic banquet, with the messianic king present, as it were, in body and blood. The apostles' eucharistic practice in the early church is, therefore, the fulfillment of Jesus' promise here that they will 'eat and drink at my table in my kingdom.' As noted above, the celebration of the Eucharist manifests the kingdom. Kingdom and Eucharist are tightly bound: it is a *eucharistic kingdom*. That is why the promise of table fellowship at the messianic banquet (v. 30a) is sandwiched between two promises of the grant of (vice)-royal authority (vv. 29b, 30b).

The link between the discussion of sitting/serving at table in verse 27 and the 'eating and drinking' at table in verse 30a was noted above. In verses 25–27, Jesus contrasted the manner of exercise of authority in his kingdom with that of Gentile kings. Unlike these kings, Jesus exercises his royal authority through *table service* (διακονία) and calls his disciples to do the same. In contrast to verse 27, no 'sitting' at table is mentioned in verse 30a. Although the apostles will 'eat' and 'drink' at Jesus' table, they will not 'sit' because they will be serving like their Lord. However, this table service is immediately juxtaposed with vice-royal authority: you will 'sit on thrones ...' (v. 30b).[103] Searching for the

---

[99] This is another indication that διατίθημι above should not be taken in a testamentary sense.

[100] See Green, *Luke*, 770.

[101] See Nelson, *Leadership*, 59.

[102] Cf. Ossom-Batsa, *Institution*, 146, 159.

[103] This juxtaposition may suggest a paradoxical equation of the two promises: it is precisely when the apostles 'eat' and 'drink' at Jesus' table in his kingdom, not sitting

scriptural background of this concept of 'thrones over the twelve tribes,' we find the Davidic imagery of Psalm 122:3–5:

> Jerusalem, built as a city which is bound firmly together,
> To which the tribes go up, the tribes of the Lord ...
> There thrones for judgment were set,
> The *thrones of the House of David.*

The connection between the two texts is firm, in light of the collocation in each of the three elements: 'tribes,' 'thrones,' and 'judgment.'[104] Psalm 122:5b makes explicit the Davidic context of the promise of Luke 22:30b. The disciples, then, are promised a share in the exercise of authority of the Davidic monarchy over all twelve tribes. The disciples' 'appointment is an anticipation of the restoration of Israel ... and [they] are commissioned to govern the renewed people of God.'[105] L.T. Johnson comments on the significance of Luke's version of this dominical saying vis-à-vis Matthew's:

> Luke decisively alters the reference point for this prediction ... In Luke the saying points forward to the role that the apostles will have within the *restored Israel in the narrative of Acts* ... These followers [will] exercise effective rule within the people gathered by the power of the resurrected prophet (see e.g., Acts 5:1–11).[106]

It is now possible to grasp the logical relationship between verses 19–20 and verses 28–30.

Jesus is the heir of the covenant with David, by virtue of which he is eternal king over Israel and the nations (Lk. 1:32–33). In Luke 22:19–20 he enacts a *new* covenant between himself and the disciples, who share in the covenant meal. This new covenant is a renewal and extension of the covenant with David: in essence, the privileges of the Davidic covenant are being extended to

---

but serving, that they are in fact 'sitting on thrones judging the twelve tribes of Israel.' Alternately, the contrast between 'eating and drinking at table' and 'sitting on thrones' may be between realized and unrealized eschatology, the 'already' and 'not yet,' respectively. In either case, when the apostles serve at table (διακονία) to host the eucharistic meal – fulfilling the command to 'do this in remembrance of me' – they exercise Davidic royal authority in imitation of the servant-king, judging (κρίνοντες) the twelve tribes. The administration of the Eucharist would at first glance not appear to be an act of 'judging,' but Paul's reference to 'eating and drinking judgment on oneself' (1 Cor. 11:31) reflects a very similar and early tradition of the judicial aspect of eucharistic participation (cf. 1 Cor. 11:27–32 and 1 Cor. 5:1–13, esp. vv. 4, 7–8).

[104] See Evans, 'Thrones.'
[105] Green, *Luke*, 770; cf. Fitzmyer, *Luke*, 1419.
[106] Johnson, *Luke*, 345–46, 349.

the apostles, as in Isaiah 55:3, 'I will make with you an everlasting covenant; my steadfast, sure love for David.' By virtue of their sharing in the covenant established in verses 19–20, the apostles, like Christ, are now heirs of the kingdom of David (v. 29a). Because they are heirs, they have filial privileges: they may eat at the royal table (v. 30a) and sit on the thrones of the royal house, judging the twelve tribes (v. 30b). The Davidic traditions form the context for the logic of the entire transaction, and it is clear that the apostles have become heirs of the kingdom and covenant of David. The ecclesiological ramifications are profound, since the twelve apostles 'are transitional figures who link the church with the ministry of Jesus (cf. [Acts] 1:1) ... [and] provide an essential foundation for the church's continuing faith and life.'[107] If the foundation is Davidic, the edifice will be Davidic as well.

The Ecclesiological Significance of the Institution Narrative in Acts

In order to grasp the ecclesiological implications of the *IN*, it is necessary to venture a little way into Acts, where it can be seen that Jesus' promise of inheritance and rule of the Davidic kingdom is manifested in the apostle's assumption of authority in the ἐκκλησία, and the promise of table fellowship is fulfilled in post-resurrection meals with Jesus and the continuing eucharistic practice.[108] Johnson remarks, 'Luke must show how in fact the apostles carry on the prophetic power of Jesus in their deeds and words, and how they are to be leaders over this restored people, "judging the twelve tribes of Israel" (Luke 22:30).'[109]

The first three narratives of Acts – concerning Jesus' last teaching prior to his ascension (Acts 1:1–11), the replacement of Judas (Acts 1:12–26), and the descent of the Spirit at Pentecost (Acts 2) – are crucial links in the chain binding Davidic Christology to kingdom ecclesiology.

Significantly, in the opening verses of Acts (1:3, 6), Jesus' topic of discussion with the apostles over forty days is *the kingdom of God*.[110] 'Kingdom' will remain a central theme throughout the book, which ends with Paul proclaiming the

---

[107] Clark, 'Role,' 190.

[108] On the important links between the end of Luke and beginning of Acts, the common Isaianic-restoration imagery behind Lk. 24:49 and Acts 1:8 (e.g., Is. 43:10–12, 49:6), and the restoration of Israel around the twelve, see Turner, *Power*, 300–301. On the church as restored Israel in Acts, see Turner, *Power*, 418–22. On the fulfillment of the promise of vice-regency to the apostles see Strauss, *Messiah*, 25; Jervell, *Luke*, 94; and Neyrey, *Passion*, 26–28.

[109] Johnson, *Acts*, 71.

[110] On the close link between the 'kingdom' in Lk. 22 and here in Acts 1:1–11, see Jervell, *Luke*, 81–82.

kingdom of God in Rome (28:31).[111] Acts 1:4 makes the connection between the kingdom and eating and drinking (cf. Lk. 22:30a) – that is, the messianic banquet – when it states that Jesus taught them over this forty-day period 'while taking salt' (συναλιζόμενος) with them, an idiom for 'eating together.'[112]

When the disciples ask Jesus, 'Lord, will you at this time restore the kingdom to Israel?' (1:6), their query may refer to Jesus' promise in Luke 22:30b that 'you will sit on thrones.' The apostles are asking, 'When will we receive the authority promised to us?' In response, Jesus discourages speculation about *timing* (v. 7), but does in fact describe the *means* by which the kingdom will be restored, namely, through the Spirit-inspired witness of the apostles throughout the earth (v. 8).[113] Jesus' geographical description of the spread of the gospel: 'you shall be my witnesses in Jerusalem and in all Judea and Samaria and to the end of the earth' is, on the one hand, a programmatic outline of the narrative of Acts, helping us to recognize that the whole book concerns the spread of the kingdom (cf. Acts 28:31).[114] On the other hand, it is a *Davidic map* that reflects the *theological geography* of God's covenant pledge concerning the extent of the Davidic empire. Jerusalem was David's city (cf. 2 Sam. 5:6–10), Judea his tribal land (2 Sam. 5:5; 1 Kgs. 12:21); Samaria represents (northern) Israel, David's nation (1 Kgs. 12:16); and 'the ends of the earth' are the Gentiles (cf. Is. 49:6), David's vassals (Pss. 2:7–8; 72:8–12; 89:25–27).[115] The kingdom of David, encompassing Jerusalemites, Jews (i.e., Judeans), Israelites, and Gentiles, will be restored as the apostles' witness extends to 'the ends of the earth' and the ἐκκλησία grows.[116]

But the apostles in the narrative of Acts 1 do not yet realize the significance of Jesus' words or understand his transformation of their expectation of a national, earthly kingdom to one that is international and, though manifest on

---

[111] 'The concept of βασιλεία τοῦ θεοῦ ... seems to give unity to the whole narrative of the Lucan two-volume work ... The whole theological project of Luke ... [is] a narrative unit with the central theme of the *basileia* as its starting point' (del Agua, 'Narrative,' 639).

[112] See LaVerdiere, *Eucharist*, 99 and L&N §23.13. BAGD acknowledges the idiomatic force of συναλιζόμενος as 'eating together,' but argues that this meaning does not fit the context of Acts 1:4 (BAGD, 783b). *Pace* BAGD, the meaning fits the context extremely well. Acts 10:41 makes explicit the implicit significance of Lk. 24:43 and Acts 1:4. Cf. BAGD, 783b: 'Ac 10:41 appears to echo 1:4.'

[113] As argued by Penney, *Emphasis*, 70; Pao, *Acts*, 95, nn. 143, 144; and Bock, 'Reign,' 45.

[114] 'The verse is programmatic in its significance for the narrative structure ... That the mission will begin in Jerusalem alludes to the restored Zion of Isaiah (Is. 2.3)' (Penney, *Emphasis*, 73).

[115] Cf. Pao, *Acts*, 95.

[116] Cf. Penney, *Emphasis*, 21, 71.

earth, essentially heavenly.[117] *The Spirit must still be poured out for the apostles to perceive the transformed kingdom.* Thus only *after* the disciples have received the power of the Holy Spirit will they become μάρτυρες, or witnesses (Acts 1:8).

Between the promise of the outpouring of the Spirit (Acts 1:8) and Pentecost (2:1–4) Luke records the restoration of the circle of the twelve by the replacement of Judas with Matthias. Here again there is a relationship to the promise of Luke 22:30b: 'the election of [Matthias] is crucial if Jesus' promise to establish the twelve on thrones governing the twelve tribes of Israel is to survive.'[118] Thus Neyrey comments:

> Luke has given us in Acts a vivid picture of apostolic governance and leadership ... which gives immediate realization to the commission in [Lk.] 22:29–30. For example ... the first act of the apostles in Acts is to replace Judas, thus signaling that the group's membership must be complete, a completeness that is irrelevant unless Luke sees it as a fulfillment of Jesus' remark that there should be *twelve* judges of the twelve tribes of Israel.[119]

After the reconstitution of the twelve, the event of Pentecost (Acts 2:1–42) marks: (1) the restoration in principle of Israel as kingdom under the Son of David; and (2) the beginning of the apostles' vice-regency over that kingdom.

First, it is clear that Luke presents us in Acts 2 with the principial fulfillment of the promised restoration of Israel. Not only are all the twelve (and presumably the 120) 'all together in one place' (2:1) – thus representing the nucleus of the restored Israel – but they address their message to 'Jews, devout men from every nation under heaven,' (v. 5) and Luke enumerates those nations (vv. 9–11). The exile and diaspora are reversed.[120]

In response to the apostolic message there is a mass conversion as three thousand of these dispersed Jews enter the messianic community. In this event, the eschatological prophecies of Joel and other prophets are fulfilled and Israel restored – not definitively, as much growth of the ἐκκλησία remains, but nonetheless 'fundamentally', as Johnson points out:

> Three thousand Jews in the city are baptized and enter the messianic community (2:41). Although Luke will be careful to note further such increments, this one is

---

[117] 'Jesus shifts the focus from "knowledge" to mission ... [this is] the real answer to the question concerning the 'restoration' of the kingdom to Israel. Jesus' answer contains a redefinition of "kingdom" and therefore of the Christian understanding of Jesus as Messiah ... The "kingdom for Israel" will mean for Luke, therefore, the restoration of Israel *as a people of God*' (Johnson, *Acts*, 29).

[118] Brawley, *Text*, 73.

[119] Neyrey, *Passion*, 27–28; cf. Denova, *Things*, 70; Fitzmyer, 'Role,' esp. 182; and Pao, *Acts*, 124.

[120] Denova, *Things*, 138, cf. 169–75.

fundamental, for in it we find the realization of the restored people of God within historic Judaism.[121]

However, we can be more precise than to say 'Israel is restored.' The restored Israel has a certain form and structure: not that of the confederated tribes at Sinai, but that of the twelve tribes within the *kingdom of David*.[122] Peter's sermon stresses the Davidic royalty of Jesus Christ (cf. 2:36).[123] He preaches to the assembled exiles of Israel that Jesus is the fulfillment of the covenant of David (v. 30)[124] and the fulfillment of David's own prophecies (vv. 25–28; 34–35).[125] He applies to Jesus the royal Davidic enthronement psalm (Psalm 110), asserting that Jesus is now enthroned in heaven ('exalted at the right hand of God') and has poured out the Spirit on the apostles as the crowd has just witnessed (v. 33). Thus, Jesus is reigning *now* in heaven, and the results of his reign are being manifest *now* in events that the people may 'see and hear' (v. 33).[126] Peter and the apostles, filled with the Spirit, have become 'witnesses,' inasmuch as they now see the nature of Jesus' kingdom and its present realization. When Peter's hearers accept the fact that Jesus is the presently-enthroned Davidic king – and thus acknowledge his rightful reign over themselves – they are incorporated into the ἐκκλησία through baptism (2:41–42; cf. 4:32–5:11, esp. 5:11).[127] Not just Israel, but *David's reign* over Israel, has been established in principle.

It is important to note, however, that the Davidic kingdom is not only restored but transformed.[128] The Son of David is not now enthroned in the earthly Jerusalem but in the heavenly, 'exalted at the right hand of God.' The kingdom has been transposed from earth to heaven, even though it continues to manifest itself on earth as the ἐκκλησία.[129] This *ecclesial* kingdom exists simultaneously on earth and in heaven. The king is enthroned in heaven, but the ministers (the apostles) are active on earth. Meanwhile the heavenly king is

---

[121] Johnson, *Acts*, 61.
[122] See O'Toole, 'Acts 2:30,' 245–58; and Bock, 'Reign,' 47: 'Although the term *kingdom* never appears in the entire chapter, the imagery of rule and the features of God's covenants are present. In fact, the chapter is saturated with such images and allusions.'
[123] Cf. Tannehill, *Unity*, 38.
[124] See Bock, 'Reign,' 49.
[125] On the Davidic background of Peter's sermon, see Bock, 'Reign,' 38–39.
[126] On the relationship of Lk. 1:32–33 and Acts 2:24–31, see Lane, *Luke*, 160.
[127] See Fitzmyer, 'Role,' 175–76; and Denova, *Things*, 138 and 169–75.
[128] Francis Martin compares ways in which the NT transforms the expectations of the OT in the very process of fulfilling them to Bernard Lonergan's concept of 'sublation,' although Martin prefers the term 'transposition' (see discussion in Martin, 'Directions,' 69–70).
[129] So Penney, *Emphasis,* 75.

united to his earthly officers and subjects by the Holy Spirit and, though it receives less emphasis, the eucharistic 'breaking of bread.'

Second, the promise of apostolic vice-regency over the Davidic kingdom (Lk. 22:30; Ps. 122:5) begins at Pentecost, when the apostles receive the 'power' (δύναμις) of the Holy Spirit, call a worldwide audience of Jews to repentance, and incorporate the respondents into the messianic community. Just as the outpouring of the Spirit is the perceptible sign of Jesus' royal enthronement (Acts 1:33), the dispensation of the Spirit thereafter through the apostle's hands is a sign of their own enthronement as vice-regents.[130] The vice-regents are sharing in the king's power to dispense the Spirit. The kingdom and Spirit are co-extensive; it is a *pneumatic* kingdom.[131] One might also call it a *sacramental* kingdom: one must enter it through baptism, and the community of the baptized devotes themselves 'to the apostle's teaching and fellowship, to *the breaking of bread* and the prayers.' The eucharistic significance of the 'breaking of bread' in Luke 9:16, 22:19, and 24:30 has been noted. The 'breaking of bread' here in Acts 2:42, as well as 20:11 and 27:35, is no simple eating but eucharistic celebration and proleptic participation in the messianic banquet. In the continuing practice of 'the breaking of bread' the apostles experience the fulfillment of the promise 'to eat and drink at my table in my kingdom' (Lk. 22:30), and the whole eschatological community shares in the fulfillment with them.

In sum, Acts 1–2, the key introductory chapters of the book, have several links to the Institution Narrative and describe the birth of the church as the restoration of the kingdom of David. The identification of the Davidic kingdom and the church is not limited to these two chapters, but occurs throughout Acts. For example, in James' concluding statements at the Jerusalem council (Acts 15), he confirms the decision to embrace Gentile converts by quoting Amos 9:11–12: 'After this I will return, and I will rebuild the dwelling (*skēnē*) of David ... that the rest of men may seek the Lord, and all the Gentiles who are called by my name' (Acts 15:13–18). The 'dwelling' or 'tent' of David referred to by Amos (Amos 9:11) is the Davidic kingdom, which at its peak incorporated Edom (cf. Amos 9:12a) and other Gentile nations (Ammon, Moab, Aram, etc.) who may be 'the nations who are called by my name' (Amos 9:12b).[132] James sees the fulfillment of Amos' prophecy – that is, the restoration

---

[130] Johnson, *Acts*, 29. Significantly, hereafter in Acts 'it is made clear that the Spirit is given only when the twelve are present, or a member of the twelve, or one of their delegates is on the scene' (Fitzmyer, 'Role,' 182).

[131] Cf. Bock, 'Reign,' 53: 'Those who share the Spirit show the influence of God in the world and reflect his work on earth, both in his powerful transformation of them and in their love toward those around them. They are a kingdom alongside other kingdoms.'

[132] Mauchline, 'Signs'; and Polley, *Amos*, 66–82.

of the Davidic *kingdom* – in the incorporation of Gentiles into the *church* as related by 'Simeon' before the whole council.[133] No one has seen this more clearly than Pao:

> The promise to rebuild and restore the Davidic kingdom is explicitly made at the point in the narrative of Acts that focuses on defining the people of God. The Amos quotation of Acts 15 shows that ... the development of the early Christian community is also understood within the paradigm of the anticipation of the Davidic kingdom. The *christological* focus of the David tradition should be supplemented by an *ecclesiological* one.[134]

Conclusion

The work that has been done on royal Davidic messianism in Luke has been excellent, but its logic must be carried forward. If Jesus is the royal Son of David, this fact has not merely christological but also ecclesiological significance. If Jesus is the Davidic King, then his kingdom is the Davidic kingdom. That kingdom is present already, because it was conferred on the disciples at the Last Supper. Their rule over Israel is manifested in their rule over the ἐκκλησία. The ἐκκλησία is the incipient, growing kingdom of David, incorporating Jews, Israelites, and the nations, under the reign of Jesus the Davidic King, which is exercised through his Spirit-empowered apostolic vice-regents.[135]

Nonetheless, while the Davidic kingdom finds historic fulfillment in the church, it also undergoes a transposition from the earthly to the heavenly sphere. The earthly Jerusalem and its temple, despite Luke's genuine respect for them, cannot be the ultimate locus of eschatological fulfillment (cf. Acts 7:48–50; Lk. 21:6). Peter makes clear that Christ's present rule is not from the earthly Jerusalem but from the heavenly (Acts 2:33a). Nonetheless his reign expresses itself in the earthly realm by what can be 'seen and heard' (2:33b). The renewed kingdom of David, of which the church is the visible manifestation, exists simultaneously in heaven and on earth, as its citizens move from one sphere to the other. To quote Durrwell:

> She [the Church] exists fully in two different periods of time ... she dwells in heaven but also journeys on earth. She does not exist somewhere between the two times, but actually in both simultaneously ... Thus the church bears the marks of two

---

[133] See Strauss, *Messiah*, 190–92.
[134] Pao, *Acts*, 138. Cf. also Penney, *Emphasis*, 74; Seccombe, 'People'; and Bauckham, 'James,' esp. 457.
[135] Cf. del Agua, 'Narrative,' 661.

opposite states. She leads a mysterious, heavenly existence, and she is also a visible, empirical reality ... In her mysterious reality the church is indeed the Kingdom of God ... but as perceived by the senses, she is only its sign and instrument.[136]

Nonetheless, the whole kingdom (i.e., the whole church) is united by the indwelling Holy Spirit and the celebration of the Eucharist, in which the King becomes present, the kingdom manifest, and the earthly citizens of the kingdom participate in the perpetual messianic banquet of the heavenly King.

---

[136] Durrwell, *Resurrection*, 270.

Bibliography

del Agua, A., 'The Lucan Narrative of the "Evangelization of the Kingdom of God:" A Contribution to the Unity of Luke-Acts,' in *The Unity of Luke-Acts* (ed. J. Verheyden; BETL 142; Leuven: Peeters, 1999), 639–62

Bailey, K.E., *Jacob and the Prodigal: How Jesus Retold Israel's Story* (Downers Grove, IL: InterVarsity Press, 2003)

Bartholomew, C., 'Biblical Theology and Biblical Interpretation', in *Out of Egypt: Biblical Theology and Biblical Interpretation* (ed. C. Bartholomew et al.; SHS 5; Carlisle: Paternoster; Grand Rapids: Zondervan, 2004), 1–19

Bartholomew, C., and M.W. Goheen, 'Story and Biblical Theology', in *Out of Egypt: Biblical Theology and Biblical Interpretation* (ed. C. Bartholomew et al.; SHS 5; Carlisle: Paternoster; Grand Rapids: Zondervan., 2004), 144–71

Barton, S.C., 'The Unity of Humankind as a Theme in Biblical Theology', in *Out of Egypt: Biblical Theology and Biblical Interpretation* (ed. C. Bartholomew et al.; SHS 5; Grand Rapids: Zondervan, 2004), 233–58

Bauckham, R., 'Anna of the Tribe of Asher (Luke 2:36–38),' *RB* 104 (1997), 161–91

—, 'James and the Jerusalem Church', in *The Book of Acts in Its First Century Setting. Volume 4: The Book of Acts in Its Palestinian Setting* (ed. R. Bauckham; Grand Rapids: Eerdmans, 1995), 415–80

Bechard, D.P., 'The Theological Significance of Judea in Luke-Acts,' in *The Unity of Luke-Acts* (ed. J. Verheyden; BETL 142; Leuven: Peeters, 1999), 675–91

Becker, O., 'Covenant', in *NIDNTT* 1:365–76

Benoit, P., 'Le Recít de la Cène dans Luc xxii, 15–20', *RB* 48 (1939), 357–93

—, *Jesus and the Gospel*, I (New York: Herder and Herder, 1973)

Block, D.I., 'My Servant David: Ancient Israel's Vision of the Messiah,' in *Israel's Messiah in the Bible and the Dead Sea Scrolls* (ed. R.S. Hess and M.D. Carroll R.; Grand Rapids: Baker Books, 2003), 17–56

Bock, D.L., *Proclamation from Prophecy and Pattern: Lucan Old Testament Christology* (JSNTSup 12; Sheffield: Sheffield Academic Press, 1997)

—, *Luke 1:1–9:50* (BECNT; Grand Rapids: Baker Books, 1994)

—, *Luke 9:51–24:53* (BECNT; Grand Rapids: Baker Books, 1996)

—, 'Proclamation from Prophecy and Pattern: Luke's Use of the Old Testament for Christology and Mission,' in *The Gospels and the Scriptures of Israel* (ed. C.A. Evans and W.R. Stegner; JSNTSup 104; Sheffield: Sheffield Academic Press, 1999), 293–94

—, 'The Reign of the Lord Jesus,' in *Dispensationalism, Israel and the Church: The Search for Definition* (ed. C.A. Blaising and D.L. Bock; Grand Rapids: Zondervan, 1992), 37–67

Brawley, R.L., 'Abrahamic Covenant Traditions and the Characterization of God in Luke-Acts,' in *The Unity of Luke-Acts* (ed. J. Verheyden; BETL 142; Leuven: Peeters, 1999), 109–32

—, *Text to Text Pours Forth Speech: Voices of Scripture in Luke-Acts* (Bloomington, IN: Indiana University Press, 1995)

Brown, R., S.S., 'Communicating the Divine and Human in Scripture,' *Origins* 22.1 (1992), 5–6

Bruce, F.F., 'The Davidic Messiah in Luke-Acts,' in *Biblical and Near Eastern Studies: Festschrift W.S. Lasor* (Grand Rapids: Eerdmans, 1978), 7–17

Chance, J.B., *Jerusalem, the Temple, and the New Age in Luke-Acts* (Macon, GA: Mercer University Press, 1988)

Childs, B.S., *Biblical Theology in Crisis* (Philadelphia: Westminster Press, 1970)

Clark, A.C., 'The Role of the Apostles,' in *Witness to the Gospel: The Theology of Acts* (ed. I.H. Marshall and D. Peterson; Grand Rapids: Eerdmans, 1998), 169–90

Collins, J.J., *The Scepter and the Star: The Messiahs of the Dead Sea Scrolls and Other Ancient Literature* (ABRL; New York: Doubleday, 1995)

Denova, R.I., *Things Accomplished among Us: Prophetic Tradition in the Structural Pattern of Luke-Acts* (JSNTSup 141; Sheffield: Sheffield Academic Press, 1997)

Durrwell, F.X., *The Resurrection: A Biblical Study* (trans. R. Sheed; New York: Sheed and Ward, 1960)

Evans, C.A., 'The Twelve Thrones of Israel: Scripture and Politics in Luke 22:24–30,' in *Luke and Scripture: The Function of Sacred Tradition in Luke-Acts* (ed. C.A. Evans and J.A. Sanders; Minneapolis: Fortress Press, 1993), 154–70

Evans, C.A., and W.R. Stegner (eds.), *The Gospels and the Scriptures of Israel* (JSNTSup 104; Sheffield: Sheffield Academic Press, 1999)

Evans, C.A., and J.A. Sanders (eds.), *Luke and Scripture: The Function of Sacred Tradition in Luke-Acts* (Minneapolis: Fortress Press, 1993)

Van Den Eynde, S., 'Children of the Promise: On the Διαθήκη-Promise to Abraham in Lk. 1,72 and Acts 3,25,' in *The Unity of Luke-Acts* (ed. J. Verheyden; BETL 142; Leuven: Peeters, 1999), 470–82

Farris, S., *The Hymns of Luke's Infancy Narratives: Their Origin, Meaning and Significance* (JSNTSup 9; Sheffield: JSOT Press, 1985), 95–96

Fitzmyer, J.A., 'The Role of the Spirit in Luke-Acts,' in *The Unity of Luke-Acts* (ed. J. Verheyden; BETL 142; Leuven: Peeters, 1999), 165–84

—, *The Gospel According to Luke, I–IX* (AB 28; Garden City: Doubleday, 1981)

—, *The Gospel According to Luke, X-XXIV* (AB 28A; New York: Doubleday, 1985)

García Martínez, F., and E.J.C. Tigchelaar (eds.), *The Dead Sea Scrolls Study Edition* (2 vols.; Leiden: E.J. Brill/Grand Rapids: Eerdmans, 1997–98)

Gese, H., *Essays in Biblical Theology* (Minneapolis: Augsburg Press, 1981)

Gordon, R.P., *1 & 2 Samuel* (Old Testament Guides; Sheffield: JSOT Press, 1984)

Green, J.B., *The Gospel of Luke* (NICNT; Grand Rapids: Eerdmans, 1997)

Horbury, W., *Jewish Messianism and the Cult of Christ* (London: SCM Press, 1998)

—, *Messianism among Jews and Christians: Twelve Biblical and Historical Studies* (New York: T&T Clark, 2003)

Hurowitz, V., *I Have Built You an Exalted House: Temple Building in the Bible in Light of Mesopotamian and Northwest Semitic Writings* (JSOTSup 115; Sheffield: Sheffield Academic Press, 1992)

Ishida, T., *The Royal Dynasties in Ancient Israel: A Study on the Formation and Development of Royal-Dynastic Ideology* (New York: de Gruyter, 1977)

Japhet, S., 'From the King's Sanctuary to the Chosen City,' in *Jerusalem: Its Sanctity and Centrality to Judaism, Christianity, and Islam* (ed. L.I. Levine; New York: Continuum, 1999), 3–15

Jervell, J., *Luke and the People of God: A New Look at Luke-Acts* (Minneapolis: Augsburg Press, 1972)

Johnson, L.T., *The Gospel of Luke* (SP 3; Collegeville, MN: Liturgical Press, 1991).

—, *The Acts of the Apostles* (SP 5; Collegeville, MN: Liturgical Press, 1992).

Juel, D., 'Review of Mark L. Strauss, *The Davidic Messiah in Luke-Acts: The Promise and Its Fulfillment in Lukan Christology*,' in *RBL*; 2000 online http://www.bookreviews.org

Karris, R.J. (ed.), *The Works of St. Bonaventure, VIII*, Part 3: *Commentary on the Gospel of Luke Chapters 17–24* (St. Bonaventure, NY: Franciscan Institute, 2004)

Kimball, C.A., *Jesus' Exposition of the Old Testament in Luke's Gospel* (JSNTSup 94; Sheffield: Sheffield Academic Press, 1994)

Koenig, J., *The Feast of the World's Redemption: Eucharistic Origins and Christian Mission* (Harrisburg: Trinity Press International, 2000)

Kruse, H., 'David's Covenant,' *VT* 35 (1985), 139–64

Laato, A., 'Psalm 132 and the Development of the Jerusalemite/Israelite Royal Ideology,' *CBQ* 54 (1992), 49–66

—, *A Star is Rising: The Historical Development of the Old Testament Royal Ideology and the Rise of Jewish Messianic Expectations* (Atlanta: Scholars Press, 1995)

Lane, T.J., *Luke and the Gentile Mission: Gospel Anticipates Acts* (Frankfurt am Mein: Peter Lang, 1996)

LaVerdiere, E., *Dining in the Kingdom of God: The Origins of the Eucharist according to Luke* (Chicago: Liturgy Training Publications, 1994)

—, *The Breaking of the Bread: The Development of the Eucharist according to Acts* (Chicago: Liturgy Training Publications, 1998)

—, *The Eucharist in the New Testament and the Early Church* (Collegeville, MN: Liturgical Press, 1996)

Levenson, J.D., *Sinai and Zion: An Entry into the Jewish Bible* (San Francisco: Harper & Row, 1985)

Marshall, I.H., *Luke: Historian and Theologian* (Grand Rapids: Zondervan, 1970)

Martin, F., 'Some Directions in Catholic Biblical Theology', in *Out of Egypt: Biblical Theology and Biblical Interpretation* (ed. C. Bartholomew et al.; SHS 5; Grand Rapids: Zondervan, 2004), 65–87

Mason, R., 'The Messiah in the Postexilic Old Testament Literature,' in *King and Messiah in the Ancient Near East: Proceedings of the Oxford Old Testament Seminar* (ed. J. Day; JSOTSup 270; Sheffield: Sheffield Academic Press, 1998), 338–64

Mauchline, J., 'Implicit Signs of a Persistent Belief in the Davidic Empire,' *VT* 20 (1970), 287–303

McKnight, S., *A New Vision for Israel: The Teachings of Jesus in National Context* (Grand Rapids: Eerdmans, 1999)

Meyers, C., 'The Israelite Empire: In Defense of King Solomon,' in *Backgrounds for the Bible* (ed. P. O'Connor and D.N. Freedman; Winona Lake: Eisenbrauns, 1987), 181–97

Moessner, D.P., *Lord of the Banquet: The Literary and Theological Significance of the Lukan Travel Narrative* (Minneapolis: Fortress Press, 1989)

Nelson, P.K., *Leadership and Discipleship: A Study of Luke 22:24–30* (SBLDS 138; Atlanta: Scholars Press, 1994)

Neyrey, J., *The Passion according to Luke: A Redaction Study of Luke's Soteriology* (New York: Paulist Press, 1985)

Nolan, B.M., *The Royal Son of God: The Christology of Matthew 1–2 in the Setting of the Gospel* (OBO 23; Göttingen: Vandenhoeck & Ruprecht, 1979)

Nolland, J., *Luke 18:35–24:53* (WBC 35c; Dallas: Word, 1993)

O'Toole, R.F., 'Acts 2:30 and the Davidic Covenant of Pentecost,' *JBL* 102 (1983), 245–58

Ossom-Batsa, G., *The Institution of the Eucharist in the Gospel of Mark: A Study of the Function of Mark 14,22–25 within the Gospel Narrative* (Bern: Peter Lang, 2001)

Pao, D.W., *Acts and the Isaianic New Exodus* (WUNT 2/130; Tübingen: Mohr Siebeck, 2000)

Penney, J.M., *The Missionary Emphasis of Lukan Pneumatology* (Sheffield: Sheffield Academic Press, 1997)

Plantinga, A., 'Two (or More) Kinds of Scripture Scholarship', in *'Behind' the Text: History and Biblical Interpretation* (ed. C. Bartholomew et al.; SHS 4; Carlisle: Paternoster; Grand Rapids: Zondervan, 2003), 19–57

Polley, M.E., *Amos and the Davidic Empire: A Socio-Historical Approach* (New York: Oxford University Press, 1989)

Priest, J., 'A Note on the Messianic Banquet,' in *The Messiah: Developments in Earliest Judaism and Christianity* (ed. J.H. Charlesworth; Minneapolis: Fortress Press, 1992), 222–38

Ravens, D., *Luke and the Restoration of Israel* (JSNTSup 119; Sheffield: Sheffield Academic Press, 1995)

Ratzinger, J., *Behold the Pierced One* (San Francisco: Ignatius Press, 1986)

Seccombe, D., 'The New People of God,' in *Witness to the Gospel: The Theology of Acts* (ed. I.H. Marshall and D. Peterson; Grand Rapids: Eerdmans, 1998), 350–72

Strauss, M.L., *The Davidic Messiah in Luke-Acts: The Promise and Its Fulfillment in Lukan Christology* (JSNTSup 110; Sheffield: Sheffield Academic Press, 1995)

Swartley, W.M., *Israel's Scripture Traditions and the Synoptic Gospels: Story Shaping Story* (Peabody, MA: Hendrickson, 1994)

Tannehill, R.C., *The Narrative Unity of Luke–Acts: A Literary Interpretation,* I: *The Gospel according to Luke* (Philadelphia: Fortress Press, 1986)

Taylor, N.H., 'Luke-Acts and the Temple,' in *The Unity of Luke-Acts* (ed. J. Verheyden; BETL 142; Leuven: Peeters, 1999), 709–21

Tuckett, C.M., 'The Christology of Luke-Acts,' in *The Unity of Luke-Acts* (ed. J. Verheyden; BETL 142; Leuven: Peeters, 1999), 133–64

Turner, M., *Power from on High: The Spirit in Israel's Restoration and Witness in Luke–Acts* (Sheffield: Sheffield Academic Press, 1996).

Vanhoozer, K.J., 'From Speech Acts to Scripture Acts: The Covenant of Discourse and the Discourse of Covenant', in *After Penetecost: Language and Biblical Interpretation* (ed. C. Bartholomew et al.; SHS 2; Carlisle: Paternoster; Grand Rapids: Zondervan, 2001), 1–49

Vööbus, A. (ed. and trans.), *The Didascalia Apostolorum in Syriac,* II: *Chapters XI–XXVI* (CSCO 408; Scriptores Syri 180; Louvain: Secretariat du CSCO, 1979)

Waltke, B.K., 'The Phenomenon of Conditionality within Unconditional Covenants,' in *Israel's Apostasy and Restoration: Essays in Honor of Roland K. Harrison* (ed. A. Gileadi; Grand Rapids: Baker Books, 1988), 123–40

12

A Canonical Approach to Interpreting Luke

The Journey Motif as a Hermeneutical Key

Charles H.H. Scobie

Introduction

Those who seek to interpret Luke's Gospel as part of Holy Scripture, the supreme rule of faith and life for believers, and at the same time to reckon with contemporary academic study of the Lukan writings, face serious problems. The dominant 'historical-critical' method, while representing a range of approaches, broadly speaking has become increasingly sceptical regarding such matters as the traditional authorship by Luke the companion of Paul, the dating of the gospel, and indeed its historical accuracy in general.[1]

It might be thought that if Luke's reputation as a historian has declined, his reputation as a theologian would have increased. In one sense this has been the case, especially since Conzelmann's pioneering *redactionsgeschichte* study, *The Theology of St. Luke.* Conzelmann assumes that Paul and the earliest Christians expected the imminent end of the world; Luke wrote in a later situation when it had become clear that this was not the case and that the church was here to stay. Without accepting all the details of Conzelmann's approach, there has been considerable agreement that Luke is not just a scissors and paste compiler; his gospel (and Acts) manifest a distinctive theological position characterized by the centrality of 'salvation history' (*Heilsgeschichte*). On this view, God works out his purpose within human history in three successive stages: the period of Israel, represented by the Old Testament; the period of Jesus' ministry, which

---

[1] See Powell, *What Are They Saying,* 5–7

comes not at the end but in the centre of history (hence the original German title of Conzelmann's book, *Die Mitte der Zeit*); and the period of the church, which is of indefinite length and stretches from the ascension to the parousia.

In terms of New Testament theology as a whole, however, Luke's distinctive theology has frequently received a very negative assessment. At this point the work of the Bultmann school casts a long shadow. Bultmann found the core of the New Testament and of the Christian faith in Paul and John (suitably demythologized, and reinterpreted with the aid of existentialist philosophy). For the earliest church and for Paul, he contends, 'the history of the world has reached its end, because in Christ the history of salvation had found its fulfilment and hence its end'.[2] Luke, on the other hand, represents a late development that betrays the original Pauline kerygma and replaces it with an ongoing 'salvation history'. Hence, in Bultmann's two-volume *Theology of the New Testament*, Luke plays a very minor role and is treated in the last section under the heading 'The Development toward the Ancient Church'.[3] Those who follow the Bultmann line see Luke as a representative of 'early catholicism' (*Fruhkatholicismus*), and they accuse him of 'historicizing'; the original kerygma that challenges hearers to existential decision and a radically new self-understanding has been replaced by a false security found in an ongoing history of God with his people. In Luke, the church has become an institution within history.

This approach to Luke has, of course, been challenged, and Luke's reputation both as a historian and as a theologian has been defended by moderately conservative scholars.[4] Nevertheless, even among scholars who evaluate Luke more positively (for example, for his ethical teaching and treatment of social issues) there is a tendency to see the Lukan writings as a prime example of diversity within the New Testament. In 1960, Ernst Käsemann cited Luke's salvation history approach as an example of 'the different theological outlooks of the Evangelists' and as evidence of 'irreconcilable theological contradictions' within the New Testament.[5] Historical-critical scholarship in the second half of the twentieth century increasingly emphasized this diversity; not only was it no longer possible to speak of a 'biblical theology', one could not even speak of a 'New Testament theology' but only of 'New Testament theologies'.

In the closing decades of the twentieth century a renewed interest in biblical theology opened up new possibilities. Without disparaging a sound historical approach, such a biblical theology would be based primarily on the final canonical form of the text and would be truly 'biblical', encompassing Old and New

---

[2] Bultmann, *Theology of the New Testament*, II, 117.
[3] Bultmann, *Theology of the New Testament*, II, Part IV.
[4] Notably by I.H. Marshall, *Luke: Historian and Theologian*.
[5] Käsemann, 'Is the New Testament Canon', 96,97,100.

Testaments together, read and interpreted as Christian Scripture. Such a canonical biblical theology can find an ally in at least some forms of the renewed literary approach to Scripture characteristic of the same period. W.S. Kurz, for example, while building on insights derived from historical criticism, develops a narrative-critical approach to Luke-Acts that focuses on the final form of the text and that seeks to deal with 'the meaning of Luke and Acts not only for the original author and intended audience but for the church through the ages and for contemporary readers'.[6] Similarly, M.A. Powell argues that while traditional historical-critical approaches focus on determining the meaning of the text in its original historical setting, narrative criticism recognizes 'transcendence of immediate context'; its purpose can be 'to engage the reader's imagination in ways that elicit faith, inspire worship, provoke repentance, or otherwise shape the perspective and conduct of those who encounter the work in a variety of life settings'.[7]

This chapter seeks to explore the interpretation of Luke's Gospel from the perspective of a canonical biblical theology, focusing in turn on: (a) the place of Luke in the New Testament canon; (b) the canonical structure of Luke; and (c) reading Luke in a canonical context, with special reference to 'the journey motif' as a key theme linking Luke with the Old Testament and with the rest of the New Testament.

The Place of Luke in the New Testament Canon

Some insight into the development of the structure of the New Testament canon may be gained from the evidence of early manuscripts; much, however, remains unknown and much remains controversial. The primary focus here, therefore, will be on the final form of the canon as recognized and accepted by the church.

(a) All versions of the New Testament known to us from manuscripts begin with the four gospels, a fact that witnesses to the central importance of the Christ event in the canon of the New Testament and, indeed, in the canon of the whole Bible. Luke's Gospel is always placed within this fourfold gospel.

The fact that the existence of four differing gospels caused problems for some in the early church is well attested.[8] Nevertheless, the church rejected the

---

[6] Kurz, *Reading Luke-Acts*, 5.

[7] Powell, 'Toward a Narrative-Critical Understanding of Luke', 342. For other literary (narrative) treatments see Aletti, *L'art de raconter Jésus Christ*, and Knight, *Luke's Gospel*.

[8] See Cullmann, 'The Plurality of the Gospels', 39–50; Morgan, 'The Hermeneutical Significance', 376.

solution of Marcion (select one gospel only, in his case a version of Luke), as well as the solution of Tatian (combine all four gospels in a harmony), and instead adopted the position of Irenaeus, who contended that Christ 'gave us the Gospel under four forms but bound together by one Spirit'.[9] This understanding is witnessed to in the headings given the gospels when they were brought together in one corpus: (the gospel) ΚΑΤΑ ΜΑΘΘΑΙΟΝ . . . ΚΑΤΑ ΜΑΡΚΟΝ . . . ΚΑΤΑ ΛΟΥΚΑΝ . . . ΚΑΤΑ ΙΩΑΝΝΗΝ ('according to Matthew ... Mark ... Luke ... John').[10]

Luke therefore deserves our respect as one of the four gospels that equally testify to the Christ event, and thus form the core of the New Testament. The structure of the canon prohibits us from privileging one gospel over another, or from excluding any one gospel from an inner 'canon within the canon'. Despite their differences the four gospels are not to be read separately and set against each other; they complement rather than contradict each other and are to be read together, recognizing that they are inspired by the one Spirit and that ultimately all testify to the one reality.[11]

(b) The order of the four canonical gospels varies in the early centuries.[12] The two commonest arrangements are the Western (pre-Jerome) order of Matthew-John-Luke-Mark, and the Eastern order of Matthew-Mark-Luke-John, the one that ultimately prevailed. The reasons for the variant orders are largely a matter of speculation. Thus it has been suggested that the Western order may be due to a desire to place first the gospels written by apostles – Matthew and John, followed by those written by disciples of apostles – Luke and Mark, while the Eastern order may be due to a desire to list the books in the supposed chronological order of writing. It will be noted that Matthew comes first in both lists; in terms of the complete biblical canon, this allows Matthew, with its strong emphasis on the fulfilment of Old Testament prophecy, to act as a hinge between the two Testaments.

In both Eastern and Western lists Luke's Gospel comes third. Why should this be the case? If chronology played any part in the order, then given the reference in Luke 1:1–2 to 'many' (πολλοί) earlier written accounts, Luke could hardly have come in first, or even second, place. In the Eastern order that prevailed John comes last, perhaps because it was believed to have been written last and/or because, as 'the spiritual gospel', it was considered most suitable to conclude the series. These factors would thus combine to place Luke third in the series.

---

[9] *Haer.* 3.2.8; see Cullmann, 'The Plurality of the Gospels', 47–53.
[10] Cf. Farmer and Farkasfalvy, *The Formation of the New Testament Canon*, 72.
[11] Cf. Cullmann, 'The Plurality of the Gospels', 52–53; contra Käsemann, 'Is the New Testament Canon', 95–97.
[12] See Gamble, 'Canon: New Testament', 855; Trobisch, *The First Edition*, 30–31.

(c) Perhaps the most striking fact about the position of Luke in the New Testament canon is the severing of the link between Luke and Acts. It is virtually the unanimous opinion (in ancient as well as modern times) that they are the work of the same author, as the opening verses of each clearly demonstrate. Luke-Acts was originally a two-volume work: the 'first book' (πρῶτον λόγον) of Acts 1:1 refers back to the gospel as volume one. Thus the placement of Luke within the fourfold gospel was accomplished only by breaking the connection with Acts. It is significant that, although the two volumes were separated, no attempt was made to disguise their original unity (as might have been done by deleting the opening verse of Acts). It should be noted that acceptance of a fourfold gospel, with John in last place, prevented a solution that could have allowed Luke to be placed with the other gospels but also kept Luke and Acts together, that is, by placing Luke in fourth place, directly followed by Acts.[13] This has important consequences for the structure of the New Testament canon.

(d) In the early centuries, the gospels always come first in the canon of the New Testament but the order of the other books varies.[14] The arrangement that eventually won out was: gospels – Acts – Pauline epistles – minor epistles – Revelation. Whatever may have been the historical process that brought this about, in the final form of the canon Luke's Gospel plays a key role. On the one hand, as noted above, it is firmly embedded within the fourfold gospel; on the other hand, it links the gospels to Acts. Acts in turn functions as an introduction to the works of four of the main characters of the New Testament – Paul, James, Peter and John – that is, in terms of traditional authorship, to virtually the rest of the New Testament.[15] Luke's Gospel is thus, in effect, the lynchpin of the New Testament canon.

To this analysis of the canonical role of Luke (and its companion volume Acts) we may add the fact that between them they occupy approximately 28 per cent of the New Testament.[16] I am not suggesting that the importance of these books be gauged purely in quantitative terms. But, when their volume is assessed alongside the fact that their position in the canon makes them virtually the glue that holds the whole New Testament together, we are justified in concluding that the Gospel of Luke (with Acts) has been seriously undervalued in most New Testament and biblical theologies.

---

[13] See Farmer and Farkasfalvy, *The Formation of the New Testament Canon*, 73.

[14] See Trobisch, *The First Edition*, 21–30.

[15] See Farmer and Farkasfalvy, *The Formation of the New Testament Canon*, 73; Trobisch, *The First Edition*, 52.

[16] Based on the word count cited in Green, *The Theology of the Gospel of Luke*, 2, n. 5.

The Canonical Structure of Luke

A canonical biblical theology is not concerned with theories regarding possible sources of Luke's Gospel (Mark, Q, L), nor with theories of composition (e.g., proto-Luke), but focuses instead on the final canonical form of the book. This involves looking at the shape of the book, at how the author structures his work and presents it to his readers.[17] In this endeavour literary analysis can be a valuable ally to the biblical theologian.

Luke's Gospel shares important structural features with the other gospels, especially with Matthew and Mark; however, the Lukan structure has two major distinctive features:

(a) The infancy narrative of Luke 1–2 and the resurrection accounts in Luke 24, consisting almost entirely of material peculiar to Luke, form *an envelope structure* for the gospel as a whole, so that, unlike the other three gospels, it both begins and ends in Jerusalem, in fact in the Jerusalem temple.[18] Luke 1 begins with Zechariah taking his turn of priestly duties in the sanctuary, while the very end of the gospel has the disciples 'continually in the temple blessing and praising God' (24:53). The emphasis on Jerusalem is typical of Luke; the city holds a central, if somewhat ambiguous place in his theology.

(b) The other major distinctive feature of Luke is the large central 'travel narrative' (*Reisebericht*), extending from 9:51 to 19:44.[19] Both Matthew and Mark have a transition from a Galilean ministry to a Jerusalem ministry, but this is accomplished in relatively short order. Luke, on the other hand, makes this journey a major feature of his gospel,[20] occupying some ten chapters (more than a third of the gospel), within which he places mostly material that has no parallel in Mark (i.e., material that source critics would assign to Q and L).

---

[17] Cf. Green, *The Theology of the Gospel of Luke*, 21, who emphasizes that Luke's 'chief contribution as a narrative theologian' includes 'his ordering and staging of the account'.

[18] There is a further element of geographical parallelism: both sections locate narratives in the hill country of Judah. Mary visits Elizabeth in 'a Judean town in the hill country' (1:39, cf. 1:65), while two disciples meet the risen Christ on the way to Emmaus 60 (or 160) stadia from Jerusalem (24:13), i.e., in the hill country. For further correspondences see Kurz, *Reading Luke-Acts*, 28.

[19] Some close the central travel narrative at Lk. 18:14 (where use of Markan material resumes) or at Lk. 19:27; but the journey notices clearly characterize this section as a journey to Jerusalem which logically concludes at Lk. 19:44 just before Jesus enters the city and the temple – so e.g. Filson, 'The Journey Motif', 71; Navone, 'The Journey Theme', 617; Resseguie, 'Interpretation', 3; Kurz, *Reading Luke-Acts*, 51–54. Aletti's analysis of the Lukan narrative strongly supports this structural division (*L'art de raconter Jésus Christ*, 111–31).

[20] Knight contends that 'the journey of Jesus from Galilee to Jerusalem is *the* major structural element in the Gospel' (*Luke's Gospel*, 64).

This section has been the focus of extensive study that has generated a large literature.[21]

The reader learns that Jesus and his disciples are on a journey to Jerusalem from a series of notices (*Reisenotizen*), beginning at 9:51 where Jesus 'set his face to go to Jerusalem', and continuing at intervals until 19:41 where 'he came near and saw the city'. These are clearly editorial in nature; Gill calls attention to the repeated use in them of πορεύομαι (a favourite Lukan word) for Jesus 'journeying' towards Jerusalem.[22] This journey has long posed problems for scholars. Much of the material in the section, it is frequently pointed out, has nothing to do with a journey at all. Moessner has characterized the problem as 'an unmitigating dissonance of form from content'.[23] Attempts to reconstruct the itinerary of the journey also produce problems. Luke 17:11 is perhaps the most difficult verse: Jesus goes through 'the region between Samaria and Galilee' (διὰ μέσον Σαμαρείας καὶ Γαλιλαίας: a difficult phrase), apparently no closer to Jerusalem than he was in 9:52. McCown, in his 1938 study, concluded that Luke shows either complete ignorance or complete indifference to Palestinian geography.[24] Some scholars have tried to reconcile Luke's account with the other gospels, including with Jesus' travels in John's Gospel;[25] today, however, the great majority of scholars see the journey as basically an editorial creation.[26] Luke's concern is not to convey detailed and accurate geographical information; he uses the journey as a framework into which he inserts a variety of material (parables, teaching, healings, conflict stories, etc.) derived from his sources. Kurz sees the journey motif as a 'plot device for gathering independent traditions'.[27]

Efforts have been made to find a single connecting thread running through the narrative. Thus Aletti argues that the theme of 'the Kingdom and the King' unifies the journey material.[28] Other suggested themes include mission, prayer, repentance, possessions, and the necessity of suffering.[29] The very variety of

[21] For bibliography see Girard, *L'Évangile des voyages de Jésus*, 5–16 (esp. for older works); Moessner, 'Luke 9:1–50', 575–76. For history of scholarship see Resseguie, 'Interpretation of Luke's Central Section'; Powell, *What Are They Saying*, 25–27.
[22] Gill, 'Observations', 200–201. πορεύομαι occurs a total of forty-nine times in Luke, twenty-five of these in the central travel narrative, and thirty-nine times in Acts.
[23] Moessner, 'Luke 9:1–50', 575.
[24] McCown, 'The Geography', 59.
[25] Girard, (*L'Évangile des voyages de Jésus*) thinks Luke used a separate source for 9:51 – 18:14 that recounted three journeys to Jerusalem.
[26] Cf. Robinson, 'The Theological Context', 20; Conzelmann, *The Theology of St. Luke*, 63; Craddock, *Luke*, 140.
[27] Kurz, *Reading Luke-Acts*, 27–28, cf. 52.
[28] Aletti, *L'art de raconter Jésus Christ*, 119–23.
[29] Trompf, 'La Section Médiane', thinks Luke has carefully constructed the section around three alternating themes: security, discipleship, and reward/punishment.

suggestions tells against finding a single unifying theme. Very broadly, however, the contents of the central travel narrative may be catalogued under two
main headings.

(1) *Christology.* Jesus is the central figure in the narrative which in part
    contributes to the Lukan Christology. Jesus is portrayed by Luke as a
    prophetic figure (Lk. 13:33). But this is far from the complete picture;[30] he
    is also Son of Man (Lk. 9:58; 11:30; 18:31; and 19:10), Son of God
    (Lk. 10:22), and Lord (Lk. 10:1, 17, 39; 11:1, etc.).[31] Luke identifies Jesus as
    Messiah (Lk. 2:11, 26; 4:41; 9:20), but this title does not occur in the central
    travel narrative; instead, the focus turns to the necessity of suffering and
    death. What distinguishes this journey from the earlier Galilean travels is
    the fact that, at the end of the journey, lies Jesus' death.[32] The final goal of
    the journey may be Jesus' 'taking up', or 'ascension' (ἀνάλημψις, Lk. 9:51),
    but the path to glory leads via the cross. The various controversies with
    opponents (Lk. 11:15–23, 37–54; 13:14–17; 14:1–6; 15:2; 16:14–15)
    presage the more deadly opposition Jesus will face when he arrives in
    Jerusalem.[33] In the central travel narrative Jesus, the traveller along the way
    and the guest at table, is the bearer and bringer of God's kingdom and God's
    salvation. A person's reaction to Jesus determines his or her destiny: those
    who welcome him and follow his teaching, like Zacchaeus, find salvation
    (Lk. 19:9); those who do not accept him, like the city of Jerusalem, face
    God's judgement because they fail to recognize the time of their visitation
    (ἐπισκοπή) from God (Lk. 19:44).[34] Jesus' hearers are summoned to a
    fundamental decision: 'Repent, or perish!' (Lk. 13:1–5).

(2) *Discipleship.* In form, much of the central travel narrative consists of teaching
    and hence has been classified as 'didactic' or 'paraenetic'. This teaching is
    directed primarily to the disciples, who will emerge in Acts as the core of

---

[30] Cf. Green, *The Gospel of Luke*, 353.

[31] Unlike Matthew and Mark, Luke frequently applies κύριος to Jesus during his min-
    istry. While in some passages the term may be simply a respectful form of address, in
    others it clearly has full christological significance. Cf. Marshall, *Luke: Historian and
    Theologian*, 166–67; Martin, 'Salvation and Discipleship', 371–72; Giles, 'The
    Church in the Gospel of Luke', 133–34.

[32] Cf. Conzelmann, *The Theology of St. Luke*, 65: 'Jesus' awareness that he must suffer is
    expressed in terms of the journey'.

[33] Kingsbury goes too far in arguing that Luke's entire narrative revolves around con-
    flict, but he is right in distinguishing Jesus' 'protracted, intermittent conversation'
    with opponents prior to Lk. 19:45 from the 'unremitting controversy' that develops
    immediately thereafter ('The Plot', 374–75).

[34] See Grundmann, 'Fragen der Komposition', 253.

the early Christian community.[35] As Green observes, 'The travel notices interspersed throughout the narrative, together with the overwhelmingly didactic content of the travel narrative, point to the Lukan concern with the formation of disciples on the journey. Clearly, a major purpose of the Jerusalem journey is to prepare for the time following Jesus' departure'.[36] Since discipleship involves community, one of Luke's main interests in the travel narrative has also been classified as 'Ecclesiastical-Functional'.[37] As Bernadicou puts it, on the journey to Jerusalem Jesus 'teaches his disciples what in turn will be expected of them and he binds them into a community by reason of their intimacy with him'.[38] The category of 'discipleship' is therefore appropriate, though only if interpreted very broadly as including material on the call to discipleship, the cost of discipleship, the mission of disciples, the lifestyle of disciples, the prayer life of disciples, and so on.[39]

That Luke chose to place this material within the framework of a journey to Jerusalem is extremely significant. The journey section clearly is closely related to the first major structural feature noted above – the prominence of Jerusalem at the beginning and at the end of the gospel. Not only does Jesus go *to* Jerusalem because that is where he is destined to suffer and die, but also because it is *from* Jerusalem that the gospel is destined to spread outwards to the rest of the known world (Lk. 24:47).

The central section of Luke is not the only instance of the journey motif in the gospel (hence we prefer to refer to it as the central travel narrative). Jesus has already been portrayed as journeying from place to place in his Galilean ministry.[40] In fact, 'Luke depicts Jesus as an inveterate traveller'.[41] Moreover, journeys are a key feature of the distinctive sections at the beginning and end of the gospel. The infancy narratives recount two journeys of Jesus to Jerusalem: the presentation visit of Luke 2:22–38, and the Passover visit of Luke 2:41–51.

---

[35] In comparison with Mark, the disciples in Luke are a much larger group, including 'all those who are in fellowship with Jesus'. This suggests that Luke wants his readers to identify with the disciples and 'to see them as a model church' (Giles, 'The Church in the Gospel of Luke', 126).

[36] Green, *The Gospel of Luke*, 397.

[37] Moessner, 'Luke 9:1–50', 577.

[38] Bernadicou, "The Spirituality of Luke's Travel Narrative', 455.

[39] See esp. the treatment of this theme in Sweetland, *Our Journey with Jesus*; and in Green, *The Theology of the Gospel of Luke*, ch. 5: '"Let them take up the cross daily": The way of discipleship'.

[40] Cf. Grundmann, 'Fragen der Komposition', 252; Bernadicou, 'The Spirituality of Luke's Travel Narrative', 456. Some of the themes that characterize the central travel narrative have already been introduced in Jesus' Galilean ministry.

[41] Giles, 'The Church in the Gospel of Luke', 139.

Thus Jesus actually makes *three* journeys to Jerusalem in Luke, with the two earlier visits placed near the beginning of the gospel prefiguring the great final journey to Jerusalem. Similarly, in Luke's distinctive resurrection narrative (Lk. 24) a journey again plays a central role: a journey of despair *from* Jerusalem (to Emmaus), followed by a journey of joy back *to* Jerusalem.[42] In short, it is the journey motif that constitutes the most marked structural feature of Luke's Gospel in its final canonical form.

With the infancy narratives (Lk. 1–2) and the resurrection accounts (Lk. 24) balancing each other, and the large travel narrative occupying the central position, the two remaining blocks of material can be seen to correspond to each other: Luke 3:1–9:50 focuses on Jesus' ministry in Galilee (preceded by preparation), while Luke 19:45–23:56 focuses on Jesus' ministry in the temple (followed by his passion). The gospel can thus be seen to be basically chiastic in structure:[43]

Preface (1:1–4)
A[1] – *The birth of Jesus* (1:5–2:52)
   B[1] – *Jesus' early ministry* (3:1–9:50)
      1. Preparation (3:1–4:13)
      2. Ministry in Galilee (4:14–9:50)
         C – *Jesus' journey to Jerusalem* (9:51–19:44)
   B[2] – *Jesus in Jerusalem* (19:45–23:56)
      1. Ministry in the temple (19:45–21:38)
      2. Passion (22–23)
A[2] – *The resurrection and ascension of Jesus* (24)

The Journey Motif in the Old Testament

The third aspect of interpreting Luke from the perspective of a canonical biblical theology involves reading the gospel in the total canonical context. The great majority of readers/hearers of Luke's gospel accept it 'as part of a larger biblical totality ... within the full biblical historiographical sweep from Genesis to Revelation, as part of the Holy Book, and in the light of the tradition and life

---

[42] See the discussion in Resseguie (*Spiritual Landscape*, 30–34), who sees the Emmaus narrative as 'a spiritual journey in which the two disciples awaken to a new way of seeing the world'.

[43] Attempts have been made to discern a more elaborate chiastic structure within the central travel narrative: e.g., a block of teaching on prayer near the beginning of the journey (Lk. 11:1–13) roughly balances a further block of teaching on prayer near the end of the journey (Lk. 18:1–14). Efforts to find a complete chiastic scheme, however, tend to be forced and have failed to convince most scholars; see Resseguie, *Spiritual Landscape*, 132, n. 44, and Craddock, *Luke*, 141.

of the church'.[44] Here we can only consider briefly the journey motif, which we have identified as a major structural feature of the gospel, first in relation to the Old Testament and then to the New Testament. At once it becomes apparent, as Filson points out, that the journey narrative is 'one of the dominant literary patterns of the Biblical story'.[45]

From the wanderings of the patriarchs, through the epic journey of the exodus, to the homeward trek of the exiles from Babylon, the journey motif has deep roots in the Old Testament. A number of scholars have proposed that Luke's central travel narrative is modelled on the exodus journey and specifically on the book of Deuteronomy. This thesis was proposed by C.F. Evans,[46] developed by a number of scholars, and has been worked out in great detail by D.P. Moessner.[47] The Lukan transfiguration narrative (Lk. 9:28–36) is a transitional passage, coming at the very end of the Galilean ministry and introducing the journey to Jerusalem that commences shortly thereafter. The undoubted Moses typology associated with the transfiguration[48] casts Jesus in the role of the Moses-like prophet (Deut. 18:15). A series of parallels in both form and content between the central travel narrative and the book of Deuteronomy are cited in support of this thesis. Just as Deuteronomy presents teaching in the framework of a journey, so the Lukan narrative is 'a Christian Deuteronomy – a handbook on the Christian life in the historical setting of a journey to Jerusalem'.[49]

This thesis has a lot to commend it, but it can only be accepted with two qualifications. First, while the central travel narrative is clearly based on exodus typology, not all of the Lukan material can be pressed into a specifically Deuteronomic mould. Luke's parallel with the giving of the Torah (Lk. 10:27), for example, cites the Shema (Deut. 6:5), but also Leviticus 19:18 as the

---

[44] Kurz, *Reading Luke-Acts*, 159. For important studies of the use and significance of the Scriptures of Israel in Luke see the contributions in this volume by Joel B. Green and Scott W. Hahn.

[45] Filson, 'The Journey Motif in Luke-Acts', 68; cf. Navone, 'The Journey Theme', 616. The bulk of Stephen's speech (Acts 7:2–44) deals with the journeys of the patriarchs and of Moses.

[46] Evans, 'The Central Section of St. Luke's Gospel'.

[47] Moessner finds numerous parallels with the Deuteronomic view of Israel's history (i.e., in the historical books as well as Deuteronomy itself), where the major themes are Israel's disobedience, God's sending of prophets to call the people to repentance, Israel's rejection of the prophets, and God's subsequent judgement (*Lord of the Banquet*, 83–211). These themes are, of course, widespread in the OT, in the prophetic as well as the historical books.

[48] See Moessner, 'Luke 9:1–50'; O'Toole, 'The Parallels between Jesus and Moses', 22–23; Turner, *Power from on High*, 234–38.

[49] Drury, *Tradition and Design*, 140.

summary of the ethical law, and if the sending out of the 70 (72) looks back to the appointment of 70 (72) elders to assist Moses, then the reference there is to Numbers 11:16–17, 24–25. The reference to 'the finger of God' in Luke 11:20 echoes Exodus 8:19.[50] The parallel between Jesus and Moses is undeniable, but it is best to see the central travel narrative as parallel to the exodus journey in general rather than restrict it to Deuteronomy.[51] The reference in Luke 9:31 to Jesus' 'exodus' (ἔξοδος), 'which he was to accomplish at Jerusalem' thus has a twofold reference: forwards to Jesus' coming death ('departure') at Jerusalem, and backwards to the Old Testament associations of the word 'exodus'.

Secondly, it is important to note that Luke's evocation of the exodus journey does not derive directly from the pentateuchal narrative; it is mediated by the prophetic promises of a new exodus, especially in Isaiah 40–55 – promises that Luke sees as being fulfilled in the Christ event. It has long been recognized that the numerous allusions to the exodus in Second Isaiah (Is. 42:13; 43:16, 17; 48:21; 51:10; 52:12, etc.) form the basis of the portrayal of the future age of salvation, on the principle that the past deliverance is a type of the future deliverance.[52] Just as God led the Israelites on the 'way' through the wilderness (Ex. 13:21; 23:20), so now the call goes out to prepare the 'way' for a new and greater deliverance and restoration of God's people (Is. 40:1–11, etc.). A number of recent studies have demonstrated how not only the key quotations of Isaiah 40:3–5 in Luke 3:4–6 and Isaiah 61:1–2 in Luke 4:18–19, but numerous other allusions in the gospel as well, evoke the Isaianic prophecies of a new exodus.[53] The parallels between the travel narrative and the exodus are to be seen in this light.

Luke presents Jesus as the prophet 'who recapitulates and consummates the career of Moses'.[54] Like Moses of old, Jesus leads his people (the disciples as representatives of Israel) on a journey, in the course of which he encounters opposition. His followers themselves can be obdurate and lacking in understanding. Despite this, he delivers teaching to the people and seeks to prepare them for the tasks that lie ahead. He appoints seventy (seventy-two) to share in his ministry. Through the power of God he carries out mighty works. And, like Moses, Jesus' 'exodus' culminates in his death, apparently before reaching his goal. But Jesus is also presented as the Isaianic Servant, anointed by the Spirit,

---

[50] It should also be noted that the Moses typology of the transfiguration narrative, while echoing Dt. 18:15, builds primarily on Ex. 24 and 34.

[51] Cf. the critique of the Deuteronomy theory in Knight, *Luke's Gospel*, 63, 198.

[52] Anderson, 'Exodus Typology'; Turner, *Power from on High*, 247; Pao, *Acts and the Isaianic New Exodus*, 45–59.

[53] See Turner, *Power from on High*, 244–50; and the summary in Pao, *Acts and the Isaianic New Exodus*, 10–17.

[54] Green, *The Gospel of Luke*, 353.

who inaugurates the promised time of salvation and calls forth the eschatological Israel into which the Gentiles will be welcomed.

The journey motif therefore represents for Luke a strong element of continuity in God's dealings with his people.

The Journey Motif in the New Testament

When we read Luke's Gospel in the light of the rest of the New Testament our view is directed first and foremost to the book of Acts, and at once it becomes apparent that a major connecting link is the widespread use of the journey motif. As Kurz notes, the 'plot device of the journey supports the dynamic view of the spread of God's word, first through Jesus in the gospel and then through the disciples in Acts'.[55] The structure of Acts starts out by resembling that of Luke. It, too, opens (Acts 1–7) in Jerusalem. But as the book proceeds, the mission of the church unfolds in a series of journeys that gradually move not *towards* Jerusalem but *away* from it. We noted that Luke's Gospel recounts *three* journeys of Jesus to Jerusalem. It is therefore significant that in Acts *three* journeys of Peter are recounted, each one beginning in Jerusalem, followed by a visit to a mission field, followed by a return to Jerusalem:

(1) Acts 8:14–25: Jerusalem, to Samaria, and back to Jerusalem.
(2) Acts 9:32–11:2: Jerusalem, to the Palestinian coast, and back to Jerusalem.
(3) Acts 12:19: Jerusalem, to Caesarea, and back to Jerusalem (see Acts 15:7).

When we come to Paul in Acts, first of all we hear of *three* visits he makes *to* Jerusalem:

(1) The education visit (Acts 7:58, cf. 22:3) – Paul, a native of Tarsus, journeys *to* Jerusalem to be educated under Gamaliel.
(2) The post-conversion visit (Acts 9:26–30) – after his conversion and a stay in Damascus Paul journeys *to* Jerusalem where he meets the apostles.
(3) The famine relief visit (Acts 11:30) – Paul (with Barnabas) journeys from Antioch *to* Jerusalem with famine relief.

Then, as the Gentile mission develops and the faith radiates outwards further and further *from* Jerusalem, Acts is structured by Paul's *three* great 'missionary journeys'. Each one begins in Antioch but, significantly, at the end of each journey comes a visit to Jerusalem.

---

[55] Kurz, *Reading Luke-Acts*, 28.

(1) First missionary journey (Acts 13–14) – after which Paul goes to Jerusalem for the council of Acts 15.

(2) Second missionary journey (Acts 15:36–18:22) – at the end of which Paul visits Jerusalem before returning to Antioch.

(3) Third missionary journey (Acts 18:23–21:17) – that concludes in Jerusalem.

The third missionary journey to Jerusalem, as has often been observed, closely parallels Jesus' last journey to Jerusalem in Luke's Gospel.[56] Like Jesus, Paul resolves to go to Jerusalem (Lk. 9:51; Acts 19:21); this despite the fact that his death is foretold (Lk. 13:33; 17:25; 18:31–33; Acts 20:22–23; 21:4, 11; cf. 21:13). Initially he has a good reception (Lk. 19:37; Acts 21:17–20); he enters the temple (Lk. 19:45; Acts 21:26); but then, like Jesus, he is arrested and undergoes four trials (Jesus: before the Sanhedrin, Pilate, Herod, and Pilate; Paul: before the Sanhedrin, Felix, Festus, and Agrippa).

As we move from Luke's Gospel to Acts, therefore, the journey motif represents a significant element of continuity in salvation history. The central travel narrative not only looks back to God's dealings with his people in the Old Testament, especially in the exodus journey; it also points forward to the ongoing journey of God's people in the post-resurrection/ascension period.

In opposition to Conzelmann's view, it has been argued that Luke does not divide God's dealings with his people into three distinct epochs; he thinks rather of 'one unfolding divine plan'.[57] This emphasizes the *continuity* of salvation history. But it is equally important to recognize that the Christ event introduces a significant *discontinuity*. The central travel narrative, as we have seen, recalls the exodus journey towards the land of promise; indeed, if Deuteronomy is at least partly in mind then it could be argued that the goal of that journey was 'the place which the LORD your God will choose' (Dt. 12:5, etc.) – that is, in a canonical context, Jerusalem and specifically the Jerusalem temple. Certainly the returning exiles headed for Jerusalem (Ez. 1:1–4), and the Psalms of Ascent (Pss. 120–134) were sung by pilgrims to Zion. Eschatological passages look for a future ingathering of Israel (Is. 49:8–21) and a future ingathering of the Gentiles (Is. 2:2–4), both of which involve a movement to Jerusalem/Zion. Jerusalem in the Old Testament is a goal, a place of security and stability, the home of a monarchy and a priesthood, a place of 'rest'. In Luke, on the other hand, Jerusalem is the goal of Jesus' journey not only because it is where he is destined to meet his fate, but also because it is *from* Jerusalem that the mission of the church is to be launched. Here, then, is a significant discontinuity and break with the exodus typology. In the Old Testament,

---

[56] Cf. Moessner, *Lord of the Banquet*, 297–99; Lane, *Luke and the Gentile Mission*, 70–71.

[57] Giles, 'The Church in the Gospel of Luke', 122.

the teaching (Torah) that Moses delivers to the people prepares them for life in the promised land. The teaching Jesus delivers during the new exodus prepares the new Israel to leave the land! In Lukan theology Jerusalem is not a place of rest but the launching pad for a difficult and daring new journey, or set of journeys, outward into the wider world. If Jerusalem dominates the structure of Luke's Gospel, Acts becomes 'a tale of two cities'.[58] The book ends, not in Jerusalem, but with one last great journey of Paul, and with the gospel being freely proclaimed in the city of Rome, the capital of the empire and the centre of the known world. As D. Marguerat has argued, Luke locates Christian identity between Jerusalem and Rome. The two cities are not simply geographical locations but religious and cultural symbols that witness to Luke's desire to portray Christianity both as the fulfilment of salvation history and as a response to the religious quests of the Greco-Roman world.[59]

The spread of the gospel is anticipated in Luke (cf. Lk. 2:32; 3:6). Unlike the other three gospels, Luke has no Galilean resurrection appearances. The disciples are told to stay in Jerusalem (Lk. 24:49) because the divine plan is that repentance and forgiveness of sins are to be proclaimed in Christ's name to all nations 'beginning from Jerusalem' (Lk. 24:47). In fact, Luke's Gospel anticipates the threefold expansion of the early Christian mission as narrated in Acts. The mission of the twelve in Luke 9:1–6 corresponds to the early chapters of Acts, where outreach is to Jews only; three references to Samaritans in the central travel narrative (Lk. 9:52–55; 10:30–37; 17:11–19) pave the way for the second-stage Samaritan mission in Acts 8:1–25;[60] while the sending out of the seventy (seventy-two), though in part a look back to the elders appointed by Moses, also anticipates the third-stage Gentile mission of Acts (seventy or seventy-two is the number of the Gentile nations in Gn. 10).[61]

Space does not allow us to trace the journey motif elsewhere in the New Testament, though a study of the Epistle to the Hebrews would reveal significant parallels to the pattern found in Luke. Hebrews emphasizes both continuity with the wandering people of God in Old Testament times (epitomized by Abraham who 'set out, not knowing where he was going', Heb. 11:8), as well as the decisive turn in salvation history brought about by the Christ event, and

---

[58] Drury, *Tradition and Design*, 426.

[59] Marguerat, 'Luc-Actes Entre Jérusalem et Rome', 70, 80. Marguerat contends that, for Luke, Rome does not replace Jerusalem; Christianity has a double identity, and its continuity with Israel is maintained even as it develops as a universal religion.

[60] See Lane, *Luke and the Gentile Mission*, 47–48. Luke does not report a ministry of Jesus in Samaria (cf. Jn. 4), unless the 'other village' of Lk. 9:56 was Samaritan, hence Navone concludes that the travel section 'prepares for but does not inaugurate the ministry to the Samaritans' ('The Journey There', 617).

[61] See Lane, *Luke and the Gentile Mission*, 85–95; Bernadicou, 'The Spirituality of Luke's Travel Narrative', 459–60; Craddock, *Luke*, 144.

summons readers to renewed commitment and costly discipleship as they continue their faith journey (Heb. 12:1–2).

Hermeneutical Implications of the Journey Motif

When Luke is read in the wider canonical context it becomes clear that, while
the central travel narrative recalls the great Old Testament journey of the
exodus, it also anticipates a surprising new turn of events: the new Israel does
not settle down to life in the land, but is sent forth, after Pentecost, on a new
series of journeys *from* Jerusalem and *from* the land. According to Acts 13:31, it
is 'those who came up with him [Jesus] from Galilee to Jerusalem' – that is, precisely those who accompanied Jesus on his journey to Jerusalem, who are to be
Christ's witnesses to the people of the wider Greco-Roman world.[62]

In one of the early *Reisenotizen* [63] Luke refers to Jesus and his disciples 'journeying along the way' (πορευομένων αὐτῶν ἐν τῇ ὁδῷ). The use of 'way'
(ὁδός) recalls the role of John, who came to prepare the way of the Lord
(κύριος = Jesus) in fulfilment of Isaiah 40:3 (Lk. 3:4). Now Jesus leads his disciples along the way (ὁδός) to Jerusalem in a new exodus that prepares them for
the role they will play in Acts where the early believers are 'those belonging to
the Way' (Acts 9:2; cf. 19:9; 19:23; 22:4; 24:14; 24:22).[64]

Again and again, the themes of the central travel narrative reappear in Acts.
The sending out of the seventy (seventy-two) in pairs (Lk. 10:1) is mirrored by
the missionary activities of Peter/John, Barnabas/Saul, Barnabas/Mark, Paul/
Silas in Acts. The warning about 'savage wolves' in Acts 20:29 recalls Jesus
sending out disciples 'into the midst of wolves' (Lk. 10:3). Jesus' teaching on
the cost of discipleship (Lk. 14:25–35; 18:28–30) and the need for fearless confession before 'the synagogues, the rulers and the authorities' (Lk. 12:8–12) is
illustrated in Acts by the fate of Stephen and the various imprisonments and
trials of Peter and Paul. John Mark's quitting during Paul's first missionary
journey (Acts 13:13) provides a negative example of Jesus' demand for no turning back (Lk. 9:57–62). Jesus' teaching on possessions (Lk. 12:13–21; 12:33–
34; 14:33; 16:14–15, 19–31; 18:18–30; 19:1–10) is illustrated positively by the

---

[62] Cf. Robinson, 'The Theological Context', 30.
[63] Lk. 9:57. ὁδός also occurs at 10:4, and near the end of the journey at 18:35 and 19:36.
It is noteworthy that Luke calls the beginning of Jesus' ministry an εἴσοδος (Acts
13:24), and the end of it an ἔξοδος (Lk. 9:31); cf. Giles, 'The Church in the Gospel of
Luke', 140. See also Green, *The Theology of the Gospel of Luke*, 102; and W.C. Robinson, who interprets Lukan theology in terms of 'the *hodos* conception of
Heilsgeschichte' ('The Theological Context', 23).
[64] On the designation of the early Christian movement as 'the Way' see Pao, *Acts and
the Isaianic New Exodus*, 59–68.

sharing of the earliest community (Acts 2:44–45; 4:32) and by the action of Barnabas (Acts 4:36–37), and negatively by the story of Ananias and Sapphira (Acts 5:1–11).

In the central travel narrative Jesus highlights what are to be the main themes of Christian preaching in Acts, such as the proclamation of the kingdom of God (Lk. 9:60; 10:9; 16:16; Acts 8:12; 14:22; 19:8; 20:25; 28:23, 31); the need for repentance (Lk. 13:1–5; 15:7, 10; 16:30; cf. 24:47; Acts 2:38; 3:19; 5:31; 11:18; 17:30; 20:21; 26:20); and faith (Lk. 12:28; 17:5–6; 18:8; Acts 6:5; 11:24; 14:27; 15:7, 9; 16:31, etc.). When the message is not received, Jesus' command to shake the dust off one's feet (Lk. 10:11) is followed to the letter by Paul and Barnabas (Acts 13:51). Jesus' ministry of healing (Lk. 13:10–17; 14:1–6; 17:11–19; 18:35–43) and exorcism (Lk. 11:14–23) sets the pattern for the early church's healings (Acts 3:1–10; 4:30; 5:15–16; 9:32–35; 14:8–10; 19:11–12; 28:8–9) and exorcisms (Acts 5:16; 8:7; 16:16–18; 19:12), including healing in the name of Jesus (Lk. 10:17; Acts 3:6; 4:10). The community is to be sustained by prayer (Lk. 11:1–13; 18:1–8; Acts 1:24; 6:6; 8:15; 9:11, etc.) and guided and empowered by the Holy Spirit (Lk. 11:13; 12:12; cf. 24:49; Acts 1:5, 8; 2:4, 33, 38; 4:8, etc.). The joy experienced by Jesus and his followers (Lk. 10:17–20; 19:6, 37) is a characteristic of the early Christian community (Acts 5:41; 8:8, 39; 11:23, etc.).[65]

Acts, we might say, is *the first interpretation of the Gospel of Luke*. As such, it points to the function of the central travel narrative in later interpretation, down to the present day, challenging readers, as individuals but also as members of the ongoing community of faith, to embark on their own journey of discipleship. As Craddock puts it, 'perhaps the real journey Luke has in mind is that of the reader who is being drawn by Luke's presentation of Jesus' journey to Jerusalem into a pilgrimage with Jesus in an unfolding and deepening way, not only to the passion but into the kingdom of God'.[66] By means of the journey motif Luke invites his readers 'to see themselves as a community on mission, always on the move, always on a journey, always in the presence of the Lord'.[67]

This hermeneutical function of the travel narrative presents a strong challenge to the Bultmannian tradition of denigrating Luke and severing Lukan theology from the rest of the New Testament and especially from Paul. In the central travel narrative Jesus challenges readers to make a radical decision and a

---

[65] See the discussion of 'The Joy of Jesus', in Bernadicou, 'The Spirituality of Luke's Travel Narrative', 460–63.

[66] Craddock, *Luke*, 142.

[67] Giles, 'The Church in the Gospel of Luke', 141. Cf. Green's emphasis on the way in which Luke invites a *response* from his readers: the gospel 'encourages its audience to recognize, and having recognized, to embrace and to serve the salvific aim of God' (*The Theology of the Gospel of Luke*, 24, cf. 35–37).

radical commitment to embark on a difficult and dangerous journey – hardly something synonymous with 'early catholicism' (in the Bultmannian sense) and the church settling down as an institution in the world! Readers are challenged to embark on a journey that is basically ongoing and open-ended. Unlike the journeys of the Old Testament, Jesus' journey only ends in Jerusalem because another journey is to start there. Paul's journeys in Acts end in Rome, but surely we are meant to see that Rome is not the end of the church's journey.[68] All roads led not only *to* Rome but also *from* Rome, from the Golden Milestone in the forum,[69] to 'the ends of the earth' and thus 'to all nations'.

Although there may be historical problems in correlating the travel data of Acts and the Pauline epistles, these epistles do correspond to Acts in giving us glimpses of the extensive journeys of Paul. How far Paul expected the imminent end of all things is very much a matter for debate. Certainly he invested a huge amount of time and effort in founding and nurturing Christian communities. Even towards the end of his active career we find him making long-term plans for further journeys, hardly something one would do if the world was to come to an end tomorrow. Most of the references to journeys in Paul's epistles are brief and occasional in nature. The one place where he presents a somewhat broader view of his travels is in Romans 15:18–29, a passage that presents a surprisingly similar pattern to that found in Luke. Paul's mission is designed 'to win obedience from the Gentiles' (Rom. 15:18, cf. Lk. 24:47); it began 'from Jerusalem' (ἀπὸ Ἰερουσαλήμ, Rom. 15:19; cf. Lk. 24:47); and although the immediate goal is to visit Rome (though only after a visit to Jerusalem!), that destination will in turn become a launching pad for even further travels as far away as Spain (Rom. 15:24, 28). Interestingly, although πορεύομαι is not a typically Pauline word, he does use it twice in this passage (Rom. 15:24, 25) with reference to his intended journeys to Jerusalem and Spain! Thus Paul in his own way sees the present as 'the time of the church'. Conversely, though Luke may lay more emphasis on the mission and expansion of Christianity, he is far from surrendering the expectation of the parousia and the end of history (see Lk. 9:26; 11:31, 32; 12:40; 18:8; 21:27; Acts 1:11; 17:31; 24:15).[70] Both Paul and Luke see themselves as living in the interval between the Christ event and the parousia; the difference between them is one of degree, not of kind. And both see the Gentile mission as a major characteristic of the interval.[71]

---

[68] Cf. Kurz's discussion of 'incompletion' as a characteristic of the ending of Acts that 'propels the narrative toward the future and the time of the intended readers' (*Reading Luke-Acts*, 31, cf. 35).

[69] Cf. Filson, 'The Journey Motif', 76.

[70] Cf. Hultgren, 'Interpreting the Gospel of Luke', 364–65; Knight, *Luke's Gospel*, 162–66. Wilson ('Lukan Eschatology') distinguishes two strands in Lukan eschatology – one emphasizing the delay of the end, the other an imminent expectation.

[71] Cf. Cullmann, *Salvation in History*, 250–54.

Granted, there are important differences between Pauline and Lukan theology, yet clearly the contrasts have been overdrawn and, in a broad canonical context, the two theologies can be seen not as contradictory but as complementary. As Cullmann in particular has argued,[72] a salvation history perspective is not lacking from Paul and John, and it is certainly not incompatible with their theologies.

As noted above, the two main themes of the central travel narrative are Christology and discipleship. The two, of course, are closely connected: to recognize Jesus and accept the salvation he offers is at the same time to answer his call to discipleship with all that this entails. Readers of Luke's Gospel are summoned to decision by the claims of Jesus. The magnitude of this decision is underscored by the repeated emphasis on the cost of discipleship. Noting how Luke edits his material to make following Jesus even more difficult and demanding, Giles argues that for Luke 'the life of discipleship, a challenge to all, involves not one act of heroic self-sacrifice but continually "being crucified with Christ."'[73] Readers are called to repentance and faith, to abandonment of trust in this world and the things of this world, and in company with the continuing community of God's people to a journey of discipleship and service to others, despite the difficulties and trials that shall surely be encountered. A salvation history perspective that views the church as the people of God journeying forward in faith is by no means incompatible with a call to decision, commitment, and a new self-understanding.[74] In fact, such a perspective is not, in principle, so different from Paul, who summoned people not just to an individual decision of faith that leads to justification and sanctification, but also to membership in the church (ἐκκλησία), the body of Christ (σῶμα Χριστοῦ), and to a life of mission and service. Thus, as Kurz contends, a canonical approach 'while recognizing the distinctiveness of the Lukan vis-à-vis the Pauline or Markan perspectives ... views the distinct contributions as complementary, not as contradictory'.[75]

Luke and the Journey of Faith

The journey motif functions as an important hermeneutical key to Luke's Gospel. When the gospel is read in its total canonical context and from the perspective of a biblical theology, readers are reminded of the continuity of

---

[72] Cullmann, *Salvation in History*, esp. 248–68 on Paul, and 268–91 on John.

[73] Giles, 'The Church in the Gospel of Luke', 135. The reference is in particular to Lk. 9:23 (cf. Mk. 8:34). Cf. also Grundmann, 'Fragen der Komposition', 256; Martin, 'Salvation and Discipleship', 378–80.

[74] Cf. Cullmann, *Salvation in History*, 20–21.

[75] Kurz, *Reading Luke-Acts*, 163.

salvation history, going back to the great journeys of faith in the Old Testament, especially the exodus. But they are also reminded of the radical new turn brought about by the Christ event which reverses the goal of the journey: God's people are called to new challenges and new risks, with each supposed goal becoming a new starting point.

Acts constitutes the earliest interpretation and application of the Gospel of Luke, and especially of the central travel narrative. However, just as Acts shows how the horizon of Jesus' journey through central Palestine was fused with that of the mission of the church in the wider Greco-Roman world of the eastern Mediterranean in the first few decades of Christianity, so contemporary readers must seek to fuse the horizon of Jesus' journey with that of their own situation in the modern world. Over the centuries, the challenge has often been to literal journeys that have involved taking the Christian mission to the ends of the earth. More recently, in line with the supposed goal becoming a new starting point, mission is not simply *to* the developing world but to and from every continent. In Christian history, pilgrimage has provided another form of journey that is both literal and spiritual. Yet the journeys of Luke's Gospel present a challenge to believers in every possible situation, regardless of whether or not they are called to embark on literal journeys. As Resseguie puts it, the journeys in Luke outline 'the itinerary of spiritual formation'; they remind us that *'journeying with a resolute purpose is a fundamental characteristic of the spiritual life'*.[76] For every Christian, even those who remain in the one spot all their lives, the life of faith constitutes a 'Pilgrim's Progress'.

Each reader of Luke, therefore, each Christian congregation, each preacher of the gospel must relate the claims of Jesus and his call to discipleship to their own situation. P.J. Bernadicou, in his study of 'The Spirituality of Luke's Travel Narrative', concludes that 'love of neighbour (10:25f.), listening to Jesus' word (10:38f.), and learning the faith-response of prayer (11:1f.) are three basics of the Christian life which Jesus' message entails for those who follow in his way'.[77] D.M. Sweetland concludes his study of discipleship in Luke-Acts with a chapter on 'The Importance of Luke-Acts for Us Today' in which he explores how Luke's presentation of Jesus and the early church can guide those who ask the question, 'What does Christian discipleship entail?' In the post-Vatican II situation he hears Luke speaking of the missionary responsibility of the entire community, of teaching authority belonging to the whole church as the people of God, of a service ethic radically opposed to the standards of this world, of the dignity of women and the importance of marriage, and of the need to be open to the possibility of change.[78]

---

[76] Resseguie, *Spiritual Landscape*, 36.
[77] Bernadicou, 'The Spirituality of Luke's Travel Narrative', 466.
[78] Sweetland, *Our Journey with Jesus*, 198–209.

Part of the attraction of Luke's narrative lies in the universal popularity and appeal of the journey motif. Educated, Greek-speaking readers of the gospel would have been familiar with Homer, and hence with one of the great examples of an epic journey. The journey motif retains its fascination for modern audiences as witness, for example, the huge popularity of *The Lord of the Rings*.

In recent decades it has become popular to speak of one's 'faith journey'. Interpreters, however, must seek always to be open to the challenge of Christ as presented in the central travel narrative. The concept of a 'faith journey' is capable of being interpreted in very individualistic and introspective terms. The journey to which Jesus calls his hearers/readers, as both Acts and the Pauline epistles so amply illustrate, involves decision and risk, but also participation in a community of faith engaged in outreach and service. It calls for total commitment, for 'no one who puts a hand to the plough and looks back is fit for the kingdom of God' (Lk. 9:62). Those who respond to Jesus' call should be under no illusions as to what this may entail; as Gill points out, Jesus' journey to Jerusalem 'is indeed a type of the Christian life, but more than that, as a journey toward suffering it gives a rationale for the difficult things in the living of the Christian life, the things that are the biggest stumbling blocks and causes of misunderstanding for the community here and now'.[79]

From the perspective of a canonical biblical theology, Lukan theology is to be recognized as a major component of the New Testament – not to be subordinated to other witnesses such as Paul, but to be interpreted alongside them. For Luke, as for Paul, Christian discipleship involves embarking on a journey guided by the Holy Spirit, sustained by prayer, living by faith, and with singleness of purpose witnessing to the gospel in ever new situations. Far from settling down and becoming comfortable in this world, Christian readers of Luke are called to be a people on the move, a people in this world but not of it, a people who do not say 'Hallelujah! I'm saved!' but a people who, because they know they have been saved, are involved in universal mission, compassionate service, and the struggle for justice and peace in the world today.

---

[79] Gill, 'Observations', 214. Conversely, as Resseguie points out, the scribes and Pharisees encountered on the journey serve as a negative foil, representing 'values and activities that hinder travel to the new promised land' (*Spiritual Landscape*, 41).

Bibliography

Aletti, J.-N., *L'art de raconter Jésus Christ: L'écriture narrative de l'évangile de Luc* (Paris: Éditions du Seuil, 1989)

Anderson, B.W., 'Exodus Typology in Second Isaiah', in *Israel's Prophetic Heritage* (ed. B.W. Anderson and W. Harrelson; New York: Harper, 1962), 177–95

Bernadicou, P.J., 'The Spirituality of Luke's Travel Narrative', *Review for Religious* 36 (1977), 455–66

Bultmann, R., *Theology of the New Testament, II* (London: SCM Press, 1955)

Conzelmann, H., *Die Mitte der Zeit* (Tübingen: Mohr Siebeck, 2nd edn, 1957); ET: The Theology of St. Luke (London: Faber & Faber, 1960)

Craddock, F.B., *Luke* (Louisville: Westminster/John Knox Press, 1990)

Cullmann, O., 'The Plurality of the Gospels as a Theological Problem in Antiquity', in *The Early Church* (London: SCM Press, 1956), 37–54

—, *Salvation in History* (London: SCM Press, 1967)

Drury, J., *Tradition and Design in Luke's Gospel* (London: Darton, Longman & Todd, 1976)

Evans, C.F., 'The Central Section of St. Luke's Gospel', in *Studies in the Gospels: Essays in Memory of R.H. Lightfoot* (ed. D.E. Nineham; Oxford: Basil Blackwell, 1955), 37–53

Farmer, W.R., and D.M. Farkasfalvy, *The Formation of the New Testament Canon: An Ecumenical Approach* (New York: Paulist Press, 1983)

Filson, F.V., 'The Journey Motif in Luke-Acts', in *Apostolic History and the Gospel: Biblical and Historical Essays Presented to F.F. Bruce on His 60th Birthday* (ed. W.W. Gasque and R.P. Martin; Exeter: Paternoster, 1970), 68–77

Gamble, H.Y., 'Canon: New Testament', in *ABD I* (Garden City: Doubleday, 1992), 852–61

Giles, K.N., 'The Church in the Gospel of Luke', *SJT* 34 (1981), 121–46

Gill, D., 'Observations on the Lukan Travel Narrative and Some Related Passages', *HTR* 63 (1970), 199–221

Girard, L.C., *L'Évangile des voyages de Jésus, ou la section 9:51 – 18:14 de Saint Luc* (Paris: Gabalda, 1951)

Green, J.B., *The Theology of the Gospel of Luke* (Cambridge: Cambridge University Press, 1995)

—, *The Gospel of Luke* (Grand Rapids: Eerdmans, 1997)

Grundmann, W., 'Fragen der Komposition des lukanischen "Reiseberichts,"' *ZNW* 50 (1959), 252–70

Hultgren, A.J., 'Interpreting the Gospel of Luke', *Int* 30 (1976), 353–65

Käsemann, E., 'Is the New Testament Canon a Basis for the Unity of the Church?', in *Essays on New Testament Themes* (London: SCM Press, 1960), 95–107

Kingsbury, J.D., 'The Plot of Luke's Story of Jesus', *Int* 48 (1994), 369–78

Knight, J., *Luke's Gospel* (London: Routledge, 1998)

Kurz, W.S., *Reading Luke-Acts: Dynamics of Biblical Narrative* (Louisville: Westminster/John Knox Press, 1993)

Lane, T.J., *Luke and the Gentile Mission: Gospel Anticipates Acts* (Frankfurt: Peter Lang, 1996)

Marguerat, D., 'Luc-Actes Entre Jérusalem et Rome: Un Procédé Lucanien de Double Signification', *NTS* 45 (1999), 70–87

Marshall, I.H., *Luke: Historian and Theologian* (Exeter: Paternoster, 1970)

Martin, R.P., 'Salvation and Discipleship in Luke's Gospel', *Int* 30 (1976), 366–80

McCown, C.C., 'The Geography of Luke's Central Section', *JBL* 57 (1938), 51–66

Moessner, D.P., 'Luke 9:1–50: Luke's Preview of the Journey of the Prophet Like Moses of Deuteronomy', *JBL* 102 (1983), 575–605

—, *Lord of the Banquet: The Literary and Theological Significance of the Lukan Travel Narrative* (Harrisburg: Trinity Press International, 1989)

Morgan, R., 'The Hermeneutical Significance of Four Gospels', *Int* 33 (1979), 376–88

Navone, J.J., 'The Journey Theme in Luke-Acts', *TBT* (1972), 616–19

O'Toole, R.F., 'The Parallels between Jesus and Moses', *BTB* 20 (1990), 22–29

Pao, D.W., *Acts and the Isaianic New Exodus* (Grand Rapids: Baker Books, 2000)

Powell, M.A., *What Are They Saying about Luke?* (New York: Paulist Press, 1989)

—, 'Toward a Narrative-Critical Understanding of Luke', *Int* 48 (1994), 341–46

Resseguie, J.L., 'Interpretation of Luke's Central Section (Luke 9:51 – 19:44) since 1856', *StudBibTh* 5 (1975), 3–36

—, *Spiritual Landscape: Images of the Spiritual Life in the Gospel of Luke* (Peabody, MA: Hendrickson, 2004)

Robinson, W.C., 'The Theological Context for Interpreting Luke's Travel Narrative', *JBL* 79 (1960), 20–31

Sweetland, D.M., *Our Journey with Jesus: Discipleship according to Luke-Acts* (Collegeville, MN: Liturgical Press, 1990)

Trobisch, D., *The First Edition of the New Testament* (Oxford: Oxford University Press, 2000)

Trompf, G.W., 'La Section Médiane de l'Évangile de Luc: L'Organisation des Documents', *RHPR* 53 (1973), 141–54

Turner, M., *Power from on High: The Spirit in Israel's Restoration and Witness in Luke-Acts* (Sheffield: Sheffield Academic Press, 1996)

Wilson, S., 'Lukan Eschatology', *NTS* 16 (1970), 330–47

13

Prayer in/and the Drama of Redemption in Luke

Prayer and Exegetical Performance

Craig G. Bartholomew and Robby Holt

A parable for reflection

There were two exegetes who prayed as they entered the library to work on understanding a biblical text. One was a biblical scholar and the other a common lay preacher. The biblical scholar, on route to deep seclusion in the collection of recent monographs, prayed like this:

'Lord, I thank you that I am not like other exegetes – the youth ministers, authors of popular devotional literature, mass production book publishers or even this lay preacher. I study the Scriptures for hours every day – in their original ... and several other languages, not to mention my work in ancient history and historiography, literary theory, social-scientific research, the most important commentaries, the most recent monographs and dissertations, and the most scholarly periodicals!'

But the lay preacher, trying to remember how to use the complicated cataloging system to find an *understandable* commentary on a passage of Scripture, prayed thus,

'God, please help me, a mere preacher, find something to help me understand your word.'

I tell you, this person – who desperately needed it – received help from the Lord. But could it have come from the eminent biblical scholar?

Introduction: Prayer and Biblical Hermeneutics

As is well known, prayer is a major theme in Luke as it is not in the other gospels. In Luke's Gospel, prayer is closely associated with the self-disclosure of Jesus. Luke's account of the transfiguration is a good example of this (9:28–36). It is *as* Jesus is praying that his true status is disclosed to Peter, James and John. Prayer here, and in many other places in Luke's Gospel, sets the context for and facilitates the disclosure of Jesus to his disciples. Thus it was that our Scripture and Hermeneutics consultation on Luke's Gospel invited reflection not only on the theme of prayer *in* Luke, but also on the theme of prayer *and* Luke. By the latter we refer to the question of whether or not the Gospel of Luke illumines the important, but much neglected, question of the relationship between prayer and biblical hermeneutics. If Luke teaches that prayer facilitates the disclosure of Jesus, and if the ultimate concern of any Christian reading of the Bible is to find hid there that priceless treasure which is Christ, then can Luke help us reengage the much neglected topic of prayer and interpretation?

This is not an easy topic to raise in a serious way in academic circles. The relationship between prayer and biblical interpretation is neglected almost across the board. A perusal of books on biblical hermeneutics indicates that prayer is hardly ever listed in indices,[1] and searches of journal databases reveal very few articles that address this topic. A major characteristic of modernity has been the privatization of religion, whereby *inter alia* the scientific nature of academic work is protected by religion being confined to the private dimensions of our lives. In biblical studies the result has often been an iron wall between biblical interpretation and theology. Christian faith resists such privatization and compartmentalization, and fortunately we are witnessing a growing desire to bridge this wall between exegesis and theology.[2] Without in any way detracting from the fundamental importance of academic exegesis, the opening up of biblical studies to theology creates the space for reengagement with such important questions as the relationship between prayer and exegesis. The Seminar has been glad to exploit such space!

In this chapter, we will therefore:

- review the distinctive aspects of prayer as a theme *in* Luke;
- examine this prayer material in the context of the drama of redemption as set out in Luke and then Acts;
- explore what this tells us about prayer *and* Luke;
- conclude with some comments about the relationship between prayer and biblical hermeneutics.

---

[1] But, as Anthony Thiselton reminded us at the consultation, there are ways in which prayer is strongly implied in biblical hermeneutics, such as in notions of self-involvement and interpretation.

[2] See, e.g., Watson, *Text, Church and World*.

Prayer *in* Luke[3]

All three synoptic gospels note Jesus' pattern of withdrawing to pray amidst his public ministry (Lk. 5:16; Mt. 14:23; Mk. 1:35), but time and again Luke foregrounds prayer in a way that the other gospels do not. Matthew and Mark write of Jesus' baptism by John, the opening of the heavens, the descent of the Spirit, and the voice from heaven. Luke narrates all of this *and adds* his reference to Jesus' prayer (3:21–22). Matthew and Mark tell us that Jesus called and sent out twelve disciples, giving them authority to cast out evil spirits and to heal. Luke narrates all of the above, though admittedly not within a single pericope as Matthew. But Luke's narration *includes* that on one occasion 'he went out to a mountain to pray, continued all night in prayer to God' (6:12) and then chose twelve of his disciples, designating them as 'apostles' (6:13). We are aware of the same difference between Luke and the others with regard to Peter's confession (9:18–20) – only Luke mentions that Jesus 'was praying alone' – and the transfiguration (9:28–36).

At the end of Luke 10, and immediately prior to the Lord's Prayer, there is the story of Jesus' visit to Mary and Martha's, material which is also unique to Luke. In this story Mary exemplifies the welcome of Jesus that is appropriate to discipleship. The fourfold repetition of 'Lord' foregrounds Jesus' authority, and Mary's position at Jesus' feet signifies submission and attentiveness. 'The welcome Jesus seeks is not epitomized in distracted, worrisome domestic performance, but in attending to this guest whose very presence is a disclosure of the divine plan.'[4] The word 'prayer' does not occur in this story, but there is a long tradition of associating Mary with (contemplative) prayer.[5] Thus Merton comments:

> Is there anything in the Gospels about the contemplative life? What is the value of the Mary-Martha story? It seems to me that the literal sense is plain, and that the superiority of contemplation over action is explicitly stated there. But as St. Thomas himself proves – and the whole life of Jesus shows – the supreme Christian life is one which shares the fruits of contemplation with others.[6]

There is a danger here of eisegesis, but if we think of prayer as that attitude according to which we 'wish to hear his word and respond to it with our whole

---

[3] The best treatments of this material include Conn, 'Theology,' Dunn, 'Prayer,' Liefeld, 'Prayer,' Marshall, 'Jesus – Example,' O'Brien, 'Prayer,' Turner, 'Prayer' and Plymale, *Prayer Texts*. Crump offers the most helpful analysis of *Wirkungsgeschichte* concerning prayer in Luke, *Intercessor*, 2–11.
[4] Green, *Gospel of Luke*, 434.
[5] On the history of interpretation see Just, *Luke*, 181–83.
[6] Merton, *Entering the Silence*, 347.

being,'[7] then it is clearly appropriate to see instruction about prayer in this story. Augustine discerns the richness of this story when he asks: 'What was Mary enjoying? What was she eating? I'm persistent on this point, because I'm enjoying it too. I will venture to say that she was eating the one she was listening to.'[8] The context confirms this impression: Mary's attentiveness to Jesus is followed by Jesus' attentiveness to the Father in prayer. Jesus' Jewish disciples had prayed since childhood. Observing something quite new and fresh in Jesus' relationship with the Father evokes their request to be instructed in prayer.

The prayer parables unique to Luke are those of the shameless, would-be-hospitable beggar-neighbor (11:5–8), the marginalized, seemingly helpless widow, persistently pursuing and receiving justice from the wicked judge, who is not at all like the God climactically revealed in Jesus (18:1–8), and the parable of the self-assured Pharisee and the appropriately humbled tax collector (18:9–14). The first of these follows Luke's account of the model prayer Jesus gave to his disciples, in this story (but not in Matthew's account) given as a response to Jesus' example of prayer. Matthew, Mark and Luke all narrate Jesus' struggle in prayer in the garden of Gethsemane. Just prior to that, Matthew, Mark, and Luke all report Jesus' prediction of Peter's betrayal, yet *only Luke* records Jesus' words of assurance to Peter, 'but I have prayed for you, that your faith may not fail. And when you have turned again, strengthen your brothers' (22:32).

Finally, as is well known, Matthew and Mark record the cry of dereliction, that is, Jesus' quotation of the first line of Psalm 22, a psalm of great hope in the midst of suffering. So also Matthew and Mark tell us that Jesus cried out at his death. But *only Luke* tells us that these last words were *prayer*, 'Father, into your hands I commit my spirit!' (23:46), a quote from another psalm (31:5 [v. 6 LXX]).[9] And *only Luke* records the earlier, remarkable intercession, 'Father, forgive them, for they know not what they do' (23:34). The one who taught his disciples to pray by word and by example, and who taught them to pray for their enemies – according to Luke alone – did just that – from the cross – and for those who crucified him.

Prayer is clearly, therefore, a major emphasis in Luke's Gospel. However, to mine Luke's theology of prayer we need not only to compare Luke with the synoptics, but also to read his discussions of prayer in the macro co-texts provided by Luke. The Gospel of Luke sets these prayers and teachings about prayer within an expansive literary co-text to which we must attend – but without ignoring the horizon of the second volume which narrates the

---

[7] Merton, *Contemplative Prayer*, 83.
[8] See Just, *Luke*, 182. For more intra-textual reflection that bears upon this and how it might relate to a general receptivity toward Jesus and his mission, see below and esp. n. 18.
[9] On this, see further below and esp. Hamm, 'Tamid.'

beginning of a new stage in God's drama, an entire *new* Act, and, significantly, an unfinished Act, in search of final resolution.[10]

Volume 1: The Gospel According to Luke

Attending to prayer within Luke's Gospel as a whole is remarkably illuminating. Indeed, the narrative of Luke's Gospel is contained within a prayer inclusio. The story begins with a priest in the temple, set apart to burn incense, and while the community *prays* outside – an angel *appears* inside – to announce the God of Israel's answer to the priest's particular prayer about his barren wife. Luke narrates this scene in such a way that hooks his story in two very important directions. The whole initial account, while looking forward (as the beginning of Luke's two-volume story of Jesus and his people), looks backward as well, brimming with allusions to very significant stories within the larger drama of the God of Israel, his covenant promises, and his plan for the nations.

The story of righteous Zechariah and Elizabeth has become the latest, critical moment in this redemptive story which is full of persons summoned to believe God's promises and play their part in God's drama. But this 'righteous' one is like so many others within the longer narrative thus far. He is somewhat of a failure. Now, Gabriel, another character from earlier parts of the larger story into which Luke fits his narrative (a herald of kingdom messages in Daniel), and more importantly 'who stands in the presence of God,' has shown up as the mouthpiece of the One who is answering Zechariah's prayers – but Zechariah is not prepared to believe. Thus Luke's Gospel begins with a priest providentially brought into the temple and then returning to God's expectant people, but he cannot speak and so cannot bless them – for unbelief has made him mute. Silence is imposed on Zechariah, as it were – a silence in which he can contemplate Gabriel's message and be prepared to name his son 'John.'

Luke's Gospel also ends with prayer – a band of overjoyed disciples returning to Jerusalem, blessing God, continually in the same temple where Zechariah fell mute. But first they *are* blessed (24:50–53). The one who identified with the sinfulness of God's covenant people when he submitted to the baptism by the son of the once muted priest, who claimed to be playing the part of Israel's Messiah, who was rejected as such by the temple authorities and the throngs gathered in the royal city, who prayed for his enemies when they crucified him, and prayed to his Father as he died at the ninth hour (the same hour Zechariah would have been in the temple to offer incense)[11] – *has risen*

---

[10] Cf. Wright, *New Testament*, 139–44; Bartholomew and Goheen, *Drama*.

[11] Hamm, 'Tamid,' 224–26; cf. Brown, *Birth*, 280–81. Kelly Kapic first drew Robby's attention to this inclusio in an excellent and stimulating paper given at the 2003 annual conference of the Evangelical Theological Society.

(24:1–8). The first volume of Luke's story ends with the risen one blessing his people[12] as he ascends into heaven, receiving worship from a new community of blessed ones who bless God (24:50–53).[13] Luke depicts Jesus as the fulfillment of Yahweh's redemptive plan which had centered upon his covenant people Israel.[14] Something has run its course. Something new has begun. A new age has dawned, and the reality of fulfillment is charged with hermeneutical significance which far surpasses categories of 'ideas' or 'religion.' A new stage in God's redemptive drama has arrived – indeed, the whole drama has reached its climax![15]

Different characters in this drama respond differently to its climaxing in Jesus. One man *at the beginning* of Luke's work, Zechariah, cannot believe Gabriel's good words. But a young girl, Mary, does believe, when the same angel visits her. Similarly, when Jesus arises *at the end* of the first volume, the word first comes to a band of women (including two Marys) from two angelic spokespersons. When the women tell these words to the eleven and all the rest, their report 'seemed like an idle tale, and they,' like Zechariah, 'did not believe.'[16]

Luke's narrative is full of people who should be prepared to understand what God is doing in and through Jesus – but they cannot, or will not.[17] But some characters *are*

---

[12] If the Tamid service is the background to Jesus' blessing, then the blessing would refer to Num. 6:24–26. See Hamm, 'Tamid.'

[13] The opening scene depicts one who has come *from heaven* (Gabriel) to the temple, rendering the providentially designated-for-service-priest (Zechariah) mute. The closing scene depicts Jesus blessing his disciples as he passes *into heaven*, with the result that they are continually in the temple blessing God. This suggests that Luke is portraying Jesus as the fulfillment of Israel and her temple by portraying him as the designated-for-service priest who can bless and who goes to serve in the reality symbolized by the earthly temple.

[14] While this is more often implicit in the first volume, the way this is explicitly declared in the preaching Luke utilizes in the second volume strongly supports our inference at this point! See n. 15, below, for specific references.

[15] Because, in Jesus, Yahweh has 'helped his servant Israel, in remembrance of his mercy' (1:54). He 'has visited and redeemed his people, raising up a horn of salvation ... in the house of his servant David, as he spoke by the mouth of his holy prophets from of old' (1:68–70; see further 1:5–2:52; 10:21–24; 24:13–49; Acts 2:14–36; 3:12–26; 13:16–41, 46–49; 15:13–19).

[16] These 'bookends' confront typical first-century reader expectations, depicting first-century men (particularly a priest and Jesus' disciples) as persons who do not respond properly to God's redemptive action and first-century women as persons who do. Given their narrative placement, this does not appear inconsequential to Luke's central purposes.

[17] Consider, just to scratch the surface: the people of Nazareth (4:16–30); the Pharisees and teachers of Torah tradition (5:17–26, 30; 6:6–11; 7:36–40; 11:37–54); and the disciples (esp. in chs. 9 and 18).

prepared and join (what they see and hear) joyfully.[18] How are the prayers of Anna (in light of her own perception; Lk. 2: 36–38), and of Jesus (in light of his disciples gaining perception: before Peter's confession, at the transfiguration, and at the table with the disciples in Emmaus) related to this aspect of Luke's story? Quite significantly, like the confession of Peter and the transfiguration, recognizing Jesus' true identity, at least for Cleopas and his companion, is tied to Jesus' prayer (24:30–31). As Crump notes,

> Luke associates the prayers of Jesus with the acquisition of spiritual insight at key locations throughout his gospel ... Luke presents Jesus primarily, though not exclusively, as an Intercessor whose prayers on behalf of the disciples serve to accomplish all that is required for successful, obedient discipleship – including their calling, illumination and perseverance ... it is in fact the prayers of Jesus which mediate ... spiritual perception.[19]

Jesus' exultation concerning what remains hidden from 'the wise and understanding' and is revealed to 'little children' (10:21–22) is a prayer of

---

[18] Interestingly, when two figures in 'dazzling apparel' (24:4) address some women, including two 'Marys' (24:10), concerning the resurrection of Jesus, 'they [the women] remembered Jesus' words' (24:8). But when they report this to the other disciples they are resistant. Likewise, Cleopas and his traveling companion relate these episodes to the resurrected Jesus, whom they do not recognize, and as they tell Jesus about the empty tomb and the report from the women, complete with references to angels (24:22–24), Jesus, not surprisingly, addresses them, 'O foolish ones, and slow of heart to believe all that the prophets have spoken' (24:25). Luke seems to go out of his way to associate contemplative responses to Jesus with *Marys* that pay attention! Mary, his mother, responds with faithfulness when his birth is announced (1:34–38) and ponders words and events concerning him carefully (2:19, 51). Mary, sister of Martha, 'sat at the Lord's feet and listened to his teaching' (10:39). Finally, the band of women from Galilee, first introduced as a group of *providers* for Jesus and his disciples (8:1–3) attend to Jesus' death (23:55–56) and, when they hear of his resurrection, they 'remembered his [Jesus'] words' (24:8). The contrast between these women and Cleopas, and also between these women and the other disciples, lies upon the surface of the text. Like Anna, here are women, second-class citizens by first-century standards, tuned into God's plan as it unfolds in the life of his Son. Luke associates these characters with attentiveness and, in Anna's case, this attentiveness is characterized by prayerfulness.

[19] In Lk. 24, Jesus explains the Scriptures to the two traveling disciples and the eleven (with others) by demonstrating that they all find their fulfillment in him. The specific language attributed to Jesus and the others narrated herein is important. When Jesus was at table with Cleopas, his companion, and presumably others, 'he took the bread and blessed it (i.e., prayed) ... and their eyes *were opened and they recognized him.*' Cf. Crump, *Intercessor*, 106–108.

thanksgiving, which similarly relates the disclosure of Jesus to the revealing work of the Father through the Son.[20]

What we must not miss is that what we have before us are more than iso-lated prayer pericopae. *Luke associates prayer with the movement of God's redemp-tive drama, with gaining or disclosing insight into the reality of that drama and its central character, and with preparation for participation in that same drama.* Thus, years before Caesar Augustus sends out his decree 'concerning all the world' (2:1), Yahweh has been preparing his covenant people for the unfolding of his worldwide redemptive plan. In keeping with his covenant promises and mani-fold prophecies, he has decided to answer Zechariah's prayer. Zechariah knows he has been asking for a child for himself and for Elizabeth. But he was not prepared, apparently, to have his prayers and God's answer drawn up into the central hopes of Israel, into that long, troubled story desperately in need of resolution.[21]

Yahweh's plan is further revealed when Joseph and Mary bring Jesus to Jeru-salem to present him to the Lord. There Simeon is *ready* to greet them as he awaits the consolation of Israel since the Holy Spirit had revealed to him that he would not die until he saw Yahweh's Messiah (2:26). Thus, taking the child in his arms, Simeon prays, blessing God for the salvation he has prepared including 'revelation for Gentiles' and 'glory for Israel' (2:22–28). A prayer of prophetic praise is a proper response to Yahweh's dramatic action. Next the aged, wid-owed prophetess Anna, who 'did not depart from the temple, worshipping with fasting and prayer night and day,' appears 'at that very hour' thanking God and telling all who are waiting for Israel's redemption about the child (2:36–39).[22] Here are two figures, ready for and responsive to God's dramatic action, charac-terized in the narrative not only as people attuned to God's purposes but also as people of prayer. Thus considering 'the way in which prayer serves to attune the will of the individual to the will of God … Luke reveals various ways in which God is already guiding salvation-history, and prayer is a means of human per-ception of, and thus participation in, what God is doing.'[23]

Moreover, while Tiberius Caesar, Pontius Pilate, Herod, and the house of Caiaphas rule over God's beleaguered people, the word of the Lord comes to

---

[20] Compare the question Jesus asks the crowds about their inability to interpret the time (meaning and significance) of Jesus' presence and activity (12:56).

[21] Likewise, in the third gospel Jesus instructs his disciples to wait for the final resolu-tion of this drama *as a people of prayer* (11:2–4; 18:1–8; 21:29–36), even as, more spe-cifically, he instructs them to wait for the gift of the Spirit (24:49; Acts 1:4–5, 8), which they did prayerfully (Acts 1:14) and, therefore, obediently (Lk. 11:13).

[22] 'Waiting' in prayer is emphasized in these early stories in Luke. See Nouwen, 'The Path of Waiting,' in his *Finding My Way Home*, 87–117.

[23] So Crump, *Intercessor*, 6, responds to problems he perceives with O.G. Harris' important but unpublished Ph.D. dissertation, *Prayer in Luke-Acts: A Study in the*

the son born as the answer to Zechariah's prayers and the fulfillment of prophecy – in the wilderness (3:1–6). Then, when John baptizes Jesus with the baptism of sinners-needing-to-repent because the day of the Lord is at hand – and *as Jesus prays* – the heavens open, the Spirit descends, and Jesus begins his public ministry of kingdom announcement, illustration, and accomplishment (3:21–22). Skipping to the end again, when Jesus is crucified – and *as Jesus prays* – the temple veil is torn in two, his spirit ascends, and he expires (23:44–46).

The specific words on these two occasions are indeed significant. At his baptism, the Father speaks, 'You are my beloved *Son*; with you I am well pleased' (3:22). At his death, the Son cries out, '*Father*, into your hands I commit my spirit' (23:46). In between these episodes, Jesus teaches his little flock to call upon his Father as *their* Father – even as he teaches them by word and by example how costly it is to be his faithful child.

Moreover, in Luke's narration of the crucifixion, his inclusion of the quote from Psalm 31:5 (v. 6 LXX), 'Father, into your hands I commit my spirit' is noteworthy, as is his omission of the cry of Psalm 22:1. This is not, of course, a simple exchange. The quote Luke supplies does not replace the quote from Psalm 22, which is simply omitted. Rather, the quote Luke supplies fills in a blank reference from Matthew and Mark about Jesus crying out at his death. Interestingly, Psalms 22 and 31 are psalms of lament which, ultimately, express 'profound hope and trust in the midst of abandonment.'[24] While the quote in Luke 23:46 is from Psalm 31:5 (v. 6 LXX), verse 18 of that psalm 'echoes the language of the Aaronic blessing uttered at the end of the evening Tamid,'[25] the twice-daily temple service. How will God's eschatological temple become the multi-national 'house of prayer' (Mt. 21:13; Lk. 19:46) Yahweh seeks (Is. 56:7) rather than a den of robbers (Jer. 7:11; Mt. 21:12–16; Mk. 11:15–18; Lk. 19:46) unless 'repentance and forgiveness of sins' is announced 'to all nations' in the name of the One who was crucified and was raised with words of blessing on his lips (24:45–51)?

Theology of Luke (Vanderbilt, 1967). Resisting a 'cause and effect relationship' proposed by Harris concerning prayer and divine action which would make prayer 'one of the tools through which God is able to act historically,' Crump prefers to assert that 'prayer is one of the tools through which an individual becomes properly aligned with God's pre-determined action and so is able to participate within God's appointed framework.'

[24] Hamm, 'Tamid,' 226. Moreover, Dennis Hamm, like many others (see Brown, *Birth*, 280–81 and the discussion there) believes that Lk. 24:50–53 is an allusion to Sir. 50:20–21 and that this allusion fits with how Luke narrates his story of Jesus, including central passages in Luke (1:5–25; 18:9–14; 24:50–53) and Acts (3:1; 10:3, 30) and further fills out our understanding of his blessing the disciples as he ascends.

[25] Hamm, 'Tamid,' 226.

Luke's narrative thus focuses upon God and his purposes reaching their climax in the life, death, resurrection, and ascension of Jesus. The good news in Luke's Gospel is that, in Jesus of Nazareth, God is keeping his word. He will no longer withhold his righteousness and justice but will reign through the crucified but now risen Jesus and through those aligned with him as witnesses to his resurrection and his kingdom (22:24–30; 24:44–49). Part of Luke's narrative aim is to summon those who hear to align themselves (or further or more faithfully align themselves) with the living Jesus (and so with his people) as the one (family) bringing God's purposes to fulfillment.[26] Throughout the narrative, prayer is consistently linked with how characters within the story apprehend and align themselves with the manner in which God's long story is reaching its climax, Jesus himself, whose words and deeds challenge shallow perceptions of who God is. Thus those who hear this story as narrated by Luke face a call concerning their present lives and God's purposes. Luke narrates characters who judge Jesus critically, typically due to prior commitments and privileges they are unwilling to relinquish, as those who fail to enter into what God is doing redemptively in the world. Having obscured the key to knowledge for others, they are therefore doomed themselves (11:37–52). But those who pray with Jesus learn to call upon the God of Israel as 'Father' and so learn to relate to him as kind, caring and benevolent toward those willing to repent of selfish, fearful, violent, slavish, destructive and dehumanizing orientations, in order further to align themselves with him and his purposes – which are clarified by Jesus' interpretation of his Father and his own messianic vocation (4:16–44; 5:27–32; 7:18–35; 8:1, 4–15; 9:1–6, 18–22, 37–44; 10:21–24; 11:2–4; cf. 6:20–38; 12:22–34; 14:15–24; 15:1–32; 18:1–8, 15–17, 18–30, 31–34; 19:1–10; 20:9–18, 41–44; 22:7–22, 28–30, 35–38; 23:39–43; 24:25–27, 30–32, 36–49).

The prayer inclusio[27] mentioned at the beginning of this section, as well as the material highlighted and related to its narrative placement thus far, is significant for our argument. For, rather than pulling Luke apart in service of our topical interest, namely prayer, our goal has been to read the entire gospel using one of Luke's discernable interests as a window into his larger narrative aims. The next section broadens the scope of this reading to include a brief engagement with the narrative flow of Luke's second volume.

---

[26] Cf. Green, *Narrative*, 11–56. Note how the criterion for the replacement of Judas as a witness to the resurrected Jesus required one who had witnessed the entire ministry of Jesus, from the baptism of John until his ascension (Acts 1:21–22).

[27] This inclusio, including most specifically 1:8–13 and 24:50–53, should be considered, further, in light of Ps. 141:2; Ex. 30:1–10; 40:26–27; Rev. 5:8 and 8:3.

Volume 2: The Acts of the Apostles

The first volume of Luke's story ends with the risen Messiah blessing his people as he ascends into heaven, receiving worship from a new community of blessed ones who bless God. But in God's economy, being blessed by God and, indeed, blessing him involves being a blessing to others.[28] In his second volume Luke narrates the initial extension of this blessing to all nations.

Luke's story begins in Jerusalem but, in the second volume, ends in Rome. The narrative begins 'in the days of Herod, *King of Judea*' (Lk. 1:5), where Yahweh moves to prepare the way for his Anointed. One is coming who 'will be great and will be called son of the Most High.' And the Lord God will give to him *the throne of* his father *David*, and *he will reign* over the house of Jacob forever, and of *his kingdom* there will be no end (from Lk. 1:5–33). The story comes to its end with Paul imprisoned in Roman custody 'proclaiming *the kingdom of God* and teaching about the Lord Jesus Christ (Messiah) with all boldness and without hindrance' (Acts 28:31). The story is thus one of movement and fulfillment; movement and mission; God and his promises to Abraham; God and Abraham's seed; God and his covenant with David; God and recalcitrant Israel; God and renewed Israel; God and *the nations he said he would bless*: for *God himself is on the move* (keeping promises, answering prayer, filling a people, working miracles, stretching out his hand, setting prisoners free, spreading his people abroad, and overseeing their participation in his redemptive mission). God is doing something new in the world – first through his Spirit-empowered servant Jesus (3:22; 4:1, 14, 18–19) and then (and now) through the Spirit-filled followers of Jesus (11:11–13; 24:48–49; Acts 1:4–8; 2:1–21). But this *new* thing is the age-old *promised* thing, the thing for which faithful Israel had for so long been waiting. The story of national Israel has reached its divinely intended climax – it is time for Yahweh's renewed temple-people to *be* a house of prayer *made up of* all nations.

As Jesus is constantly narrated in the first volume as on mission for God and tuned into God's plan *through prayer*, so in his second volume Luke portrays the disciples of Jesus as being in continuity with Jesus, as Joel Green notes, 'particularly with regard to the practice of prayer.'[29] Thus 'In Acts, prayer is (1) a means by which God's aim is disclosed and discerned, and (2) the means by which people get in sync with and participate in what God is doing.'[30] Green cites 'parallels [between the two volumes] which seem quite deliberate' such as Jesus and the disciples praying before their reception of the Spirit for ministry

---

[28]   The call of Abraham could serve as a supreme example of this point (Gen. 12:1–3).

[29]   Green, 'Persevering,' 188.

[30]   Green, 'Persevering,' 194. Cf. Crump, *Intercessor*, 6, cited above, and O'Brien, 'Prayer,' 121–27.

(Lk. 3:21; Acts 1:14; 2:1–4; 8:15–17), Jesus and his disciples praying before they select 'apostles' (Lk. 6:12; Acts 1:24), and Jesus and Stephen praying 'in the face of death for the forgiveness of one's persecutors' (Lk. 23:34; Acts 7:60). Citing much more evidence, including more than thirty references to prayer throughout Acts, as well as the presence of prayer within very significant narrative summaries, one of Green's central points is that:

> Luke establishes Jesus' followers as persons who continue to model the piety of Jesus … the devotion of these disciples speaks volumes about their fundamental orientation to the purpose of God, their alignment with the will of God, and their conviction that God will hear and respond to their prayers.[31]

The kingdom activity of prayer is a fitting way for disciples to participate in God's kingdom power because, while prayer is a dual confession of our weakness and God's power (Acts 4:24–28), genuine acts of prayer assume that this powerful God has invited our participation (4:29–31; cf. 20:46–47).[32] To pray as one summoned into kingdom service is to take up a serious and strategic role and prepares one to participate further as a disciple *of* the King *as* the King works his holy but often mysterious will.[33]

Thus, while prayer is not a technology to make God act or a hidden hermeneutical key, it is a reminder to us that God invites our participation in his redemptive plans. 'Throughout Acts, prayer provides an opportunity for the disclosure of God's purpose.'[34] Christians pray to gain a grasp of God's purposes (or to be grasped by them), to take up our part in doing God's will and to express our faith, hope, and longing to see it done in the world.

In Luke's two volumes, aligning oneself with God's purposes clarifies not only God's will for the moment, but also the meaning of the Scriptures. And to this end, prayer in these two volumes is a practice presented to us that we might embrace, discern, persevere in and be transformed by the good news of God's kingdom.[35] In Luke's second volume, particularly:

---

[31] Green, 'Persevering,' 189.

[32] For different ways of construing how our prayers-as-participation relate to the unfolding of God's purposes compare Crump with Goldingay, 'Logic,' 266.

[33] Consider the answer to the prayer of the gathered believers in Acts 4. Increased boldness came *with* increased persecution, arrests, threats, and death rather than because these things diminished.

[34] Green, 'Persevering,' 193.

[35] Likewise, devotion to other basic commitments and resisting God's agenda obscures, for those who fail to see and hear, the good news announced in God's name (Lk. 4:16–30; 7:18–35; 8:1–21; 9:51–53; 10:13–24; 11:34–35, 37–53; 12:54–56; 13:10–17; 14:1–6, 25–33; 16:14–17; 18:18–25; 20:19–44; Acts 4:1–22; 5:17–42; 6:8–15; 7:51–8:3; 12:1–5).

Prayer is put forward as one of the ways in which God's will becomes manifest, both in the sense that in prayer the divine will is disclosed and in the sense that in prayer humans align themselves with God's will.[36]

Prayer and Luke

In Luke's narrative, prayer is inseparable from the disclosure of Jesus and understanding/participating in the divine drama. But Luke narrates a particular moment within this redemptive drama. This raises interesting questions about the relationship between the story Luke is narrating and our interpretative purposes. What implications for our interpretation of Luke, of the Scriptures as a whole, and indeed of the meaning of our lives, follow from Luke's narrative focus upon prayer? If Luke is narrating a particular act in an ongoing drama – and pointing to prayer as a practice which clarifies the meaning of that drama, its central figure, and roles within that drama – what would happen if we extended Luke's teaching on prayer to Scripture as a whole?

Theologically, we would argue that Scripture announces and interprets the good news of God's redemptive drama.[37] As it does so, it functions as God's agent, spreading the effects of God's redemptive work, clarifying its past, present, and future implications, and incorporating those who hear the report and entrust themselves to its interpretation into that very drama. The word that announces and interprets God's redemptive work is the word that sets apart and transforms a people for God's redemptive purposes in the world, making them disciples. If, then, we perceive Scripture announcing and interpreting this drama with multiple acts, climaxing in Jesus' vocation as Messiah of Israel, and including those who believe as those narrated into the drama *as disciples*, what hermeneutical comportment best fits these convictions?

Since Scripture does not merely inform us, but also incorporates us as participants into God's redemptive drama, prayer becomes, we suggest, essential to the interpretation of Scripture. *For*, prayer is a God-given and therefore indispensable means to grasp and live within this drama. Since Luke narrates Jesus as Messiah as the center of this drama, and since, as Luke reminds us, prayer is basic to the disclosure of Jesus as the Messiah, prayer cannot be an addendum to exegesis or theological reflection. Luke is not a lone voice in Scripture urging us to reorient our lives around God's plan coming to fulfillment in Jesus. Luke has a keen interest in presenting prayer as an indispensable practice for any seeking this reorientation. So what if Luke's interest is valid? What if prayer is an indispensable part of having one's whole life continually

---

[36] Green, 'Persevering,' 189–90.

[37] See Bartholomew and Goheen, *Drama*, and Vanhoozer, 'Company' and 'Voice' for a defense of this approach.

reoriented around God's plan, and of receiving and acquiring the understanding, character formation and sanctified performance apart from which no meaningful 'knowledge' of God or his ways is possible?[38]

If Luke narrates the prayers of Jesus and his first followers – not so much to give us religious trivia but because he believes that similar commitments will have desirable effects upon those who hear and respond in faith to his narrative presentation of Jesus – what hermeneutical implications ensue if we do not share his convictions or, further, if we do not become shaped by them? If, as Luke seems to imply, prayer is an essential ingredient in the disclosure of God's purposes, and if the Scriptures are centrally bound up with the person of Jesus and how he fulfills God's word through his Torah, Prophets, and Writings (24:13–49), then the lacuna mentioned at the outset of this chapter is a serious deficiency in biblical hermeneutics.

How much confidence, then, should a person (or a community) have concerning one's grasp of any portion of Scripture (not to mention the whole), no matter how learned one might be, if that person (or community) is not a person (or community) devoted to prayer? Why should any person who is *not* part of a community whose 'fundamental orientation' *is* devotion to God's redemptive purposes announced and interpreted *in Scripture* have any hermeneutical confidence when it comes to interpreting the Scriptures?[39] One may be able to exegete Jesus' demand that one lose one's life in order to find it. One may even be able to work backward from textual variants of Greek narratives to surmise how Jesus may have said something like this in an Aramaic tongue. But how might one become able to lose one's life (Lk. 14:25–33)? It is one thing to assent to an ancient articulation concerning God's purposes – but it is quite another to become a faithful participant within those purposes and have one's whole life reoriented accordingly.

Perhaps one thing we can learn from the way Luke narrates the two-volume story of Jesus and his people fulfilling God's redemptive mission is that we need to recommit ourselves to a corporate comportment before Scripture –

---

[38] See Ps. 119:33–40, 97–104; Jn. 7:14–18; Eph. 4:17–24; Col. 1:9–11. Further, we do not participate as 'helpers' by virtue of our own strength of character, wisdom, powers, or intellect. Rather, we must *not only* become like children to enter (Lk. 18:15–17), and mature in God's economy; we must *also* enter beating our chests (18:9–14) and empty handed (18:17–30). Prayer is an ideal God-given way to take our humbled, child-like part, the part of expectant servants, repentant and ready to hear and then follow another. But all of this language assumes that there is a God with a redemptive plan. This is because, to take up the practice of prayer, to speak and live as one present to the God who presents himself to us as a Father, is to adopt, practice, and seek formation into and within a particular worldview.

[39] This is not an argument that only devout Christians have contributions to make. See below.

with prayerfulness literally and metaphorically at its center – where research, teaching and reading are (self-consciously Spirit-dependent) tasks on the way to faithful kingdom reception, participation, and performance.[40] This in no way implies an abandonment of the tools and benefits of historical and critical research. It merely seeks to place those endeavors in a wider context – to see scholarly methods as tools meant to open texts for communities of faith in light of the church's vocation to receive, celebrate, and display the realities to which the Scriptures bear witness. The church has a God-given task: to perform our role in this present act of God's drama.[41] Contemporary scribes must ask ourselves how we can best serve that vocation, lest we find ourselves, like the scribes of the first century, filled with knowledge but shut out of God's kingdom.[42]

With respect to exegesis and interpretation, *diligence* in historical, grammatical, linguistic, philosophical, social-scientific, and theological matters *is perpetually helpful* in any hermeneutics of mutual respect where the otherness of the other is taken seriously.[43] But to exalt ever more 'learning' above humble

---

[40] Cf. Lash, 'Performing'; Barton, 'New Testament Interpretation'; and Vanhoozer, 'Voice.'

[41] The church is to be a hermeneutic of the gospel for the world (Newbigin, *Gospel*). Our ecclesiology (including the missiological assumptions we carry and the explicit decisions we make) represents concrete interpretations of Scripture (Lash, 'Performing'; Stiver, 'Theological Method'; Goheen, 'A Critical Examination of David Bosch's Missional Reading of Luke' in the present volume; and Vanhoozer, esp. 'Company').

[42] Or, as Paul put it, 'always learning but never able to come to a knowledge of the truth' (2 Tim. 3:7).

[43] A good example of one particular kind of diligence, and its potential for hearing the other well, is the very brief but corrective article by Klyne Snodgrass, '*ANAIDEIA*' – so brief, it appears merely within the 'Critical Notes' section of *JBL*. Snodgrass shows quite conclusively and powerfully that this *hapax legomenon* in Lk. 11:8: (1) would have meant 'shamelessness' to Luke's readers; (2) would not have carried any positive connotation; (3) could not have connoted 'persistence' (a very common ET); and (4) ought to cause us to rethink what the parable teaches about prayer and God. Snodgrass argues (512–13) that the parable is contrastive rather than comparative, arguing from the weaker to the greater. Noting the prayer request for bread in the immediate cotext (11:3) and the '"how much more" argument ... explicit in 11:13,' Snodgrass believes 'the whole point of the parable ... is that God is *not* like the sleeper in that God is not reluctant but is eager to respond' (512). Thus, readers should conclude that if 'a human will respond to the request of a rude friend for bread, how much more will God provide bread in response to the requests of his people?' Snodgrass's method, including diligence in lexical research particularly, but also translation comparisons and the consultation of authorities within the professional guild, has produced something beneficial *for* all interpreters of Luke's Gospel.

prayer for understanding is to play the part of the self-sufficient Pharisee in Luke 18. Having done all the work required of us, we should rather remember that we are mere servants and, beating our chests like the tax collector, keep asking for hermeneutical wisdom.[44] Prayer is essential to the interpretation of Scripture because acceptable prayer is the opposite of self-sufficiency (Lk. 18) and, since the Scriptures are revelation, no one has access to them apart from God's gracious gift (Lk. 2:25–32, 36–38; 10:21–22; 16:19–31; 24:13–49; Acts 10; 13:44–49; 16:14).

For this reason alone, then, prayer should be associated with the interpretation of Scripture. That is, prayer is a fitting activity through which to participate in the drama rendered in Scripture. Hermeneutically speaking, prayer is neither a 'trick' nor a 'key' nor a 'technology' that, in and of itself, achieves interpretive goals – especially when those goals are reduced to obtaining merely the right information. Rather, *prayer is a necessary means of opening oneself to God and aligning oneself with his redemptive mission,* apart from which meaningful interpretation of the Bible *as Scripture* is impossible.[45]

Prayer and biblical hermeneutics

Luke's Gospel, in our opinion, thus entails a serious reexamination of the role of prayer in biblical hermeneutics. Although this is a much neglected topic, there are significant contemporary voices exhorting us in this direction. John Paul II asserts that,

---

He has provided a crucial corrective step toward understanding the text by clarifying the semantic range of a single term within its historical context without ignoring its literary cotext.

[44] Indeed, Joel Green, in his capacity as editor, pointed out the 'historically situated' nature of these methodological concerns. We agree. This does not mean that they serve no purpose. Any 'method' that helps us hear Luke's voice is helpful and welcome, lest our own historically situated concerns drown out his narrative aims entirely. But, as Green rightly pointed out in editorial correspondence, we, the authors, are more interested in 'comportment vis-à-vis the Scriptures' than we are with modernist preferences for 'method/technique'.

[45] In general, in both of Luke's volumes the religious leaders of Israel resist God's redemptive plan. In the first volume, the Pharisees and the Scribes 'knew' Jesus told parables about them, but they could not respond properly (Lk. 20:9–19). Jesus castigated the lawyers (νομικοῖς) because they had 'taken away the key to knowledge.' How? They 'did not enter' into the new thing God was doing in and through his servant Jesus – that is, the kingdom, the new stage of God's drama announced, redefined, and inaugurated by Jesus – and so, implicitly by their negative example and explicitly by their opposition to Jesus, they 'hindered those who were entering' (11:52).

to arrive at a completely valid interpretation of words inspired by the Holy Spirit, one must first be guided by the Holy Spirit and it is necessary to pray for that, to pray much, to ask in prayer for the interior light of the Spirit and docilely accept that light, to ask for the love that alone enables one to understand the language of God, who 'is love' (I Jn. 1:8, 16).[46]

The most thorough exploration of this topic we have come across is that by Clifton Black in an excellent article entitled 'Exegesis as Prayer.' Black's work connects with John Paul's point about inspiration. Reflecting on Otto Piper's work on prayer in the Bible, Black asserts that the enduring contribution of Piper was to see that

> prayer was not a religious auxiliary, a pietistic nod before getting down to the serious business of biblical exegesis … When proceeding in alignment with the same Spirit that animated scripture's creation and canonization within the church, *exegesis is an expression of prayer.*[47]

In this light Black suggests three prayerful dispositions that are indispensable for the exegete today, namely, a capacity for holiness; a transfigured affection, and a disposition for thankful praise.[48] This type of exegesis requires a community of prayer and a community of interpretation, and the two should overlap:

> The practices of these two communities, however, do not always overlap. In our time, we are sad to say, much training in biblical scholarship occurs in settings where prayer has been severed from its task and responsibility, where the nurture of a faithful church is a *non sequitur.* Visits to the religious aisles of Barnes & Noble have become for me chilling summonses before the bar of judgement: much of what I find among the biblical resources are speculative fantasies, whether by Tim LaHaye or the Jesus Seminar. To my shame there is comparatively little that invites the church's laity or even curious passersby into the mysterious world of biblical faith that questions us, little to remind a reader that exegesis, like prayer, is not a cold conjecture but a relationship with God so madly in love with us and the world that only the foolishness of the cross makes sense (1 Cor. 1:18–31). Cruciform exegesis resembles petitionary prayer in this respect: if serious, its practitioner is inextricably bound up with its fulfillment (Mt. 25:31–46).[49]

Our examination of prayer in/and Luke leads us to conclude that John Paul II and Black are right. Prayer, both as quiet contemplation and as active participation, is an indispensable condition for the disclosure of Jesus, and so too,

---

[46] John Paul II and the Pontifical Biblical Commission, *Interpretation,* 19f.
[47] Black, 'Exegesis as Prayer,' 138 (emphasis original).
[48] Black, 'Exegesis as Prayer,' 139.
[49] Black, 'Exegesis as Prayer,' 143.

therefore, for the exegete who seeks to find his or her imagination transformed by the drama announced and interpreted in and by Scripture. Prayer, in the sense of being present to the Father in dependence and thankfulness, is utterly basic to responding to the invitation to participate in the great drama of the Bible. Thus prayer will also be basic to understanding that drama and living it out today. This, we are afraid, turns common hermeneutical agendas upon their heads! The goal is not to grasp the distant, objective meaning of the text for our purposes. On the contrary, our aim is to seek transformation, in prayer, via the claims and aims of the text as they announce and interpret God's purposes.

Since Luke situates his story of Jesus and his followers within the grand narrative of God's redemptive drama, and since prayer is a way to participate in what God is doing, we must ask ourselves if we are willing to find our life within this larger story – and so be led (among other ways, prayerfully) by Luke and the power and influence of the Spirit highlighted by Luke – or if we are looking for insight or limited wisdom to fit within some other story. Further, since God's redemptive drama has different acts, our prayer must take into account the act in which we are called to perform our role and the posture most fitting for kingdom participants.

Part of what is revealed in the unfolding drama of God's redemptive plan is increased understanding of God. In the third gospel Jesus' ministry has a focus: God's kingdom. Central to Jesus' kingdom activity is his prayer. Central to Jesus' kingdom teaching, both in general and specifically with respect to prayer, is his unveiling the utterly benevolent, trustworthy, and generous 'Fatherness' of God.[50] Thus *one prays most properly when one takes one's place in the unfolding drama of redemption, and one prays most sensibly when one perceives how the new stage of God's drama renders God most fully.* According to the New Testament as a whole, and not least the resurrected Jesus of Luke 24, Jesus stands at the center of Scripture and is the climax of God's self-revelation.[51]

In Luke's narrative, shortly before Jesus teaches his disciples the *pater noster* (Lk. 11:1–4), he exults in the hiddenness and the present unveiling of his

---

[50] This language is not meant to imply that Yahweh had never made himself known as Father to Israel or that God the Father is mere metaphor. The point is how Jesus magnifies the *goodness* of his Father's 'fatherness.'

[51] Comparatively, when Abraham intercedes for Sodom, God's *character* is central to the discussion between God and Abraham (Gen. 18:16–33). When Moses intercedes for Israel after coming down the mountain to find the children of Israel worshipping the golden calf, *fullness of revelation concerning Yahweh* is central to his request (Ex. 33 – 34). Daniel rests his great prayer for Israel upon *God's mercy, covenant faithfulness and identification with his people* (Dan. 9). Finally, the prayer report in Jn. 17 wraps requests for first-century disciples and all those who come after them in faith inside Jesus' claim to have manifested God's name/character and his intention to continue doing so (Jn. 17:6, 26).

identity as the Son and his Father's identity as Father (10:21–22). Then Jesus turns to his disciples to express how *blessed* they are to be witnesses to the particular dramatic moment in which they are taking part:

> Blessed are the eyes that see what you see! For I tell you that many prophets and kings longed to see what you see, and did not see it, and to hear what you hear, and did not hear it.

According to Jesus, then, this story has reached a moment of enormous anticipation. If Joel Green is correct when he writes, 'Luke's Model Readers will embrace this narrative as their own, and seek to continue it in their lives,' taking up our roles 'by embracing, indwelling, and embodying the divine story,'[52] one of the primary ways Luke signifies this is to narrate Jesus, those waiting for his first arrival, and those living in the wake of his 'exodus,' as people dedicated to prayer (Acts 1:14; 2:42). That is, these are people who relate to God as a kind and merciful Father and thereby openly accept his 'narration' of themselves into the same drama *as his children* (Lk. 18:15–17), with a growing awareness of the significance of the times (Lk. 12:54–56; Acts 2:14–40; 3:24; 13:16–41; cf. 1 Cor. 10:1–11; Heb. 1:1–2:4; 1 Pet 1:10–12, 17–21).

Thus our prayer is more fully eschatological in comparison to Simeon's and Anna's. They prayed for the consolation of Israel – that God would keep covenant faithfulness. Knowing Jesus, we know the covenant faithfulness of God and our prayers look back toward this fulfillment even as they look forward to consummation (see Lk. 18:1–8 and 21:34–36 in light of 22:14–23; cf. Acts 3:17–21 with 3:24).[53] Moreover, our prayer is characterized by a freedom and boldness of access into God's presence only typified by the tabernacle and temple(s), and now realized through the self-offering of Jesus – a more competent priest than Zechariah! Luke ends – and Acts begins – with the ascended Jesus blessing and directing his people. The second volume interprets these blessings and this guidance as eschatological. That is, the risen Jesus blesses and

---

[52] Green, 'Learning Theological Interpretation from Luke,' 66.

[53] The parable about the widow and the unjust judge is offered to encourage the weak among God's people to pursue justice, but in a manner driven by hope. Or, better yet, since the widow in the story is the one with whom we are intended to identify, this parable helps us to view ourselves appropriately: as weak servants – unless, of course, we are more like the heartless judge! So why is it that Jesus' disciples should pray continually and *not become discouraged*? What is implied about discipleship that would tempt us toward discouragement? Alternatively, what realities will sustain our hope in pursuing justice, even when we are in seemingly desperate situations? Finally, how will we become the kind of people God intends if we avoid the pursuit of justice and the dispositions required and acquired by adopting this pursuit?

guides through the ministry of the promised Spirit of restoration.[54] But already in Luke's first volume, the Spirit is a 'gift' available to people who know God as a better Father than earthly fathers who are evil (11:11–13).

> According to the apostolic witnesses, Jesus is our way to communicate with God at the turn of the ages (1 Cor. 1:4–9). When we acclaim him *Kyrios* or address him as such, we are already speaking from an experience of the power, presence, and praise of God. But we are also asking, in his name, to enter more deeply into God's new creation, to take our own unique part, through prayer and action, in the final act of the divine drama.[55]

Conclusion: 'When you pray, say: "Father …"'

Jesus, the Messiah, in whom we are blessed and who brings the age of the Israel-specific temple to a close, invites us to share in his prayer life, that is, to 'know' the goodness of God[56] and relate to him the way he did – as our Father. He who knows the Father uniquely (Lk. 10:21–22) invites us to call upon his Father as our 'Father' (11:2b). Thus the model prayer given by Jesus is a prayer befitting those who come to God like little children (10:21; 18:15–17). The true Son (3:22, 38; 4:3, 9; 9:35; 10:21–22; 23:46) who magnifies his Father's name (10:21) invites us to orient our lives for the same purpose: 'Father, may your name be regarded as sacred.' We are to identify God as 'Father' and consecrate ourselves as his true children by setting his name apart for honor.[57]

The inaugurator of the kingdom – because he is the eschatological Son of David, Israel's true King who must reign over the nations until all his enemies are put under his feet – teaches us to pray for its consummation (11:2c).[58] That

---

[54] Numerous papers at least this long could be dedicated to how Luke associates prayer and the Spirit which, among other things, also informs us concerning the eschatological nature of the drama in which prayer involves us. Conn, 'Theology'; Smalley, 'Spirit, Kingdom and Prayer'; and Turner, 'Prayer' are good essays with which to begin.

[55] Koenig, *Rediscovering*, 11–12.

[56] Perhaps disciples of Jesus need to work toward embracing an epistemology of self-abandonment. For to 'know' the Father as Jesus did is to relinquish one's life for his purposes and therein to discover what otherwise would be lost.

[57] According to 9:46–48, living as children of the Father as revealed in Jesus opens disciples up to practices such as hospitality and self-orientations such as meekness. Moreover, the forms that this kind of life can take – loving, doing good toward and blessing enemies and persecutors (6:27–34) – results in emulating and therefore exegeting the Father's character (6:35–36).

[58] When, importantly, he will return all things over to his Father (1 Cor. 15:20–28).

is, again, we must learn to see ourselves as children who want their Father's authority to spread rather than recede.

The one who taught concerning the reliability of the Father, who taught of his unfathomable beneficence and of our great worth in his estimation (11:11–13; 12:22–32), teaches us to ask his and our Father for our daily bread (11:3). Only those who know him as a kind and merciful Father will be able to live like Jesus' brothers and sisters and as the Father's true children (6:27–36; 8:21; 9:46–48; 12:22–32; 23:34, 46).

He who calls tax collectors to be close associates (6:27–28), eats with sinners (6:29–32; 7:31–35; 15:1–2; 19:1–10), comes 'to call sinners to repentance' (6:32) and 'to seek and to save what was lost' (19:10), narrated himself as one 'numbered with the transgressors' (22:37). Moreover, this One, crucified between two criminals as he intercedes for the forgiveness of his enemies, is the One who teaches us to ask for the same for ourselves and to release others from any indebtedness (11:4). The one who teaches us to ask the Father for forgiveness is the One who established the new covenant with his blood even as he shared the table with his betrayer (22:20–21) and announced Simon's future failure *and recovery* through a reference to his intercession (22:31–32). Indeed, the One who teaches us to ask our Father for forgiveness is the Father's true Son in whose name 'repentance and forgiveness of sins' is to be proclaimed to all nations (24:47; cf. Acts 2:38; 5:31)!

This One who sent out his disciples like lambs before wolves (10:3) teaches us to turn to our Father in light of potential πειρασμοὶ (11:4). Whether these are *our trials* that might tempt us to turn faithless, *our temptations* to turn away more generally, or *our unbelief* that might put God to the test, the remedy remains the same – Jesus teaches his disciples to depend upon God *our Father.*[59] That is, 'the Lord's prayer is an invitation to share Jesus' own prayer life – and with it his agenda, his work, his pattern of life, his spirituality.'[60] Jesus is inviting us to identify the God of Israel freshly revealed in and by himself as our Father and to be identified as his children.

According to the author of these two volumes, Jesus is Israel's Messiah, come at last, who ushers in a new day, even a new day of prayer for a new community who gathers in his name, calls upon God as 'Father', and is filled with the gift he said his Father would give to those who ask (11:11–13).[61] Thus,

---

[59] Perhaps, then, the most dangerous temptation, test, or trial remains the tendency to doubt either God's identity as our kind and merciful Father or our identity as his beloved children (4:3, 9).

[60] Wright, 'Lord's Prayer,' 138. See further Wright's discussion of the possibility that the 'testing' we are prayerfully to avoid is our testing of God, so that we do not emulate the stiff-necked wilderness generation (137–38, 144–47).

[61] Of course, one is instantly mindful of Paul's reflection upon these things in Rom. 8 and Gal. 4, where calling God 'Abba' is now a privilege of Gentiles who, recognizing

Luke's narration of Jesus' example and teaching about prayer – as well as his depictions of the earliest Christian community devoted to prayer – may do more than teach us about prayer or Luke's redactional hand.

Luke's telling of this story is his narration of *the climax* and the beginning of *the act of resolution* of God's redemptive story. This telling of the story – with this practice of prayer underscored again and again – may serve to expand and sanctify our theological horizons. Therefore, attending to and responding to Luke's prayer-filled story may alter not only our views of God's plan (may it do so), and not only our perception of our role within this great drama (may it do so), but also our knowledge and experience of God the Father, Jesus Christ his Son, and God the Holy Spirit, who intercedes *in and for us,* transforming and maturing us as his holy children, in order that God's will would be done *in and through* us unto the fulfillment of his purposes and thereby the blessing of his Name.

We are well aware that such assertions raise many questions. Indeed, at our Oxford consultation we had to extend our discussion period because of the multitude of questions raised in response to this chapter. Questions ranged from 'how precisely does prayer affect exegesis?' to 'how should we form coming generations of biblical interpreters if this perspective is right?'[62] There is also the intriguing question of how academic exegesis relates to a devotional reception of the word as typified, for example, in *lectio divina.* This latter question will be taken up at our consultation in Rome on canon and exegesis. Suffice it to note, for now, that if we take Luke's Gospel seriously, then we need to reengage the relationship between prayer and exegesis as a matter of urgency. Our aims in this chapter will have been achieved if it stimulates further reflection on this crucial topic.

Jesus as Lord, have been confirmed in doing so by the Spirit of promise (cf. Wright, 'Lord's Prayer,' 151–53). As Jesus taught his disciples about God as their Father, 'your Father knows your needs … it is your Father's good pleasure to give you the kingdom' (Lk. 12:22–32), so the Spirit who searches the deep things of God unveils and clarifies God's radical generosity to his children 'that we might understand the things freely given us by God' (1 Cor. 2:12) precisely through the Spirit-empowered proclamation of this same Jesus.

62 See in this respect Francis Martin's fascinating account of his own formation in his 'Reading Scripture in the Catholic Tradition.'

Bibliography

von Balthasar, H.U., *Prayer* (San Francisco: Ignatius Press, 1986)
—, 'Toward a Theology of Christian Prayer,' *Comm* 12.3 (1985), 245–57
Barr, J., 'Abba, Father,' *Theology* 91.714 (1988), 173–79
Bartholomew, C.G., 'Uncharted Waters: Philosophy, Theology, and the Crisis in
    Biblical Interpretation,' in *Renewing Biblical Interpretation* (ed. C.G.
    Bartholomew, C. Greene and K. Möller; SHS 1; Carlisle: Paternoster; Grand
    Rapids: Zondervan, 2000), 1–39
—, and M.W. Goheen., 'Story and Biblical Theology,' in *Out of Egypt: Biblical
    Theology and Biblical Interpretation* (ed. C.G. Bartholomew, M. Healy, K. Möller
    and R. Parry; SHS 5; Carlisle: Paternoster; Grand Rapids: Zondervan, 2004),
    144–71
—, and M.W. Goheen, *The Drama of Scripture: Finding our Place in the Biblical Story*
    (Grand Rapids: Baker Academic, 2004)
Barton, S.C., 'New Testament Interpretation as Performance,' *SJT* 52 (1999),
    179–208
Beauchamp, P., 'Prayer,' in *DBT* (trans. J.J. Kilgallen; ed. X. Léon-Dufour;
    Ijamsville, MD: The Word Among Us Press, 2nd edn, 1982), 445–49
Black, C.C., 'The Education of Human Wanting: Formation by Pater Noster,' in
    Character and Scripture: Moral Formation, Community, and Biblical Interpretation
    (ed. W.P. Brown; Grand Rapids: Eerdmans, 2002), 248–63
—, 'Exegesis as Prayer,' *PSB* 23 (2002), 131–45
—, 'Inquiring after God When Meditating on Scripture,' in *Inquiring after God:
    Classical and Contemporary Readings* (ed. E.T. Charry; Blackwell Readings in
    Modern Theology; London: Basil Blackwell, 2000), 207–31
Blomberg, C., 'Messiah in the New Testament,' in *Israel's Messiah in the Bible and
    the Dead Sea Scrolls* (ed. R.S. Hess and M.D. Carrol R.; Grand Rapids: Baker
    Books, 2003), 85–101
—, *Interpreting the Parables* (Downers Grove, IL/Leicester: InterVarsity Press, 1990)
Bock, D.L., 'Luke,' in *The Face of New Testament Studies: A Survey of Recent Research*
    (ed. S. McKnight and G.R. Osborne; Grand Rapids: Baker Books, 2004),
    349–72
—, *Luke 1:1 – 9:50* (BECNT; Grand Rapids: Baker Books, 1994)
—, *Luke 9:51 – 24:53* (BECNT; Grand Rapids: Baker Books, 1996)
—, 'The Gospel of Luke,' in *Dictionary of Jesus and the Gospels* (ed. J. Green, S.
    McKnight and I.H. Marshall; Downers Grove, IL: InterVarsity Press, 1992),
    495–510
Brown, R.E., *The Birth of the Messiah: A Commentary on the Infancy Narratives of
    Matthew and Luke* (Garden City: Doubleday, 1977)
Conn, H.M., 'Prayer for the City – Then and Now,' *Urban Mission* 12.3 (March
    1995), 3–6

—, 'Luke's Theology of Prayer,' *Christianity Today* (1972; facsimile)

Conzelmann, H., *The Theology of St. Luke* (trans. G. Buswell; New York: Harper & Row, 1960)

Crump, D.M., *Jesus the Intercessor: Prayer and Christology in Luke-Acts* (Grand Rapids: Baker Books, 1999)

Cullmann, O., *Prayer in the New Testament* (London: SCM Press; Minneapolis: Fortress Press, 1995)

Dunn, J.D.G., 'Prayer,' in *DJG* (ed. J.B. Green, S. McKnight and I.H. Marshall; Downers Grove, IL: InterVarsity Press, 1992), 617–25

Goldingay, J., 'The Logic of Intercession,' *Theology* (1998), 262–70

Green, J.B., *The Theology of the Gospel of Luke* (Cambridge: Cambridge University Press, 1995)

—, *The Gospel of Luke* (NICNT; Grand Rapids: Eerdmans, 1997)

—, 'Persevering Together in Prayer: The Significance of Prayer in the Acts of the Apostles,' in *Into God's Presence: Prayer in the New Testament* (ed. R.N. Longenecker; Grand Rapids: Eerdmans, 2001), 183–202

—, and M. Pasquarello, III (eds.), *Narrative Reading, Narrative Preaching: Reuniting New Testament Interpretation and Proclamation* (Grand Rapids: Baker Books, 2003)

Hamm, D., 'The Tamid Service in Luke-Acts: The Cultic Background behind Luke's Theology of Worship (Luke 1:5–25; 18:9–14; 24:50–53; Acts 3:1; 10:3, 30),' *CBQ* 65 (2003), 215–31

Huebner, H., 'The Politics of Memory and Hope,' *The Mennonite Quarterly Review* 76.1 (2002), 35–48

John Paul II and the Pontifical Biblical Commission, *The Interpretation of the Bible in the Church* (Boston: St. Paul Books and the Media, 1993)

Johnson, A.F., 'Assurance for Man: The Fallacy of Translating *Anaideia* by "Persistence" in Luke 11:5–8,' *JETS* 22.2 (1979), 123–31

Just, A.A., *Luke* (ACCS, NT III; Downers Grove, IL: InterVarsity Press, 2003)

Keesmaat, S.C., 'Strange Neighbors and Risky Care (Matthew 18:21–35; Luke 14:7–14; Luke 10:25–37),' in *The Challenge of Jesus' Parables* (ed. R.N. Longenecker; Cambridge/Grand Rapids: Eerdmans, 2000), 263–85

Koenig, J., *Rediscovering New Testament Prayer: Boldness and Blessing in the Name of Jesus* (San Francisco: Harper & Row, 1992)

Lash, N., 'Performing the Scriptures,' in *Theology on the Way to Emmaus* (London: SCM Press, 1986), 37–46

Liefeld, W.L., 'Parables on Prayer (Luke 11:5–13; 18:1–14),' in *The Challenge of Jesus' Parables* (ed. R.N. Longenecker; Cambridge/Grand Rapids: Eerdmans, 2000), 240–62

—, 'Prayer,' *ISBE*, III (ed. G.W. Bromiley; Grand Rapids: Eerdmans, 1986), 931–39

Loughlin, G., *Telling God's Story: Bible, Church, and Narrative Theology* (Cambridge: Cambridge University Press, 1996)

Marshall, I.H., 'Jesus – Example and Teacher of Prayer in the Synoptic Gospels,' in *Into God's Presence: Prayer in the New Testament* (ed. R.N. Longenecker; Grand Rapids: Eerdmans, 2001), 113–31

—, *Luke: Historian and Theologian* (Grand Rapids: Academie Books, 2ⁿᵈ edn, 1989)

—, *Commentary on Luke: A Commentary on the Greek Text* (NIGTC; Grand Rapids: Eerdmans, 1978)

—, and D. Peterson (eds.), *Witness to the Gospel: The Theology of Acts* (Grand Rapids: Eerdmans, 1998)

Martens, A., 'Salvation Today: Reading Luke's Message for a Gentile Audience,' in *Reading the Gospels Today* (ed. S.E. Porter; Grand Rapids: Eerdmans, 2004), 100–26

Martin, F., 'Reading Scripture in the Catholic Tradition,' in *Your Word is Truth: A Project of Evangelicals and Catholics Together* (ed. C. Colson and R.J. Neuhaus; Grand Rapids: Eerdmans, 2002), 147–68

Merton, T., *Contemplative Prayer* (London: DLT, 1969)

—, *Entering the Silence: Becoming a Monk and Writer, The Journals of Thomas Merton, II (1941–1952)* (ed. J. Montaldo; San Francisco: HarperSanFrancisco, 1996)

Migliore, D.L. (ed.), *The Lord's Prayer: Perspectives for Reclaiming Christian Prayer* (Grand Rapids: Eerdmans, 1993)

Newbigin, L., *The Gospel in a Pluralist Society* (Grand Rapids: Eerdmans, 1989)

Nouwen, H., *Finding My Way Home: Pathways to Life and the Spirit* (New York: Crossroad, 2001)

O'Brien, P.T., 'Prayer in Luke-Acts,' *TynBul* 24 (1973), 111–27

Packer, J.I., 'The Bible in Use: Evangelicals Seeking Truth from Holy Scripture,' in *Your Word Is Truth: A Project of Evangelicals and Catholics Together* (ed. C. Colson and R.J. Neuhaus; Grand Rapids: Eerdmans, 2002), 59–78

Plymale, S.F., *The Prayer Texts of Luke-Acts* (American University Studies Series VII, Theology and Religion 118; New York: Peter Lang, 1991)

Porter, S.E. (ed.), *Reading the Gospels Today* (Grand Rapids: Eerdmans, 2004)

Reid, B.E., 'Beyond Petty Pursuits and Wearisome Widows,' *Int* 56.3 (July 2002), 284–94

Resseguie, J.L., *Spiritual Landscape: Images of the Spiritual Life in the Gospel of Luke* (Peabody: Hendrickson, 2004)

Ridderbos, H.N., *When the Time Had Fully Come: Studies in New Testament Theology* (Jordon Station: Paideia Press, 1957)

Scott, D., 'Speaking to Form: Trinitarian-Performative Scripture Reading,' *AThR* 77 (1995), 137–50

Smalley, S., 'Spirit, Kingdom, and Prayer in Luke-Acts,' *NovT* 15 (1973), 59–71

Snodgrass, K.R., '*ANAIDEIA* and the Friend at Midnight,' *JBL* 116 (1997), 505–13

Stiver, D., 'Theological Method,' in *Postmodern Theology* (ed. K.J. Vanhoozer; Cambridge: Cambridge University Press, 2003), 170–85

Tan, B.O.S., 'The Parable of the Pharisee and the Tax-Collector in Luke 18:9–14: A Study in the Practice of Prayer,' *AJT* 14.2 (2000), 286–303

Turner, M.M.B., 'Prayer in the Gospels and Acts,' in *Teach Us to Pray: Prayer in the Bible and the World* (ed. D.A. Carson; Exeter: Paternoster, 1990), 58–83

Vanhoozer, K.J., 'Evangelicalism and the Church: The Company of the Gospel,' in *The Futures of Evangelicalism* (ed. C. Bartholomew, R. Parry and A. West; Leicester: InterVarsity Press, 2003), 40–99

—, 'The Voice and the Actor: A Dramatic Proposal about the Ministry and Minstrelsy of Theology,' in *Evangelical Futures* (ed. J.J. Stackhouse, Jr.; Grand Rapids: Baker Books), 61–106

Waetjen, H.C., 'The Subversion of "World" by the Parable of the Friend at Midnight,' *JBL* 120.4 (2001), 703–21

Walton, S., 'Acts: Many Questions, Many Answers,' in *The Face of New Testament Studies: A Survey of Recent Research* (ed. S. McKnight and G.R. Osborne; Grand Rapids: Baker Books, 2004), 229–50

Watson, F., *Text, Church and World* (Edinburgh: T&T Clark, 1994)

Wright, C.J.H., 'Mission as a Matrix for Hermeneutics and Biblical Theology,' in *Out of Egypt: Biblical Theology and Biblical Interpretation* (ed. C.G. Bartholomew, M. Healy, K. Möller and R. Parry; Carlisle: Paternoster; Grand Rapids: Zondervan, 2004), 102–43

Wright, N.T., 'The Lord's Prayer as a Paradigm of Christian Prayer,' in *Into God's Presence: Prayer in the New Testament* (ed. R.N. Longenecker; Grand Rapids: Eerdmans, 2001), 132–54

—, *The Lord and His Prayer* (Grand Rapids: Eerdmans, 1996)

—, *Jesus and the Victory of God* (London: SPCK, 1996)

—, *The New Testament and the People of God* (London: SPCK, 1992)

—, 'How Can the Bible Be Authoritative?,' *VE* 21 (1991), 7–32

Issues in Reception History
and Reception Theory

14

The Reception and Use of the Gospel of
Luke in the Second Century
François Bovon

Several scholars have investigated the way various New Testament writings were received and used in the second century. Elaine Pagels and Jean Michel Poffet, for instance, investigated the reception and use of the Gospel of John.[1] Andreas Lindemann and Ernst Dassmann pursued reception of the Pauline corpus, while Edouard Massaux and Wolf Dietrich Köhler tracked the Gospel of Matthew.[2] Some scholars dared to trace the development of the synoptic tradition as a whole, while others attempted to detect the earliest traces of the book of Acts.[3] But apart from interest in Marcion, only a few scholars have investigated the reception and use of the Gospel of Luke in the second century since Edouard Zeller's work in 1848.[4]

Zeller's work produced a number of conclusions and findings. He agreed with Ritschl's thesis that Marcion did not rewrite the Gospel of Luke but Luke's primary source. He noted the absence of any reference to the third gospel in the Apostolic Fathers and demonstrated that Justin used both the

---

[1] Pagels, *The Johannine Gospel in Gnostic Exegesis*; Poffet, *La Méthode Exégétique d'Héracléon et d'Origène*; Kaestli, Poffet, and Zumstein, *La Communauté Johannique et son Histoire*.

[2] On the Pauline corpus see Lindemann, *Paulus im ältesten Christentum: Das Bild des Apostels und die Rezeption der Paulinischen Theologie in der frühchristlichen Literatur bis Marcion*; and Dassmann, *Paulus in frühchristlicher Frömmigkeit und Kunst*. On the Gospel of Matthew see Massaux, *Influence de l'Évangile de Saint Matthieu*; and Köhler, *Die Rezeption des Matthäusevangeliums in der Zeit vor Irenäus*.

[3] On the synoptic tradition see Koester, *Synoptische Überlieferung bei den apostolischen Vätern*; France and Wenham (eds.), *Gospel Perspectives*; Sevrin, *The New Testament in Early Christianity*; and Peterson (ed.), *Gospel Traditions*. On the book of Acts see Haenchen, *The Acts of the Apostles*; Bovon, *De Vocatione Gentium*; and Bieder, *Die Apostelgeschichte in der Histoire*.

[4] Zeller, 'Die älteste Überlieferung.'

final version of the third gospel as well as Luke's major source. He further concluded that the *Epistle to Diognetus* does not contain any reference to Luke.
Zeller claimed that there is evidence to support that the *Pseudo-Clementines*,
like Justin, had access to Luke and his principal source. Zeller deduced from
Irenaeus that the gnostics – the Valentinians in particular – used the Gospel of
Luke. He also established that the pagan philosopher Celsus, as well as the
apologist Theophilus, both knew the third gospel. With regard to the book
of Acts, Zeller considered that this book was unknown to Justin and is
clearly attested only by Irenaeus. Finally, Zeller concluded that the final
version of the Gospel of Luke was written between 130 C.E. – that is, after
the time of Marcion, who did not know of it – and before Justin, who clearly
uses it.

Between Zeller's paper in 1848 and today I can only mention the eight
pages of John Martin Creed's introduction to his commentary on the Gospel of
Luke[5] and a study I discovered after the first version of this chapter was written
– Andrew Gregory's fine dissertation. Creed, who did not refer to Zeller's
paper, detected evidence of the Gospel of Luke in the *Didache*, a text that was
not available to Zeller; but Creed believed that the references to Luke belong
to a later interpolation (*Did.* 1.3 – 2.1). Creed did not find any influence of the
third gospel in Ignatius, Barnabas, or Hermas, but he felt there was evidence
that the writer of the *Gospel of Peter* (another text that was unavailable to Zeller)
was somewhat familiar with it. He detected Lukan influence in Justin,
Theophilus and the so-called gnostics, in Basilides, who seems to know the
parable of Lazarus and the rich man (Lk. 16:19–31), and in Ptolemaeus and
Heracleon, as they are known to us through Irenaeus and Clement of Alexandria. Creed concluded that the influence of our final version of Luke on
Marcion is clear; thus he does not address Ritschl's and Zeller's hypothesis.
After mentioning Tatian's use of the third gospel in his *Diatessaron*, Creed men-
tions the *Epistula Apostolorum* (yet another text that was discovered only after
Zeller's time),[6] and claims that the author of the *Epistula Apostolorum* knew the
four gospels.

Creed arrived at three conclusions with respect to our four canonical gospels. First, he concludes that, because they were thought to have been written
by apostles, Matthew and John were the most popular gospels in the second
century. Second, Creed claimed that Mark, whose material is almost completely integrated into Matthew and Luke, dropped into the background. And
third, Creed thought that because of the extent of the special material in Luke,
particularly the parables, this gospel occupied an intermediate position.

---

[5] Creed, *The Gospel According to St. Luke*, XXV–XXXII.
[6] Creed follows Schmidt's date and location of that text: Asia Minor around the year
160 C.E.; see Schmidt, *Gespräche Jesu mit seinen Jüngern nach der Auferstehung*.

Andrew Gregory's dissertation *The Reception of Luke and Acts in the Period before Irenaeus*[7] deals explicitly with my topic, as the title indicates. It contains an excellent bibliography and goes into much greater depth and detail than the present chapter. Gregory's general conclusions, often agrees with mine on negative results. For example, in orthodox writings it is impossible to prove the use of the Lukan redaction of Jesus sayings until Justin and Irenaeus.[8] Concerning Marcion, he writes, 'Marcion is instead the first witness to the sustained self-conscious exclusive use of any single text concerning Jesus.'[9] I agree also with his judgment relative to Justin Martyr, namely, that 'Justin must be considered to depend on *Luke*.'[10] These major agreements between us are important, and I am pleased to mention them since this scholar also responds to this chapter.

There are still – even after having read Andrew Gregory's work – questions regarding Luke's Gospel that remain unanswered to this day, which leave us wondering about this gospel's destiny in the early patristic period. Which groups or communities, for example, possessed the Gospel of Luke in the second century? How was this gospel transmitted? Why are there different textual forms of this gospel (and of Acts)? Who decided to dissociate the gospel from the book of Acts? What was the earliest interpretation of Luke's Gospel? When and by whom was it considered Holy Scripture? How early in the second century can traces of Luke's Gospel be detected? These intriguing questions demand that the investigations of Zeller, Creed, and Gregory be reopened and that historical answers be found.[11]

New research tools and methods also compel fresh inquiry. The volumes of *Biblia patristica*[12] made information about Luke's Gospel much more accessible than it had previously been. Recent critical editions of second-century Christian literature promise more reliable results than nineteenth-century scholarship could have achieved. New discoveries, such as the *Gospel of Thomas*, have opened up new possibilities for studies. Thus it is time, as Andrew Gregory[13] notes, that this lamentable lacuna in Lukan studies be filled. How was Luke's Gospel received and used in the second century?

---

[7] See Gregory, *Reception*.

[8] Gregory, *Reception*, 171–72 and 293–98.

[9] Gregory, *Reception*, 210.

[10] Gregory, *Reception*, 291.

[11] I demonstrated my interest in the history of reception of Luke's Gospel in the second century C.E. at the end of my paper 'Le Récit Lucanien de la Passion,' esp. 416–20; see the ET published in my *Studies in Early Christianity*, 74–105, esp. 98–101.

[12] J. Allenbach, et al., *Biblia patristica*.

[13] Gregory, *Reception*, 22.

But before we attempt to answer this question, we must consider another. How should we proceed with our investigation? There are a number of possibilities. One could imagine, for instance, the theological problems and ecclesiastical quarrels that took place during this time period and then evaluate the role of Luke's Gospel in these discussions. For example, how might Luke 1:35 have been a response to questions about Jesus' birth?[14] Or how might Luke 24:39 have influenced developing thought about the resurrection?[15] But this path is uncertain since it risks abandoning the concrete, historical plane and embarking upon an abstract, theological one that has no solid footing. Or, one could employ socio-geographical categories and investigate the status of Luke's Gospel in Asia, Rome, or Antioch.[16] But since the original setting of so many early Christian texts is uncertain, this path has little to recommend it.

One could follow the Gospel of Luke itself and examine successively the way second-century writers understood Jesus' birth, his parables and miracles, his passion and resurrection. One might discover a significant interest in the ethical (love of enemies) and eschatological (the parousia) aspects of Jesus' teaching, with a corresponding lack of interest in his miracles. But the drawback to this procedure is that it attributes the same value to each Lukan passage.

In light of the documents now at our disposal, I shall propose another course. Namely, what was the attitude of second-century authors who were confronted with Luke's Gospel? How did they receive it? How did they make use of it? My research indicates that there were two different lines of response in the second century. Some authors adopted Luke as a source for their own gospels. For them, his writing was a ready reserve for their own retelling of stories about Jesus and his disciples. For other authors, Luke's text became an authoritative document. It became their scripture, something to be preserved and interpreted.

Luke as a Source for New Writings

One response to Luke's Gospel was to view it merely as a source for further narration. It came as a surprise to me to discover that Luke the *historian* (the anonymous author of a διήγησις, Luke 1:1) was used as a source by many anonymous authors of the second and third centuries. New storytellers read and drew from this ancient storyteller as if there had been a familiarity between them. But here one must exercise caution, for just as Luke was not the first storyteller (cf. Lk.

[14] See Brock, 'The Lost Old Syriac at Luke 1:35.'
[15] See Bovon, 'Le Récit Lucanien de la Passion,' 419.
[16] Apparently Polycarp was unaware of Luke's Gospel in Asia, just as *1 Clement* and *Hermas* suggest no knowledge of it in Rome; likewise, Ignatius of Antioch seemed to be unacquainted with Luke's Gospel.

1:1), the possibility that some second-century authors did not use Luke himself so much as one of his sources should not be dismissed. And what is true of the stories is all the more true of the words attributed to Jesus.

It appears that the authors of the following texts had knowledge of passages of Luke's Gospel that are unique to him and have no synoptic parallels:

(a) The *Gospel of the Ebionites* is a very old gospel harmony known only through quotations found in Epiphanius. This gospel is probably older than Tatian's *Diatessaron*, since, unlike the latter, it melds only three gospels. Knowledge of Luke's Gospel is revealed in the affirmation that John the Baptist was from priestly roots: 'It was said that he [John the Baptist] was from the descent of the priest of Aaron, son of Zacharias and Elizabeth.'[17]

(b) Several quotations from the *Gospel of the Nazarenes* are preserved in the works of Jerome as well as in a medieval manuscript entitled *Historia passionis Domini*. While most of these quotations are related to the Gospel of Matthew,[18] two of them reveal unmistakable knowledge of the Gospel of Luke: the Lukan episode (Lk. 22:43–44) where an angel appears to comfort Jesus when, seized by anxiety in the garden, he begins to sweat clots of blood (*Hist. pass. Dom.*, fol. 32ʳ);[19] and Jesus' final words on the cross ('Father, forgive them, for they know not what they do,' Lk. 23:34[20]). These two passages, which are unique to Luke, seem to indicate that the author of this gospel was well aware of the Gospel of Luke.

(c) Two passages from the *Gospel of Peter* must also be considered. The first affirms that Herod was present and active during Jesus' trial (*Gos. Pet.* 1:1–2:5), which is also stated in Luke 23:6–12 and Acts 4:27–28. It is most likely in this instance that the *Gospel of Peter* does not depend directly upon the Gospel of Luke but shares with it a common oral tradition.[21] The same holds true for the utterance of the good robber crucified along with Jesus (*Gos. Pet.* 4:13).[22]

(d) The fragments of Papyrus Egerton 2, the so-called 'Unknown Gospel,' sound very Johannine, but they also echo Luke. For example, the attempt

---

17 This quotation is preserved by Epiphanius, *Pan.* 30.13.6. For an ET see Schneemelcher, *New Testament Apocrypha*, I, 169.

18 The *Gospel of the Nazarenes* is similar to the Gospel of Matthew in that both are orthodox Judeo-Christian gospels.

19 The Latin text is available in Aland, *Synopsis*, 457. Justin Martyr (*Dial.* 103.8) also knows of this episode.

20 Preserved by Jerome, *Epist.* 120.8; PL 116.934.

21 Pace Massaux, *Influence de l'Évangile de Saint Mathieu*, 377.

22 The good robber's rebuke (ἡμεῖς διὰ τὰ κακὰ ἃ ἐποιήσαμεν οὕτω πεπόνθαμεν, οὗτος δὲ σωτὴρ γενόμενος τῶν ἀνθρώπων τί ἠδίκησεν ὑμᾶς; see Aland, *Synopsis*, 484; cf. Schneemelcher, *New Testament Apocrypha*, I, 223), is similar to that found in Lk. 23:41.

to arrest Jesus[23] includes statements very similar to those found in John
5:39, 45–46. But the use of the term 'lawyer' (νομικός) is more Lukan; the
term is found seven times in Luke but only once in Matthew, and it is
absent from the Gospels of Mark and John. Also, the participle στραφείς
depicts a frequent gesture of Jesus that is found primarily in Luke; the
gesture is found eight times in Luke, twice in Matthew, once in John, and
is absent from Mark. And in the next episode, the story of the leper,[24]
much of the language resembles that found in Luke 5:12–14 and 17:14.
Finally, Luke is the only New Testament evangelist who uses terms such as
συνοδεύω, συνεσθίω, and παντοχεῖον.[25]

(e) In the *Gospel of Thomas* there are at least seven verses that have parallels
only in the Gospel of Luke:

Gos. Thom. 3:	The kingdom of God is within you and outside you (cf. Lk. 17:21).
Gos. Thom. 10:	I have cast fire upon the world (cf. Lk. 12:49).
Gos. Thom. 39:	The Pharisees and scribes have received and hidden the keys of knowledge (cf. Lk. 11:52).
Gos. Thom. 63:	The parable of the rich man (cf. Lk. 12:16–21).
Gos. Thom. 79:	An apothegm in the form of a dialogue with two beatitudes (the woman: blessed is the womb; Jesus: blessed are those who have heard the word; cf. Lk. 11:27–28, mixed with an apocalyptical sentence known only by Luke (Lk. 23:29).
Gos. Thom. 95:	Do not lend money at interest (cf. Lk. 6:34–35).
Gos. Thom. 113:	On what day does the kingdom come? The kingdom does not come so that one can expect it (cf. Lk. 17:20–21)

---

[23] See Papyrus Egerton 2, fol. 1ᵛ (Aland, *Synopsis*, 200, 323; cf. Schneemelcher, *New Testament Apocrypha*, I, 98).

[24] See Papyrus Egerton 2, fol.ʳ (Aland, *Synopsis*, 60; cf. Schneemelcher, *New Testament Apocrypha*, I, 98).

[25] Massaux, *Influence de l'Évangile de Saint Matthieu*, 331–33, 339.

There may be other parallels, but the common elements between Luke and the *Gospel of Thomas* listed above are indisputable. And even if one were to try to dismiss these parallels as being due to a common source (either oral or written tradition), there is one instance among them where the final redaction of the *Gospel of Thomas* depends on the final redaction of the Gospel of Luke: the disposition of a loan without interest (*Gos. Thom.* 95 = Lk. 6:34–35; cf. Mt. 5:42).

(f) Clement of Alexandria mentions in *Stromata* 2.45.4, 3.26.3, and 7.82.1 a non-canonical work called the *Traditions of Matthias*. In *Stromata* 4.6.35.2, he attributes the decision made by Jesus' interlocutor in the gospel ('Here, Lord, I give half of my possessions to the poor,' Lk. 19:8) to Zacchaeus, knowing that some claim these words came from Matthias's lips. The Savior's response to this promise was, 'The Son of Man has come σήμερον [cf. Lk. 19:10 and 13:15, 'today'] to find what had been lost.'[26]

(g) Papyrus Cairensis 10735 (sixth or seventh century, but the text may be much older) contains a very fragmentary birth narrative.[27] Here again we have either a parallel story or an instance of free usage of Luke (and Matthew): on the recto of the fragment there is the account of the flight into Egypt (cf. Mt. 2:13) and on the verso the story where Mary receives as a sign the message of John's conception in Elizabeth's womb (cf. Lk. 1:36).

(h) In the *Ascension of Isaiah*, an early Christian apocalypse (probably early second century), the prophet shares with Luke (and with Luke only, Lk. 12:37) a special hope: in the kingdom, Christ the Lord will be a servant and will give food to the elect and blessed ones (*Asc. Isa.* 4:16).[28] The author may have used Luke's redaction or even the parable in its original form.

(i) The *Questions of Bartholomew*, a very strange text (probably second or third century C.E.), seems to rewrite quite freely a chapter from Luke's Gospel. As a way of explaining Jesus' conception the author lets Mary herself tell the story of the annunciation:

> And when they had done that, she began: 'When I lived in the temple of God and received my food from the hand of an angel, one day there appeared to me one in the form of an angel; but his face was indescribable and in his hand he had neither bread nor cup, as had the angel who came to me before. And immediately the veil of the Temple was rent and there was a violent earthquake, and I fell to the earth, for I could not bear the sight of him. But he took me with his

---

[26] There is also the memory of a Zacchaeus in the Pseudo-Clementines; see *Recognitiones*, Preface 14; 1.20.1; 1.21.2; 1.72.3; 1.72.4; 1.73.1; 1.74.1; 2.1.2; 2.19.1; 2.19.3; 3.65.5; 3.66.3; 3.66.4; 3.66.5; 3.67.2; 3.68.1; 3.68.5; 3.74.1; 7.33.3; 9.36.5.
[27] Aland, *Synopsis*, 4, 17; cf. Schneemelcher, *New Testament Apocrypha*, I, 101.
[28] Schneemelcher, *New Testament Apocrypha*, II, 609.

hand and raised me up. And I looked toward heaven; and there came a cloud of dew on my face and sprinkled me from head to foot, and he wiped me with his robe. Then he said to me: 'Hail, you who are highly favored, the chosen vessel.' And then he struck the right side of his garment and there came forth an exceedingly large loaf, and he placed it upon the altar of the Temple, and first ate of it himself and then gave to me also. And again he struck his garment, on the left side, and I looked and saw a cup full of wine. And he placed it upon the altar of the Temple, and drank from it first himself and gave it also to me. And I looked and saw that the bread did not diminish and the cup was as full as before. Then he said: 'Three years more, and I will send my word and you shall conceive my son, and through him the whole world shall be saved. But you will bring salvation to the world. Peace be with you, favored one, and my peace shall be with you forever.' And when he had said this, he vanished from my eyes and the Temple was as before. (*Quest. Bart.* 2:15–21)[29]

(j) The *Epistula apostolorum*, a very old text, combines pseudepigraphy and apocalyptic inspiration from a catholic perspective, to combat Simon and Cerinthus. With this purpose in mind, the author quotes and rewrites quite freely the four gospels, which for him are *not yet canonical*. In a summary of Jesus' miracles the author mentions the story of the woman with a hemorrhage and quotes an utterance of Jesus that is unique to Luke: 'I have noticed that strength went out of me' (Lk. 8:46; *Ep. apost.* 5 [16]).[30] In another passage the author demonstrates knowledge of the birth stories, particularly the annunciation (*Ep. apost.* 14 [25]; cf. Lk. 1:26–35).[31] Here we have a Christian keen to defend orthodox views, possessing good knowledge of the four gospels but not yet regarding them as canonical, holy writings.

(k) Similarly, the scribe who added the long ending to the Gospel of Mark also knew the Gospel of Luke, or its source. In any case, he profits from the story and uses the appearance of the resurrected Christ to the eleven in his effort to provide a conclusion to Mark's Gospel. While the sequence Mark 16:12–13, 14–15 suggests knowledge of our Gospel of Luke, the

---

[29] Schneemelcher, *New Testament Apocrypha*, I, 544–45. Note that in this story there are three years between the annunciation and Jesus' birth, just as in *Prot. Jas.* 8:2 and 12:3.

[30] This story was popular in gnostic circles.

[31] Note also the allusion to Lk. 16:23, the parable of Lazarus and the wicked rich man, in *Ep. Apost.* 27 [38] and the allusion to Lk. 24:37, 39, the resurrection scene where the disciples are encouraged to touch Jesus and verify that he is not a ghost, in *Ep. Apost.* 11 [22]. There is also a passage in *Ep..Apost.* 31 [42] which reveals knowledge of the book of Acts. See finally, in *Ep. Apost.* 35 [46], Jesus' words about the two disciples on the road to Emmaus being slow of heart (Lk. 24:25).

summary of the Emmaus story (Mk. 16:12–13) seems to depend upon a traditional oral narrative.[32]

(l) Apparently in the second century the responsibility of the scribe could cohabit with narrative freedom. Only such a conclusion could account for the many variations within the textual tradition itself. Some scribes used their freedom in a cautious, conservative way, trying to bring Luke's Gospel closer to Matthew's.[33] The most unusual example is found in one of the genealogies: Codex Bezae (siglum 'D' or 05) transforms the Lukan genealogy of Jesus into the Matthean but respects Luke's logic by beginning with Jesus and working backwards. Scribes also liked to develop novel details or episodes; Codex Bezae, for example, supplies an incident in Luke 6:4, where Jesus confronts someone working on the Sabbath day. This tendency is well known, but I would set it within the context of a broad and free movement in the second century, a movement of continual rewriting that actually originated in the first century. And in light of the way Luke used his own sources, he himself is already a witness to this tendency.

(m) A most impressive free use of Luke's Gospel appears in the *Protevangelium of James*. The author's intention was to write the life of Jesus' mother for purposes of defending her virginity.[34] In so doing, he freely integrates the birth stories from both Matthew and Luke:

> And she took the pitcher and went forth to draw water, and behold, a voice said, 'Hail, thou art highly favored, the Lord is with thee, blessed art thou among women.' And she looked around on the right and on the left to see whence this voice came. And trembling she went to her house and put down the pitcher and took the purple and sat down on her seat and drew out (the thread). And behold an angel of the Lord (suddenly) stood before her and said, 'Do not fear, Mary, for you have found grace before the Lord of all things and shall conceive his Word.' When she heard this she doubted in herself and said, 'Shall I conceive of the Lord, the living God, (and bear) as every woman bears?' And the angel of the Lord came and said to her, 'Not so, Mary, for a power of the Lord shall over-shadow you; wherefore also that holy thing which is born of you shall be called the Son of the Highest. And you shall call his name Jesus, for he shall save his people from their sins.' And Mary said, 'Behold, (I am) the handmaid of the Lord before him: be it to me according to your word.'

---

[32] In Mk. 16:12 the two disciples are going εἰς ἀγρόν ('into the country'); in Lk. 24:13 they are going εἰς κώμην ('to a village').

[33] Note the frequent occurrence of the siglum 'p' in the apparatus of the Nestle-Aland edition of the NT.

[34] The oldest known title of this work is γένεσις Μαρίας found in the third-century papyrus Bodmer V.

And she made (ready) the purple and the scarlet and brought (them) to the priest. And the priest took (them) and blessed Mary, and said, 'Mary, the Lord God has magnified your name, and you shall be blessed among all generations of the earth.' And Mary rejoiced, and went to Elizabeth her kinswoman, and knocked on the door. When Elizabeth heard it she put down the scarlet, and ran to the door and opened it, (and when she saw Mary) she blessed her and said, 'Whence is this to me, that the mother of my Lord should come to me? For behold, that which is in me leaped and blessed thee.' But Mary forgot the mysteries which the (arch)angel Gabriel had told her, and raised a sigh toward heaven and said, 'Who am I, (Lord), that all the women (generations) of the earth count me blessed?' And she remained three months with Elizabeth. Day by day her womb grew, and Mary was afraid and went into her house and hid herself from the children of Israel. And Mary was sixteen years old when all these mysterious things happened (to her). (*Prot. James* 11.1–12.3)[35]

(n) The author of the *Infancy Gospel according to Thomas* demonstrates a similar enterprise. His intention is to tell the stories of Jesus as a boy, in order to demonstrate that the divine power was already in him at that time. Chapter 19 of this gospel is present in some of the oldest forms of the text and must be original. It retells the story of Jesus in the temple at the age of twelve (Lk. 2:41–52) with an interesting expansion, a dialogue between the scribes and Mary:

But the scribes and Pharisees said, 'Are you the mother of this child?' And she said, 'I am.' And they said to her, 'Blessed are you among women, because God has blessed the fruit of your womb.' (*Inf. Gos. Thom.* 19:4; cf. Lk. 1:42)[36]

(o) An impressive free usage of gospel writing in the second century is found in the *Apocalypse of Peter*, a text preserved only in Ethiopic. Since it is more than a rewriting – indeed it constitutes a commentary on the text as well as reasoning with the text – we shall return to examine this passage in the second half of this chapter.

(p) The only Greek fragment of the *Diatessaron*[37] (found at Dura Europos) reflects knowledge of Luke 23:49–51 (of the Lukan redaction, and not only of the tradition used by Luke).

(q) *Sibylline Oracles* 8.478–80 gives a three-verse summary of the Lukan story of Jesus' birth:[38]

---

[35] See Schneemelcher, *New Testament Apocrypha*, I, 430–31.
[36] See Schneemelcher, *New Testament Apocrypha*, I, 449.
[37] See Metzger, *Canon*, 115.
[38] Another text, *Odes Sol.* 19, discusses the virgin birth. See Franzmann, *The Odes of Solomon*, 146–52. It is clear that this ode is dependent on Matthew and Luke.

478	And when Bethlehem became the homeland of the Word through God's choice
479	The child, wrapped up in the crib, was presented to those who obey God,
480	Shepherds who look after cows, goats, and lambs.

While one might dismiss this instance on the basis of its late date,[39] it is nevertheless a poetic witness to the continuous narrative power that did not stop with the written form of our canonical New Testament gospels but carried on in both oral and written traditions well into the second century and even later.

Luke as a Normative Text for Preservation and Comment

Irenaeus tells us that the Ebionites used only the Gospel of Matthew, the Valentinians primarily John, and Marcion an amputated version of Luke (*Haer.* 3.11.7). It is not my intention here to concentrate on Marcion, except to mention that his theological mind made more use of philology than exegesis. Even if we are unsure of the extent to which his *Antitheses* attempted an exegetical analysis of Luke,[40] we can be certain that his understanding of the written gospel coincided with a rewriting, not with a scholarly commentary. In one sense Marcion's attitude toward Luke's Gospel was not so different from that of the apocryphal writers – aside from his historical and philological pretensions and his preference for emendation rather than interpolation. Instead of extratextual exegesis, Marcion preferred an implicit understanding, embedded in a manipulation of the text. As it stood after the restoration, after the glosses had been erased, the text was clear – according to him anyway – and did not need any commentary. Marcion was opposed to allegorical interpretation and is not the originator of New Testament exegesis. Having a special, indeed religious, respect for the Gospel of Luke is not the same as intentionally writing commentaries on it. As for Marcion, orthodox Christians may have canonized Luke's Gospel without feeling any need to give a written explanation of it. But as time went on, New Testament exegesis arose. Why?

---

[39] The latest possible date for this part of book 8 is provided by Lactantius (ca. 260 C.E. to ca. 330 C.E.), who quotes from it extensively. But Johannes Geffcken argues for a date toward the end of the second century; see Geffcken, *Komposition und Entstehungszeit*, 44.

[40] Harnack believed Marcion's *Antitheses* contained much exegesis and commentary on his amputated version of Luke; see von Harnack, *Marcion*, 76. I remain convinced that it was more doctrinal in nature.

The *Acts of Peter* provides a double clue to the answer to this question. First, the work attests – as does Justin Martyr's *First Apology* 67.3, written about the same time – to the liturgical reading of New Testament texts during Christian worship, followed by someone preaching upon the same text. Thus in *Acts of Peter* 20,[41] as Peter enters the house of Marcellus he comes upon some Christians reading the story of Jesus' transfiguration in 'the gospel,' and so begins to expound upon the text and explain the significance of that event. Within the context of the second century (cf. 2 Peter), the sermon served a polemical purpose. Liturgical necessity together with polemics kindled oral comment on the New Testament, and particularly on Luke's Gospel.

But there was another reason for the production of the first Christian exegeses, especially in written form: the divergences among the gospels. As soon as a plurality of gospels[42] was accepted, for ecumenical and ecclesiastical reasons, it became imperative to harmonize their contradictions and differences. A good part of the five books of Papias entitled Λογίων κυριακῶν ἐξηγήσεις[43] may have been devoted to this special exegetical task.

In my commentary on the Gospel of Luke[44] I tried to follow the very rational and – at the same time – fundamentalist explanation that Julius Africanus gives for the divergent genealogies of Jesus in Matthew and Luke.[45] Julius Africanus enlists the aid of an apocryphal family story involving levirate marriage in his effort to harmonize the differences.[46] There is similar reasoning and exegesis in Irenaeus when he tries to harmonize the book of Acts with the Pauline epistles.[47] Irenaeus' conclusion is very similar to that of Julius Africanus, who claims that the gospel is true and there are no contradictions among the different texts. He further states, 'So Paul's preaching and Luke's witness to the apostles are converging and more or less identical.'[48] 'Und die Bibel hat doch recht!'[49]

One archaic way of exegeting Luke's Gospel lay midway between the use of Luke as a source and the use of Luke as normative Scripture. According to this method, exegesis took the form of pseudepigraphical revelation whose beneficiary and witness, supposedly an apostle, provided the right

---

[41] See Schneemelcher, *New Testament Apocrypha*, II, 303–304.
[42] I believe that our four canonical gospels were accepted by several churches ca. 120 C.E.
[43] Eusebius, *Hist. eccl.* 3.39.1.
[44] See Bovon, *Luke 1*, 135.
[45] On Julius Africanus see Eusebius, *Hist. eccl.* 1.7.1–16.
[46] Eusebius, *Hist. eccl.* 1.7.16.
[47] Eusebius, *Hist. eccl.* 3.13.1.
[48] Eusebius, *Hist. eccl.* 3.14.1.
[49] 'And nevertheless the Bible is right!' See Keller, *Und die Bibel hat doch recht.*

interpretation of New Testament traditions. Such an exegetical path was possible in orthodox circles only as long as the gospels were not fully canonical. This phenomenon was actually a transmission of the gospel story into a hermeneutical perspective and was not yet an exegetical explanation of the gospel text. The *Didache*, the *Epistula apostolorum*, and the *Apocalypse of Peter* contain such authoritative apostolic comments on Jesus' teaching. The most impressive case is that found in the *Apocalypse of Peter*.[50]

The framework of this apocalypse is the dialogue between Jesus and his disciples on the Mount of Olives; Matthew 24:3 helps create the scenario. The question that disturbs the disciples (meaning that the church during the author's time asks this question) concerns the parousia and the signs that accompany it. The Savior responds first with the short synoptic parable of a fig tree, where the first leaves announce the coming of summer.[51] After a new question from Peter, the Savior pursues this explanation with a different parable of a fig tree, known only from Luke 13:6–9. Interestingly enough, the author responds to the question with an allegorical interpretation: 'Have you not understood that the fig tree is the house of Israel?' (*Apoc. Pet.* 2). The parable he quotes has a form that is parallel to the one in our canonical Luke, but there are significant differences that seem to imply that he is using the parable at its oral, pre-Lukan level.[52]

Allegorical interpretation is already present in the synoptic tradition itself. The Gospels of Mark, Matthew, and Luke are written witnesses to the application of this method to the oral form of the parables. This method is developed further in the *Apocalypse of Peter*. Later, nothing will prevent the use of allegorical interpretation in exegeting the written form of the gospel.

There is patristic evidence for such an exegesis of the parable of the Good Samaritan. One of Origen's homilies on Luke, preserved in Jerome's Latin translation, remembers the witness of a so-called 'elder.'[53] This man, according to Origen, gave a christological interpretation of the parable,[54] an interpretation shared by Irenaeus, whose respect for the 'elders' is well known. The so-called 'elders,' or πρεσβύτεροι, in the second century may have carried out the first orthodox allegorical interpretation of the gospels.[55]

Another surprise in this study was the discovery that, while the Gospel of John has always been characterized as the favorite among the gnostics, Luke the

---

[50] See Bauckham, 'Two Fig Tree Parables'.

[51] See Mt. 24:32–36; Mk. 13:28–29; and Lk. 21:29–33.

[52] See Schneemelcher, *New Testament Apocrypha*, II, 626.

[53] Origen, *Hom. Luc.* 34.3.

[54] Cf. the catena attributed to Titus of Bostra in Cramer, *Catenae graecorum patrum*, II, 87–88.

[55] In any case Irenaeus regards the elders as the oldest and best interpreters of the NT (*Haer.* 4.26.2).

historian also attracted their attention. Nearly all the gnostic schools had an ongoing interest in Luke's Gospel. According to the Ophites, Elizabeth and Mary represent two ways of human procreation: 'Prounikos functioned through Jaldabaoth – though he was ignorant of what she was doing – and emitted two men, one from the sterile Elizabeth and the other from the Virgin Mary.'[56]

If Carpocrates refused to believe in the gospel birth stories,[57] Ptolemaios tried to respect them while rejecting a strict incarnation.[58] He used a famous explanation: the psychical Christ, son of the demiurge, attested by the prophets, went through Mary 'like water through a pipe.'[59] The Savior, who is pneumatic, came upon him in the form of a dove at baptism.

Irenaeus gives us insight into the gnostic exegesis of Luke's Gospel and specifies that the gnostics applied the biblical passages to events that occurred outside the pleroma but were connected with it.[60] The daughter of Jairus was an image of Achamoth. The lost sheep is also the lost Achamoth, searched for by Christ the shepherd, while the woman looking for her lost drachma is the superior wisdom looking for ἐνθύμησις (intuition). Simeon is a figure of the demiurge, who, at the coming of the Savior, learns that he has to change his location, and so he praises the ἄβυσσος. Anna the prophetess is a figure of Achamoth.

The gnostics considered the numbers twelve and thirty to be significant. They interpreted the story of Jesus at the age of twelve in the temple as the emission of the twelve eons.[61] Other evidence suggests the popularity of this story in the second century.[62] According to Marcos' disciples, the episode demonstrates the way Jesus announced the unknown God. This dangerous interpretation – from an orthodox point of view – had to be refuted: Origen devoted no less than four sermons to this story.

Typical also of the double reception of Luke's Gospel in the second century is the importance attributed to the age of Jesus ('thirty years old') when he begins his ministry. This information is provided only by Luke (3:23). These thirty years are accepted not only by apocryphal writers but also became the foundation for allegorical interpretation among gnostic theologians.[63]

---

[56] Irenaeus, *Haer.* 1.30.11.
[57] Irenaeus, *Haer.* 1.25.1.
[58] Cf. Irenaeus, *Haer.* 1.7.2.
[59] Cf. Tardieu, 'Comme à travers un tuyau'.
[60] Irenaeus, *Haer.* 1.8.2.
[61] Irenaeus, *Haer.* 1.3.2.
[62] See *Inf. Gos. Thom.* 19:1–5 (Schneemelcher, *New Testament Apocrypha*, I, 449–49).
[63] See Irenaeus' discussion of Ptolemaios in *Haer.* 1.1.3 and 3.1. Later, in 1.16.1, Irenaeus chides that the gnostics interpret everything according to numbers.

Other so-called gnostic interpretations that reflect knowledge of Luke's Gospel include the following:

(a) The Roman officer at Capernaum (Mt. 8:5–13//Lk. 7:1–10)[64] is understood as a figure of the demiurge, because he learns his real identity only upon meeting the Savior. The meaning of his statement on obedience and his dialogue with the Savior is that the demiurge will lead the economy of this world to the prescribed moment for the sake of the church he is responsible for and because he knows his future reward: his transfer to the place of the mother.

(b) Jesus' words on reconciliation before two people take their dispute to court (Lk. 12:58–59) have been used by gnostic allegorical interpretation to justify belief in metempsychosis.[65]

(c) Heracleon gave an interesting interpretation of Jesus' teaching on confessing one's faith (Lk. 12:8–9). He attempted to show that the heart is more important than the lips and conviction more decisive than words alone. Orthodox writers accused him of giving this explanation in order to avoid any real confrontation with judges during a time of persecution.[66]

(d) Another logion received special attention: the so-called Johannine passage on mutual knowledge between the Father and the Son (Jn. 10:15; 17:25–26). Several writers of the second century, particularly the gnostics, used a reading from the gospel text (Lk. 10:22; Mt. 11:27) that is different from our canonized version. Our text reads, 'No one knows who the Son is but the Father, and who the Father is but the Son.' The gnostic reading was, 'No one knows who the Father is but the Son, and who the Son is but the Father.' As they read it, they were comforted in their belief that the unknown God was revealed only through the Savior.[67]

(e) The three logia of the call to discipleship in Luke 9:57–62 were used by gnostics to distinguish three human races: the man who receives the reply that 'foxes have their holes …' represents material (*hylic*) humanity; the man who receives the reply to 'leave the dead to bury their dead' represents spiritual (*pneumatic*) humanity; and the man who desires first to go and say goodbye to his family represents living (*psychic*) humanity.[68] But

---

[64] Irenaeus, *Haer.* 1.7.4.

[65] Irenaeus, *Haer.* 1.25.4.

[66] Clement of Alexandria, *Strom.* 4.71–73; see van den Hoek, 'Clement of Alexandria,' esp. 330–31.

[67] See the long discussion by Irenaeus in *Haer.* 1.20.3 and 4.6.1. It is gratifying to see that such an important second-century reading was finally included in the critical apparatus of Nestle-Aland, *Novum Testamentum Graece* at Mt. 11:27 (p. 28); it is, however, still lacking at Lk. 10:22 (p. 192).

[68] Irenaeus, *Haer.* 1.8.3.

while the Lukan text surely lies behind the gnostic interpretation, the gnostic order differs from that which is found in our Luke, indicating that perhaps the gnostic text of Luke had another sequence: Luke 9:57–58 (*hylic*), 61–62 (*psychic*), and 59–60 (*pneumatic*).

(f) According to Irenaeus, some gnostics also used the story of Zacchaeus in their classification of humanity: Jesus' reply ('Make haste and come down, for today I must stay in your house,' Lk. 19:5) was applied to the pneumatic human being.[69]

(g) The gnostics could accept the passion of Jesus but they refused to read it historically. Instead, they understood it allegorically and discovered in it the fate of the one who fell under the passion.[70]

Other gnostic references to Luke could be gathered from the Nag Hammadi Library and Clement's *Excerpts from Theodotus*, but these examples are sufficient to demonstrate the honored position that second-century gnostics gave to the Gospel of Luke. These theologians competed against one another as to the best spiritual, allegorical interpretation of Luke's stories and Jesus' words. Surely such comments were a polemical response against orthodox readings, since Irenaeus systematically reproaches them for several exegetical deficiencies. According to him, the gnostics brought non-canonical materials into their exegesis, twisted the meaning of biblical texts to support their own doctrines, disturbed the sequence of word order in the Scriptures, and freely transferred and transformed the words of the Lord to suit their own purposes. Irenaeus believed that when the Bible is interpreted correctly it is a beautiful mosaic depicting a king. But the gnostics only see an image that looks like a dog or a fox.[71]

Through their allegorical readings, these gnostic readers compelled orthodox readers to ask themselves whether their simple harmonizing exegesis was sufficient and whether their common-sense, plain-meaning explanations could satisfy the intellectual needs of converts. As we have seen, in orthodox circles the second century was also a century of preaching on the gospel's narrative, a century of harmonizing discrepancies between the synoptic gospels and – under the leadership of the 'elders' – a century of allegorical interpretation.

---

[69] Irenaeus, *Haer.* 1.8.3. Irenaeus does not say more about this, and his text remains obscure.

[70] Irenaeus, *Haer.* 2.20.4.

[71] Irenaeus, *Haer.* 2.20.4.

Conclusion

The presence of the Gospel of Luke in the second century is irregular and surprising. The epistles from Paul's disciples and bishops do not show any trace of it. What remains from early apologetical works is silent. Justin Martyr is the first apologist who demonstrates evidence of contact with Luke's Gospel and with Lukan traditions; there is, for example, an allusion to the annunciation in the *First Apology* 33.4–5.[72] In his *Dialogue with Trypho* there are several points of contact with Lukan passages that have no synoptic parallels.[73]

For the words of Jesus, Justin seems to rely not only on our written gospels but also upon an oral tradition that is still alive. The same is probably true for *2 Clement*, as *2 Clement* 4:5 is similar to Luke 13:27 ('Go away, you workers of injustice!'), but it is an oral version of the logion. *2 Clement* 5:2–4 is an apocryphal dialogue between Jesus and Peter that is similar to Luke 10:3 ('I am sending you out like sheep among wolves') and 12:4–5 ('Fear him who after death has power over body and soul'; the wording here differs from our Lukan text). *2 Clement* 6:1 ('No servant can serve two masters') follows the text of Luke 16:13 rather than Matthew 6:24. But most authors and apologists, especially those who were educated and orthodox, suggest no knowledge of the Gospel of Luke until the middle of the second century. None of the Pauline churches reflect any familiarity with it.

The situation was different for storytellers and visionaries, for the authors of gospel harmonies as well as the authors of pseudepigraphical revelations used Luke's Gospel.[74] Among the apocryphal acts of the apostles, the *Acts of Andrew*, the *Acts of John*, the *Acts of Peter*, and the *Acts of Paul* show no indication of contact with Luke's Gospel. Only the *Acts of Thomas*, the youngest of the five, mentions episodes or words known only from the Gospel of Luke; for example, the sending out of the 70 in Luke 10:1 and the logion of Jesus in Luke 9:62 ('No one who sets his hand to the plough ...').[75]

---

[72] See also the following echoes from the synoptic tradition: 'Love your enemies' (*1 Apol.* 15–16); 'Give to Caesar the things that are Caesar's' (*1 Apol.* 15.17); 'He who hears you hears me' (*1 Apol.* 63.3); 'No one knoweth the Father, but the Son' (*1 Apol.* 63.13); 'Things impossible for man are possible for God' (*1 Apol.* 19.6).

[73] E.g., the statement that Elizabeth is barren (*Dial.* 84.4), that Jesus is thirty years old (*Dial.* 88.2), the annunciation to Mary (*Dial.* 100.5), and Herod at the passion (*Dial.* 102.4). In *Dial.* 105.5 Justin quotes Lk. 23:46. In *Dial.* 106 his belief in the prophecy of the Scriptures is similar to that found in Lk. 24:25–27. Massaux (*Influence de l'Évangile de Saint Matthieu*, 556–60) mentions several other passages, in particular *Dial.* 76.6a; 81.4; 100.3; 49.3; and 53.5.

[74] Cf. Massaux, *Influence de l'Évangile de Saint Matthieu*, 329.

[75] *Acts Thom.* 6.3 and 147.1.

It is possible that Marcion received the Gospel of Luke in his homeland of Pontus; in Rome he began reading Paul's epistles. Rome does not seem to know the third gospel until the middle of the century; *1 Clement* and *Hermas* show no knowledge of it at all. Marcion's task was to simplify the gospel into an earlier, more authentic and literal form. The gnostics, who also knew the Gospel of Luke, dared to emphasize strongly the figurative meaning of the parables and to extend an allegorical significance to historical events. In so doing they were the antipode of Marcion.

But what place do we give the scribes who copied Luke's Gospel in the second century?[76] Is Christian-Bernard Amphoux correct in connecting their work with the first orthodox schools of theology in Asia and Egypt?[77] Confronted by various attempts to produce a harmony from the plurality of gospels, the teachers of these schools may have wished for a fixed text of Luke, since they would have rejected gnostic allegories and Marcion's philological equations.

Thus there were two ways of receiving Luke's Gospel in the second century: either as a source for authors wishing to create new stories or as a fixed text for commentators to interpret and explain. And these two categories must be subdivided even further since preachers and theologians often used different methods of exegesis. There are even differences among theologians, since some were attempting to reconcile the four gospels by harmonizing their wording, while others were merely trying to draw spiritual teachings from them through allegorization. Similarly, the storytellers may have had various intentions: some were writing a gospel for their own communities – just as Matthew and Luke were attempting to do – while others who were confronted with our three synoptic gospels or with all four of our canonical Gospels felt compelled to bring them to a unity. Still others added complements to the gospels, filling in the lacunae about the life of Jesus' mother and the childhood of Jesus.

Thus there is evidence that the orthodox reading of Luke's Gospel was established in stages. In its final outcome, such a reading meant to accept the whole gospel and to receive it with the three others; to use the creed[78] as a normative reference point to avoid wild interpretations; to use logic, grammar,[79] and a historical method to ensure the integrity of the text and safeguard its

---

[76] P^4 (the same ms. as P^{64} and P^{67}) probably dates from the third century, as do P^{45} and P^{69}. P^{75} falls between 175–225 C.E.

[77] See Amphoux, 'Les Premières Éditions de Luc, I' and 'Les Premières Éditions de Luc, II,' esp. 48.

[78] That is, the rule of faith received at baptism; see Irenaeus, *Haer.* 1.9.4.

[79] Irenaeus, *Haer.* 3.8.1; Irenaeus uses a philological argument to explain the meaning of the Semitic word 'mammon.'

cohabitation with the other, now canonical, gospels; to explain obscure passages by means of clear passages (that is, not only intertextuality but also intratextuality within the normative Scriptures); and to ask the ancients for help in receiving the spiritual, apostolic meaning of Jesus' teaching. It is only then, 'through the polyphony of the texts,' writes Irenaeus, that 'only one harmonious melody will sound in us, praising in song the God who created everything.'[80]

---

[80] Irenaeus, *Haer.* 2.28.3.

Bibliography

Aland, K., *Synopsis quattuor evangeliorum* (Stuttgart: Deutsche Bibelgesellschaft, 13th edn, 1984)

Allenbach, J., et al., *Biblia patristica* (7 vols.; Paris: Editions du Centre National de la Recherche Scientifique, 1975–91)

Amphoux, C.-B., 'Les Premières Éditions de Luc, I: Le Texte de Luc,' *ETL* 67 (1991), 312–27

—, 'Les Premières Éditions de Luc, II: L'Histoire du Texte au IIe Siècle,' *ETL* 68 (1992), 38–48

Bauckham, R., 'The Two Fig Tree Parables in the *Apocalypse of Peter*,' *JBL* 104 (1985), 269–87

Bieder, W., *Die Apostelgeschichte in der Histoire: Ein Beitrag zur Auslegungsgeschichte des Missionsbuches der Kirche* (Zurich: EVZ Verlag, 1960)

Bovon, F., 'Le Récit Lucanien de la Passion de Jésus (Lc 22–23),' in *The Synoptic Gospels: Source Criticism and the New Literary Criticism* (ed. C. Focant; BETL 110; Leuven: Leuven University Press/Peeters, 1993), 393–423

—, *De Vocatione Gentium: Histoire de l'Interprétation d'Act 10,1–11,18 dans les Six Premiers Siècles* (BGBE 8; Tübingen: Mohr Siebeck, 1967)

—, *Luke 1: A Commentary on the Gospel of Luke 1:1–9:50* (trans. C. Thomas; Hermeneia; Minneapolis: Fortress Press, 2002)

—, *Studies in Early Christianity* (WUNT 161; Tübingen: Mohr Siebeck, 2003)

Brock, S.P., 'The Lost Old Syriac at Luke 1:35 and the Earliest Syriac Terms for the Incarnation,' in W. L. Petersen, *Gospel Traditions in the Second Century: Origins, Recensions, Text, and Transmission* (Christianity and Judaism in Antiquity 3; Notre Dame, IN: University of Notre Dame Press, 1989)

Cramer, J.A., *Catenae graecorum patrum in Novum Testamentum* (8 vols.; Oxford: Oxford University Press, 1844)

Creed, J.M., *The Gospel According to St. Luke: The Greek Text with Introduction, Notes, and Indices* (London: Macmillan, 1957)

Dassmann, E., *Paulus in frühchristlicher Frömmigkeit und Kunst* (Geisteswissenschaften Vorträge/Rheinisch-Westfälische Akademie der Wissenschaften G 256; Opladen: Westdeutscher Verlag, 1982)

France, R.T., and D. Wenham (eds.), *Gospel Perspectives* (6 vols.; Sheffield: JSOT Press, 1980–86)

Franzmann, M., *The Odes of Solomon: An Analysis of the Poetical Structure and Form* (NTOA 20; Fribourg: Universitätsverlag; Göttingen: Vandenhoeck & Ruprecht, 1991)

Geffcken, J., *Komposition und Entstehungszeit der Oracula sibyllina* (TU 23; Leipzig: Hinrichs, 1902), 44.

Gregory, A., *The Reception of Luke and Acts in the Period before Irenaeus: Looking for Luke in the Second Century* (WUNT 2.169; Tübingen: Mohr Siebeck, 2003)

Haenchen, E., *The Acts of the Apostles: A Commentary* (Philadelphia: Westminster Press, 1971)

van den Hoek, A., 'Clement of Alexandria on Martyrdom,' *StPatr* 26 (1993), 324–41, esp. 330–31.

von Harnack, A., *Marcion: Das Evangelium vom fremden Gott: Eine Monographie zur Geschichte der Grundlegung der katholischen Kirche* (TU 45; Leipzig: Hinrichs, 2nd edn, 1924; repr. Darmstadt: Wissenschaftliche Buchgesellschaft, 1960)

Kaestli, J.D., J.M. Poffet, and J. Zumstein, *La Communauté Johannique et son Histoire: La Trajectoire de l'Évangile de Jean aux Deux Premier Siècles* (Geneva: Labor et Fides, 1990)

Keller, W., *Und die Bibel hat doch recht: Forscher beweisen die historische Wahrheit* (Düsseldorf: Econ, 1955)

Koester, H., *Synoptische Überlieferung bei den apostolischen Vätern* (TU 65; Berlin: Akademie Verlag, 1957)

Köhler, W.D., *Die Rezeption des Matthäusevangeliums in der Zeit vor Irenäus* (WUNT 2.24; Tübingen: Mohr Siebeck, 1987)

Lindemann, A., *Paulus im ältesten Christentum: Das Bild des Apostels und die Rezeption der Paulinischen Theologie in der frühchristlichen Literatur bis Marcion* (BHT 58; Tübingen: Mohr Siebeck, 1979)

Massaux, E., *Influence de l'Évangile de Saint Matthieu sur la Littérature Chrétienne avant Saint Irénée* (BETL 75; Leuven: Leuven University Press/Peeters, 1986)

Metzger, B.M., *The Canon of the New Testament* (Oxford: Clarendon Press, 1987), 115.

Nestle-Aland, *Novum Testamentum Graece* (Stuttgart: Deutsche Bibelgesellschaft, 27th edn, 1993)

Pagels, E.H., *The Johannine Gospel in Gnostic Exegesis: Heracleon's Commentary on John* (SBLMS 17; Nashville: Abingdon, 1973)

Peterson, W.L., (ed.), *Gospel Traditions in the Second Century: Origins, Recensions, Text, and Transmission* (Christianity and Judaism in Antiquity 3; Notre Dame, IN: University of Notre Dame Press, 1989)

Poffet, J.M., *La Méthode Exégétique d'Héracléon et d'Origène: Commentateurs de Jn 4: Jésus, la Samaritaine et les Samaritains* (Paradosis 28; Fribourg: Editions Universitaires, 1985)

Schmidt, C., *Gespräche Jesu mit seinen Jüngern nach der Auferstehung: Ein katholisch-apostolisches Sendschreiben des 2. Jahrhunderts* (TU 43; Leipzig: Hinrichs, 1919)

Schneemelcher, W., (ed.), *New Testament Apocrypha* (2 vols.; Louisville: Westminster/John Knox Press, 1991–92)

Sevrin, J.M. (ed.), *The New Testament in Early Christianity* (BETL 86; Leuven: Leuven University Press/Peeters, 1989)

Tardieu, M., '"Comme à travers un tuyau": Quelques remarques sur le mythe valentinien de la chair céleste du Christ', in B. Barc (ed.), *Colloque international sur les textes de Nag Hammadi (Québec, 22–25 août 1978)* (Bibliothèque copte de Nag Hammadi, Études 1; Québec: Les Presses de l'Université Laval, 1981)

Zeller, E., 'Die älteste Überlieferung über die Schriften des Lukas,' *Theologische Jahrbücher* 7 (1848), 528–72

15

Looking for Luke in the Second Century

A Dialogue with François Bovon

Andrew Gregory

François Bovon's discussion of the second-century reception and use of Luke[1] is a helpful resource both for historians and for theologians. Not only does Bovon cover a remarkable breadth of texts in a refreshingly brief compass, he also offers a suggestive and illuminating analysis of the historical evidence that he presents. I have offered my own discussion of the second-century reception of Luke elsewhere,[2] so in what follows I restrict myself to larger methodological and theological issues rather than discussing matters of historical detail or offering close readings of particular passages. As befits the volume and series in which this discussion appears, I concentrate on hermeneutical issues. Two issues are of particular interest. First, the way in which contemporary readers approach early Christian texts in an attempt to determine if and how their authors have drawn on Luke. Second, the way in which such evidence that we may find of that earlier appropriation might impact the way in which Christians seek to read Luke as Scripture today.

My focus is on Luke, but I cannot altogether avoid issues to do with the formation of the New Testament canon and of the transmission of Acts. This is because the evidence strongly suggests that although Luke originated as the first of two volumes, it appears to have been transmitted quite separately from Acts, at least from the time when its transmission may be traced. Few second-century

---

[1] Bovon, 'The Reception and Use of the Gospel of Luke in the Second Century', Chapter 14, above 379–400.

[2] Gregory, *Reception*. The range of texts that I have discussed is not identical to that addressed by Bovon, but the conclusions that each of us reaches are of a broadly similar nature.

Christians may be shown to have been conscious of its status as part of the two-volume work to which modern scholars refer as Luke-Acts.[3]

The following discussion centres on three observations. The first reflects on the method that Bovon has followed in establishing his results, and on the historical and theological issues that this method raises. The second concerns his analysis of his findings in which he differentiates between those who used Luke as a source and those who used Luke as an authoritative document. The third relates to Bovon's suggestion that the orthodox reading of Luke is one in which Luke is read as part of the fourfold gospel. I shall consider each in turn, beginning with the method that Bovon has employed.

What Constitutes Evidence of the Use of Luke in the Second Century?

Luke introduces his narrative with a preface in which he refers to other authors who have already undertaken to compile a narrative of the matters concerning which he writes – 'the things that have been accomplished among us' (Lk. 1:1). He refers to traditions that have come down from those who were 'eyewitnesses and ministers of the word' (1:2), and he suggests that his own narrative or orderly account is dependent on what he has received from them (1:3). Luke also implies that what he is telling Theophilus is not altogether new: his purpose in addressing him and therefore in writing this orderly account is that Theophilus may know the truth concerning the things of which he has already been informed (1:4). Whether Luke implies that he has drawn on the written narratives of his predecessors is unclear, but there is no doubt that he claims to have drawn at least on existing oral traditions. His claim is consistent with the widely accepted axiom that Luke has drawn almost certainly on Mark, and very probably (or perhaps even almost certainly) on Q, a postulated source that Matthew is likely also to have used.[4] It has also been suggested that Luke may have drawn on one or more other sources that are sometimes detected behind his text. These include postulated sources that might lie behind the canticles of the infancy narratives, the single tradition of the travel narrative and also a postulated pre-Lukan passion narrative in addition to that of Mark. In its most

---

[3] Cadbury coined this double title, 'Luke-Acts'. For discussion and references, see Maddox, *Purpose*, 3–6. His reference to Cadbury is on p. 3. For a recent assessment of the unity of the two volumes, see Verheyden, 'Unity'. On the lack of any evidence that the two volumes circulated together in the period before Irenaeus, see Gregory, *Reception* 2–3, 352; cf. below, 410–11.

[4] For an important discussion by one of the leading advocates of the Q hypothesis, see Kloppenborg Verbin, *Excavating Q*.

developed forms, this suggestion has led to the hypothesis of a proto-Luke,[5] and also to the hypothesis of a largely recoverable written source, sometimes referred to as *L*.[6] Such source-critical hypotheses are logically independent of the claims that Luke makes in his preface, but each is consistent with the other. Therefore both the very strong likelihood that Luke drew on written and/or oral traditions and the strong possibility (perhaps the probability) that Luke included in his narrative very little that was not known elsewhere, at least among others with whom he may have shared some of the traditions to which he was privy before he committed them to writing, require that great caution be exercised in seeking to find evidence of the reception and use of Luke in Christian writings of the second century.

We do not know for how long or how widely pre-Lukan written sources and/or traditions may have continued to circulate even after Luke had incorporated some of them into his narrative, so it is possible that parallels to Luke in other early Christian writings are not necessarily allusions to or quotations from Luke. Unless they show clear evidence of Luke's fingerprints, they may come from some of the sources on which he drew. Further, if we grant the possibility that much of what Luke narrates has its basis in events outside his text – that it refers to things which were actually said and done – then it is also possible that others may have known of such sayings and deeds quite apart from any knowledge, direct or indirect, of the narrative of the third gospel.

This is an issue of which Bovon is aware. He notes explicitly that 'the possibility that some second-century authors did not use Luke himself so much as one of his sources should not be dismissed',[7] and he implies that parallels alone are not sufficient to demonstrate a literary dependence between two texts when he appeals to the presence of Lukan redaction in Thomas[8] and in the Dura-Europos fragment[9] to substantiate the case for their dependence on Luke. It appears therefore, at least in these instances, that Bovon makes use of the widely used methodological principle that the use of one text in another may be established most securely when the later text includes material that is thought to originate in the redactional work of the earlier author and therefore cannot be explained on the hypothesis that each has drawn independently on a common tradition or source. This method is not without its limitations,[10] not

---

[5] For a survey and critical assessment of the theory see Harrington, *Passion Narrative*.

[6] For a recent survey of scholarship, and a proposal about the extent of *L*, see Paffenroth, *Story*.

[7] Bovon, 'Reception', 383.

[8] Bovon, 'Reception', 385.

[9] Bovon, 'Reception', 388.

[10] For a full discussion see Gregory, *Reception*, 5–15; and Gregory and Tuckett, 'Method'.

least of which is that the absence in a later text of any redactional material from
an earlier writing is never sufficient reason to conclude that the former is independent of the latter. But should such redactional material be present, this criterion offers extremely strong evidence to suggest that a later text is dependent
on the earlier text to which it is parallel, at least in the instance where such
redactional material is present.

In most of the instances of the use of Luke in second-century writings that
Bovon adduces, these later writings contain material that is parallel to tradition
found only in Luke. This is problematic in the light of the possibility that Luke
may have drawn on earlier sources or traditions, for it is precisely in single tradition that it is most difficult to identify what is tradition and what is redaction.
Bovon does note instances where second-century sources contain words that
are found nowhere else in the New Testament than in Luke, but it is difficult to
see why this indicates dependence on Luke rather than on a postulated source
(assuming that such a hypothesis is granted) unless such words may be shown
not only to be characteristic of Luke but also rare in other literature of the
period, not just in the small sample of writings that were included in the New
Testament.

As Bovon implies in his comments on a motif in a parable that is found in
both Luke and the *Ascension of Isaiah*,[11] identifying what is redactional and what
is not is not always straightforward. But something fundamental is at stake, and
it points to a significant tension in what might be labelled loosely as conservative (and particularly evangelical) approaches to the composition and early
reception of the writings of the gospels.[12] On the one hand, conservative scholars are often keen to emphasize the historical reliability of the gospels, by
which is often understood their historicity, a direct and detailed correspondence between the gospel accounts and the people and events external to but
portrayed in their texts.[13] On the other hand, there is also an apologetic interest
in establishing that the gospels were in circulation at a relatively early date.[14]

---

[11] Bovon, 'Reception', 385, where he notes that the author 'may have used Luke's redaction or even the parable in its original form'.

[12] This critique, I must emphasize, does not apply to the work of François Bovon, but my discussion of issues arising from his chapter offers a convenient and appropriate place in which to introduce it.

[13] E.g., C. Blomberg, *Historical Reliability of the Gospels* and *Historical Reliability of John's Gospel*. For an argument that the authority of the New Testament is not dependent on historicist notions of historical reliability, see Greene, 'Taking Soundings'.

[14] E.g., the claim of Baker (*Two Testaments,* 34): 'For the Apostolic Fathers the two Testaments formed one Bible. Both Old and New Testaments were accepted as Scripture, though the limits of the canon had not yet been finally defined'. See also Bock, *Luke,* 5, who presents as if it were uncontroversial the claim that Luke was alluded to by *1 Clement.* Cf. Gregory, *Reception,* 125–29.

The former conviction logically implies that any number of sources or traditions might witness to an event or to a saying if it originated in a public context and was retold by different individuals who witnessed or were informed of it, whereas the latter conviction often appears to drive those who are keen to establish that the presence of materials parallel to Luke or to another gospel indicate the influence of that text. A case in point is the story of a resurrection appearance recounted in Ignatius of Antioch's letter to the Smyrneans. Its affinities with the resurrection appearance recounted in Luke 24 are clear, but its differences are also significant. Therefore I am convinced that this passage is not evidence of the use of Luke, at least in the form that we know it.[15] Thus this is a further example of an instance in which Bovon[16] and I agree in the negative results that we reach in our respective discussions of the reception of Luke.[17] Bishop Lightfoot's words are apposite, for they restate rather than resolve the issue: 'The reference [in Ignatius] is plainly to the same incident which is related in Luke xiv.36 ... The words however, in which it is told, are different.'[18]

What, then, are we to make of second-century parallels to Lukan single tradition or to other material found only in his account of the synoptic tradition? On a historical-critical level, the problem is how we assess the degree to which Luke as an author has shaped or composed the material that he shares with neither Matthew nor Mark. If such material originates with Luke, then 'parallels' in later texts may reflect dependence on his account. If Luke reproduces earlier traditions, such 'parallels' may reflect the independent use of shared traditions, not the dependence of a later author on Luke. Both possible conclusions are illustrated in Bovon's discussion, insofar as there are some instances where he attributes parallels to Lukan single tradition to the use of shared traditions, but others where he attributes such parallels to the use of Luke itself.[19] But much more significant on a wider hermeneutical level is the challenge that this

[15] For a full defence of this conclusion see Gregory, *Reception*, 70–75.
[16] Bovon notes that 'Ignatius of Antioch seemed to be unacquainted with Luke's Gospel' ('Reception', 382, n. 16); and in the previous note ('Reception', 382, n. 15) he refers the reader to an earlier publication, noting that Ignatius may be one of a number of patristic witnesses who refer not to Luke's account of the appearance of the risen Jesus, but to the source on which he draws. Cf. 'Reception' n. 31, where Bovon finds that the author of the *Epistula Apostolorum* alludes to Luke 24:37, 39, not to its source.
[17] But see below, where I emphasize that I understand a negative result to mean an instance where the evidence available is not sufficient to demonstrate the use of Luke, not that it is possible to demonstrate that a given author did not know Luke.
[18] Lightfoot, *Apostolic Fathers*, 294.
[19] For the former, see Bovon, 'Reception', 383, on the Gospel of Peter; for the latter, 'Reception', 383, on the Gospel of the Nazarenes.

difficulty raises for readers who wish to reflect on how they form their conclusions, or perhaps their presuppositions, about the degree to which the single tradition of an evangelist is considered to originate in the theological creativity of that author or in the use of sources or traditions that other evangelists either did not know or did not use.

It may appear conservative, at least to a Protestant, whose attitude to tradition may be very different from that of a Roman Catholic, to assume that second-century parallels to Lukan single tradition imply the early use of that gospel, for the former may be much less willing to rely on apostolic tradition than on texts later considered to be Scripture.[20] Yet such a presumption logically implies that Lukan single tradition should be treated as if it originates largely in Luke's own creative composition, not in the way in which he shapes and presents traditions that he has received of incidents or teaching from the ministry of Jesus. This is a conclusion with which those of more conservative instincts may be very uncomfortable. If Luke's single tradition is not his own composition in the strongest sense of that term, arguing for the use of Luke on account of early parallels with his single tradition is very difficult indeed. I agree with Bovon that we cannot demonstrate that many second-century authors knew Luke, and I am perhaps more cautious than he is on this question. But the fact that second-century authors may not leave evidence that allows us to demonstrate their use of Luke does not mean that they did not use it.[21]

This is a point that I cannot emphasize enough. Some scholars have inferred that their inability to demonstrate the presence of redactional material from an earlier text in a later one means that they can argue that the later author was unaware of the earlier writing, but this is an argument from silence. It is an inappropriate use of the criterion, but it does remind us of the limitations on its use. Just because modern scholars are unable to demonstrate that an ancient author was familiar with an earlier text does not allow us to infer that he was

---

[20] For a classic expression of a Roman Catholic perspective on tradition and its relationship to Scripture, see Congar, *Tradition and Traditions*. The official position of the Roman Catholic Church is presented in the *Catechism*, 23–26, §§73–84. Important recent evangelical re-engagements with tradition include Williams, *Retrieving* and *Evangelicals and Tradition*. Still important is Bruce, *Tradition*.

[21] Cf. Bovon, 'Reception', 382, n. 16. I agree that *1 Clement* and *Hermas* evince no knowledge of Luke, but this need not imply that they did not know it – though the use of what appears to be a non-canonical source of synoptic tradition in *1 Clement* indicates that he saw no need to draw on either Matthew or Luke's version of these sayings if he was aware of them (see above, n. 14). Something similar applies to Ignatius, for his use of a source parallel to but distinct from Luke suggests that he felt no compunction to use Luke's version of this incident if in fact he knew it (see above). I am agnostic about whether or not Polycarp knew Luke, but I see no positive reason to believe that he did so (see Gregory, *Reception*, 129–36).

not. Perhaps the ignorance of which we should be most certain is our own, and there is virtue in acknowledging that we may have reached a point beyond which we cannot go on the basis of such evidence and critical methods as are currently available.

Luke as a Source or as an Authoritative Text?

Bovon suggests that there are two main ways in which the early use of Luke might be classed: as a source for authors wishing to create new stories;[22] or as a normative, authoritative and fixed text for commentators to preserve and explain.[23] In between these approaches is another that appeals to a pseude-pigraphical revelation as the basis for the correct interpretation of Lukan traditions.[24] Bovon suggests that this appeal to pseudepigraphical revelation was possible in orthodox circles only so long as the gospels were not canonical, and he implies that this was true also of those who treated Luke 'merely' as a source. Both approaches stand in contrast to those instances where Luke appears to be treated as an authoritative text that might be said in some sense to be evidence of its reception as Scripture or as part of an emerging canon. The distinction is suggestive, but I wonder whether questions might be raised not only about the evidence on which it is based but also about the terminology with which it is expressed. Is it clear that there is enough evidence to say that some authors used Luke as a source rather than as an authoritative text, since (as we have seen) most of the evidence for this type of use is drawn from parallels between single tradition in Luke and in later sources that might be explained on the basis of the latter using sources or traditions shared with Luke rather than using Luke itself? If such parallels are not strong evidence for the use of Luke, it may be more accurate to make the more cautious claim that such parallels with Luke indicate that the authors of these texts show an interest in the world 'behind the Lukan text'[25] rather than in Luke as a source.

This is not only perhaps a more accurate if less precise description of the phenomena that Bovon observes, but it also leaves open the question of which other authors gained access to the world behind the Lukan text by means of Luke itself, and which gained access to that world by means of sources and tra-ditions on which Luke himself might also have drawn. This primary interest in

---

[22] Bovon, 'Reception', 382. Cf. Bovon, 'Reception', 382, where he refers to Luke understood '*merely* as a source for further narration' (emphasis mine).

[23] Bovon, 'Reception', 382, 389–94.

[24] Bovon, 'Reception', 390f.

[25] Here I refer to the events external to the text to which its author claims that it refers, not to the preoccupations or agenda of its author.

the world behind the text – the story of Jesus in general rather than the particular form in which that story and impact is portrayed by one particular evangelist – might then be contrasted with those who treated Luke as an authoritative text, and who might therefore be characterized as being interested in the world of the text itself. The former, to use Bovon's terminology, are storytellers who draw on Luke or his sources (or a combination of both) in order to inform their own retelling of stories about Jesus and his disciples, whereas the latter are those for whom Luke may be seen to have become an authoritative document and therefore something to be preserved and interpreted.

If it is correct that those whom Bovon characterizes as being interested in Luke merely as a source are in fact primarily interested in the story of Jesus and of his impact on those who followed him, rather than in any records of that impact as a means in themselves, it is hardly surprising that they would show little clear and indisputable evidence of the use of Luke in their writings. This would not mean that their use of Luke is precluded,[26] but it would suggest that their primary interest in the story of Jesus would encourage them to draw on whatever sources were available – Luke, his sources, or quite independent traditions – and to reorder them in the light of their own interests and concerns. While on one level that might be following the practice that Luke himself claims to have adopted (cf. Luke 1:1–4), there is little evidence to suggest that such writers had any consciousness of Luke as a text. We cannot be confident that they had any consciousness of Luke as a fixed, distinct and continuous text rather than as one of many collections of material to do with Jesus nor, even if they did know such a narrative *in extenso*, that they associated it with Luke or that they used his name as part of its title. Nor, therefore, do we know if they associated it with Paul if such associations depend on the identification of Luke as author of Acts and companion of Paul.

Debates continue as to when gospels were first called gospels and when the traditional names of the evangelists were associated with each text,[27] but even the bookish Justin Martyr, whose knowledge of Luke seems clear, never refers to it by its traditional title,[28] just as he does not refer to that of any of the other gospels. That his preferred title 'memoirs of the apostles' is co-extensive with those texts to which he refers also as gospels seems clear, but we do not know what individual titles he would have used to differentiate between individual

---

[26] See above, n. 21.

[27] Gregory, *Reception*, 45–53.

[28] Bock's claim (*Luke,* 5) that Justin 'speaks of Luke writing a "memoir of Jesus"' in Dialogue 103 may be a legitimate inference from this text, but it certainly goes beyond what Justin states explicitly. Nor does Justin note that any of the evangelists were associates of Paul – only that some were followers of the apostles. The first references to a written gospel explicitly associated with the name of Luke come in Irenaeus and in the Muratorian Fragment. See Gregory, *Reception*, 32–54, esp. 45–54.

gospels, nor whether the gospels that he used included other texts in addition to Matthew, Mark, Luke and (perhaps) John. Even Marcion, whose exclusive use of something similar to an abbreviated form of Luke is not to be denied, appears to have referred to that text only as the gospel, not as a gospel in any way associated with or according to Luke.

It is possible, of course, to use a text without any knowledge of the identity of its author, and it is possible that those who first show any signs of interest in Luke as a text may have done just that: they may have used our third gospel, but not under our title, the Gospel according to Luke (nor, perhaps, were they even aware of any association at all with Luke). We do not know which, if any, of the so-called Gnostics whose early use of Luke Bovon discusses knew the text under its traditional name, but their interest in Luke as a text rather than as a window onto the world behind that text seems clear. Thus their interest in numerology demonstrates an interest in the text as a resource out of which or into which to read theological concerns, for their theological concerns are grounded in the details of the text rather than in an appeal to, and interpretation of, external events that it claims to narrate. But the very fact that it is so-called Gnostics whose interest in the text may be demonstrated at an early stage is important. It is not necessarily that Gnostics were the first to use Luke, as it is sometimes claimed that they were the first to use John.[29] Rather, they were among the first to use Luke in such a bookish or exegetical way that we can see clear signs of their use and be confident that the focus of their interest was Luke as a text rather than his sources or the story that he portrays. Here we see a link with my earlier observations on method, for it is only when second-century Christians use Luke in such a way as to reveal dependence on his text rather than on what might lie behind that text that we can be confident that it was Luke that they used.

Yet there is also a further conclusion that might be drawn. Namely, interest in Luke as a text in its own right rather than as an authoritative witness to the world behind the text to which it testifies may be to understand and to appropriate the text in a way that is at odds with its author's explicit statement of the purpose for which he composed his account. Thus whereas Luke's preface makes clear that his narrative was intended to show its readers the truth concerning the things of which they had already been informed (Lk. 1:4), subsequent use of Luke as a text from which to extract hidden meanings suggests that it could become an obstacle to the understanding of Jesus that Luke claimed to have received from others and to preserve in his written account. This may seem a surprising conclusion, especially to those who today would value the canonical gospels as a primary place of encounter with the living Lord to whom

---

[29] For an important and powerful response to this perception, see Hill, *Johannine Corpus*.

they bear witness. But it is a salutary reminder that he is to be found not in the text but behind the text, and that a Christian reading of Luke must treat it as pointing to something behind its text rather than as an end in itself. Here we are reminded that our reading of Luke cannot be the same as that of second-century Christians, indebted to them though we are for the transmission of this text. The very fact that it is so difficult to tell whether so many second-century parallels with Luke are evidence of interest in his narrative or in the world behind his text indicates that this was a time when the text of the gospels was not yet 'between' Christians and their understanding of Jesus, for theirs was a period when texts such as Luke were recognized to be authoritative precisely because they were in agreement with the living and apostolic tradition, not vice versa. Luke was already aware of the need to preserve in writing the story of Jesus for others like him who were not eyewitnesses of Jesus' ministry from his baptism to his ascension (Acts 1:21–22; Luke 1:1–4), but yet more time would pass before his narrative and others like it would become the primary means by which the story of Jesus' life and its significance would be transmitted to posterity.

This conclusion leads neatly to my third point of engagement with Bovon's discussion of the reception of Luke, namely, its emergence and subsequent transmission as part of the fourfold gospel.

Luke as Part of the Fourfold Gospel

The final emergence of an orthodox reading of Luke, notes Bovon, included the key requirements that it be read in its entirety and as part of the fourfold gospel, and that it be interpreted in light of the rule of faith.[30] This is first clearly, explicitly and unambiguously evident in the writings of Irenaeus,[31] and in the approximately contemporary Muratorian Fragment.[32] Irenaeus notes that Luke is the first of a two-volume work – and he is the first identifiable author who can be shown to have done so, though it seems unlikely that this connection was lost on Theophilus or the other earlier readers to whom Luke first offered his work – but he presents it as one part of the fourfold gospel. The author of the Muratorian Fragment does likewise, referring to Luke as the third

---

[30] Bovon, 'Reception', 396, with particular reference to n. 78. For one contemporary application of the rule of faith in contemporary hermeneutics, see Wall, 'Reading'.

[31] For arguments for an earlier origin, see Stanton, 'Fourfold Gospel'; Hengel, *Four Gospels*, summarized in 'Four Gospels'. In support of a late second-century date, Bovon, 'Synoptic Gospels'.

[32] For a recent and substantial defence of its traditional (second-century) date, see J. Verheyden, 'Canon Muratori'.

of four gospels, turning next to the fourth gospel, and only then introducing Acts, which he also ascribes to Luke.[33] We cannot be certain whether or not its testimony is independent of that of Irenaeus, but the similarities between the two are clear. A single author writes Luke and Acts, but each is placed independently of the other in the collection of authoritative texts that Irenaeus and the author of the Muratorian Fragment each discuss.

The end of the second century and the beginning of the third is also the period from which our manuscript evidence for the New Testament begins to emerge, and the evidence of these remains is consistent with the evidence from Irenaeus and the Muratorian Fragment, although again it is difficult to know whether their evidence is independent of that of Irenaeus and his insistence on one fourfold gospel. P^{75} (usually dated late second or early third century) and P^4, P^{64}, P^{67} (probably third century) each contain fragments of Luke and are usually thought to have come from a codex that contained the fourfold gospel. P^{45} (also probably third century) contains the fourfold gospel and Acts.[34] Thus the physical remains of these manuscripts cohere with the accounts of Irenaeus and the Muratorian Fragments in rejecting not only Marcion and others who read only one gospel, but also Tatian and others who compiled harmonies such as the *Diatessaron*. Thus Luke as it is known to modern readers is available only as it has been transmitted within the fourfold gospel: not as a text that circulated independently by itself or even as part of a two-volume work by one author. It may be only an accident of history that we have no direct access to Luke in any form earlier than the form in which it was transmitted as part of the fourfold gospel – there is no reason to believe that earlier 'stand alone' copies were ever suppressed – but the point remains that Luke as it has been transmitted to us has been transmitted only as part of a construct of the second-century church.[35] Further, as Bovon perhaps implies, this was a construct that arose because the four gospels to which it gave such privileged status were considered to be in accord with the rule of faith to which they may have contributed but by which they were also judged.

This is a point of the utmost importance. Just as Luke is a narrative written on the basis of what was handed down to its author by those who were eyewitnesses and ministers of the word, so the form and context in which Luke has been transmitted to subsequent generations depends on decisions made by subsequent Christians who decided that his portrait of Jesus was in harmony with others that presented an authentic presentation and interpretation of the impact that Jesus of Nazareth made on those who followed him by his life, his death

---

[33] On the Muratorian Fragment and its testimony to Luke and Acts see Gregory, *Reception*, 40–43.

[34] See Gregory, *Reception*, 27–32.

[35] See Gregory, 'Oral and Written Gospel?', 7–8.

and his resurrection. Just as Jesus lived, died and rose before the gospels were
written, so already there was a living tradition – an early rule of faith? – on
which Luke drew in order to write his orderly account and on account of
which his gospel was considered to be one of four authoritative narrative testaments to Jesus as he was remembered, understood and worshipped by those
who followed him. This is not merely to make the historical point that the
canonical gospels are our only primary sources of historical evidence about
Jesus that go beyond the skeletal outline that may be drawn from the letters of
Paul,[36] nor that those gospels are available only as they were transmitted in the
context of the fourfold gospel from the late second century. Both points are
important, but they may be made within a theological context that affirms that
neither presents any historical or theological obstacle to those who would continue to use these texts as evidence for the life and teachings of Jesus of Nazareth and as a source of encounter with the living Jesus today. Christian faith is
based on beliefs concerning what God has done in the Jesus to whom the fourfold gospel is a primary witness, not on an ever-changing historical Jesus who is
a construct of different phases in contemporary scholarship.[37] Certainly the
Christian faith claims that there is continuity between Jesus born of Mary and
Jesus who was raised from the dead and remains alive today, but the two are not
the same, and neither is identical to the historical Jesus whose life and teachings
historians seek to reconstruct today.

The Jesus on whom Christian faith in God is centred and based is the Jesus
testified to by Luke and the other evangelists whose writings were recognized
as consistent and in continuity with the faith of those to whom the risen Lord
first appeared. Thus although the fourfold gospel emerges clearly only in the
latter half of the second century, nevertheless the Jesus to whom it bears witness
is the same Jesus whose impact gave rise to the living traditions which these
four gospels were recognized to preserve, to articulate, to safeguard and to
transmit. There was an oral gospel before there were written gospels, and there
was a continuing oral gospel and developing rule of faith before the fourfold
gospel, of which Luke is a part, can be shown clearly to have been established.

---

[36] Here I assume that other gospels that were not included in the canon were probably
   written later than the canonical texts, and that they derive at least in part from them.
   This does not preclude the possibility that some non-canonical gospels may be our
   only source of some traditions that do go back to Jesus or to his earliest followers, but
   such 'authentic' traditions that they might contain are unlikely to alter substantially
   what can be known of Jesus from the accounts in the fourfold gospel. For fuller
   defences of the primacy of the four canonical gospels, especially the synoptics, as
   sources for the historical Jesus, see Meier, *Marginal Jew*, 112–66; and (with some
   slight qualifications) Charlesworth and Evans, 'Jesus'. Klauck, *Apocryphal Gospels*,
   offers an excellent discussion of many non-canonical gospels.
[37] Johnson, *Real Jesus*.

Thus the establishment of the fourfold gospel is not only a constraint upon the number of windows through which those who maintain the faith of the great church may look in their search for authentic Christian testimony to Jesus[38] but also a constraint upon the pool of evidence available for the non-confessional historian whose interest is in Jesus rather than in the early Christians who in the second century fashioned new accounts of some or all of his impact.[39] But it is not only a historical constraint, for it offers also an opportunity for continuing theological reflection, not least the recognition that the fourfold gospel is both a historical construct and a theological necessity.[40] It is not only that we have few other early and reliable witnesses to Jesus to whose testimony we may turn; it is also that this is what has been bequeathed to us by the great church, such that those who claim to stand in its traditions can read Luke within the fourfold gospel not as a constraint but as a gift.[41]

---

[38] 'When is a gospel not "Gospel"? when it is a set of Jesus traditions out of kilter with the faith of the church' (so Stanton, *Jesus*, 4).

[39] Even if early Christian beliefs about which gospels were authentic witnesses to Jesus were mistaken, nevertheless such beliefs have had profound consequences for which texts have been preserved until today.

[40] Cullmann, 'Plurality', 50.

[41] Stanton, 'Fourfold Gospel', 341–46; repr. (with minor revisions) in *Jesus*, 86–91; Burridge, *Four Gospels*; Morgan, 'Hermeneutical Significance'.

Bibliography

Baker, D.L., *Two Testaments, One Bible: A Study of the Theological Relationship between the Old and the New Testaments* (Leicester: InterVarsity Press, 1991)

Blomberg, C., *The Historical Reliability of the Gospels* (Leicester: InterVarsity Press, 1987)

—, *The Historical Reliability of John's Gospel* (Leicester: InterVarsity Press, 2001)

Bock, D.L., *Luke 1:1 – 9:50* (BECNT; Grand Rapids: Baker Books, 1994)

Bovon, F., 'The Synoptic Gospels and the Non-Canonical Acts of the Apostles', *HTR* 81 (1988) 19–36

Bruce, F.F., *Tradition Old and New* (Exeter: Paternoster, 1973)

Burridge, R.A., *Four Gospels, One Jesus?* (London: SPCK, 1994)

Catechism of the Catholic Church (London: Geoffrey Chapman, rev. edn, 1999)

Charlesworth, J.H., and C.A. Evans, 'Jesus in the Agrapha and the Apocryphal Gospels', in *Studying the Historical Jesus: Evaluations of the State of Current Research* (ed. B. Chilton and C.A. Evans; Leiden: E.J. Brill, 1994)

Congar, Y.M.-J., *Tradition and Traditions: An Historical and a Theological Essay* (London: Burns & Oates, 1966)

Cullmann, O., 'The Plurality of the Gospels as a Theological Problem in Antiquity', in *The Early Church* (ed. A.J.B. Higgins; London: SCM Press, 1956)

Greene, C.J.D., 'Taking Soundings: History and the Authority of Scripture: A Response to Peter van Inwagen', in *'Behind' the Text': History and Biblical Interpretation* (ed. C. Bartholomew, C.S. Evans, M. Healy, and M. Rae; SHS 4; Carlisle: Paternoster; Grand Rapids: Zondervan, 2003), 131–40

Gregory, A., *The Reception of Luke and Acts in the Period before Irenaeus: Looking for Luke in the Second Century* (WUNT 2.169; Tübingen: Mohr Siebeck, 2003)

—, 'An Oral and Written Gospel? Reflections on Remembering Jesus', *ExpTim* 116 (2004), 7–12

—, and C. Tuckett, 'What Constitutes the Use of the New Testament in the Apostolic Fathers? Reflections on Method', in *The Reception of the New Testament in the Apostolic Fathers* (ed. A. Gregory and C. Tuckett; Oxford: Oxford University Press, 2005)

Harrington, J.M., *The Lukan Passion Narrative: The Markan Material in Luke 22,54–23,25. A Historical Survey: 1891–1997* (NTTS 30; Leiden: E.J. Brill, 2000)

Hengel, M., *The Four Gospels and the One Gospel of Jesus Christ* (London: SCM Press, 2000)

—, 'The Four Gospels and the One Gospel of Jesus Christ', in *The Earliest Gospels: The Origins and Transmission of the Earliest Christian Gospels – The Contribution of the Chester Beatty Gospel Codex P45* (ed. C. Horton; London: T&T Clark, 2004)

Hill, C.E., *The Johannine Corpus in the Early Church* (Oxford: Oxford University Press, 2004)

Johnson, L.T., *The Real Jesus: The Misguided Quest for the Historical Jesus and the Truth of the Traditional Gospels* (New York: HarperSanFransisco, 1996)

Klauck, H.J., *Apocryphal Gospels: An Introduction* (London: T&T Clark, 2003)

Kloppenborg Verbin, J.S., *Excavating Q: The History and Setting of the Sayings Gospel* (Edinburgh: T&T Clark, 2000)

Lightfoot, J.B., *The Apostolic Fathers: Clement, Ignatius, and Polycarp. Revised Texts with Introductions, Notes, Dissertations, and Translations*, II.2 (London: MacMillan, 1889–90; Peabody, MA: Hendrickson, repr. 1989)

Maddox, R., *The Purpose of Luke-Acts* (Edinburgh: T&T Clark, 1982)

Meier, J.P., *A Marginal Jew: Rethinking the Historical Jesus, I: The Roots of the Problem and the Person* (New York: Doubleday, 1991)

Morgan, R., 'The Hermeneutical Significance of Four Gospels', *Int* 33 (1979), 376–88

Paffenroth, K., *The Story of Jesus according to L* (JSNTSup 147; Sheffield: Sheffield Academic Press, 1997)

Stanton, G.N., 'The Fourfold Gospel' *NTS* 43 (1997) 317–46, on 341–46; repr. (with minor revisions) in Jesus and Gospel (Cambridge: Cambridge University Press, 2004)

—, *Jesus and Gospel* (Cambridge: Cambridge University Press, 2004)

Verheyden, J., 'The Unity of Luke-Acts: What Are We Up To?', in *The Unity of Luke-Acts* (BETL 142; Leuven: Leuven University Press/Peeters, 1999)

—, 'The Canon Muratori: A Matter of Dispute', in *The Biblical Canons* (ed. J.-M. Auwers and H.J. De Jonge; BETL 163; Leuven: Leuven University Press/ Peeters, 2003)

Wall, R., 'Reading the Bible from within our Traditions: The "Rule of Faith" in Theological Hermeneutics', in *Between Two Horizons: Spanning New Testament Studies and Systematic Theology* (ed. J.B. Green and M. Turner; Grand Rapids/ Cambridge: Eerdmans, 2000)

Williams, D.H., *Retrieving the Tradition and Renewing Evangelicalism: A Primer for Suspicious Protestants* (Grand Rapids: Eerdmans, 1999)

—, *Evangelicals and Tradition: The Formative Influence of the Early Church* (Grand Rapids: Baker Books, 2005)

16

Illuminating Luke

The Third Gospel in Italian Renaissance and Baroque Painting

Heidi J. Hornik and Mikeal C. Parsons

Introduction

This chapter is part of a larger three-volume project entitled *Illuminating Luke*. In this larger study we have identified scenes unique to the Gospel of Luke which were also popular subjects during the Italian Renaissance and Baroque periods (1300–1700).[1] The methodology we employ is stylistic, historical and hermeneutical. The stylistic and historical dimensions require assessing the object's formal features, as well as situating it within its historical and cultural contexts. To understand the meaning of the symbolism, or iconography, in religious painting it is necessary to discover the sources and precedents of these elements, as well as to attend to how the artist and the audience appropriated this culturally conditioned symbolism in their interpretation of both the visual image and the biblical scene which it depicts.

Our methodology is also explicitly hermeneutical. We are interested in how this 'visual exegesis' might enrich our understanding of Luke's Gospel. Several generations of biblical scholars have been trained in the 'two-step'

---

[1] Earlier versions of sections of this chapter (from the Introduction and Leonardo) appeared in Heidi J. Hornik and Mikeal C. Parsons, *Illuminating Luke: The Infancy Narrative in Italian Renaissance Painting* (Valley Forge, PA: Trinity Press International, 2003) and used with the permission of Morehouse Publishing, and some of the material on Caravaggio appeared in *Christian Scholars Review* 28.4 (1999), 561–85, copyright 1999 by Christian Scholar's Review; reprinted by permission. Appreciation is expressed to the editors of these publications for permission to use those materials in the present chapter.

hermeneutic of 'what it meant/what it means.'[2] In this model, the biblical scholar explicated what a biblical text meant in its original context, and the theologian, building on these insights, discerned what the text now means in contemporary terms. Among the many difficulties with this model is the fact that this construal has operated from the assumption that we need only understand the context of the first century in which most New Testament texts were produced and the twentieth century in which these texts are read.[3] Between the original communication, 'what it meant,' and the contemporary interpretive context, 'what it means,' however, lies a largely neglected element, 'what it *has* meant' at critical moments in the text's reception history. Scholars today including Brevard Childs and David Steinmetz write of the importance of patristic, mediaeval, and reformation hermeneutics, but they have limited their vision to literary texts.[4]

We propose to include examples of visual interpretations as part of the *Nachleben*, the 'afterlife' (what Thiselton calls the 'post-history') of these stories as they are reconfigured for a different time and place. Of course, we are not the first to examine visual depictions of religious art for their theological content. The efforts of Jaraslov Pelikan and Margaret Miles, for example, to track the development of the Christian tradition through analysis of both verbal *and* visual texts have been rightly lauded, but unfortunately seldom followed.[5] One exception is the recent work of John Drury, who examines the religious meaning of various works of art from the National Gallery, London.[6] Our project, while deeply indebted to the approach of Pelikan and Miles, differs from theirs and Drury's in scope and emphasis. We attempt to trace portrayals of individual artists of specific scenes unique to Luke's Gospel. This limited scope has enabled us to examine our topic in much more detail, and it hopefully has prevented us from making some of the overgeneralizations often associated with such interdisciplinary studies.

By seeking to reclaim visual aspects and material culture of the historic Christian tradition, we seek to join the larger project aimed at retrieving the larger historic and catholic tradition for contemporary liturgical practice and theological reflection, especially among the heirs of the Free Church tradition.[7]

---

[2] See Stendahl, 'Biblical Theology, Contemporary,' 1.432; also his recent reaffirmation of this approach in *Meanings*.
[3] See also Sugirithajah, *Voices from the Margin*, for another critique of this model.
[4] See Childs, 'The *Sensus Literalis* of Scripture,' 80–93; Steinmetz, 'The Superiority of Pre-critical Exegesis,' 65–77.
[5] See Pelikan, *Jesus through the Centuries* and Miles, *Image as Insight*.
[6] Drury, *Painting the Word*.
[7] See, e.g., the following series: The Church's Bible project by Robert Wilken et al., the Ancient Commentary on Christian Scripture by Tom Oden et al., and especially the work of our colleague Daniel H. Williams, *Retrieving the Tradition*.

We also join the growing number of scholars interested in the reception history and the *Wirkungsgeschichte* of the biblical text and the way this 'history of influence' shapes our contemporary reading of Scripture.[8]

Luke is an appropriate subject, not only because it contains some of the most vivid and memorable scenes in the New Testament (think, for example, of the Parables of the Good Samaritan and the Prodigal Son), but also because from early on in the Christian tradition, Luke was believed to be a painter himself, having painted a 'true picture' of the Virgin Mary and subsequently was known as the patron saint of painters. In some cases, the traditions of Luke as physician and painter coalesced in a most remarkable way around the image of the Virgin and Child in S. Maria Maggiore.[9] In the *Golden Legend*, Jacobus de Voragine (1229–98) reports that St. Gregory the Great (ca. 540–604) carried St. Luke's portrait of the Virgin through the city streets in an effort to stop the plague (Figure 1, p. 420):

> The plague was still ravaging Rome, and Gregory ordered the procession to continue to make the circuit of the city, the marchers chanting the litanies. An image of the blessed Mary ever Virgin was carried in the procession. It is said that this image is still in the church of Saint Mary Major in Rome, that it was painted by Saint Luke, who was not only a physician but a distinguished painter, and that it was a perfect likeness of the Virgin. And lo and behold! The poisonous uncleanness of the air yielded to the image as if fleeing from it and being unable to withstand its presence: the passage of the picture brought about a wonderful serenity and purity in the air … Then the pope saw an angel of the Lord standing atop the castle of Crescentius, wiping a bloody sword and sheathing it. Gregory understood that that put an end to the plague, as, indeed, it happened. Thereafter the castle was called the Castle of the Holy Angel.[10]

---

[8] Anthony Thiselton, 'Exegesis and Reception History in the Patristic Era,' has helpfully traced the origins of the term *Wirkungsgeschichte* in philosophical hermeneutics, especially the work of Gadamer, and of reception history (or *Rezeptionsgeschichte*) in reader-response theory, especially the work of Jauss and Iser. On the history of reception theory and especially on the contributions of Jauss and Wolfgang Iser to its theoretical foundations, see Holub, *Reception Theory*. On the art-historical side, see the work of Shearman, *Art and the Spectator in the Italian Renaissance*. Despite their differences, Thiselton (214) maintains that both regard: 'the text as "potential" until it is "performed", like a script or score that finds its "reality" in the play or the concert that performs it interactively with an *audience* as an *event*.' On *Wirkungsgeschichte* in biblical studies, see the pioneering work of Ulrich Luz on Matthew (who also includes a limited selection of art as part of Matthew's history of influence) and now the Blackwell's Commentary on the Bible series. Appreciation is expressed to Professor Thiselton for sharing this article with us in manuscript form and for providing the appropriate reference numbers in the printed version.

[9] On the history of this painting, see Henrietta Irving Bolton, *The Madonna of St. Luke*.

[10] De Voragine, *The Golden Legend*, 1:174.

In this scene, Luke's work of art becomes itself a vehicle of healing. The number of icons traditionally attributed to Luke number literally in the hundreds, testimony to the deep ways in which this tradition has taken root in the imaginations of Christians across the centuries.

Eventually Luke was also revered as a patron saint. Florentine painters belonged to the Guild of Doctors and Pharmacists not only because they ground their colors as pharmacists ground materials for medicines, but also because painters and doctors enjoyed the protection of the same patron saint, St. Luke.

We have treated the works of art we focus on as an extension of Luke's own rhetorical and theological artistry and have thus tried to understand the work in its historical, cultural, and religious context. Our 'visual exegesis' of these works attends to a brief overview of the biblical text and its subsequent reception in ecclesiastical circles, to the life of the artist producing the work, the commission and original location of the painting, the work's likely sources and precedents, its iconographic program, and a brief hermeneutical reflection on how the contemporary community of faith might incorporate the insights of the painting in its liturgical practices and theological reflection in order to hear afresh the word of God through the pages of Luke and the art they inspire. We have chosen two examples, one from the high Renaissance in Florence and the other from the Baroque period in Rome. We have focused our remarks in this essay on the iconography of the paintings as examples of 'visual exegesis.'

Leonardo's Uffizi *Annunciation*

As an example of our work, let's look briefly at Leonardo's *Annunciation* (Figure 1, p. 420). The painting, of course, is based on the annunciation story in Luke 1:26–38. Most commentators are agreed that this passage draws heavily on similar epiphany scenes found in the Jewish Scriptures (cf. Ex. 3:2–12; Judg. 6:11–21). Known in literary circles as a 'type scene' (cf., e.g., Robert Alter, Robert Tannehill), these commissioning stories contain five elements, and Luke 1:26–38 shares in all of them: (1) the appearance of an angel (Ex. 3:2; Judg. 6:11; Lk. 1:26–28); (2) the reaction of the recipient of the epiphany (Ex. 3:6; Judg. 6:13; Lk. 1:29); (3) the angel's message/commission (Ex. 3:7–10; Judg. 6:14; Lk. 1:30–33); (4) objection to the message (Ex. 3:11; Judg. 6:15; Lk. 1:34); (5) the giving of a sign (Ex. 3:12; Judg. 6:17–21; Lk. 1:36). This commissioning type scene is found also in the Lukan annunciation of the birth of John the Baptist (Lk. 1:11–20). The audience familiar with the convention will realize that Zechariah and Mary stand in a long tradition of those who have been assigned a particular task by God – a tradition that includes Moses and Gideon.

Figure 1. *The Anunciation of the Virgin* painting is Credit: Alinari/Art Resource, NY

Figure 1. *The Anunciation of the Virgin* painting is Credit: Alinari/Art Resource, NY

In subsequent interpretation, the Annunciation is a pivotal point, marking as it does a new start for humanity. From early on in Christian interpretation, the Annunciation was seen as the moment when Mary, the 'second Eve,' reversed the havoc wrought by the first Eve (in much the same way that Christ, the 'second Adam,' provided a solution to the sin of the first Adam). Irenaeus (taking his cue from Paul's typology of Adam and Christ in Romans 5) framed his interpretation of the Annunciation in this way: 'as the former [Eve] was led astray by an angel's discourse to fly from God after transgressing his word, so the latter [Mary] by an angel's discourse had the gospel preached unto her that she might bear God, in obedience to his Word. And if the former was disobedient to God, yet the other was persuaded to obey God, that the Virgin Mary might become an advocate for the virgin Eve' (*Haer.* 5.19.1; also Justin Martyr, *Dial.*). In the widely popular thirteenth-century work the *Golden Legend,* Jacobus de Voragine continues and expands this comparison of the Annunciation scene with the fall.

Leonardo's *Annunciation,* one of his earliest attributed works, also reflects the second Eve typology but moves beyond it in significant ways. Though there is no documentation extant for the commission and original location of Leonardo's *Annunciation* (it has been in the Uffizi collection since 1867), it appears to have been owned and perhaps commissioned by the monks of St. Bartolomeo at Monte Oliveto, outside Florence. The scene is deceptively simple, consisting only of Gabriel and Mary (behind a lectern) against an uncluttered landscape. For the sake of space we will focus on the figure of Mary, drawing on features of the landscape and Gabriel only to assist us in our 'visual exegesis' of the Virgin.

Art historian Michael Baxandall has shed considerable light on the visual tradition of depicting the Annunciation.[11] He cites a fifteenth-century sermon by Fr Roberto Caracciolo da Lecce on the Annunciation as being typical of the theological categories through which visual depictions like that of Leonardo's may have been viewed by the original audience.[12] In the third mystery of the Annunciation, Fr Roberto attributed five successive spiritual states to Mary, which correspond to details in the text: (1) *Conturbatio* (Disquiet) – 'she was troubled'; (2) *Cogitatio* (Reflection) – 'she cast in her mind what manner of salutation this might be'; (3) *Interrogatio* (Inquiry) – 'How shall this be ...?'; (4) *Humiliatio* (Submission) – 'Behold the handmaid of the Lord'; (5) *Meritatio* (Merit) – 'the angel departed from her' (and, according to Fr Roberto, the Virgin 'at once had Christ, God incarnate, in her womb').

We are not, of course, suggesting that Leonardo or his audience heard this particular sermon of Fr Roberto – it was, after all, published some twenty years

---

[11] Baxandall, *Painting and Experience,* 49–56.

[12] Caracciolus, *Sermones de laudibus sanctorum,* cxlic r.–cliii r.

after the Uffizi *Annunciation* was completed. We do, however, wish to argue that Fr Roberto's sermon, far from a unique or idiosyncratic interpretation of the Annunciation, rather represented the conventional thinking about this text in fifteenth-century Italy. Further, as Baxandall has observed: 'Most fifteenth-century Annunciations are identifiably Annunciations of Disquiet, or of Submission, or – theses being less clearly distinguished from each other – of Reflection and/or Inquiry. The preachers coached the public in the painters' repertory, and the painters responded within the current emotional categorization of the event.'[13]

Leonardo's *Annunciation* depicts the initial moment of the encounter between Gabriel and Mary and fits within the first category of *Conturbatio* ('Disquiet'), though as many commentators have observed, the 'disquiet' of Mary is of a rather 'quiet' sort! Leonardo was not given to excesses of emotional display, as was the case with some of his contemporaries (see, e.g., Botticelli's Cestello *Annunciation*, 1489, Uffizi, Florence). In fact, the portrayal of Mary here corresponds with Leonardo's own observations about tendencies toward the violent mode in other artistic renderings of the Annunciation: 'some days ago I saw the picture of an angel who, in making the Annunciation, seemed to be trying to chase Mary out of her room, with movements showing the sort of attack one might make on some hated enemy; and Mary, as if desperate, seemed to be trying to throw herself out of the window. Do not fall into errors like these.'[14]

The gesture of Mary, then, seems to be one more of affirmation or welcome than disquiet (and thus is similar to the gesture of Venus welcoming spring in Botticelli's famous *Primavera*, ca. 1482, Uffizi, Florence). The gesture also recalls a typical priestly blessing. This priestly component is reinforced by other details in the painting. Mary is seated behind a lectern with a book. By the fourteenth century, this image of Mary behind a lectern had almost universally replaced the depiction of Mary holding a spindle (inspired by *Protevangelium of James* 11 and *Pseudo-Matthew* 9). This lectern has been variously identified as a sepulchral urn, a sarcophagus, or a Roman altar. Too large, however, to be an urn and too square to be a sarcophagus, the lectern is best understood as an altar, thus contributing to the understanding of Mary's priestly role in humanity's salvation. This interpretation of Mary as priestess had already been suggested in the writings of Antonino Pierozzi, archbishop of Florence, whose *Summa Theologica* would have been available by the 1460s. Furthermore, the port and ships in the landscape reflect Mary's title of 'star of the Sea' (underscored in the mediaeval hymn, *Ave Maris Stella*) and 'Port of the Shipwrecked,' another allusion to her important intercessory role in redemption.

---

[13] Baxandall, *Painting and Experience*, 55.
[14] Leonardo, *Treatise on Painting*, I.58, II33 r.

Leonardo uses other details of the Annunciation to complete the picture of Mary. On the lectern rests a book whose fluttering pages (presumably because of the recent arrival of Gabriel, whose wings are still extended!) are stilled by Mary's extended fingers. Especially interesting for understanding the role of the book is the thirteenth-century *Meditations on the Life of Christ* (written by a Franciscan monk in Tuscany), which suggests that Mary may have been reading Isaiah's prophecy of the virginal birth at the moment Gabriel appeared. While it is impossible to make out the words on the page where Mary has stopped, it is reasonable to expect that the fifteenth-century beholder, knowing traditions like that of pseudo-Bonaventure's *Meditations on the Life of Christ*, would have imagined that Mary had marked the place in Isaiah which reads, 'A virgin shall conceive and bear a son' (cf. Is. 7:14). The lily that Gabriel holds, likewise, is a traditional symbol of Mary's purity. Mary's impending role as mother is seen in the royal blue mantle draped over her lap, subtly emphasizing the separation of her thighs and knees, a typical birthing metaphor. This emphasis on Mary as mother dovetails with her role as second Eve, a role further suggested by the garden of grass and flowers in which Gabriel kneels (recall also the literary tradition which ties the fall and the Annunciation closely together, as we saw above).[15]

The result is a rich theological interpretation of the Annunciation that draws on visual and literary sources to emphasize Mary's role in salvation history and, in many ways, enriches our reading of the Lukan text itself. Leonardo has captured the initial moment of *Conturbatio* (in his other *Annunciation*, 1478–85, Louvre, Paris, he depicts Mary with arms crossed in what Fr Roberto calls the spiritual state of *Humiliatio*). But rather than depicting her as troubled or surprised by Gabriel's greeting, he shows her to be an obedient recipient of the divine message, a willing priestess to intercede on humanity's behalf by becoming the mother of God, by assuming the role of the second Eve. This rendering of Mary's 'troubled' state fits well with Fr Roberto's statement that Mary was not 'troubled' at seeing an angel 'since she was used to seeing angels and marveled not at the fact of the Angel's apparition' but rather 'from wonder … at the lofty and grand salutation, in which the Angel made plain for her such great and marvelous things, and at which she in her humility was astonished.'

Later in the tradition of the church, the words of Gabriel to Mary recorded in the Vulgate as *Dominus tecum* ('the Lord is with you') were slightly revised, changing the 'you' from singular to plural. They became the beginning of the liturgy for Holy Communion where the leader spoke '*Dominus vobiscum*,' thus preserving these assuring words of God's presence, originally spoken to Mary (and earlier Gideon) for the community of faith.

---

[15] For more on the traditions of Mary as a 'second Eve,' see Anderson, *The Genesis of Perfection*, 75–97.

Unfortunately, in most English translations, these words are rendered, 'The Lord be with you!' to which the congregation responds, 'And also with you.' Both the Latin and Greek are missing the verb, and as W.C. van Unnik has pointed out, in such cases it is customary to supply 'is.'[16] This shift has profound theological implications. Whereas the translation 'the Lord be with you,' in the minds of many congregants, may suggest nothing more than a mere wish or pious hope, the phrase *Dominus vobiscum*, 'the Lord *is* with you' 'announces the indispensable prerequisite that God's Spirit is given to people to enable them to do the work of God.'[17] Leonardo's *Annunciation* also serves as a powerful visual reminder of the humble astonishment that we, no less than Mary, should experience when we hear those powerful words: *Dominus vobiscum*. The Lord *is* with you!

Caravaggio's London *Supper at Emmaus*

Let us turn now to consider Caravaggio's London *Supper at Emmaus* (Figure 2). Caravaggio was one of the founders of the Baroque. The term 'Baroque' was originally coined to disparage the very style it designates. According to Ann Southerland Harris:

> As a term applied to seventeenth-century visual arts, it was used pejoratively in the later eighteenth century by supporters of classical architecture who saw Francesco Borromini's imaginative transformation of its forms as distortions of long-established perfection. Instead of a perfectly spherical pearl, Borromini offered the equivalent of a distorted one; the French term 'barrocco,' meaning a pearl of irregular shape. What began as an insult has become a more positive word associated with energy, emotion, drama, even extravagance, qualities believed to be especially characteristic of the arts of seventeenth-century Europe. Thus the word is often adopted to embrace all seventeenth-century art, whether or not it exemplifies these qualities.[18]

It is generally agreed that, although it began in Rome around the 1590s, the Baroque style is best defined regionally. Therefore, the *Italian* Baroque style often expresses the spirit of the Counter Reformation, which, of course, was well underway by the seventeenth century. Catholicism had recaptured much of its former territory, and Protestantism was on the defensive, so neither side had the power any longer to upset the new balance.

The *Supper at Emmaus* is an oil painting on canvas and is located in the National Gallery, London. The painting was commissioned around 1600–

---

[16] van Unnik, 'Dominus Vobiscum,' 270–305.

[17] Kolden, 'Dominus Vobiscum,' 456.

[18] Harris, *Seventeenth-Century Art and Architecture*, xxi.

1601 and is documented as being paid for by Ciriaco Mattei on January 7, 1602. The provenance, or history of the painting's ownership, is fairly well established. It was in the Borghese Gallery in Rome by 1650. In 1801 Prince Camillo Borghese sold it, and by 1831 it belonged to an English collector, who gave it to the National Gallery in London eight years later.

Caravaggio, thirty years old at the time of painting, used the standard Venetian central type of composition derived from Titian (as seen in the 1535 *Supper at Emmaus* today in the Louvre), and included an innkeeper as well as Christ, Cleopas and his traveling companion.

Caravaggio's attention to the still life draws from his fascination with, and previous experience of, incredibly realistic detail of fruit and vegetables. As we look more carefully at the still life we observe that some of these formal details are directly related to the iconographical content of the painting. There is a double meaning in the objects – not only in the eucharistic grapes, wine and water, but also in the apples, symbolic of the fall of man, and in the bursting pomegranate, symbolic of the crown of thorns.[19] Moir continues by suggesting that Caravaggio included the Ushak pattern on the tablecloth to suggest the Near Eastern locale of the event. This pattern was a commonplace in North Italian painting of the sixteenth century on both rugs and table linens.[20]

The dramatic tenebrist light, which originated from a source outside the painting, was used by Caravaggio in this painting as well as in his earlier works of the 1590s and became a characteristic of the Baroque. Caravaggio's use of color and light has long been the topic of discussion. Giovanni Pietro Bellori (1613–96), the first biographer of Caravaggio in 1672, made a distinction between the excessive naturalism of Caravaggio's unselective models and the naturalness of his color.[21] Bellori admired Caravaggio's color because of its closeness to nature, yet he criticized Caravaggio's figures. The patrons found the dirty and torn clothing to be indecorous. 'Bellori recognizes that the strong, dark shadows and the restricted areas of light were practices that gave great relief to the figures, and did imitate one particular natural situation: a windowless room, with a lamp placed very high, shining directly onto the figure. Such a light would strongly illuminate one part of the figure leaving the rest in shadow'.[22]

The *Supper at Emmaus* is traditional in composition. But the lighting, the close-up view of dramatically posed, half-length figures set against an impenetrable dark background, and the beardless Christ are all novel.[23] In this

---

[19] Moir, *Caravaggio*, 82.

[20] Moir, *Caravaggio*, 82.

[21] Bellori, *Le vite de' pittori, scultori et architetti moderni*, 163.

[22] Bell, 'Appraisals of Caravaggio's Coloring,' 123.

[23] Hibbard, *Caravaggio*, 75.

composition, the raking light accentuates the right side of the beardless face of Christ and the white coloring of the mantle which drapes his left shoulder. Christ's down-turned eyes direct us to the table and to his hand gesture of blessing the bread.

The beardless Christ and the moment Caravaggio chooses to depict in the narrative directly relate to the biblical text. There are four parts to the Lukan narrative relating to the bread. Christ: (1) takes the bread; (2) blesses the bread; (3) breaks the bread; and (4) gives the bread to the disciples. The recognition of Christ by the disciples occurs in Luke at the *third* scene described above – the breaking of the bread.

There are several examples from the sixteenth century that show the image of Christ blessing the still unbroken bread on the table (scene 2). Jacopo Bassano's (1510–92) work dates from 1538 and is owned by the Kimbell Museum of Art, Fort Worth, Texas. Christ is shown with his left hand on the yet unbroken bread and his right in the blessing gesture. The disciples appear to be in conversation and still unaware of the event. There is no sign that they recognize Christ yet.

Veronese, around 1560–70, also depicts this second scene, as Christ blesses the unbroken bread. The disciples' excitement is apparent as one follows their gaze at the bread on the table, away from his face, without a sign of recognition.[24]

Finally, Pontormo's work of 1525 also depicts this second scene, the blessing of the bread. One disciple gazes at Christ blessing the loaf, while the other concentrates on pouring red wine. Christ stares at us, as do the onlookers behind him – the contemporary Carthusians of the convent for which the work was painted.[25] There is still no recognition by the disciples. All three of these examples are consistent with the Lukan text, in which the recognition occurs at the breaking of the bread (scene 3).

Why, then, does Caravaggio allow the moment of recognition to be moved one scene earlier, to the third scene of the blessing of the bread? Because it further emphasizes the Counter Reformation issue, transubstantiation, which was being defended by his patron Cardinal Mattei. The eucharistic reading of Emmaus already had a doctrinal role to play in the Counter Reformation.[26] That the account was viewed as having eucharistic overtones during Caravaggio's time is clear. In the 1593 Jesuit book of engravings *Evangelicae Historiae Imagines*, meant to accompany Ignatius' *Spiritual Exercises*, Jerome

24 Gilbert, *Caravaggio*, 144.
25 Rearick, *The Drawings of Pontormo*, 226–30.
26 See Gilbert, *Caravaggio*, 146. Gilbert cites Caravaggio's contemporary, biblical commentator Lapide (1567–1637). Lapide's volume on the gospels gained approval from his Jesuit superiors in 1636 and was published posthumously in 1638 with a dedication to Cardinal Francesco Barberini.

Nadal uses the Supper at Emmaus to prefigure the Mass, in which Christ distributes the broken bread to the disciples. 'As Christ holds the bread out to a disciple, the disciple leans forward to take it, extraordinarily, in his mouth, as in Communion.'[27] Augustine, in the *Harmony of the Gospels*, besides asserting that the breaking of bread led to the recognition, had also brought in the text of 1 Corinthians 10:17 about our being all one bread and one body, to deduce that 'Christ wished to be known only to those who took part in his body, that is, in the church, whose unity in the sacrament of the bread Paul commends.' Augustine's conclusion reiterates the point: Satan had kept the disciples' eyes closed 'until the sacrament of the bread,' after which, through participation in his body, they could recognize him.[28]

Part of the stylistic problem of this 'moment of recognition' in the painted visual document is how to portray a Christ who is not recognizable. The Gospel of Mark says that Christ 'appeared in a different guise to two of them as they were walking, on their way into the country' (Mk. 16:12; the Vulgate translates the Greek for 'in a different guise' as *in alia effigie*).[29] This point in Mark made its way into the comment on Luke 24 in the *Glossa Ordinaria*, so that anyone consulting the gloss about the Supper at Emmaus would encounter this reference to *alia effigie*, without ever having to turn the page to the comments at the end of Mark's Gospel. Several scholars have noted this passage and agree that Caravaggio has indeed found a way to visually depict Christ in an other-than usual way.[30] For Caravaggio, *in alia effigie* translates into a beardless Christ. Although Christ appears bearded in all other Supper at Emmaus paintings, and Caravaggio himself paints a *Supper at Emmaus* scene later in 1606 maintaining this bearded tradition, there exist artistic precedents for a beardless Christ.[31] The most famous work is Michelangelo's Christ figure in the *Last Judgment* of the Sistine Chapel, 1534–41. The sarcophagus of Junius Bassus was unearthed in Rome in 1595. Christ appears beardless in several earlier works of art such as the marble sarcophagus ca. 359 C.E., *Entry into Jerusalem*. Both Caravaggio and his audience would have known these visual sources.[32]

Of the three remaining figures in the portrait, there is little controversy about two of them. The figure on the left is typically identified with Cleopas,

27 Gilbert, *Caravaggio*, 146.

28 Augustine, *Harmony of the Gospels*, III.25.72.

29 Hibbard, *Caravaggio*, 85.

30 Hibbard, *Caravaggio*, 75.

31 See Moir, *Caravaggio*, 133.

32 Hibbard, *Caravaggio*, 77, states: 'A beardless Christ is found in paintings by two artists in whom Caravaggio had particular interest. A Salvator Mundi long attributed to Leonardo, which was presumably then as now in Rome, shows him beardless; (another such picture, now in the Ambrosiana in Milan, was owned by Cardinal Borromeo)'.

the named pilgrim in our story. The only real point of contention about this figure is whether or not his gaze is fixed on Christ and the role that would play in identifying this scene as one of 'recognition.'[33]

About the innkeeper, more has been said. Though his gaze is clearly fixed on Christ, his covered head is taken by some not as a simple sign of irreverence,[34] but rather as an indication that if there is epiphany here, the innkeeper simply does not participate in it.[35] 'Even ... the innkeeper, who sees and understands nothing, represents the world of pagans and heretics who do not recognize Christ and his Church. Nevertheless the innkeeper casts a shadow that seems to form a negative halo around the brilliant head of Christ, as if to indicate that we honor the Savior even while ignoring or denying him'.[36]

To be sure, the figure on the right is the most intriguing. In the biblical account, of course, this traveler is left unnamed.[37] That has not stopped biblical scholars across the centuries from attempting to identify him! Some fascinating proposals have been tendered: Luke himself, Philip the deacon and, more recently, Cleopas' wife. In a tradition that goes back at least to Eusebius (citing Hegesippus), Cleopas was the uncle of Jesus, the brother of Joseph, and the unnamed companion is his son, Simeon, later leader of the church in Jerusalem.[38] Finally, and for our purposes most importantly, Origen no less than seven times identifies Cleopas' companion as Simon Peter. In *Contra Celsum*, Origen writes:

> It is written in the gospel of Luke that after the resurrection Jesus took bread and blessed and brake and gave it to Simon and Cleophas, and when they took it, 'their eyes were opened and they knew him; and he vanished from their sight.' (II.68)

Origen simply asserts this identification; he does not feel compelled to argue for it – a point that has vexed scholars since. The most likely suggestion is that

---

[33] See Gilbert, *Caravaggio*, 147.

[34] So Caravaggio's earliest critic, Bellori seems to suggest; see *Le vite de' pittori, scultori et architetti moderni,* 164.

[35] Scribner, 'In Alia Effigie,' 376. Scribner further observed (376): 'The covered head deliberately underscores the servant's exclusion from the miracle of divine revelation.'

[36] Hibbard, *Caravaggio*, 80.

[37] Both disciples are left unnamed in what appears to be the earliest reference to the Emmaus account in Tertullian, *Praescr.*, 22 ('And were they ignorant to whom also after His Resurrection He deigned to "expound all the Scriptures" as they journeyed?'), though one might infer, as does Annand ('He Was Seen of Cephas,' 181,), that given the context of the citation, Tertullian considered that at least one of the travelers was a member of the twelve.

[38] See Eusebius, *Hist. eccl.* iii, 32.

Origen, well-known for his text-critical interests, may have been following a manuscript tradition which read *legontes* (nominative plural) rather than *legontas* (accusative plural) in Luke 24:34 where the Emmaus pilgrims meet the 11 apostles. At stake is who is making the statement, 'The Lord has risen indeed, and has appeared to Simon!' The use of the nominative plural (*legontes*) would assign the statement to the Emmaus disciples and would imply that Simon Peter was the other (to this point unnamed) disciple. In fact, this reading is found in the major witness to the Western tradition of manuscript evidence, Codex D (Cantabrigiensis), a fifth-century, bilingual manuscript.[39] Origen could have known a precursor to this text (the Coptic version, for example, reflects a tradition that would have predated Origen) and felt no need to defend his textual reading.[40] We shall return to this literary tradition of identifying Cleopas' companion momentarily.

First, though, let us survey the various proposals for the figure on Jesus' left in Caravaggio's *Supper at Emmaus*. The suggestions from the art-historical side, though fewer, are no less imaginative. Some identify the disciple simply as a 'pilgrim,' taking the shell to be symbolic of travelers. Others have identified him as James the brother of Jesus.[41] Finally, a number of scholars have identified this disciple as Peter, though often with little or no supporting comment.[42]

In agreement with this last view, we contend that: (1) Caravaggio was instructed by his patron to identify the 'other' disciple as Peter, and the literary source for this identification was ultimately Origen; (2) Caravaggio employed symbols and gestures in this figure so that his educated audience would have been led to identify the disciple with the Apostle Peter; and (3) finally, such an identification served further the pro-papacy apology already identified in this painting.

---

[39] Crehan, 'St. Peter's Journey to Emmaus,' 421, also cites the Sahidic and Bohairic Coptic in favor of this reading. The Latin *dicentes*, since it is both nominative and accusative in form, is ambiguous on this point. The omission in Codex D of Luke 24:12, where Peter visits the empty tomb, goes hand-in-hand with this variant in 24:34, since Simon Peter could not have discovered the tomb empty and also be, as Codex D presumes, one of the disillusioned Emmaus disciples.

[40] For the evidence that Origen knew these various text traditions see Crehan, 'St. Peter's Journey to Emmaus,' 422. At any rate, Bruce Metzger's claim that the variant in D represents a simple 'transcriptional error' is brought into serious doubt (see Metzger, *A Textual Commentary*, 186). Rather, this variant seems to fit D's general tendency to 'heighten' Peter's status. See Acts 1:23, where D replaces 'they put forward' (*estesan*) with 'he put forward' (*estesen*), indicating that it was Peter alone, and not the apostles as a group, who selected the two replacement candidates for Judas.

[41] See Hibbard, *Caravaggio*, 79–80.

[42] See Friedländer, *Caravaggio Studies*, 164; with a sympathetic reading by Scribner, 'In Alia Effigie,' 381, n. 44.

Since Origen is the only known author who explicitly identifies Cleopas'
companion as Simon Peter, we must ask if the works of Origen were known
during Caravaggio's time. Given Origen's rather checkered reception by
fellow ecclesiastics during his own lifetime and his even more tumultuous post-
humous history, one might expect a negative answer. For example, Origen's
interpretation is missing altogether from the comments on Luke 24 in the
Glossa Ordinaria. And perhaps with good reason. After all, Origen was forced to
leave Alexandria over a quarrel with Demetrius; in the third and fourth centuries his work came under sharp attack by Methodius of Alexandria; he was con-
demned by the emperor Justinian and his domestic synod, and apparently also
by the Fifth Ecumenical Council in 553.[43]

Nevertheless, Origen was better received in the West than in the East, and
his works continued to be read into the high Middle Ages.[44] Reformers like
Calvin and Luther made Origen, and especially his notion of the 'spiritual
sense' of Scripture, the object of much derision. Luther, for example, wrote:
'Jerome and Origen contributed to the practice of searching only for allegories.
God forgive them.'[45] During the Renaissance, however, Origen inspired some
of the greatest humanists, including Erasmus.

Not unexpectedly, we find a number of scholars coming to Origen's
defense, including Cardinal Robert Bellarmine (1542–1621).[46] Bellarmine was
one of the great minds of the later Catholic Counter Reformation and a long-
time colleague of Cardinal del Monte.[47] He came to Rome in 1576 and from
1586–93 served as Professor of Controversial Theology. In 1599, he was
appointed Cardinal by Clement VIII. In *De Verbo Dei* 1.3 he offers a vigorous
defense of Origen's exegetical method, in the course of which he cites *Contra*

---

[43] On the life and thought of Origen, see Crouzel, *Origen*.
[44] On mediaeval attitudes toward Origen, see de Lubac, *Exégèse Médiévale*, 221–304.
[45] See Luther, *Table Talk*, no. 5285, 406. On Calvin, see *Commentaries*, 107.
[46] On Bellarmine's life, see Brodrick, *Robert Bellarmine*. On Bellarmine's role in refut-
ing Protestant arguments, and especially those of Calvin, see Evans, *The Road to the
Reformation*, 24–25, 32–33, 47, 72–73, et passim.
[47] See Brodrick, *Bellarmine*, 207–208, who reports a conversation between the two
that both preserved in their papers. They often consulted on matters political and
theological, especially related to Galileo (see Brodrick, *Bellarmine*, 346, 359, 370).
Upon Bellarmine's death, Del Monte wrote in tribute: 'Often enough the whole
Congregation of Rites, which numbered upwards of fourteen cardinals, abandoned
or changed decisions that had been reached by common agreement, solely out of
respect for the learning and authority of this one man' (see Brodrick, *Bellarmine*,
303). It is reasonable to infer that Cardinal Mattei was well aware of Bellarmine's
work, and Caravaggio himself had no doubt made his acquaintance during his time
in Cardinal Del Monte's palazzo. Therefore, we may conclude that, through
Bellarmine, Origen's views were accessible to both painter and patron.

Celsum. Thus Origen and his work, specifically *Contra Celsum*, were well known in Rome at the end of the sixteenth century – at least among the educated clerics engaged in pro-papacy apologetics, of whom Cardinal Bellarmine was one and Caravaggio's patron, Cardinal Mattei, was another.

For someone interested in placing Peter at the Emmaus scene, the literary sources, specifically Origen's writings, were available and known. The problem here for Caravaggio was similar to the one he faced with the *alia effigie* issue: how to translate the literary source into a visual representation?

The shell on the disciple's breast is often identified as an attribute for St. James, and had this painting been composed in Spain, where the cult of St. James was so dominant, there would be little doubt as to its function. But the shell in Italian Baroque was not universally or univocally attributed to James; rather, it could be viewed as a symbol for pilgrims in general.[48] Here we assume that it signifies Peter's role as one of the Emmaus 'pilgrims' who has journeyed to and from Jerusalem for the Passover feast.

Furthermore, as Scribner observes: 'If Caravaggio's disciple seated at the right in the London painting is Saint Peter, then his violent gesture may allude not only to Christ's Crucifixion but also to his own eventual martyrdom.'[49] This point gains weight when one realizes that, at about the same time, Caravaggio completed *The Crucifixion of St. Peter* in the Cerasi Chapel, Santa Maria del Popolo, Rome. Not only are the outstretched arms of the martyr strikingly reminiscent of the Emmaus disciple's gesture, but the facial resemblance between our disciple and the now older Peter is remarkable. There is a 'Peter type' into which both of these depictions easily fit. The use of the same type in the *Crucifixion* may very well have been intended to strengthen the identification of Simon Peter in the *Supper*.

Furthermore, the basket of fruit casts a shadow in the shape of a fish on the right side.[50] Of course, the fish may simply allude to the traditional ICHTHUS symbol for Christianity or to the feeding of the multitudes with bread and fish. But the fish is also a well-known symbol for Peter, as seen in the Hampton Court copy of Caravaggio's *Walk to Emmaus* in which the foremost disciple carries a catch of fish, and is most usually identified as Saint Peter. Thus Caravaggio's identification of Cleopas' companion finds confirmation in another of his works. If this seems too subtle, remember that the cardinal's intended audience consisted of his fellow ecclesiastics, who would visit his living quarters and who would presumably have the leisure to puzzle over the

---

[48] See Kaftal, *Iconography*, 1187.

[49] Scribner, 'In Alia Effigie,' 381.

[50] Noted by Warma, 'Christ, First Fruits, and the Resurrection,' 583. The potential meaning of shadows in this painting has already been suggested by the shadowy halo behind Christ's head.

painting, not to mention unmediated access to its patron. In other words, Caravaggio and his patrons were involved in apologetics, in which the audience could be presumed to share the viewpoint of the artist/patron, as opposed to protestant polemics, where a hostile audience might dismiss the identification of Peter as the unnamed disciple as biblically unwarranted.

If the viewer is led to identify the disciple on the right as Peter, what is its purpose? What better way to defend the papacy than to depict the risen Christ revealing himself, through the liturgical gesture of blessing the bread, to the first pope, Peter? Peter's gaze is fixed on the blessing hand while his own hands are outstretched – not only reminiscent of the Christ, but also foreshadowing his own martyrdom. The continuity between Christ the high priest and Peter the first communicant of the first post-resurrection Eucharist is clear and powerful.

Susan Warma has observed: 'since its completion nearly four hundred years ago, Caravaggio's London *Supper at Emmaus* has provoked, bewildered, delighted, and involved the spectator.'[51] The involvement of the spectator is what keeps this chapter from being purely a historical exercise in visual exegesis. As we saw earlier, Caravaggio does indeed enjoy involving the viewer in his paintings. The bowl of fruit, precariously perched on the edge of the table, ready to fall at the viewer's feet, the outstretched arms of both Christ and Peter invading the viewer's space, the play of light drawing the viewer's eye to the gesture of blessing, all invite the viewer to his or her own moment of epiphany. So while Caravaggio is closing the text on the one hand by naming the unnamed disciple Peter for pro-papacy purposes, he opens the text, on the other hand, by painting a scene that invites the viewer to enter.

In so doing, Caravaggio reenacts the rhetoric of Luke. Commentators have been too busy trying to identify the other Emmaus disciple or arguing that the naming of Cleopas lends credibility and authority to the story to realize that leaving the other unnamed is an invitation to the reader to participate in its story – to inscribe him or herself into the narrative. Such rhetorical strategy in Luke is not always edifying as here; one need only think of the rich man and Lazarus in this light! But in Emmaus the reader enters a world where the mood shifts from afternoon despair to meal-time epiphany!

Conclusion

The title of our larger project, *Illuminating Luke*, is, of course, an allusion to the practice among mediaeval scribes of visually illustrating the manuscript being copied. These illuminations provided additional interpretive resources to the

---

[51] Warma, 'Christ, First Fruits, and the Resurrection,' 583.

reader. We hope also to illumine the reader with regard both to the message of Luke's Gospel and Luke's subsequent 'career' at specific moments in its reception history, that is, 'what it *has* meant.' Here we agree with Anthony Thiselton's conclusion: 'Wrestling with *Wirkungsgeschichte* or reception history opens the door to exegesis as explication: an explication that permits us to see dimensions of meaning that *successive contexts of reading bring into sharper focus* for our attention.'[52]

By understanding how the artists and audiences of Renaissance and Baroque religious art 'translated' Luke in culturally and religiously appropriate ways, we may detect some clues about their explication and appropriation in our contemporary context, about how to hear God's word afresh. It is our prayer that these visual texts will assist us in apprehending God's redemptive work through the person of Jesus Christ in both word ('The Lord *is* with you') and sacrament ('how he was made known to us in the breaking of the bread'). Our desire is that our efforts here, and in our larger project, not only further clarify the interpretive history of each of these Lukan stories at some of their most critical moments, but also assist, as it were, in illuminating Luke!

---

[52] Thiselton, 'Exegesis and Reception History in the Patristic Era,' 228. Paolo Berdini, an art historian, writes in a similar vein of the artist 'actualizing' the text, or more precisely, a reading of the text: 'Painting is not the simple visualization of the narrative of the text but an expansion of that text, subject to discursive strategies of various kinds' (*Painting as Visual Exegesis,* 35).

Bibliography

Adams, J.E., 'The Emmaus Story, Lk. XXIV.13–25: A Suggestion,' *ExpTim* 17 (1905–06), 333–35

Anderson, G., 'Mary as Second Eve,' in *The Genesis of Perfection: Adam and Eve in Jewish and Christian Imagination* (Louisville: Westminster/John Knox Press, 2001), 75–97

Annand, R., '"He Was Seen of Cephas": A Suggestion about the First Resurrection Appearance to Peter,' *SJT* 11 (1958), 180–87

Augustine, *Saint Augustine, Sermon on the Mount; Harmony of the Gospels; Homilies on the Gospels* (Grand Rapids: Eerdmans, 1956)

Baxandall, M., *Painting and Experience in Fifteenth-Century Italy* (Oxford: Oxford University Press, 1988)

Bell, J., 'Some Seventeenth-Century Appraisals of Caravaggio's Coloring,' *Artibus et Historiae* 14.27 (1993), 103–29

Bellori, G.P., *Le Vite de'Pittori, Scultori e Architetti Moderni* (ed. E. Borea; intro. G. Previtali, Turin: G. Einaudi, 1976)

Berdini, P., *The Religious Art of Jacopo Bassano: Painting as Visual Exegesis* (Cambridge: Cambridge University Press, 1997)

Bolton, H. I., *The Madonna of St. Luke: The Story of a Portrait* (New York: G. P. Putnam, 1895)

Brodrick, J., *Robert Bellarmine: Saint and Scholar* (Westminster, MD: Newman Press, 1961)

Buser, T., 'Jerome Nadal and Early Jesuit Art in Rome,' *Art Bulletin* 58.3 (1976), 424–34

Calvin, J., *Calvin – Commentaries* (ed. and trans. J. Haroutunian, with L. Pettibone Smith; Philadelphia: Westminster Press, 1958)

Caracciolus, R., *Sermones de laudibus sanctorum* (Naples 1489)

Charlesworth, C.E., 'The Unnamed Companion of Cleopas,' *ExpTim* 34 (1922–23), 233–34

Childs, B., 'The *Sensus Literalis* of Scripture: An Ancient and Modern Problem,' in *Beiträge zur Alttestamentlichen Theologie* (ed. H. Donner, et al.; Göttingen: Vandenhoeck & Ruprecht, 1977), 80–93

Crehan, J.H., 'St Peter's Journey to Emmaus,' *CBQ* 15 (1953), 418–26

Crouzel, H., *Origen: The Life and Thought of the First Great Theologian* (San Francisco: Harper & Row, 1989)

Drury, J., *Painting the Word: Christian Pictures and Their Meaning* (New Haven: Yale University Press, 1999)

Evans, G., *The Language and Logic of the Bible: The Road to the Reformation* (Cambridge: Cambridge University Press, 1985)

Friedlaender, W., *Caravaggio Studies* (Princeton: Princeton University Press, 1955)

Gadamer, H.-G., *Truth and Method* (London: Sheed & Ward, 2nd rev. edn, 1993)

Illuminating Luke   435

Gilbert, C., *Caravaggio and his Two Cardinals* (University Park, PA: Penn State Press, 1995)

Harris, A.S., *Seventeenth-Century Art and Architecture* (Upper Saddle River, NJ: Prentice Hall, 2005)

Hibbard, H., *Caravaggio* (New York: Harper & Row, 1983)

Holub, R.C., *Reception Theory: A Critical Introduction* (London: Methuen, 1984)

Hornik, H.J., and M. C. Parsons, *Illuminating Luke: The Infancy Narrative in Italian Renaissance Painting* (Valley Forge, PA: Trinity Press International, 2003)

—, 'Caravaggio's Supper at Emmaus: A Counter-Reformation Reading of Luke 24,' *CSR* 28.4 (1999), 561–85

Huffman, N., 'Emmaus among the Resurrection Narratives,' *JBL* 64 (1945), 221–26

Iser, W., *The Act of Reading: A Theory of Aesthetic Response* (Baltimore: Johns Hopkins University Press, 1978)

Jauss, H.R., *Toward an Aesthetic of Reception* (Minneapolis: University of Minnesota Press, 1982)

Kaftal, G., *Iconography of the Saints in Tuscan Painting* (Florence: Sanson, 1952)

Kolden, M., '"Dominus Vobiscum": Luke 1:26–31,' *CurTM* 21 (1994), 455–57

Leonardo da Vinci, *Treatise on Painting* (ed. A. P. McMahon; 2 vols.; Princeton: Princeton University Press, 1956)

de Lubac, H., *Exégèse Médiévale* (Paris: Aubier, 1959)

Luther, M., *The Table Talk of Martin Luther* (ed. T.S. Kepler; New York: World Publishing, 1952)

Luz, U., *Matthew 1 – 7: A Commentary* (Edinburgh: T&T Clark, 1989)

—, *Matthew 8 – 20* (Philadelphia: Fortress Press, 2001)

Metzger, B.M., *A Textual Commentary on the Greek New Testament* (London/New York: United Bible Societies, 1971)

Miles, M.R., *Image as Insight: Visual Understanding in Western Christianity and Secular Culture* (Boston: Beacon Press, 1985)

Moir, A., *Caravaggio* (New York: Harry N. Abrams, 1982)

Pelikan, J., *Jesus through the Centuries* (New Haven: Yale University Press, 1985)

Rearick, J., *The Drawings of Pontormo* (Cambridge, MA: Harvard University Press, 1964)

Sawyer, R.D., 'Was Peter the Companion of Cleopas on Easter Afternoon?', *ExpTim* 61 (1949–1950), 91–93

Scribner, C., 'In Alia Effigie: Caravaggio's London *Supper at Emmaus*,' *The Art Bulletin* 59 (1977), 375–82

Shearman, J., *Only Connect ... Art and the Spectator in the Italian Renaissance* (Princeton: Princeton University Press, 1992)

Steinmetz, D., 'The Superiority of Pre-critical Exegesis,' in *A Guide to Contemporary Hermeneutics* (ed. D. K. McKim; Grand Rapids: Eerdmans, 1986), 65–77

Stendahl, K., 'Biblical Theology, Contemporary,' in *The Interpreter's Dictionary of the Bible,* I (ed. G. A. Buttrick; 4 vols.; Nashville: Abingdon, 1962), 418–32

Sugirithajah, R.S. (ed.), *Voices from the Margin: Interpreting the Bible in the Third World* (Maryknoll: Orbis/SPCK, 1995)

The Book of the Bee, in *Anecdota Oxoniensia* (ed. and trans. E. A. Wallis Budge; Semitic Series I.ii; Oxford: Clarendon Press 1886)

Thiselton, A., 'The Holy Spirit in 1 Corinthians: Exegesis and Reception History in the Patristic Era,' in *The Holy Spirit and Christian Origins: Essays in Honor of James D. G. Dunn* (ed. G. N. Stanton, B. W. Longenecker, and S. C. Barton; Grand Rapids and Cambridge: Eerdmans, 2004), 207–28

van Unnik, W.C., '*Dominus Vobiscum*: The Background of a Liturgical Formula,' in *New Testament Essays: Studies in Memory of T. W. Manson* (ed. A. Higgins; Manchester: Manchester University Press, 1959), 270–305

Voragine, J. de, *The Golden Legend* (trans. W. G. Ryan; New York: Longman, Green, and Co., 1941)

Warma, S.J., 'Christ, First Fruits, and the Resurrection: Observations on the Basket in Caravaggio's London "Supper at Emmaus,"' *ZKunstG* 53 (1990), 583–86

Williams, D.H., *Retrieving the Tradition and Renewing Evangelicalism* (Grand Rapids: Eerdmans, 1999)

Afterword

Interpretation, Reflection, Formation: Unfinished Business
Joel B. Green

How do we read the Gospel of Luke as Christian Scripture so as to hear God's address? This is the question before us in the Scripture and Hermeneutics Seminar, and for most of us it is a strange one. Whether in seminary or graduate school, or in other advanced biblical studies, the methods of choice have generally focused elsewhere. In the past, we attended to the voice of the reconstructed historical Jesus, the voice of the redactor of the gospels, or the voice of the 'community' behind the text. More recently, some have learned to heed the voice of the implied author or the narrator, or the cacophony of voices ricocheting around the echo chamber of the text, or have focused on the text as an instrument of power – whether giving voice to the voiceless or silencing voices; or, perhaps, in the absence of an 'author,' on our own voices as these are energized by the text before us. However, we have not given ourselves much to the sketching of approaches or development of means that would tune our ears to the voice *of God*.

This is not to say that we were necessarily uninterested in hearing from God, however. As the liturgy says,

> This is the Word of the Lord.
> Thanks be to God.

The question, rather, is how to access the divine word.

In the modern biblical theology movement, as typified in Krister Stendahl's famous essay in the *Interpreter's Dictionary of the Bible*,[1] God's voice could be known to us only indirectly – mediated not so much *textually* as through the medium of biblical scholarship. With its accredited practices and certified practitioners, the latter moved to the forefront on account of its presumed capacity to explicate what the biblical text *meant* at the moment of its historical

---

[1] Stendahl, 'Biblical Theology, Contemporary,' *IDB* 1:418–32.

generation, thus providing the raw materials from which we might extrapolate what it *means*. The text can never *mean* what it never *meant*, we are often told. Despite the cleverness of the slogan – from 'what it meant' to 'what it means' – this hermeneutic has died a thousand deaths at the hands of a virtual phalanx of opponents from across the theological spectrum. For example, the guiding assumption of the historical-critical paradigm has been that it would enable the discovery of the (one, single) meaning of a biblical text through careful analysis of the text within its historical context. However, in fact, historical criticism*s* (plural!) abound, so that the historical-critical paradigm is not so much one approach as a family of related methods capable of yielding an array of historical meaning*s*. Scholars press other questions, too. What are we to make of the diversity between and among the biblical materials? How are we to engage in the work of 'translating' the ancient meaning into its modern application? What are we to make of the claims to scientific neutrality that necessarily fund the descriptive task of Stendahl's brand of biblical theology? Does historical-critical analysis actually give us what we need, theologically, or is its yield more often not so much a coherent theological vision as layers of tradition and deposits of disparate data[2] – or, as N.T. Wright cleverly put it, 'the mountain of historical footnotes' now expected 'to give birth to the mouse of theological insight'?[3]

The questions keep coming. In theological method, is the Bible's role best construed as historical foundation? Does this sort of theological method not reduce the theological significance of texts to what can be made of them through the application of the historical-critical method?[4] That is, does not theological exegesis begin with the presumption that what is before us is *sacred* text rather than (simply) *ancient* text, with the result that, from this perspective, the historical-critical paradigm misconstrues from the outset the object in view? Brevard Childs complains: Why should a correct *theological* interpretation of a biblical text be dependent upon first reconstructing its original setting? How does historical inquiry 'address the basic hermeneutical issue of the function of the church's canonical literature in providing its own normative interpretive context which is not necessarily to be identified with the original author's intention'?[5] What are we to make of the problematic theological presupposition of this hermeneutic – namely, its failure to take seriously that *the church is one*? Does not the unity of the one people of God across time and space

[2] See Watson, *Text, Church and World*, 46–59.
[3] Wright, 'The Letter to the Galatians,' 206.
[4] See, e.g., Ollenburger, 'What Krister Stendahl "Meant"'; Green, 'Scripture and Theology' and 'Modernity, History'; Cummins, 'Theological Interpretation.'
[5] Childs, *New Testament as Canon*, 251; see pp. 249–51; see also Fowl and Jones, *Reading in Communion*, 29–83.

render problematic a hermeneutic grounded in a failure to acknowledge that those who received this divine word and those who now seek to interpret it comprise the same community?[6]

To give one final example, although most would agree with the adage, 'a text without a context is little more than a pretext,' the question remains: Which context? The historical-critical paradigm pointed unwaveringly to the context of the ancient world (though, then, to a plurality of contexts, whether to the mind of the author, or to the communities within which traditions took shape, or to some other stable thing-in-the-past), but a range of positions regarding the location of meaning is now championed.[7] Indeed, long before Stendahl's essay, Karl Barth, without absolving readers of the Bible from doing their historical homework, had nonetheless insisted that the context for understanding the Bible could not be identified with its historical milieu. For him, 'the fact that "the whole Bible authoritatively proclaims that God must be *all in all*" meant that God Himself, that revelation, was the actual context in which the Bible was to be understood.'[8]

If the approach articulated by Stendahl and developed by his heirs has been repeatedly assayed and found wanting, how do we explain its staying power? Two answers come to mind. First, most of us recognize at one level or another the nature of biblical texts as cultural products, whatever else they are, which derive from and bear the marks of their respective histories. Attention to these histories thus seems an inescapable constant in any hermeneutical formula. Does this not imply a *descriptive* task as precursor to a *constructive* or *normative* one? If not, then how otherwise might we who engage biblical texts account for their own, self-evident character as documents from another time and place? Second, simply put, among the alternative approaches championed, none is as yet fully developed or, at least, none has yet proven itself. But if the regnant paradigm is misshapen, how might we achieve our goal of reading the Bible so as to hear God's address? Not without good reason, we may easily conclude that we do not know what to do, those of us who share this goal.

This conclusion may seem pessimistic in the extreme, but it actually signifies hope, since those of us who sound this note are able to do so only because we have begun to give ourselves to this hermeneutical work. Realizing that old paths need to be rediscovered or new trails opened is surely a necessary first step. Haltingly, we have begun to explore hitherto unknown terrain, chart the frontiers, and map the topography. Even when we do not know how to span them, we have identified some of the main fault lines; even when we do not yet

---

[6] See, e.g., Jenson, 'The Religious Power of Scripture'; McClendon Jr., *Systematic Theology*, I: *Ethics*, 31–34.

[7] See Fowl, *Engaging Scripture*.

[8] Burnett, *Karl Barth's Theological Exegesis*, 101.

know how to achieve them, we have identified some of the more prominent landmarks. My aim here, then, is to name some of these in the form of questions, so as to point toward areas where more work is needed.

What is the Role of Canonical Context in Theological Interpretation?

Study of the Gospel of Luke, for the most part, has focused on the gospel itself or on the gospel in its relationship to the Acts of the Apostles, without primary reference to its canonical location. Redaction criticism located the Gospel of Luke in relation to the other synoptic gospels, but this pressed backward in time to presumed literary relations between or among the Gospels of Matthew, Mark, and Luke; or to their purported sources, whether literary (Q, L, M, *Urmarkus*, et al.) or oral; and not to their canonical juxtaposition. Since Cadbury, the Gospel of Luke has been read in relation to the Acts of the Apostles (Luke-Acts), an approach that takes seriously the 'unity' of Luke and Acts, while allocating little if any attention to the plain reality that Luke and Acts do not appear side-by-side in the biblical canon. Not without good reason, then, Mikeal Parsons and Richard Pervo complained about imprecision in claims regarding the unity of Luke-Acts, and Robert Wall has urged that, from a canonical perspective, Acts must be read in relation to the fourfold gospel (Matthew, Mark, Luke, and John) on the one hand, the epistolary collections on the other.[9] 'If Acts is read in its current canonical placement rather than as the second volume of Luke-Acts, then the reader will naturally reflect upon its narrative as continuing the story of Jesus presented by the four Gospels.'[10]

The theological issues at stake on this issue should not be minimized. Thirty-five years ago, James Dunn complained that Pentecostals based their presumption of a second experience of the Spirit, subsequent to and distinct from the new birth, on a problematic hermeneutic, one which reads Acts 2 as the 'second experience' following the 'first' in John 20:22 (and in light of additional Johannine material in John 13–16). 'This appeal to John's Gospel raises a basic methodological issue: Are we to approach the NT material as systematic theologians or as biblical theologians and exegetes?'[11] Compare this with Wall's apparent claim that Acts provides a sequel better suited to the Gospel of John than to the Gospel of Luke itself: 'the importance of retaining the final shape of the NT rather than combining Luke and Acts as a single narrative is indicated

---

[9] Parsons and Pervo, *Rethinking the Unity of Luke and Acts*; Wall, 'The Acts of the Apostles.'

[10] Wall, 'The Acts of the Apostles,' 29.

[11] Dunn, *Baptism in the Holy Spirit*, 39.

by the significant roles performed by Peter and the Holy Spirit in Acts where Jesus is absent – roles for which Luke's Gospel does not adequately prepare the reader of Acts. Peter's rehabilitation at the end of John (John 21:15–17) as well as the teaching about the Spirit's post-Easter role by John's Jesus (John 14–16) signify the important role that John's Gospel performs in preparing the reader for the story of Acts.'[12]

Clearly, here is an area in which more investigation is necessary, but the terms of the discussion should not be narrowed too quickly. It is arguable, for example, that canonical position is not the only factor worth considering in a decision about whether Luke and Acts ought to be read, as Christian Scripture, as Luke and Acts or as Luke-Acts. What is one to make of the ways in which Acts 1:1–11 seems actually to urge that we read Acts in relation to the Gospel of Luke (see, e.g., the connections formed by references to the 'former book, Theophilus' [Luke 1:1–4 // Acts 1:1], the promise of the Father [Luke 24:49 // Acts 1:4], the mission to all nations [Luke 24:47 // Acts 1:8], and the ascension [or exaltation] as the hinge of the Lukan narrative enterprise [Luke 24:50–53 // Acts 1:9–11]). A decision in favor of reading Luke and Acts as a unity would not close the door on other canonical readings, however, including the possibilities of Acts as a bridge from gospel to letter (that is, from 'gospel' to its [pastoral] articulation and appropriation in particular settings) and of Acts as a narrative authorization of Paul and the 'pillars' (Gal. 2:9) represented in the epistolary collections.

Quite different questions about a canonical reading remain as well. For example, what of the relation of Luke and Acts to the whole of Scripture, from Genesis to Revelation? The narrative of Luke-Acts is illustrative of the hospitality of narrative to all sorts of literary forms – for example, parables, speeches, letters, summary accounts – and, thus, the capacity of narrative to enfold these narrated elements within a web of significance. The analogical question is how Luke's location in the canonical narrative, from creation to new creation, Genesis to Revelation, shapes the theological significance of Luke's work. Given the way the third evangelist has written the story of Jesus into the story of the Septuagint, the way he has written the story of the early church into the story of Jesus, and the way he has reached an end to his narrative without bringing closure to the story of the actualization of God's purpose in history may provide us with clues as to how best to read canonically in this way. At the very least, this important issue presses us to strike out into forms of enquiry about the relationship between the Old Testament and Luke that move us beyond the parameters of more typical explorations of the use of the Old Testament by the third evangelist.[13]

---

[12] Wall, 'The Acts of the Apostles,' 30.

[13] Typified, e.g., by Bock, *Proclamation from Prophecy*; see the counter-argument in Litwack, *Echoes of Scripture*.

What Is the Place of Historical Criticism in Theological Interpretation of Christian Scripture?

Unfortunately, the choices too often presented to us have been *either* history *or* theology, with the result that historical criticism has tended to eschew theological interests, and theological interpretation has sometimes seemed to rub elbows with an historicism, or even antihistoricism, that is problematic to a Christian faith concerned with 'God's mighty acts *in history*.'[14] The reasons for such dichotomous thinking are not difficult to identify. One thinks immediately of the ways in which ecclesial and dogmatic interests have overruled actual engagement with biblical texts, with the result that Scripture was made to play the role of mannequin to the ecclesial master; or of a scientific historicism consumed with 'what actually happened,' and, thus, with a Rankean notion of the historical enterprise: secure the remains of the past, assess them critically, and synthesize them into a whole that reflects transcendent principles.[15] Irrespective of motivations, the reality before us is largely that, in spite of the progress made in the philosophy of history in the last thirty years, and the concomitant innovations in the academic field of historiography, biblical studies in the historical mode has generally continued on the basis of an 'old historicism' not identical with, but with close ties to, the historical positivism of the nineteenth century. Perhaps this is not surprising, given Stephen Neill's assessment of the need in New Testament research for a nuanced theology of history, taken up again and lamented by N.T. Wright: 'But where are the scholars sufficiently familiar with actual history-writing, sufficiently at home in philosophy and the history of ideas, and sufficiently committed to the study of the New Testament, to undertake the task?'[16]

Recent work in the philosophy of history pushes us in the direction of a historical reading of Luke that would shift our attention away from concerns with *validation* (Did it happen in just this way?), in the direction of concerns with *signification* (What might this mean?). Is the role of Luke's narrative within the church endangered or enhanced by this shift of emphasis? First, a focus on the question of the status of Luke-Acts within the Christian Scriptures does not turn attention away from the need for historical investigation. If Scripture purports to narrate human-divine relations, then Scripture itself invites historical questions. Having said this, however, it is important to realize that historical study cannot accomplish what has often been desired of it, at least generally – namely, that Luke's narrative might be proven to be true. Historical study can and should explore our 'beginnings,' together with the sociocultural

---

[14] Cf. Green, 'Narrative and New Testament Interpretation.'
[15] See the survey in Breisach, *Historiography*.
[16] Neill and Wright, *Interpretation of the New Testament 1861–1986*, 366.

conditions of the rise of the Jesus-movement. But the 'meaning' or 'truth' of these texts can never be reduced to the results of historical study. Historical study alone cannot speak to such questions as whether Jesus of Nazareth is both Lord and Christ, whether Jesus' resurrection signaled the restoration of God's people and the ushering in of the new era, or any of a number of other claims that are central to the witness of Luke's work. And, in the end, this means that the meaning, truth, and authority of Luke's narrative cannot be tethered to, or made dependent on, modernist notions of history or historical veracity. Instead, as with other biblical narratives, the essential truth-claim with which we are concerned in our reading of Luke lies above all in the claim of this narrative to speak, as it were, on God's behalf—that is, to interpret reality in light of God's self-disclosure of God's own character and purpose working itself out in the cosmos and on the plain of human events. In this sense, the authority of this text, read as Scripture, rests in its status as revealed history.

If we were to take seriously this perspective on history/writing, what sequela would follow? First, the interests underwriting the historical-critical enterprise would be shifted away from the question 'Did this thing happen?' or 'Did it happen in just this way?' Instead, we would see that the most important contribution of the quest for Jesus and the first-century missionary church would be our enhanced access to Luke and Acts *as cultural products* – that is, as a narrative that speaks both out of and over against the world within which it was penned. This would allow us a sharper image of how Luke himself has pursued his task of shaping the identity of a people through shaping their history at the same time that it would mitigate our impulses toward domesticating the narrative of Luke-Acts by locating it within our own cultural commitments, as though it embodied and authorized our cherished dispositions. Second, we would attend more pointedly to the persuasive art of the narrator of Luke-Acts, and particularly to what he has chosen to include, how he has ordered his material, and into what plotline he has inscribed the whole. Like any historiographer or biographer, Luke's work presumes not only the availability of 'facts' (i.e., 'low-level interpretive entities unlikely for the moment to be contested'),[17] but also a story line into which Luke's story is inscribed; this story line includes a beginning and end, expectations and presumptions, which tacitly guide the actual narrativizing process. Readerly discernment around these issues would help to define the interpretive task for those of us who want to engage Luke-Acts as history/writing. Third, the narrative before us would materialize again as a subject in the work of interpretation, as narratives in general are wont to do. That is, it would be heard again to extend its invitation for people to embrace this story as their own, to indwell it, to be transformed in living it. Not inconsequently, this perspective would find support from within

---

[17] Haskell, 'Objectivity Is Not Neutrality,' 157.

the pages of Luke itself, concerned as this narrative is with assigning meaning to 'the events that have been fulfilled among us' (Lk. 1:1).

Other approaches to the question of history in theological interpretation may present themselves. Howard Marshall's helpful recognition that Luke is both historian and theologian,[18] however, presses the question: How are history and theology to be seen as coexisting not only in the same book, but in each sentence of that book? How does theological interpretation of Luke account for this primary quality of history/writing, that verification and rhetoric 'run inescapably together,' as Albert Cook puts it, so that each descriptive account, when correlated with others in historiography, carries an interpretive as well as a documentary force?[19]

What is the Relationship Between Bible and Creed?

Christian theological interpretation of Scripture cannot escape the question of the relationship between those ecumenical creeds that define the faith of the church and this canonical collection we embrace as Scripture. For many, this relationship must be explored in terms of source and continuity: Can these biblical documents, by themselves, support the theological weight placed on them by later creedal formulations? For example, can we find in the texts of the Bible adequate foundation for the later, explicit, confessional claims of Jesus' divinity? More pressing at the hermeneutical level, however, is that, taken on their own terms and without recourse to a history or community of interpretation, these texts are capable of multiple interpretations. Thus, even if we want to affirm that scriptural engagement is inescapable for the Christian community, *sola scriptura* can never guarantee that one is Christian. Irenaeus (*ca.* 130 – *ca.* 202) noted how Gnostics made use of biblical exegesis in their arguments, but he insisted that they did not read the Scriptures aright on account of their disregard of the 'order and connection' of Scripture; failing to understand the Bible's true content, they put the pieces of the biblical puzzle together in a way that turned a royal personage into a hound or fox (*Haer.* 1.8.1). The 'order and connection' to which Irenaeus referred was the rule of faith, a summary of the Christian kerygma that measured faithful interpretation of Scripture. Writing of this stage in the church's history, William Abraham observes,

> the development of a scriptural canon was utterly inadequate to meet the challenge posed by the Gnostics. The Gnostics had no difficulty accepting any canon of Scripture which might be proposed; being astute in their own way and eclectic in

---

[18] Marshall, *Luke*.

[19] Cook, *History/Writing*, 55.

their intellectual sensibilities, they simply found ways to use Scripture to express their own theological convictions. *This should come as no surprise to anyone. A list of diverse books merely by the sheer volume involved is susceptible to a great variety of readings.*[20]

The church has long recognized the need, then, for a 'ruled reading' of its canonical texts, and this presents us with the following question: How does Scripture function vis-à-vis doctrine (and, more broadly, the teaching office of the church)? Yet, today, biblical and theological studies seem to speak the same language only rarely. Indeed, theology today often seems quite capable of carrying on its work sans any need to draw on or check in with biblical studies, and vice versa.

A specifically Christian theological reading of Scripture cannot escape such conversation, however. Let me press further, to insist that, for a Christian theological reading of Scripture, the measure of validity in interpretation cannot be taken apart from the great creeds of the church, and thus a concern with the Rule of Faith. This way of putting things need not waylay 'a close reading of the text' nor historical spadework, since these enable the text its robust voice as a subject (rather than an object) in theological discourse. Another caveat is necessary, too – namely, the Rule of Faith may be a necessary insurance that our reading of Scripture is *Christian*, but is itself insufficient to guarantee such a reading. This is because a Christian reading of Scripture must be concerned with the incarnation of the divine word within the community of God's people and not only with the prospect of (disembodied) truth claims. The ecclesial context of Christian interpretation of Scripture, including both the historical and global dimensions of that context, and the ecclesial formation of those interpreters, are pivotal in theological interpretation.

What is the Relationship Between Exegesis and Christian Formation?

If, as James L. Resseguie has recently argued, 'Luke challenges us to think critically about the spiritual life and its implications for everyday living,'[21] how is it that so little attention has been paid in Lukan scholarship to this challenge? True, we can point to contemporary studies of Luke's perspective on spirituality and discipleship,[22] but this is not quite the issue. Notice Ressequie's words: 'Luke challenges *us*' (and not only Luke's first readers). A commitment to dispassionate exegesis following the contours of the scientific method has proven

---

[20] Abraham, *Canon and Criterion in Christian Theology*, 36 (emphasis mine).

[21] Ressequie, *Spiritual Landscape*, ix.

[22] E.g., Sweeland, *Our Journey with Jesus*; more broadly, Barton, *The Spirituality of the Gospels*.

itself capable of segregating study of Luke's work from an encounter with the God of Luke's narrative. But Luke's own perspective is that prayer is crucial to the work of discerning Jesus' identity and God's purpose,[23] so how can a reading of Luke faithful to the Lukan enterprise not be a prayerful one? Is it possible genuinely to understand ('stand under') a narrative concerned so manifestly with the marginal if we are not ourselves engaged in friendship with the marginal? Might we not formulate a theological version of the hermeneutical circle (or hermeneutical spiral) in terms of putting into play (or performing) the message of Luke's Gospel as a means for understanding it better?

Undoubtedly, this set of questions is tied into another. Namely, how do we take the measure of the 'effects' of a text and its interpretation? One way to get at this question is to inquire into the history of Luke's reception. Another, not unrelated, approach would be to query what a community would look like were it to embody (or to have embodied) the word of God as this is heard in the Gospel of Luke. This approach to *Wirkungsgeschichte*, or to the history of the influence of the Lukan narrative, would press us beyond the imperialism of 'presentism,' toward the recognition of the canonical status of this book, toward the recognition that there is only one church (*that* community of interpretation includes us), and toward the recognition of 'the end' of exegesis as embodiment in community. It would also underscore the political and embodied nature of our study and build a bridge between biblical studies and theology/ethics. Study of this nature has hardly even begun.

Are We Ready to Sacrifice Some of the Sacred Cows We Have Inherited?

By 'sacred cows,' of course, I refer to some of the commitments that operate at such a taken-for-granted level that they hardly even seem to be commitments; they are simply 'the way things are.' Two come to mind as of special importance in biblical studies. The first is the priority of 'right method.' The second is the presumption of the 'singularity of meaning.'

Already in the Reformation era, handbooks were produced to guide exegetical performance; in the early days, these emphasized grammar and philology, while more recently they have expanded considerably, perhaps even exponentially, to embrace any number of exegetical approaches: tradition criticism, rhetorical criticism, new historicism, postcolonial interpretation, guerrilla exegesis, and more. My concern is not with method per se; indeed, given the plethora of approaches available in the biblical studies marketplace today, my sense is that, the more disciplined one can be in reporting one's

---

[23] So Crump, *Jesus the Intercessor.*

methodological commitments, the better. Nor is my concern that different methods almost by default generate different meanings; indeed, it is especially for this reason that I so confidently cast my vote in favor of full disclosure regarding what approach(es) one will take to biblical texts. The problem lies, rather, with our presumption that the answer to our dilemma lies with finding the right method, as though good interpretation were a matter first and foremost of good technique. The veneration of technique so much a part of conventional wisdom encourages us either to formulate a method or to set out sentries to scan the horizons for a method that will lift us out of the quagmire in which we find ourselves, as if our hope could be found in a four-step process. The kind of hearing we are after – reading the Bible so as to hear God's address – is less about methods and techniques, however, and more about comportment and sensibilities. Theological interpretation demands more of the interpreter than good technique. In a quite different context, novelist Ursula K. LeGuin puts it helpfully: 'To learn a belief without belief is to sing a song without the tune. A yielding, an obedience, a willingness to accept these notes as the right notes, this pattern as the right pattern, is the essential gesture of performance, translation, and understanding.'[24] We might formulate a hermeneutical motto along these lines: We orient ourselves toward a theological interpretation of Christian Scripture first in terms of our dispositions in relation to Scripture, 'a yielding, an obedience, a willingness to accept these notes as the right notes, this pattern as the right pattern'; here 'is the essential gesture of performance, translation, and understanding.'

Again, without disparaging our attentiveness to issues of method, we should recognize that no particular method can insure theological interpretation. At the same time, some methods are more theologically friendly than others. In addition to approaches that situate the voice of Scripture socio-historically, of special interest in theological interpretation would be modes of analysis that struggle in some way seriously with the generally narrative content of Scripture; the theological unity of Scripture, which takes its point of departure from the character and purpose of the God of Israel and of Jesus Christ, and which gives rise to the historical unity of Scripture as the narrative of that purpose being worked out in the cosmos; and the final form and canonical location of the biblical texts.

The second sacred cow is the presumption of the singular meaning of a biblical text, which has led to waves of crusades in search of that one meaning, a quest now documented in the rows of commentaries now adorning our bookshelves. That scholars of Luke's Gospel have been unable to achieve unanimity on *the* meaning of key Lukan texts ought already to suggest the wrongheadedness of the quest. How can this be so? My own entry point into this

---

[24] LeGuin, *The Telling*, 97–98 (emphasis original).

discussion was helped by the publication in 1990 of Umberto Eco's aptly named monograph, *The Limits of Interpretation*, in which the author introduces his brief by noting that 'no text can be interpreted according to the utopia of a definite, original, and final historical meaning. Language always says more than its unattainable literal meaning, which is lost from the very beginning of the textual utterance.' However, to say that a text is capable of multiple meanings is not to open the door to unbridled subjectivism or an infinite range of valid readings; rather, 'the limits of interpretation coincide with the rights of the text' (which, for Eco, does not mean with the rights of its author).[25]

An openness to a plurality of meanings from a single text raises the question: How do we know when an interpretation is valid? This is controverted territory! Today, we work on the hermeneutical frontier, with some continuing to argue for a singular meaning tied to authorial intent and others, at the opposite end of the spectrum, imagining from no less a critical stance that meaning has no limits. My own view is that a theological reading of Scripture, in order to be regarded as valid, would account: the text in its final form; the text as a whole; the cultural embeddedness of all language (rather than assuming that all people everywhere and in all times construed their life-worlds as we do); the canonical address of the text, particularly with reference to the location of particular biblical witnesses within the grand mural of the actualization of God's purpose; and the witness of Scripture as seen in its effects within and among the community of God's people, including in the distillation of Scripture's message in the great creeds of the church which confess and proclaim and worship the Triune God.

The Road(s) Ahead

Wesley Kort has recently asserted, 'At one time people knew what it meant to read a text as scripture, but we no longer do, because this way of reading has, since the late medieval and reformation periods, been dislocated and obscured.'[26] This collection of essays on reading the Gospel of Luke theologically demonstrates not so much our incapacity to read a text as Scripture as it demonstrates how this way of reading has been obscured. In its own way, each essay in *Reading Luke* brings to the forefront different interests, problems, and commitments that occupy Christian interpreters of Luke, thus demonstrating the lack of consensus both on the nature of the problem before us, we who want to read Luke so as to hear God's address, and the path before us that must be cleared and more clearly marked.

---

[25] Eco, *The Limits of Interpretation*, 2, 6–7.

[26] Kort, *'Take, Read'*, 1.

In the end, then, *Reading Luke*, with its problems and proposals, is an invitation for persons within the church to engage the Scriptures for *interpretation, reflection,* and *formation*. The nature of the task before us is multilayered, equally important for postgraduate researchers and small group Bible study groups. The hermeneutical work has only begun. Old paths need to be rediscovered and new trails opened as we explore little-known terrain and chart the frontiers of engaging Scripture so as to tune our ears to the voice of God.

Bibliography

Abraham, W.J., *Canon and Criterion in Christian Theology: From the Fathers to Feminism* (Oxford: Clarendon Press, 1998)

Barton, S.C., *The Spirituality of the Gospels* (Peabody, MA: Hendrickson, 1992)

Bock, D.L., *Proclamation from Prophecy and Pattern: Lucan Old Testament Christology* (JSNTSup 12; Sheffield: JSOT Press, 1987)

Breisach, E., *Historiography: Ancient, Medieval, and Modern* (Chicago: University of Chicago Press, 2nd edn, 1994)

Burnett, R.E., *Karl Barth's Theological Exegesis: The Hermeneutical Principles of the Römerbrief Period* (Grand Rapids: Eerdmans, 2004)

Childs, B., *The New Testament as Canon: An Introduction* (Philadelphia: Fortress Press, 1984)

Cook, A., *History/Writing: The Theory and Practice of History in Antiquity and in Modern Times* (Cambridge: Cambridge University Press, 1988)

Crump, D., *Jesus the Intercessor: Prayer and Christology in Luke-Acts* (WUNT 2.49; Tübingen: Mohr Siebeck, 1992).

Cummins, S.A., 'The Theological Interpretation of Scripture: Recent Contributions by Stephen E. Fowl, Christopher R. Seitz, and Francis Watson,' *CBR* 2 (2004), 179–96

Dunn, J.D.G., *Baptism in the Holy Spirit: A Re-examination of the New Testament Teaching on the Gift of the Spirit in Relation to Pentecostalism Today* (Philadelphia: Westminster Press, 1970)

Eco, U., *The Limits of Interpretation* (Advances in Semiotics; Bloomington, IN: Indiana University Press, 1990)

Fowl, S., and L. Gregory Jones, *Reading in Communion: Scripture and Ethics in Christian Life* (Grand Rapids: Eerdmans, 1991)

Fowl, S.E., *Engaging Scripture: A Model for Theological Interpretation* (Oxford: Basil Blackwell, 1998)

Green, J.B., 'Modernity, History, and the Theological Interpretation of the Bible,' *SJT* 54 (2001), 308–29

—, 'Narrative and New Testament Interpretation: Reflections on the State of the Art,' *LTQ* 39 (2004), 153–66

—, 'Scripture and Theology: Uniting the Two So Long Divided,' in *Between Two Horizons: Spanning New Testament Studies and Systematic Theology* (ed. J.B. Green and M. Turner; Grand Rapids: Eerdmans, 2000), 32–34

Haskell, T.L., 'Objectivity Is Not Neutrality: Rhetoric versus Practice in Peter Novick's *That Noble Dream*,' in *Objectivity Is Not Neutrality: Explanatory Schemes in History* (Baltimore: Johns Hopkins University Press, 1998), 145–73

Jenson, R.W., 'The Religious Power of Scripture,' *SJT* 53 (1999), 89–105

Kort, W.A., *'Take, Read': Scripture, Textuality, and Cultural Practice* (University Park, PA: Penn State University Press, 1996)

LeGuin, U.K., *The Telling* (New York: Harcourt, 2000)

Litwack, K.D., *Echoes of Scripture in Luke-Acts: Telling the History of God's People Intertextually* (JSNTSup 282; London: T&T Clark, 2005)

Marshall, I.H., *Luke: Historian and Theologian* (Grand Rapids: Zondervan, 2nd edn, 1989)

McClendon Jr., J.W., *Systematic Theology*, I: *Ethics* (Nashville: Abingdon, 1986)

Neill, S., and T. Wright, *The Interpretation of the New Testament 1861–1986* (Oxford: Oxford University Press, 2nd edn, 1988)

Ollenburger, B.C., 'What Krister Stendahl "Meant" – A Normative Critique of "Descriptive Biblical Thought,"' *HBT* 8 (1986), 61–98

Parsons, M.C., and R.I. Pervo, *Rethinking the Unity of Luke and Acts* (Minneapolis: Augsburg Fortress Press, 1993)

Ressequie, J.L., *Spiritual Landscape: Images of the Spiritual Life in the Gospel of Luke* (Peabody, MA: Hendrickson, 2004)

Stendahl, K., 'Biblical Theology, Contemporary,' *IDB* I, 418–32

Sweeland, D.M., *Our Journey with Jesus: Discipleship according to Luke-Acts* (GNS 23; Collegeville, MN: Liturgical Press, 1990)

Wall, R.W., 'The Acts of the Apostles: Introduction, Commentary, and Reflections,' in *The New Interpreter's Bible* (ed. L.E. Keck, et al.; vol. 10; Nashville: Abingdon, 2002), 1–368

Watson, F., *Text, Church and World: Biblical Interpretation in Theological Perspective* (Grand Rapids: Eerdmans, 1994), 46–59

Wright, N.T., 'The Letter to the Galatians: Exegesis and Theology,' in *Between Two Horizons: Spanning New Testament Studies and Systematic Theology* (ed. J.B. Green and M. Turner; Grand Rapids: Eerdmans, 2000), 205–36

University of Gloucestershire

The University of Gloucestershire is delighted that this further volume is now published. It confirms the continuing vitality of the Scripture and Hermeneutics Seminar.

However, our delight is not only in the health of the Seminar. It is also in the significant nature of the book's content. The Seminar involves academics in serious debate but this is not, and should never become, an exercise separate from grappling with the Scriptures themselves. Certainly much has been written about the Gospel of Luke over the centuries since it was first written, but the task of interpretation and application is not complete, even with the publication of this volume. Nevertheless, we thank the contributors for their fine work and also the editors for their part in bringing the book to publication.

I also want to thank Rosemary Hales for her continuing support of the Seminar as its Administrative Manager, and I am sure I speak on behalf of all those involved in the Seminar. Rosemary's patience and persistence are a great asset to the Seminar. She makes arrangements for each Consultation with meticulous care. Her willingness to move to Canada in 2004, to see the Seminar through to the completion of the present phase in 2006/7, is remarkable. I readily acknowledge her ongoing contribution.

The University continues to be committed to supporting the Seminar in the coming years. We look forward to the publication of the two remaining volumes, in 2006 and 2007.

Dr Fred Hughes
School of Humanities
University of Gloucestershire
Francis Close Hall
Swindon Road
Cheltenham
Gloucestershire GL50 4AZ
UK

The British and Foreign Bible Society

The Scripture and Hermeneutics Seminar on the Gospel of Luke held in Oxford in 2004 made a fitting contribution to the bi-centenary of the British and Foreign Bible Society. Bible Society remains the major sponsor of this ground-breaking project and we have been delighted to welcome Redeemer University College as an official partner alongside Baylor University and the University of Gloucestershire.

We would also like to acknowledge the work of Paternoster and Zondervan as the publishers of the volumes. This volume on Luke promises to be no less distinguished than its predecessors. It reflects the excitement of the dialogue that emerged from focusing the application of various hermeneutical tools on one gospel in the context of doxology and prayer.

The discussion on Luke attracted some of the most prominent Lukan scholars. Outstanding discourse continues to be a feature of the Scripture and Hermeneutics Seminar and we look forward to completing the initial series of volumes with our meetings in Rome in 2005 and Texas in 2006. Taken together, the partners in this project prayerfully hope that this unique collection of thoughtful Christian work will significantly influence the way that the Bible is understood and explained.

Our hope is that work such as this reinvigorates the confidence of those working in the church and the academy in relation to the credibility of the Bible as the Word of God.

Ann Holt OBE
Director of Programme
British and Foreign Bible Society
Stonehill Green
Westlea
Swindon
Wiltshire, SN5 7DG
UK

Baylor University

Baylor University is honored to be able to join with the British and Foreign Bible Society, the University of Gloucestershire, and Redeemer University College in supporting the Scripture and Hermeneutics Seminar as a North American partner. As a university community with 160 years of commitment to Christian higher education, we are deeply interested in the kinds of issues the Seminar pursues. As the largest Baptist university in the world, we have a particular interest in the themes of the present volume as the work of the Seminar is brought to bear on a specific biblical text, namely the Gospel of Luke. Baptists have always believed that the Bible is central for Christians, not just for theology but for Christian existence in its entirety.

It is fitting that this work on Luke emerges out of a Seminar which is interdisciplinary in character. Interdisciplinary scholarship is an increasingly necessary and highly productive feature of academic life generally, and it is particularly important when the goal is to produce theology and biblical interpretation that will support the life of the church. The Christian intellectual community at Baylor places particular value on such work, and we strive to make Baylor a place where such an integrated approach is encouraged. We relish occasions during which Christian philosophers can talk with biblical scholars, theologians, missiologists, social scientists, and other intellectuals concerned about the vitality of Christian faith in the contemporary world.

We congratulate the editors and contributors to the present volume on the vigor and quality of their exchange of views. This volume makes evident that biblical interpretation should not be identified solely with the critical methodology which so dominantly characterized the discipline throughout much of the twentieth century. Rather, biblical interpretation is a work prefaced by prayer, imbued with the spirit of *lectio divina*, and ultimately focused back upon the worship life of the churches. This full-bodied opus has always been, and should always be, central to the intellectual life of Christian scholars. We look forward to working with the Seminar in the years ahead and to hosting a Consultation here in 2006 on the campus at Baylor University.

David Lyle Jeffrey,
Distinguished Professor of Literature and Humanities and Provost Baylor University
One Bear Place
P.O. Box 97404
Waco, TX 76798–7404, USA

Redeemer University College

Redeemer University College has been honored in the past year to give a 'home' to the Scripture and Hermeneutics Project as the sixth volume in its series on Scripture and hermeneutics, *Reading Luke*, has been prepared for publication. We have been glad to work together with the other partners – the British and Foreign Bible Society, the University of Gloucestershire, and Baylor University – who have given support to this important international project.

It has been a delight to see this volume come together from the pre-planning stage, through to the consultation in Jesus College, Oxford, in September 2004, to the framing of a volume of essays that capture the interdisciplinary flavor of study of the book of Luke. The authors come from various countries and a number of disciplines. Together they examine a gospel that begins in the temple with Zechariah and Elizabeth hearing the announcement of the expected birth of John the Baptist, to the conclusion of the assumption of Christ to heaven followed by the disciples returning to the temple to praise God. This volume examines in an interdisciplinary way what comes in between, using the most recent scholarly and hermeneutical tools to shed light on the gospel message.

Redeemer University College is proud to identify with this project and to do its modest share to push it forward. Redeemer University College is a confessional university – rooted firmly in the catholic creeds of the Christian church and the distinctive features of the Reformed theological tradition. Open and confident about its moorings, Redeemer is committed to engaging the intellectual currents in our culture. This is what this volume, and the entire Scripture and Hermeneutics series, is committed to doing. We are confident that this fresh scholarship will enable our culture to see even more clearly the light that has come to the world through the Gospel of Luke.

Jacob P. Ellens, PhD
Vice-President (Academic)
Redeemer University College
Ancaster
Ontario
Canada

Scripture Index

Old Testament

Genesis
2:4 63
2:7 284
4:4–5 204
5:1 63
10 341
18:16–33 367
21:12 204
22:2 136
25:28 204
28:13–15 204
29–45 204
37:27 67
38:1 67
50:24 140

Exodus
2:13 306
3–4 204
3:2–12 419
3:16 140
8:19 277, 338
13:19 140
13:21 338
15 68
23:20 338
24 338
24:6–8 310
30:1–10 359
32:27 306
33–34 367
34 338
40:26–27 359
40:35 273

Leviticus
19:18 306, 337

Numbers
6:24–26 355
11:16–17 338
11:24–25 338

Deuteronomy
1:37 140
3:26 140, 143
3:27 140
4:21–22 140
6:5 337
12:5 340
18:15 337–38
21 137
32:5 68
34:5 140

Joshua
15:63 300

Judges
1:21 300
5 68
6:11–21 419
9:1–57 301
19:10–21 300

1 Samuel
2 68
14:52 301
16:6 303
16:13 300

24:6 303
31:1–7 301

2 Samuel
2:11 298
5:1–5 301
5:5 316
5:6–10 316
5:6–12 300
6:19 308
7 296
7:1–7 297
7:8–16 300
7:9–16 303
7:11–13 300
7:13 312
7:14 295, 300, 312
7:16 301
8:11–12 301
9:7 308
9:9–13 298
9:10 308
9:13 308
10:19 301
12:1–4 31
12:30 301
19:21 300
22:51 300
23:1 300, 303
23:5 300–301

1 Kings
1:33 298
1:38–39 300
2:7 308, 313

Names Index

Subject Index

RENEWING BIBLICAL INTERPRETATION

CRAIG BARTHOLOMEW, COLIN GREENE, KARL MÖLLER, EDITORS

Renewing Biblical Interpretation is the first of eight volumes from the Scripture and Hermeneutics Seminar. This annual gathering of Christian scholars from various disciplines was established in 1998 and aims to reassess the discipline of biblical studies from the foundation up and forge creative new ways for reopening the Bible in our cultures.

Including a retrospective on the consultation by Walter Brueggemann, the contributors to *Renewing Biblical Interpretation* consider three elements in approaching the Bible—the historical, the literary and the theological—and the underlying philosophical issues that shape the way we think about literature and history.

Zondervan: ISBN 0-310-23411-5   Paternoster Press: ISBN 0-85364-034-3

AFTER PENTECOST: LANGUAGE AND BIBLICAL INTERPRETATION

CRAIG BARTHOLOMEW, COLIN GREENE, KARL MÖLLER, EDITORS

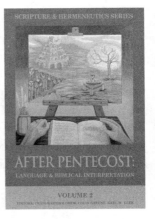

After Pentecost is the second volume from the Scripture and Hermeneutics Seminar. This annual gathering of Christian scholars from various disciplines was established in 1998 and aims to reassess the discipline of biblical studies from the foundations up and forge creative new ways for reopening the Bible in our cultures.

The Seminar was aware from the outset that any renewal of biblical interpretation would have to attend to the issue of language. In this rich and creative volume the importance of linguistic issues for biblical interpretation is analyzed, the challenge of postmodernism is explored, and some of the most creative recent developments in philosophy and theology of language are assessed and updated for biblical interpretation.

CONTRIBUTORS INCLUDE:

Mary Hesse

Ray Van Leeuwen

Kevin Vanhoozer

Nicholas Wolterstorff

Anthony Thiselton

Zondervan: ISBN 0-310-23412-3   Paternoster Press: ISBN 1-84227-066-4

PATERNOSTER PRESS

bible society

ZONDERVAN™

GRAND RAPIDS, MICHIGAN 49530 USA

WWW.ZONDERVAN.COM

UNIVERSITY OF GLOUCESTERSHIRE

A ROYAL PRIESTHOOD?

CRAIG BARTHOLOMEW, JONATHAN CHAPLIN,
ROBERT SONG, AL WOLTERS
EDITORS

A Royal Priesthood? is the third volume from the Scripture and Hermeneutics Seminar. This annual gathering of Christian scholars from various disciplines was established in 1998 and aims to reassess the discipline of biblical studies from the foundations up and forge creative, new ways for reopening the Bible in our cultures.

Any attempt to open the Book in new and fresh ways for our cultures at the start of the third millennium must explore how to read the Bible ethically and politically. This volume looks at the obstacles to such a process and, in dialogue with Oliver O'Donavan's creative work in this regard, looks in detail at how to read different parts of the Bible for ethics and politics. A unique element of the book is Oliver O'Donavan's fourteen responses to individual chapters.

Zondervan: ISBN 0-310-23413-1   Paternoster Press: ISBN 1-84227-067-2

PATERNOSTER PRESS

BAYLOR
UNIVERSITY

bible society

ZONDERVAN™
GRAND RAPIDS, MICHIGAN 49530 USA
WWW.ZONDERVAN.COM

UNIVERSITY OF
GLOUCESTERSHIRE

"BEHIND" THE TEXT

CRAIG BARTHOLOMEW, C. STEPHEN EVANS, MARY HEALY, MURRAY RAE
EDITORS

Volume 4 of the Scripture and Hermeneutics Seminar is orientated to the crucial role exercised by the philosophy (or philosophies) of history that continually infiltrate the world of biblical interpretation. A contemporary understanding of the nature of historiography cannot ignore any of these earlier developments in epistemology, hermeneutics, and linguistics. *"Behind" the Text: History and Biblical Interpretation* demonstrates the importance of not cutting short any of these interdisciplinary conversations, if we are to understand what it is about history that continually bears down on us when we engage with the biblical text.

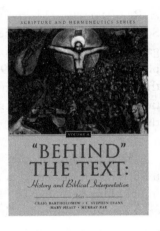

Zondervan: ISBN 0-310-23414-X   Paternoster Press: ISBN 1-84227-068-0

PATERNOSTER PRESS

BAYLOR
UNIVERSITY

bible society

ZONDERVAN™
GRAND RAPIDS, MICHIGAN 49530 USA
WWW.ZONDERVAN.COM

UNIVERSITY OF
GLOUCESTERSHIRE

OUT OF EGYPT:
BIBLICAL THEOLOGY AND
BIBLICAL INTERPRETATION

CRAIG BARTHOLOMEW, MARY HEALY,
KARL MÖLLER, ROBIN PARRY;
SERIES EDITORS
CRAIG BARTHOLOMEW, ANTHONY C. THISELTON

Biblical theology attempts to explore the theological coherence of the canonical witnesses; no serious Christian theology can overlook this issue. The essays in the present volume illustrate the complexity and richness of the conversation that results from attentive consideration of the question. In a time when some voices are calling for a moratorium on biblical theology or pronouncing its concerns obsolete, this collection of meaty essays demonstrates the continuing vitality and necessity of the enterprise.

Richard B. Hays, George Washington Ivey Professor of New Testament, The Divinity School, Duke University, USA.

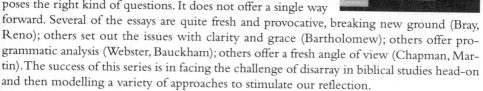

This volume on biblical theology jumps into the fray and poses the right kind of questions. It does not offer a single way forward. Several of the essays are quite fresh and provocative, breaking new ground (Bray, Reno); others set out the issues with clarity and grace (Bartholomew); others offer programmatic analysis (Webster, Bauckham); others offer a fresh angle of view (Chapman, Martin). The success of this series is in facing the challenge of disarray in biblical studies head-on and then modelling a variety of approaches to stimulate our reflection.

Christopher Seitz, Professor of Old Testament and Theological Studies, St. Andrews University, UK

Zondervan: ISBN 0-310-23415-8

Paternoster Press: ISBN 1-84227-069-9

PATERNOSTER PRESS

BAYLOR
UNIVERSITY

bible society

ZONDERVAN™
GRAND RAPIDS, MICHIGAN 49530 USA
WWW.ZONDERVAN.COM

UNIVERSITY OF
GLOUCESTERSHIRE

We want to hear from you. Please send your comments about this book to us in care of zreview@zondervan.com. Thank you.

GRAND RAPIDS, MICHIGAN 49530 USA

WWW.ZONDERVAN.COM